DEADLY FORCE:

What We Know

A Practitioner's Desk Reference on Police-Involved Shootings

William A. Geller
Michael Scott

Police Executive Research Forum

Washington, D.C.

© 1992 by Police Executive Research Forum
Cover Design by Fitzgerald & Swaim
Library of Congress Catalog Number 92-61461
ISBN 1-878734-30-X

POLICE EXECUTIVE RESEARCH FORUM
2300 M Street, N.W., Ste. 910
Washington, D.C. 20037
(202) 466-7820

PERF Midwest Office:
2116 Thornwood Ave.
Wilmette, IL 60091-1452

This book is dedicated to dedicated individuals:

■ *The men and women of America's police departments who have given what President Abraham Lincoln, in his Gettysburg address, called "the last full measure of devotion."*

■ *And the citizens—civilians and police alike—who are determined to be peacemakers, determined to find better ways to resolve human conflict nonviolently.*

Foreword

When a police officer kills someone in the line of duty—or is killed—it sets in motion a series of internal and external reviews and public debate that normally does not end until several years later when the civil and criminal court trials are over. In this process a number of questions are usually raised. Does the police department have an appropriate deadly force policy? Did the officer comply with that policy? Was the officer properly trained? Supervised? What is the officer's background? What is the subject's background? What are the races of the officer and the individual killed? How does the police department's record compare with others that serve similar communities in the number of officers killed and citizens killed? Do police shoot minorities more frequently than whites? Could the situation have been handled another way? Should criminal charges be filed? What should the police department say to the community? The officer? The victim's family and friends? Police department employees? The questions are almost endless—and, often, the answers never quite seem to satisfy the full range of legitimate interests in these incidents.

What do we know about situations in which the police use deadly force? Bill Geller and Mike Scott in *Deadly Force: What We Know* have done a masterful job of answering that question. Between the covers of this book one will find over 600 information packed pages on police-involved shootings. It is the most comprehensive, well researched volume on the subject ever published in America. The authors present and discuss information on all of the previous non-legal research on this subject as well as data they collected about and from 13 large American cities and counties. Their examination of these jurisdictions offers new insight and understanding into this complex area. Not only do Geller and Scott answer the question of what we know about officer-involved shootings, they address that equally important question of what we don't know.

Police-involved shootings have always presented police executives with one of their most difficult challenges to manage. Like the circus tightrope walker 100 feet above the ground without a net, the police executive must maintain perfect balance. One misstep by either can turn a complicated situation into a disaster. In the aftermath of a police-involved shooting, the police executive plays a critically important role. Both the community and the officers must be assured the department is doing the proper things. And what is proper is not always easy to determine. I recall a few years ago when the Dallas police chief was roundly criticized by officers for using the word "unfortunate" rather than "tragic" in remarks following the killing of an officer. The community is equally interested in what the chief says and how it is said.

In the past few years the chiefs in Kansas City, Missouri; Portland, Oregon; and San Diego have gone through extensive reviews of their policies, practices, and procedures following several officer-involved shooting incidents within relatively short time frames. Had

Deadly Force: What We Know been available to them, their inquiry into these issues could have been completed more thoroughly, quickly, and at less cost.

Deadly Force will be a valuable resource for police executives in the future. It addresses the limitations of current information and why it is useful to understand the problems with data collection and analysis. Geller and Scott present information on both the shootings of civilians by police and of police officers. They explore the context of shooting incidents and offer valuable insight on a wide range of variables. They also examine strategies to control shootings—this discussion includes policy development, policy enforcement, training, and weapons and equipment. In the final chapter of the book the authors discuss the importance of values in setting standards of conduct, maintaining high standards of conduct while providing officers with the much needed support from the top, and the areas where more research is needed.

Geller and Scott have made a tremendous contribution to our knowledge and understanding of the circumstances around officer-involved shootings that will be helpful to anyone who has an interest in this important public policy area. Those in the academic community will gain new insight into police-involved shootings from the perspective of the issues police executives need to consider. *Deadly Force* can provide local government CEOs a full education into the complexity of managing government's authority to take a life that is vested in the hands of a 21-year-old police officer who exercises that authority under circumstances that would test the mettle of those much older and wiser. The book should also be required reading for those in the news media who report on these situations and those who edit their work. If it were, I believe the quality of reporting on these situations would be substantially improved.

If I had my way, *Deadly Force* would have been published over a year ago. At that time the draft was a couple of hundred pages shorter—but in my mind better and more comprehensive than anything I had ever read on police-involved shootings. Bill kept working on it though and, as we reached the end of 1991, he argued that it would not be complete without the 1991 data from the 13 jurisdictions that were studied. Collecting the data, analyzing it, and working it into the volume took a few additional months of hard work. In the meantime, the volume grew as he tinkered with one chapter, then another. The result is a book that will make a substantial contribution to PERF's mission of improving policing in America.

So even though *Deadly Force: What We Know* is a bit later than I would have preferred, I am confident that most readers will agree with me that it was well worth the wait. This important issue needs the depth of discussion and understanding that Bill Geller and Mike Scott have given it—even at the risk of a PERF-involved shooting...

Darrel W. Stephens
Executive Director
Police Executive Research Forum

Preface

Much of what appears in the body and appendixes of this book will seem somewhat academic in spite of our efforts to inject a sense of the real-life tragedy and terror of police-involved shootings. As the friends, families, and colleagues of officers and civilians laid to rest as a result of a police-involved shooting know (see Stillman 1987), our efforts still fall short of conveying the true sense of grief and anger.

Death at the hands of the police prompts confusing emotions for the victims' families, fellow police officers, government officials, and the public who must stand in judgment of the event. Given that the highest calling of police duty is to protect life, a sense that something has gone wrong is appropriate, even if the death proves to have been legally justifiable. Many are left to wonder whether there was not some other way the situation could have been resolved and whether the shooting was absolutely necessary. Killings by the police rarely produce the sense of swift and sure justice that Hollywood producers seem able to manufacture. The death itself is anything but the final act in the real-life drama; it is but the beginning of a long and agonizing period of much reviewing, grieving, judging, condemning, reflecting, and redressing. And when the death proves not to have been justifiable, doubt turns to outrage and security turns to fear.

During the early preparation of this book, one of us (Scott) attended his second funeral of a Fort Pierce, Florida, police officer killed in the line of duty. The deaths of both officers were particularly brutal. And as this book neared completion, in March 1992, our lead author watched still another Chicago police officer laid to rest, whose badge will become the 405th placed in that agency's star case commemorating officers killed in the line of duty. In one sense, we are fortunate; others have attended more police funerals than us or were more closely associated with the slain officers. Our feelings were the same at each of the funerals: more sad than angry, more empty than full of rage; scared to be reminded of our mortality, and frustrated by the seeming futility of the death. It was painful to see the officers' close friends and families suffer as they did. And we know that the friends and families of citizens killed by the police feel similarly.

Recalling how we felt at those funerals, wishing we could have done something to prevent those deaths, it occurs to us that understanding, writing about, teaching, and implementing the recommendations contained in books such as this one are among the things that those of us in research and administration can do to minimize the suffering. Perhaps even in the safer confines of administrative and academic offices, armed only with facts and figures, we can make real contributions to the safety of those who live and work amid the passion and pain of violence.

We also have obligations of citizenship, of course, and among the most gratifying experiences one can have in our field is facilitating efforts that tangibly reduce violent injuries during police encounters with suspected offenders. Ten years ago, our lead author (Geller) co-chaired a fund-drive in Chicago that provided an opportunity for thousands of citizens to show their concern for officer welfare and public safety by raising enough money ($1.5 million) to purchase soft body armor for the 12,500 officers of the Chicago Police Department. Attending the ceremony several years later in which the first dozen Chicago police officers were inducted into the International Association of Chiefs of Police/DuPont Kevlar Survivors' Club (their lives having been saved by the vests bought through public donations) was a sweet counterbalance to the sorrow of attending other officers' funerals.

Nor could we have developed this book, of course, without getting out of our cloistered settings and spending a fair amount of time with police officers discussing tactical, philosophical, and other professional concerns. Each of us has logged innumerable hours with both police administrators and working cops learning a great deal about their perceptions, attitudes, hopes, dreams, fears, and talents. We remember many of those officers as we write: an officer who shot a man who first shot at him with a shotgun, and who then rendered first aid to save the man's life; an officer who stayed awake all night in a vigil for a man he shot; an officer who tackled a man in the dark, sparing another officer from shooting him; an officer wresting a knife from a deranged man while his partner distracted the man; an officer who calmed an infuriated colleague who otherwise might have needlessly shot a suspect; an officer who only noticed he had been stabbed but saved by his soft body armor while undressing after his shift. And we think about the officers, depicted as cold statistics in this book, who would be alive today if they had put on their bullet-resistant vests along with the rest of their uniforms before beginning their appointed rounds.

We also recall the numerous holes in the station ceilings and walls, and in the squad cars, testimonials to the dangers of accidental firings of police weapons. And we reflect on the officers who would probably be alive today if they had not made tactical mistakes—mistakes that are often difficult for fellow officers to acknowledge and learn from given the understandable impulse to avoid appearing disrespectful to a fallen colleague and his or her survivors.

As we conclude this writing, an officer in Florida tells us of the terror she felt when a man pointed a gun in her face only hours ago. Chicago police on this late July Saturday morning try to sort out the still foggy details of an off-duty fracas last night in a northwest side tavern that left one officer stabbed to death, another shot nonfatally, and a civilian killed. The deceased officer was the second slain this year in Chicago; his partner was the 17th shot nonfatally. And officers in Los Angeles contemplate how, with the help of their new chief, they will best protect the citizenry and themselves as they continue picking up the pieces three months after the most calamitous American riot of this century. Thankfully, most of the current generation of American police as yet do not know first hand the terror and tragedy of urban rioting. But many have been involved in potentially lethal encounters—experiences that bring a pulsing reality to what otherwise might seem like abstract discussions on these pages. We hope that in some small way this work will help make these experiences less common for police and civilians alike.

TABLE OF CONTENTS

Chapter 5: SHOOTING CONTROL STRATEGIES ... 247

APPENDIXES:

LIST OF TABLES AND FIGURES

TABLES

Tables in Appendixes

FIGURES

Figures in Appendixes

Acknowledgments

This book began as a 30-page update of a chapter in *Thinking About Police: Contemporary Readings*, 2nd edition, edited by Carl Klockars and Stephen Mastrofski, published by McGraw-Hill (1990). We are grateful to Carl Klockars for editorial advice on drafts of that chapter. As that chapter for the McGraw-Hill volume began to grow into this volume, we were most fortunate to receive data and insightful critique from many people around the nation. Thus, we gratefully acknowledge the assistance provided by officials in various police agencies that furnished previously unpublished data to us:

- in the Atlanta Police Department, the office of Chief Eldrin Bell and Deputy Chief Beverly Harvard;
- in the Chicago Police Department, former Superintendents Fred Rice, Jr. and LeRoy Martin, the Office of Professional Standards (Chief Administrator Gayle Shines, former Chief Administrator David Fogel and executive secretary to the Chief Administrator Joanne Kenner), the Research and Development Division (former Commander—and now Joliet, IL Police Chief—Joseph Beazley and statisticians Deo Dantes and Patricia Williams), former Department General Counsel—and current detective division deputy chief—Gerald Cooper, current General Counsel John Klein, and the Public and Internal Information Division (Commander Nelson Baretto);
- in the Dallas Police Department, Chief William Rathburn, Assistant Chief Marlin Price, and former Chief Mack Vines;
- in the Houston Police Department, former Chief (and incoming chief in Austin) Elizabeth Watson, staff Sergeant Les Mayo, and Internal Affairs Division Lieutenant Jerry Williams;
- in the Los Angeles Police Department, the office of former Chief Daryl Gates, Deputy Chief Mark A. Kroeker, Commander Michael J. Bostic of the Personnel and Training Bureau; Sergeant Len Hundshamer of the Office of Operations; and Sergeants Chuck Urso and Bruce Bogstad of the Training Bureau's Use of Force Review Section;
- in the Kansas City Police Department, Chief Steven Bishop, former Chief Larry Joiner, Major Ron Smith, and Sergeants Louis Zacharias and Jan Zimmerman;
- in the Metro-Dade County, FL Police Department, Director Fred Taylor, former Deputy Director Eduardo Gonzalez (now Chief of the Tampa Police Department), and Homicide Lieutenant Robert Lengel;
- in the New York City Police Department former Police Commissioners Lee P. Brown and Benjamin Ward, the Police Academy's Firearms and Tactics Section (Deputy Inspector John Cerar, Commanding Officer, and civilian data analyst Gina Goehl), Deputy Chief Michael A. Markman, the Office of Public Information (headed by Suzanne Trazoff), and Lieutenant William Chimento in the Crime

Analysis and Program Planning Section;

- in the New York City Transit Police Department, former Chief William Bratton (now Superintendent-in-Chief of the Boston Police Department), legal counsel Dean Esserman (now Deputy Chief in the New Haven Police Department), and Chief of the Inspectional Services Division Bill Wiese;
- in the Philadelphia Police Department, former Commissioner Willie Williams (now Chief of the LAPD), Deputy Commissioner Thomas Nestel, Internal Affairs Division Lieutenant Jerry Levins, and former Internal Affairs Division Sergeant John Ferry;
- in the Portland, Oregon, Police Department, training division Captain Roy Kindrick;
- in the Saint Louis Metropolitan Police Department, Chief Clarence Harmon, former Chief Robert Scheetz, Lieutenant Don Ebner, Captain John Siebenman (former Commander of Planning and Development), and the five-member Board of Police Commissioners, especially Board President David Robbins;
- in the San Diego Police Department, Chief Robert Burgreen, Assistant Chief Norman Stamper, Lieutenant Lawrence Moratto of the Internal Affairs Division, and Ms. Kimberly Glenn of the Crime Analysis Unit; and
- in the Santa Ana, CA Police Department, Training Section Lieutenant Greg Cooper.

The FBI's Uniform Crime Reporting program User Services Section (Ms. Nancy Carnes and Editor Victoria L. Major) and Training and Program Development unit were also most helpful in providing us with unpublished data concerning justifiable homicides by American police. FBI UCR program Analyst Loretta Behm, who compiled the 1991 edition of *Law Enforcement Officers Killed and Assaulted*, was kind enough to take time to share with us updated data on American police killed and assaulted in the years 1990 through 1992. In addition Professor Geoffrey P. Alpert of the University of South Carolina generously shared previously unpublished data analyzing officer-involved shootings in both the Metro-Dade Police Department and the Dallas Police Department.

Insightful comments on drafts were provided by several current or former police chiefs: Dennis Nowicki from Joliet, Illinois (now executive director of the Illinois Criminal Justice Information Authority); Chief Elizabeth Watson from Houston; Clarence Harmon from St. Louis; Peter Ronstadt from Tucson; Eduardo Gonzalez from Metro-Dade and, more recently, Tampa; and others.

Gary W. Sykes, Director of the Southwestern Law Enforcement Institute, offered helpful comments as the book took shape and provided us access, through teaching risk management seminars at the Institute, to talented police executives from throughout the nation with whom we could discuss cutting-edge issues pertaining to officer-involved shootings. Similarly useful suggestions were made by University of Nebraska-Omaha Criminal Justice Professor Samuel Walker, by Robert Wasserman of Harvard University's John F. Kennedy School of Government, and Police Executive Research Forum (PERF) staff members John Eck and Darrel Stephens. Without the continuing support—beyond sound substantive advice—of PERF executive director Darrel Stephens and the board of directors, this book would not have been possible.

The editorial blue pencil—readily recognizable by an author as a dangerous weapon—was wielded adroitly and graciously by Peter Slavin; John Urbik heroically tackled the mind-altering task of proofing the index; Connie Moy and colleagues at Editorial Experts, Inc.

proofread everything else; and Martha Plotkin of the PERF staff managed the entire production process with her usual skill and equanimity. We are very grateful to all for their assistance. Thanks, too, to John Scardino for his reliable and effective technical support with computer equipment.

Finally, we are indebted to songwriter Julie Shannon (aka Julie Geller), who took one look at the pages of statistics contained in an early draft of this volume and said, "If you really want to put the readers in the shoes of the people that all these numbers represent, give them some real-life *stories* along with the statistics." So we have included capsule anecdotes concerning police-involved shooting encounters as "sidebars" throughout the book in the hope of helping the reader and ourselves never lose sight of the human consequences—for officers and others—of the policy and procedural subjects addressed in these pages. To paraphrase a dedication in a recent report on police use of force (Meyer 1991: iv), the officers in each of the thousands of incidents on which we report statistical information in these pages saw what most should never see, learned what most will never know, and did what most could never do.

Appreciative for Julie Shannon's suggestion that we include the sidebars found throughout this volume—and as evidence of the proposition that no good deed goes unpunished—we imposed on her to proofread the entire volume. Whether marital bliss can survive this ordeal remains to be seen.

The usual acknowledgment page disclaimers apply: All deserved praise is shared widely and all harsh critique must fall on the authors' shoulders. As they say, success has many fathers and failure is an orphan.

Chapter 1:

INTRODUCTION

"No one knows about the hundreds of instances when a police officer decides not to shoot. Perhaps no one cares. After all, people say, we're trained to handle such things, as if training somehow removes or dilutes our humanity." —Santa Monica Police Officer

"Defusing potentially explosive situations is the key to good police work. No smart cop wants to fight with crooks." —San Francisco Police Officer

One of the first thoughts that races through a police chief's mind when the telephone rings in the middle of the night is: Oh God, one of my officers has shot someone or has been shot. Former Minneapolis Police Chief Anthony Bouza, interviewed recently by a reporter about police-community conflict (Bouza 1992), added that in most urban centers in the United States, when the police chief is called "at 3:00 in the morning and told, 'Chief, one of our cops has just shot a kid,' the chief's first questions are: 'What color is the cop? What color is the kid?' " "And," the reporter asked, "if the answer is, 'The cop is white, the kid is black'?" "He gets dressed," replied Bouza.

The importance of police-involved shootings stems not so much from their frequency (they are rare compared with the hundreds of thousands of encounters each year between police and persons suspected of violating the law) but from their potential consequences. Any experienced police officer knows the potentially devastating effects of even justified shootings by police—loss of life and bereavement, risks to an officer's career, the government's liability to civil suits, strained police-community relations, rioting and all the economic and social crises that attend major civil disturbances.

While many of our readers will hardly need a recitation of the civil disturbances ignited in America over the past several decades by controversial police uses of deadly and nondeadly force and related pressures, listing prominent examples of these clashes may help those who did not live through them to consider recent instances of collective violence in a broader context. Riots precipitated by racial tensions stemming from police shootings and other problems for which the police were held at least partially responsible flared in August 1943 in the Harlem neighborhood of New York City (Weiner 1991) and during the years 1964-67 in such cities as San Francisco, St. Louis, New York, Los Angeles, Chicago, Detroit, Durham (North Carolina), Memphis, Omaha, Cleveland, Dayton, Atlanta, Cambridge (Massachusetts),

Rochester (New York), Cairo (Illinois), and the New Jersey cities of Newark, Jersey City, Paterson, New Brunswick, Englewood, and Elizabeth (see, e.g., President's Commission 1967: 189-90; Sherman 1980a: 93; *New York Times* 1992; Upton 1985). The riots of the summer of 1967 were particularly bloody; and as we write exactly 25 years later we are struck by both how much and how little has changed in America.

> *"The use of the word 'riot' to describe racial disorders in this country may tell us something about our racial fault lines and our sense of history. We tend to use 'riot' in situations we fear or want to characterize pejoratively, whereas what we see as part of our hallowed national tradition may be given more appealing names. The Boston Tea Party, for example, sounds almost decorous"* (Northwestern University Professor Michael Sherry, quoted in Galloway 1992: 1; see also Sipchen 1992).

> *"Thousands...thronged around City Hall today, swarming through police barricades to rally on the steps of the hall and blocking traffic on the Brooklyn Bridge for nearly an hour.... [T]he protesters [jumped] barricades, tramp[ed] on automobiles, mobb[ed] the steps of City Hall [and took] over the bridge. * * * [Police Benevolent Association President Phil] Caruso said the protesters who stormed the bridge had got out of hand. He said he did not sanction their actions, but he added that their anger was understandable and warned that 'the administration better wake up to what's happening' "* (McKinley 1992). Those who recall Caruso's criticism of civil rights and civil liberties advocates might find his charitableness toward the protesters inexplicable—until they learn that the protesters were 10,000 off-duty officers, angry over Mayor David Dinkins' support for a civilian review board and handling of a police-involved shooting in the Washington Heights neighborhood (McFadden 1992a). The **New York Times** (1992y, 1992z) called the protest a police "riot." Mayor Dinkins said the lawless behavior of the protesting officers and the racial slurs by some helped explain why some segments of the community distrust police (McKinley 1992a), adding: "[I]f black New Yorkers had come to protest at City Hall and made a similar disturbance, Phil Caruso...'would have said lock 'em up—no question' "* (Purdum 1992).

Not all of the disturbances noted in this chapter stemmed from controversial police shootings; some were sparked by other forms of deadly force (e.g., life-threatening beatings with batons or other weapons). We are not aware of riots having been precipitated by animosity over high-speed police pursuits that end in fatal crashes (which some observers characterize as deadly force), but it is certainly conceivable that there have been or will be such disturbances. Though a book on police use of deadly force might properly address in detail life-threatening force by means other than guns, the issues surrounding *shootings* by and of officers are sufficiently complex as to justify our focusing in this volume almost exclusively on that form of deadly force. Still, to appreciate community tensions over police shootings, one needs to be familiar with conflicts that have arisen around uses of other types of force and to understand that people often draw general conclusions from such cases about police propensity to use or misuse their firearms.

Among the most devastating of the community uprisings over police use of force was the riot in the Watts neighborhood in south central Los Angeles of August 11-17, 1965, which claimed 34 lives, injured 1,032 people, and destroyed property valued at more than $182 million. The riot sprang from a police-civilian confrontation: Los Angeles police stopped black motorists Marquette and Ronald Frye on suspicion of drunken driving (Stone 1992; Cook 1992). Their pregnant mother, Rena, and others interceded to challenge the police, and the situation rapidly escalated as blows were exchanged and rumors circulated through the neighborhood that the officers had brutalized Mrs. Frye.

The "arrest and beating of a black cab driver" sparked a riot in Newark, New Jersey over the six days July 12-17, 1967. When the smoke had cleared, 26 were dead and 1,500 were injured. Property losses were estimated at nearly $58 million (Stone 1992). Less than a week later, on July 23, Detroit erupted in six days of rioting, prompted by a police raid of an illegal bar in a black[1] neighborhood. Until the Los Angeles riot of 1992, Detroit held the sad distinction of the bloodiest insurrection in modern times: 43 slain, 2,000 injured. More than 1,700 stores were looted and 477 buildings burned. Property damage was pegged at over $162 million (*ibid.*; Cook 1992).

During the period April 4-11, 1968, following the assassination of Dr. Martin Luther King, Jr., mass violence erupted in approximately 125 cities coast to coast, taking 46 lives and injuring over 2,600 (*New York Times* 1992). In Washington, DC alone, from April 4 to 9, 1968, 10 people died and 1,202 were injured; property damage exceeded $45 million (Stone 1992). Sherman (1980a: 93) observes that less violent but nevertheless strident protests over police shootings occurred in the 1970s in New York, Houston, Los Angeles, Dallas, Newark, and other cities, citing the *New York Times* (1977a, 1977b, 1978a, 1978b).

The Newark riot of 1974 occurred over the Labor Day weekend and involved mostly Puerto Ricans, with some "other browns, blacks and whites joining in." The first rioting over perceived police brutality since the eruptions that swept the country after Dr. King's assassination, the Newark conflict began "after two mounted policemen overturned a picnic table in a park [during a Puerto Rican fiesta] while breaking up a dice game and one of their horses accidentally struck a little girl." The incident sparked four days of "firebombing, window smashing and looting...; [s]poradic outbursts of violence continued for weeks afterwards. Thirty-five civilians and 37 policemen and firemen were injured during the four days of disorder and 84 arrested." Police were also accused of killing two Puerto Rican men during the conflict. The president of the Greater Newark Urban Coalition, commenting on the turmoil, noted that "he had been predicting for three years that eventually Puerto Rican and Chicano problems were going to explode in the country's face. 'Newark is not isolated,' he [said]. 'It just happened here first. It's going to happen in New York, Chicago, Philadelphia.... It may not be a riot but at some point the Spanish-speaking community is going to let everyone know they have some problems' " (Slavin 1974).

During the 1980s, Miami erupted in rioting three times. The first—an eerie precursor to the event that triggered the Los Angeles riot in 1992—came during May 18-20, 1980, in the Liberty City section of town over the acquittal of four white Metro-Dade police officers for the 1979 beating death of black traffic violator Arthur McDuffie; it resulted in 18 fatalities, more than 400 injured, and $100 million in damage (Grogan 1992). Then, in December 1982 in the Overtown neighborhood of Miami, rioting flared again, causing two

---

[1] The terms "black" and "African-American" are both used by most of our colleagues of color, and we will do likewise throughout this volume. Moreover, an early 1991 national opinion poll conducted by the Joint Center for Political and Economic Studies, a Washington, D.C.-based think tank specializing in black issues, found that, at least at that time, 72 percent of black Americans preferred to be referred to as "black" (*New York Times* 1991c).

Similarly, we use the term "Hispanic" in this book and mean no offense by it to those who would prefer such terms as "Latino" and "Latina" (Weaver 1992: 6). Among other uses, the word "Hispanic" is part of such organizational names as the Hispanic-American Police Command Officers Association.

deaths and more than 25 nonfatal injuries. And in January 1989, again in the Overtown section, there were disorders after the shooting by a Hispanic officer of a black motorcyclist
being pursued by police for reckless driving; unrest broke out again, and six people were
injured and 30 buildings burned (*New York Times* 1992; Cook 1992; *Chicago Tribune* 1992;
Crime Control Digest 1992m).

Perhaps police-citizen clashes have erupted so readily in Miami because multi-racial
tensions seem never to be far from the boiling point there. In mid-1990, a group of black
Miami attorneys, angered that local Cuban leaders snubbed South African leader Nelson
Mandela by failing to welcome him officially to town on his celebrated American tour,
organized a reasonably successful boycott of their city by major conventions. The Cuban
power structure in Miami resented a remark by Mandela on an American television talk show
shortly before his planned visit to Miami, in which the South African freedom fighter
expressed appreciation for the support of Yasir Arafat, Muammar Qaddafi, and Fidel Castro.
Castro is detested by the Miami Cuban community as an enemy of human rights. By the end
of 1990, the boycott organizers had persuaded a dozen conventions to cancel their Miami
bookings, costing the city up to $12 million (Schmich 1991). Even more than the immediate
economic costs, city leaders worried that "the emotional rift created by the action could last
for years." The chair of the Greater Miami Chamber of Commerce said he saw no end in
sight: "The longer this goes on, the deeper the lines are drawn in the sand" (*ibid*.: 24).

In this atmosphere, Miami was hit once again with a riot prompted by dissatisfaction
with police and the criminal justice system. On December 3, 1990, a federal jury acquitted
six members of the Miami Police Department's street narcotics squad, known as the "Jump-
Out Squad," who had been charged under federal civil rights laws with beating a Puerto Rican
drug dealer to death in December 1988. Federal prosecutors accused the officers—one white,
two Hispanic, and three black—of "pummeling..., stomping, * * * and beating [the deceased]
over the head with a nightstick or flashlight." The jury's acquittal came on charges of assault
and conspiracy to violate the victim's civil rights by killing him; it deadlocked on murder-
related civil rights charges against all the defendants and on assault charges against one.
Within hours of the verdict, in the predominantly Puerto Rican neighborhood of Wynwood
(Holmes 1990),

> "scores of black and Hispanic youths, many with their heads covered with
> scarves and paper bags, rampaged through [the] neighborhood just north of
> Miami's business district, setting fires, throwing rocks at cars and looting stores.
> * * * Cars were overturned and youths hurled stones and bottles at police patrol
> cars. Several businesses were also destroyed..." (*Law Enforcement News* 1990c).

The destruction continued with impunity for more than three hours, until police could
muster riot squads numbering about 300. City officials estimated the fire and other damage
at $2.5 million. In contrast to previous riots in Miami, this time there were no serious injuries
(other than the roughing up of two news photographers), and there were no shots fired and
only a few (about 15) arrests (*ibid*.; Holmes 1990). Since the accused officers were of several
races/ethnicities, the fatal beating was not being characterized "in strictly racial terms. The
resentment expressed...was against the police, not against a particular racial group" (Holmes
1990). Police, as with previous and future riots, cited the opportunism of many of the
participants, characterizing them as

> "neighborhood toughs whose sole motive was to cause trouble and steal. 'All
> these criminals saw this demonstration taking place and they started taking

advantage of it,' said Sgt. David Rivero, spokesman for the Miami Police Department. 'You had hoods, dope dealers, alcoholics, dope users who decided to have a good time' " (Holmes 1990).

In a pattern of post-riot finger-pointing that would recur again and again,

> "several residents and merchants criticized the police for responding too slowly to the violence. The police acknowledged...that they did not expect [this] traditionally tranquil Puerto Rican community to become violent. As a result, there was only a normal complement of officers on duty when the disturbance began around 6 P.M., several hours after the verdict was announced. * * * Mr. Rivero, the police spokesman, said that any police presence in Wynwood before the arrival of the riot squads could easily have resulted in more people being hurt, as outnumbered officers without tear gas or riot gear might have had to resort to firing their weapons to protect themselves" (*ibid.*).

In another familiar pattern, community leaders, mindful of their neighborhood's ranking as one of Miami's poorest, cited the riot as a squeaky wheel that might now be greased: "[T]he community is getting recognition of its needs. Before, people didn't really know where Wynwood was. They didn't know there was a Puerto Rican community" (*ibid.*).

A candlelight vigil by 1,000 youths in Teaneck, New Jersey, on April 11, 1990, protesting the killing of a black teenager, who had been shot in the back by a white officer the previous evening, turned violent when police from the 88-member suburban New York City department appeared in riot gear to try to disperse the crowd. Women and children were trampled by the frightened crowd, and some of the protesters smashed windows in patrol cars, overturned the cars, broke windows at police headquarters and in area stores, and looted the stores. Charges flew from the African-American community (which constitutes 25 percent of this town of 39,000) that the youth was shot in the back while raising his hands to surrender. Police retorted that they had been summoned to the scene by a call of "a youth in a red jacket brandishing a gun" and that the deceased, while being patted down by responding officers, ran away. Thinking they had felt a gun during the pat-down, the officers pursued on foot. At some point, police say, the youth "turned and reached toward his pocket." Thinking he was reaching for a gun, one of the officers fired, striking him fatally in the back. A year later, the officer, who had been suspended with pay after the incident, was still awaiting trial on charges of manslaughter (Hanley 1990). In February 1992 the 32-year-old officer was acquitted of reckless manslaughter and in August 1992 was given a disability pension, on the condition he never again work as a police officer in New Jersey (*New York Times* 1992p).

The indictment was especially controversial among police because an earlier grand jury hearing the matter decided the officer should not be charged, but New Jersey Attorney General Robert J. Del Tufo, citing "a major error in forensic and medical analysis by the Bergen County Medical Examiner" (*ibid.*), took the unusual step of dismissing that grand jury and convening a second one, which returned the indictment. Breaching the rules of secrecy governing grand juries, a majority of the first grand jury publicly criticized the attorney general's decision to disregard their verdict as an "injustice" to the families of both the slain youth and the police officer (*ibid.*). A Teaneck Police captain said that the agency's

> "officers had always prided themselves on being restrained and nonconfrontational and that they were embittered after the shooting about charges that they had harassed teenagers, particularly blacks. 'We thought we were doing well and

we had no inkling the community at large, including the black community, thought the way we were doing our job was unsatisfactory. There's a conflict between people calling for service and the rights of individuals they're complaining about. It's a Catch-22' " (Hanley 1991; see also Hanley 1990; Wakin 1990).

While the killing of a black youth with a shot in the back by a white Minneapolis police officer on December 1, 1990 did not produce civil disturbances, it led to a protracted series of police-community hostilities, charges and counter charges of racism, including threats and attempts to shoot police. In mid-February 1991, less than three weeks prior to the Rodney King beating, Minneapolis Chief John Laux reported that "[r]elations between police and the black community 'are certainly as tense as it's ever been here.... There's no time in my 23 years that it has been any greater" (Harrison 1991).

On May 5, 1991, in the nation's capital, a black-Hispanic clash again prompted rioting—this time after the nonfatal shooting of a Salvadoran immigrant by a rookie black District of Columbia policewoman in the Mount Pleasant neighborhood. The suspect reportedly brandished a knife during his arrest for public intoxication, but doubts among the local Hispanic community about that version of events[2] prompted violent protest (*Crime Control Digest* 1991h: 8). Some alleged that, when shot, the immigrant was in handcuffs; police denied the allegation, saying that he was shot for lunging at the officer with a knife (Ayres 1991: A10). As dawn approached, more than 30 stores had been looted (Spolar and Wilgoren 1992), 10 police officers injured—one critically—and cars and trucks set afire (Ayres 1991: A10).

> *"In the first half of this century there were 30 major ['race riots'], more than 20 from 1915 to 1920, which was before, during and after World War I. The worst was in Chicago in 1919. In almost all, whites were the aggressors and blacks were attacked. What changes in the 1960s is that African-Americans become the aggressors. The Watts riot of 1965 exemplifies this change. And it's that image that most Americans have embedded in their minds because of the nearness in time and modern media technology"* (Timothy Gilfoyle, Assistant Professor of History, Loyola University-Chicago, quoted in Galloway 1992: 4; see also Sipchen 1992: A18).

The Metropolitan Washington, D.C. Police Department's clash with residents of the Mount Pleasant neighborhood was renewed on May 11, 1992 after police arrested a Hispanic man for fighting in a restaurant. For about four hours a multi-ethnic crowd of several dozen

---

[2] Some of the questions about official versions of the encounter may have stemmed from transplanted skepticism concerning police abuse and government cover-ups (see Krauss 1991). A Salvadoran was shot fatally by National Guard members stationed in Los Angeles to restore order after the south central Los Angeles riot in 1992. Family members of the decedent questioned the National Guard's insistence that the soldiers shot to protect their lives as the Salvadoran immigrant attempted to run them down with his car. Their skepticism was heightened when Los Angeles officials made them wait several days to see their relative's body. "It was not unusual," one of the family members said,

> "for army officials in [El Salvador] to falsify autopsy reports to cover up atrocities against civilians. * * * Sometimes the authorities would get the doctors to bathe the bodies to wash away all signs of having been shot at close range.... If my brother-in-law truly did try to attack them, for whatever reason, then I will be the first one to say that he was at fault. But if they only shot him to shoot him, then I don't believe that is correct" (Newman 1992).

youngsters fought police, threw rocks and bottles, started several fires, and looted a neighborhood convenience store (*New York Times* 1992f).[3]

In 1992, shortly before this book went to press, south central Los Angeles, site of the devastating 1965 Watts riot, again erupted in a wave of arson, murder, vandalism, and looting that surpassed the 1965 insurrection in personal and property losses. Again, the spark was community resentment of police use of force. By the end of the third night of chaos, the Los Angeles County Coroner put the death toll attributable to the rioting at 44 people, 10 more than the casualties in Watts 27 years earlier (CBS network radio broadcast, May 2, 1992). Despite cloudless skies for the first three nights of turmoil, it was not until the third night, Friday, May 1, that the smoke from what were then estimated to be more than 6,400 arson fires had cleared enough for Angelenos to see the moon (CBS network radio broadcast, May 2, 1992; *Crime Control Digest* 1992g: 2).

The rioting subsided by May 3, but in the days following a number of people hospitalized earlier succumbed to their injuries. By May 22, nearly three weeks after the killing subsided, the coroner's office reported that 60 people died in riot-related violence, including 9 or 10 shot fatally by police or the National Guard (Reinhold 1992: 1; Stevenson 1992; Cannon and Smith 1992; Horrock 1992; *Crime Control Digest* 1992g: 2).[4] On May 6, the *Los Angeles Times* (Zamichow 1992: B12) reported the ethnic and gender mix of 58 people said to have perished as a result of the riot. Twenty-five (43 percent) were black, 19 (33 percent) were Hispanic, 10 (17 percent) were white, 2 (4 percent) were Asian, and 2 (4 percent) were of unknown heritage (total exceeds 100 percent due to rounding). Of the same 58, 50 (86 percent) were male, 7 (12 percent) were female, and one body (2 percent) was so badly burned that its gender could not be determined. The May 18, 1992, issue of *Newsweek* magazine profiled each of 54 persons whose deaths had been attributed to the rioting, of whom 10 were said to have been shot fatally by Los Angeles Police Department (LAPD) officers, Los Angeles County Sheriff's deputies, or the National Guard (*Newsweek* 1992). At about the same time, the *Washington Post* reported that "police killed nine rioters," adding, "...but rioters killed no police" (Norris, et al. 1992: A1). An additional 2,300 people were estimated to have been injured (Cannon and Smith 1992; *Law Enforcement News* 1992d: 7).

Besides running the daily casualty figures, the national media were rightly beginning to question them, cautioning that "some of the...deaths [may have resulted not from] rioting [but from] the normal violence endemic to large cities" (Taylor and Cannon 1992: A1; see also Norris, et al. 1992). By early June 1992, official sources (the County Coroner) and media analysts (principally the *Los Angeles Times*) had begun to suggest that some of the 60 deaths earlier ascribed to the riot were in fact unrelated (Zamichow 1992). Newspaper analysts said as many as 15 of the 60 died under circumstances not linked to the rioting (Mydans 1992a). A riot death toll of 45, analysts observed, would still mean that the L.A. riot had eclipsed the 1967 Detroit riot's record casualty toll of 43 (*ibid.*). In mid-August, the Coroner issued a new estimate: 51 people had died as a direct result of the riot (Lacey 1992; *New York Times* 1992s). One commentator called this "the most violent American civil disturbance since the

---

[3] One police official linked the disturbance to the tense atmosphere in many communities across America following the acquittal of Los Angeles officers for beating Rodney King. The widespread effects of that verdict are discussed below in the text.

[4] One news outlet (Horrock 1992) reported *19* slayings by police, but this may have been a typographical error, since no other newspaper, news magazine, or broadcast news story we could locate ever repeated so high a number.

Irish poor burned Manhattan in 1863" (Davis 1992: 743; see also Sipchen 1992: A18).

Dollar estimates of property damage fluctuated as well but were consistently described in the *hundreds* of millions. As the night-time curfew was lifted by the City, services began to be restored to the affected areas, property damage estimates rose to as much as $1 billion (Stevenson 1992; Reinhold 1992; *Law Enforcement News* 1992d: 7; some even suggested *3 billion* in damages—*Chicago Tribune* 1992a). Estimates of how much of the losses would be covered by insurance ran from only about $200 million (Crenshaw 1992) to $775 million (Kerr 1992: section 3, p. 6). Official reports on the number of arson fires set during the several days of rioting fluctuated wildly, beginning in the hundreds during the height of the chaos; rising about a week after the insurrection ceased to several thousand fires that were said to have destroyed approximately 5,200 buildings (*Crime Control Digest* 1992g: 2); and finally, by early June, being revised downward to 750 (Mydans 1992a; *New York Times* 1992d). The revision from over 5,000 to less than 1,000 was explained by local fire department officials as based on taking "into account multiple emergency calls and multiple visits by firefighters to the same fires" (Mydans 1992a). The later estimate of 750 arson fires packed into about four days the number of arsons Los Angeles would normally experience in about 60 days and overwhelmed the City fire department's squad of 17 arson investigators (*New York Times* 1992d).

Nobody reading this book in 1992 will need to be reminded what triggered the late April-early May rioting in Los Angeles: the verdict on April 29 acquitting the four officers charged with criminally assaulting Rodney King in March 1991,[5] a videotaped beating that was later broadcast worldwide. Urban watchers, who recalled that Miami's riots of May 1980 and December 1990 were both sparked by community outrage over the acquittal of police for allegedly using excessive force, could only shake their heads over the playing out of the adage that those who ignore the mistakes of history are bound to repeat them. Anger over the Los Angeles verdict fanned the embers of local grievances in other cities, too, producing a melange of violent protests and opportunistic crimes in the days following the verdict. Even the protests were an uncertain mixture of spontaneous outrage over the courtroom outcome and demonstrations whipped up by what *U.S. News and World Report* once called "provocateurs [who twist police brutality] into racial morality plays" (Witkin, et al. 1990: 34). Among the communities hit with a range of attacks on police officers or police property, racially motivated assaults by citizens on one another, arson, vandalism, and looting that observers connected to the Los Angeles verdict were Atlanta, Las Vegas, Tampa, Seattle, San Francisco, St. Louis, San Diego, New York, San Jose, Madison (Wisconsin), Toledo, Gary (Indiana), Charleston (South Carolina), Omaha, Minneapolis, Pittsburgh, Montgomery County (Maryland), Mobile and Birmingham (Alabama), New Rochelle (New York) and others (*Crime Control Digest* 1992h: 4; CBS network radio broadcasts, May 1 and 2, 1992; K. Sullivan 1992; Smothers 1992; Richardson 1992; Coates 1992; *Law Enforcement News* 1992d: 11; Johnson 1992a, 1992b). Violent protests were not confined to the United States. Chanting Rodney King's name, demonstrators protesting the May 2 killing of a black man by a Toronto undercover police officer smashed store windows and looted when a peaceful May 5 rally turned violent (*Washington Post* 1992; *Law Enforcement News* 1992d: 11).

To be sure, in Toronto, Los Angeles, and many other cities, there is reason to believe,

---

[5] The facts of the Rodney King beating in March 1991 are set forth near the end of Chapter 2. We also address in detail in Chapters 2 and 6 some steps that police departments might take to deal with the credibility problems created for law enforcement agencies everywhere by the King beating and the April 1992 state court acquittal of the officers involved.

as suggested above, that the looting was perpetrated by a mixture of people infuriated over the injustice of the King verdict and career criminals—persons who may have had Rodney King's name on their lips but almost assuredly had larceny in their hearts. Thus, the City Attorney's office in Los Angeles, having run criminal history checks on persons arrested for looting and having reviewed the nature of the goods being looted as order began to be restored in early May 1992, concluded that "a major element of professional criminals were involved in the preliminary aspect to this civil disobedience" (Thomas-Lester 1992).

The fact that some business establishments in south central Los Angeles were looted and torched by black offenders despite the hastily posted signs in the windows proclaiming the businesses to be "black owned" (Whitaker 1992: 118) is probably testament both to the larcenous intentions with which some of the rioters acted and to the illiteracy of others. The latter possibility is a poignant emblem of the helplessness that can turn anger into anarchy.

As the summer of 1992 began, there were some clashes around the country that police said were delayed reactions to the acquittals of the officers for beating Rodney King. We noted above the May 11 disturbances in the Mount Pleasant community of Washington, D.C. In Chicago, when celebrations of the Bulls winning the National Basketball Association championship on June 15 turned violent in several locations (including looting, arson, the injury of 95 police officers, damage to more than 60 police vehicles, and the shooting of one man by police for threatening an officer with a gun), Police Superintendent Matt Rodriguez linked the trouble to three factors: "warm weather, the tight economy and the tense environment in the aftermath of the Los Angeles riots" (Terry 1992; Fountain and Kates 1992; compare Clark 1992, reporting the Chicago Superintendent's account of how his city avoided rioting in the immediate aftermath of the verdict acquitting the L.A. officers of beating Rodney King).

> "When Rumor Mixes with Rage:
>
> "MINNEAPOLIS—The gunfire rang out at dusk. A 14-year-old black youth lay bleeding next to his bicycle. Word spread fast: The cops did it—white cops.
>
> "Hostilities boiled to a rage. Hundreds of people chased up and down the street. The time had come for vengeance. A house was firebombed. Two television journalists were pelted with bricks.
>
> "But the rumor was false. A boy had been shot, but he had been shot by an elderly black man.
>
> "Yet, in these days of anger and mistrust, even a rumor can start a fire. In the aftermath of the verdict in the Los Angeles police brutality case, rage is filling the streets of black neighborhoods like a river of gasoline, waiting for a match, even here in the middle of America" (Johnson 1992a).

Whether linked to the Rodney King affair or not, police shootings continued in the summer of 1992 to demonstrate a capacity to ignite violent community protest. In New York City on July 6 in the predominantly Hispanic Washington Heights neighborhood in upper Manhattan a group of Dominicans, accusing police of having killed an "unarmed and possibly unconscious" man on July 3, broke out of a peaceful protest march led by a city councilman and attacked police, turned over cars, and set fire to numerous cars and several buildings. One man was killed in the conflict when he fell from a rooftop while fleeing from police (residents claim police pushed him); 20, including seven officers, were injured on July 6 (*New York Times* 1992i). Violent protests continued for six days, leading to 139 arrests, the one death that occurred the first night, and 90 injuries—74 of them to police officers. Fourteen buildings were set afire and 121 vehicles were damaged by the time the violence subsided (Sullivan 1992: A15).

Police disputed the protesters' accounts of the shooting, stating that the slain individual, Jose Garcia, was carrying a loaded revolver and was killed as he struggled with an officer (*New York Times* 1992i; Sullivan 1992). The situation was further complicated by community allegations, which authorities promised to investigate, that the officer who shot the Dominican man may have been engaged in illegal activity—trying to shake down drug dealers—at the time of the struggle (Dao 1992; Goodstein 1992). The director of the Mayor's Office for Latino Affairs' said Garcia's death was "the drop that made the cup overflow.... The Latino community is the poorest in the city, has the highest unemployment and the highest rate of dropouts.... I suspect [the riot] is the culmination of a number of frustrations, unemployment being the biggest after the issue of police brutality" (Goodstein 1992; see also Gonzalez 1992; Giuliani 1992; Alexander 1992). Fearing a resumption of rioting if the officer at issue was not indicted by the grand jury, City Hall officials, police, and representatives of the Manhattan District Attorney's Office planned a multi-faceted approach to preventing collective violence in Washington Heights, including meetings with community leaders and deployment of hundreds of officers to stand watch and make a show of force in the affected Dominican neighborhood. The grand jury's decision declining to indict, evidently well-grounded (McFadden 1992; *New York Times* 1992w), was suppressed for several days while such preventive measures were taken and was revealed publicly on September 10 (Sullivan 1992).

In Tyler, Texas, on July 10, 1992, a grand jury of eight whites and two blacks declined to indict a white officer for accidentally shooting and killing an 84-year-old black woman during a "botched" drug raid in the nearby Smith County town of Kilgore on January 29, 1992. The fatal shooting of Annie Rae Dixon aroused the anger of the local black community, which planned protest demonstrations over the course of the summer, citing other instances of alleged police abuse of force (Suro 1992).

"Try to imagine what it must feel like to know that the closest anyone will come to respecting you is to be afraid of you. If you had other resources, you might try to relieve their fear in order to be seen as a worthwhile human being. But if the threat of violence is your only currency..." (Columnist William Raspberry 1992, commenting on the connection between what he termed the "outrageous Simi Valley verdict [acquitting the officers who beat Rodney King] and the outrageous violence that followed it").

Often in America, protests over police action have been skirmishes in larger battles over local and national socio-economic policy. Commenting on the spring 1992 L.A. riot, Davis (1992: 743) observed:

> "An analysis of the first 5,000 arrests from all over the city revealed that 52 percent were poor Latinos, 10 percent whites and only 38 percent blacks.... [T]he nation's first multiracial riot was as much about empty bellies and broken hearts as it was about police batons and Rodney King."

An important effect of the skirmishes on the police has been to substantially elevate their public profile. As Walker (1976: 702-03) observed,

> "A related series of social crises—urban racial disorders, anti-war political protest, and the emergence of a widespread drug culture—thrust the American policeman to the forefront of national attention.... In some instances it became apparent that the conduct of police officers served to perpetuate and even escalate the violence."

The perception of the police as guardians of society's status quo arrangements is, of course, not new and not entirely inaccurate. In a number of respects, police protection of the status quo is entirely proper and well within the police oath of office. Still, there are times when defense of the status quo is unprofessional. This nation's (and other nations') sordid histories of *de facto* and *de jure* race, class, and religious discrimination repeatedly thrust the police into the role of enforcing injustice, sometimes with brutality and caprice that lingers long in the memories of its victims and their descendants (Williams and Murphy 1990). Regardless of his or her *personal* appraisal of current national and local progress in redressing past institutional inequities, no American police administrator can afford to adopt a *professional* stance that denies the influence on current day attitudes and, perhaps, behaviors of past hatred and hate violence.[6]

Sadly, holding responsible views and a track record of behaving honorably will not necessarily immunize a police force, its leadership, or its community from violent protest when outrages such as the April 1992 acquittal of Rodney King's assailants lay spark to the kindling of accumulated social discontent. The local police for some people have become a readily available symbol of other oppressors and of oppressive public and private institutions generally. Among the cities suffering violence in the days following the Rodney King verdict were those with police executives and elected leadership

"Asked once about his distaste for the forward pass, Ohio State's legendary coach Woody Hayes replied that three things could happen when you throw the ball and two of them were bad. The announcement [two days ago] of federal indictments of four Los Angeles police officers in the Rodney King case evokes a similar reaction.

"A number of things could happen as a result of this case, most of them bad. * * * One negative result is certain to be a widespread public impression that the constitutional protection against double jeopardy has been set aside to allow the four officers to be tried again.... This impression will persist despite the fact that the principle of separate federal and state sovereignty in such cases is well established....

"Another negative result will be to place jurors in the federal case—assuming an impartial jury can be assembled—under enormous pressure to convict. Having seen the results of the verdict of acquittal in the state trial—60 people dead and $850 million in damage in the worst urban riot of the century—the jurors would have to be intimidated by the prospect of a repetition. * * *

"Nothing seems certain any longer in this case that once looked so certain. But one thing ought to be clear: Whether or not the four officers can be shown to have been responsible legally, Rodney King suffered a grievous moral wrong and grievous bodily injuries on the streets of Los Angeles. * * * [T]he City of Los Angeles will [quite likely] pay handsomely in damages—as it should. Would that could be the end of it. Unfortunately, the new indictments ensure that it will not be" (Chicago Tribune *1992c*).

whose sensitivity to race relations and dedication to overcoming past institutional racism and police abuse are beyond question.

As a long series of riot-study commissions have concluded, our society's simmering

---

[6] We shall return in Chapter 4 to the question of what the available data might tell us about the motivations—racial and otherwise—with which police and civilians shoot one another in the United States.

socioeconomic and political problems are so potent that even the most respectful and vital police-community partnerships cannot keep the American melting pot from periodically boiling
over in violent outbursts. Indeed, if improved policing is thought of simply as a way to keep
the lid more securely on society's cauldron, the heroic efforts of current-day police reformers
such as Herman Goldstein, Mark Moore, Darrel Stephens, Lee Brown, Cornelius Behan, and
others will have been in vain. They may even have unwittingly insulated our nation from a
shattering awareness of the need to deal promptly and profoundly with the emergency of
social-economic injustice. Fortunately, there are indications that a majority of the American
public is beginning to realize that police cannot be expected by themselves to ensure domestic
tranquility. In a *New York Times*/CBS News national poll conducted May 6-8, 1992, in the
immediate aftermath of the Los Angeles riot, "majorities of both whites and blacks said that
investing in jobs and job training programs is a better way of preventing future turmoil than
strengthening police forces" (Toner 1992: A1).

> *"Justice without force is powerless; force without justice is tyrannical"* (17th Century French philosopher Blaise Pascal, quoted in Peter 1979: 194).

As calls rang out for the appointment
of yet another riot-study commission after
the Los Angeles insurrection of 1992—and
as former FBI Director William Webster
and Police Foundation President Hubert
Williams were named to head an investigative panel[7]—observers recalled Judge A.
Leon Higginbotham, Jr.'s admonition in
1968 on release of the Kerner Commission report that he co-authored. Judge Higginbotham
cautioned the nation against its impulse to convene "temporary study commissions to probe
the causes of racism, or poverty, or crime or the urban crisis." America, in his view, should
"not [appoint] more commissions to study the same problems, but [instead should] prompt[ly]
implement...their many valuable recommendations" (McAllister 1992). As the sounds of
gunfire, looting, and vandalism died out in south central Los Angeles in May 1992, Los
Angeles Urban League President John Mack pled, "I sincerely hope that this time around,
people will learn a lesson that apparently was not learned following the 1965 Watts
rebellion.... The solution is not simply to jail the looters and restore order to the streets of Los
Angeles. I believe...democracy is on trial" (Stone 1992). To paraphrase a commentator who
lamented the seeming blindness of some politicians to the relationship between the rioting and
long-standing neglect of urban problems, as a nation we need to better understand the
connection between what we deplore and what we ignore. For some among us, it is clearly
too late. Scholar William Julius Wilson, after the chaos subsided in Los Angeles in early May
1992, commented on how much had changed in three decades for destitute, young black males

---

[7] Webster and Williams in May 1992 "were named special advisers to the Los Angeles Police
Commission and asked to examine the LAPD's preparedness before the riots and its response once the
violence erupted April 29..." (L. Berger 1992a: B1). The Webster panel on August 27 released as an
interim report the results of a public opinion survey exploring whether the LAPD shares responsibility
for the devastation of the city (because of poor departmental preparation for quelling any civil
disturbance that might follow acquittal of the LAPD officers for assaulting Rodney King and slow and
inadequate response once the violence began). Among other issues, the survey also explored the
community's views about the adequacy of the Department's staffing to properly police the City; 82
percent of the 1,000 respondents "believed that the LAPD was understaffed" (*ibid.*: B8). It seemed
relatively clear to many observers that one of the central objectives of the Webster panel was going to
be making the case to a recession-plagued electorate that the LAPD is "under-resourced in terms of
personnel and infrastructure," as a panel staff member put it. A final report to the Police Commission
was expected in October 1992, according to L.A. lawyer Richard J. Stone, "general counsel and chief
of staff to the probe's chairmen" (*ibid.*: B1, B8).

living in America's cities: "In his time, Martin Luther King could still have a dream. These kids can't even imagine a future" (Wilson 1992).

American police agencies and their service populations have been confronted with riots and the other risks associated with controversial uses of deadly force ever since police in this nation, after nearly 75 years without sidearms, first started routinely carrying them during the late 1850s (Miller 1975; Sherman 1980a: 75; Kennett and Anderson 1975: 91). For example, during a 10-month period in 1857 and 1858, four New York City police officers were killed in the line of duty, and, in the tense aftermath, a city policeman shot and killed a fleeing suspect in an unrelated case. A *New York Times* editorial was sharply critical, declaring, "If a policeman needs to defend his life, the use of force is permissible, but if he is chasing a suspect, he has no right to shoot the man." More than 130 years later, these events and the debate over them continue with only slight variation on the theme (the U.S. Supreme Court's 1985 ruling in *Tennessee v. Garner*, as we shall discuss, has narrowed the scope of controversy over official policy to a certain extent).

The factors that for generations have placed police use of deadly force high on the civic policy agenda include crime problems, the public's ready access to handguns, conflicting community perceptions and values, the limited technology available to police for the immediate apprehension of fleeing suspects, and, as noted earlier, the potential of questionable and even proper police actions to provide a catalyst for community turmoil.

More is known now about the nature and frequency of shootings in which police are involved, although we have nothing resembling a comprehensive, continuous national picture of these violent police-civilian encounters. Even *police* insight into the nature, extent, causes, and prevention of police shootings tends to draw on anecdotal rather than systematic information, and insight is highly localized. Tactically useful knowledge about how to apprehend potentially dangerous criminal suspects with a minimum of bloodshed remains rudimentary.

This state of affairs poses a dilemma for public policymakers, who do not have the luxury of waiting for systematic data or tactical advances before making concrete decisions about how the police are supposed to conduct themselves. The atmosphere surrounding the "deadly force debate" is charged with emotion, fear, entrenched assumptions, class- and race-based suspicions, and virtually intractable value conflicts. For some partisans, the controversy is part of a larger quest to "handcuff" or "unhandcuff" the police. Virtually any deadly force policy decision is likely to be challenged by one constituency or another—although the observer must be careful not to allow his or her own prejudice to produce overly simplistic notions of how the different constituencies are likely to line up on any particular deadly force issue. Debate over police use of deadly force raises issues that no responsible public official can disregard:

- If we clamp down too strictly on police use of deadly force, will we endanger the police and the public by permitting rapists, robbers, and murderers to evade arrest?

- If we are too lax in our controls, will we imperil the police and the public by allowing needless killing or maiming (some of it motivated by prejudice), discouraging the community cooperation necessary for effective police work, provoking retaliatory violence against the police and, in particularly volatile situations, even providing the spark that rekindles the embers of community conflagrations?

SIGNIFICANT RIOT COMMISSIONS 1917-82*

■ *Special Committee Authorized by Congress (1917, East St. Louis, Illinois). Appointed by the House of Representatives, chaired by Ben Johnson. Published* Report of the Special Committee Authorized by Congress.

■ *Chicago Commission on Race Relations (1919, Chicago). Appointed by Governor Frank Lowden, chaired by Edgar A. Bancroft. Published* The Negro in Chicago: A Study of Race Relations and a Race Riot.

■ *Mayor's Commission on Conditions in Harlem (1935, New York City). Appointed by Mayor Fiorello La Guardia, chaired by Charles Roberts. Published* The Negro in Harlem: A Report on Social and Economic Conditions Responsible for the Outbreak of March 19, 1935.

■ *Governor's Committee to Investigate Riot (1943, Detroit). Appointed by Governor Harry Kelly, chaired by Herbert J. Rushton. Published* Final Report of the Governor's Committee to Investigate Riot.

■ *Governor's Commission on the Los Angeles (Watts) Riots (the "McCone Commission," 1965, Los Angeles). Appointed by Governor Edmund Brown, Sr., chaired by former CIA director John A. McCone (Serrano 1992b: B8) and vice-chaired by Warren Christopher, who later chaired the commission appointed after the Los Angeles Police Department's beating of Rodney King. Published* Violence in the City—An End or a Beginning?

■ *National Advisory Commission on Civil Disorders (1968, Washington, D.C.). Appointed by President Lyndon B. Johnson, chaired by Otto Kerner. Published* The Kerner Report.

■ *Governor's Select Commission on Civil Disorders (1968, New Jersey). Appointed by Governor Richard J. Hughes, chaired by Robert D. Lilley. Published* Report for Action.

■ *Chicago Riot Study Committee (1968, Chicago). Appointed by Mayor Richard J. Daley, chaired by Richard B. Austin. Published* Final Report of the Chicago Riot Study Committee.

■ *National Commission on the Causes and Prevention of Violence (1970, Washington, D.C.). Appointed by President Lyndon B. Johnson, chaired by Milton S. Eisenhower. Published* To Establish Justice, To Ensure Domestic Tranquility.

■ *National Commission on Campus Unrest (1970, Washington, D.C.). Appointed by President Richard M. Nixon, chaired by William W. Scranton. Published* The Scranton Report.

■ *U.S. Civil Rights Commission (1982, Miami, Florida). Appointed by President Ronald Reagan, chaired by Clarence Pendleton. Published* Confronting Racial Isolation in Miami.
* *Based on McAllister (1992) and Platt (1971).*

No wonder reasonable people differ on when police should be allowed to use their firearms and on how to interpret the conduct of an officer and a suspect that often occurs out of public view and under ambiguous circumstances. Indeed, the debate rages as vehemently *within* the police world as it does across the police-civilian boundary. This is sometimes obscured by simplistic, monolithic perceptions of the police profession, and by the tendency of many police practitioners to close ranks when criticized by the news media, community groups, or other "outsiders." The aim of this book is not to resolve this perennial debate but to inform it by surveying the hard data available.

On what issues would empirical information be helpful? Several come to mind:

- How much shooting—not only *by* police but *of* police—is there now and what does the track record of the past few decades look like?
- Who gets shot, why, and by whom?
- Is the picture significantly different from city to city?
- Is the current level of shooting too high? What yardstick do we use to answer that question? And what values influence our selection of a particular yardstick?
- What rules govern officer discretion to shoot?
- How controllable are shootings of and by police? What techniques seem to work?
- What social costs might these techniques impose?

These and related questions have been addressed by a growing body of operational and academic research over the past 15 to 20 years. This empirical research[8] has been conducted partly as a reaction to the findings of riot-study commissions and partly in response to the research funding that became available as public and private grant-making institutions attempted to increase the knowledge on which key public policy decisions are based.[9]

As the U.S. Department of Justice undertook a multi-faceted examination of use of force by police after the March 3, 1991, videotaped beating of motorist Rodney G. King by Los Angeles police officers, one of the components that DOJ's National Institute of Justice (NIJ) quite sensibly included was research on killings *of* police officers (National Institute of Justice 1991: 36-40; 1992). Separate NIJ-sponsored studies will be conducted during 1992 by the FBI and the Police Foundation and will involve interviews with both victims and offenders in deadly weapon assaults on officers as well as case studies in police departments to explore the factors associated with police killings and their prevention. As is implied by NIJ's sponsorship of research on officer victimizations at the same time that the Institute has commissioned studies on curtailing police abuse of force, attempting to examine use of force by police in isolation from the use of force against police, or vice versa, is, in our view, a poor methodology. Doing so would eliminate from the analysis a crucial part of the dynamics of police-civilian violence.

The deadly force debate and the violent encounters that fuel it also have spawned a considerable body of legal commentary, litigation, and training guides. The most casual

---

[8] By "empirical" we mean research that is not merely theoretical but attempts to portray and understand police field and administrative work based on observation or review of records describing the activity.

[9] Compare Cordner's (1985) propositions about the limited ways in which research findings actually influence significant policy decisions. He argues, among other things, that most policymakers employ research to support a decision they wish to make anyway rather than being led to their decision by the empirical evidence.

perusal of any police magazine or trade show today reveals a host of offerings in the realm of "officer survival" simulation training, risk-management seminars focusing on police use of firearms and high-speed pursuits, and the like. The Supreme Court's pronouncement in the landmark case of *Tennessee v. Garner* (1985) did not put police practices litigators on the unemployment lines. The pages of such newsletters as *Liability Reporter* (published by Americans for Effective Law Enforcement) and *National Bulletin on Police Misconduct* (prepared by Quinlan Publishing) continue to be filled with accounts of civil litigation charging that police shootings stemmed from deficient policy, negligent selection, training, and supervision of police personnel, and so forth.

This book makes no effort to report systematically on developments in the *legal* commentary or *court* decisions. Where mention of legal issues is essential for an understanding of the policy environment in which shooting patterns have emerged (e.g., in the period following the *Tennessee v. Garner* ruling), we will offer brief references to court cases. But the reader interested in the evolution of legal doctrine on the use of deadly force by police should turn to other sources, many of which are cited in the Supreme Court's opinion in the *Garner* case and in subsequent court decisions. The reader also can contact any of the widely publicized liability-management training programs offered by various professional organizations for information on both the evolution and current status of legal doctrine. Also, one of the most current and most cogent summaries of the evolution of deadly force policy in the United States is contained in Alpert and Fridell's recent volume *Police Vehicles and Firearms* (1992).

What we attempt in this book is a relatively thorough survey of the empirical research in an effort to describe the present state of knowledge about the use of deadly force by and against police in the United States.[10] As implied earlier, it is not merely a spirit of "being balanced" that causes us to combine information about shootings *by* and *of* police in a single inquiry. Rather, we believe that an essential ingredient in any analysis of why police shoot people is an effort to appreciate the risk that police run of being shot or otherwise seriously

---

[10] Most of the English language deadly force empirical research focuses on police-involved violent confrontations in the United States. Perhaps the earliest empirical study of shootings of and by police was of the Shanghai, China, Police Force in the 1930s and 1940s by British-trained police captains Fairbairn and Sykes (1987 reprint of 1942 study). Their recommendations for handgun shooting technique were based on analysis of 666 armed encounters between members of the 6,000-officer Shanghai Department and suspects over 12½ years, in which 42 police were killed and 100 were wounded and 260 suspects were killed and 193 were wounded (*ibid.*: 8, 12). It is safe to assume that, as the British police today increasingly equip themselves with firearms (see, e.g., Waddington 1988; Harper 1992; Woollons 1992), operational research in the United Kingdom will pay more attention to deadly force policy and practice.

For discussion of the findings of a judicial inquiry into the slaying of 17 Palestinians by Israeli police during a clash in Jerusalem in 1990, see Brinkley (1991). Elliot (1979) focuses on use of deadly force by police in Australia, and Swanton and Psaila (1986) study fatal and nonfatal shootings *of* Australian police during the period 1964-83. Whittingham (1984), using United Nations and Statistics Canada data, examines killings of police in Canada and 13 other nations, finding that Canada had the fourth highest rate of officer murders (0.16 per one million population), with 73 officers slain in 65 incidents during the period 1961-80 (the United States' rate of police murders during the same 20-year period was 0.41 per one million population). Janssen and Hackler (1985) also studied killings of police in Canada; and Chappell and Graham (1985) studied the use of deadly force *by* Canadian officers, focusing intensively on 13 cases in which British Columbia officers killed suspects from 1970 through 1982. The International Criminal Police Organization (INTERPOL) (1969) contains data on police-involved shootings in various nations.

injured in the line of duty.

Besides summarizing a great deal of published data, this report also presents some previously unpublished, reasonably current data concerning the use of firearms by and against police in several large agencies:

- the Atlanta Police Department
- the Chicago Police Department
- the Dallas Police Department
- the Houston Police Department
- the Kansas City, MO Police Department
- the Los Angeles Police Department
- the Metro-Dade County, FL Police Department
- the New York City Police Department
- the New York City Transit Police Department
- the Philadelphia Police Department
- the Saint Louis Metropolitan Police Department
- the San Diego Police Department
- the Santa Ana, CA Police Department

We make no claim that these cities are a nationally representative sample and therefore characteristic of the patterns of officer-involved shootings in other agencies. We have sought and obtained data from these departments largely based on our prior professional associations with the chief or other key departmental officials. We also chose to seek data from fairly large agencies so that the numbers of officer-involved shootings might be large enough to permit some generalization about patterns over time. Some researchers have cautioned that

> "[p]olice agencies which allow researchers access to their files are probably more progressive and more committed to eliminating abuses in...[the] area [of deadly force]. In addition, they probably have less to hide from the public" (Blumberg 1983: 299; see also Alpert and Fridell 1992: 54).

If our participating departments are atypically good, so be it. Surely some readers might question that characterization of one or more of the agencies. In any event, given the sorry state of affairs in national record keeping on police decisions to employ lethal force—a problem about which we will have more to say in Chapter 2—groups such as the Police Executive Research Forum have tried to do the best we can on a shoe-string budget to take some sort of national snapshot of the prevalence and nature of extreme police-civilian violence.

Another element in this "snapshot" we offer is previously unpublished FBI data on justifiable homicides by police nationwide and in major cities throughout the nation. These data cover the period 1985 through 1990 and thus supplement the important work published by Sherman and Cohn (1986) covering the period from 1970 through 1984. Moreover, we go beyond Sherman and Cohn's use of the FBI data by employing the information not only to portray the frequency of deadly force incidents (and the continuing problem with inadequate national tallies) but also to provide a national picture of the race/ethnicity of the officers who took the lives of criminal suspects and the race/ethnicity and "precipitating conduct" of those suspects.

Although reporting the new FBI data and the shooting tallies from the major cities listed above makes a contribution by providing analysts and practitioners with access to information they otherwise might not have an opportunity to compile, we are well aware that enumerating a jurisdiction's shooting cases is merely the first step in attempting to understand the causes and control methods for police-involved shootings. We use demographic information (e.g., levels of homicide and arrests for violent offenses) to place the shooting tallies in some broader context, but for the most part we have not had the opportunity to explore the *details* of the shootings—"mobilizing" events, tactical efforts to defuse tense confrontations, officers' reasons for shooting, administrative control measures such as training and policy, and so forth. Behind every shooting that is presented as a two-dimensional statistic is a complex human story that must be understood if one is to make genuine progress in devising feasible systems for safeguarding police and their clientele. Fortunately, some of the research

The officer "swears he saw the bullet leave the gun, even though he knows nobody really can.... 'I saw his shirttail fly up when the bullet went through him. He was going down and I swear he was getting bigger. It's amazing: After all these years it's difficult to talk about. You know that you're killing someone. You think, My God! You want him to stop. To drop the knife. I could actually see the trajectory of the bullet. I've shot millions of rounds and never seen one before. It's a physical and psychological phenomenon that cops go through when they shoot' " (Petrillo 1990b).

conducted over the past 25 years has begun to penetrate to this level of understanding, and we are able to report these findings both for the guidance they might offer and as illustrations of the kind of inquiries that probably should be made to follow up the presentation of new shooting tallies in this volume.

Still another previously unpublished (indeed, virtually unknown) data set that receives its first public discussion in these pages is in a study completed in 1978 by two Chicago police sergeants, Dennis Nowicki and Bernie Stahl (Nowicki and Stahl 1978). (Nowicki has since gone on to become a nationally respected police chief and, more recently, executive director of the Illinois Criminal Justice Information Authority.) The Nowicki-Stahl study is not only of high caliber, it is also historically important, for it represents one of the first comprehensive and candid looks at the hard questions surrounding police use of deadly force. Completed *before* then-New York City Police Department Sergeant James Fyfe's landmark study on shots fired by New York City officers (Fyfe 1978), the Nowicki-Stahl report employs data on shots fired (hits as well as misses) and does not shy away from addressing highly sensitive questions. Among the topics they explore are racism in police use of deadly force, dishonesty in the reporting of missed shots and accidental discharges as "warning shots," the danger posed to police officers by their own guns and their colleagues' guns, the quality of psychological screening of police recruits, the adequacy of training in deadly force decision making, and the sufficiency of departmental data collection on police-involved shootings.

In almost any major American police department in the 1990s, a report of the quality written by these Chicago sergeants would be a matter of pride and would represent some daring on the part of the authors and the administrators who allowed the report to be produced. For this report to have been written 14 years ago is remarkable. It is a shame Department administrators did not allow it to be published in its day (they ordered it suppressed lest it prove embarrassing to them). Had it been published upon completion, the Nowicki-Stahl report would have taken its place among the landmarks in early deadly force research alongside the work of Larry Sherman, Jim Fyfe, the Police Foundation, the Chicago

Law Enforcement Study Group, and a few other individuals or organizations. We are proud to be able to include data and observations from the Nowicki-Stahl report in our book.

The most recent prior report on police use of deadly force in major cities is Sherman and Cohn's 1986 publication, which covers only *killings* by police through 1984. As such, the present volume is the first comprehensive examination of deadly force questions since the *Tennessee v. Garner* decision in early 1985 and since much of the nation was hit by the crack cocaine epidemic in 1984 and 1985. Many in the criminal justice policy community believe that, more than any other single development, the emergence of crack has altered the level of violence in the nation (see, e.g., Police Foundation President Hubert Williams quoted in Horrock 1992: 1).[11] Add the violent propensity of persons under the influence of crack (and PCP) to the increased prevalence of semi-automatic and automatic weapons in the hands of citizens with little to lose, and the nation's police are understandably frightened. As a first effort to explore the level of shootings of and by American police in the second half of the 1980s and in the early 1990s, this book may shed light on the impact of crack and the police-civilian "arms race"—and on the efforts of police to minimize the resulting bloodshed. Much more research needs to be done to attempt to isolate the possible effects of crack, the arming of civilians, and other factors in changing the level of police-involved shootings in America.

This book is intended as a quick-reference tool for police practitioners, other government administrators, and journalists who might need information about various cities' experiences with police-involved shootings. Accordingly, the volume contains a detailed table of contents and index designed to help the reader needing information on a particular subject to locate it rapidly. This report is also intended for the reader who wishes to conduct more extensive and detailed analysis using the large and growing body of empirical literature on deadly force. Hence, we have frequently provided parenthetical or footnote references to useful studies. Full bibliographic information on all cited publications appears in the "References and Bibliography" section. Appendix C shows studies conducted over the past several decades that the reader may consult to find additional data or further discussion on officer-involved shootings for specified big cities.

Because, as we shall discuss, it is difficult to compare findings in most of the empirical studies of police-involved shootings, providing an overview of the collected learning in this body of work is a tricky business (Blumberg 1989; Binder and Fridell 1984). Simply tallying the findings on key issues from the different studies does not qualify as "accumulated wisdom," any more than mashing together a bunch of apples, oranges, and other fruit—some ripe, some rotten—makes great applesauce. Nevertheless, presenting an isolated abstract of each study without some cautious comparison is of little help to the reader. Mindful of the

---

[11] Chapman (1992) argues that the

"biggest reason for the escalating violence [in urban America] isn't drugs—it's the effort to eradicate them. With the spread of crack, the competition for drug turf has gotten more intense. In Chicago, [for example,] police commonly estimate that at least half of all murders are tied to the drug trade—usually gang members shooting it out to decide who gets to sell in that park or on this corner. That doesn't include the people killed during armed robberies and muggings committed by addicts in need of money to finance their habit. Tougher law enforcement isn't the answer: It's the problem. Every policy offensive has the perverse effect of driving up drug prices—raising the profits of the drug dealers who survive and increasing their incentive to expand sales through violence. When one dealer is arrested, bloody battles ensue to determine who gets his old business."

analogy to Winston Churchill's view of democracy ("the worst possible system, except for all the alternatives"), we have organized this volume's discussion of what is known about police-involved shootings according to the four principal tasks that many of the studies undertake:

- *counting* (efforts to identify with some precision the prevalence of police-involved shootings—Chapter 3);

- *describing* (characteristics of shooting incidents and their participants—Chapter 4);

- *explaining* (why certain shooting patterns emerge—Chapter 4); and

- *controlling* (identification and assessment of strategies for reducing the number of shootings of and by police—Chapter 5).

Before moving through the findings of earlier studies and reporting our own data in this fashion, however, Chapter 2 addresses the various challenges entailed in attempting to study the use of deadly force by and against police personnel. An understanding of these challenges will help the reader critically assess the research findings reported in this book and other studies and appraise decisions made by criminal justice administrators and other public officials aimed at reducing police-civilian violence.

A Note on the Accuracy of Data in and the Scope of this Book

We have made every effort in the preparation of this volume to be as accurate and complete as possible in presenting data. In obtaining information on police-involved shootings from departments or the FBI, for instance, we have checked, double-checked, and often triple-checked—both in writing and follow-up phone calls—to be sure we and those furnishing the data were communicating clearly concerning the meaning of the numbers being exchanged.

Still, it is inevitable in an effort like this, with literally thousands of numbers reported based on hundreds of calculations, that best efforts will not prevent all errors—mathematical or cerebral. We apologize to you, dear reader, for the few inevitable mistakes and enlist your assistance in identifying and correcting any errors you discover. If this volume proves to be of value to police practitioners, researchers, journalists, policymakers, and others, we anticipate preparing updated editions in the future.

Please call all numerical offenses and methodological misdemeanors to the attention of the lead author, who can be reached in the Police Executive Research Forum's Midwest Office. We would also welcome any suggestions readers might have for making this volume more "user friendly" for those with schedules that match their heavy responsibilities. This includes topics we have failed to address that you believe would be of broad interest to our diverse readership, topics you think we need to cover more completely, and index entries that would make it easier to locate needed information quickly. Thank you in advance for your help!

Chapter 2:

STUDYING THE USE
OF DEADLY FORCE

I. Why Practitioners Need to Understand Some Basic Problems in Data Collection and Analysis

The main audiences for whom this book is intended are police executives, public policymakers, and journalists—those who need quick access to accurate information on a wide array of topics concerning police-involved shootings. Criminal justice students and academicians will find some of the data and methodological discussions useful as part of their more intensive explorations of the role of police in a democratic state. Although *researchers* may have an interest in the methodological questions we touch on early in this volume, the *practitioner* using this book may reasonably ask why he or she should wade through a discussion of the difficulties of studying the use of deadly force by and against police. Several reasons come to mind:

■ Police over the past couple of decades have increasingly come to appreciate that well-designed research—on police tactics, on community perceptions, and so forth—is one of the important tools of professional planning, operations, and analysis (see, e.g., Eck 1984).

■ More specifically, police officials may find that, on short notice and in the context of community dissension over a police-involved shooting, they have to conduct a quick survey of the literature and of other law enforcement agencies to see what is known about a particular aspect of deadly force. In that situation, the police researchers will want to be able to frame their survey questions so as to identify precisely the information they are seeking. Having at hand a description of the most diversely used and most frequently misunderstood terms on the subject of deadly force should prove beneficial.

■ In addition, the police charged with providing background briefings to policymakers will want to be able to itemize efficiently the factors that may make casual generalization and quick and dirty comparison among police forces unreliable and irresponsible.

■ Finally, a police department may be confronted with a recently published study or news release that raises questions about the agency's professionalism in deadly force policy, training, practice, and administrative review. Although such criticism could be accurate to some degree, it is also possible that the critic has knowingly or accidentally taken a "cheap shot," based on a flawed method of comparing one police agency or one community with another.

What follows is *not* a highly technical discussion laden with statistical jargon. Indeed, our effort throughout this book is to present a vast array of research findings in language that speaks clearly to nonresearchers and researchers alike. Yogi Berra, when asked what the key to success in baseball is, answered without hesitation: "Baseball is 90 percent mental. The other *half* is physical." While Yogi might get lost in some of the tables and figures that follow, our interaction over the years with police executives and other policymakers gives us some confidence that we have struck an appropriate balance between precision and user friendliness.[1] When we touch on abstract, theoretical propositions, we have tried to discuss their practical implications. Perhaps a comedian best captured the way we hope in these pages to bring philosophical or other abstractions down to earth so that their implications for day-to-day decision making by practitioners become evident. In a metaphysical mood one day, the comic reflected, "What if everything is an illusion and nothing exists? In that case, I definitely overpaid for my carpet" (Knight-Ridder Newspapers 1991).

II.   *Some General Cautions*

The first and most general warning for the policymaker is to exercise caution in drawing broad conclusions about the use of deadly force by and against the police from the empirical literature. The research conducted to date has various limitations (some externally imposed). While there are great variations among the studies, the research generally suffers from several kinds of flaws: incompleteness and inaccuracy of the data sources, narrow scope of inquiry, inadequacy of analytic methods, and incomparability of findings across studies. Most studies have focused on fatal shootings by the police and less on other significant incidents, such as shootings *of* police officers, nonfatal shootings, missed shots, and "averted shootings" (i.e., incidents in which officer skill or other circumstances made it unnecessary for an officer to fire at a subject against whom use of deadly force might have been justifiable). In many published studies, the sample sizes available to the researchers are too small to generate statistically significant findings, an analytic misfortune but a societal blessing.

Furthermore, because the official records analyzed by researchers are primarily compiled for the purpose of an official investigation into possible officer culpability, a great deal of potentially useful information about shootings and near shootings either is not collected or is not candid enough to support administrative decisions concerning policy, tactics, and training. For example, officers possibly facing departmental rebuke for violation of policy or procedure may be understandably reluctant to volunteer information about an honest error in perception or judgment or a personal skill deficiency. They may also be reluctant to point out a defect in agency policy, procedure, training, or equipment that they believe leaves officers at a tactical or other disadvantage in potentially violent encounters. This reluctance will be especially strong in agencies that have failed to articulate clearly their interest in acquiring

---

[1] At the same time as we have tried to keep the quantitative presentations readily understandable for nonmethodologists, we have attempted to convey in plain language any theoretical perspectives that may help police administrators understand assessments of police-involved shooting patterns. Still, this book clearly is *not* a review of the various criminological theories that might help explain police conduct (see Sherman 1980b for an excellent overview of what is known about the "causes of police behavior").

such suggestions from the workforce and in agencies that send mixed messages (e.g., asking for suggestions but then routinely ignoring them or penalizing the officers who make them for calling attention to problems). Thus, interviews with officers in the wake of shootings when administrative, civil, and criminal investigations are pending are extremely unlikely to elicit their most insightful and candid judgments about the avoidability of such shootings in the future. Shooting review files may also contain incomplete or inaccurate information on matters of interest to researchers, because the pertinent information was not of immediate operational or investigative importance.

"The statistics for injuries and fatalities tell us that policing is a relatively safe occupation compared with fire fighting, shipbuilding, or forestry. The incidence of fatal injuries and injuries involving days lost from work for police is reported as 2.37 events per 100 workers for 1987. The national (U.S.) rate for all industries was 1.86. But policing was safer than fire department work (5.36); ship and boat building (4.20); or forestry (4.10).

"But it is not so much the accident level as the perceived degree and frequency of threat that affects behavior and attitudes. Most industrial accidents are totally unexpected. By contrast, police are forever anticipating violence. Police work feels dangerous" (Sparrow, et al. 1990: 143; see also National Safety Council 1989: 44-45).

III. Multi-jurisdictional Data Hampered by Divergent Definitions

Perhaps the greatest pitfall in interpreting studies on the use of deadly force is attempting to compare data from different jurisdictions. The reporting categories of different police agencies vary, and the methodologies and definitions of key terms and events differ or are unstated in many studies. For example, it may be impossible to compare jurisdictions accurately because of ambiguities or differences among them concerning what constitutes deadly force, the categories used to report officers' reasons for firing their weapons, or the characterization of the event that mobilized police and eventually led to a shooting.

Some degree of definitional uniformity has probably resulted from police departments adjusting their record keeping to facilitate reporting to the FBI's Uniform Crime Reporting (UCR) system. Nevertheless, there are still vast differences between agencies concerning what a term such as "police use of deadly force" means. There is general agreement that the term means force reasonably capable of causing death or great bodily harm. But some departments include only certain segments of such force in their deadly force tallies, while others are more expansive in their identification and recording of lethal force incidents.

Thus, some agencies report as instances of police use of deadly force only events involving police firearms, excluding, for instance, high-speed pursuits in which the police intentionally ram the suspect's vehicle[2] or threats to life produced by tactical use of

[2] Yet, there is no doubt that when a suspect intentionally rams a police vehicle this is a form of deadly force (see, e.g., a Newark case described in *New York Times* 1992aa). The forms of force likely to cause serious bodily harm or death that police sometimes use in high-speed pursuits include firearms discharges; ramming, bumping (optimistically called "precision immobilization" by Pearson [1992]), or boxing the fleeing vehicle; setting a "spike strip" in its path to puncture its tires; and establishing a roadblock (see, e.g., Schofield [1990: 77]; Alpert and Anderson [1986]; Nugent, et al. [1989: 13]; Alpert and Fridell [1992]; and *Crime Control Digest* [1992q]). In *Brower v. County of Inyo* (1989), the U.S. Supreme Court addressed a practice that some who used it had come to call the "dead man's roadblock":

incendiary devices. Other agencies explicitly acknowledge the potentially lethal consequences of certain high-speed pursuit tactics. For instance, the St. Petersburg, Florida Police Department's pursuit policy declares that ramming a fleeing vehicle should be considered deadly force (St. Petersburg Police Department 1984; Nugent, et al. 1989: 32). The best known, and most tragic, use of incendiary devices in recent history was the Philadelphia Police Department's effort to smoke the radical group MOVE out of their stronghold on May 13, 1985, which sparked a fire that consumed 61 rowhouses and resulted in millions of dollars in civil liability for the municipality (*New York Times* 1992a; Nemeth 1991; Hinds 1992). By some, although not most, police agency definitions, fatal chokeholds, fatal TASER shocks, or fatal attacks by police dogs might be classified following investigations as official uses of deadly force (see Hall 1992: 26, 31).

Narrow definitions of deadly force (e.g., those limited to the discharge of firearms at persons) run counter to the terminology used by the UCR system. It asks police agencies, in completing the "supplementary homicide report" form, to include justifiable homicides committed by peace officers regardless of the weapon used (FBI 1990). Some departments' tabulations of deadly force include only on-duty incidents. Others will incorporate off-duty incidents in the count only when the lethal force was in furtherance of a police enforcement effort (thus, shootings during a personal dispute or accidental misfire while cleaning a weapon might be excluded).

Moreover, some agencies will include in tallies their officers' use of deadly force *outside* the police department's service area (e.g., if a city police officer shoots someone in a suburb). Where agencies do not count such out-of-jurisdiction shootings, the explanation sometimes offered is that the department only compiles data on uses of deadly force that fall within its *investigative* jurisdiction. While this is entirely appropriate (and, indeed, is required) in furnishing data to the FBI's UCR system, it seems dubious policy for an agency to decline to investigate or report locally on an officer's continuing fitness for duty or entitlement to hometown gratitude just because the officer fired a weapon while outside his or her jurisdiction of employment. If a city department that permits officers to reside outside the jurisdiction excluded from its deadly force tallies shots-fired incidents occurring in suburbs, the agency might significantly undercount its officer' off-duty involvement in deadly force.

Some agencies would understand the term "shooting by a police officer" to mean only shots that strike a person (fatally or nonfatally), perhaps calling off-target shots "firearm discharges." Other departments, however, would interpret "firearm discharges" to be all shots fired, including those that produce personal injury and those that do not. Thus, a multi-jurisdictional survey requesting a count of firearm discharges (without precisely defining the term) could produce radically unmatched data sets from different cooperating sources. Further, many agencies' or researchers' counts gloss over the distinction between *incidents* in which police officers discharged their weapons and the number of *persons* (criminal suspects, bystanders, fellow officers, etc.) at whom shots were fired or who were struck by off-target or accidental shots. Thus, in a comparative study, researchers may count incidents (some of which may have produced multiple shooting victims) for one agency and individuals for another, unaware of the inconsistency. In collecting new data for this study, we have typically had at least two written communications and two or more telephone conversations with reporting agencies clarifying and confirming our mutual understanding of the precise meaning of the terminology

---

A substantial roadblock, such as police vehicles, was established just over the crest of a hill or just beyond a blind curve, and pursuing officers allowed the fleeing suspect to run headlong into the obstacle at high speed.

used in the data request and response.

In our discussion of deadly force in this volume, we have concentrated on the use of firearms by police officers (regardless of whether the rounds fired strike a person) and the use of all manner of deadly force *against* officers. Such data, as hard as they are to acquire at times, are still the simplest to get and engender the broadest interest in the field. Alpert and Fridell (1992) and a few other researchers have argued mightily that, in the years ahead, the police world and the criminal justice policy community in general should begin to encompass high-speed pursuits in their conceptions and record keeping on police use of deadly force. The casualty record, they argue, suggests that vehicle chases produce death or serious bodily injury frequently enough they should be considered a police tactic reasonably capable of causing death or serious injury.

IV. Lack of Contextual Information About the Department or Community

As the FBI is very careful to point out in the introductory material to its annual *Crime in the United States* (see, e.g., FBI 1989a: iii, v), interpreting measures of police activity and criminal activity in the absence of reasonably sophisticated contextual information is likely to prove misleading. The FBI's caution against simplistic rank ordering of American police departments and communities according to their reported crime rates has many parallels when one thinks about appraising a particular department's patterns of using deadly force, especially when one attempts to compare police-involved shooting rates across jurisdictions.

A. Information About the Department

Beyond the disparate definitions one encounters of such basic terms as "use of deadly force," studies frequently lack important information about the characteristics of the police agencies or their personnel. Although many studies fail to report even basic descriptive information about the subject police agencies, almost all omit the kind of profiles of the departments that would help the reader understand the challenges and opportunities facing the police and the public in the locale being reviewed. Information of this sort might include:

- the actual (as opposed to authorized) sworn strength of the police agency

- the percentage of officers assigned to street duty

- the career experience and personal characteristics of officers in various assignments—among the relevant personal characteristics would be officer age, time on the job, education, gender, race/ethnicity, and assignment history[3]

- the nature and duration of special proactive enforcement initiatives against potentially violent suspects

- the way in which discretion not to arrest is exercised

---

[3] Later in this book, we report some Chicago data that suggest why black officers do *not* have substantially higher on-duty shooting rates than their white colleagues *despite* the disproportionate assignment of black officers to high-crime districts.

- the nature, timing, and scope of attendance at "officer survival" training sessions (and, specifically, whether the officers involved in a deadly force incident had been given such training prior to the encounter)

- the issuance of different weapons and/or ammunition departmentwide or for selected units (this would include not only firearms but "less-than-lethal" weaponry) and whether the officers involved in the shooting incident had such weapons or equipment available

- the issuance of soft body armor departmentwide or to personnel in selected units, along with any order mandating that officers wear it under specified circumstances (e.g., while executing search warrants or while on routine patrol)[4]

- the presence (and troop strength) in the police agency's jurisdiction of other armed police forces (e.g., some cities have a park police, housing police, transit police, or armed private security patrols, which sometimes employ off-duty public police personnel). These forces may affect the number of potentially dangerous encounters to which the general force is exposed)[5]

- the assignment practices used during the period of study. Relevant practices might include whether first-responder personnel are assigned to one- or two-officer cars or to foot beats; whether rookies are assigned to the jurisdiction's highest crime areas and, if so, what type of in-service supervision they receive from partners and/or patrol sergeants; whether officer partners are paired for long periods of time so they can get to know each other's skills and develop predictable teamwork techniques for approaching and handling crime and arrest scenes;[6] whether officers

---

[4] In Chapters 3 and 5 we report the latest available data on the number of officers whose lives have been saved by soft body armor and the circumstances in which those officers were saved.

[5] It would be overly simplistic to assume that a city with multiple armed police agencies necessarily exposes the general service department to a lower level of potentially dangerous encounters than it would otherwise experience. For example, consider a municipality with a housing authority police force that typically does *not* attempt to serve as a first responder on crime-in-progress calls (e.g., the Baltimore, Philadelphia, and Chicago housing police). The preventive and investigative activities of the housing police in the generally high-crime public housing neighborhoods in such a city might very well *increase* the housing residents' willingness to tip the police about criminal activity (drug dealing, armed intimidation, etc.). Thus, the net effect could be that the general police force was summoned to *more* potentially violent incidents than they would be in the absence of the intelligence-gathering activities of the specialized forces. See, for example, Weisel (1990); Flanagan and Maguire (1990); Bureau of Justice Statistics (1988).

[6] The U.S. Border Patrol's Agent Survival Course, described in P.M. Smith (1990), emphasizes the knowledge that agents must have not only concerning their own skills and weapons but those of their partners. For example, agents are trained to review a mental checklist at the beginning of each tour of duty, including the questions:

- "Do you know the capabilities and limitations of yourself and each of your weapons?"
- "Are your weapons clean and functional?"
- "Are they loaded? How are they loaded (one in the chamber or not)? What type of ammunition are they loaded with? Does your partner know the answers to these questions?"

work fixed shifts or rotate among shifts over time (important since some violent police-civilian encounters in many cities may be concentrated in afternoon or night shifts); and whether officer beat assignments are stable for reasonably long periods (as in "community policing" or "problem-oriented policing"), allowing officers to get to know the law-abiding and criminal populations on their beats, as well as the safest ways to approach specific buildings and other sites.

- the specific type of assignments that identified categories of officers are working in different geographic areas (e.g., if one wanted to estimate the likelihood that experienced officers will become involved in deadly force incidents, it would be important to know not only the distribution of such officers among low-, medium-, and high-crime areas but also whether, within such areas, these officers were working on the street missions or at desks [see Fyfe 1981d]).

- residential patterns of agency personnel (this could help predict the likelihood of officers becoming involved in off-duty deadly force encounters).

- the administrative climate during the period of study. Failure to identify and accurately describe formal *and informal* messages being sent to street officers by the command concerning the circumstances under which deadly force may be used and, more generally, concerning the values that the command wants officers to adhere to can severely limit a researcher's insight into possible causal factors for changing patterns of the use of deadly force.[7]

Knowing about these and other departmental or work force characteristics all would contribute to a sophisticated understanding of the organizational and individual attributes that one might expect to influence the way in which potentially violent police-civilian encounters arise and are handled by the participants.

B. *Information About the Community*

Almost as often as they overlook or fail to report significant features of police agencies, deadly force researchers omit important details about the community in which the shootings occurred. Thus, a deadly force study might give scant attention to the community's

- reported crime levels

- actual criminal victimization rates (often such data are available only on a national or regional basis, largely due to the cost of the victimization surveys that produce these data)

---

[7] In Dallas in 1987-88, for example, an otherwise unexplainable sudden drop in shootings (and, perhaps, certain types of arrests) of suspects by police may be substantially attributable to the highly publicized termination of an officer for misuse of fatal force (Dallas Police Dept. 1990). By the same token, a strong administrative initiative such as this does not always accurately predict the future likelihood of deadly force incidents. Thus, the termination of another Dallas officer for rash use of deadly force in the summer of 1989 was not followed over the next 10 months by a drop in the number of intentional firearms discharges by Dallas officers (Dallas Police Dept. 1990). This pattern is particularly interesting in light of dramatic off-the-record declarations by the rank and file to the effect that, for more than a year following this officer's termination by the agency, not only firearms discharges but aggressive, productive arrest activity by Dallas officers nearly ground to a halt.

- prior police-community rapport or tension that may help explain patterns of incidents

- climate and other natural or designed architectural factors that facilitate or discourage certain types of street-crime patterns (e.g., structures, hills, or growths of shrubbery that shield armed robberies or drug deals from public view)

- diversity in racial, ethnic, age (especially youth concentration), gender, income, education, unemployment, housing pattern, and other characteristics

- transience or residential stability among the general population or subgroups

- residential versus actual population (e.g., a relatively small community's residential population figure may give little indication of the way the daytime population swells due to the presence of a factory, other work centers, or shopping malls and the way the nighttime population increases due to concert arenas, amusement parks, bars, other entertainment establishments, or work centers employing night-shift personnel)[8]

- degree of tensions or rapport between groups (e.g., racial tensions over school or housing desegregation)

- prevailing family structures within particular geographic areas (e.g., single-parent families in which children may receive insufficient adult supervision from relatives or family friends to protect them from recruitment by violent gangs)

- dependence on neighboring jurisdictions for various public services and economic support

- transportation system (within the community and between it and nearby communities)

- concentrations of special populations (e.g., military bases, mental health facilities, corrections institutions) or attractions (such as nightclubs or taverns) that draw predictable populations and problems

- presence or absence of "informal social control" institutions other than the family (religious, educational, athletic, artistic, etc.)—that is, institutions capable of subtly or overtly providing guidance on acceptable forms of behavior and productive activities to occupy the time and talents of community members who might otherwise get in trouble and wind up in confrontations with the police

- likelihood of having known violent offenders at large and level of supervision they will have by enforcement bodies

---

[8] FBI crime rate information, often presented as the number of crimes of a particular type per 100,000 inhabitants, fails to adjust for actual population swells due to employment and entertainment patterns. Thus, a small town with a metropolitan area's largest shopping mall may look like it has an unexplained wave of larceny and theft from autos unless the reader of Uniform Crime Reports understands the type and amount of activity generated by the shopping mall.

- citizen and criminal subgroup attitudes toward the police (e.g., the extent to which the police could reasonably rely on the public to assist them in a critical incident and the extent to which the police could reasonably predict that, despite professional police techniques, different types of criminal suspects would nevertheless engage the police in violent confrontations).

The lack of such organizational or community information, added to the likely inconsistencies in counting the uses of deadly force, heightens the difficulty of making meaningful comparisons among jurisdictions. Police officers around the nation frequently assert that every deadly force incident is unique and therefore incomparable with others, even within their own agency, let alone with critical incidents from other jurisdictions. At some level, of course, such a statement is irrefutable. No two incidents will have precisely the same participants under precisely the same environmental, organizational, community, and behavioral circumstances. Nor will the emotional, physical, and liability aftermath of any two deadly force incidents be identical for their participants and their loved ones and colleagues.

But at a level that is of more immediate importance for policymakers, it is *not* true that it is impossible to make helpful comparisons and generalizations about the circumstances in which police officers shoot others and are themselves shot in the performance of their duties. The crucial point is that one's ability to draw meaningful conclusions about changing patterns of officer-involved shootings over time or across service areas or police agencies will be highly dependent on having a rich understanding of the involved personnel, their organizations, and communities. This understanding will come from awareness of the kinds of factors listed above.

Nevertheless, we generally agree with those researchers and law enforcement executives who have taken the position in published studies that *extreme* differences between cities' use of deadly force rates are likely to be indicative of genuine differences in practice, regardless of any minor methodological flaws in the reporting and analysis of such data. For instance, one department's members may be 20 times more likely (based on troop strength, violent crime arrests, or some other factor) to use deadly force than officers in another department. Moreover, in the absence of contextual factors that might help explain the reported shooting patterns, such findings of large shooting rate variations between agencies often serve as evidence that the two agencies have different administrative climates concerning what is acceptable use of deadly force.

But it is equally important to realize that *marginal* shooting rate variations, even over long periods of time (such as five or more years), should not be used to conclude that one city's rate of deadly force is higher than another's (Sherman and Cohn 1986). Even an absolutely accurate difference between departments' shooting rates, if relatively small, generally should be taken as offering no meaningful distinction. As they say, a difference that makes no difference makes no difference.

V. Researchers' Access to Data

For many years it was extraordinarily difficult for researchers or the general public to gain access to police department records concerning shootings by police (Geller 1979; Fyfe 1980b). Occasionally, police agencies would not even disclose to the public or city council members their deadly force *policy* for fear such disclosure would prove tactically useful to criminals (see Dallas Police Dept. 1990; Brumley 1988; Iannello 1988). Because of the unavailability of official information in many locales in earlier periods, some of the studies conducted in the 1970s (e.g., Kobler 1975b; Public Interest Law Center of Philadelphia 1975, 1979) relied on newspaper accounts of police-involved shootings—a methodology that almost certainly skews the sample in the direction of incidents that help sell papers rather than incidents that illustrate the diversity of police-civilian violent encounters (Blumberg 1989).

But access problems were not limited to citizen watchdog groups or Ph.D. candidates. Even the International Association of Chiefs of Police (IACP), in the early 1980s, had only a 42 percent response rate by major city police departments when the IACP conducted its first national survey of justifiable homicides by police (Matulia 1982; Sherman and Cohn 1986). When data on shootings *were* available, sometimes demographic data were deemed too sensitive to disclose. For instance, when Fyfe conducted his ground-breaking study of shots fired from 1971 through 1975 by New York City police, to address persistent questions about the race/ethnicity of officers involved in shootings, he circumvented official channels. A sergeant in the New York City Police Department (NYPD) at the time he began his research, Fyfe, having twice been denied access to the information by superiors, used an informal network of colleagues assigned throughout New York's five boroughs to learn, by word of mouth, the race/ethnicity of more than 1,000 shooting officers (Fyfe 1981d: 369).

Another indication of the trouble facing police employees who dared hold a mirror up to their agency's deadly force policies and practices in the 1970s was the chewing out that Chicago sergeants Dennis Nowicki and Bernie Stahl received from Department brass for recommending ways to improve the agency's deadly force training and control systems (Nowicki and Stahl 1978). In contrast to Fyfe's circumventing direct orders barring him from using officer racial/ethnic identifications, however, Nowicki and Stahl produced a report that was fully authorized by—indeed, was commissioned by—the Department's senior leadership. Even though the Chicago study breached no directives, those administrators who disliked its message minced no words in trying to hold the messengers responsible for its unwelcome truths.

Official reticence to disclose shooting incident information and pertinent demographic data to responsible in-house and external researchers is much less common today than it was a decade ago.[9] Sherman and Cohn's 1986 study of justifiable homicides by police, begun under the auspices of the Police Foundation and published by the Crime Control Institute some years later, enjoyed a 93 percent response by the nation's 59 cities with populations exceeding 250,000. Moreover, many departments maintain and will provide to researchers under proper circumstances (confidentiality guarantees, measures to prevent subpoena of officers' names from researchers, etc.) detailed data on all woundings and killings by officers.

---

[9] Take the NYPD, for example. Its reluctance to disclose the race/ethnicity of its officers has decreased. Its annual "Firearms Discharge Assault Report" indicates the races of Department members involved in firearms discharge incidents. Still, a review of unpublished FBI UCR data on justifiable homicides by officers indicated that, in contrast to most other local police agencies, the NYPD, as recently as 1990, left blank the portion of the UCR "supplementary homicide report" calling for data on officer race, ethnicity, and age. Except for this idiosyncratic reticence in reporting to the FBI, however, the NYPD's continuing self-studies of the causes and prevention of police-involved shootings (e.g., Cerar 1990) are exemplary efforts to understand more fully such violence. More recently, under Chief Clarence Harmon, the St. Louis Metropolitan Police Department has begun conducting ambitious and insightful inquiries into its officers' firearms discharges (see, e.g., St. Louis Metropolitan Police Department 1992). A few other agencies publish information on officer-involved shootings in their annual reports (see, e.g., Indianapolis Police Department 1992: 8).

Although we did not seek current police-involved shooting data from a large number of agencies for this volume, it is a sign of the new openness of American police agencies to responsible deadly force research that not a single agency from which we sought data declined to cooperate fully. This includes such agencies as those in New York City, Philadelphia, Chicago, Dallas, Houston, St. Louis, Atlanta, Kansas City (Mo.), Dade County (Fla.), Santa Ana, and Los Angeles. Some departments maintain extensive, detailed information on all firearm discharges by their officers, including those that produce no personal injury. A few agencies routinely analyze this information to search for patterns and trends. For example, each year the New York City Police Department, under the direction of Captain John Cerar of the Police Academy's Firearms and Tactics Section, produces one of the outstanding examples of an internal statistical report on officer-involved shootings. If most big city police agencies prepared reports comparable to this one on a regular basis, without waiting for a critical incident to push the department into a reactive and necessarily rushed inquiry, the profession's knowledge about the nature and frequency of police-involved shootings in America would be far ahead of where it is today.

> *"It is about 11:00 P.M. on a weekend. Two uniformed police officers working the 3rd watch in a district patrol vehicle observe a street robbery in progress. While attempting to arrest the offender, a 19-year-old black male, one of the officers, a 27-year-old white male, fires two rounds at the offender from his service revolver in self-defense. Neither the officer nor the offender is injured. There are no other witnesses to the gunfire. This is the only time in his seven-year tenure that the officer has fired his weapon outside of a pistol range. He will not fire his weapon again during the next 20 years.*
>
> *"The offender is arrested and charged with robbery. A check of his previous criminal history finds three arrests and one conviction. He has served less than one year in jail as a result of this prior conviction. Court proceedings result in the offender being convicted of a felony and sentenced to one to two years in the penitentiary. The Department's internal investigation finds that the officer was justified in his use of a firearm and no disciplinary action is taken.*
>
> *"The preceding incident never took place exactly as stated. It is a profile of the typical incident involving the use of firearms by [police officers in many urban departments]" (Nowicki and Stahl 1978: v).*

A smattering of agencies even try to maintain records that provide insight into officer decisions to *avert* shootings. For example, the Charleston, South Carolina Police Department has officers report the *pointing* of their sidearms at any person (Greenberg 1990). This allows the Department to identify a large portion of the situations in which officers thought deadly force might be necessary and to explore which tactics were used to resolve the encounters. A Canadian study indicated that some (unspecified) agencies are routinely directing officers to file reports "where the use of lethal force was avoided with a less violent option" (Jamieson, et al. 1990: 30).

To say that American police agencies are individually keeping ever improving records on their officers' decisions to fire weapons, however, does *not* suggest that our capacity to present an accurate and policy-relevant *national* picture of police use of deadly force is improving—a point to which we shall return shortly. Nor is the openness shown by many local police departments on the subject of use of deadly force mirrored in the federal arena. Unless there is a particular need to marshall data in support of an agency objective, it is rare for the FBI or other federal police agencies to reveal the frequency with which their agents are called upon to use deadly force.[10] Assaults on federal agents are, however, typically reflected in published FBI reports (e.g., the annually released *Law Enforcement Officers Killed and Assaulted*). Individual cases of lethal force used by federal agents may, of course, receive news coverage (see, e.g., *Crime Control Digest* 1992e; *New York Times* 1992x).

VI. Major Data Sources and Their Limitations

Like data on assaults against federal agents, information on assaults on local, county, and state police is reported with reasonable completeness in publicly accessible FBI documents (in Long Beach and some other jurisdictions, it has been alleged that some officers file false claims of injuries—*Law Enforcement News* 1992f: 4). In preparing its annual report, *Law Enforcement Officers Killed and Assaulted*, the FBI goes to great lengths to get accurate information about every police officer slain in America. Besides receiving official reports on officer victimizations in monthly submissions by police departments to the Uniform Crime Reporting program, the FBI monitors newspaper accounts of police fatalities. These two data sources can be compared by the FBI with claims for survivors' benefits filed with the Justice Department on behalf of the families of slain officers pursuant to the federal Public Safety Officers' Benefit Program (see Stillman 1987: 510). This program, which covers all federal, state, and local public safety officers who die from line-of-duty injuries, provided $114,235 in death benefits (for eligible deaths occurring from October 1, 1990, through September 30, 1991—an increase over the prior benefit). In January 1991, the IACP reported that since the benefits program began in 1977, "approximately $172 million has been awarded to the eligible survivors of 3,000 public safety officers killed in the line of duty" (IACP 1991: 20).

As indicated earlier, access to accurate and complete information concerning the use of deadly force *by* law enforcement personnel can be considerably more difficult to obtain. In the absence of access to police departments' files on use of deadly force by officers, some researchers have turned to public health records. For many years, the U.S. Public Health Service's National Center for Health Statistics (NCHS) has maintained records furnished by coroners and medical examiners to state health departments concerning "deaths by legal

---

[10] During a recent controversy over the FBI's announced intention to amend its current "defense-of-life" shooting policy, a Bureau spokesperson provided a rare public indication of the frequency with which agents' use deadly force. To bolster the argument that agents are well disciplined and unlikely to abuse a relaxed deadly force policy, the spokesperson reported that "weapons have been fired by its agents less than 30 times in the last five years" (*Law Enforcement News* 1990: 5). Of course, sometimes data on federal agencies' use of force become available through means other than official announcements. For instance, the Associated Press wire service in 1991 obtained a copy of a report by the U.S. Justice Department's Inspector General, which identified the need for additional deadly force training for agents with the Immigration and Naturalization Service (INS) and the U.S. Border Patrol. According to a summary published in *Law Enforcement News* (1991c),

> "nearly half of the immigration and border guards who fired their weapons on duty last year [1990] were not qualified in their use. The report...said 28 of the 62 [INS and Border Patrol] agents...who fired their weapons had not been properly trained. INS was criticized for inadequate policies governing firearms use, training and disciplinary action. An INS spokesman said the lack of firearms training did not violate agency policy, but added that INS training procedures are being modified."

For a listing of the approximately 50 federal law enforcement agencies whose personnel are routinely armed and possess arrest powers, see Geller and Morris (1992).

intervention of police" (NCHS 1967). These records, however, generally are incomplete and inaccurate as measures of the police use of deadly force.[11] NCHS data, published in the *Vital Statistics of the United States* (e.g., U.S. Department of Health and Human Services 1991), report approximately 200-350 civilians killed each year by "legal intervention," a numerical range that researchers estimate *under*reports justifiable homicides by police by up to 50 percent at the state and national levels and by as much as 75 percent in certain cities (Sherman and Langworthy 1979).

A study commissioned by the governor in New York State discovered that public health records only accurately reported 38 percent of a sample of known homicides by the police (New York State Commission on Criminal Justice 1987). Among the inaccuracies is that coroners' records may attribute legal intervention killings to the police agency in the deceased's community of *residence*, regardless of where the death occurred. Moreover, public health records may not capture in the "legal intervention" category fatalities caused *accidentally* by police during line-of-duty activities.

As an alternative to the death certificate records maintained by the NCHS, some researchers have used data on justifiable homicides by police compiled by the FBI since 1940 under the Uniform Crime Reporting system (see, e.g., a study by James Fox, co-director of Northeastern University's National Crime Analysis Project, commissioned by the *New York Times* (Malcolm 1990a). These data, whose submission by local agencies is voluntary (although some states *mandate* local agency submission—Matulia 1985), are furnished to the FBI on UCR "supplementary homicide report" forms (Sherman and Cohn 1986). FBI data, available through the User Services Section of the FBI's UCR unit, have enabled researchers both to begin to profile the use of deadly force nationwide and to enumerate its frequency in police agencies that have been unwilling to disclose pertinent information directly to other agencies or to researchers.

But, as with the public health records, there is reason for concern about both the accuracy and completeness of these UCR data.[12] For instance, Sherman and Cohn (1986) noted a discrepancy rate of 54 percent between the total number of justifiable homicides reported for identical time periods by the same big-city police agencies to the FBI and to them. Although the discrepancies for which any one police department was responsible may not have been very large, if enough agencies inaccurately report their tallies, this can produce a substantial *national* miscount. For instance, for the years 1980-83 the nation's 59 largest municipal police departments reported 66 *fewer* deaths to the FBI and IACP (as published in Matulia's 1985 study) than they reported to Sherman and Cohn.

---

[11] For discussion of the reasons for the defects in these records, see Sherman and Langworthy (1979); Matulia (1985); Sherman and Cohn (1986); New York State Commission on Criminal Justice—hereafter NYSCCJ—(1987, vol. I); and Blumberg (1989).

[12] We, too, have provided at various places in this book some previously unpublished, FBI-collected data on justifiable homicides by police and by civilians. We do so in an effort to shed light on national patterns during the late 1980s because no other study has yet published national data for these years. We caution the reader, however, that such data generally are less complete than data furnished to us and other researchers directly by individual police agencies.

Our own comparison of Sherman and Cohn's data with FBI data furnished to us[13] showed an even larger discrepancy for the year 1980. In 1980 Sherman and Cohn (1986) reported data on justifiable homicides by police officers in 55 big cities. The FBI tallies of the number of "felons killed [justifiably] by peace officers" in 1980 differed (either higher or lower) from Sherman and Cohn's tallies in 40 (73 percent) of those 55 cities. In 1981 different tallies by the FBI and Sherman and Cohn appeared in 26 (47 percent) of those 55 cities. The specific discrepancies for 1980 and 1981 are shown in Table E-10 in Appendix E. We assume, without knowing, that the same kind of discrepancies render only marginally useful the data collected from the FBI by Professor Fox for the *New York Times* depicting the number of persons killed justifiably by police from 1976 through 1987 (Malcolm 1990a).

Sherman and Cohn offer a number of plausible explanations (in addition to the possibility of clerical error) for the larger number of deaths reported to them than to the FBI. The principal reason, they say, is that the UCR data—which are supposed to include both homicides by the general public and by police officers—are compiled by police crime reporting units, which in some departments do not count off-duty, justifiable, or unprosecuted homicides among the homicides recorded for the FBI. By contrast, special requests from independent researchers or other law enforcement agencies for data on all fatalities caused by police typically are fulfilled by agency personnel outside the crime reporting unit (e.g., from the internal affairs division, firearms and tactics section of a training academy, or the chief's office), whose records more often include all deaths at the hands of department members investigated internally.

Moreover, in accordance with UCR reporting procedures, the data compiled by any given agency's crime reporting unit and forwarded to the FBI on the supplementary homicide report would include justifiable homicides by peace officers that occurred *within* the reporting agency's jurisdiction. This means, for example, that the Chicago Police Department's supplementary homicide reports would notify the FBI about killings of suspects within Chicago's city limits committed, on or off duty, by Chicago, Cook County, Illinois State Police, and other agency personnel permanently stationed there or merely visiting.[14] The Chicago reports to the FBI would exclude any justifiable homicides committed by Chicago officers outside Chicago's borders.

---

[13] The FBI data were furnished in the form of computer printouts showing, for specified years, the number of justifiable homicides of felons by peace officers or by civilians in every city reporting such data to the UCR program.

[14] UCR policies directing that cooperating law enforcement agencies report all killings of felony suspects by peace officers within the reporting agency's jurisdiction might, one would guess, lead to FBI overcounts of these justifiable homicides for agencies such as the Metro-Dade County Police Department (MDPD), whose county includes major city departments (in this instance, Miami). But the data reported in the FBI's unpublished UCR file listing showed, for instance, that in the period January 1984 through June 1988, peace officers justifiably killed six felony suspects in the MDPD's jurisdiction (one each in 1984 and 1985, the other four in 1987). A private, unpublished consulting report (Alpert 1989a), drawing data directly from various sources within the MDPD, reports that during this same 4½-year period, Metro-Dade officers themselves fatally shot 18 individuals, three times the tally apparently reported to the FBI by Metro-Dade. Our own data collection yielded still a different tally: We were informed by the MDPD of 15 civilians shot fatally by MDPD personnel during the *full* five-year period, 1984-88, so obviously the 4½-year period through June 1988 could not have yielded the tally of 18 derived by Alpert. Although one might expect both overcounts and undercounts in the FBI compilations, undercounts seem to be much more common. The reasons for this are not clear.

Thus, there are various plausible explanations for discrepancies between the data Sherman and Cohn (1986) received directly from big-city police departments and the data compiled by the FBI. The discrepancy that Sherman and Cohn found more difficult to explain, however, was between the total count of justifiable homicides furnished by police departments in response to *their* special research request and the total count furnished by the identical agencies in response to the *IACP's* special request (Matulia 1985). Here, the discrepancy rate was 23 percent. Sherman and Cohn's only speculation about the reasons for this discrepancy was that different agency personnel responding to the two different surveys a year apart may have exercised different levels of care or have had different understandings of the definitions of deadly force called for in the two surveys (Sherman and Cohn 1986). It should be noted also that, although the *total* number of criminal suspects killed by police over a block of years was higher in the reports sent to Sherman and Cohn than in the same agencies' reports to either the IACP or the FBI, the discrepancy ran in the opposite direction for a few of the years (lower counts were sent to Sherman and Cohn).

So what? That is, of what practical significance is it to know with any greater precision than we currently do how many criminal suspects are slain nationally by big-city

The youth's "family gathered his favorite sports jerseys, baseball cards and photographs on Monday in preparation for his funeral, their grief mitigated by anger over what they believe was the unjustified weekend shooting of the 12-year-old by [an undercover] police officer. Meanwhile, police officials defended the action by [the] Gang Crimes Officer...who shot the 7th grader three times after the youth allegedly pointed a .22-caliber revolver at the officer during a chase. [The officer who fired] and his partner first suspected they saw [the youth] had a gun in the playground where the incident began and were able to confirm it when they moved closer. It was then that [the youngster] fled and [one of the officers] chased him....

"The youngster's age was irrelevant, given his possession of the loaded gun, [a violent crimes police commander said], and the officers did not have any other options to stop him. 'He's as dangerous as anybody else with a gun,' [the commander] said. * * *

"But [the youth's] family members insist that the shooting could have been avoided. * * * [The officer], a 19-year veteran..., is still on active duty and has no history of using excessive force in previous cases, authorities said. However, he was involved in two previous shootings of suspects, according to news reports..." (Stein 1992a).

"Police said [the youth], who was left-handed, was holding a revolver in his right hand and pointing it at the officer when shot. The medical examiner's spokesman, also left-handed, said it is not unusual for left-handers to use their right hand for important tasks" (O'Connor 1992).

"A handgun that authorities say a 12-year-old boy pointed at a police officer who then shot him to death in a South Side alley did not reveal any fingerprints from the youth, police officials said Tuesday. 'One partial print was found on the gun; it did not match the boy or the police officer....' The family of [the youngster] had contended since the shooting Saturday that police planted the gun, found in a flower garden near the 7th grader's body. [A violent crimes sergeant] said the lack of fingerprints on the gun does not mean the youth was not carrying the weapon. * * * 'Someone could hold a gun and still not register prints for any number of reasons,' said [an] FBI Special Agent...in San Francisco. 'You have to have 12 points of a fingerprint to positively identify it. If it's smudged, it's useless. Anything can smudge a print—moving a gun around or sweat or dirt could have something to do with it. It happens lots of times' " (Kates and Papajohn 1992).

police departments? Perhaps the simplest answer is that researchers such as Sherman and Cohn and the IACP (Matulia 1982, 1985), who have reported long-term national trends in the frequency of extreme police-civilian violence, may unwittingly be misleading the public and the police profession about either the direction of change or (more likely) the magnitude. As Sherman and Cohn (1986) note, they have probably *understated* the amount of restraint American police have been showing in use of deadly force in recent years, because their more recent data (1980-84) come from police agencies' internal affairs divisions (IADs), while their data for the earlier years (1970-79) come from the less complete FBI records.

But there are reasons other than creating accurate national counts of police justifiable homicides why the limitations of the official data sources should cause concern for policymakers. For instance, the Christopher Commission (Independent Commission on the Los Angeles Police Department 1991), convened to investigate the Los Angeles Police Department in the aftermath of the March 1991 videotaped beating of Rodney King and chaired by former U.S. deputy secretary of state Warren Christopher, reminded the profession and the nation of the importance of keeping track of *patterns* of police conduct or misconduct that might suggest the need for employee assistance, retraining, reassignment, or discipline. Using the LAPD's own automated data retrieval systems, the Christopher Commission staff demonstrated that there were some officers currently employed by the Department who had large numbers of excessive (but not necessarily *deadly*) force allegations against them but no serious attention had been given to exploring whether these allegations, even if found to be unprovable by agency investigators, nevertheless were indicative of patterns of problematic officer conduct. The LAPD was not alone, of course, in this pattern of review and supervision. In many respects, the LAPD is in much better shape than other large agencies, because it has the technical capacity rapidly to retrieve and analyze use of force information by *individual* officers. By contrast, other agencies have not automated even their records on police officers' use of *deadly* force (Chicago is but one example—Rodriguez 1991).

When we were told by officials in one big-city agency that it had officers (presumably very few) who had in their careers been involved in as many as 17 shots-fired incidents (some in which no injuries resulted), we inquired of another department—Chicago's—whether they had officers with similarly high rates of involvement in lethal force incidents. The answer was that no data on officers' use of firearms in combat was available for any years other than the most recent four. Furthermore, answering the question about officers with multiple shooting involvement even for the past four years would entail painstaking manual review of documents, searching for the names of officers in large stacks of firearms use reports (Rodriguez 1991).[15]

If the Chicago Police Department is at all representative of major city agencies in America, a significant limitation of existing authoritative data sources (namely, police departments) is that they are unable to provide high quality information beyond the past half dozen years or so concerning any officers involved in multiple shooting incidents. One could probably find out by a quick survey of different unit supervisors which officers had

---

[15] It's not always difficult finding officers or ex-officers who have been involved in large numbers of shootings. Once in a while, they parlay their experience into successful careers as tactical advisors. For instance, Devallis Rutledge, during his police and military career, was "shot at more than 300 times." And, he reported, "I've shot more than 30 people" (Rutledge 1988: 273). He went on to author a number of books on "officer survival" techniques, to acquire a law degree, and become a prosecutor in Orange County, California (*ibid.*: 4).

reputations for repeated use of lethal force. But such an informal poll can hardly substitute for the accurate information an agency's management needs to ensure that (a) employees are given state-of-the-art guidance and assistance, (b) government attorneys have the information they need to properly handle officer-involved shooting litigation, and (c) the community at large is being well served and protected.

Among the explanations departments have offered for maintaining only short-term deadly force records are storage space limitations (which should no longer pose a problem in a day of low-cost, high-quality personal computers) and labor-management contracts (or officers' statutory bills of rights) that require the purging of certain internal affairs information from officer personnel files after a stated time period. While officers need to be treated with respect and trust befitting the enormously complex and challenging work they are asked to do, it seems odd indeed that management would agree to blind itself to highly influential, critical incidents in the professional (and personal) life of its employees in the spirit of fairness to workers. If any equitable, professional psychological appraisal could demonstrate that, as a general proposition, police officers' current thinking and behavior are uninfluenced by early-career involvement in life-threatening confrontations, then perhaps there might be a persuasive basis for pruning departmental records to delete early deadly force encounters from an officer's permanent record. Unless and until such proof can be offered, it seems to us that it is essential for departments, as standard operating procedure, to maintain current, readily accessible documentation on the frequency (and nature) of every officer's *entire* career experience with the use of deadly force.[16]

At the same time that researchers find it relatively easy to point out the flaws in official data sets, it is certainly true that there is wide variation in the quality of *research* conducted using those data. Sherman (1980b: 71) has said of the body of research on extreme police-civilian violence that "all studies are [not] of equal value...and conclusions based on a 'democratic vote' of the available studies on each issue would clearly be inappropriate." In the future, as well, the value of empirical research on police-involved shootings will vary considerably. It will depend on the researchers' ability and willingness to ask the right questions, on their access to adequate data, on their analytic insight and skill, and on the cooperation and collaboration they receive from practitioners who see operational research as an effective way to advance policing.

VII. How Incomplete Data Can Mislead Policymakers

In the absence of solid evidence to the contrary, we choose to be optimistic and accept Sherman and Cohn's supposition that, nationwide, justifiable homicides by police have been

---

[16] Theoretically, it might be possible for researchers or investigators to reconstruct an officer's career experience with extreme violence by interviewing the officer and verifying the information provided through additional interviews with supervisors, professional peers, family members, friends, social service providers, and others. Even if the officer declined to answer questions about his or her history of using firearms, some of these other sources might prove illuminating. This approach is sometimes used in the study of others who cannot be interviewed personally—homicide and suicide victims; such interviews are culled to produce a "psychological autopsy" of the deceased (see, e.g., Marzuk, et al. 1992: 3182, 3183). Any such approach to reconstructing an officer's career involvement in shooting incidents would, of course, prove enormously more complicated and expensive than a system in which the police department maintained permanent records. Such records might also be useful to officers who claim stress disabilities.

falling dramatically—even more dramatically than official data indicate. But suppose they are wrong not only about the *magnitude* of change but about the *direction* of change? Wouldn't that have some important public policy implications?

To explore this question we were provided unpublished data from the FBI representing the number of "felons killed by peace officers" for the period 1985-89 and reported as such to the Bureau by local, county, and state police departments nationwide. These data come from the same source relied upon by Sherman and Cohn for much of their pre-1980 findings (Sherman and Cohn 1986: 18). We also were provided data on the same subject for the years 1985-89 by selected big city police departments, in Chicago, Dallas, Kansas City (Mo.), and Philadelphia. The San Antonio, Texas Police Department provided data for a multi-city survey conducted by the *San Diego Union* newspaper (O'Connell 1990), which we have incorporated into our analyses. We discovered, as Sherman and Cohn (1986) had earlier, very substantial discrepancies between the FBI data and those furnished to us directly. Indeed, collectively, for the five-year period, the five cities reported 88 justifiable homicides by police to the FBI but 171 justifiable homicides by police to us and to the *San Diego Union*. This represents a *49 percent undercount reported to the FBI*. If this rate of undercounting applied across all 50 cities that Sherman and Cohn and we studied, current shooting levels would have taken a distinct upward turn.

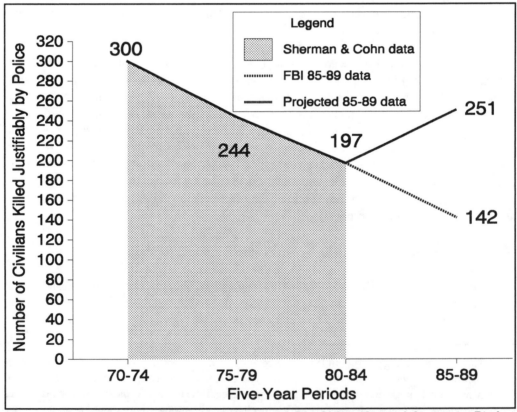

Figure 1: Justifiable Homicides by Police in 50 Big Cities (Annual Averages During Five-Year Periods, 1970-84, and Alternate Possibilities for 1985-89)

Figure 1 shows the dramatic downward trend reported by Sherman and Cohn for justifiable killings by police during the period 1970-84 and the two very different, more recent *alternative* findings. These alternatives are based on different assumptions about the completeness of city department reports to the FBI. The figure shows successive five-year annual averages as a way of minimizing the possibly misleading effects of year-to-year reporting errors (Sherman and Cohn 1986 used the same method for presenting their data). If one takes the data furnished to us for 1985-89 by the FBI as complete, the average annual number of killings by police in all 50 cities during 1985 through 1989 would have been 142.[17] But if the aggregate undercount of 49 percent we found for five cities reflects undercounts for the remaining 45 cities represented in the figure, then the reality is that the late 1980s produced an upswing in justifiable homicides by police in these 50 large cities to an aggregate annual average of 251 fatalities.[18]

Three other illustrations will help demonstrate some of the other ways that *incomplete* data can be misleading to police and other policy makers.

First, suppose one knew only the number of civilians shot *fatally* by two different departments—Chicago and Los Angeles—during a given time period. During the five-years 1974 through 1978, Chicago police officers fatally shot 132 persons, while their colleagues in the Los Angeles Police Department fatally shot 139 persons (Geller and Karales 1981a; Meyer 1980a). One might assume, therefore, that Chicago and LAPD police experienced a reasonably similar number of encounters in which they felt compelled to use their firearms in the line of duty. Indeed, taking into consideration the fact that the LAPD at the time had roughly half the number of sworn personnel as Chicago, one might surmise that officers in Los Angeles are considerably more likely than those in Chicago to fire at criminal suspects. But Table 1 shows that a different picture emerges when shots-fired data are examined.

Now it becomes reasonably clear that Chicago police fired at more than three times as many suspects as Los Angeles police fired at over this five-year period. What accounted for the roughly similar number of fatal police shooting victims was the different rates at which officers in both agencies struck and killed those at whom they reported firing. Chicago officers during this period struck 18 percent of the persons at whom they shot; LAPD personnel hit 43 percent. Whether the difference might be accounted for by such factors as average number of shots fired per incident, type of standard service weapons, or average number of hours of in-service firing range practice are among the key questions that police and researchers might pursue.

---

[17] In an unpublished study obtained by the *New York Times*, Sherman and colleagues at the Washington, D.C.-based Crime Control Institute compiled data on killings by police in the nation's 57 largest cities during the period 1985-88. The number of such slayings, reportedly, "held steady in the 160-170 range in each year" (Malcolm 1990a). Besides the fact that the 1985-88 data cover 57 cities and the earlier data collected by Sherman and Cohn pertain to just 50 cities, the major limitation we have in interpreting the more recent numbers is not knowing from the *Times* article whether the data were taken from the FBI's incomplete files or from the generally more complete records of each of the 57 police agencies.

[18] This 251 figure was calculated based on a total 50-city number of 646 justifiable homicides by police reported to the FBI on supplementary homicide report forms. We multiplied 646 by 1.94 (which corrects for a 49 percent undercount) and derived 1,253, which, divided by the five years covered, produces an average annual number of 251.

Table 1:
**Civilians Fired at, Struck, and Missed by Police
in Chicago and Los Angeles, 1974-78**

Category of Civilians	Number		Percent	
	Chicago	LAPD	Chicago	LAPD
Wounded	386	238	13%	27%
Killed	132	139	5%	16%
Injury unknown	5	0	0.2%	---
Total struck	523	377	18.2%	43%
Total missed	2,353[1]	491	82%	57%
Total fired at	2,876[1]	868	100%[2]	100%

Sources: Geller and Karales (1981a), Meyer (1980a).
[1] *Estimates based on Chicago Police Department shots-fired data for 1975-77.*
[2] *Does not total 100 percent due to rounding.*

As a second example of how incomplete data tell only part of a story that may be important to a particular police department and its community, suppose a police department was criticized for killing civilians needlessly. Suppose further that the evidence offered by the critic was what might be called a "comparative body count"—the ratio of officers killed feloniously to civilians killed by police.

Such body counts are common in wartime, of course, as a way of estimating who's winning the war. Although most reasonable people would be appalled at gauging the success of police in fighting crime by reference to such body counts, it is not inconceivable that a given community's more strident police watchdogs might present the mayor's office with such multi-city data, suggesting "trigger happy" performance by the local police. Those who might resort to comparative body counts as a way of estimating police professionalism could rarely be expected to have more than intermittent access to authoritative deadly force data; they probably could be counted upon to present publicly only such data as happened to support their preconceptions. Thus, knowing what questions to ask (i.e., what data to collect) and being able to go to pertinent data sources is important for those who may on short notice have to place apparently damaging information in a broader and more relevant context.

For example, consider the two portraits of "comparative body counts" that emerge from two different data sources—the FBI's *national* data and a private research firm's report on justifiable homicides in 50 U.S. cities with populations exceeding 250,000 (FBI, various years; Sherman and Cohn 1986).[19] As Figure 2 shows, for the six years 1979-84, the 50 big cities

---

[19] It is common for criminal justice analysts to use a 250,000 population figure as the dividing line between the nation's largest cities and other municipalities. For instance, in FBI UCR reports, six population groups are used to report crime, arrest, law enforcement employment, and other data. These groups include cities with populations of 250,000 or more (Group I); cities of 100,000 to 249,999 (Group II); cities of 50,000 to 99,999 (Group III); cities of 25,000 to 49,999 (Group IV); cities of 10,000 to 24,499 (Group V); and cities with populations under 10,000 (Group VI) (FBI 1989a: 238).

collectively had a ratio of one police officer slain feloniously for every 11.8 civilians justifiably killed by their police. But the FBI's national data produces a distinctly different ratio of 1 to 4.4.

Since the FBI's data attempt to depict the entire national experience, one might reasonably hypothesize that smaller agencies lose more officers in relation to civilians killed by police than do larger agencies (one would also assume substantial differences *among* big-city departments in these "body count" ratios). Whether such a pattern, if it is accurate, might be associated with different qualities of officer "survival training," supervision, shooting policies, or the availability of protective apparel and other equipment (*Crime Control Digest* 1992a) in large, medium, and small cities are among the interesting questions that policymakers and others might wish to pursue if they were intrigued by the difference in the fatality ratios reported by the FBI and by the Sherman and Cohn study.

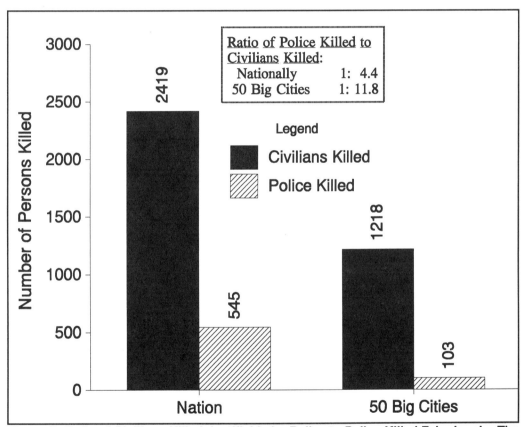

Figure 2: Ratio of Civilians Killed Justifiably by Police to Police Killed Feloniously: The Nation Compared with 50 Big Cities (over 250,000 pop.), 1979-84

The FBI's national data may be accurate, but the unwary reader could overlook a relatively technical but nonetheless potentially crucial methodological aspect of this comparative national count: To a certain extent, the national data are comparing apples with oranges. That is, the data on civilians killed justifiably by the police come from a little more than 9,000 police agencies that voluntarily report such incidents, if and when they occur, to the FBI under the UCR program. Given reports that there are over 15,000 police and sheriff's agencies in the United States (*Crime Control Digest* 1992b), the data on justifiable homicides by police could potentially represent only about 60 percent of these violent police-civilian encounters.[20] By contrast, the data on law enforcement personnel feloniously killed are very likely to be nearly complete. The FBI goes to great lengths to capture information concerning the felonious slaying of any law enforcement officer, whether employed by a local, state, or federal agency. Even in a jurisdiction where the police agency has long refused to cooperate voluntarily with the UCR program by furnishing crime statistics, the FBI will collect detailed information on the felonious death of police through FBI field offices, searches of newspapers, federal Bureau of Justice Assistance information on death benefits applied for by slain officers' survivors, and other means (FBI 1989b: 1).

Thus, to take a hypothetical example based on the numbers shown in Figure 2, let us assume that the 545 law enforcement officers indicated as feloniously killed in the nation during the six years from 1979 through 1984 is an accurate and complete count. But let us assume, since only a little more than 9,000 police departments furnished data on civilians killed justifiably (and the FBI takes no steps to garner such information other than waiting for police departments to furnish it), that the 2,419 civilians shown as killed justifiably by police during this same time period is only 60 percent of the total. Thus, there would have actually been 4,032 civilians killed by police during the six years. Using this higher number, the comparative body count produces a ratio of 1:7.4 (4,032 divided by 545). This still does not match the 50 big-city ratio, but it is far closer than the ratio obtained using the data furnished by the FBI. This is not intended as a criticism of the FBI. It is responsibly reporting what information it has. Indeed, the Bureau would probably be criticized if it attempted to provide "guesstimates" on matters as sensitive as police-caused deaths. But the illustration stands as a reminder to police executives and other policymakers that, when using data to *reach* or (as more commonly happens) to *support* a policy decision (see Cordner 1985), one needs to understand exactly what the data do and do not mean.

A third illustration of how deadly force data can be misused to create an erroneous impression of police work could be offered in the context of judicial review of police search and seizure activities. One important line of U.S. Supreme Court decisions concerns the right of police to search motor vehicles they have stopped for various reasons. A decision that helped frame police and civilian rights and responsibilities in such field contacts came in 1977 in *Pennsylvania v. Mimms*. One of the factors that the Court cited in support of its decision was the portrait of officer endangerment in car stops presented in the social science data offered in the litigants' briefs. What the Court did, however, was to look at the *number* of officers injured or killed annually when making car stops without attempting to calculate the *rate* at which officers are injured during car stops, given the mammoth number of car stops made by American police each year.

To illustrate the point, five officer deaths resulting from vehicle stops mean one thing if drawn from a universe of 100 stops and quite another thing if drawn from a pool of one million such police-civilian contacts (see Sherman 1980c: 8; Geller 1985a: 156). Lest the

---

[20] There is no easy way to derive a more precise estimate than the 60 percent figure. One approach, potentially time consuming, would be to explore the pattern of agencies (by size of jurisdiction, violent crime rates, etc.) that typically do and do not report justifiably killing crime suspects to the FBI. In such an effort, however, one could not safely generalize about justifiable homicide rates based on such simplistic factors as agency size or community violent crime rates. Instead, a more complex basis for estimation would need to be derived.

reader think we are straining to make a point with unrealistic numbers, a single law enforcement agency, the California Highway Patrol, reports that it makes "over 4 million vehicle enforcement stops" *each year* (Abbott 1988: 7; see also Nemecek 1990: 30). The loss of an officer's life in a vehicle stop is no less tragic, of course, regardless of the underlying number of vehicle stops made by the officer's agency. But the two contrasting situations hypothesized here—officer victimization rates of 5 percent versus 0.0005 percent—certainly would send significantly different messages to the risk-manager and police trainer, who need to target limited training budgets to those topics that merit the most attention. There are also different implications of the two risk rates for the policymaker, who needs to strike a reasonable balance between officer safety and positive police-civilian rapport in assessing how police should conduct themselves during vehicle stops. (We do not mean to imply by this discussion that police should be less cautious than they typically are in approaching stopped vehicles. Nor do we disregard the fact that different categories of vehicle stops present vastly different levels of risk to the involved officers. Indeed, we wish to emphasize the need for developing much more finely tuned estimates of the risks posed to officers by different types of activities under varying circumstances.)

Two U.S. Justice Department analysts, Garner and Clemmer (1986), have explored the question raised by our hypothetical concerning vehicle stops, deploying a number of different data sets to attempt to portray the hazard levels of different types of police activities. We will examine their findings in some detail later in this volume. But for now we note their conclusion that, considering the FBI's traditional categories of circumstances in which police are slain feloniously (responding to disturbances, attempting arrests for various felonies, civil disorders, handling prisoners, investigating suspicious persons, ambush, dealing with mentally deranged persons, and traffic pursuits and stops), "the traffic category ranks as the least dangerous when used with two out of three studies of officer deaths" (*ibid.*: 2, 5).

Moreover, Bayley and Garofalo (1989: 12), engaged by the New York State Commission on Criminal Justice and Use of Force to study potentially violent police-civilian encounters and the nature and extent of violence when it resulted, found that, even in some of the highest crime precincts in New York City, police-civilian traffic encounters rarely erupted in violence. Out of 467 "police-citizen encounters that had at least some possibility of resulting in violence" (*ibid.*), including in this definition "intervention by the police to apply the law against specific individuals" (*ibid.*: 5)—a definition that resulted in the inclusion in the study of 154 vehicle stops made by officers (*ibid.*: 7)—"[t]raffic stops never sparked the use of force by either officers or citizens" (*ibid.*: 12).

In concluding this discussion of the difficulties of accurately and insightfully studying the use of deadly force by and against law enforcement officers, three points should be stressed. First, those who turn to deadly force studies to inform their policymaking and other administrative decisions should be especially careful to avoid comparing apples with oranges. Second, they should stress, to the media, city hall, officers, and anyone else who will listen that great care must be exercised in making assumptions about police conduct not directly addressed by the available data.

The third point, elaborated immediately below, is that the profession of policing deserves and should demand a better intelligence base on which to frame policy decisions that profoundly affect the lives of police officers and the communities they serve.

VIII. Call for a National Deadly Force Reporting System

The kind of inaccurate *national* deadly force data on which both academic and law enforcement-based researchers have had to rely thus far (which today leaves us unsure whether, since 1984, total killings by American police are up or down) led Sherman and Cohn (1986) to observe:

"[I]t seems appropriate for democracies to keep careful track of how many citizens are killed by the government. No matter how justifiable those deaths may be, the government cannot be held fully accountable for the use of its powers unless the public has access to reliable information. That is not the case now, in most states or nationally."

They note, additionally, that government takes the national pulse in the area of public health in many ways, such as by counting deaths due to alcohol-related auto accidents and lung-cancer deaths of long-term smokers. Our knowledge concerning the prevalence of many public health risks is far superior to what we know about the level of police-involved violence.[21]

Moreover, as Americans for Effective Law Enforcement pointed out in calling for "a national reporting system on use of force [and] police misconduct," (*Crime Control Digest* 1991e: 1),

"reporting on subjects of public interest is a common practice in the business world. For example, members of the public can read the number of complaints

---

[21] The medical profession increasingly considers interpersonal violence a public health problem and urges studying and addressing it as an epidemic. Attempting to deal with the special contribution of firearms to the American plague of violence, doctors writing in the *Journal of the American Medical Association* decried the absence of useful, detailed, *national* data on firearms-related deaths and called for the creation of a central repository of information:

"A Firearm Fatality Reporting System is needed. One can be patterned after the Fatal Accident Reporting System (FARS), which is maintained by the National Highway Traffic Safety Administration and which has reported on all motor vehicle-related fatalities since 1975. FARS collects uniform data from the states and reports on up to 90 different data elements characterizing each fatal crash and the vehicles and people involved in that crash. In 1989, FARS collected data on 45,555 fatalities involving 40,718 crashes. The annual budget for FARS is approximately $3.5 million.

"The FARS data have been used, for example, to evaluate seatbelt laws, child restraint laws, and changes in speed limit laws; to detect vehicles that are at high risk for injury involvement; to monitor trends in motor vehicle safety; and to monitor the role of alcohol in highway fatalities. The existence of the FARS database has been crucial to the development of highway safety.

"As is the case with highway fatalities, gun deaths are routinely investigated by medical examiners or coroners and by police. A good deal of information, therefore, is currently collected at the state and local levels, but this information is not uniform, nor are the medical data reported to a national repository. A Firearm Fatality Reporting System, which might best be located within the Centers for Disease Control, could rely on data currently collected at the state and local levels in much the same way FARS does. Information maintained at the federal level need not contain identifiers, so that the confidentiality interests of involved parties are protected" (Teret, et al. 1992: 3074).

filed against a named airline per 10,000 passengers, and even compare the on-time performance of one airline versus another. Sadly, a police chief or sheriff does not have a benchmark to judge the number of citizen complaints per 100 officers of his department [in comparison] to other agencies in the same state or nationwide. While assaults and line-of-duty deaths of police officers are meticulously reported, the frequency of police use of firearms and nonlethal force is not nationally known or readily available for comparison purposes."

Our picture of the state of the nation would be more complete if we conscientiously kept track of the need that law enforcement personnel have to slay civilians.

Several leading commentators, practitioners, and interest groups, covering the entire political spectrum and including groups that tend to meet mostly on opposite sides of court cases (e.g., the American Civil Liberties Union and Americans for Effective Law Enforcement), have expressed support for a national police use-of-force reporting system. Meeting in former NYPD Commissioner Lee Brown's office just weeks after the Rodney King beating in 1991, police chiefs from large cities throughout the nation joined former Commissioner Brown (then also the president of the IACP) in calling on the federal government to develop "a national system to gather information about the use of force similar to the Uniform Crime Reporting System" (James 1991). In 1985 former NYPD Commissioner Richard Condon, in a report to Governor Mario Cuomo on police use of deadly force in New York State, recommended a centralized, statewide reporting system on the discharge of firearms by police (Condon 1985).

*After more than a year's study, a task force appointed in 1991 by the New Jersey Attorney General to make recommendations concerning the control of police abuse of force "said it was hard to obtain statewide statistics on the use of force because of a lack of common definitions and standards for recording complaints.... * * * The task force said law enforcement agencies should be required to report all incidents where force was used to county prosecutors and the Attorney General's office, and to make the reports available to the public" (Sullivan 1992).*

In Sherman and Cohn's (1986) conception, a central registry would be a "national system of reporting all deaths caused by law enforcement officers, for whatever reason, at whatever location, whether on duty or off." The system, in their view, should obligate the agency *employing* the officer who produced the death (as opposed to the jurisdiction of occurrence) to forward pertinent information to the U.S. Department of Justice. They would include federal agencies whose agents are authorized to carry firearms in the reporting obligation (see Geller and Morris 1992 for a tally of those 50 agencies). At present the FBI compilation of "justifiable homicides involving law enforcement officers" includes only city, county, and state agencies (FBI 1990). For its part, the Justice Department under the Sherman-Cohn proposal would conduct certain surveys (e.g., of newspaper reports of police-involved killings) as a check on data accuracy and completeness and would publish annually a national profile of deaths caused by federal, state, and local law enforcement personnel. Other writers have echoed Sherman and Cohn's recommendations (e.g., Blumberg 1989: 460).

In the Americans for Effective Law Enforcement (AELE) proposal, initially made some time ago but repeated in the wake of the national furor over the Rodney King incident in Los Angeles, the repository for a national reporting system would be the Justice Department, and data could be forwarded through the Uniform Crime Reporting system (*Crime Control Digest* 1991e: 10). AELE Executive Director Wayne Schmidt recommended that

> "the reporting system minimally include the number of citizens versus officer complaints, by type of allegation; number of officer versus officer complaints, by type; disposition of complaints by percentage, for each type of allegation; number of times officers have resorted to lethal and nonlethal weapons to defend themselves and/or overcome resistance" (*ibid.*).

It is striking that, despite substantial advances made over the past several decades in police telecommunications systems and automated data processing networks, the United States still does not have a reliable data base that reports precisely how many people are killed, let alone wounded or shot at but missed, by the police nationwide.[22] Moreover, we certainly lack data—even at the individual department level—that would give the profession and the public some appreciation of the frequency with which police *could have* legitimately discharged their weapons but, through competence and responsible restraint (and, sometimes, with a measure of good luck), found a less violent way to resolve the encounters (Geller 1985a; Blumberg 1989). The big-city data sets on which most of the existing studies are based are almost certainly not representative of the total population of the nation (Fyfe 1988b); nor are big-city officers' working environments and responses to those conditions likely to present an adequate profile of officer hazards and actions in other types of locations (see, e.g., our Figures 46 and 47 and accompanying discussion in Chapter 3). Both the volume and quality of city-by-city data are improving such that some general policy conclusions can be drawn from even the flawed data available. But more specific policy choices—particularly those that might affect medium and small agencies or federal agencies—are difficult to make using current information.[23]

The nation and police profession would be well served by a national deadly force reporting system that not only captures shots fired by police that strike individuals and, further, produce death, but that tabulates all instances in which police departments become aware that their officers have discharged their firearms. As experienced police know full well, whether a bullet, fired in combat, strikes a person or not and kills or merely wounds is often strictly a matter of chance—which makes the decision to pull the trigger the key operational event to monitor. Thus, we are more comfortable with the scope of the AELE recommendation than with Sherman and Cohn's more modest proposal.

If the Justice Department were designated by Congress or took it upon itself to begin collecting timely and reasonably complete information on the use of deadly force by American police, one information-gathering system that potentially could be used, consistent with the

---

[22] Some *states* have required centralized compilation of data on the use of deadly force by police. Sherman (1980a: 93) reports that Minnesota, under legislative mandate, centrally collects such information (Minn. Stat. sec. 609.066 [1976]).

[23] A number of questions pertaining to small- and medium-size law enforcement agencies have been substantially disregarded by deadly force researchers thus far. We have attempted to provide what little data are currently available about extreme police-civilian violence in smaller jurisdictions in appropriate places throughout this volume. But there is an urgent need for attention to the special needs of smaller police departments concerning police-involved shootings and their possible special *opportunities* to advance the state of the art concerning the control of police-civilian violence (see our discussion of small agencies in Chapter 6).

AELE proposal, might be the new incident-based crime reporting system being
developed by the FBI and the Justice Department's Bureau of Justice Statistics.
This system, although still based on voluntary reporting, conceivably could improve
the level of detail about police shootings of
civilians, if not the completeness and consistency of city-by-city counts (see, e.g.,
Clede 1990; FBI 1990f). Although there
are no plans at present to capture detailed
data on shootings by the police in the
National Incident-Based Reporting System
(NIBRS) (Vaugh 1991), this system's focus
on compiling better descriptive information
about local and state criminal justice activities would be consistent with that system's
use for collection of a national deadly force
data base.

State crime reporting systems that
complement the enhanced national UCR
system conceivably could also be used to
further improve reporting in this area.[24]

"Responding to a report of automatic gunfire inside a school, two officers were advised that a juvenile had just fled carrying an 'Uzi' type machine pistol. Searching the backyards of nearby homes, the officers confronted the 14-year old, who ignored their commands to stop and drop the weapon. A foot chase ensued, lasting several blocks. During his flight, the youth turned on repeated occasions, pointing the weapon in the direction of the pursuing officers. In his continued efforts to escape, the juvenile fled through a small crowd, leaving a nearby sports facility, and was finally cornered in a parking lot by the two officers. They subsequently were able to affect the arrest without firing a single shot. At the time of the apprehension, the Intratec Scorpion .22 calibre semi-automatic weapon carried by the youth still contained 17 live rounds" (Sweeney 1991).

Knowledgeable FBI personnel estimate that all state and local agencies that are willing to
participate in the incident-based reporting system probably will be "on-line," feeding pertinent
information about criminal incidents to the FBI, sometime in the mid-1990s. But some
jurisdictions still are likely not to participate. At present, eight states do not generally
participate in the Uniform Crime Reporting program (FBI 1990f).

Although it would seem to make sense for the U.S. Department of Justice to be the
central clearinghouse for data on police-involved shootings in the United States (see, e.g.,
Fridell 1989), if that did not prove feasible, there might be other options. One possibility
would be for the government to underwrite the creation of a national deadly force data center,
affiliated with one or more of the national police membership organizations and/or with a
university-based criminal justice research center. An analogy might be the federally funded

---

[24] Centralized reporting systems for officially identified uses of force by police should not be
confused with efforts to also create repositories for systematically identifying the prevalence of citizen
allegations of police misconduct. For instance, as this volume went to press, legislation was
pending—and being strenuously opposed by police groups and the State Department of Justice—in
California that would create, among other things, a statewide "uniform system for reporting, handling
and publicizing police misconduct complaints" (*Crime Control Digest* 1992i). At the federal level,
Congress was considering the "Police Accountability Act," introduced by Representative Don Edwards
(D-California), that, among other things, would require the Attorney General to create standardized
reporting guidelines for local officials to employ in forwarding to the U.S. Department of Justice data
on excessive force complaints made by the public (*Crime Control Digest* 1992j). Although certain
aspects of the Police Accountability Act are controversial, in a 1991 survey of its members (chief
executive officers of large police agencies), the Police Executive Research Forum found that 92 percent
supported the bill's creation of a Department of Justice-based national repository for complaints about
police abuse of authority (Police Executive Research Forum 1991: 4).

annual publication, *Sourcebook of Criminal Justice Statistics*, compiled by university-based criminal justice experts. Another possible central repository might be the National Center for Injury Prevention and Control, a branch of the U.S. Department of Health and Human Services' Centers for Disease Control in Atlanta. Established on June 25, 1992, the National Center for Injury Prevention and Control has among its principal objectives "to reduce accidents and violence" and, in particular, to "reverse a rise in the number of deaths among young people, an increase largely propelled by a sharp upturn in the homicide rate among blacks" (*New York Times* 1992g).

Regardless of which entity might sponsor or operate a national reporting system for the use of deadly force by America's publicly employed police (and perhaps its enormous cadre of armed private security personnel as well[25]), among the earliest questions that will need attention are how to define specifically the types of incidents to be reported, precisely where the data should be reported, and whether reporting is voluntary or mandatory (and, if mandatory, what enforcement mechanisms would be available to ensure compliance). If reporting is to be voluntary (as with the Uniform Crime Reporting program), then it will be crucial to identify appropriate incentives for faithful reporting and to allocate sufficient resources for the data collecting authority to perform the follow-up that would certainly be needed to elicit complete and accurate information from the thousands of reporting agencies.

At this early juncture, it seems to us that a voluntary but proactively administered reporting program, parallel to that used by the FBI to capture data on American police who are killed or assaulted each year, would be appropriate. The FBI does not sit passively waiting to be told by state, county, or municipal agencies that one of their officers has been killed in the line of duty. Instead, the Bureau monitors news reports and other data sources and dispatches agents in person where necessary to ensure that full and accurate descriptions of the events leading to an officer's felonious death are collected. Then, each year, after confirming and reconfirming all facts, the FBI publishes and disseminates to all interested parties a numerical report on officers killed and assaulted (feloniously and accidentally), together with thumbnail descriptions of the circumstances in which police were feloniously slain.

Moreover, the FBI deploys some of its best talent to analyze the behavioral and other aspects of violent encounters in which police have been slain in the hope of developing tactical and other insights that can be disseminated throughout the occupation to avert future tragedies. One might think, given the career risks that can follow a peace officer's having to use deadly force (whether ruled justifiable or otherwise, it is not uncommon for a police officer's fatal use of deadly force to start a chain of events that cuts short an officer's career and afflicts his personal health and family life), that federal authorities would devote similar resources to debriefing and analyzing fatal shootings *by* American police officers. One could justify such federal intervention on the basis of a legitimate federal interest in both governmental risk management and the health and welfare of public safety employees. The federal government admirably provides survivors benefits to the families of local police slain in the line of duty. Tracking, attempting to more fully understand, and proposing strategies for reducing the instances in which local police need to resort to lethal force to fulfill their

---

[25] Some state regulatory agencies overseeing the private security industry require that armed security guards who have discharged their weapons in the line of work file a firearms use report with the regulatory body. One example is the Georgia Board of Private Detective and Security Agencies (see Georgia Board 1992).

sworn duties could be an equally humanitarian and public-spirited initiative—which could command an equally broad base of public and law enforcement support, if presented by national leaders in a forthright and sensitive fashion.

Although the incentive structure for such meticulous data collection would need to be different if the FBI were to be charged with annually profiling the use of deadly force *by* America's police, there can be little doubt that the Bureau has much of the know-how that would be useful in operating an effective national clearinghouse of information on changing levels and patterns of police use of lethal force. Still, the methods required to identify the killing *of* police officers would seem to be much easier to implement than the methods required comprehensively to identify *officers'* use of deadly force. When police are slain, there is extensive internal and external communication, including the media coverage of the fatal encounter and the funeral. When the police kill someone, generally there likewise will be extensive media coverage that could be used to alert authorities to the need to capture data. But when an officer wounds a person or fires at but misses a person, there is a good chance that data collection authorities will be at the mercy of the parent police agency to identify the incident.

This is not to imply that one should expect universal or even widespread resistance from police agencies to participating in such a reporting program. While the filing of information on justifiable homicides by peace officers as part of the UCR program is somewhat haphazard, a great number of agencies do routinely send the requested information to the FBI. The data are compiled in the Bureau's unpublished supplementary homicide report file listings. As Americans for Effective Law Enforcement staff head Wayne Schmidt observed in calling for national reporting of uses of force by police and complaints about such tactics,

> "Many law enforcement agencies now publish this data in department annual reports. All of it is available, by subpoena, to persons who sue a police agency. There is no way to keep this information secret in a courtroom.... Why not publish it on a national basis? It would be of enormous value to police executives, most of whom have dedicated their careers to fair and responsible enforcement of the law" (*Crime Control Digest* 1991e: 10).

The challenges in mounting a national reporting system for police use of deadly force may be substantial. But to us and many others the effort seems essential. In the absence of an authoritative national repository for data at least on fatal encounters between police and those they attempt to arrest, the unfortunate reality, as we saw in Figure 1, is that public policymakers do not even know from available FBI information whether homicides by American police have gone up or down since the mid-1980s.

IX. *Establishing the Credibility of Police Versions of Disputed Shooting Incidents After the "Rodney King Beating" and April 1992 Acquittal of the Officers*

Although public policymakers may, as just discussed, lack the "big picture," they are painfully familiar with the problem of facing a "small picture"—a single dramatic and problematic incident—that looms so large for the moment that it obscures their vision of other important matters and preempts their efforts to move ahead with other crucial items on the public policy agenda. Nearly every community's police can recall one or more such occasions when their world seemed to turn topsy turvy in the wake of a controversial police decision to use force. But the events of March 3, 1991, in Los Angeles presented what many commentators and police leaders consider to be a "defining moment." The power of this "moment" to define and defile American policing and the American justice system was intensified on April 29, 1992. On that fateful day, the LAPD officers who clubbed and kicked the prone Rodney King were acquitted of criminal wrongdoing. Their attack on King is considered by some police leaders to be an example of *deadly* force even though the batons used are normally intended to be less-than-lethal weapons. Any tool may be misused and, they would argue, batons in this instance were used not in the fashion and with the restraint called for by most police agencies' policy, procedures, and training.

The April 29 verdict set in motion days and nights of rage and devastation in predominantly black south central Los Angeles and other areas of the city, lesser but still violent protests in more than a dozen other cities, and declarations from throughout the world by people representing every socioeconomic stratum that the American justice system, too often, seemed incapable of doing justice.

The events of March 3, 1991, can be summarized briefly, for they were burned almost indelibly into the consciousness of the nation by virtue of the chance that a bystander happened to have a videocamera handy. After what LAPD officers reported as a lengthy high-speed car chase of black motorist Rodney G. King and a fellow (black) passenger, several LAPD officers and officers from other agencies finally brought King's car to a halt. Once King was out of his car, a prolonged, group beating of the sort that Americans normally associate with totalitarian nations was administered by three LAPD officers (with a sergeant assisting), as 20 fellow officers from a number of agencies stood by and watched. Reportedly, none of the officers who participated in the violence or observed it were black. The LAPD sergeant on the scene fired a TASER[26] at King and, over the course of the 81 seconds

"As the nation reacted convulsively to the verdict in the King trial [acquitting the four LAPD officers], few people in Atlanta viewed the case through so intimate a prism as the black police officers who have lived for years with the conflict of being black and blue. For the nearly 400 black officers meeting here today [for the convention of the National Black Police Association], virtually all of them wearing black armbands to protest the beating and verdict, there was anger at the verdict and worries about what the case would do to their own relationship with the officers they work with and the communities they serve.

'I think it's barbaric,' said Calvin Tucker, a 10-year veteran of the Atlanta Police Department. 'You ask yourself how anyone could come up with a not guilty verdict and the only answer I can find, trying to look at it intelligently and without bias, is that as long as you're beating a black man, it's O.K.' " (Applebome 1992).

that were captured on videotape, went to some effort to keep the TASER's wires from becoming tangled and the TASER's electrodes from pulling out of King as the black man lay sprawled on the ground, attempting in vain to roll or crawl out of the path of the other officers' swinging clubs and kicks.

We must note that some, including the 12 jurors (none black) who found the LAPD officers innocent of assault and use of excessive force,[27] would disagree vehemently with our interpretation of the facts. Their interpretation is that Rodney King's movements on the

---

[26] The TASER and other less-than-lethal weapons are discussed in Chapter 5.

[27] Some of the jurors after the verdict reported that they had been pressured into their conclusions by the majority of the jury (Daniels 1992).

ground were not vain defensive efforts to shield himself from some of the 56 baton blows delivered within 81 seconds and captured on videotape. Instead, his motions were aggressive efforts to try to rise from the ground and assault one or more of the two dozen officers surrounding him. Indeed, one of the jurors, interviewed by a Los Angeles television station while portions of that city burned with flames of rage, insisted that, the way the jury viewed the videotape, Rodney King " 'was in full control' of the situation that resulted in his beating" (Daniels 1992).

This reading of the videotape was in sharp contrast to what the eyes of most Americans, including President George Bush (Reinhold 1992a; Spetalnick 1992), told them the tape plainly showed. A poll conducted for *USA Today* the day after the officers charged with assaulting King were acquitted revealed that 86 percent of white Americans and 100 percent of black Americans said "the verdict was wrong" (Marshall 1992: 1A, 4A). Most of the national news magazines conducted polls in the same time period and reached similar results.

Night after night for weeks after the March 1991 beating, and again in the days of rage following the LAPD officers' acquittals of criminal charges, segments of the short but shocking home videotape were beamed into America's living rooms on local and national TV news. Although blurry at times, the images were clearer than might have been expected for an amateur video shot at night, mostly owing to the presence of a police helicopter that took part in the vehicle chase and then hovered overhead during the beating, illuminating the area with its floodlight.

The event transformed the LAPD in the minds of many into a metaphor for brutality. And, for some, it may have transformed the simple baton into an implement of deadly force. To be sure, as we have noted, the baton and any other normally nonlethal implement can be deployed, rightly or wrongly, as a weapon of death or serious bodily injury. If use of a simple stick of wood, hard plastic, or metallic compound can be understood as deserving sophisticated interpretation, it is surely more important that an entire police agency—here the LAPD but next time a different department—be understood as far too complex and diverse to be accurately captured in any sweeping generalization. The reality is that placing any complex organization—police or otherwise—"under the microscope" typically will reveal it to be far better in some ways and far worse in others than outsiders believed it to be.

But what is significant for our present purposes is that the behavior of four Los Angeles police officers (notwithstanding their acquittal of criminal charges in April 1992) threatened to unravel the delicate fabric of trust that many police agencies from coast to coast had spent two decades—since the civil rights and antiwar riots of the 1960s—weaving with their communities, especially their minority communities (Serrano 1992b). In print and electronic news stories in literally hundreds of jurisdictions for months after the King beating was shown, arrestees claimed that their arresting officers had beaten them too, the only difference being that nobody happened to be standing by with a videocamera to corroborate the allegations.

In many departments police voiced apprehension that it would be nearly impossible for some time to come for officers' versions of disputed incidents to be taken with as much credibility as in the past (Katz 1992: A20). The media, the general public, judges, and juries were all said to be so shaken by the idea that American police officers would savagely beat a defenseless person that they would have a new inclination to doubt police testimony about what had happened in low-visibility encounters. Few who made these predictions in the months following the March 1991 beating could have conceived that even *with* seemingly incontrovertible videotape evidence of police excesses, the culpable officers would not be held accountable in a court of law.

At press time only the state charges against three LAPD officers had been resolved. Other proceedings were pending: The L.A. County prosecutor planned to retry Laurence M. Powell for using excessive force, the one charge on which the jury deadlocked in April 1992; but the trial judge said he would hold that trial in abeyance pending the outcome of a federal prosecution of Powell and his three colleagues—and might dismiss the charges outright, deferring to the federal criminal and civil courts for dispositions of the matter (*The New York Times* 1992l; Moran 1992, 1992a). The

> *"The type and level of force must be tailored to its necessity. Once a particular level of force is no longer required, it must be discontinued, despite the fact that an officer's normal passions of anger, fear, or frustration may be aroused through a suspect's efforts to thwart or evade a seizure" (Hall 1992: 27).*

four were indicted by a federal grand jury on August 5, 1992 for violating Rodney King's civil rights by summarily punishing him (Newton and Berger 1992; Reinhold 1992a; Spetalnick 1992; Nasser and Lovitt 1992; Newton 1992; Newton and Malnic 1992; see also Johnston 1992a). Also pending was an $83 million civil damage suit filed by King, which observers believed would end in a settlement (*Law Enforcement News* 1992d: 11). Probably the last allegations that would be adjudicated, after all others were resolved, would be any administrative charges that the LAPD would file against the three officers suspended for the beating (the fourth who had taken part in the baton swinging was a probationary officer, and he was fired shortly after the incident).

Undertaking a federal prosecution seemed a popular thing to do: A national poll conducted the day after the officers' acquittal revealed that 79 percent of whites and 95 percent of blacks in the United States believed "the officers in the King trial should be tried on federal civil rights charges" (Marshall 1992: 4A). While praise flowed for the indictments, however, the difficulty of proof entailed in federal prosecutions of police officers for civil rights violations suggests that the federal forum may not provide the relief sought by those outraged over the verdict in late April (Stolberg 1992b; Reinhold 1992a: A12; Spetalnick 1992; *The New York Times* 1992q; Mydans 1992c; also see our discussion in Chapter 5 of criminal prosecutions of officers to redress unlawful shootings).

Of the polls we have seen that were conducted after the beating and the verdict, none asked what effect these events had on the trustworthiness of American police generally. Thus, without any way at hand to prove or disprove the perception that American police credibility had, along with Rodney King, been a victim of the swinging nightsticks on March 3, let us suppose for purposes of this discussion that the perception is accurate. What, then, is a police department and a community to do in the aftermath of a disputed shooting by police? The answer, we believe, is that there is painfully little that a department can do that will have substantial effect on the public mind if the department *first begins* the effort to restore credibility in the crisis atmosphere following an alarming incident. To be sure, there are better and worse ways of managing a crisis (see, e.g., Gonzalez 1992). For example, a police agency to which one of us (Geller) was called in the wake of a racially divisive shooting had compounded its problems over the course of several years by the chief's standard practice of refusing to comment in any way whatsoever to the public during a post-shooting investigation. "I cannot comment on a pending investigation" was the refrain with which the chief unwittingly dug himself and his agency a deep hole.

As we discuss further in Chapter 6, a far better way to deal with the obligation not to compromise an on-going investigation, in our view, is for the chief or other department spokespersons proactively to address the public—through the news media, community groups (U.S. Department of Justice 1986: 15), and other appropriate vehicles—and to clearly explain

- the investigative process that has begun;

- how that process will fully and fairly investigate the incident;

- how long the investigation is likely to run and what factors will affect its duration;

- what the public or any possible eyewitnesses can do to assist the investigation; and

- the kinds of preventive measures the department is considering to avert such difficult situations in the future (see Gonzalez 1992).[28]

Further, departmental officials should understand the public's need (or at least the need of important segments of the public) for

"Two police officers arrested a man for marijuana possession. In the course of the arrest, the arrestee was hit on the head with a flashlight by one of the officers, who said he had to do so to prevent the arrestee from hitting the other officer in the face. The arrestee was convicted of the drug offense. A local musician accused the officers, in letters and through picketing, of using excessive force in the arrest.

"The officers sued the musician for libel. A jury awarded one officer $75,000 in compensatory and $100,000 in punitive damages, and the other $40,000 in compensatory and $60,000 in punitive damages, for a total award of $275,000. The attorney representing the officers stated that the verdict indicates that local citizens are 'sick and tired of seeing our police officers give their best and be libeled or slandered.' Headlee v. Shaffer, *Green County Circuit Court, Springfield, Missouri"* (AELE Liability Reporter 1991: 43).

reassurance that their worst fears about the department are untrue. Without purporting to address specific allegations or aspects of the questioned incident, it should be possible to describe a *hypothetical* event that raises the kinds of issues on the public's mind and to comment, in clear and decisive terms, what the department's values, policies, and procedures require in such a hypothetical situation. Presumably, most of the difficulty associated with a police leader commenting on the pending case is that its facts have not yet been determined. Naturally, an administrator may feel he or she is confronting a no-win situation, even after the facts have been settled—a virtual certainty of alienating either the majority of the officers or much of the community, depending on the disposition of charges against the officers. Without meaning to sound flip, such are the burdens of leadership. The true "artists"—and the truly lucky—among police leaders may occasionally find a way to capitalize on an apparent disaster and use it as an opportunity to advance long-standing objectives for the department and the community (see Sherman and Bouza 1991; Sherman 1983; Nieves 1992). We have seen a number of police executives effectively define the values of their organiza-

---

[28] Among the most recent initiatives being taken in some locales that departments might do well to mention as an indication of their sincere interest in advancing the state of the art of violence reduction are "intervention training" (in which police are guided in how to intervene to help their colleagues avoid blowing their cool in a stressful encounter) and a nonlethal chemical spray called "capsicum." These and other violence-reduction tactics and tools are discussed in Chapter 5. While the provision of less-than-lethal weapons may not be legally required, there is a strong line of case law saying that failure of officers to intervene to stop their colleagues from violating someone's constitutional rights can subject the "nonactor(s)" to both civil and criminal penalties (Spector 1992).

tions in such moments of crisis by announcing publicly that good police officers—like the vast majority employed by their agency—detest the lack of discipline and lack of professionalism represented by a brutal or corrupt cop. Often, however, even the most esteemed police leaders must settle for simply trying to minimize the long-term damage done to their organizations and their communities.

The ability to avert such long-term damage depends in good part on the reputation a department has built for integrity and decency *before* the critical incident. As one police executive put it, "when a difficult situation occurs, that's the time the department needs to have something in the bank—the bank of goodwill." If the reputational coffers are empty or, worse, overdrawn, a single crisis can prove disastrous. Moore and Stephens (1991a: 64) suggest that the best way to build a cushion of trust is to forge mechanisms of accountability to the community consisting not so much of civilian review boards but of ongoing, mutually responsive relationships between the police and those they serve. These relationships, they believe, are the centerpiece of the community policing and problem-oriented policing movements:

> "Strong mechanisms of external accountability are a key to legitimacy. Unless police organizations work hard to cultivate a constituency by expressing a commitment to important values and demonstrating that they can operate consistently with those values, there will be no one to support them when they are threatened" (Moore and Stephens 1991a: 64).

The recent Kolts Commission investigation of alleged abuse of force by the Los Angeles Sheriff's Department (discussed at more length in Chapter 5) agreed, declaring:

> "[W]e view the immediate, Department-wide implementation of community policing as our single most important recommendation for reduction of excessive force cases. * * * It means devolving real power to the unit commander to organize a community-specific partnership as he or she sees fit. It means fashioning ways to hold the unit commander accountable for failures and to reward him or her for successes. * * * [W]e believe it would lead to less abrasion between the police and those segments of the community from which complaints are most often voiced" (Kolts, et al. 1992: 285, 292, 293).

While we, too, believe in the enormous potential of community policing and problem-oriented policing to transform police effectiveness and to build a foundation of police-community trust capable of withstanding the inevitable tremors of police-civilian confrontations, we do not dismiss the supplementary utility of certain types of external oversight bodies. One of the most sensible proposals along these lines was made some years ago by Kerstetter (1985; see also Perez 1992); he suggested drawing on the particular strengths of both police organizations and the community to achieve effective accountability and credibility. In brief, he proposed that police departments ought to investigate alleged police wrongdoing internally, using the skills of trained police investigators to ferret out the details of incidents, something the police can do much better than civilian investigators. In turn, an external civilian body would audit the internal investigative process as often as it believed necessary to assure themselves and the public that the department fully and fairly investigates allegations of misconduct. The audit would typically entail unannounced spot checks of particular investigations to examine whether all reasonable leads were being developed and all parties were receiving a fair hearing. The external body would not, as a matter of routine, receive specific allegations of police wrongdoing; nor would its auditors generally conduct full investigations of alleged police misconduct.

Police "Bashers" Beware

"Officer Awarded $2 Million Against Woman Who Falsely Accused Her of Shooting at a Suspect"
The girlfriend of a man convicted of burglary, felonious restraint (for having taken a hostage), and possession of a concealable firearm by a convicted felon falsely accused one of the officers who was on the scene of shooting at her boyfriend during the arrest. The officer sued for defamation, and she was awarded $2 million after the girlfriend failed to answer the complaint.
"While the judgment might be difficult to collect, the officer stated, the lawsuit should put people on notice that officers 'have rights, too, and we're going to defend ourselves' against false accusations. Wyatt v. Sanders, Green County Circuit Court, Springfield, Missouri, reported in *The News-Leader, p. 1B, May 17, 1991" (Americans for Effective Law Enforcement 1991c: 122).*

Although such a conception of internal/external accountability obviously would need to be tailored to the particular circumstances and needs of any given jurisdiction, we believe there is great merit in the allocation of responsibilities that Kerstetter recommends. Followed faithfully, we believe his scheme would help many police organizations reduce the friction and heal the wounds that typically surround a questionable police-civilian encounter.

Any apparatus for fostering police accountability and public credibility should take it as a given that police work, by its nature, will occasionally generate controversy. Police departments exist because society wishes someone other than the general public to use force, when necessary, to ensure domestic tranquility and secure the other blessings of liberty. People deprived of their liberty through arrest or other police action will, not surprisingly, sometimes dispute the police officers' judgment as to how much force was needed against them. Sometimes they will be right. Sometimes, too, arrestees will fabricate allegations of police abuse in an effort to improve their bargaining position in plea negotiations, trials, or civil litigation.

Whether a police force is likely to suffer in the aftermath of false or exaggerated claims of police abuse often depends on whether the past practices of the agency lend credence to the current accusations. A striking illustration is the Watts riot in Los Angeles in 1965 (see also Katz 1992: A20). We do not intend, by selecting this example to further single out the Los Angeles Police Department; the illustration is simply so illuminating that we are drawn to it. It could have emerged from any one of a number of other police agencies in America.

According to many in the Watts community, the Watts riot was sparked by a brutal beating of a pregnant black woman by a white LAPD officer. Rumors spread like wildfire, prompting real fires and countless other acts of aggression. To be sure, underlying the riot were long-standing grievances concerning police abuse and a host of other examples of individual or institutionalized racism in America. Yet, the kindling that had been spread around the Watts community for years needed a spark. The problem with the spark in this instance is that, by all available evidence, assembled by prestigious and diligent investigatory commissions after the riot, the alleged beating of the pregnant woman never occurred (President's Commission on Law Enforcement and Administration of Justice 1967: 147-148; Governor's Commission on the Los Angeles Riots 1965: 12). How the rumor began is not known. What is crucial to understand, however, is that the rumor had the power to transform the Watts neighborhood into a battleground because the LAPD's track record in Watts gave the allegation a surface plausibility for a "critical mass" of citizens (see also Katz 1992: A20).

Establishing an organizational culture that causes police and citizens to consider abusive police action as an aberration from normal police work is clearly an essential foundation for a healthy working relationship between the police and the community. Many insightful practitioners and students of policing have written in recent years about the importance and methods of leading police organizations in accordance with basic democratic principles (e.g., Brown 1991; Delattre and Behan 1991; Delattre 1989; Moore and Stephens 1991a, 1991b). Moore and Stephens (1991a: 64-65), elaborating on a point we noted earlier, identify community accountability as one of the essential methods for police departments to foster internal accountability:

> "Strong external accountability is...an important instrument of police leadership. This strikes many as a paradox. In their view, the strength of police leaders is measured by their independence and their ability to protect their spheres of professional competence. A strong police executive is one whose legitimacy is founded on his or her individual expertise and vision. That view is the legacy of Progressive Era reforms that sought to improve police management by separating police administration from politics and placing the responsibility for management in the hands of professionally competent executives. The reality, however, is that when the police were separated from politics, police leaders were not made more independent. They simply became more dependent on the last remaining group that was interested in and capable of influencing police operations, namely, the police officers themselves. Without external accountability, the leverage police executives have over their organizations is limited.

> "Thus, one of the important ways that police leaders can bolster their leadership and find an effective basis for challenging their own organizations is to create and animate their accountability to the broader public. That is one of the important lessons that has been learned by those who first sought to professionalize the police and eliminate corruption and who are now trying to steer the police toward a strategy of community policing. Without public demands for less corruption or improved policing, stimulated through external accountability, police executives have limited power to lead."

The good news is that a police agency need not undergo a complete and profound cultural transformation before it can begin reaping the benefits of efforts to stimulate better public interaction and understanding. Even in the Los Angeles Police Department's bleakest recent hours—in the aftermath of the Rodney King beating, when all men and women of the LAPD were being painted as thugs with the broad brushes of partisan critique—officers in some neighborhoods were benefitting from their prior investment in communication and power-sharing with the community.[29] D.C. Anderson (1992) cites a practice in the

---

[29] U.S. Department of Justice (1986: 15) discusses the importance of establishing strong lines of communication between police and community organizations so that when critical incidents arise neither party needs to scramble to figure out whom to contact about collaborating to avert or reduce any misunderstandings or violence. Kolts, et al. (1992: 287-288) describe two protest demonstrations on the same subject—failure of the state government to adopt legislation protecting the civil rights of gays and lesbians—which occurred on the same day in October 1991 within a few blocks of each other. One erupted in a violent police-protester clash. The other of remained calm. They attribute the differences largely to different police tactics employed not only at the demonstration sites but in advance of the expected demonstration. The agency handling the calm demonstration had been communicating proactively with representatives of the gay and lesbian community for months on a wide range of issues and for several days before the anticipated protest held focused meetings with the groups to determine how the protesters could carry off their demonstration without risking violence. The other agency,

Wilmington neighborhood of L.A. in which about 30 officers, community activists, elected officials, school principals, and other leaders had been meeting every week to discuss and address neighborhood problems. The mutual understandings that evolved, and the lines of communication this series of meetings afforded, enabled "participants...to spike inflammatory rumors that police had murdered a suspect—who in fact had choked to death trying to swallow a stash of drugs." How similar to the rumors that many credit with triggering the Watts riots 25 years earlier! Still, the officers who had the wisdom to persist in this series of meetings must have found their efforts to maintain a trusting relationship with their service population impeded by what their brothers in blue did to Rodney King.

So while it is possible for pockets of excellence to grow and survive in the midst of an unacceptable organizational culture and a pattern of administratively tolerated behaviors that reinforce the worst aspects of that culture, surely it is going to be easier for the vast majority of well-intentioned officers and community members to collaborate successfully for mutual goals in the context of a broad-based, salutary set of departmental values that infuse the daily work of the organization.

In the wake of the Rodney King beating, some respected police practitioners and commentators offered the alarming view that the ability of American police executives to provide progressive leadership was set back two decades by that single brutality incident. Doubtless, their pessimism was fueled by the acquittal of the involved officers in April 1992 and the resulting death and destruction on the streets in south central Los Angeles.

Although we may be swimming against the stream of conventional wisdom, we resist subscribing to this bleak view. We readily concede, however, that the jobs of police executives everywhere have been

> *"Responding to a call of a man discharging a shotgun, two officers were advised the subject had come outside his basement apartment with a sawed-off, double barrel shotgun and, after threatening to kill several individuals, fired that weapon into nearby houses. The officers entered the subject's apartment to find him standing in the middle of the room with the shotgun pointed at them. Taking cover, they ordered him to drop the weapon. Instead, he backed out of the room, trying to exit the house via the front door.*
>
> *"One of the officers exited the house via the rear door and caught up to the fleeing subject in the middle of the street. There he ordered the subject to stop and drop the weapon. Instead, he turned around and broke the shotgun open, pulled the shells from his pocket, and began to reload it. The officer again asked him to drop the weapon. In the last attempt, the officer spoke to the subject in Spanish, saying, 'Don't put the shells in the gun. Put it down. I don't want to shoot you.' Only then did he drop the shells and the shotgun to the ground"* (Sweeney 1991).

---

handling the nearby gathering that turned violent, apparently had not had any significant discussions or attempted to build positive working relationships with the gay and lesbian community in this locale prior to the demonstration. The Los Angeles Police Department handled the violent protest, and the Los Angeles Sheriff's Department policed the calm one. The LAPD's demonstration was in Los Angeles just a few blocks from the City of West Hollywood; the LASD's protest was in West Hollywood, a community where a fifth of the population has declared itself to be homosexual (Kolts, et al. 1992: 289-291). The Los Angeles Police Department's effective, long-term communication with neighborhood leaders in the *Wilmington* area of town, discussed next in the text, offers an instructive contrast in policing style to the reported lack of communication, at least surrounding the gay and lesbian community, by the same organization in the LA neighborhood adjoining West Hollywood.

further complicated by the events of March 1991 and April-May 1992 in Los Angeles. Still, we believe that this brutality incident will affect police agencies differently depending on whether they have been paying lip service to building partnerships with their community over the past several years or have really been doing the hard work of constructing those partnerships. We do not believe that a police agency and a service population, many of whose members have generally come to know and respect one another as true collaborators over time, will, because of the tragic occurrences in Los Angeles, develop more than momentary rifts in their relationships.[30] To the contrary, we hope and expect that those communities and police agencies genuinely sharing the burdens of trying to reduce crime, drugs, and other problems will seize the opportunities presented by the LAPD incident and jury verdict to try to get additional crime-fighting and order maintenance resources. The U.S. Justice Department and other funding/technical assistance organizations have stated their intention to devote new resources to police issues because of the national furor that arose over the beating of Rodney King.

We have no quick fixes to offer the agency confronted by new credibility problems because of the heightened public consciousness about police brutality engendered by the King beating. As with any solution, the first step generally is acknowledging the existence of a problem. Despite the verdict in criminal court in Ventura County, there can be little question that the L.A. videotape will be cited to (and by) many police executives and courts in the months and years ahead as one of the few incontestable illustrations of an allegedly pervasive problem of police brutality. Some of these allegations will also claim that the confrontational conduct of persons shot by police was, in reality, self-defense measures designed to avert the sort of beating given to Rodney King.

The veracity of such allegations that police were bent on *punishing* an arrestee will almost certainly be interpreted in light of the individual officers' and the police force's reputation for restraint in the use of force. If the track record a police department has with its community makes believable—in public discourse and in litigation—the notion that the police would have gratuitously beaten the individual had he or she not fought back, then the police department has much larger problems than simply defending against allegations of improper shootings. The department also has fundamental problems getting the information and cooperation from citizens that are needed day in and day out to maintain order and prevent and solve crimes. The department that will weather the inevitable storms arising out of the coercive nature of police work is the department that attends proactively to building a principled organizational culture. This culture must be one that demonstrates in meaningful ways to police and community alike that force is exercised with restraint and that all people—police officers, the public at large, and criminal suspects—are treated by the agency with the basic respect due any human being.

---

[30] Isolated acts of a vandal cannot, of course, be taken as symbolic articulation of an entire community's or neighborhood's views. Nevertheless, we were struck by the irony that several of the towns in which violence in apparent protest of the LAPD officers' acquittals surfaced were those with the most enlightened, most community-oriented police leadership and police operational initiatives. That police in these centers of progressive reform should suffer even slightly for the sins of officers and jurors in a remote location is a difficult pill to swallow.

Chapter 3:

THE PREVALENCE
OF SHOOTINGS

I. Shootings of Civilians[1] by Police

A. Illustrative Counts in Big Cities

Fyfe (1988), extrapolating from available big-city data, has estimated that the number of justifiable homicides by police nationwide has probably exceeded 1,000 deaths per year during recent decades. A simple extrapolation is probably not methodologically sound, since the majority of American police agencies may have different use of deadly force rates (either lower or higher) than the big-city agencies thus far studied. Even if the 1,000 figure is too high, however, it is probably safe to assume that the true annual figure is considerably higher than the 250-300 deaths reported by the National Center for Health Statistics (Sherman and Langworthy 1979). So, too, as we saw in Chapter 2, is the true number higher than the 300-500 justifiable homicides by peace officers reported annually to the FBI's UCR program by local, county, and state law enforcement agencies (see Table E-5 in Appendix E).

---

[1] Studies and police records use various terms to designate the nonpolice participants in police-involved shootings. Among these are "suspects," "offenders," "perpetrators," "subjects," and "citizens." Although "civilians" may place more emphasis than we intend on the militaristic aspects of policing, we dislike "citizens" because the term implies that police are not citizens and that they lack the concerns, rights, and responsibilities of other citizens. Some of the other terms inaccurately portray the criminal culpability of some individuals whom police engage in deadly force encounters (e.g., persons shot unintentionally who were not even suspected of a crime or persons thought to be suspects but found to have been the subject of a mistaken identity shooting). The term "offender" implies a level of certainty about legal guilt that rarely exists at the time of a police-involved shooting (unless the person shot is a convict escaping from a correctional facility). Similarly, in discussing shots at fleeing persons, we favor the phrase "fleeing *felony suspect*" over "fleeing *felon*."

Prior efforts to estimate national levels of police-involved shootings based on the available literature (e.g., Geller 1986: 2) have taken as working figures approximately 600 criminal suspects slain per year, another 1,200 suspects shot *non*fatally, and an additional 1,800 individuals fired at but missed by law enforcement personnel per annum. Our inability to know with confidence whether Fyfe's estimate of 1,000 suspects killed per year or Geller's estimate of about 3,600 suspects shot at (with varying consequences) per year are high or low underscores the inadequacy of the current state of knowledge.

Some things are reasonably certain, however. For instance, compared with the total number of contacts police officers have with civilians, police-civilian shootings are extremely infrequent (Sherman 1980a; Fyfe 1981b; Scharf and Binder 1983; Reiss 1971a; Malcolm 1990a).[2] For example, the average police officer working in Jacksonville, Florida (a city that reports a comparatively high rate of police-civilian violence) would have to work 139 years before he or she statistically could be expected to shoot and kill a civilian (Sherman and Cohn 1986), 42 years before nonfatally shooting a civilian (given average rates at which shots fired by police cause death) (Blumberg 1989), and probably about 10 years before discharging a firearm at a civilian (calculated based on average rates at which shots fired by police hit and miss their targets). Most cities report lower rates of police-civilian violence than Jacksonville. Hence, for an average officer statistically to be expected to kill a suspect in the line of duty, he or she would have to work the following number of years in these cities:

- 193 years in Portland, Oregon (Snell 1992b, reporting data for 1988-91);
- 198 years in Dallas;
- 594 years in Chicago;
- 694 years in New York City;
- 1,299 years in Milwaukee; and
- 7,692 years in Honolulu.[3]

Except where indicated otherwise, the preceding rates were computed based on data reported

---

[2] Sherman (1980a: 94), employing the highly emotional phrase "execution without trial," nevertheless emphasizes the infrequency of homicides by police:

> "The available evidence strongly suggests that police homicide is inflicted in a trivial number of the cases in which it is legally available.... Unlike convictions for capital offenses, there are no records kept of the number of felony suspects whose actions make them legally vulnerable to execution without trial. The fact that the rate of police homicide was only one per 6,822 Part I Index arrests in 1975, however, provides a reasonable inference that the sanction is rarely used even when it is available, since the rate of flight per attempted arrest seems likely to be much larger."

Sherman further observes that "[n]oninvocation of available legal penalties is the common practice in American policing, as extensive research [on police discretion] has shown, and police homicide is no exception" (1980a: 94) (citations omitted).

[3] Comparable figures can be calculated to represent the rarity with which police officers are killed in the line of duty. For instance, in Dallas, where on average an officer would have to work 198 years in order to face a situation in which he or she committed a justifiable homicide, that same officer would need to work 674 years to be killed in the line of duty. Another way to think about such a calculation is in terms of an average 25-year police career. In Dallas each officer could work more than 26 full careers consecutively without being shot to death.

by Sherman and Cohn (1986: i) for the years 1980 through 1984.

A study of New York City patrol officers concluded that the officers who were observed used physical force of any sort in less than one-tenth of 1 percent of all police-civilian encounters and that the use of firearms by the police against civilians was extremely rare. It occurred only 5 of the 1,762 times the observers saw officers resort to any form of physical force (New York State Commission on Criminal Justice 1987, Vol. I).

Even if one uses the prevalence of serious felony arrests—the incidents that may be most likely to give rise to police-civilian violence[4]—as a comparison, police use of deadly force is infrequent. For example, in Chicago during the period 1974 through 1989, officers made 164,175 arrests for murder, nonnegligent manslaughter, criminal sexual assault, robbery, or aggravated assault, and Chicago police shot 1,300 civilians fatally or nonfatally. Thus, the number of persons shot represent less than 1 percent of the total number of persons arrested for the indicated offenses. This percentage would drop further if we could eliminate from the tally of persons shot those not being arrested for one of these violent felonies at the time of the shooting. Observational studies from the 1960s and 1970s suggested that "police only draw their weapons once in every hundred citizen encounters...and [that] patrol cars in many large cities average no more than ten encounters in eight hours." This led Sherman (1980a: 97) to suggest that it would typically require two weeks of observation to capture one drawing of a weapon (citing Reiss 1971a, 1971b; and Cruse and Rubin 1972).

Big-city data published in studies during the mid-1980s suggested a general downward trend in the use of deadly force by police officers over the past two decades (although Sherman and Cohn 1986 reported that a few cities experienced increases in absolute numbers or rates of justifiable homicide by police between 1970 and 1984). Our own data collection from several big-city departments shows that some have experienced marked, sustained decreases in shooting by police over time but that others have different track records. The Chicago profile of fatal and nonfatal shootings over time, depicted in Figure 3, exemplifies a rather sustained decrease since the mid-1970s. In 1991 the Department's personnel shot approximately one-third the number of civilians shot in 1975.

Figures 4 through 12 show the annual tallies of shootings by police in Kansas City (Mo.), Dallas, New York City, Los Angeles, Philadelphia, Houston, Atlanta, St. Louis, and San Diego, respectively.

Recent data from a few jurisdictions suggest that in the late 1980s the frequency with which firearms were used by police began to increase (Kansas City in Figure 4, New York City in Figure 6, Philadelphia in Figure 8, Houston in Figure 9, and San Diego in Figure 12[5] are examples). While it is too early to declare with confidence that the long-standing downward trend in use of deadly force by American police in most big cities has begun any substantial reversal, it may be that increasingly violent offenders—whose misdeeds are

---

[4] Some would quarrel with the notion that serious felony arrests accurately portray the events in which police are most likely to use their weapons. For example, Sherman (1980a: 96) asserted that, prior to 1980, "most police shooting incidents [arose] out of situations in which the initial criminal offense [was] clearly not an Index crime."

[5] While the number of shots-fired incidents in San Diego rose through the late 1980s, it also fell dramatically from 1989 to 1991.

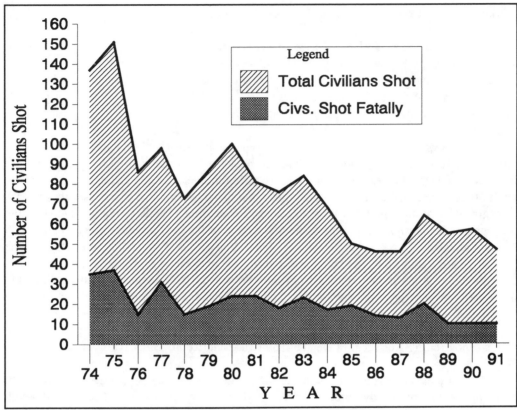

Figure 3: Shootings of Civilians by Chicago Police, 1974-91
Source: Chicago Police Department.

reflected partly in the soaring murder rates in the nation—have started to affect police shooting rates despite the special efforts of many police administrators to foster restraint in the use of lethal force by officers. It may be, too, that the public's increasing frustration with criminal violence and its effect on their life in many communities has led to a climate in which influential segments of communities are expressing their hope for and approval of police "taking the gloves off" and "showing the hoodlums and gang bangers who's boss." Such an environment, in which Dirty Harry-like officers become folk heroes, is one that strains even the most imaginative and dedicated efforts at administrative control in a police agency. Ironically, the Rodney King beating in Los Angeles in early 1991 may have provided a useful item of evidence for police administrators nationwide who were struggling against the currents of popular sentiment to maintain professional standards in police use of force.

The upward turn in the frequency of police-involved shootings in several major American cities during the late 1980s is important news in its own right. Perhaps even more important news, however, is the fact that not all major cities suffering substantial violent crime problems experienced comparable increases in the number of shootings by their officers. As does research in earlier decades, this suggests that there are powerful forces, outside of the ebb and flow of violent crime, that help shape the patterns and the numbers of police-involved shootings. In Chicago, Dallas, and St. Louis, for instance, which certainly experienced their share of drug and violent crime problems throughout the 1980s, the number of persons shot by police (Figures 3, 5, and 11, respectively) have not surged upward in the past few years. The same is true for the Metro-Dade (Fla.) Police Department (see Table E-42 and Figure 56). If one examines patterns over a longer period of time, say from 1980 through 1991, then the

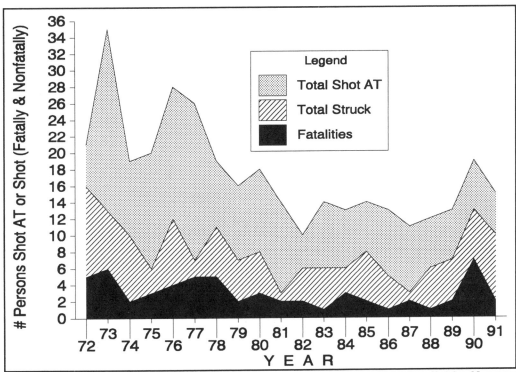

Figure 4: Civilians Shot at (Intentionally) and Shot (Fatally and Nonfatally) by Kansas City, MO Police, 1972-91

Source: Kansas City Police Department.

New York City Police Department also has experienced a decrease in suspects shot (from 126 to 108) despite the enormous crime challenges faced by police in that jurisdiction. The conditions and control mechanisms that historically have been thought to affect the nature and extent of police-involved shootings are discussed in Chapters 4 and 5.

Later in *this* chapter, data are presented on fatal encounters between police and criminal suspects—data that, as we have seen, may be substantially undercounted if national data repositories are used as the source. Here, we can offer a few additional illustrations of police department-furnished data on shootings (nonfatal as well as fatal and, in some cases, off-target shots as well as hits) that demonstrate the trends in number of shootings at the end of the 1980s and through 1991.

The reader is cautioned that a surge or precipitous drop in shootings over one or two years may not signal the beginning of a long-term trend. On the other hand, developments over a year or so *may* indeed signal the beginning of longer term success or difficulties. A successful pattern may have begun recently in Kansas City, where Police Chief Steven Bishop inherited controversy over a substantial increase in police use of lethal force that had occurred in the several months before he took office in March 1990. Upon installation, Bishop undertook a series of administrative efforts (discussed later in this volume) that were followed by a decrease in shootings by officers. Kansas City officers intentionally discharged their weapons at suspects (striking or missing them) in seven incidents during the first quarter of 1990 and in six during the second quarter (Bishop's first several weeks as chief). But the next two quarters had three incidents each, and there were only five incidents in which officers discharged their weapons intentionally in the first *half* of 1991. Table E-4 in Appendix E

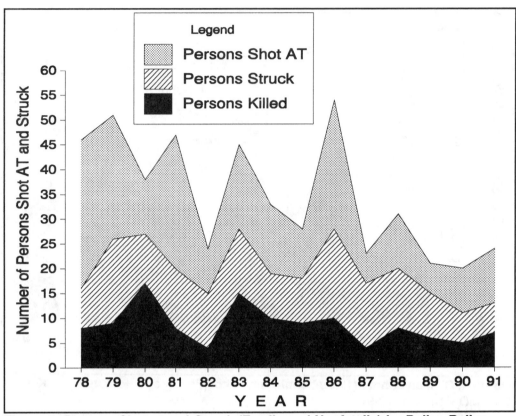

Figure 5: Persons Shot at and Struck (Fatally and Nonfatally) by Dallas Police, 1978-91 *Sources: Dallas Police Department (1990, 1991, 1992).*

displays the Kansas City Police Department quarterly shooting tallies for a number of years, including the period before and since Bishop assumed command.

This same potential to reverse increases in the frequency of violent police-civilian encounters exists in other cities as well. The important point, as we shall discuss at some length later, is that both experience and empirical research suggest strongly that, despite the host of environmental threats presented to police officers everyday, it is possible for strong police leaders to take a variety of steps to help reduce lethal violence between police and the public.

The New York City data, shown in Figure 6, show both the long-term dramatic decrease in shootings by police and the upturn at the end of the 1980s. (Note that the number of persons struck by police bullets decreased slightly from 1990 to 1991, but the number of persons fired upon without being hit moved slightly upward.) This pattern is the opposite of the change from 1989 to 1990. Slight changes such as these do not generally reflect anything other than random variations in hit rates. We do not mean, of course, to minimize the very real consequences of shootings for the participants and their families and loved ones, but merely to caution against a hasty conclusion that relatively small changes in the number of shooting incidents from one year to the next represent evidence of shooting *trends* or evidence of the impact or lack of impact of shooting control efforts or other variables.

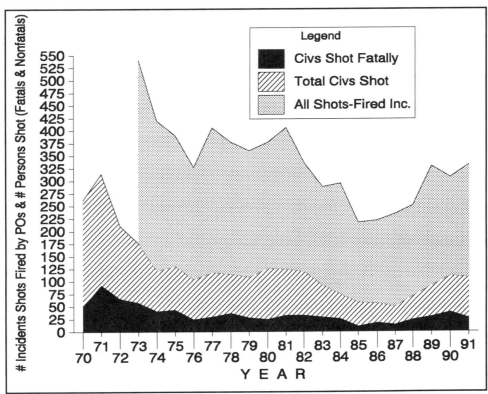

Figure 6: Shots-Fired Incidents and Adversaries Shot by NYPD Officers, 1970-91   *Sources: Cerar (1989, 1990, 1991).*

Data on shots-fired incidents[6] were not available from the NYPD prior to 1973 because that agency's Firearms Discharge Review Board, which initiated the collection of such data, was established in 1972.

The Los Angeles Police Department data, displayed in Figure 7, show a reasonably slow but steady upturn in total persons shot (fatally and nonfatally) from 1986 through 1990, with a decrease in 1991. The number of shots-fired incidents (including both hits and misses), depicted as the top layer in the figure, show no clear upward or downward trend over the years covered. There is also a remarkable consistency over the period 1980 through 1991 in Los Angeles in the number of persons slain by LAPD personnel, with the obvious exception of 1990.

The Philadelphia Police Department data, displayed in Figure 8, show a fairly steady increase in shots-fired incidents since 1987, with a drop between 1990 and 1991 in all categories except fatal shootings.

---

[6] In Figures 6 and 12, the reference in the legend to "all shots-fired inc." refers to *incidents*, rather than *persons* involved in those incidents.

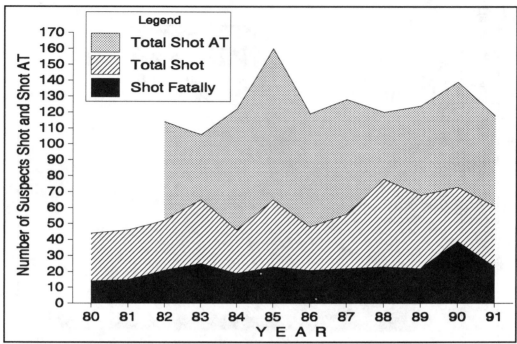

Figure 7: Suspects Shot at by Los Angeles Police Department, 1980-91
Sources: LAPD (1991, 1992).

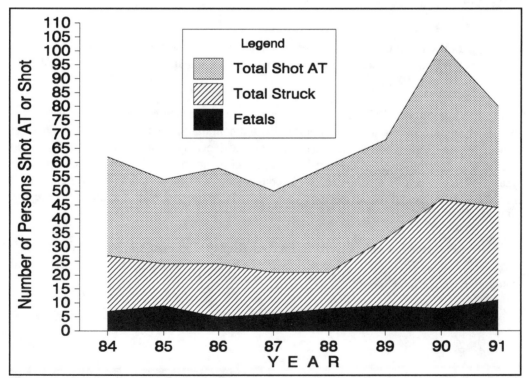

Figure 8: Incidents with Persons Shot at and Shot (Fatally and Nonfatally; Int. & Acc.) by Philadelphia Police, 1984-91
Source: Philadelphia PD.

The Houston data, in Figure 9, and the Atlanta data, in Figure 10, both show upturns in recent years in the frequency of shots-fired incidents by police. In Houston the increase in shots-fired incidents includes both more fatal shootings and more accidental firearm discharges than in some previous years (see Table E-20 in Appendix E); but without data on subcategories, we would be unaware of the decrease between 1989 and 1990 in total persons struck by police bullets (from 35 to 30 individuals) (see Figure 9). In Atlanta precisely the same pattern appears in Figure 10: More total persons fired *at* (including misses), a slight increase in persons shot fatally, but a decrease between 1989 and 1990 in the total number of persons shot (i.e., fewer persons were shot *non*fatally). The parallel in patterns between Houston and Atlanta continued from 1990 to 1991, where the number of persons shot fatally and the total number shot (fatally and nonfatally) increased slightly, but the number of persons fired on without being hit decreased.

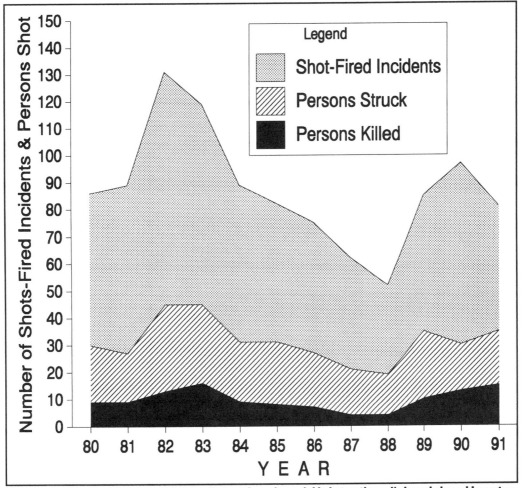

Figure 9: Shots-Fired Incidents (Intentional and Unintentional) Involving Houston Police, 1980-91
Source: Houston Police Department.

After a six-year continual decline in shots-fired incidents (1983-88) in Houston, these incidents began to rise rather steeply in 1989 and 1990. The multi-year decline (from 131 incidents in 1982 to 52 in 1988) represents a 60 percent decrease over six years. The subsequent increase, however (from 52 incidents in 1988 to 97 in 1990), constitutes an 87 percent increase in just two years. The Houston pattern of shots-fired and shootings offers a clear lesson that policymakers need to watch *shots-fired* trends as an early warning of possibly greater harm, for the *decrease* in persons *struck* by police bullets from 1989 to 1990 could lull an administrator into thinking that police use of deadly force was on the decline. Similarly, the *increase* in incidents with persons struck by police bullets from 1990 to 1991 could lead one to mistakenly assume that shots-fired incidents without injuries were up as well.

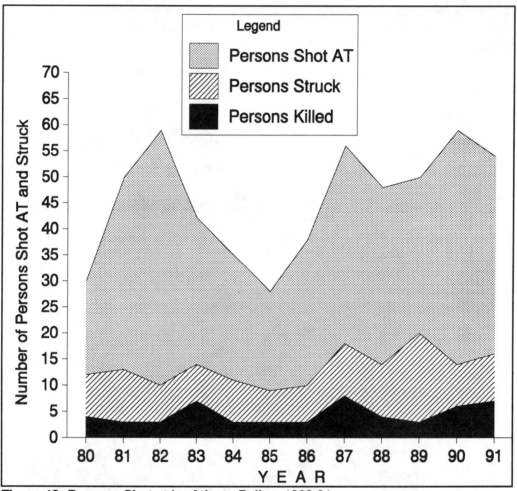

Figure 10: Persons Shot at by Atlanta Police, 1980-91
Source: Atlanta Police Department.

Figure 11 depicts the number of civilians intentionally shot at, struck, and killed by officers of the St. Louis Metropolitan Police Department from 1984 through 1991. Compared with other jurisdictions for which we obtained data, the number of civilians struck (fatally and nonfatally) by St. Louis Metropolitan Police bullets in relation to general population homicides (a standard measure of community violence) is rather large, as we shall see later. (The homicide-based shooting rate in San Diego is even higher, as we will also discuss later.) But on its own terms, the St. Louis experience over the eight years shown in Figure 11 represents a general downward trend in persons shot fatally and nonfatally by police. Incidents with off-target shots generally have risen and fallen parallel to the annual changes in numbers of persons shot, with the exception of the change from 1990 to 1991.

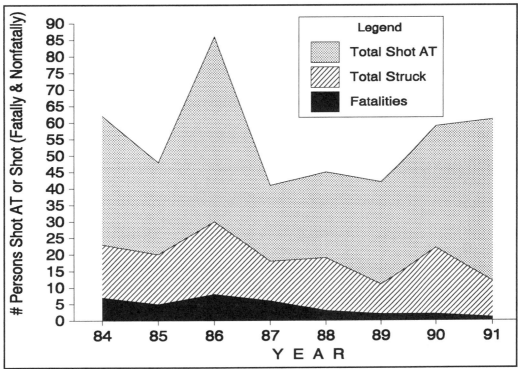

Figure 11: Civilians Shot at Intentionally by St. Louis Police, 1984-91
Source: St. Louis Metropolitan Police Department.

The shots-fired incidents displayed in Figure 12 for San Diego include both intentional and accidental firearms discharges at citizens, but shots at animals are not included. Note that Figure 12 includes not only counts of *persons* shot ("total persons struck") and killed but counts of *incidents* in which shots were fired (both on and off-target). Although this makes the calculation of numbers of *persons* shot at *but missed* difficult, this is the format in which the Department had collected the data that it generously shared with us and we did not impose on officials to recalculate their tallies. (We were also at the mercy of other agencies' particular data collection formats as we prepared this volume, a circumstance that will continue to confront researchers until the federal government or some other entity develops a workable national data repository on police use of deadly force—see our discussion in Chapter 2.)

An interesting pattern begins in San Diego in 1987, when the number of shots-fired incidents begins to rise, followed by a rise in 1988 in total persons struck by police bullets and then by a rise again from 1989 to 1990 in both persons shot fatally and total persons shot. There is a rather precipitous drop in shots-fired incidents from 1989 to 1991, with similarly steep drops in persons shot and persons killed from 1990 to 1991.

B. How Much Shooting Is Too Much?

Before presenting more detailed data on shooting patterns and their variations across time and geography, it is worth pausing to think about the yardstick the reader might use as he or she thinks critically about the frequency or infrequency with which police use deadly

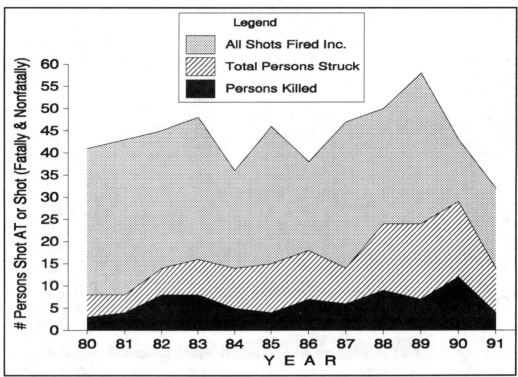

Figure 12: Shots-Fired Incidents (Intentional & Unintentional) and Citizens Shot by San Diego Police, 1980-91   *Source: San Diego Police Department.*

force or have it used against them in this nation. What is one to make of the estimated 3,600 people whom American police shoot at each year? Is that too many? What does it mean in relation to the average of 5,800 persons who die every *day* from all causes in the United States (Malcolm 1991)? How do we think about that question with some objectivity?

To be sure, objectivity in such matters is very difficult. In fact, at some level, objectivity is impossible, and the only relevant question is whether our own lives or the lives of our loved ones and colleagues have been touched by a deadly force incident. As an economist once said in explaining the difference between a recession and a depression, "A recession is when my neighbor is out of work. A depression is when *I'm* out of work." Statistics become meaningless abstractions compared to a single critical event that changes our lives and our communities. As CBS Radio commentator Charles Osgood observed in contemplating a U.S. war against Iraq's Saddam Hussein, computer-generated estimates of potential casualties mask the fact that "every soldier is someone's son or daughter, perhaps someone's father or mother, the 'sun and the moon' to somebody" (Osgood 1990). A defense analyst during the same military action assured reporters that our troops would not get cocky over the fact that casualties were light. They know, he said, that "if you're one of the casualties, they're not light" (Wilson 1991).

Nevertheless, the singular importance and unique aspects of each dramatic event obviously should not deter policymakers from attempting to use all available evidence to evaluate and devise public policy. Differences over time and across geography in *patterns* of police-involved shootings can indeed be crucial information for shaping police policy, procedure, training, equipment, accountability mechanisms, and public information campaigns.

One approach to thinking about the meaning of 3,600 annual "human targets" in America is to ask: 3,600 compared to what? One's choice of comparison very likely will be rooted in personal and group values that in turn are the product of complex and lengthy histories of experience, knowledge, and belief. For instance, as we suggested earlier, the 3,600 people could be compared to the millions of serious offenders encountered annually by America's more than one-half million publicly employed police.

To take an example from one city (Chicago), Nowicki and Stahl (1978: v) report:

"In 1977, 90 offenders and 24 police officers were injured by gunfire during police actions. These injuries are of extreme importance to those involved and to the general public but, when viewed as a percentage of total police responses, represent a minute figure. The Chicago Police Department dispatched at least one unit to 2,489,604 calls for service in 1977."

"[M]ost police officers think that sometime they may have to shoot somebody. 'Driving around, you think what if this would happen?... Finally it happens to you and a lot of things you thought would happen don't. You imagine a blazing gun battle after which you go over and roll him over with your foot and blow the smoke from your gun'.... What really happened is that when this officer had to shoot a man, it took four rounds from his .357 Magnum before the suspect dropped. The officer then grabbed some gauze from the first aid kit and tried for fifteen minutes to resuscitate the victim" (Russell and Beigel 1990: 368).

The number of dispatches excludes, of course, contacts with civilians that officers initiated on their own or at the behest of someone in the field. A more recent example was cited by a task force appointed by the New Jersey Attorney General to explore avenues for stemming abuse of force by police. It noted that 502 of the 543 law enforcement agencies in the state responded to its survey and reported that, in 1990, they collectively answered about 8.5 million calls for service and collectively "fired guns in 167 incidents" (J.F. Sullivan 1992).

Naturally, nobody would expect violence, let alone *lethal* violence, in an average officer-civilian contact. But could one use as a yardstick to appraise the level of police-involved shootings in America the frequency of incidents in which use of force (lethal or nonlethal) either by or against officers might be expected? Some researchers[7] have studied the prevalence of potentially violent encounters between police and civilians. How prevalent potentially violent contacts between police and their service populations are found to be will vary of course, depending on how a particular study defines the phenomenon.

Generally, however, the definition used is broader than just arrests encounters. For instance, Bayley and Garofalo (1989) included as potentially violent encounters "police-citizen encounters that had at least some possibility of resulting in violence" (*ibid.*: 4) "all police-citizen encounters involving disputes, intervention by the police to apply the law against specific individuals, and all police attempts to question suspicious persons" (*ibid.*).

---

[7] See, for example, Black and Reiss 1967; Reiss 1971a; Lundman 1974; Friedrich 1980; Sherman 1980b; Whitaker 1982; Sykes and Brent 1983; McIver and Parks 1983; Bayley 1986; Fyfe 1988c; Bayley and Garofalo 1989.

Bayley and Garofalo conducted observational research in New York City, having "mature students" ride as observers with officers in some of the NYPD's high-crime precincts. In a study designed to ferret out instances of police-civilian violence, they found that

> "patrol officers rarely face violence in encounters with the public. They are only occasionally called to situations where it has occurred; it is seldom directed against them; and it produces few serious injuries either to police or the public. * * * In three-quarters of the 467 potentially violent incidents to which police responded, whether initiated proactively or through radio dispatch, there were no indications of violence, such as fighting, weapons, or criminal injuries. Since we studied only potentially violent mobilizations (PVMs), the proportion of mobilizations with indications of violence among all patrol jobs is even lower" (Bayley and Garofalo 1989: 6).

They added:

> "This does not mean, of course, that attention should not be given to such events, nor that precautions should not be taken against them. Even a single act of violence may have catastrophic consequences. But it does mean that the dangers of patrolling occur very episodically" (*ibid.*).

Another way to try to estimate the frequency with which police officers feel justified in weighing deadly force as a tactical option would be to simply ask officers to recall their experiences. In an enterprising study, a Portland, Oregon, newspaper (*The Oregonian*) conducted a mail survey of sworn personnel in the Portland Police Bureau.[8] Asked "Over the last two years, how many times do you believe that you could have shot someone, with full justification, but chose not to?" 14 percent of the respondents said none, 28 percent said once, another 28 percent said twice, 8 percent said three times, and 23 percent said four or more times (Snell and Long 1992a). If these responses are close to accurate and can be extrapolated for the entire police force, then Portland officers felt they would have been justified in discharging their firearms several hundred times during 1990 and 1991. In fact, according to Police Department data furnished to us (Tercek 1992), over these two years Portland officers discharged their weapons in 13 incidents—which involved a total of 22 sworn Portland personnel (*ibid.*).

Among the many other fascinating questions posed in the newspaper's survey which may prove helpful in thinking about the yardsticks to use in appraising "how much shooting is too much shooting" was "In the past couple of years, about how often have you found it necessary to draw and point your service weapon at someone?" Overall, 26 percent of the respondents answered "about once a week"—with a sharp differentiation depending on nature of assignment (29 percent of uniformed officers, 41 percent of plainclothes officers, and 0 percent of detectives reported needing to draw their weapons about 52 times per year).[9]

---

[8] The newspaper sent mail surveys to 841 members of the Portland Police Bureau, receiving responses from 238 (a return rate of 28 percent). Some respondents did not answer every question. The respondent group's array of ages, experience, gender, and job assignments "very closely matched the actual demographics of Police Bureau personnel, indicating that it reflects the opinions and experiences of a broad range of officers" (Snell and Long 1992a).

[9] The breakdown across assignment types comes from unpublished survey data furnished to us.

The remaining answers among the entire group of respondents were every other week (12 percent), about once a month (17 percent), three to four times a year (22 percent), twice a year (8 percent), once a year (2 percent), less than once a year (5 percent), and never (8 percent) (Snell and Long 1992a). Thus, according to unpublished data from this survey, the 220 Portland officers—a fraction of the force—who responded to this particular question reported drawing and pointing their weapons at someone during the single year of 1991 over 4,300 times. Yet, only 15 officers pulled the trigger that year (in 8 incidents)[10] (Tercek 1992). One could respond, of course, that it is methodologically unsound to use the frequency with which officers in any department draw and point guns to place in perspective how frequently officers discharge weapons. Doing so, the argument would hold, poses the risk of using one set of overly aggressive acts as a yardstick against which to measure another set. While that could be true, still it seems worthy thinking about that officers have their guns at the ready (at least in Portland and very likely in most jurisdictions) hundreds of times for every occasion on which they actually employ deadly force.

Still another comparison that might be offered to the number of people at whom police shoot in an average year is the number of persons arrested for crimes of personal violence. This number probably is considerably smaller than the number of potentially violent encounters as that concept has been understood by such researchers as Bayley and Garofalo (1989: 5). During 1990, the nation's police, according to an FBI estimate, made 705,500 arrests for violent felonies (murder, forcible rape, robbery, and aggravated assault), an additional 19,100 arrests for arson, and 1,014,100 for persons on the basis of "other assaults" (FBI 1991c: 174). Hence, in 1990 over 1.7 million persons were arrested by American police on accusations that, if true, demonstrated the arrestees' willingness, at least in the past, to threaten or inflict physical injury on another person.

The number of intended police shooting victims could also be viewed against the backdrop of the violence that has characterized America from its revolutionary birth.[11]

---

[10] The nature of some of these incidents in 1991 brought the involvement of special tactical unit personnel, whose use of automatic weapons skews the overall picture. Collectively the eight incidents in 1991 produced a total of 79 rounds fired by officers. But this number drops to 24 if just two incidents are excluded from the group, which involved 19 rounds fired by four officers and 36 rounds fired by three officers, respectively (Tercek 1992).

[11] Considered across some national cultures, the exposure of American police to violent death is remarkable. For instance, one early study of British and American police fatalities revealed that from 1946 through 1966, 1,014 American police were killed on the job, compared with 10 of their British counterparts (see Geller 1986: 3). Even adjusting for population size differences, the hazards confronting cops and bobbies differed dramatically during these early decades. The shifting culture of violence in the United Kingdom in recent times, and the accompanying increase in arms among the British police, have been the subject of discussion among police practitioners and analysts around the world (see, e.g., Southgate 1992; Home Office 1986; Mirrlees-Black 1992; Sampson 1989; and Waddington 1988, 1991).
By contrast, compare the death of approximately 150 American police (from both felonious assaults and accidents) per year over the past decade to the job-related death rate of police in the Republic of South Africa, estimated to be more than 180 per year: "Every other day a policeman dies, often gunned down in a township" (Keller 1992; see also Ndibongo 1990). With 114,000 sworn South African police (Keller 1992a), the annual death rate there is 15.8 officers killed per 10,000 employed; in the U.S.A. the rate is 2.6 (150 deaths compared to 588,334 personnel—see Table E-46)—a six-fold difference. The differences are similar when population-based rates are calculated: Mid-1991 national population estimates are that South Africa had 40,600,000 residents and the United States, 252,800,000 (Johnson

Former U.S. Surgeon General C. Everett Koop, calling violence in America "a public health emergency," reported the effects of gunfire on America's future—its youngsters: "The leading cause of death in both black and white teenage boys in America is gunshot wounds" (Koop and Lundberg 1992: 3075; see also Prothrow-Stith and Weissman 1991, and for a discussion of the influence of television violence, see Anderson 1992a). Against the backdrop of either the prevalence of police-civilian contacts or our nation's violent heritage, it may seem remarkable that the average American police officer goes through an entire 20-plus-year career without ever firing his or her gun, except in target practice.

From another perspective, the 3,600 shootings could be considered examples of lawful governmental decisions to kill and could be compared to the number of individuals who, after lengthy court consideration, are given capital punishment each year (see Sherman 1980a). In 1989, 251 persons were sentenced to death by American courts and placed in penal institutions pending their execution (Maguire and Flanagan 1991: 677). By year's end, 2,250 inmates were under sentence of death and awaiting execution (*ibid.*: 676). But in 1989 just 16 persons were executed in the United States. During the 13 years from 1977 through 1989 (the Supreme Court having reinstated the death penalty in 1976) 120 prisoners had their death sentences carried out (Maguire and Flanagan 1991: 681-683).

During a single year (1989), of the prisoners in this nation "removed from death row" (Maguire and Flanagan 1991:

> *"All of a sudden the patrol car radio began spewing forth a series of 'in progress' reports that highlighted life at its worst in [many high-crime areas]:*
> *• Shots fired, Club 666; persons hit; check to see if there is someone who knows about a baby left in a baby carriage. One of the victims was its mother.*
> *• Shots fired; tavern; amphetamine robbery; several persons; roll both a unit and two ambulances to the location; looks like same guys on job before; check license 790 Love Victor Utah, New York; four black males; older model Olds or Ford.*
> *   Finally:*
> *• Car 127 has observed a car matching that description; Eighth and Avon; three or four males seen to be inside; they are in pursuit; all cars please assist" (Scharf and Binder 1983:5-6).*

681), only 16 (14 percent) were "removed" in the form of execution. Of the other 102, 6 died before they could be killed and 94 (80 percent of the 118 total) were removed through either commutation, the vacating of their death sentences, or the vacating of both the sentence and the conviction for which capital punishment was imposed (*ibid.*) While the judicial system thus has a rather large window of opportunity to reconsider and change its decisions about imposing death, police officers, of course, enjoy no such opportunity to "take back their bullets."

Or the 3,600 annual shootings could be considered in light of the findings of the various national riot commissions (see Chapter 1) that even a single instance of questionable police use of force can be enough to trigger an urban rebellion and tarnish the good image a police

---

1991: 133). Thus, police in the U.S. die in the line of duty at the rate of 6 per 10 million residents; in South Africa the rate is 44 per 10 million—more than seven times higher. For discussion of killings by South African police, see *New York Times* (1992k) and Keller (1992a).

department has painstakingly built through countless positive contacts with the citizenry.[12] In our day, the name "Rodney King" has become a metaphor for the capacity of injustice to breed injustice. In the eyes of many, the LAPD officers who pummeled Rodney King in March 1991 took the law into their own hands, as did the Simi Valley jury, which, in a classic instance of "jury nullification," on April 29, 1992 voted to exonerate the officers of state criminal charges in the face of proof beyond a reasonable doubt of their guilt. The verdict and the violence, on this view, were both examples of the public following the police lead and taking the law into their own hands. Whether subsequent state and federal proceedings against the officers would end differently remained to be seen as this volume went to press.

Figure 13 presents a variety of other data against which the prevalence of shootings by police can be considered. It compares the frequency with which various violent crimes, injuries of police officers, and shootings by police occur in the United States every 24 hours. The numbers presented in this "Violence Clock" are averages based on data showing the occurrence of each event annually during 1988 or 1989. Naturally, crimes and other violent encounters occur in a variety of hourly, daily, seasonal, and geographic clusters rather than being spread out evenly across time and space.

"In summary, on the basis of research designed to increase the amount of conflict observed, we found that patrol officers [working high-crime areas in a major American city] arrived at the scene of ongoing conflict about once every four and one-half working days, and most of that conflict was verbal only. Officers became involved in incidents in which either they or members of the public used physical force against each other about once every eight and one-third working days, and that force consisted mostly of grabbing, shoving, pushing or restraining" (Bayley and Garofalo 1989: 8).

Yet another way to consider the question of how much shooting is too much might be to consider the effects of shootings on the careers, health, and family lives of individual police officers. Post-traumatic stress disorder, discussed in Chapter 5, has inhibited the productivity of officers, led to early retirement, divorces, and even suicides of officers involved in even a single shooting incident. What is one to make of departments that leave officers in assignments in which they have shot a dozen or more people? A strong argument could be made, we believe, that transfer to a less active assignment in such circumstances is humane rather than punitive.

Sometimes, police with multiple shootings become local folk heros, as with Filipino police captain Feynaldo Jaylo. Head of the "Reaction Group, the crack anti-narcotics raiders of the National Bureau of Investigation...Jaylo and his gun *Batas* (Justice) [were featured in a popular film that] portrayed them as exterminators of wicked racketeers." Equipped with a laser sight (" 'a gift from my American friends to give me an edge on the hoodlums,' Jaylo said proudly"), *Batas* and Jaylo killed 40 alleged drug dealers in gunfights in a two-year period. (Schmetzer 1991: 9). Defending his record, Jaylo said: "Nobody ever talks about the

---

[12] To be sure, how much benefit of the doubt any particular police department might enjoy in its community when police engage in questionable conduct—and how a single instance of clearly improper police work will be appraised—will depend profoundly on the reputation of the agency and its personnel. We have discussed in Chapter 2 and will discuss a bit further in Chapter 6 approaches that might be taken by police agencies for disseminating public information in the aftermath of highly visible police-involved shootings. We suggest that a department's public information policy can play an important role in shaping the department's reputation for fairness, trustworthiness, and decency.

more than 100 drug barons I have arrested without shooting any of them. Everyone always talks about the 40 who pulled a gun on me" (*ibid.*: 22). With a ratio of 40 killed to 100 arrested, commentators in the Philippines might be forgiven for their preoccupation.

The Violence Clock in America
Every 24 hours in the U.S.A. there are...

- 4,771   **aggravated assaults (2,618 reported)**
- 2,871   **robberies (1,571 reported)**
- 349   **forcible rapes (240 reported)**
- 60   **reported murders**
- 2,740   **persons who die prematurely as a result of intentional homicide or suicide**
- 1,258   **arrests for aggravated assault**
- 452   **arrests for robbery**

- 107   **arrests for forcible rape**
- 61   **arrests for murder/nonnegligent manslaughter**
- 170   **assaults on police officers**
- 60   **officers injured from these assaults**
- 0.2   **police officers slain feloniously**
- 8.3   **suspects shot at by police**
- 4.2   **suspects struck by police bullets**
- 1.4   **suspects killed by police bullets**

Figure 13: The Violence Clock in America
Sources: FBI (1989a, 1989b), Flanagan and Maguire (1990), Koop and Lundberg (1992), Geller estimates.

Finally, one might think about whether the national and local frequency of police shootings facilitates or impedes the various police missions—preventing, detecting, and solving crimes; ameliorating community crime and disorder problems; protecting human life; providing a host of emergency services; and protecting Constitutional rights (which Delattre and Behan [1991] call "enforcing freedom"). Could these objectives be accomplished as well or better, without undue risk to police officers, if the number of shootings were lower—or higher?

Only the most rudimentary and spotty information is currently available for this difficult cost-benefit analysis, virtually assuring that interpretations of the data will reflect the interpreters' predispositions. To be sure, these predispositions need not be denigrated, for they may reflect the noblest

"We reviewed dozens and dozens of cases in which it was very obvious that the officers were restrained. There were times when they could have fired and they would have been within department guidelines but they still held their fire. And tragically, there were even cases where officers were injured or killed in those circumstances" (former NYPD Commissioner Patrick V. Murphy, commenting on the findings of the Firearms Policy Review Committee, a five-member panel on which he served that was appointed by NYPD Commissioner Lee P. Brown in 1990 to appraise the Department's policies and practices concerning use of deadly force—quoted in Law Enforcement News *1990a: 3).*

of principles (Delattre 1989; Delattre and Behan 1991). Indeed, it could be argued that a "cost-benefit" analysis has no place in the framing of public policy governing life and death decisions.

Thus, we recognize that the data in this volume will lead readers holding different values and beliefs to radically different conclusions concerning the level of success that American police institutions have achieved in controlling police-involved shootings. Our purpose is not so much to place our own marks on the report card of American policing as it is to provide as clear and reliable an indication as possible of some of the data that ought to play a key role in national and local discussions and debates. That our own values inevitably will guide our presentation is a fact of life we cannot avoid and do not regret.

C. Comparing Neighborhoods, Police Districts, and Cities

1. Comparing Neighborhoods and Police Districts

Earlier we briefly indicated (and later will discuss in more detail) that there has been a general national decline in the use of deadly force by police over recent decades (with what may be the beginning of an upward trend starting in the late 1980s). But the reported frequencies of the use of deadly force vary considerably across neighborhoods and police patrol areas within the same city (Geller and Karales 1981a; Geller 1988, 1989; Nowicki and Stahl 1978: 14) and across cities within the same state (Horvath and Donahue 1982; Horvath 1987), exposing residents and law enforcement personnel in different communities to vastly different risks regarding police shootings.[13] Because few methodologically robust studies comparing neighborhoods or cities have been conducted, there is a lack of hard social science

---

[13] As we shall discuss later, generalizations about the risk level that officers will encounter based on the reputation of an area and its populace—and based on the reputation of particular types of assignments or missions—must be made with great care, lest they become self-fulfilling prophecies.

evidence to help policymakers depict and explain most of the differences across geographical areas in officer endangerment and use of deadly force.

That there are differences, however, seems evident. Nowicki and Stahl's (1978) data on shots-fired incidents in Chicago during 1976 and 1977 illustrate the variation in shooting rates across the 23 patrol districts then existing in Chicago. The base they used to calculate shooting incident rates was the number of persons arrested in each of the districts during 1976 and 1977 who were found with any type of firearm (regardless of whether that firearm had been displayed by the arrestee prior to the arrest). Their findings are presented in Figure 14.

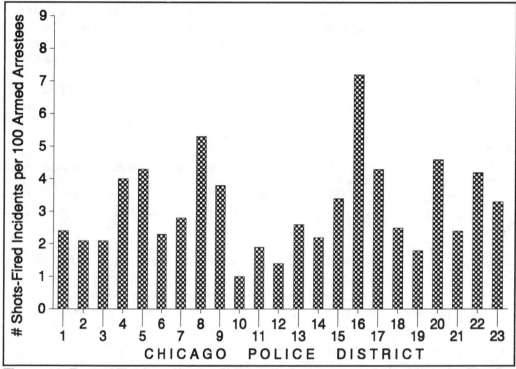

Figure 14: Rate of Firearms Use by Chicago Police per Armed Arrestees, by District, 1976-77 *Source: Nowicki and Stahl (1978: 14).*

This figure, considered together with the underlying data (in Table E-19 in Appendix E), is a good reminder of the importance, when doing deadly force research, of getting good contextual information about a police agency and the community it polices. Considering raw numbers of shots-fired incidents and of gun confiscations (the numbers on which the rates in Figure 14 are based) can be misleading. That is why rates are often constructed by researchers. For instance, the Chicago police district with the largest number of shots-fired incidents (the 2nd District, with 52 reported incidents over the two-year period) had one of the lower shooting rates based on arrests of gun-toting suspects (2.1, as shown in Figure 14). This is half the rate of the 5th District, which had nearly an identical raw number of shots-fired incidents (50).

Another contrast underscores the importance of calculating shooting rates to reveal what might otherwise be imperceptible patterns. The district that leaps out of Figure 14 as having the highest shooting rate is the 16th, with 7.2 shots-fired incidents per 100 armed arrestees. But a police commander looking only at the raw numbers (reported in Table E-19) might not give the 16th District a second thought, for this district has one of the lowest tallies of shots-fired incidents (15 over two years) in the City, and it has *the lowest* tally of any district in arrestees armed with guns (208 in two years). When researchers get to know a city and begin to acquire good demographic information, they may begin to offer useful speculations on such patterns. For instance, in Chicago, two police districts, the 8th and the 16th, contain the largest residential concentrations in the city of Caucasian municipal employees, including police officers. Thus, although there are relatively few armed suspects arrested in the 16th District and relatively few instances in which police shoot at them, nevertheless the possibility of police encountering armed opponents in a fashion that prompts a shooting (especially when the officers are off duty) may be considerably higher in the 16th District than in many others.

As discussed more fully in the note to Table E-19 in Appendix E, the district (the 10th) that Figure 14 shows to have the lowest shooting rate in the City (1.0 incidents per 100 arrestees possessing guns) is distinguished as the district with the largest number of arrestees reportedly armed with firearms (2,477 over two years, far outdistancing most other districts). Although the 10th District might seem, therefore, to cry out for research on how police can successfully avert shootings in potentially violent encounters, for reasons explained in Appendix E the data for District 10 may not be reliable.

2. *Comparing Cities*

We next discuss intercity variations before painting the national portrait of police-involved shootings, because we believe it will be useful to the reader, as he or she thinks about national indicators of police-civilian violence, to remember that local realities may be markedly different. We noted previously that comparisons of rates of deadly force among cities may be unreliable due to discrepancies in data supplied for different studies (Sherman and Langworthy 1979; Sherman and Cohn 1986). Nevertheless, as Fyfe (1981c) and

> *"The data from the present study [pertaining to the racial distribution of persons shot at by police in Miami, Florida], which examines a seven-year period, appear to be consistent with the findings of other studies.... We concur with William Geller's (1983: 322) conclusion that, '...it seems that a community's culture of violence is the best available explanation for variations across cities in levels of police shootings'"* (Alpert 1989b: 490).

Sherman and Cohn (1986) argue, the disparities between shooting frequencies in different cities are so great in some instances that genuine variation must exist despite flawed data. By the same token, *small* or even *moderate* differences between cities in use of deadly force rates generally should be viewed as unreliable indications of actual differences in the incidence of violent police-citizen encounters. Thus, rank orderings of police departments according to their degree of firearms restraint—rankings that could operate to the public relations advantage or disadvantage of any given department—often exaggerate the importance of marginal differences between agencies.

Many researchers have sought (with varying degrees of caution) to appraise whether a wide variety of societal factors might correlate either over time or across jurisdictions with differing levels of deadly force. For instance, controlling for population differences alone has not helped explain the variations. Sherman and Cohn (1986) found that during 1970-1974 civilians in Atlanta were killed by police at a rate per 100,000 residents that was 44 times higher than that in Oklahoma City. During 1980-1984, the rate in New Orleans was 52 times higher than it was in Honolulu (Sherman and Cohn 1986).

Moreover, neither the size of the police force nor the ratio of police officers to residents, which one might expect to be better indicators than population size of shooting incidents, had provided adequate explanations for the differences (Sherman and Cohn 1986; Milton, et al. 1977).

Levels of crime and arrest, while far from full explanations of discrepancies among cities, may be better indicators of the level of police exposure to potential violence (see Milton, et al. 1977; Fyfe 1979b; Alpert 1989b; Alpert and Fridell 1992). Justifiable killings of civilians by police in the largest cities, however, continue to vary significantly, even when one takes into account the general homicide rates (Sherman and Cohn 1986). Early research led analysts to believe that general homicide rates *were* a useful predictor of the rate at which police would kill civilians, because the studies demonstrated a statistically

> *"Police officers drill for that split second when they shoot to kill to protect their own life or the lives around them. True, police officers live through that split second, but they carry their wounds on the inside. The officers who have been there say that the dead never let them go"* (Petrillo 1990b).

significant correlation between different cities' rates of general population homicide and police justifiable homicide (e.g., Sherman and Langworthy 1979; Kania and Mackey 1977; Jacobs and Britt 1979; Fyfe 1980b). But, as Sherman and Cohn (1986) observe, none of these correlations "were observed as changes over time."[14] When Langworthy (1986) showed that monthly changes in homicides by police and by citizens were not correlated over time in New York City, he, Sherman and Cohn (1986), Fyfe (1988b), and others expressed doubt about the earlier declaration that homicides among the citizenry could be used to predict the level of police use of deadly force.

Obviously, more remains to be studied on this question. In Chicago, although the all-time record in homicides within the civilian population was set in 1974 (a time when shootings by Chicago officers were much more numerous than is true today), long-term trends in general population homicides and in civilians shot by Chicago police do not present the kind of correlation that would justify declaring that one or more societal events have a role in causing—or at least predicting—the occurrence of others. Figure 15 shows the number of general population homicides in Chicago from 1969 through 1991 and the number of civilians shot (fatally or nonfatally) by Chicago police officers from 1974 through 1991. Figure 16 combines the general homicide data and the tally of shootings by police into an annual rate of shootings by police per 100 community homicides. In a graph such as the one in Figure 16, the flatter the line, the more closely associated are the changes in the two sets of numbers from year to year.

Rates of shootings based on the number of general population homicides have also been calculated for other jurisdictions, with data furnished to us by police agencies. Figures 17 through 27 show, for the 12-year period 1980 through 1991, the shooting rates in Atlanta, Chicago, Dallas, Houston, Kansas City, Los Angeles, Metro-Dade County (Fla.), New York City, Philadelphia, St. Louis, and San Diego. These figures show that, as Sherman and Cohn

---

[14] Stated in more technical terms, a number of researchers have demonstrated in various contexts that "there is no guarantee that causal conclusions based on cross-sectional data will be supported when examined longitudinally" (LaFree, et al. 1992: 158, citing Lieberson 1985: 181; Byrne and Sampson 1986: 17; and Cohen 1981: 158).

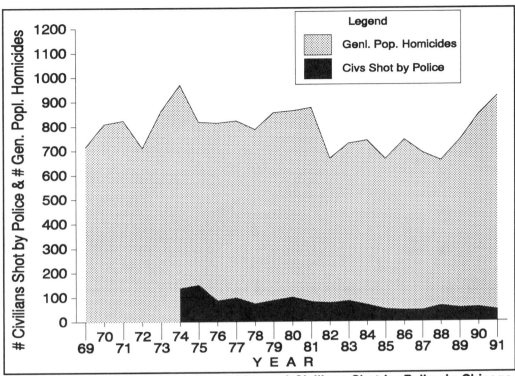

Figure 15: General Population Homicides and Civilians Shot by Police in Chicago, 1969-91

Sources: Chicago Police Department, Recktenwald and Myers (1991).

(1986) observed, general population homicide levels continue to be a weak predictor of police shooting rates over time. If it were otherwise, the graphs contained in these figures would be flatter than they are.

We present Figures 17 through 27, as well as Figure 28, for another reason besides showing the weak predictive value of general population homicides in estimating shootings by police. These figures also allow the reader to make some cautious comparisons between the use of deadly force experiences in different cities, because they provide a common denominator (general population homicides) and thus put shootings from city to city on a common scale.

Where the shooting rates are close, as we observed earlier, the discrepancies between cities should not be taken as meaningfully different. But where one city's police have shot people at two, three, four, or even five times the rate of police in another jurisdiction, it is reasonably safe to assume that there are genuine differences in the likelihood of shootings between the jurisdictions.[15] Figure 28 shows the shooting rate differences between several

---

[15] Observing differences in the likelihood of shootings does not necessarily suggest differences in the quality of a police operation. Ironically, among the agencies from which we obtained deadly force data, the one with the highest homicide-based shooting rate is the San Diego Police Department, which for years has been widely acknowledged for its enlightened and successful implementation of a problem-oriented policing strategy. Indeed, one manifestation of this agency's dedication to continuous improvement through problem solving was the rigorous fashion in which it addressed what Department officials saw as an unacceptably high rate of officer-involved shootings in the late 1980s and early

jurisdictions. The reader will also find additional data with which to compare these jurisdictions cautiously in various tables in Appendix E. In those tables, rates are calculated per year based not only on general population homicides but on resident population levels, police force size, and the number of violent crime arrests in each city.

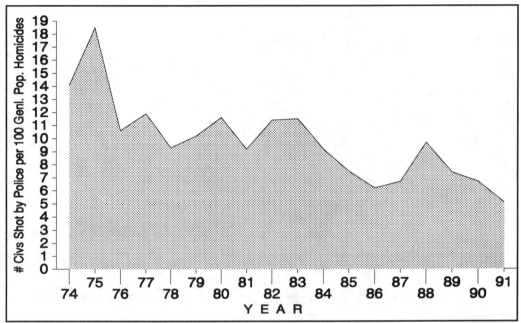

Figure 16: Civilians Shot by Chicago Police Compared with General Pop. Homicides, 1974-91 *Sources: Chicago Police Dept., Recktenwald and Myers (1991).*

The reader should note that the increases in police use of firearms that appeared during the late 1980s and in the early 1990s in some of the earlier graphs may not show in some of the graphs that follow. In the case of Atlanta and Houston, for instance, this is not so much because controlling for levels of community homicides removed the previously shown increases but because the principal increases displayed earlier were not in the number of persons *struck* by police bullets (the numbers shown in the following graphs) but in the number of persons fired at and *missed*.

As noted earlier, if fluctuations over time in general population homicide levels *were* substantially parallel to fluctuations in the number of police-involved shootings (e.g., as civilian homicides rose, so did police shootings), then controlling for changing homicide levels would greatly "flatten" the patterns depicted in Figures 16 through 27.

1990s. A multi-city study of successful policy, training, and other initiatives was conducted, and a substantial number of organizational steps were taken to afford officers better protection from the physical and career risks associated with potentially dangerous encounters.

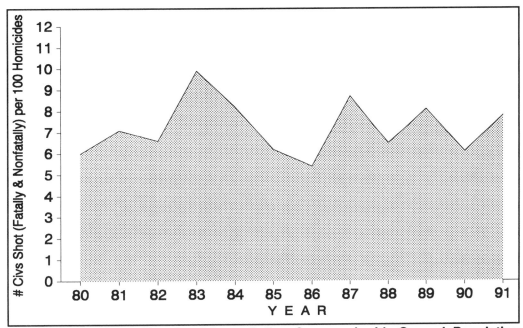

Figure 17: Civilians Shot by Atlanta Police Compared with General Population Homicides, 1980-91   *Source: Atlanta Police Department (1991, 1992).*

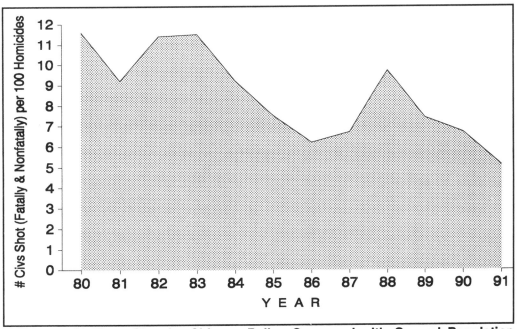

Figure 18: Civilians Shot by Chicago Police Compared with General Population Homicides, 1980-91   *Source: Chicago Police Department (1991, 1992).*

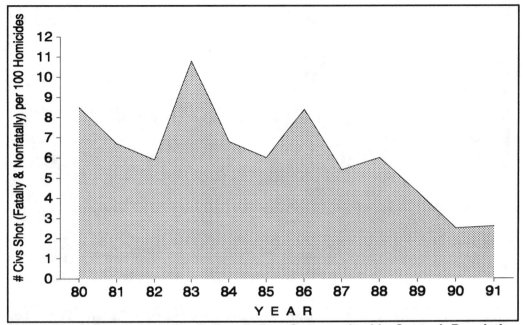

Figure 19: Civilians Shot by Dallas Police Compared with General Population Homicides, 1980-91   *Source: Dallas Police Department (1991, 1992).*

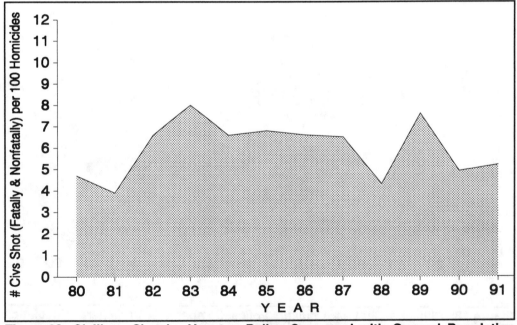

Figure 20: Civilians Shot by Houston Police Compared with General Population Homicides, 1980-91   *Source: Houston Police Department (1991, 1992).*

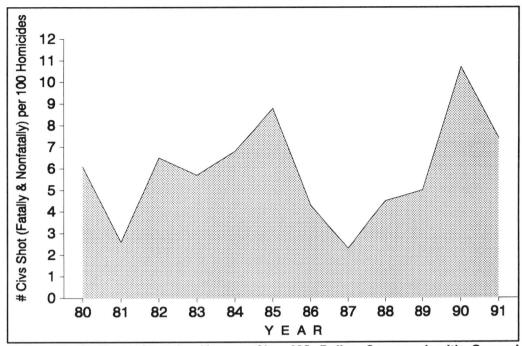

Figure 21: Civilians Shot by Kansas City, MO Police Compared with General Population Homicides, 1980-91   *Source: Kansas City Police Dept. (1991, 1992)*

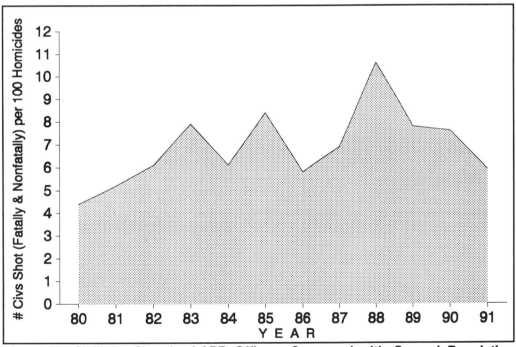

Figure 22: Civilians Shot by LAPD Officers Compared with General Population Homicides, 1980-91   *Source: Los Angeles Police Department (1991, 1992).*

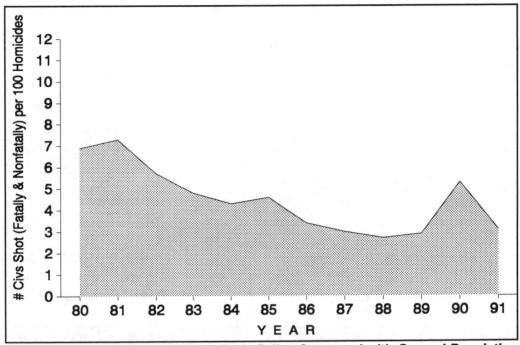

Figure 23: Civilians Shot by Metro-Dade Police Compared with General Population Homicides, 1980-91   *Source: Metro-Dade Police Department (1991, 1992).*

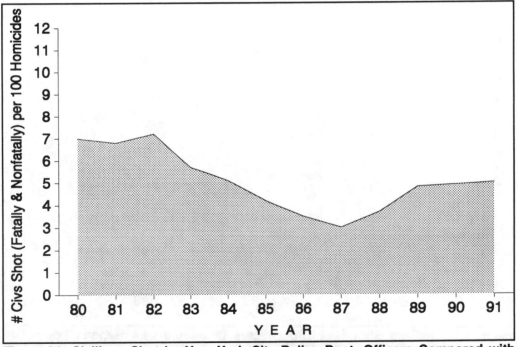

Figure 24: Civilians Shot by New York City Police Dept. Officers Compared with General Population Homicides, 1980-91   *Source: NYPD (1991, 1992).*

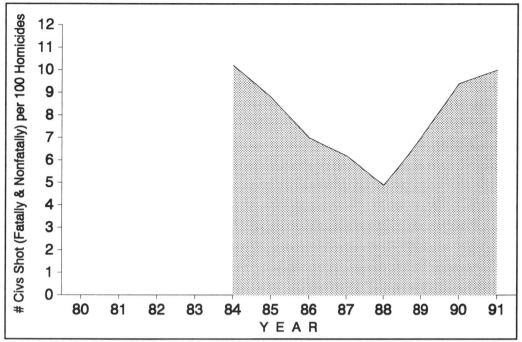

Figure 25: Civilians Shot by Philadelphia Police Compared with General Population Homicides, 1984-91 *Source: Philadelphia Police Dept. (1991, 1992).*

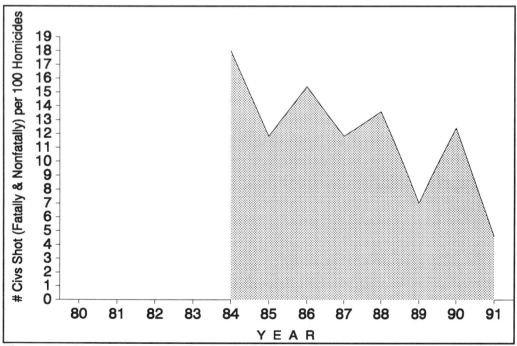

Figure 26: Civilians Shot by St. Louis Police Compared with General Population Homicides, 1984-91 *Source: St. Louis Metropolitan Police Department.*

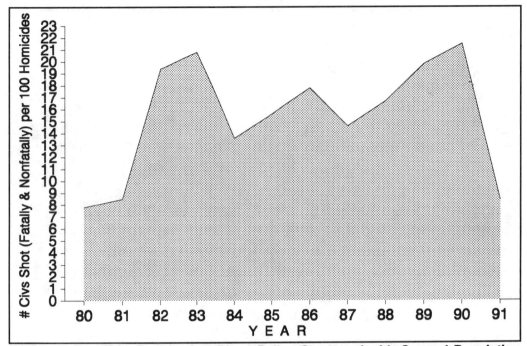

Figure 27: Civilians Shot by San Diego Police Compared with General Population Homicides, 1980-91   *Source: San Diego Police Department.*

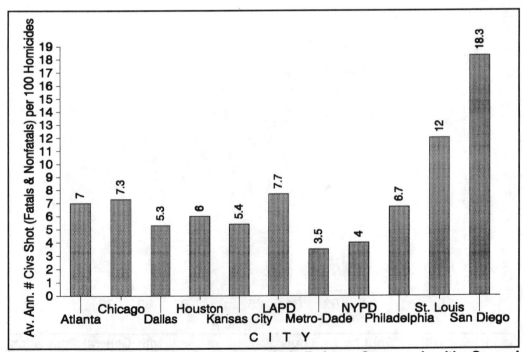

Figure 28: Shooting Rates in Various Jurisdictions Compared with General Population Homicides, 1986-90   *Sources: police departments.*

3. *Possible Explanations of Different Shooting Rates in Different Cities*

Although the principal discussion of possible explanations for shooting frequencies and shooting patterns appears in Chapter 4, it may be helpful to the reader to discuss some of the ideas offered in the research literature at this point, while the data on the differing shooting rates across cities are fresh in mind.

Doubting that different communities' "subcultures of violence" (Wolfgang and Ferracuti 1967)[16] helpfully explain varying levels of police use of lethal force,[17] some researchers

---

[16] Theorists have developed three, sometimes competing theories to explain changing patterns of extreme violence (e.g., homicide) among community members across time and geography. Some adhere to Wolfgang and Ferracuti's (1967) "subculture of violence" concept, which holds that there exist in different communities "subculture[s] with a cluster of values that support and encourage the overt use of force in interpersonal relations and group interactions" (Wolfgang and Zahn 1983: 853). But critics contend that the "subculture of violence" analysis does not adequately explain "how or why the subculture emerged and why some who are exposed to it become violent but others similarly exposed do not" (*ibid.*: 854). In turn, advocates of the subculture of violence model challenge their critics' evidence on methodological grounds (*ibid.*).

The two competing explanatory theories have been dubbed the "structural" and "interactional" models. Structural theory asserts that "broad-scale social forces such as lack of opportunity, institutional racism, persistent poverty, demographic transitions, and population density determine homicide rates. These forces operate independently of human cognition and do not require individual learning to explain their impact" (*ibid.*). Readers wishing to read more about this view may find helpful discussions in Cloward and Ohlin (1960) and Van Den Berghe (1974). Critics of the structural theory argue that it fails to specify "the conditions under which these variables lead to homicide rather than to other possible outcomes, such as passivity" (Wolfgang and Zahn 1983: 854).

The "interactional" theory "focuses on the character of relationships that escalate into homicide.... Homicide [is seen] as resulting from the interaction process itself; [theorists] examine how the act of a participant precipitates the acts of another and how escalating conflict culminates in homicide" (*ibid.*). Expressions of the interactional theory can be found in Gelles (1972) and Luckenbill (1977).

[17] As we shall note later in our discussion of the shooting *of* law enforcement officers, one must consider critically the measures used to depict a given jurisdiction's "culture of violence." Thus, as we shall show, while *homicides* set new and frightening records in many cities in 1990 and then broke them again in 1991, over the past decade all other types of violent crime (as measured not by UCR records but by Justice Department national "victimization" surveys) have registered *decreases* (Bureau of Justice Statistics 1990, 1992; *Crime Control Digest* 1990b: 1-2). The Bureau of Justice Statistics (1992: 3), reporting on victimization data collected since the early 1970s, in February 1992 revealed: "Since 1981, the peak year for victimizations, there has been a trend toward decreasing levels of violent crime, theft, and household crime. The [National Crime Victimization Survey] measured at least 18 percent fewer household crimes and personal thefts and 8 percent fewer violent crimes in 1990 than in 1981...." Moreover, neither the number of homicides nor the *rate* of homicides per 100,000 inhabitants in the United States has escalated steadily over the past decade; the upsurge has been only since 1987. The FBI's *Crime in the United States* 1989 and 1991 editions provide the following annual tallies of reported murder/nonnegligent manslaughter in the United States:

Year	Number	Rate per 100,000 inhabitants
1980	23,040	10.2
1981	22,520	9.8
1982	21,010	9.1
1983	19,310	8.3

(e.g., Sherman and Cohn 1986) began to credit most variation in police shootings to administrative control postures (also see Sherman 1983; Fyfe 1979b, 1988b). (We will discuss this proposition and the data bearing on it later in assessing control strategies.) Sherman and Cohn (1986) allowed the possibility that varying levels of violence *against the police* might help explain some of the differences in the number of shootings by police over time or across cities, but they were constrained in their analysis because their only measure of police jeopardy was *killings* of police officers. They did, indeed, observe a parallel over time between the number of killings of and by big-city police; but the rarity with which police are killed in the line of duty makes data on felonious killings of police of unknown value in explaining police decisions to pull the trigger. Future analysis employing city-by-city and month-by-month data on serious (but not necessarily lethal) assaults on police and data on firearms discharges by police could present numbers sufficient to reach more convincing conclusions.

It is still possible—and, indeed, intuitively plausible—that some *combination* of factors related to general levels of violence in communities helps to explain some of the variation in the rates at which police shoot or shoot *at* criminals from city to city and over time (Alpert 1989b: 490 concurs). The Dallas Police Department (1990) has made this argument in explaining levels of shootings by Dallas police and in appraising their restraint in the use of force despite rising violent crime rates. (The rates of crimes employed by the Dallas police pertain to crimes *reported to the police*, not violent crimes committed in Dallas—a limitation that would apply to any city police force using reported crime data to place in context its shooting experience.)

Geller's Chicago data reveal, however, that over a 17-year period (1974-1990), there is very little correlation between the number of civilians shot by police (fatally and nonfatally) and the number of "forcible felony" arrests by Chicago police. The forcible felony (or violent felony) arrest categories employed in this analysis to represent the community's culture of violence and potential officer jeopardy were murder/nonnegligent manslaughter, criminal sexual assault, robbery, and aggravated assault.[18] The rate of shootings by Chicago police

1984	18,690	7.9
1985	18,980	7.9
1986	20,610	8.6
1987	20,100	8.3
1988	20,680	8.4
1989	21,500	8.7
1990	23,438	9.4
1991	24,703	9.8

Both the FBI and independent researchers have long expressed the view that, of all categories of reported crime in America, homicides are consistently the most accurately and completely reported, due to the value that our society places on human life and the consequent difficulty of concealing homicides.

[18] For those wishing the statistical evidence, the p-value we derived was .219, and the Pearson's correlation coefficient was .3146. Figure 29, which is reproduced in Chapter 5 as Figure 71 for the reader's convenience, depicts Chicago's 17-year shooting experience. The reader will see a decrease in the Police Department's reported shooting rate from 1987 to 1989. This phenomenon is probably driven by a number of factors. They include tight administrative controls on shootings, increased command pressure for stepped-up arrest activity, plus a change in police definitions of assaults. The change in definition resulted in characterizing as aggravated assaults (a forcible felony) for the years 1988 and 1989 several thousand assaults that in previous years had been characterized as simple assaults. Further

per 1,000 forcible felony arrests (1974-90) is displayed in Figure 29 (comparable data for other cities—using the functionally similar category of "violent crime" instead of "forcible felony" arrests—appear in tables in Appendix E).

As the general downward trend in shooting rates over time suggests, the level of violent felony arrest activity clearly is not, by itself, a very powerful predictor of shooting levels. If it was, the line in graphs such as Figure 29 would be much flatter over time.[19] What this figure demonstrates, however, is that, like other big-city police, officers in Chicago have been able over time to cut down on shootings without also cutting back on arrests for serious felonies.[20] Indeed, the sharp decline in the rate of civilians shot per 1,000 forcible felony arrests from 1983 to 1984, during the administration of Superintendent Fred Rice, Jr. (1983-87), illustrates the positive effects that can be achieved by police leaders dedicated to the

---

discussion of this point, as well as a table containing the pertinent data, appears in Appendix E. In generating shooting rates for the Chicago Police Department, we selected arrests as a base for several reasons: As with most major cities, local victimization data are not available; arrests much more precisely than reported crime provide a reflection of the frequency with which police and civilians become engaged in potentially violent encounters; and, historically, serious questions had been raised about the accuracy of Department record keeping on reported crimes (the problem became a media and political *cause célèbre* known locally as the "killing crime scandal").

[19] The data for Figure 29 can be used to illustrate how a rate can change based on the interaction of its components. For instance, Figure 3 (earlier in this chapter) shows that the *number* of persons shot by Chicago police from 1987 to 1988 rose slightly. Yet, the *rate* of shootings, based on forcible felony arrests, as depicted in Figure 29, dropped from 1987 to 1988. This is because there was a dramatic *increase* between these two years in the number of forcible felony arrests. When the rate is computed (by dividing the number of shootings by the number of arrests) this results in a drop in shooting rate. A decrease in the rate might also be accomplished with a steady level of arrests and a reduction in shootings. Or, if the number of arrests decreased slightly and the number of shootings decreased dramatically, the rate would still show a decrease. For there to be a close positive correlation between shootings and arrests, there would need to be a pattern in which the number of arrests and shootings each rose and fell in roughly similar proportions from one time period to the next. If that occurred, the graph would be relatively flat because the increases or decreases in one number would counteract the changes in the other number for each time period. To take simple hypothetical numbers, if in 1985 there were 50 shootings and 12,000 arrests, that would yield a shooting rate of 4.2. If in 1985 there were 60 shootings and 15,000 arrests, the rate would be 4.0. If in 1986 there were 70 shootings and 17,000 arrests, the shooting rate would be 4.1. Finally, if in 1987 shootings dropped to 40 but for some reason arrests also fell dramatically to 10,000, again the shooting rate would be 4.0 per 1,000 arrests. This illustrates what we mean when we say that the graphs would be much flatter (less year-to-year upward and downward fluctuation) if the factors used to calculate the shooting rate—arrests, general population homicides, and such—were strong predictors (close correlates) of shooting frequency.

[20] There is hardly enough data on the relationship between shooting restraint and arrest activity to tender this proposition as anything more than an encouraging preliminary indication. Even that much encouragement may not be warranted, however, concerning the nexus between arrest levels and restraint in police use of *non*lethal force. It was argued in the wake of the March 1991 Rodney King debacle in Los Angeles, for instance, that the atmosphere of scrutiny surrounding police use of force resulted in a marked decrease in *misdemeanor* arrests (Stolberg 1991). And even arrests for violent felonies in Los Angeles decreased slightly between 1990 and 1991, after years of substantial *increases* (Geller 1992). One commentator offered an interpretation of the decline in misdemeanor arrests by the LAPD in the second quarter of 1991: This "probably is attributable to the end of 'street-sweep' arrests for Part II offenses, in which a great number of people were arrested but not charged. This was the end of an unconstitutional practice rather than a decline in appropriate aggressiveness" (Fyfe 1992).

principle that there can be "safety with justice."[21] We will return to the subject of fostering aggressive arrest activity, officer safety, and shooting restraint in discussing control strategies.

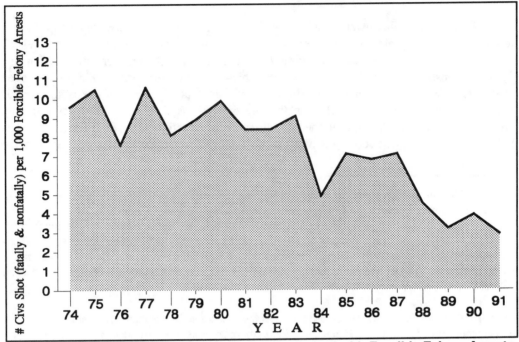

Figure 29: Civilians Shot by Chicago Police Compared with Forcible Felony Arrests, 1974-90 *Source: Chicago Police Department.*

Adding credence to the notion that there is a relationship between a geographic area's "dangerousness" and the use of deadly force by police in that area is Sherman and Langworthy's (1979) finding of a significant positive correlation between homicides by police and gun density within the community. Different rates of shootings may be a function of different numbers of firearms in cities, of different levels of police aggressiveness in confiscating firearms (see Brill 1977), or of variations in different populations' willingness to shoot it out with police (Fyfe 1981c). Police in many urban areas have expressed the view that today's criminals display what Witkin, et al. (1990: 36) called a "new bellicosity"—a greater willingness "to tangle with the law." A 25-year Cleveland Police Department veteran told a reporter, "You used to go to a party and say, 'Break it up....' Now they throw beer bottles at you and smash the windows of your patrol car" (*ibid.*). Studying with some care how police across America's cities are trying to protect themselves and their beats, and what those protective measures imply for the level of police-involved shootings, is a matter of considerable importance. It is also an inquiry stymied by the lack of a national reporting system for instances of police use of deadly force (see the discussion in Chapter 2).

---

[21] The subsequent track record during the tenure of Superintendent Rice's successor, LeRoy Martin (1987-92), may stand for the same proposition, although the issue is clouded by the previously mentioned "paper" increase in arrests for aggravated assaults. Without that "accounting" modification, shooting rates calculated on the basis of arrest tallies would not have declined as substantially from 1987 to 1989.

Correlations between shootings and economic, social, or political indicators have been hypothesized and, occasionally, established (Jacobs and Britt 1979; Kania and Mackey 1977; Fyfe 1981c; Peterson and Bailey 1988; Mendez 1983; Sherman and Cohn 1986). Among the indicators examined in these and other studies have been income inequality; level of food stamp and welfare receipt; measures of "social cohesion," including rates of divorce, unemployment, and suicide; and black political empowerment as exemplified by the election of big-city black mayors or city council members, the election or appointment of black local judges, and other measures.

Chamlin (1989), exploring the relationships between killings of police and various social factors, discovered that, contrary to his expectations, there was little correlation between the killings and income inequality. But he did find some support for the hypothesis that there is a correlation between murders of police and two other factors: increases in the proportion of racial minorities and of poor people. Chamlin argued that as the percentage of racial/ethnic minorities and economically disadvantaged people in a jurisdiction rose, there was an increase in "mutually suspicious interactions" between officers and civilians, with a consequent rise in the rate at which police were slain. Where correlations have been found, however, Sherman (1980b) has argued that they are difficult to assess in the absence of any systematic theory that would explain the presumed causal relationships.

At the same time, even where statistically significant correlations have *not* been found—as in the National Urban League's (Mendez 1983) assessment of the relationship between black elective power and police killings of civilians—researchers have presented plausible arguments for a nexus between a social factor and police shooting rates.

For instance, Sherman and Cohn (1986) argue that "while the relative presence of elected black officials may make little difference," this does not mean that minority empowerment measured by some other yardstick does not have a profound influence on police self-restraint in the use of lethal force. Indeed, the historical record presents powerful evidence (even if it cannot be quantified and analyzed statistically) that elected officials and police executives of *all* races began during the 1970s and 1980s to restrain police use of deadly force. In many instances these administrative actions very likely were ambivalent responses to pressure from a wide array of civil rights organizations. In a few cases, the mayors or police chiefs took policy initiatives based on their own prior commitment to reforming societal conditions and rules that unfairly disadvantage racial, ethnic, and religious groups.

An officer responding as backup to a disturbance call in an apartment building fatally shot a suspect who lunged at a fellow officer with a knife. The shooting officer, now a sergeant, reported that she often relives the incident: "You get into that morality play with yourself—It's not my job to take somebody's life—but then you tell yourself, but I had to do it" (Petrillo 1990b).

Sherman and Cohn (1986), reflecting on the Urban League's ten-year analysis, acknowledge that the correlation between killings by police and the presence of a black mayor was not statistically significant. But they observe,

"There are many examples in our data of the election of a black mayor being followed by dramatic reductions in the total numbers of citizens killed. In the early 1970s, Atlanta (see Sherman, 1983) and Detroit elected black mayors who had campaigned against police killings, and moved swiftly to restrict them once elected.

"But the Urban League findings suggest that it was not only black mayors who were politically sensitive to the racial disparities in citizens killed by police. The rising percentage of black voters in big cities meant that few mayors could ignore the issue, no matter what their race. While mayors vary in their degree of influence over police practices, even constitutionally weak mayors have been able to push successfully for fewer police killings of citizens.

"Thus, while the relative presence of elected black officials may make little difference, it still seems likely that the influence of black political power was an important factor. Massive protests in many black communities after killings of unarmed youths posed a political problem for many mayors, and provided a continuing source of pressure for restraint in shootings at blacks" (Sherman and Cohn 1986: 11).

Fyfe (1988b) points out that, of course, not all mayors or other city officials responded in a similar fashion to the civil rights protests. He notes that during the years 1970-1979, when Frank Rizzo was Philadelphia police commissioner and mayor, his decisions to *relax* departmental firearms use guidelines were followed by prompt and dramatic *increases* in the number of fatal shootings per 1,000 Philadelphia sworn officers. These higher levels of shootings *dropped* substantially after Rizzo retired in 1979 and remained lower for the balance of Fyfe's study period (through 1983).

4. A Caution About Generalizing the Dangerousness of Neighborhoods, Cities, or Groups

As practitioners reflect on the various research efforts to draw correlations between officer-involved shooting patterns and the demographics of particular communities, it is crucial to remember the reason for such analysis. It is part of an effort to understand the contexts in which officers shoot and get shot and, if possible, to generate ideas for violence-reduction strategies. Strategies that could be framed based on assessment of patterns of shootings might entail adjustments in the activity of entire units (e.g., redeployment of officers among beats, adjustments—up or down—in the percentage of one-officer cars responding to certain types of events, modification of buy-bust practices among narcotics interdiction task forces), or adjustments in the tactical handling of individual calls for service.

At the same time, practitioners need to be aware that research drawing correlations between shooting patterns and community demographics is *not* an effort to rationalize or justify individual officers' decisions, in the past or the future, to fire their weapons. Drawing broad generalizations that shootings of and by police are almost inevitable in a given community in light of its demographics (poverty, income inequality, social class, unemployment, race, religion, politics, past crime levels, etc.) can become a disastrous, self-fulfilling prophecy.

It would be foolhardy, of course, for officers to ignore anything they know about a neighborhood and its residents when appraising the hazards they may face on the job.[22] Yet

---

[22] Indeed, with the recent popularity of community-oriented and problem-oriented policing, new emphasis has been placed on officers having as much information as possible that will help them accurately appraise both the crime and disorder conditions in a given neighborhood and the capacities

assumptions about strangers' propensity for violence can lead to unnecessary officer and civilian injuries. Two simple examples may illustrate the countless others that police everywhere could offer to show that the reality of street conditions can differ sharply from what our intuition suggests will be true.

First, assumptions are often made—by police, politicians, the media, and the public at large—about the inevitability of extreme police-civilian violence in so-called high-crime areas. To almost anyone familiar with New York City, for instance, the term "Spanish Harlem" has become nearly synonymous with a number of conditions, including narcotics-related violence. Thus, it may be surprising to many, as it was to us, to learn about NYPD undercover narcotics officers who have spent as many as 12 years engaged in such traditionally high-risk

"It is important that the public understand that just as citizens have a heightened perception of danger shaped by personal experience and the print and electronic media, so too are police officers affected by similar perceptions. The media continually tell us that we live in a terribly dangerous society, where people have no respect for the rights and sanctity of others, that life is cheap in today's market, and yet we expect police officers responsible for responding to this danger, night after night, not to feel and suffer similar perceptions. They are just ordinary individuals who are often thrust into extraordinary situations. They are dedicated public servants who have chosen to serve their community as professionally as possible" (Bishop 1991a: J-4).

activities as "buy-bust" operations in Spanish Harlem without ever being shot at or needing to fire their weapons at suspects (Palermo 1990).

A second counter-intuitive finding comes from a recent national survey of the frequency with which Americans of different racial, economic, religious, social-economic, and other characteristics have ever been involved in a physical fight. The results are reproduced in Table 2.

Table 2:
Americans Who Have "Ever Been Punched or Beaten by Another Person," as Reported in a 1989 National Survey

Characteristics of Respondents	"Have Been"	"Have Not Been"
Total National Sample	36%	64%
SEX: Male	54%	46%
Female	23%	77%
RACE: White	38%	62%
Black/Other	30%	70%

neighborhood groups have to collaborate with police in reducing such conditions. Many veteran law enforcement personnel tend to misunderstand this aspect of community problem solving. They think, mistakenly, that community problem solving means police should practice social work and display sympathy toward all elements of a community—good, bad, and indifferent. In fact, this strategic approach to policing means working more intelligently and more effectively with those in the community who can help attain legitimate police objectives.

Characteristics of Respondents	"Have Been"	"Have Not Been"
EDUCATION: College	39%	61%
High School	37%	63%
Grade School	23%	77%
OCCUPATION: Professional/business	41%	59%
Clerical	28%	72%
Manual	40%	60%
Farmer	25%	75%
INCOME: $15,000 and over	38%	62%
$10,000 to $14,999	42%	58%
$7,000 to $9,999	29%	71%
$5,000 to $6,999	37%	63%
$3,000 to $4,999	19%	81%
Under $3,000	30%	70%
AGE: 18 to 20 years	36%	64%
21 to 29 years	53%	47%
30 to 49 years	43%	57%
50 years and older	21%	79%
RELIGION: Protestant	33%	67%
Catholic	38%	62%
Jewish	53%	47%
None	51%	49%
POLITICS: Republican	35%	65%
Democrat	31%	69%
Independent	43%	57%

Source: Flanagan and Maguire (1990: 270), based on data provided by the National Opinion Research Center and made available through the Roper Public Opinion Research Center. The survey question asked of a representative group of American adults was "Have you ever been punched or beaten by another person?" [23]

---

[23] If the portrait of bruised and abused Americans hinted at in this table is accurate, pity the 21- to 29-year-old white Jewish businessman who graduated from college, earns between $10,000 and $15,000 per year, and votes Independent!

Although, admittedly, this example may be a bit off our central focus on *extreme* violence, we submit that, in subtle but important ways, a police officer's appraisal of strangers' propensity for physical confrontation[24] will be based on assumptions about the group of which the stranger is a member. We believe that such appraisals will, in turn, play a role in officer use-of-force decisions. The point we wish to emphasize here is that, while a correlation between a neighborhood's social circumstances and officer-involved shooting patterns may be absolutely accurate, it should serve as the basis for *critically testing* our assumptions, not as a pedestal on which to exalt our prejudices. That is, we must guard against overestimating the dangerousness of a neighborhood for its police officers based solely on such criteria as the concentration there of poor people, people of color, or adherents of a particular religion. Such broad generalizations about the factors that endanger officers can become self-fulfilling prophecies.

D. Fatality Rates and Hit Rates

1. Fatality Rates

The prior studies show a fairly wide range of fatality rates in large cities. For example:

- 18 percent of the civilians struck by police bullets died from their wounds in Philadelphia in 1975-78 (Fyfe 1988a, 1988b), 20 percent died in 1986 (Pate and Hamilton 1991: 140), and in 25 percent of the *incidents* in which Philadelphia officers' bullets struck persons, the individuals died over the six-year period 1986 through 1991 (Geller and Scott data collection—Table E-12);

- 18 percent of the suspects hit by gunfire in Baltimore during 1991 were killed (4 out of 22) (Dallas Police Department 1992a: 17);

- 19 percent of the civilians shot by Detroit police during 1986 died (Pate and Hamilton 1991: 140);

- 20 percent of the 59 civilians shot by members of the Washington, D.C., Metropolitan Police Department during 1989 and 1990 died from these shootings (Jennings 1991a: A9);

- 20 percent of those shot by Indianapolis police in 1991 died as a result (2 out of 10) (Dallas Police Department 1992a: 17) (see below for the rate over 22 years);

- 22 percent of persons shot by the St. Louis officers over the eight years from 1984 through 1991 were shot fatally (Geller and Scott data collection—Table E-52);

- 23 percent of the civilians shot by Chicago police officers during 1986 died as a result (Pate and Hamilton 1991: 140) and 25 percent over the 18-year period 1974 through 1991 (Geller and Scott data collection—Table E-1);

---

[24] We recognize that the data in this table concern persons who have been beaten, not necessarily persons who have taken the initiative in a physical altercation. Nevertheless, enough elements in the table seemed to us contrary to popular expectations that we believe the table still serves as a helpful reminder not to generalize precipitously. The child's saying—"When you *assume,* you make an 'ass' out of 'u' and 'me' "—contains important lessons for police and those with whom they deal on the streets.

- 27 percent (64) of the 238 suspects shot by Indianapolis officers during the 22-year period 1970-91 died as a result (see Table E-70);

- 29 percent of the 21 civilians shot by on-duty officers in the Prince George's County, Maryland, Police Department during 1989-90 died (Jennings 1991a: A9);

- 31 percent of the civilians shot by Houston officers during 1986 died (Pate and Hamilton 1991: 140), a percentage that applied as well to the 12 years 1980 through 1991 (Geller and Scott data collection—Table E-20);

- 33 percent of the civilians shot by Los Angeles County Sheriff's Deputies from 1975 through 1978 died (51 out of 156) (Meyer 1980a: 28);

- 34 percent of those shot by Atlanta police officers from 1980 through 1991 suffered fatal wounds (Geller and Scott data collection—Table E-21);

- 37 percent of the civilians shot by Los Angeles City officers from 1974 through 1979 died (153 out of 409) (Meyer 1980a: 15), 38 percent died in 1986 (Pate and Hamilton 1991: 140), and, showing remarkable consistency, 38 percent died over the 12-year period 1980 through 1991 (Geller and Scott data collection—Table E-17);

- 37 percent of those shot by Kansas City (Mo.) officers over the 20-year period 1972-91 died (Geller and Scott data collection—Table E-46);

- 39 percent of the civilians shot by San Diego officers from 1980 through 1991 died (77 fatalities out of 199 civilians struck by bullets—Table E-60) (cf. Petrillo 1990a: A-1, which reported nearly the same number of persons shot during a considerably shorter period);

- 40 percent of the civilians shot by New York City Police Department officers during 1986 died from those wounds (Pate and Hamilton 1991: 140), but over the 22-year period 1970 through 1991, 29 percent of all "adversaries" shot by NYPD officers succumbed (Geller and Scott data collection—Table E-14);

- 40 percent of those shot by Memphis police in 1991 did not survive (6 out of 15) (Dallas Police Department 1992a: 17);

- 42 percent of the suspects shot intentionally by Dallas police officers during the period 1980-89 died from these wounds (91 deaths out of 216 civilians struck by police bullets) (Dallas Police Department 1990) and 39 percent of the 446 civilians struck by Dallas police bullets from 1970 through 1991 died as a result of these wounds (Geller and Scott data collection—Table E-6);

- 50 percent of the suspects shot intentionally by Portland, Oregon, officers from January 1, 1988, through February 7, 1992, died as a result (11 out of 22—one additional suspect was shot unintentionally and succumbed to his wounds) (Kindrick 1992);

- 50 percent of the persons shot by police in San Antonio in 1991 did not survive (3 out of 6) (Dallas Police Department 1992a: 17);

- 58 percent of those at whom Metro-Dade police fired from January 1984 through June 1988 died (18 out of 31) (Alpert 1989a);

- 67 percent of the suspects shot by San Francisco officers in 1991 died (4 out of 6) (Dallas Police Department 1992a: 17);

- 75 percent of the people struck by Phoenix police bullets during 1991 succumbed to their wounds (6 out of 8) (Dallas Police Department 1992a: 17);

- 75 percent of those shot by police in San Jose in 1991 died (3 out of 4) (Dallas Police Department 1992a: 17); and

- 88 percent of the suspects shot by Milwaukee police in 1991 died (7 out of 8) (Dallas Police Department 1992a: 17).[25]

Thus, the fatality rates reported for different agencies over different time periods vary widely (from 18 percent in Philadelphia during the second half of the 1970s and in Baltimore during 1991 to 88 percent in Milwaukee approximately 15 years later). Fatality rates may be driven by a variety of factors, all of which may vary across jurisdictions and within jurisdictions over time. These factors include officer marksmanship, type of ammunition, location and number of wounds, and the availability of prompt, high quality emergency medical care.[26] A Chicago violent crimes detective noted that recent homicide records are all the more alarming because "many more people are surviving gunshot wounds.... [M]any of the wounded would have died 20 years ago in a police wagon or waiting for the wagon to arrive. But the modern ambulence is almost equivalent to an emergency room 20 years ago" (Crimmins 1992).

"While on special assignment in East Los Angeles, [three deputies] of the Los Angeles...Sheriff's Office came upon a carload of gang members preparing to commit a drive-by shooting. Observing the deputies, the suspects immediately fired upon them and then sped away. The deputies pursued the vehicle, exchanging gunfire with the gang members. When the suspects' car collided with another sheriff's vehicle that joined the pursuit, the gang members' car rolled onto its roof and burst into flames. As live ammunition inside the burning vehicle exploded, [the deputies] worked to save those who, moments before, had fired upon them. Because of the deputies' actions, four of the youths were saved" (FBI 1992d).

The number of wounds may well be expected to vary with the number of shots fired by officers at any given opponent. Some data are available that portray the number of wounds inflicted during shootings by police. For instance, in Dade County, Florida, of the 31 persons struck by police bullets from 1984 through mid-1988, 55 percent were struck by one bullet,

---

[25] For other studies of fatality rates, see New York City Police Academy 1971; Milton, et al. 1977; Fyfe 1978, 1980a; Meyer 1980a; Geller and Karales 1981a, 1981b; Geller 1988; O'Connor 1988; Temkin 1988; and NYPD 1988, 1989, 1990.

[26] Vogel (1990) argues that police officers downed during gunfights would probably have a higher survival rate if their colleagues were trained in providing first aid for gunshots. Such training for officers probably would also improve the survival chances of civilians whom police shoot. For discussions of the relevance of medical resources to lethality in gunshot victims, see Doerner (1983, 1988) and Doerner and Speir (1986).

the remaining 45 percent by between two to nine rounds (Alpert 1989a). An internal study by the Portland, Oregon, Police Bureau, released to the local media, found that, in the words of a newspaper reporter,

"There is a strong relationship between the volume of shots fired by police and the probability of killing the suspect. In 17 incidents in which police fired three times or less, only two persons died. In 12 incidents in which four or more shots were fired, nine persons died" (Snell 1992b).

Moreover, "of 11 persons fatally shot by Portland police during the [period 1988-91]...the average number of bullet strikes was 9.3" (*ibid.*).

2. *Hit Rates*

The numbers of wounded and slain criminal suspects in the United States pale by comparison to the numbers shot at but missed by police. Of 1,585 suspects whose conduct prompted police to discharge a firearm in a sample of 155 police agencies in Michigan during the period September 1976-August 1981, officers missed their targets almost 60 percent of the time. About 27 percent of the time, the civilian opponent was either wounded or killed. Officers reported firing only a warning shot in the presence of the remaining 13 percent (Horvath 1987; Horvath and Donahue 1982).

Sometimes officer characterizations of their off-target shots as warning shots are considered unreliable by police executives. This skepticism, combined with the potential hazards of warning shots, has led many departments to prohibit them (Matulia 1982, 1985: 71). The FBI, in mid-1990, announced plans to amend its firearms policy in various ways, including permitting warning shots when bystanders would not be jeopardized (Ostrow 1990). We shall discuss the FBI's policy reconsideration—and reaction to it—later, in connection with various policy questions.

Los Angeles Police Department data showed that an average of 28 percent of known police firearm discharge incidents from 1980 through 1988 resulted in either the death or wounding of a civilian (LAPD 1989). This is a sharp decrease from the LAPD's 56 percent hit rate during the 1970s (Meyer 1980a: 14-15 reports 733 civilians shot at by officers from 1974 through 1979, of whom 409 were struck); but it closely parallels the recent hit rates in the New York City Police Department. In 1987 and 1988 officers of the NYPD reported hit rates of 26 and 31 percent, respectively (NYPD 1988, 1989) and, in 1990, 23 percent (Cerar 1990: 7).

A number of other agencies for which shots-fired data are available fall somewhere between the current New York/Los Angeles hit rates and the hit rates exceeding 50 percent of LAPD officers in the 1970s.[27] For instance, Pate and Hamilton (1991: 139) present data

---

[27] There are undoubtedly exceptions to this range of hit rates of which we are unaware. One startling exception, reported in the *Washington Post* apparently is the Prince George's County, Maryland, Police Department. If accurately reported, this agency had 21 on-duty incidents over the course of 1989 and 1990 in which their officers fired at civilians, with a *100 percent* hit rate (Jennings 1991a, 1991b). Even if true, such a hit rate must be considered in light of the comparatively small number of incidents involved; over a longer time period and a greater number of cases, this hit rate is unlikely to hold. Moreover, interesting questions might be asked about the number of rounds fired by officers, the proximity between officers and adversaries, and other circumstances in these encounters in Prince George's County.

for the nation's six largest police agencies, reporting that, in 1986, the percentages of civilians struck by police bullets (calculated by comparing civilians wounded or killed to the number of firearms discharge incidents) was 24 percent for police in New York City, 25 percent for Detroit, 26 percent for Chicago, 33 percent for Philadelphia, 42 percent for Los Angeles, and 43 percent for Houston. Alpert (1989b: 488) reports that 31 percent of the 50 incidents in which Miami police officers intentionally fired their weapons at others over the seven years 1980-86 resulted in fatal or nonfatal injuries to citizens.

Our own data collection revealed the following additional hit rates:

- 46 percent of the persons reportedly shot at *intentionally* by Kansas City (Mo.) police officers over the 20 years 1972 through 1991 were struck by one or more police bullets (162 persons struck out of 349 shot at) (Table E-4);

- 49 percent of the suspects fired at by LAPD officers during the ten years from 1982 through 1991 were struck (Table E-17);

- 69 percent of the suspects fired at intentionally by Portland, Oregon, police officers from January 1, 1988, through February 7, 1992, were struck by at least one bullet (22 out of 29—one additional person was shot unintentionally) (Kindrick 1992: 3);

- 56 percent of those shot at by Dallas officers over the 14 years from 1978 through 1991 were struck (Table E-56); and

- in several cities (e.g., Houston, Atlanta, St. Louis, and San Diego), we have only data on the number of *incidents* in which officers fired their weapons and data on the number of *persons* struck by the rounds fired, which prevents the calculation of either "person" or "incident" hit rates (see Tables E-20, E-21, E-52, and E-60; also see Table E-46 containing Kansas City data).

A Dallas Police Department survey of major city police agencies disclosed additional hit rates during the year 1991. According to police reports, the percentages of *persons* struck who were fired at that year were:

- 25 percent in Memphis (15 out of 61);

- 40 percent in El Paso (2 out of 5);

- 50 percent in Austin (5 out of 10);

- 50 percent in Seattle (1 out of 2);

- 51 percent in Baltimore (22 out of 43);

- 53 percent in Milwaukee (8 out of 15);

- 53 percent in Phoenix (8 out of 15);

- 56 percent in Indianapolis (10 out of 18);

- 60 percent in Oklahoma City (3 out of 5);

- 67 percent in Cincinnati (2 out of 3);

- 67 percent in San Jose (4 out of 6);

- 100 percent in San Antonio (6 out of 6); and

- 100 percent in San Francisco (also 6 out of 6) (Dallas Police Department 1992a: 17).

A St. Louis Metropolitan Police Department study of police firearms discharges completed in May 1992 documented *incident* hit rates for several jurisdictions for the years 1987 through 1990. The annual average hit rates identified were:

- 29 percent in Washington, D.C. (persons were struck in 23 out of 79 incidents per year—based on data only for the years 1989 and 1990);

- 37 percent in St. Louis (persons were struck in 15.8 out of 42.8 incidents per year);

- 50 percent in Baltimore (persons were struck in 18.5 out of 36.8 incidents per year); and

- 60 percent in Seattle (persons were struck in 2.7 out of 4.5 incidents per year) (St. Louis Metropolitan Police Department 1992: 32-33).

The same study also reported a *suspect* hit for one additional agency:

- 54 percent in Cleveland (9.5 out of 17.5 persons fired at per year were struck during the period 1987-90) (St. Louis Metropolitan Police Department 1992: 32).

There is a difference between the percentages of persons struck who are fired at by NYPD officers and by officers of their "sister" agency, the New York City Transit Police Department (NYTPD). In contrast with the hit rates for the NYPD, which have ranged in recent years from 24 to 31 percent, the NYTPD's hit rates have ranged from 32 to 86 percent (New York City Transit Police Department 1991). The numbers on which the Transit Department's rates are generated are considerably smaller but nonetheless noteworthy. From 1985 through 1990, Transit officers fired intentionally at suspects in a total of 114 incidents, striking 55 of their targets, for a six-year average hit rate of 48 percent. The numbers on which this rate was calculated are flawed (*incidents* are compared with *persons* rather than persons fired at being compared with persons struck), but these are the only data readily available. The year with the highest Transit police hit rate (86 percent) was 1987, when offices struck 12 people they fired at in 14 incidents (NYTPD 1991).

Why should there be such differences in the experience of Transit police and City police in New York's five boroughs? After all, for years, both sets of officers have received a substantial portion of their basic training side by side in the NYPD's academy (the initial stage of basic training was identical for City police, Transit police, and Housing police). Thereafter, the Transit Police officers went though a three-week specialized training program administered by the Transit Police Department. Since 1990 the Transit Police Department has assumed a much larger responsibility for basic training of its recruits (Bratton 1991).

One possible reason for the differences in officer-involved shooting experiences between City and Transit police could be differences in working environments. It is plausible, for instance, that the confined spaces of subway stations and subway cars produce hit rates (both of and by officers) higher than elsewhere. Indeed, we will see later in this section that the *bullet* hit rate (number of *rounds* fired that strike their target) was higher for Transit than for City police during comparable periods in New York (Bratton 1990a; NYPD 1989).

As plausible an explanation as differences in their working environments might seem, data show that a substantial majority of the shootings by Transit officers occur "off system," that is not on property (subway or elevated train stations, trains, or yards) owned by the Transit Authority (Bratton 1991; NYTPD 1991). Of 168 incidents in which Transit officers discharged their firearms (intentionally and accidentally, including both persons struck and off-target shots) from 1985 through 1990, in 74 percent of the incidents the officers were "off system" (NYTPD 1991). Sometimes this occurs because of an encounter that begins on Transit Authority property and continues onto city streets; but often the explanation for the large percentage of off-system firearms discharges is that the involved Transit officers are off duty. Of the 168 incidents from 1985 through 1990, officers were off duty in 91 (54 percent) (NYTPD 1991). Even though only a small portion of shootings occur in subway cars, stations, and on other Transit Authority property (26 percent over the years 1985 through 1990), high hit rates in those incidents may help account for the Transit Police Department's comparatively high average hit rates in all shootings.

Other factors, too, may help explain the rate at which Transit officers strike offenders when they shoot. For instance, the deployment of Transit officers is such that most of the time a lone officer will have to handle whatever incident he or she enters. In contrast, of the NYPD members who were involved in 757 reported incidents during 1990 in which they either discharged their firearms or were seriously assaulted or both, only 19 percent were unaccompanied by other officers at the time (Cerar 1990: 5).[28] By working alone—and working with a woefully inadequate radio communications system—Transit officers know that there is little chance they will receive backup during a critical incident. It is possible that they hit offenders at whom they fire at elevated rates in part because the officers know that their own proficiency with the weapon may be the only thing that keeps them alive in a dangerous encounter. As Bill Wiese, chief of inspectional services for the Transit police, put it (1991), "As a Transit cop, once I commit to something, it's *me* that has to conclude it. I can't just hold on for a minute and have another officer arrive."

Two officers *"responded to the report of an armed man who had taken a child hostage and barricaded himself in a residence. As the officers took positions near the house, the subject appeared on the back porch and fired two shots into the yard. He then told the psychiatric counselor with whom he'd been speaking by telephone that he intended to kill the first officer to arrive. However, [these two officers] successfully talked the distraught man out of the house and convinced him to surrender his weapon without incident"* (FBI 1992b: 33).

---

[28] A recent study of firearms discharges by police in Portland, Oregon, disclosed that, over the four years from January 1, 1988 through February 7, 1992, "police who fired when they were alone...fired fewer shots than when other officers took part. The 21 lone officers fired 57 shots, or 2.7, on average. The 22 who fired as part of a group shot 129 times, averaging 5.9" (Snell 1992b).

In an experience more akin to that of the NYPD, officers in the Metro-Dade (Fla.) Police Department struck 31 percent of the civilians at whom they fired purposefully from January 1984 through June 1988 (31 out of 100 subjects fired at) (Alpert 1989a). Alpert offers an intriguing finding from Metro-Dade: "There is no relation between shots fired that hit their targets and the officer's qualifying score" (1989a: 5). With a wide variety of range practice conditions used by different police agencies, some directly relevant and some barely relevant to street conditions (Matulia 1985: 76-78), it is possible that a careful comparative study would show that range qualification scores correlate much more closely with field combat skills in some locales than in others.

Aside from the challenges of obtaining complete and accurate reports from officers about off-target shots, one must be cautious in comparing hit rates across cities or studies. No methodologically sound comparative study has yet been done on this topic. One conclusion that can be derived from studies of hit rates is that the rates debunk the Hollywood-generated myth that police can shoot a handgun under combat conditions accurately enough to "wing" rather than kill a suspect (Geller and Karales 1981a, 1981b). The myth often surfaces when people call in the wake of a fatal shooting for an officer's dismissal because he aimed, in accordance with training, at the suspect's torso rather than a less vulnerable body part. For instance, told that an officer had fired only to disarm her teenage brother, a Newark woman demanded, "Then why didn't he shoot him in the arm instead of the chest?" (J. Sullivan 1992b). The IACP was emphatic about correcting this myth:

> *Although marksmanship under combat conditions often is very limited, stories abound of officers at least attempting to shoot suspects in ways that will stop but not slay them. Sometimes they succeed: A sergeant in the Military Police "responded to the report of gunfire in a base housing area. [He] was taking information from a witness when a man carrying two firearms approached them. The gunman fired two rounds, narrowly missing [the sergeant] and shattering the windshield of his patrol vehicle. When [the sergeant] identified himself and ordered the man to drop his weapons, the man fired upon him again. [The sergeant] refrained from returning fire until a clear shot was available, then shot at the assailant's legs to immobilize him. The gunman was then taken into custody" (FBI 1992a: 33).*

> "Television and the movie screen have generally portrayed the wild west sheriff and the contemporary police officer as a sharp shooter who could shoot the eye out of a gnat. Whereas in reality many police officers have a difficult time meeting departmental qualification standards at the firing range, let alone during a combat situation" (Matulia 1985: 69).

A related myth of Hollywood's making is that officers, in combat, can invariably accomplish their tactical objectives with a single shot. While cases with large numbers of bullet wounds to suspects certainly bear particular scrutiny for a range of obvious tactical and political reasons, still the public and media sometimes make overly simplistic assessments of police capabilities to stop a lethal threat by an adversary with a single shot. We do not pretend to have the information necessary to judge the shooting on its merits, but a May 1992 fatal shooting by New York City police officers generated a public reaction that illustrates our point. Friends of the decedent, a Dominican night club owner, challenged the police assertion that the deceased had precipitated the shooting by attacking the police. One angry friend of the nightclub proprietor told the *New York Times*: "There were six police officers. Be for real here. If you're going to shoot someone, shoot him one time" (Lorch 1992).

Citing findings about hit rates ranging from 18 to 62 percent in Michigan (Horvath and Donahue 1982), Los Angeles (Meyer 1980b), and Chicago (Geller and Karales 1981a), the IACP declared:

> "These results are probably typical of our nation's police officers' ability to hit a live target under combat conditions. The results certainly dispel any potential to 'shoot the gun out of the assailant's hand,' 'shoot a leg or arm" or 'shoot to wound.' Officers have traditionally been trained to shoot at center body mass. It is now time to place the training standard in policy statements. Such a policy should increase the hit rate and [better protect] the officer [because] the shooting will stop the assailant" (Matulia 1985: 69).

Particularly when there is an exchange of gunfire between an officer and a civilian, the probability that *either* shooter will hit his or her target appears rather low from existing studies. In recent years, NYPD members hit suspects during shoot-outs with only 18 percent of their shots (treating shotgun rounds as a single shot) (NYPD 1989). In 1990 the bullet hit rate for NYPD officers in gunfights was 19 percent (Cerar 1990: 9).

But rates in this range are higher than the mere 8 percent of suspects' shots that hit NYPD officers during the mid-1980s and their 6 percent hit rate in 1990 (Cerar 1990: 9), presumably due at least in part to superior police firearms training. Another factor worthy of analysis across a number of police agencies is whether a higher *person* (as distinguished from *bullet*) hit-rate for shots fired by police than by their adversaries in shoot-outs might be related to a difference in the number of shots fired by each. For instance, in New York City in 1990, during gunfights, suspects fired an average of 2.8 rounds per incident, while NYPD officers discharged their weapons an average of 4.4 times (Cerar 1990: 9).

Computations of the hit rate for *bullets fired* or *persons fired at or struck* should not be confused with *incident* hit rates. In any given *incident*, police may shoot at more than one *person* and may fire more than one *bullet*.[29] As a result, the incident hit rate might be higher than the bullet hit-rate in any particular jurisdiction. For example, officers of the Metro-Dade Police Department fired a single shot in 88 (52 percent) of 169 incidents for which such data were available during the 1980s; two shots were fired in 32 (19 percent) of these encounters; and three or more shots were fired in 49 (29 percent) incidents. More than six shots were fired by Metro-Dade officers in only one out of these 169 incidents (0.6 percent) (Alpert 1989a). The Metro-Dade *incident* hit rate of 31 percent compares with a reported *bullet* hit rate of 16 percent (Alpert 1989a: 5). Sometimes the incident and bullet hit rates will be relatively similar. In Portland, Oregon, for instance, during the sightly more than four years from January 1988 through February 7, 1992, the incident hit rate was 69 percent (at least one round struck the suspect in 20 out of 29 incidents). And the *bullet* hit rate in the same encounters was 60 percent (112 hits out of 186 shots fired) (Snell 1992b; Kindrick 1992). But this similarity between the incident and bullet hit rates does not hold up when a longer period is analyzed in Portland. Over the slightly more than nine-year period from January 1, 1983, through February 7, 1992, the agency experienced an *incident* hit rate of 65 percent (suspects where struck in 41 of the 63 firearms discharge cases) but a *bullet* "hit potential" (hit rate)

---

[29] For instance, in ten shoot-outs between police and offenders, 16 officers might be confronted with 19 opponents, and the officers might fire 32 rounds and be fired at 50 times. With two officers wounded and eight suspects shot, three different rates would emerge for bullet hit rates, incident hit rates, and individual hit rates.

of just 50 percent (149 rounds struck suspects out of 296 rounds fired) (Kindrick 1992).

Incident hit rates vary from city to city, just as bullet and individual hit rates differ. In contrast with Metro-Dade's 31 percent incident hit rate, the Dallas Police Department over the ten years from 1980 through 1989 reported a 60 percent hit rate (345 incidents of officers intentionally firing weapons, striking one or more civilians in 207 of these incidents) (Dallas Police Department 1990). As in all agencies, the hit rate varied from year to year in Dallas, ranging from a reported low during the 1980s of 43 percent to a high (in 1987) of 74 percent (17 persons struck out of 23 fired at) (Dallas Police Department 1990). In Philadelphia over the six years from 1986 through 1991, in the 417 *incidents* in which officers fired (either intentionally or accidentally) at others, their bullets struck a person in 59 percent of the *incidents* (Geller and Scott data collection—see Table E-12).

During the 1970s, the *bullet* hit rate of police in Chicago was 14 percent (Geller and Karales 1981a, 1981b, 1982) and in Los Angeles was 30 percent (Meyer 1980a: 33). During the period January 1, 1988 through October 31, 1990, members of the New York City *Transit* Police Department fired a total of 216 rounds at suspects. Of this number, 68 (32 percent) bullets either wounded or killed a person (Bratton 1990a).

On average, the big-city officers discussed in the published and unpublished studies fire between two and four bullets per shooting incident (Meyer 1980a: 22; Geller and Karales 1981a; NYPD 1988; Cerar 1990: 7).[30] This figure might be expected to increase as semi-automatic and perhaps even fully automatic weapons assume a more prominent role in policing (Ostrow 1990; *Law Enforcement News* 1990; Krajick 1990; Edwards 1991a, 1991b; McCauley and Edwards 1990).

3. The Possible Effects of Revolvers Versus Semi-automatic Pistols on Hit and Fatality Rates

The experience thus far has been mixed. In the NYPD, which has been experimenting with several hundred Glock 19 semi-automatic pistols since mid-1989 (*Law Enforcement News* 1990a: 9; Cerar 1989, 1990, 1991; Brown 1992), early results did *not* point to a significant

---

[30] Meyer (1980a: 33-34), in a consulting report commissioned by the Los Angeles Board of Police Commissioners in the wake of a highly controversial L.A. police shooting, compared the average number of rounds fired per incident and the resulting hit rates by LAPD and New York City police officers during the 1970s:

> "Los Angeles Police officers appear to shoot more accurately than New York Police Department officers. Of 2,432 rounds fired at suspects in Los Angeles from 1974 to 1978, 722, or 30 percent, struck their targets. Of 7,394 rounds fired at suspects in New York City from 1971 to 1975, 1,130, or 15 percent, actually hit their targets.... Los Angeles Police officers fired more rounds *per incident* than their counterparts in New York did in the period prior to 1976. Over the 1971-75 interval, an average of 3.28 bullets was fired per incident by New York officers. Los Angeles Police officers fired an average of 4.42 rounds per incident from 1974 through 1978."

In 1990 the average number of rounds fired by members of the NYPD was 3.83 per incident, compared with an average of 2.41 shots fired per incident by those who used firearms against NYPD officers—in a total of 138 incidents (Cerar 1990: 7). In 1990, the average number of rounds fired intentionally by officers of the New York City *Transit* Police Department was 3.5, up from an average of 3.0 in 1989 and an average of 2.1 in 1988 (New York City Transit Police Department 1991).

increase in average number of rounds fired per incident. As Table E-66 in Appendix E of this volume shows, during the period May 1989-December 1991, in which NYPD officers intentionally shot at other persons in 22 incidents, the average number of rounds fired per incident was 5.5. This compares with an average of 3.7 rounds fired per incident with revolvers during recent years (Markman 1992: 1).

Former NYPD Commissioner Lee P. Brown, who had been resisting rank-and-file pressure to adopt semi-automatics departmentwide,[31] said in 1992 that some research shows a doubling of the average number of rounds fired per incident when officers switch from revolvers to semi-automatics (Verhovek 1992). An NYPD deputy chief reported in mid-1992 that, since the beginning of the Department's trial use of semi-automatic weapons in May 1989 (mostly with narcotics enforcement personnel), these officers had "been involved in 7 shootings involving armed adversaries. The officers fired a total of 59 rounds of ammunition or 8.4 per incident" (Markman 1992: 1). (Some of the incidents in which Glocks were employed did not involve "armed adversaries.")

In Los Angeles an internal LAPD study of the average number of shots fired by its officers in shooting incidents found that officers using semi-automatic pistols (the Department authorized use of 9 millimeters in 1986) averaged just one more shot fired per encounter than officers using revolvers. This was reported eventually in the popular media (Krajick 1990: 58). The Portland, Oregon, Police Bureau reported data showing that, over a four-year period (January 1, 1988-February 7, 1992), the 12 officers who discharged revolvers at suspects fired an average of 2.6 rounds each, while the 19 officers who discharged semi-automatic pistols shot an average of 4.6 rounds each (Snell 1992b). But longer study periods revealed that Portland officers using semi-automatics shot an average of only one-half round more per incident than officers using revolvers (Kindrick 1992). The periods analyzed were January 1, 1983-January 5, 1990, for officers firing revolvers and July 21, 1984-February 7, 1992, for officers discharging semi-automatic pistols; but this study was limited to shooting incidents involving *lone* officers. The average number of rounds fired per officer was 2.39 for the revolver shooters and 2.93 for those officers using semi-automatics (*ibid.*).

Another early indication of the effect of using semi-automatics on number of rounds fired per incident comes from a survey by the New York City Transit Police Department (Bratton 1990a). In exploring the feasibility of switching its standard issue sidearm from a revolver to a 9-millimeter semi-automatic,[32] the Transit Police compiled data on shots fired per incident in a few agencies that had already taken this step. These data show an average

---

[31] This pressure included an effort by the New York State legislature to *mandate* that the NYPD adopt such sidearms (Verhovek 1992; Fritsch 1992, 1992a) and a Patrolmen's Benevolent Association campaign that ended on June 15, 1992, in a compromise by which then-Commissioner Brown agreed to allow 1,000 additional officers to use semi-automatics and the legislation was withdrawn from consideration (Lyall 1992).

[32] The New York City Transit Police initiative has both strong supporters and opponents within the criminal justice policy community and the political community in New York City (see Steisel 1990a, 1990b; Kiley 1990a, 1990b; *Law Enforcement News* 1990a: 9). As a consequence, former Transit Police Chief William Bratton and his staff compiled a useful set of materials and position papers outlining in clear terms the issues presented when considering the revolver versus the semi-automatic pistol. Although the documentation and argumentation were all marshalled in support of a strong position favoring the shift (over two or three years) from revolvers to semi-automatics, the administration took care to identify and attempt to meet a wide variety of possible objections to the weapons change.

increase in the number of shots fired per shooting incident following adoption of semi-automatic weaponry of less than one round (Bratton 1990, 1990a). More recently, as part of a public relations and legislative campaign to describe the benefits of maintaining revolvers as the standard police service weapon, the NYPD has noted: "In 1990 the Transit Authority Police Department issued Glock semi-automatic pistols to officers on patrol. In 4 incidents the TAPD officers fired 43 rounds or an average of 10.7 rounds per incident" (Markman 1992: 1). We do not know whether these four incidents represent *all* Transit Police shootings with semi-automatics after Chief Bratton succeeded in adopting them.

Even assuming that research shows that the increase in rounds fired per incident after adoption of semi-automatics averages one or two rounds, practitioners and commentators may still differ in their interpretations of such findings. Some would express concern over any increase in number of shots fired per incident, while others would emphasize that an increase of one shot is well within tolerable bounds given the advantages they see for semi-automatics over revolvers.[33] Exploring what would be "tolerable bounds" should certainly involve an appraisal of what pattern of results may flow from even a relatively small increment in shots fired per incident. For instance, does an increase in shots fired result in a higher hit rate and so in a higher fatality rate among those whom police engage in gun battles?

In Portland, Oregon, officers firing revolvers from January 1, 1983, through January 5, 1990, struck adversaries with 24 rounds out of 67 fired (a hit rate of 36 percent); Portland officers firing semi-automatic pistols from July 21, 1984, through February 7, 1992, struck adversaries with 19 rounds out of 44 fired (a hit rate of 43 percent) (Kindrick 1992). And as we noted earlier, the Portland study of deadly force encounters from 1988 through 1991 suggests that firing more shots results in more suspect fatalities (Snell 1992b). The IACP (Matulia 1982: 169; 1985: 73) reported that, in the 1970s and early 1980s, agencies using semi-automatic weaponry (or at least permitting officers to elect to use it) experienced a somewhat higher rate of justifiable homicides by officers than agencies equipped primarily or exclusively with revolvers.

In its 1982 report the IACP offered little explanation that might soften the interpretation of what it characterized as "a significantly high justifiable homicide rate" in the studied big-city departments permitting use of semi-automatics (Matulia 1982: 169). But in revisiting this issue in 1985 the IACP was careful to caution that a variety of factors might be associated with an elevated justifiable homicide rate in agencies employing either large calibre handguns or semi-automatics:

"(1) the higher calibre weapon has more stopping/killing power;
(2) agencies which are more prone to shoot tend to prefer the larger calibre;
(3) the more expert shooters can better handle the more difficult weapons and thus hit their target more often" (Matulia 1985: 73).

The impetus for many agencies that are considering switching from the revolver to a

---

[33] Either way, the 1988-91 experience of the Portland Police Bureau (with a much smaller number of deadly force encounters per year than occur in larger jurisdictions) stands in contrast to the other findings because officers using semi-automatics shot an average of two rounds more per incident during the same time period as their colleagues using revolvers (Snell 1992b). But the data from the longer study periods counterbalance this finding, revealing that the average number of rounds fired per incident was only about one-half round higher for officers using semi-automatics than for officers firing revolvers (Kindrick 1992).

semi-automatic weapon is multi-faceted but typically includes improving marksmanship and expanding the number of rounds available to officers in combat situations. Police marksmanship with the Glock 19s being used on a trial basis in the NYPD since mid-1989 has not changed appreciably. The *bullet* hit rates discussed above in this chapter can be compared with the fact that, over the past several years in New York City, officers shooting intentionally at other persons struck them with 33 percent of the rounds fired from the Glocks (see Table E-66 in Appendix E).

As suggested above, a number of police executives have misgivings about the police participating in this "arms race" with the criminal population (e.g., L. Martin 1990;[34] see also Krajick 1990), but few would contest that improvements of various types are needed in the revolver, which has changed surprisingly little since Samuel Colt invented his six-shooter in 1836. We will discuss the operational and administrative issues surrounding choice of police service weapon further in Chapter 5.

4. A Caution on Calculating Average Number of Shots Fired Per Incident and Calculating Bullet Hit Rates

As with other computations and intercity comparisons, deadly force analysts must be careful when calculating the average number of rounds fired per incident that they understand the nature of the incidents from which a given time period's data are derived. For instance, Meyer (1980a: 6), studying shots fired incidents in Los Angeles during 1974-1979, was careful to note where his findings might mislead the reader who failed to understand the impact of a single incident during the study period: In May 1974 the shootout with six members of the Symbionese Liberation Army prompted Los Angeles police to fire more than 5,000 rounds, "more rounds than the total fired in the remaining 912 officer-involved shootings analyzed." Meyer properly excluded this incident in analyzing the average number of shots fired by police during violent encounters with suspects. Similar care would need to be exercised if one analyzed rounds fired by police in Philadelphia during 1985. In the May 13, 1985, shootout with the group MOVE, besides using water cannons, tear gas, and a smoke bomb that engulfed the block in flames, "the police alone fired 10,000 bullets" during the 11-hour confrontation (Hinds 1992).

Another consideration facing researchers—and particularly police supervisors and trainers—is how to help officers control the number of shots they fire in incidents so that they discharge their weapons no more than necessary to resolve encounters.

In this regard, Alpert (1987b: 32) offers interesting findings from a survey of Dallas police officers who fired their weapons during the 1980s: "Only 61 percent of the officers remembered how many shots they fired. Twenty-six percent did not hear the noise of the shot(s). Of those who did hear the shots, most remembered the noise as muffled." Similarly, in his study of shots fired by Miami, Florida, officers, Alpert (1989b: 491) surveyed officers about their recollections of their participation in shootings during the period 1980-83. He found that "[o]nly...64 percent [18 officers] reported the shots as being loud. In fact, two officers reveal that they never heard the shots." Officers can generally figure out after an

---

[34] Former Chicago Police Superintendent LeRoy Martin finally relented in his opposition to authorizing officers who qualify with semi-automatics to carry such weapons as their primary sidearms, but he continued to resist particular semi-automatic weapons whose design he believed presented undue risks of accidental discharges due to light trigger pull, short length of trigger pull, or other features (Spielman 1992, 1992a).

incident how many rounds they fired by checking the number of live rounds left in their weapon(s). But the prospect of officers having perceptual and memory problems during the heat of an encounter may complicate analysis of *when* during a complex encounter, perhaps covering multiple locations, specific numbers of rounds were fired.

E. Number of Fatal Shootings of Civilians

1.   Shootings in American Cities; Shootings by Police in Other Nations

Prior to our review of FBI data for 1985 through 1990, the most recent *national* study of justifiable homicides by police was that conducted by Sherman and Cohn (1986). That study showed a sharp reduction in the total number of civilians killed over time by big-city police agencies. (In that study, "big-city agency" was defined to mean a department serving a population exceeding 250,000.) In their 15-year study (covering 1970 through 1984), the peak year was 1971, when 353 civilians were reported killed. The low year was 1984, with 172 reported civilian fatalities.

"In yet another violent encounter involving car theft, a Newark teen-ager was shot and wounded [in Belleville, NJ] early today as he tried to hit three police officers with a stolen car, the authorities said. The youth, who was shot three times, is the fourth occupant of a stolen car to be killed or wounded by police gunfire in the last eight days in and around Newark, the police said" (Hanley 1992).

Five-year averages were used to minimize the effect of potential inconsistencies in counting methods from year to year, thereby revealing a more valid picture of trends. Nevertheless, the reader must take care to understand that only the 1980s data in Sherman and Cohn's study were collected directly by them from the participating police agencies. For many of the earlier years, data reported by police agencies to the FBI were used; we discussed earlier the undercounting that such data typically present.

Figure 30 depicts the combined 50-city experience over 15 years, showing the annual aggregate of justifiable homicides by police. Figure 31 shows, for these same 50 cities, the aggregate change from one block of five years (1970-74) to another (1980-84). Figure 32 and Table 3 show the changes in various cities between the same two blocks of five years.

Thus, for instance, New York City dropped from an annual average of 63 civilians killed during 1970-1974 to 35 during 1980-1984, and San Antonio dropped from 4 to 2. Los Angeles also dropped from 21 to 19, a seemingly less substantial decrease. But if population growth and increases in general population homicides have any bearing on raising the number of shootings by police (a proposition which has not been statistically demonstrated but which some analysts find plausible), then the reduction in killings in Los Angeles may be comparable to the reductions in New York and Philadelphia. Los Angeles had 332,256 more residents in 1984 than in 1970,[35] and homicides jumped from 395 in 1970 to 759 in 1984 (see also Matulia 1982, 1985). By the same token, increases in homicide levels in other locales, including New York and Philadelphia, may heighten the meaning of reductions in justifiable homicides by police in those agencies.

[35] The 1970 Los Angeles population was 2,812,000 and its 1984 population was 3,144,256, according to the FBI's annual publication *Crime in the United States.*

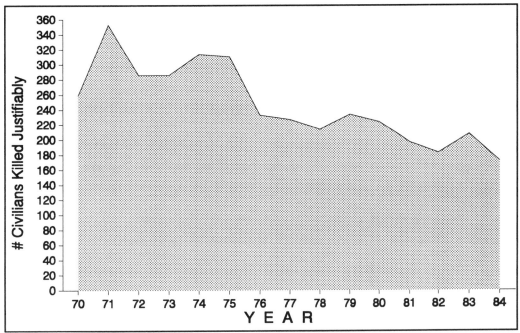

Figure 30: Civilians Killed Justifiably by Police in 50 Big Cities, 1970-84
Source: Sherman and Cohn (1986).

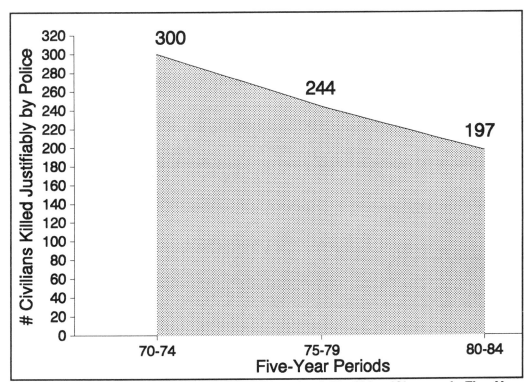

Figure 31: Civilians Killed Justifiably by Police in 50 Big Cities (Changes in Five-Year Annual Averages), 1970-84
Source: Sherman and Cohn (1986).

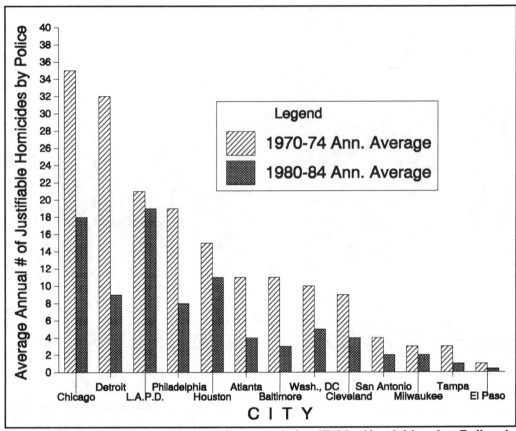

Figure 32: Decreases in Average Ann. # of Justifiable Homicides by Police in Selected Big Cities for 1970-74 vs. 1980-84

Source: Sherman and Cohn (1986).

Table 3:
Changes in the Average Annual Number of Justifiable Homicides by Police in Selected Big Cities During 1970-74 and 1980-84

City Department	1970-74 Ann. Av.	1980-84 Ann. Av.
Departments with Decreases		
Atlanta	11	4
Baltimore	11	3
Chicago	35	18
Cleveland	9	4
Detroit	32	9
El Paso	1	0.4
Houston	15	11
Los Angeles	21	19

City Department	1970-74 Ann. Av.	1980-84 Ann. Av.
Milwaukee	3	2
New York City	63	35
Philadelphia	19	8
San Antonio	4	2
Tampa	3	1
Washington, DC	10	5
Departments with No Appreciable Change		
Columbus, OH	4	4
Memphis	5	5
Miami, FL	4	4
San Jose	2	2
Departments with Slight Increases		
Austin	1	2
Charlotte, NC	1	2
Dallas	8	10
Fort Worth	1	2
Oklahoma City	0.2	3.6
Phoenix	1	2
Rochester, NY	0.4	1
San Diego	1	4

Source: Sherman and Cohn (1986).

As shown in Table 3, a few agencies experienced virtually no change in the number of civilians killed justifiably by officers between these two five-year blocks. Thus, in both the early 1970s and early 1980s, Memphis police killed an annual average of five civilians. The Memphis Police Department, of course, was the agency whose use of fatal force provided the occasion for the U.S. Supreme Court in 1985 to invalidate nearly half the states' deadly force statutes (*Tennessee v. Garner*). San Jose, too, where Joseph McNamara was named chief in 1974 after a much publicized campaign to reduce officer use of deadly force in Kansas City,[36] showed no appreciable change in fatal shooting rates. San Jose officers justifiably

---

[36] Later, in our discussion of the empirical studies of policy and policy enforcement, we examine the findings of one study that suggested that shootings by Kansas City officers increased following Chief McNamara's departure due to a deterioration in the agency's "administrative climate."

killed an annual average of two civilians during the periods 1970-74 and 1980-84. One cannot, of course, place much meaning on increases, decreases, or stability of police-involved shootings without knowing far more than is presented here about the environment over time in a given city.

A few of the major cities experienced a slight *increase* in justifiable homicides by their officers from the 1970-74 period to the 1980-84 period. Largest among these agencies was the Dallas Police Department, whose annual average went from eight civilians slain justifiably to 10 (Sherman and Cohn 1986: 16-17). But, as Figure 5 showed earlier, after a peak in 1986, shootings by Dallas police have followed a general downward trend. The other major cities with increases between the 1970-74 and 1980-84 periods have very few justifiable homicides, so one must expect random changes from year to year—that is, changes unrelated to agency leadership, policy, procedure, recruitment, training, or disciplinary initiatives.

Differences between five-year averages may be indicative of meaningful trends, but we cannot say too often that the reader must still exercise caution to place an agency's shooting experience in a proper context. For instance, as mentioned above regarding Los Angeles, a number of the cities noted here experienced both rising populations and rising violent crime rates between the 1970s and 1980s. In such a department, a slight increase in shooting rates might be understandable; a level trend-line might be indicative of admirable restraint in the face of mounting problems; and a decrease in shooting rates might represent a remarkable accomplishment indeed.

To attempt to place justifiable homicides of citizens by the police in a context of changing levels of violence in the community, Sherman and Cohn (1986) calculated rates of justifiable homicides based on homicides in the general population. They found that among the nation's big cities (250,000 population or more), general population homicides by 1980 had risen 38 percent over the 1970 level. With decreases in the number of justifiable homicides by police, substantial rate reductions resulted:

> "[T]he proportion of all intentional killings in these cities caused by police has dropped dramatically. In 1971, for example, policed committed almost 5%, or one in twenty, homicides in these cities. By 1984, that figure had dropped by more than half to 2.4%, or one out of every 42 homicides" (*ibid.*: 3).

They observe that the police contribution to civilian death tallies in the United States stands in sharp contrast to the pattern in at least some other "high crime" nations:

> "Jamaican police, for example, were recently reported to have committed 288 of the 808 homicides in that country in 1984, or 36% of all homicides (Treaster 1986)—a rate 15 times as high as that of big city American police" (*ibid.*: 3).

More recent research (Chevigny 1990: 405-406) confirms the persistence of this rate of police contribution to death in Jamaica. Chevigny reports a slightly higher percentage of total homicides attributable to the Jamaican authorities for the year 1984, because he differs on the total homicide count (288 killings at the hands of Jamaica's 6,000 constables and approximately 2,000 auxiliaries out of a total of *772* general population homicides, or 37 percent). Over the ten-year period 1979-88, Chevigny (1990: 405) attributes 2,083 homicides to the Jamaican Constabulary, an average of 208 per year—this for a force smaller than the Los Angeles Police Department (which over the ten years from 1980 through 1989 killed 205 suspects, for an average of 20.5 per year) (see Table E-17). New York City has just over twice the resident population and three times the police officers of Jamaica. Yet, during the same ten years Chevigny examined (1979-88), NYPD personnel fatally shot 241 persons, an average of two dozen per year (see Table E-14).

Chevigny (1990: 406) concludes that over the ten years he examined, the Jamaican police "account for nearly one-third of all homicides in the island." He adds: "Official figures for the number of civilians killed and wounded are available only for 1988. During that year, 98 persons were wounded; 188 were killed"—the reverse of the general pattern in cities in the United States, in which more persons typically are wounded than killed from police shootings. A similar pattern of police employment of deadly force was discovered in metropolitan Buenos Aires in Argentina, whose population is approximately 10 million (Chevigny 1990: 414):

> "Police statistics for the period December 1983-July 1985 indicated that 304 civilians were killed by the police * * * and 199 'criminals' were injured. In other words...three fifths of all police shootings resulted in death. During the year 1984 alone, the police accounted for over a quarter of all homicides."

Nearly twice the size of New York City, the state of São Paulo, Brazil, over the six years 1982-87 accounted for 2,394 known deaths by police, an annual average of 399. An additional 1,008 persons were shot nonfatally, an annual average of 168 (Chevigny 1990: 418). Chevigny, a New York University law professor, (at 419, 425) indicates that, while police reforms are being implemented in Brazil,

> "some police homicides in Brazil, as in Jamaica, are summary executions of suspects, many of whom are black youths. The [police] tend to dispose of criminals in this way not in major cases but in fairly routine ones involving drugs or theft, in which the victims are anonymous. * * *

> "When we consider a variety of indicators concerning the disproportionate use of deadly force by police—the ratio of civilians killed to those wounded, the ratio of civilians killed to police killed, and the ratio of police killings to the total homicide rate—the statistics, both official and unofficial, for Jamaica, Buenos Aires, São Paulo, and Rio de Janeiro all point toward the conclusion that the police are summarily executing suspects in routine, nonpartisan cases. * * * [V]irtually all police killings are justified [in Jamaica, Argentina, and Brazil] to the public as acts of self-defense, typically in the context of shoot-outs. This justification appears to be essential for organizing public opinion even though, for at least some people at all socioeconomic levels, summary executions, like vigilantism, are considered the proper punishment for alleged crimes" (see also Brooke 1990).

While American police account for a relatively small portion of all homicides in the United States, it has long been the case that the American populace kills one another at rates far above those in most other nations of the world. For instance, a National Center for Health Statistics study compared homicide rates in 22 industrial countries during 1986 and 1987. The NCHS concluded that the United States was in a class by itself: Its overall murder rate was between 2.6 and 8 times the murder rate in such countries as Austria, Japan, West Germany (before reunification), Scotland, New Zealand, Israel, Norway, Finland, Canada, and Sweden.

In specific age categories (e.g., 15-24), Americans slaughtered one another at rates 74 times as high as the Austrian rate, 73 times the Japanese rate, and 22 times the West German rate. Compared with the average rate in this age bracket of the 21 other nations in the study, the U.S. murder rate was nearly 12 times as high. The U.S. rate in the 15-24 age group was 21.9 murders for every 100,000 citizens (*Law and Order* 1990: 5). Figure 33 displays the differences in murder rates per 100,000 for the 15-24 age groups in several nations.

For American police to have exercised continuing restraint in fatal shootings of civilians and for felonious killings of law enforcement personnel to have generally fallen in the face of this nation's escalating level of community homicides is an attainment that deserves considerable study and public discussion.[37] It is easy, in the face of pressing day-to-day business and new challenges, to overlook the remarkable strides that have been made in the professionalization of American policing. At the same time, it is easy occasionally to forget to demand restraint and the exercise of mature wisdom on the part of American police when newspaper headlines and TV news broadcasts portray much of American society as gripped by nearly paralyzing fear of drug-related violent crime.[38]

As indicated, the most dependable published data available on justifiable homicides by police in the nation's largest cities depict patterns only through 1984. These were reported in Sherman and Cohn (1986) and were provided to them directly by police agencies. We have obtained comparably reliable, more current data from selected big-city agencies and have reported them as appropriate throughout this volume.

We also have compiled more current data from unpublished FBI tallies and offer them in the interest of updating the profession's knowledge. But, for all the reasons discussed in Chapter 2, we urge the reader to exercise caution in interpreting these updated FBI data. This is because Sherman and Cohn's research and our own (see Appendix E, Table E-10) have demonstrated that, almost always, counts of justifiable homicides reported to the FBI and reported by the same police agencies to researchers conducting deadly force studies differ, sometimes dramatically. Figure 34 incorporates the data shown earlier in Figure 31 and adds the average annual number of justifiable homicides in the nation's 50 biggest cities as reported to the FBI for the period 1985-89.

---

[37] Among the ways in which police may have helped reduce their own victimization is through better tactical training, conflict management training, and the wearing of soft body armor. These initiatives are discussed in Chapter 5.

[38] For a police perspective on how media and political rhetoric, particularly metaphorical references to a *"war* on drugs," can inhibit professional restraint by police officers, see G. Williams (1991). Despite the impression one might take from news stories and Hollywood fiction, the emergence of semi-automatic and fully automatic weaponry among criminals in the United States and the soaring murder levels among the general population may be only tangentially related. *U.S. News and World Report*, in an otherwise alarmist portrait of crime and the plight of police in America, reported (Witkin, et al. 1990: 38) that "contrary to widespread belief, the number of murders committed with firearms has remained fairly steady for at least 15 years:

Murders with guns:	
1974:	12,470
1980:	13,650
1983:	10,895
1986:	11,381
1989:	11,832."

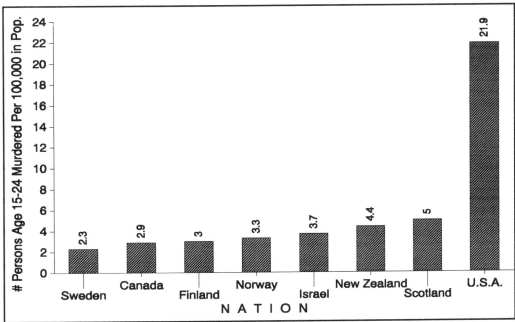

Figure 33: Murder Rates in Various Nations for Victims Aged 15-24, 1986-87
Source: Law and Order (1990: 5).

Figure 34 is identical to Figure 1, presented to make a methodological point in Chapter 2. It is reproduced here for the convenience of the reader. As explained in Chapter 2, the consequence of not having an authoritative central national repository for information on police-involved shootings is that we cannot say with confidence what was the average annual number of justifiable homicides by police during the 1985-89 period or any other period. Was it as reported by the FBI or higher as we have projected, knowing the substantial undercounts reported for some cities in the FBI's unpublished supplementary homicide report file listings?

2.   *Line-of-Work Shootings by Private Security Personnel: An "Invisible" Factor in the Rise and Fall of Shootings by Public Police?*

Another, related gap in accurate reporting of police shootings also contributes to an extremely unreliable national data base on which to build responsible national and local public policy. This second gap concerns the frequency with which private security personnel, who far outstrip public police in numbers, use deadly force against criminals. The leading recent reports on private security in America (Cunningham and Taylor 1985; Cunningham, et al. 1990; Cunningham, et al. 1991) provide what little current information there is about the arming of private security personnel and their use of firearms in the line of duty (also see Behar 1992).

In surveys conducted in the early 1980s, Cunningham and Taylor (1985: 93-94) discovered that, nationwide, nearly 10 percent of all security personnel routinely carried firearms on the job. They suggest that, due to sampling methods, the 10 percent estimate was low. Even so, the gun-carrying rate for private security in the 1980s seemed considerably lower than a Rand Corporation study (Kakalik and Wildhorn 1971) had discovered at the beginning of the 1970s: At that time, "50 percent of both contract and proprietary guards carried firearms at least a quarter of the time" (Cunningham, et al. 1991: 4).

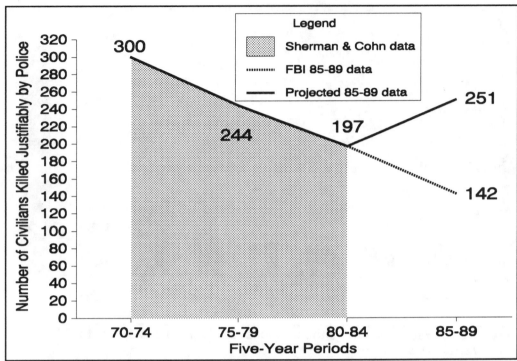

Figure 34: Justifiable Homicides by Police in 50 Big Cities (Annual Averages During Five-Year Periods, 1970-84, and Alternate Possibilities for 1985-89)

Since experts suggest that the nation by the early 1990s had approximately 1.5 million private security personnel,[39] a conservative estimate would be that, in the early 1990s, approximately 200,000 private security personnel carried firearms as part of their employment. Interestingly, despite the topsy-like growth of private-sector security, Cunningham, et al. (1991: 4) predict that, "the rise in insurance premiums and liability litigation suggests that by the year 2000 perhaps only 5 percent will be armed." Cunningham and Taylor (1985: 94) found that, in two sites (Baltimore County, Maryland, and Multnomah County, Oregon), of the private security personnel who carried firearms on the job, anywhere from 11 to 75 percent reported having "used" their firearms (with unspecified and unquantified effects).

Thus, although it is impossible to guess how many crime suspects may have been fired upon, hit, and killed during any given time period by private security personnel, it does seem likely that some portion of the violent criminal population who in prior years might have been shot by public police are now being shot by private security. Presumably, such shootings, when fatal, would be included among the FBI's annual tallies of justifiable homicides ("felons killed by citizens") but without any special indication that the shooter was a security guard. Such justifiable homicides would not, presumably, show up in the FBI unpublished file

---

[39] Cunningham and Taylor (1985: 113) estimated the number of private security personnel during the *early* 1980s at 1.1 million (see also McCrie 1988: 32). By 1990, Cunningham, et al. (1991: 1) reported that there were 1.5 million persons employed as private security personnel, and they predicted that by the year 2000 this number will swell to approximately 1.8 million. The annual growth rate for the private security industry during the balance of this century is seen as about 8 percent—roughly twice the growth rate for the public police industry (Cunningham, et al. 1991: 2).

listings of "felons killed by *peace officers*." An exception might be if the security guards were public police officers working secondary employment, whose employing police departments required them to report such off duty shootings.

There are apparently at least some states in which the potential exists to capture and analyze data on uses of lethal force by private security personnel. In Georgia, for instance, the state Board of Private Detective and Security Agencies requires that licensed security agencies submit to the Board within 10 business days a "weapons discharge report form" when their employees fire guns in connection with their job responsibilities (*Law Enforcement News* 1991b: 14; Rules of the Georgia Board of Private Detective and Security Agencies, section 509-4.05; a copy of the reporting form appears in Appendix K of this book). Staff in that regulatory agency indicated, however, that they do not generally compile tallies or conduct analyses of the shooting reports (Georgia Board of Private Detective and Security Agencies 1992).[40]

Cunningham and Taylor (1985: 94), although unable to enumerate the use of nondeadly or deadly force by the private security industry, leave little doubt that the policy issues deserve attention by criminal justice practitioners and public policy analysts:

"One inescapable fact is that firearms tend to be used when they are carried.... Overall, the potential for firearms abuse seems to be greater in proprietary security, because of the larger number of firearms and more opportunities for exposure, notwithstanding the amount and quality of training. Before any firm conclusions could be drawn, as to the greater firearms abuse potential, a much larger sample of both contract and proprietary security would have to be drawn from similar distributions of work environments."

3. *Rates of Fatal Shootings Based on General Population Homicides*

How do the current fatal shooting data we have obtained from several large cities compare with patterns observed by Sherman and Cohn (1986) through the year 1984? By analyzing data presented in a number of tables in Appendix E, we can provide an overview of the relative rates of fatal shootings by police in a dozen major American jurisdictions (due to data availability, 12 cities are represented in Table 5 but only 11 are shown in Table 4).

Thus, Table 4 shows the number of killings by police and rates of killings (based on general population size, police force size, and the general population homicide rate). The jurisdictions and agencies represented in the table are Atlanta, Chicago (the City Police Department rather than the Chicago Housing Authority Police Department, founded in 1990), Dallas, Houston, Kansas City (Mo.), Los Angeles (the LAPD as distinguished from the L.A. Sheriff's Department), Metro-Dade County, Florida (the Metro-Dade County Police Department), New York City (the City Police as opposed to the Housing Police or Transit

---

[40] The *Security Law Newsletter*, published monthly by the Crime Control Institute in Washington, D.C., is potentially another source of information on the use of deadly force by armed private security personnel. It contains capsule summaries of litigation over performance by security personnel, including cases in which security guards were accused of misusing lethal force. Since the newsletter commenced publication in 1981, however, it has not attempted to compile data on the frequency with which security personnel around the nation employ deadly force.

Police), Philadelphia (excluding the Housing Police), St. Louis (the Metropolitan St. Louis Police Department), and San Diego (the City police rather than the County Sheriff's Department). Table 5 shows the same categories but uses annual averages for the number of killings, population sizes, police force sizes, and homicide levels in each jurisdiction. The annual averages were computed for the five-year period 1985-89 to facilitate comparison with previous analysis conducted by Sherman and Cohn (1986) of earlier five-year periods.

Table 4:
Number and Rates of Killings by Police in 11 Jurisdictions, 1990

City	# Persons Killed	Rate per 1,000 POs	Rate per 100,000 Pop.	Rate per 100 Homicides
Atlanta	6	3.9	1.5	2.6
Chicago	10	0.8	0.4	1.2
Dallas	5	1.8	0.5	1.1
Houston	13	3.2	0.8	2.1
Kansas City, MO	7	6.0	1.6	5.8
LAPD	39	4.6	1.1	4.0
Metro-Dade	7	2.8	0.7	2.6
NYPD	39	1.4	0.5	2.1
Philadelphia	8	1.2	0.5	1.6
St. Louis	2	1.3	0.5	1.1
San Diego	12	6.6	1.1	8.9

Sources: Police departments, FBI (annual reports).

Table 5 shows rates that are less subject to the effects of random fluctuation and sporadic reporting error than does Table 4. The reader is reminded that Tables 4 and 5 show rates based only on the number of persons shot *fatally* in these jurisdictions. Figure 28, earlier in this chapter, graphically depicts the different shooting rates among the 11 cities shown in both Tables 4 and 5 when both fatal and nonfatal shootings are included in the comparison.

Thus, that figure revealed, even more clearly than it appears in Tables 4 and 5, that the rate of shootings by officers (calculated based on community homicide levels) in St. Louis and in San Diego in the past several years has been rather different than in the other nine jurisdictions. Whether this is due to a more confrontational criminal element, training, policy, procedural, equipment, or organizational culture differences among the various agencies, we

Table 5:
Average Annual Number and Rates of Killings by Police
in 12 Jurisdictions, 1985-89

City	Ann. Av. # Persons Killed	Rate per 1,000 POs	Rate per 100,000 Pop.	Rate per 100 Homicides
Atlanta	4.5	3.1	1.0	2.1
Chicago	14.3	1.3	0.5	2.2
Dallas	7.0	3.2	0.7	2.2
Houston	7.7	1.5	0.4	1.6
Kansas City, MO	2.5	1.4	0.4	1.3
LAPD	25.0	3.0	0.7	2.8
Memphis	3.8	3.1	0.6	2.6
Metro-Dade	2.6	1.1	0.3	1.0
NYPD	22.7	0.7	0.3	1.2
Philadelphia	7.3	1.1	0.5	2.1
St. Louis	4.8	3.1	1.1	3.0
San Diego	6.6	4.1	0.7	5.9

Sources: Police departments, FBI (annual reports), Sparger and Giacopassi (1992: 21, Table 5).

do not know.[41] But when an organization seems to be an "outlier"—that is, exceptional—on an important dimension of police work such as officer-involved shootings, the profession would do well to explore the reasons and any lessons to be learned by other agencies.

---

[41] Officials in San Diego suggest that analysis of that city's police-involved shooting rate needs to take into account the agency's efforts to cope with high levels of violent crime involving persons illegally crossing the Mexican-U.S. border into San Diego. The San Diego Police Department's Border Crime Intervention Union (BCIU), established in 1974 in conjunction with the Immigration and Naturalization Service's Border Patrol (*Crime Control Digest* 1990g), has, during the more than 16-year period 1974-May 1990, fatally shot 33 people and wounded another 48; 12 were "run over and injured or killed by Border Patrol vehicles" (*ibid.*). From 1984 through 1991, BCIU members shot 19 percent of all the civilians shot nonfatally by San Diego officers (19 individuals out of 122 shot) and 28 percent of those shot fatally by SDPD personnel (15 decedents out of 77 shot). Of the 375 incidents in which San Diego police officers intentionally discharged their weapons at civilians during 1984-91, BCIU personnel officers took part in 32 (13 percent) of these incidents (San Diego Police Department 1992). Hence, the presence of the BCIU in departmental shooting tallies is increasingly out of proportion to the percentage of the force assigned as one examines, in turn, off-target shots, nonfatal shootings, and fatal shootings. Representatives of San Diego officers and Border agents, responding to criticism over these shooting rates, argued that these personnel show "restraint [in the face of] 'hostile crowds of people [that] hurl rocks, bottles and insults at Border Patrol agents who venture close to the border'" and "ruthless bandits (who) prey upon the undocumented aliens venturing through the no-man's land" at the border (*Crime Control Digest* 1990g).

II. *Shootings of Police*

A. *Number of Officers Killed or Shot Nonfatally*

Just as the swelling ranks of private security guards armed and using weapons in the line of duty may be contributing to the reduction in use of deadly force by public police, so too may the line-of-duty deaths of private security personnel be contributing to the general downward trend in felonious killings of public law enforcement officers. Privatizing policing in America also means, to an unknown extent, privatizing police-involved shootings. As noted earlier, however, some of those employed as private police are off-duty public police officers, and their victimization while working second jobs might be tallied by their full-time employers as assaults or slayings of public police personnel.

Although studies of the use of deadly force by and against private security personnel are not available in the published literature, gaining access to data on shootings of *public* police officers is relatively easy. For instance, data on police officers killed in the line of duty have been collected by and available from the FBI since 1961 in the Bureau's annual *Uniform Crime Reports* (FBI 1989b: ii) and, more recently, in separate annual reports titled *Law Enforcement Officers Killed* (between 1972 and 1981) and *Law Enforcement Officers Killed and Assaulted* (since 1982) (see Garner and Clemmer 1986:7).[42] Figure 35 and Table 6 show the annual number of American police (employed by federal, state, and local agencies) who were killed feloniously (as distinguished from *accidentally*) from 1960 through 1991. The data presented include officers killed by *all* types of weapons, not only firearms. As this volume went to press, the FBI informed us that, as of September 18, 1992 it had received reports of 34 American police having been slain feloniously in 1992 (Behm 1992). The Bureau also learned that some of its published reports had undercounted felonious deaths by 1 in 1990 and 2 in 1991 (*ibid.*); the necessary corrections have been made throughout this volume. If the preliminary count of 34 for the first three quarters of 1992 is accurate (information on some deaths could be missing), 1992 would be considerably behind the pace of felonious killings for 1990 and 1991. For the first *two* quarters of those years, the numbers of officers slain were 42 and 41, respectively (*Crime Control Digest* 1991q: 1).

---

[42] A few researchers have attempted to compile long-term historical counts of police killed in the line of duty. For example, Margarita (1980a) used New York City Police Department and other records to attempt to portray not only the number of fatalities but the precipitating factors for all officer duty-related deaths from 1844 through 1978. More recently, both the National Law Enforcement Memorial project (which constructed a Washington, D.C., monument to American police killed in the service of their communities) and a similar effort by the Roselle, Illinois-based Law Enforcement Memorial Foundation have made a determined effort to identify every police officer killed in the line of duty throughout American history. Indeed, the Illinois effort predates American history and reportedly has identified 34,000 police officers killed (both intentionally and accidentally) in the American colonies and the U.S. since 1724, when Constable Peter Symons, "went out [near Charleston, South Carolina] to arrest suspects accused of violating colonial religious laws.... [and] didn't return alive" (McRoberts 1992; Van Raalte 1990). The leadership of the National Law Enforcement Memorial project believes this estimate is high by several thousand (Floyd 1990).

Another compilation of police killed in the line of duty that experts find high is that released in early 1991 by the Miami-based American Police Hall of Fame and Museum. That group asserted in a news release that, nationally, 189 police were killed in the line of duty during 1989 and that 119 were killed during 1990. The Miami group further claimed that, of the 1989 deaths, guns accounted for 72 (38 percent) and that in 1990 guns claimed the lives of 51 (43 percent) of the slain officers (Associated Press 1991).

Figure 35: American Law Enforcement Officers Killed Feloniously, 1960-91
Sources: FBI (annual reports).

Figure 36 presents the same data contained in Figure 35 (with the exception of 1990 and 1991 data) but shows the average annual number of American law enforcement personnel killed feloniously during five-year periods from 1960 through 1989. As with similar data presented earlier on the number of justifiable homicides committed by police, presenting multi-year averages helps to mask the sometimes misleading effects of fluctuating reporting errors from year to year and also makes it easier to see long-term trends.

Another way to think about the frequency with which American law enforcement personnel have been feloniously slain over the past several decades is to look not at the actual numbers of slain officers but at the *rate* at which they were killed (the number compared to some other variable). Thus, Figures 37 and 38 display the changing *rates* at which officers were killed over approximately the same time period shown in the earlier figures. The rates in Figures 37 and 38 are based on the total number of sworn police in the nation each year (excluding from the denominator federal law enforcement personnel but including municipal, county, and state police—the numerator *includes* federal as well as nonfederal law enforcement personnel who were slain). As a result, these graphs suggest the likelihood that American police had of being killed in any given year based on the number of officers employed.

Table 6:
American Law Enforcement Officers Killed Feloniously, 1960-91

Year	# of Law Enforcement Officers Killed	Year	# of Law Enforcement Officers Killed
1960	28	1977	93
1961	37	1978	93
1962	48	1979	106
1963	55	1980	104
1964	57	1981	91
1965	53	1982	92
1966	57	1983	80
1967	76	1984	72
1968	64	1985	78
1969	86	1986	66
1970	100	1987	74
1971	126	1988	78
1972	112	1989	66
1973	134	1990	66[1]
1974	132	1991	71[2]
1975	129		
1976	111	Total	2,635

Sources: IACP (1971), FBI (1974, 1982, 1988, 1989b, 1991a, 1991b, 1992g), Behm (1992).
[1] *The FBI's report,* Law Enforcement Officers Killed and Assaulted—1990, *indicates that 65 American law enforcement personnel were killed feloniously. By September 1992, that figure had been revised by the FBI to 66 (Behm 1992).*
[2] *The FBI's report,* Crime in the United States—1991 *(page 290), indicates that 69 American law enforcement personnel were killed feloniously in 1991. By September 1992, that figure had been revised by the FBI to 71. The explanation offered was that local officials were slow to notify the FBI of the felonious deaths of two Puerto Rican police officers (Behm 1992).*

In 1990, when 11.1 American police were feloniously slain per 100,000 officers, the murder/nonnegligent manslaughter rate for the general population was 9.4 per 100,000 (Table E-63 in Appendix E; FBI 1991c: 8). In 1991, the rates changed to 11.9 for police slain and 9.8 for general population homicides (Table E-43; FBI 1992g: 13). Compared in this way, police were approximately 1.2 times more likely than other Americans to be murdered in 1990 and 1991—a relatively small difference. This difference was larger a decade ago, due to a higher level of victimization for officers (24 per 100,000); the national murder rate, in fact, was slightly higher in 1980 (10.2) than in 1990 and 1991 (Table E-43 in Appendix E; FBI 1981a: 7). So in 1980 police were 2.4 times more likely than other Americans to be murdered.

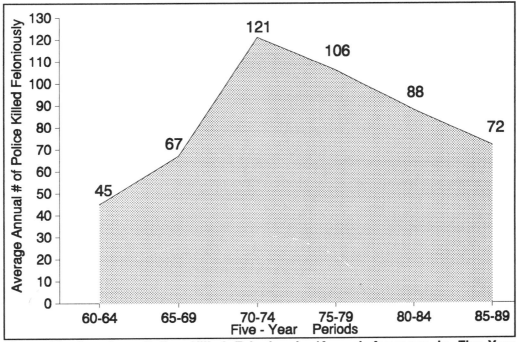

Figure 36: American Police Killed Feloniously (Annual Averages in Five-Year Periods), 1960-89

Sources: FBI (annual reports).

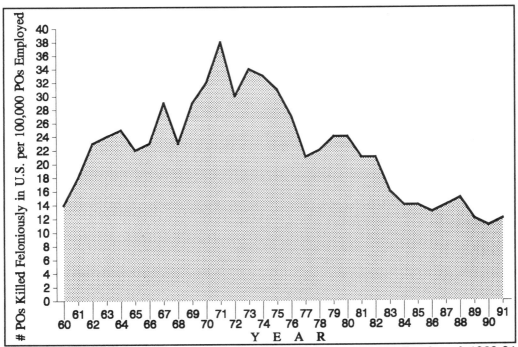

Figure 37: Rate at Which American Police Were Slain per 100,000 Employed, 1960-91

Sources: FBI (annual reports).

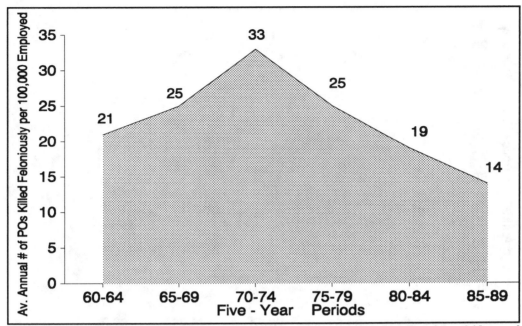

Figure 38: Rate at Which American Police Were Slain per 100,000 Employed (Annual Averages for 5-Year Periods), 1960-89   *Sources: FBI (annual reports).*

Table 7:
Average Annual Rates at Which American Police Were Killed
Feloniously, During Five-Year Periods, 1960-89

Years	# Killed per 100,000 Officers Employed	# Killed per 100,000 Violent Crime Arrests[1]	# Killed per 10,000 Homicides[2]	Actual Number of Officers Killed (Ann. Av.)
1960-64	21	36	51	45
1965-69	25	36	54	67
1970-74	33	34	65	121
1975-79	25	24	54	106
1980-84	19	18	42	88
1985-89	14	13	35	71
1960-89	23	27	50	83

[1] *Includes arrests for murder/nonnegligent manslaughter, rape/aggravated sexual assault, robbery, and aggravated assault.*
[2] *Includes reported murders and nonnegligent manslaughters.*
Sources: FBI (annual reports).

The employment levels of sworn officers is only one way to think about the relative chances that police have of being killed in the line of duty at any given time. Another way is to examine the number of violent crime arrests—arrests for murder/nonnegligent manslaughter, forcible rape/aggravated sexual assault, robbery, and aggravated assault. Still another way, which likewise attempts to represent the changing levels of violence in American culture over time, is to compare the slayings of police with the number of homicides in the nation each year. Table 7, based on Table E-43 in Appendix E, shows the average annual rates of American police killed feloniously during blocks of five years, displaying rates based on police employment levels, violent crime arrests, and reported homicides (murders and non-negligent manslaughters).

What becomes clear from Table 7 and from Figures 37 and 38 is that, as of 1989 and 1990, using each of these measures of opportunity for violent encounters between police and civilians, American police were less likely to be killed in the line of duty than at any time in the past three decades. In 1960, when 28 officers were slain by felons (compared with 66 slain in 1990), 14 officers were killed for every 100,000 employed in the nation. After a peak rate of 38 killed per 100,000 employed in 1971, the rate had dropped by 1989 to 12 and by 1990 to 11 (it rose to 12 again in 1991) (see Table E-43). Looking at the annual averages during five-year blocks shown in Figure 38 reveals that the rate (based on employment levels of officers) in the 1960-64 period (when 225 officers lost their lives feloniously) was 21 officers killed per 100,000 employed. By contrast, the rate during the 1985-89 period (when 356 officers died feloniously) was 14 officers killed per 100,000 employed. Comparing Figures 36 and 38 shows graphically what these numbers mean. Although the annual average *number* of officers killed feloniously (Figure 36) has generally decreased in recent years, two time periods—1960-64 and 1965-69—had lower annual average death tolls than the most recent period. But we see from Figure 38 that the average annual *rate* at which police were feloniously killed, based on their numbers in the nation's police departments, was never lower over the past three decades than it was in the most recent five-year period.

The National Law Enforcement Officers' Memorial Fund, in researching the names of American law enforcement personnel (including both police and corrections officers) slain in the line of duty since the nation's founding, has reported that:

- *"The first line of duty death was Robert Forsyth, a U.S. Marshal shot and killed in 1794 while serving an arrest warrant.*
- *The oldest officer killed was 84.*
- *The youngest officer killed was 19.*
- *The state with the most deaths is California with 1,055 officers killed, followed by New York with 955 deaths.*
- *The states with the fewest deaths are North Dakota and Vermont with 12"* (Memorial News *1990:3*).

As Table 7 shows, parallel findings are derived regardless of which rate is used. Thus, if the number of officers employed at any given time, the number of violent felony arrests that officers make, and the number of general population homicides all seem to be plausible indicators of the likelihood from year to year that police will become engaged in life-threatening confrontations, then American police were better protected from the hazards of their work as the nation entered the last decade of this century than they were in the preceding 30 years. This is not to say that police work has become less dangerous. It may simply be that better protections have been afforded to officers, as we discuss in the next subsection.

The 1989 and 1990 FBI reports on *Law Enforcement Officers Killed and Assaulted* reveal that 791 police officers were feloniously killed *by firearms* during the 11 years from 1980 through 1990, ranging from a high of 95 in 1980 (the 1979 figure was 100) to a low of 56 in 1990 (Behm [1992] indicates the revised number may be 57). During this same period, 866 law enforcement officers were feloniously killed by offenders using all types of weapons. But in 1991, 68 American police were slain with *firearms*; three others were killed with other weapons—one each by a bomb, vehicle, a flashlight (Behm 1992).

It is unclear, of course, whether the relatively steady, long-term decline in fatal attacks on American law enforcement personnel will continue throughout the 1990s. While the 1990 death toll documented by the FBI was 66 sworn personnel, in 1991 71 law enforcement personnel were killed feloniously (and another 52 died accidentally) (Behm 1992, correcting erroneous data in FBI 1992g: 290). Of course, one year's increase (in 1991) amid a long-term general decline does not indicate a change in the trend.

Despite the long-term *national* decline in the number of police officers shot, particular cities naturally have various patterns of officer victimization. In New York City, for instance, as Figure 39 shows, there is no discernible continuing decrease in officers shot through the 1980s (although there was a dramatic decrease from 1973 to 1976 of 80 percent—see Table E-15). Indeed, from 1987 through 1989, there was a rather steep increase in officers shot. Then, the number

> In 1989, "for the second year in a row, no Canadian police officers were killed on duty. However, in 1989, the number of homicides in the country increased 13 percent to 649." The 1989 national homicide rate was 2.48 for 100,000 Canadian residents (Law and Order 1990b).

dropped again in 1990 and remained at the same level in 1991. As noted above, even a dramatic change from one year to the next, while important in human and perhaps political dimensions, can hardly be taken as indicating a trend, since police-involved shootings are extremely rare events and thus are highly subject to random fluctuation from one time period to the next.

B. Deadly Weapon Assaults on Police and Number of Officers Who Might Have Been Killed but for Soft Body Armor

The earlier discussion and graphs make clear that there has been a national downward trend in the number of felonious *killings* of police since the mid-1970s. But is this because fewer assailants are attempting to kill police or because police are better protected—with soft body armor, with tactical skills, and with conflict management training and other safeguards?

Figure 40 shows the annual numbers of American police officers assaulted with deadly weapons from 1978 through 1990 (the earliest and most recent years for which pertinent data were available from the FBI). The deadly weapons used include firearms, knives or other cutting instruments, and "other dangerous weapons." The final category does *not* include "personal weapons"—hands, feet, teeth, and such.

Figure 40 reveals that, in contrast to the dramatic downturn in the number of American police slain since the mid-1970s, there was, until 1990, a remarkably steady level of deadly weapon assaults on police (as reported each year by police agencies to the FBI through the Uniform Crime Reporting program). Similarly, the number of deadly weapon assaults resulting in *nonfatal injuries* to the officers remained very steady over this same time period, with a

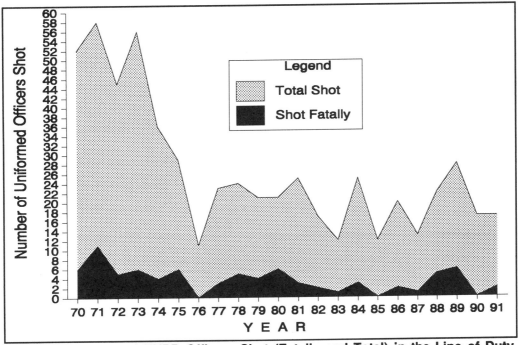

Figure 39: Uniformed NYPD Officers Shot (Fatally and Total) in the Line of Duty, 1970-91   *Source: Cerar (1989, 1990, 1991).*

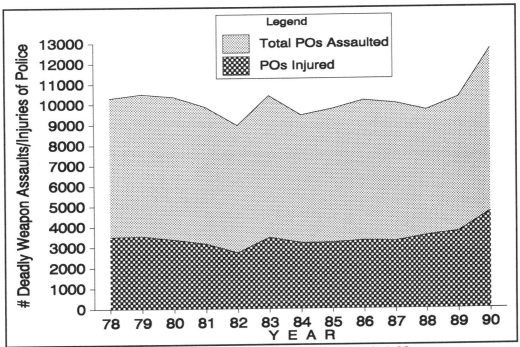

Figure 40: Deadly Weapon Assaults on American Police, 1978-90
Sources: FBI (annual reports).

slight increase from 1984 through 1989 (from national totals of 9,464 to 10,311). But in 1990 the number of officers who reported having been assaulted increased to 12,693.

To display these officer assault data in a fashion that minimizes the effect of year-to-year random fluctuations and the effect of fluctuating reporting error, Figure 41 shows the average annual number of American law enforcement personnel subjected to deadly weapon attacks during blocks of three years (through 1989).

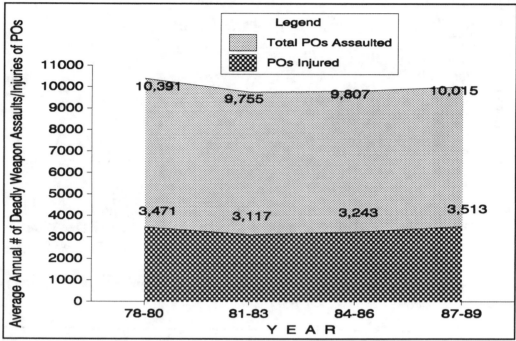

Figure 41: American Police Assaulted/Injured with Deadly Weapons (Annual Averages for 3-year Periods), 1978-89
Sources: FBI (annual reports).

When one considers the steady number of assaults against the backdrop of gradually increasing numbers of sworn law enforcement personnel in the nation, however, it becomes clear that officers were not only less likely (based on their numbers on police forces) to get killed over time; they were less likely to be assaulted with the variety of guns, knives, and other dangerous weapons represented in the preceding graphs. During the most recent three-year period displayed, however, there was a slight increase in the likelihood that assaulted officers would be *injured*.

Thus, Figure 42 shows the annual averages during the same three-year periods as shown in Figure 41, but this time the deadly weapon assaults on officers are expressed as a rate—the number of officers assaulted per 100,000 employed in the nation. The numbers used to generate this graph are in Table E-44 in Appendix E.

Figure 43 presents only the *firearms* assaults (with and without injury to officers) that are included along with other deadly weapon assaults in Figures 40 and 41. Even though an officer would have ample justification for using deadly force against an assailant who menaced him or her with *any* type of deadly weapon, most officers would concur that firearms assaults present a special level and type of threat (e.g., endangering officers over greater distances than do cutting instruments or other dangerous weapons). Hence, it is important to understand that, although the overall number of deadly weapon assaults on officers and the number of *noninjury firearms* assaults on officers did not vary appreciably over most of the

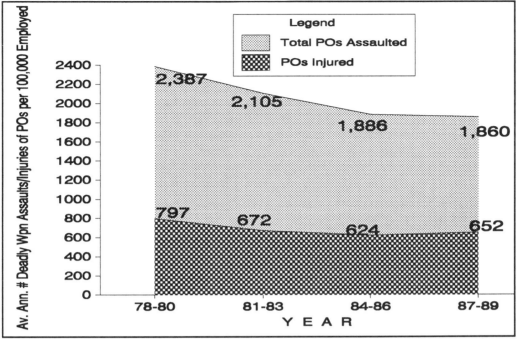

Figure 42: Rate of Deadly Wpn Assaults/Injuries of U.S. Police per 100,000 Employed (Ann. Avs. for 3-Year Periods), 1978-89
Sources: FBI (annual reports).

1980s, the number of officers *injured* (as well as the total number assaulted) with assailants' firearms *did* increase during the late 1980s and again in 1990.[43] This increase probably consists in part of officers who suffered bruises when shot while wearing soft body armor (officers who have been saved by protective apparel from gunshots say the impact feels like getting struck with a hammer—IACP 1990c). The reporting of such nonfatal injuries is highly

---

[43] Just as firearms assaults against officers vary over time, they vary from city to city. A St. Louis Metropolitan Police Department survey of a few agencies revealed the following range of rates at which officers were assaulted with firearms (meaning that firearms either were fired at officers or were displayed in a confrontational situation) (St. Louis Metropolitan Police Department 1992: 34). All of the rates listed below reflect the annual average number of officers assaulted with firearms per 1,000 officers on the police force (during the years 1987-90, except for the Los Angeles Police Department, whose rate is based on data for 1989 and 1990):

Washington, D.C.	0.15
Detroit	8.0
Chicago	12.5
Cleveland	15.0
Los Angeles	16.5
Seattle	20.3
Dallas	21.6
Baltimore	25.2
St. Louis	44.8

The study expressed the belief that the unusually low assault rate in the Washington, D.C., Metropolitan Police Department might be based at least partly on reporting rather than actual differences between it and some of the other agencies listed (*ibid.*: 34).

encouraged by the IACP/DuPont Kevlar Survivors' Club, which has a very effective national marketing campaign designed to publicize as role models those officers whose foresight in wearing soft body armor allowed them to survive otherwise fatal encounters.

When one considers the raw number increase in nonfatal firearms injuries of American police officers since 1984 in light of the rising level of sworn police employees in the nation, the increase is tempered. Based on data presented in Tables E-22 and E-45 in Appendix E, during 1978 American police were injured in firearms assaults at the rate of 127 victims per 100,000 police employed in the nation. In 1989 the firearms injury rate had risen to 174 per 100,000 officers employed and by 1990 the rate was 183. The increase in rate from 1978 to 1990 was 44 percent—a substantial increase, but far less than the 97 percent increase in the raw number of injurious firearms assaults (from 546 in 1978 to 1,077 in 1989). Working police officers coast to coast with whom we have talked in training sessions almost uniformly say that the streets have become increasingly dangerous for them in the 1980s and into the 1990s.

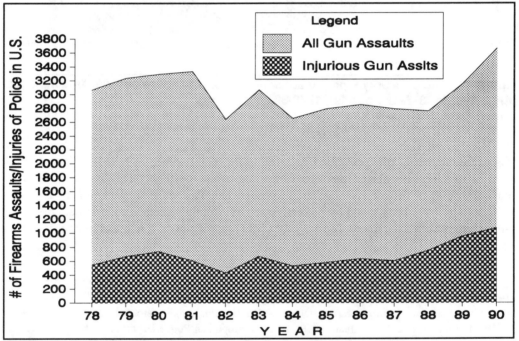

Figure 43: Firearms Assaults/Injuries of American Police, 1978-90
Sources: FBI (annual reports).

A formal mail survey of 238 members of the Portland (Ore.) Police Bureau in 1992 revealed that 80 percent of the respondents believe "that the level of violence directed at [them]...has increased in the past year or two" (Snell and Long 1992a). Moreover, 84 percent said they believe "that street officers generally are in greater danger today than five years ago" (*ibid.*). Asked to be more specific, 65 percent of the Portland personnel said they are "having to fistfight, wrestle, etc. with subjects more than in the past." The officers offered their own appraisals of the societal factors that "are most responsible for the current level of violence." "Drugs" was the principal explanation, selected by 88 percent of the respondents. The next most frequently chosen reason was "alcohol," selected by 60 percent of the officers. "Decline of the family" was cited by 50 percent, "criminals readier to use guns, etc." was offered by 48 percent, "mental illness" by 26 percent, "criminals are better armed" by 21 percent, "violence in the media" by 16 percent, and "other" explanations by 11 percent[44] (*ibid.*).

If officers *believe* that the streets are more dangerous—and there is evidence that this is true—then the question remains why the *rate* of *fatal* assaults against police is down in recent years (through 1990, with no change or slight increases in 1991 depending on the rate one examines—see Table E-43). Is it because fewer civilians attempted to assault them or because police got better at preventing such assaults and particularly at preventing life-threatening injuries? Is it possible that, through tactical and equipment choices (particularly the wearing of soft body armor), police in recent years survived potentially lethal assaults at a higher rate than in the past?

Figure 44 explores this question by adding to the previously presented number of American law enforcement personnel killed feloniously each year the number of police whose lives have been saved from felonious assaults because they wore soft body armor. The number of "saves" was documented by the IACP/DuPont Corporation "Kevlar Survivors' Club"; they have tracked officer "saves" due to soft body armor since the equipment was first made generally available in 1972. More data on officers whose lives have been saved with soft body armor appear in Chapter 5.

It is noteworthy that, without soft body armor, there would have been an aggregate additional 795 American police slain *feloniously* during the period January 1, 1972 through September 21, 1992. (As of that date, the total number of documented saves—from both assaults and accidents—was 1,448—Slavin 1992a.) After a start-up period from 1972 through 1974, when police were first becoming acquainted with soft body armor for routine operational use, the number of additional felonious slayings that would have resulted each year but for the protective apparel has ranged between 24 and 70. Experts believe that other cases exist that have not been documented by the Survivors' Club.

Experts also estimate that less than half the nation's sworn police personnel are equipped with soft body armor, a state of affairs generally attributed to cost considerations (*Crime Control Digest* 1992a: 5). *Wear* rate, of course, is an entirely different question than *availability* rate. Wear rate may be related in part to whether a police administration *requires* officers to use soft body armor in all or selected field assignments or leaves that decision to their discretion (see *Crime Control Digest* 1992b: 7; IACP 1990c). In 1991 the John Jay College of Criminal Justice in New York City conducted a national survey of 3,500 police officers in jurisdictions with populations of 25,000 or more and found that "72 percent of front-line police say they wear bullet resistant vests * * * all the time when on the street and clearly identifiable as a police officer." Moreover, "younger officers were more inclined to wear vests: * * * 97 percent of all front-line officers under 30 years of age will wear soft body armor while only 25 percent of front-line and management police over 50 wear it." The fact that a large number of agencies do not provide protective apparel to their officers is significant because, according to the survey, "police in departments where the body armor is provided are more likely to wear [it] than in departments with no vest program" (*Crime Control Digest* 1991o; see also *Law Enforcement News* 1991).

---

[44] Since the officers could check up to three causal factors, the percentages sum to more than 100 percent.

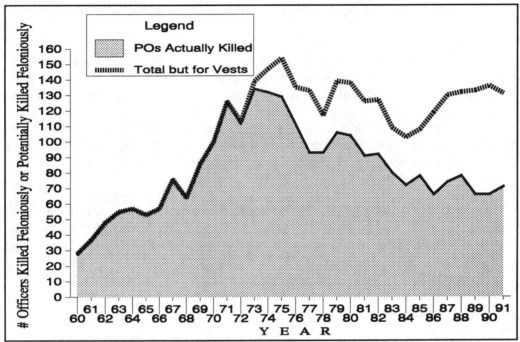

Figure 44: American Police Slain and Nearly Slain (Saved by Soft Body Armor), 1960-91   *Sources: FBI (annual reports), IACP/DuPont (1992).*

Figure 44 shows that from 1984 to 1991 the actual number of officers feloniously killed in the nation decreased by one (from 72 to 71). But during this same period, the number *potentially* killed (derived by adding the documented "saves" each year to the number of slain officers) *increased* by 27 percent (from 103 to 131). As Figure 44 makes clear, the number of officers who might have died feloniously in 1990 if soft body armor were not available would have been among the highest in the past 30 years, exceeded only twice, in 1975 and 1979. It is also noteworthy that, in 1989 and 1990, for the first time ever, the number of documented saves with soft body armor during felonious assaults (67 and 70, respectively) exceeded the number of officers slain feloniously (66 in each year).

The *rate* at which officers might have been killed feloniously in the absence of soft body armor (computed on the basis of sworn police employment levels in the nation) is displayed in Figure 45. As Figure 45 makes clear, when correcting for the number of sworn police personnel in America, we find that the likelihood of police being feloniously slain in recent years and the likelihood that police would have been slain in recent years in the absence of soft body armor is somewhat less than suggested by the raw numbers in Figure 44. (Remember that the rates shown in Figure 45 are the number slain *per 100,000* publicly employed police.) Visual comparison of Figures 44 and 45 will reveal that in some years the magnitude or direction of change differ as between the raw numbers and rates. The rate of officers who, but for soft body armor, might have been killed by felons rose between 1984 and 1988. Still, in the most current year for which data on rates are available, 1991, the rate of potential officer deaths (22.0 per 100,000 employed in the nation) was considerably lower than in most of the earlier years since soft body armor became available. Thus, if soft body armor were *not* available, the chances of American police officers dying in 1991 at the hands of assailants still would have been lower than at most other times in the past 20 years. One has to go back to 1960 and 1961 to find an appreciably lower rate of officers being murdered.

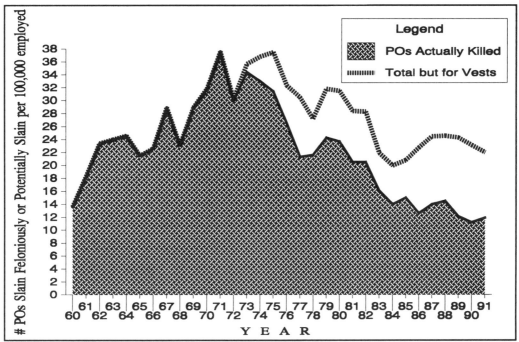

Figure 45: Rate at Which American Police were Slain and Nearly Slain (Saved by Soft Body Armor), 1960-91 *Sources: FBI, IACP/DuPont (various years).*

C. Hit Rates and Fatality Rates for Officers Who Are Shot

We saw earlier that the hit rates and fatality rates for civilians fired at by police vary considerably from jurisdiction to jurisdiction. This may be true as well for shootings *of* police, although pertinent data are not easy to find. The New York City Transit Police Department provided data for a six-year period, which might serve as an interesting yardstick against which other agencies could calculate the rate at which their own personnel are struck when fired upon in combat situations. These data are presented in Table 8.

Table 8:
New York City Transit Police Fired Upon and
Struck (Fatally and Nonfatally), 1985-90

YEAR	Total # Fired Upon	# Actually Hit	Hit Rate
1985	9	0	0%
1986	7	0	0%
1987	2	1	50%
1988	4	1	25%
1989	3	0	0%
1990	8	2	25%
TOTAL	33	4	12%

Source: New York City Transit Police Department (1991).

With numbers of the size shown in this table, it would be unwise to draw conclusions from year-to-year variations in the hit rates. Even the six-year totals present a relatively shaky basis for statistical analysis. But it is reasonably clear that offenders are not very likely to strike New York City Transit officers when they fire at them. This conclusion holds as well for the Transit officers' colleagues in the NYPD. Members of the NYPD were hit by adversaries' bullets in 12 percent of the incidents (17 out of 138) in which they were fired upon during 1990 (Cerar 1990: 7, 12). The rate of *bullets* fired by perpetrators at NYPD officers that found their mark during 1990 was 6.2 percent, compared with a 23 percent hit rate for bullets fired by officers at adversaries (Cerar 1990: 7). On a related issue, Transit Police officials report that, per capita, Transit Police officers are shot more often than NYPD officers (Wiese 1991).

The Dallas Police Department also furnished recent data on the frequency with which their officers are fired upon and struck by adversaries. In 1990, 45 Dallas police were shot at but only 1 was struck by bullets (nonfatally). These numbers produced a hit rate of a scant 2 percent. But in 1991 27 Dallas officers were fired upon[45] and 7 were struck (nonfatally), a hit rate of 26 percent. This shows how variable experiences can be from one year to the next and how small numbers almost inevitably produce wide percentage fluctuations over time.

In Philadelphia, data were available on *incidents* in which officers were fired at *and* were able to return fire (no data were available for incidents in which assailants fired at officers but the officers did not fire). Of the 58 Philadelphia incidents on which we obtained data, covering the five years from 1987 through 1991, in 16 (28 percent) incidents the officers were struck by adversaries' bullets (see Table E-13 in this volume).

Data from many other agencies are needed to shed more light on the rate at which police are struck when fired upon. It is hoped that the research the National Institute of Justice commissioned in mid-1991 on the circumstances in which American police are slain feloniously (NIJ 1991) will provide further insight into the reasons why officers in different departments are struck by adversaries' bullets at significantly different rates.

Differential *hit* rates should not be confused, of course, with differential *survival* rates (or, the flip side of the coin, *fatality* rates) for officers, which could be related to various other factors beyond those that affect hit rates. In New York City, over the 22 years from 1970 through 1991, 81 (14 percent) of the 584 uniformed members of the NYPD who were shot died from their wounds. The annual fatality rates ranged from a low of 0 percent (i.e., no officers died) in 1976, 1985, and 1990 to a high of 29 percent in 1980 (see Table E-15 in Appendix E). In Houston, over the 12 years from 1980 through 1991, no officers were slain in half of those years, although the lowest number of officers shot nonfatally in any one year during this period was three. The combined 12-year felonious fatality rate for Houston sworn personnel was 10 percent (9 officers killed out of 94 shot) (see Table E-20).

In Chicago, over the nine years from 1974 through 1982, of the 143 police officers shot by civilians, 23 (16 percent) succumbed to their wounds (Geller and Karales 1985). During

---

[45] An additional officer was mistakenly fired upon and struck fatally by fellow officers during an undercover drug raid. This incident produced a great deal of organizational self-examination and outreach to other departments for advice on how to safeguard officers from "friendly fire."

this period, there were years with no officers killed, and one year (1982) in which 60 percent of the 10 officers shot by assailants died as a result of their injuries (*ibid.*). More recently, over the five years from 1985 through 1989, of 50 officers shot by assailants, 11 (22 percent) died (Chicago Police Department 1990a).

Nationally, in 1990, 1,077 police officers were shot nonfatally (taking the FBI's figures on law enforcement personnel assaulted with firearms and injured as a result—FBI 1991b: 46),[46] and 57 officers were shot fatally (Behm 1992). Thus, the total number of officers shot in 1990 across the United States was 1,134, and the fatality rate was 5 percent. Over the period 1981-90, 6,851 officers were shot nonfatally and 697 were shot fatally, for a total of 7,548 total officers struck by assailants' bullets over these 11 years and a fatality rate of 9 percent (*ibid.*). Fatality rates for officers will vary, of course, as they will for civilians shot by officers, depending on such factors as number and type of rounds fired, location and number of wounds, the availability of prompt and pertinent medical care, whether the victim officers wore protective apparel, and other variables.

D. Accidental Deaths of Officers

Over the past two decades, the FBI reports an average of 48 officers per year have been killed *accidentally* in the line of duty. Accidental deaths include those that were the result of

"At approximately 1535 hours, during a buy and bust operation, two detectives and one [State] Police investigator were involved in a gunfight with two perps. The incident [began] in a hallway, where one perp pulled a .357 Magnum revolver, one detective struggled with perps and was severely beaten and bitten on the forehead. The detective pulled his off duty revolver and accidentally discharged one round hitting himself in the leg, then fired three times at the two perps who were fleeing down the hallway. The State Police investigator assigned to the buy and bust entered the hallway facing [the detective, with the perps running towards the state investigator]. At this time [the state investigator] fired twice, and at the same time the detective was firing (crossfire). [A second detective] was outside of the building; he observed the perps fleeing and fired seven times at the perps...while the [State] Police investigator turned towards the perps but did not fire at the fleeing perps [a second instance of] crossfire. One perp fired once [but did not hit anyone]. A .357 Magnum revolver was recovered. One [State] Police investigator was shot and killed during crossfire. One detective shot in leg, second detective shot in both legs, and two perps were shot and injured" (Cerar 1990: 17).

such incidents as vehicle accidents, drownings, falls, and shootings (including mistaken identity and self-inflicted shootings, training mishaps, and crossfires). In 1984, for the first time since the reporting of these data began in 1962, more police officers died accidentally than feloniously (Garner and Clemmer 1986). In 1989, when 66 law enforcement officers were feloniously slain in the line of duty, accidents occurring while performing official duties claimed the lives of an additional 79 officers (FBI 1989b: 45). The numbers of felonious and accidental deaths were much closer in 1990, when 66 police personnel were slain feloniously and 67 lost their lives in job-related accidents (FBI 1991b). In 1991, 71 officers were killed

---

[46] Note that the total number of officers assaulted with firearms (both those injured and those not reportedly injured), as tallied in FBI annual publications, cannot be equated with the number of officers *fired at*, because menacing an officer with a gun would probably be tallied by some departments, if not most, as a firearms assault on an officer, even though the assailant's gun was not discharged.

feloniously, and 52 died in accidents (Behm 1992, correcting figures in FBI 1992g: 290).

Gunfire figures much more prominently in the *felonious* killing of law enforcement personnel (causing 93 percent of these fatalities nationwide from 1979 through 1988) than in their *accidental* line-of-duty deaths (causing 9 percent of these fatalities nationally over the same ten-year period) (FBI 1988). In 1990 of the 67 police accidentally killed, 5 were shot accidentally (8 percent) (FBI 1991b: 4), while 57 (86 percent) of the 66 officers killed feloniously succumbed to gunshot wounds (Behm 1992; FBI 1991b). Additional discussion of the circumstances in which American police have lost their lives in the line of duty appears in the next chapter.

E. Use of Deadly Force Against Police in Smaller Jurisdictions

Due to the relatively small number of police-involved shootings that occur during given time periods in small- and medium-size localities, deadly force analysts and police administrators especially concerned about officer effectiveness and safety and public welfare in such jurisdictions have a particularly difficult time deriving empirically based guidance. As we note in Chapter 6, there is an important, as yet unaddressed research agenda pertaining to the use of deadly force by and against police in smaller police agencies.

One of the few sources that consistently presents relevant data for small towns is the FBI's annual publication *Law Enforcement Officers Killed and Assaulted*. Although it is difficult to draw statistically meaningful conclusions about patterns of events in small jurisdictions from the data on officers *killed*, the data presented on officers assaulted comprise numbers large enough that some patterns begin to emerge. Perhaps the clearest pattern is that, according to recent FBI data (for the years 1989 and 1990), the likelihood of officer nonfatal injuries due to assaults in the line of duty decreases as the size of

"In an era of widespread gang violence, readily available guns and battles over drug turf, it comes as no surprise to most urban dwellers that city police are facing heightened dangers on the street. * * * But what may be more surprising is that violence against suburban police—once nearly a contradiction of terms—is keeping pace this year. In 1991, two suburban officers [in the Chicago area] were shot. Already this year, four have been shot.... * * * Between 1982 and 1992, 18 Chicago police officers were slain...[and] five [suburban] officers were killed.... * * * There have been at least 15 suburban [nonfatal shootings of] police since the mid-'80s, according to news reports. * * * 'It's not all Chicago's fault,' [a suburban police chief] said. 'It's society's problem. Society as a whole has gotten more violent. There's less respect for human rights and values and nature. It's a very dangerous trend.' * * * 'I think (we) had the attitude, well, we're in the suburbs,' said [another suburban chief], a 25-year veteran of that northwest suburban department. 'But the whole attitude has changed' " (Goering and McRoberts 1992: 1, 20).

In 1990, in suburban Chicago and "downstate" Illinois, "nine police officers were threatened with firearms or shot.... That compares with 218 Chicago officers who faced guns during calls. [Still,] the image of the suburbs as a safe haven for police officers is changing, said Cornell Smith, deputy director of the Illinois State Police. Smith seconds the notion of the Chicago City Council that police officers should always wear bulletproof vests—even in the suburbs" (Carr 1992).

the policed population decreases.[47] Figures 46 and 47 display this pattern for jurisdictions ranging in size from over 250,000 residents to under 10,000. There is remarkable consistency in the patterns shown for both years, with the only variation being that in 1990 the assault rate on officers working in suburban counties rose slightly above the assault rate for officers working in small municipalities (populations less than 25,000).

> *Maywood, a 1.2-square-mile city seven miles south of downtown Los Angeles, "buried its first slain police officer [on June 4, 1992] in an intensely personal ceremony befitting its 34-member police force and the affable, small-town ways of Officer John A. Hoglund. * * * Hoglund, 47, was fatally shot May 29 when he responded to a silent alarm and encountered five armed robbers fleeing a neighborhood market. He had been riding alone—as patrol officers typically do in [Maywood]—and had no chance to draw his gun.*
>
> *"A 16-year police veteran who left accounting because he loved the streets more than numbers, Hoglund is the first officer shot to death in the line of duty in the Maywood Police Department's 68-year history. Chief Ted Heidke said...that another Maywood officer died on duty in 1944, in a motorcycle accident. * * * Even in deceptively safe Maywood, Hoglund was aware of his job's risks but still found the work irresistible, a friend a co-worker told mourners. 'There's a love only a police officer can experience and savor—the love he has for the streets,' said Sgt. Ed Robison, his voice breaking. 'The lover can be cruel and harsh. She will knock you down, beat you up and make you wonder why you come back to it day after day. Last Friday, John Hoglund put on his badge and his gun and went out to meet his lover for the last time.'*
>
> *"'This has been a very difficult time at Maywood,' [Chief Heidke] said. 'We're all really, truly a family'"* (L. Berger 1992).

As we have noted elsewhere, in appraising the circumstances confronting police in any given jurisdiction one must see if the actual population policed on any given tour of duty is approximately the same as the resident population. Many factors might produce important differences between the Census Bureau's count of resident population for a jurisdiction and the number of people whom police must serve there. One factor is a miscount by the Census Bureau, which might be skewed along income or racial/ethnic lines in ways that were widely discussed in the popular media and professional journals when the 1990 Census was being prepared. Another, more easily identified discrepancy could be that a given residential area empties out during the day as residents go elsewhere to work. Conversely, a business, shopping, or entertainment area may swell to many times its residential population due to the influx of nonresidents to work, shop, or play.

---

[47] If one examines only *killings*—felonious slayings of police and justifiable homicides *by* police—there is evidence that big-city police slay about half of all the civilians killed by police in the nation but constitute less than one-fifth of the law enforcement personnel slain by criminals. We derive this by analyzing, for the period 1979 through 1984, data in Sherman and Cohn (1986) on citizens and police killed by one another; data in annual FBI reports on law enforcement officers killed and assaulted, showing the total number of police killed in the nation each year; and unpublished FBI supplementary homicide report data on the number of citizens killed justifiably each year by the nation's police. We offer this finding cautiously because, as we discussed in Chapter 2, the unpublished FBI data on justifiable homicides by police are notoriously incomplete. With more complete tallies of justifiable homicides by all police in the country, the Sherman and Cohn data on killings by *big-city* police (which the researchers obtained directly from police agencies) would constitute something less than 50 percent of all justifiable homicides by American police.

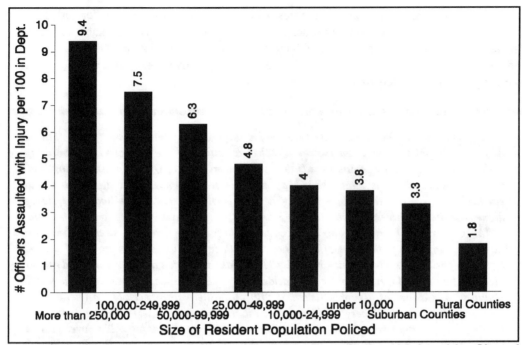

Figure 46: Rate at Which American Police Were Assaulted and Injured by Size of Jurisdiction, 1989 *Source: FBI (1989b).*

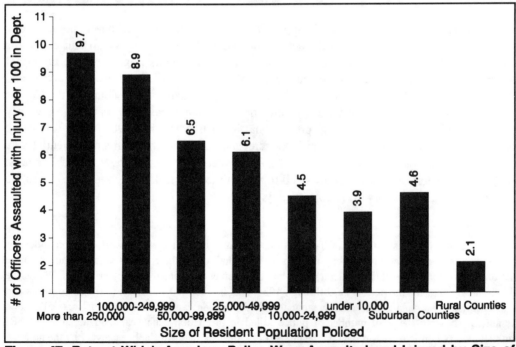

Figure 47: Rate at Which American Police Were Assaulted and Injured by Size of Jurisdiction, 1990 *Source: FBI (1990).*

F. The Long-term National Trend and a Note on Counting Methods

Just as the number of civilians killed justifiably by police has been generally decreasing over the past two decades (at least according to data on large cities), the number of police officers feloniously killed in the line of duty generally decreased during the 18 years from 1973 through 1990 (FBI annual reports), with a slight increase in the 1991 preliminary count (FBI 1992c). National data are much more revealing of statistically significant trends than data from individual police agencies, which (fortunately) have relatively few line-of-duty deaths and accordingly show larger fluctuations from year to year.[48]

"While it is true that blacks form a significant portion of the homeless population and the food bank population, the media have done a tremendous disservice by equating poverty with being black. Although blacks are over-represented among the poor, the majority of poor people in this country are white. The majority of food stamp recipients are white. The majority of welfare recipients are white. The majority of recipients of AFDC are white. The media helps us to see what we look for and we look for what we see!" (Blackwell 1992: 19).

Before leaving our discussion of the *frequency* with which police are shot, a methodological point about counting should be made. Police administrators have sometimes criticized the accuracy of outside researchers' reports on use of deadly force by their officers. Similarly, the FBI's characterizations of trends in police officer deaths occasionally have been subject to challenge by private researchers. In 1974 the FBI's reports of alarming increases in killings of police were called misleading by some researchers (e.g., Takagi 1974). Based on data for 1963 through 1971, during which time the annual number of police deaths rose

---

[48] Sporadic data from earlier periods of American history are available for certain cities. Bowman (1984) reports the toll that the "roaring twenties" and 1930s took on Chicago police: In the 10-year period from 1924 through 1933, 114 Chicago policemen gave their lives (some through accidental deaths, many through felonious attacks). In 1924, 1925, and 1928, 13 officers died while on duty. In 1933, 14 on-duty officers died. Bowman portrays the type of circumstances in which these officers died:

"One of the 14 Chicago policemen killed in the line of duty in 1933 was shot with his own gun in a tavern when he refused to drink wine offered by his assailant. Another died after a beating by a mob protesting the high price of bread at a nonunion bakery. A third was machined-gunned by mail robbers. A fourth was shot by a prisoner escaping from the Criminal Courts Building."

In 1934 10 Chicago officers were killed; five were killed in 1935, and five in 1936. "From 1937 [through 1984]—except 1982 when five policemen died—no more than four were killed in any year and several years passed with no line-of-duty fatalities" (*ibid.*). The two-digit fatality figures for Chicago police during the 1920s and 1930s are even more shocking when one considers the size of the City's resident population and police force then and more recently. For instance, the City's population in 1930 was 376,438 (Chicago Public Library Information Center 1984), but by 1980 it had grown to 3,005,072. In 1933, when 14 on-duty officers died feloniously, the force had 6,285 personnel (Chicago Police Department 1992); in 1979, when two officers were killed feloniously, the sworn complement numbered 13,293. Thus the rates of officer fatalities (numbered killed per 1,000 officers in the Department) were 2.23 in 1933 and 0.15 in 1979, meaning that Chicago Police in 1933 were nearly 15 times as likely to be killed feloniously as they were in 1979. (In 1980 no Chicago officers died in the line of duty.)

*"The FBI found that the nature of youth crime shifted in the 1980's away from crimes against property...to violent crimes against people.... The erupting violence in the 1980s coincides with the dramatic rise in the use of crack cocaine, which can provoke violent behavior in its users. The FBI study, which tracks arrests but not individual offenders, said that arrests for murder by the young increased 332 percent, from 2.8 per 100,000 in 1965 to 12.1 per 100,000 in 1990. * * * Disputes once settled with fists 20 years ago are too commonly resolved today in gunfire, said Renee Wilson-Brewer, project director of the National Network of Violence Prevention Practitioners, in Boston" (Marriott 1992b).*

from 55 to 129, Takagi argued that while the *number* of police killed had indeed risen, the *rate* of killing had not, for there had been an increase of more than 50 percent in the number of sworn police officers in the country and an increase in the number of agencies reporting to the FBI during the period studied.

In this chapter we have presented a wide array of data drawn from both prior studies and our own research. The tallies of civilians shot by officers and of officers shot reported here are but the beginning of any serious analysis. The next crucial steps are to attempt to describe the circumstances in which these violent encounters arise and to explore possible reasons for some of the patterns that emerge over time and across geography. These are the tasks of the next chapter.

Chapter 4:

DESCRIBING AND EXPLAINING SHOOTINGS OF AND BY POLICE

Most of the empirical studies from the past three decades support the following broad generalization:

The most common type of incident in which police and civilians shoot one another in urban America involves an on-duty, uniformed, white, male officer and an armed, black, male civilian between the ages of 17 and 30 and occurs at night, in a public location in a high-crime precinct, in connection with a suspected armed robbery or a "man with a gun" call.

Although this statement is generally accurate for big cities with sizable black populations, by itself it provides little insight into efforts to make police officers and civilians safer and the use of force free from racial bias. Indeed, taken out of context, this statement could be misused in an attempt to justify racially prejudicial conduct either by or against police officers. Columnist Carl Rowan captured the point nicely in a critique of the national media for feeding racial tensions in America by mindless and continual reference to the involvement of minorities in crime (see Rowan 1989).

To reduce the risk of casual generalizations, in the next several sections of this chapter we examine in some detail the characteristics of situations in which police officers use deadly force and are shot, as well as the characteristics of the officer and civilian participants in these incidents.

I. "Mobilizing Events" (Situations that Escalated into Shootings by Police) and Mode of Mobilization

The crimes or other situations that immediately preceded and escalated into shootings of civilians by police (what Sherman [1983] called the "pre-intervention situation") have been reported in various studies. They may be summarized using some standard classifications. Table 9 presents data from Fyfe's study of New York City, the Police Foundation's seven-city study, Geller and Karales' Chicago study, and the State of New York's examination of justifiable homicides by police throughout that state.

Table 9:
Various Studies of Situations Preceding Shootings by Police

Situations Preceding Shootings*	Percentages of Shootings by Police Reported in:			
	Fyfe (1978) *N.Y.C.*	Milton et al. (1977) *7 Cities*	Geller and Karales (1981a) *Chicago*	NYSCCJ (1987) *N.Y. State*
Robbery	39%	21%	27%	---
Disturbances (domestic and nondomestic)	25%	32%	39%	28%
Traffic stops/pursuits	12%	8%	7%	3%
Burglaries	7%	20%	15%	---
PO's personal business (horseplay, dispute, accident, etc.)	---	4%	4%	4%
Crimes against persons	---	---	---	36%
Property crimes	---	---	---	10%
Suspicious activity	6%	---	---	10%
Narcotics arrest	---	---	---	6%
Other situations	---	11%	8%	2%
TOTAL	89%	96%	100%	99%

* *The studies used slightly different classifications.*

Later in this book we will present additional data that separate the "disturbance" category into domestic and nondomestic disturbances and thus help clear up long-standing confusion in the profession about the level of violence likely to occur in various kinds of disturbances.

At this point, Table 9 helps illustrate an important distinction made by many of the studies—the distinction between the events that prompted police intervention with the civilian and the behavior that directly precipitated the shooting. Table 9 contains types of events that prompted police intervention. For instance, a police officer may have made what seemed like a routine traffic stop, only to be confronted by an armed passenger in the stopped car (for discussion of a Los Angeles Sheriff's traffic stop that escalated to a life-and-death struggle, see Katz 1992). If the passenger aimed the weapon at the police officer and the officer fired, this incident would be characterized in many studies both as a traffic stop (the mobilizing event) and as an armed assault on an officer (the action that prompted the shooting).

By the same token, many other relatively trivial incidents (e.g., shoplifting, a weaponless domestic dispute) could escalate to the point where a suspect jeopardized the responding officer's life. It is more likely, however, that persons suspected of certain types of violent crimes (especially armed robbery) will respond to police intervention by attempting to injure an officer.

The reason both police tacticians and researchers make a special effort to document not only the civilian conduct that directly precipitated a shooting but also the criminal events that initially drew police into contact with the civilians they shot is straightforward. Searching for patterns of incidents that mobilized police intervention in what eventually became shootings is one important way the studies may be able to contribute to improved training, policy, procedure, equipment, and tactics that will help police do their work with minimal jeopardy to themselves and those they encounter.[1]

There has probably been some change over time in the mix of calls for service that led to shootings by police, especially in the wake of the 1985 Supreme Court decision in *Tennessee v. Garner*, which, as a practical matter, precluded officers from shooting at most

"[A deputy sheriff] was interviewing a witness to an apartment complex disturbance when he was shot by an assailant who had just robbed a nearby convenience store. Saved by his safety vest, [the deputy] returned fire, wounding the suspect. The individual was placed under arrest and later convicted of his crimes" (FBI 1990b: 33)

fleeing *burglary* suspects. The reader should keep in mind, accordingly, that the studies referenced in Table 9 all report data from the pre-*Garner* period. Such data are included in this volume partly because they are available but mostly because current police administrators and others interested in understanding the issues that drive public policy on officer discretion to take another's life should be familiar with the police shooting experience in prior decades that the Supreme Court found inconsistent with fundamental constitutional principles.

One would expect that more recent data from most cities concerning the mix of mobilizing crime incidents would show considerably less than the 20 percent figure derived by Milton, et al. (1977) and the 15 percent figure found by Geller and Karales (1981a) for burglary-related shootings by police.

As distinguished from the *events* that mobilized officer intervention in potentially violent situations, the *mode* of mobilization refers to the source of the officer's knowledge that his or her service is needed. Traditional categories of officer modes of mobilization include dispatch, on-view (officer notices a need for intervention while in the field), and citizen complaint (a citizen hailing an officer in the field rather than calling central dispatching). Some departments analyze modes of mobilization in more discrete categories.

Thus, for instance, in New York City during 1991, of 370 incidents in which NYPD members either discharged their weapons or were attacked with lethal weapons (these exclude 69 cases of shots fired accidentally by officers and police suicides), the Department specified "how members became involved" in these incidents: 104 (28 percent) were "radio runs"; 90

---

[1] As we will discuss in Chapter 5 (in connection with a section on the myth of the "split-second decision"), cutting edge thinking about tactics, training for violence reduction, and post-incident investigation takes the position that neither the mobilizing event nor the "final frame" danger posed by the officer's opponents are sufficient basis for appraising the *inevitability* of a given encounter ending in bloodshed. Instead, the view is that, in the interest of preventing career-threatening injuries or liabilities for officers and needless harm to others, it is important to consider whether police decisions taken minutes or even seconds in advance of a shoot/don't shoot determination may unwittingly paint an officer and his or her civilian adversary into a corner from which the officer's only reasonable option often is to shoot first and sort things out later.

(24 percent) were mobilized by a "complainant or pick up job"; 49 (13 percent) took the initiative to intervene after "observation" of a situation requiring police attention; 16 (4 percent) of the incidents arose while officers were "making [an] arrest"; 4 (1 percent) during car stops; 13 (3.5 percent) during "investigation" of some matter; 54 (15 percent) did not involve a planned intervention, in the sense that the officer was a "victim of assault"; 15 (4 percent), relatedly, entailed a "sniper/ambush attack"; and 25 (7 percent) involved "other" ways in which officers became involved (Cerar 1991: 11). The level of detail provided by the NYPD is helpful for various analytic purposes. There is a risk of using this type of categorization for analysis, however, because it mixes in some places what are best thought of as modes of mobilization (officer's own decision, a decision prompted by other police personnel, or a decision prompted by a field request for assistance by a civilian) with what we think should more properly be conceptualized as the events that eventually escalated into a lethal-encounter (e.g., the NYPD categories of "making arrest" and "car stop").

By "backing up" in time from the "split-second" decision to pull or not pull the trigger, some researchers have charted a course for a new body of research on "averted shootings." Averted shootings are situations with potential to escalate into use of deadly force by police but that, through officer skill or other circumstances, are resolved without the officer(s) firing a weapon. Much of the best police tactical training literature for many years has focused on how officers, through proper approaches to and handling of suspects, can apprehend potentially dangerous persons with minimal risk.[2]

---

[2] Some of the difficulties of handling suspects during arrests so as to reduce the potential threat they pose to police came jarringly to light in Chicago in January 1991, when two tactical police officers were shot in the back of the head (one fatally) in their squad car by a prisoner turned informant. The culprit had been arrested earlier in the day on a narcotics possession charge, handcuffed behind his back, transported to the police station for booking and, after his offer to show officers where his supplier operated, was placed back in the unmarked car by his arresting officers, handcuffed in front of his body so that he could smoke, and driven toward the location he had specified (Silverman and Copeland 1991; Hermann 1991; Reardon and O'Connor 1991; O'Connor 1991; O'Connor and Myers 1991). At this writing it was still not clear precisely where the offender had obtained or hidden the .38-caliber snub-nosed revolver he used (Petacque and Casey 1991), but the best thinking was that he had it concealed in his crotch under two layers of long underwear (we also discuss this incident and two related ones involving other agencies in Chapter 6 in the section on "the wisdom to study successes and the courage to study 'failures' ").

Then-Chicago Police Superintendent LeRoy Martin observed that this incident raised questions about handcuffing procedures for persons just arrested and persons being worked as informants (Kupcinet 1991; Petacque and Casey 1991). Moreover, it raised questions about the adequacy of searching procedures. It has long been a challenge in numerous jurisdictions to ensure that police conduct complete protective searches. There are several reasons for this, but a leading one is reflected in former Chicago Police Assistant Deputy Superintendent Raymond Risely's assessment of the circumstances that led to the shooting of the two Chicago officers: "[A]pparently [the arresting officers] didn't search the guy's crotch" (Petacque and Casey 1991). Different but related problems are posed when male officers have to search female arrestees. The annals of policing also contain examples of women arrested for prostitution drawing weapons on officers while being transported in the back seat of police cars to stationhouses for booking.

In recent years, officer fear about contracting AIDS through accidentally being stuck with a contaminated needle hidden in a suspect's pocket or elsewhere in his or her clothing has exacerbated the difficulties of saving officer lives and averting shootings by officers; they may suddenly be placed in grave jeopardy by a suspect whom they thought they had adequately searched for weapons. For an excellent summary of the reasonable and misplaced fears officers have about contracting AIDS during encounters with suspects, see Blumberg (1989a: 210-212). Chicago Police Superintendent Matt

Among the deadly force research that has also begun to study officer violence-reduction techniques (techniques for averting shootings) are Reiss (1980), Scharf and Binder (1983), Geller (1985a), and Jim Fyfe's work for the Police Foundation (1988) (see also Fyfe 1986b). We will briefly discuss in Chapter 5 some of the recommendations for police training that emphasize the *sequence* of decisions (or decision opportunities) that often precede an officer's "final frame" determination to shoot or not shoot at another person.

Naturally, no reason other than the inherent value our culture places on human life is needed to justify studying how to better protect officers and those whom they engage in high-risk encounters. Nevertheless, the experience of the past several decades has taught the police community and our society that special sensitivities exist concerning the use of deadly force against minorities. In turn, these sensitivities, whether one credits them as legitimate or not, have indisputably been among the chief sources of tension between police and the communities they serve. Hence, special attention is paid throughout the deadly force literature to racial aspects of police-involved shootings.

II.   The Race/Ethnicity of Civilians Shot or Shot at by Police and of Civilians Who Killed Police

The racial distributions of civilians fired upon by police have been reported in numerous studies. A sampling is presented in Table 10 (also see Figures E-3, E-4, E-6, and E-7 in Appendix E). Data on Hispanic civilian shooting victims are considerably harder to get than data on black victims of shootings. This reflects the difficulty the U.S. Census Bureau and others continue to have designing simple ethnic classifications as well as the relative political clout of African Americans and Hispanics in the United States in recent decades. As a result, one should have little confidence that consistent classification systems have been used across police agencies and across deadly force studies when considering the shooting involvement of civilians or police officers having Spanish surnames.

Virtually all of the studies that have examined the race of civilian victims of shootings by the police have shown that blacks are shot in numbers significantly disproportionate to their proportion of the local population (see Table 10).

Using population figures to standardize the number of civilians shot or shot *at* by police in different jurisdictions (that is, creating rates showing the number of shootings per 100,000 population), researchers have found that

- blacks in Chicago were 3.8 times more likely than whites to be shot by police during the 1970s (Geller and Karales 1981a, 1981b) and, as we found in research conducted for this book, 6.2 times more likely in 1991 (see discussion later in this section of this chapter);

- blacks were six times more likely than whites to be shot by NYPD officers during the 1970s (Fyfe 1981a);

Rodriguez (1991) succinctly summarized various reasons that officers sometimes fail adequately to search suspects and challenged the profession to deal candidly and proactively with the problem (see also Stein 1992b: 2).

- blacks were 4.5 times more likely than whites to be shot by police during the 1970s and 1980s in Dallas (Dallas Police Department 1990: III-11);

- blacks in St. Louis were 7.7 times more likely than whites to be shot *at* by Metropolitan Police Department officers during 1987-91 (28 whites and 204 blacks shot at; 1990 Census data show 202,085 white and 188,408 black residents) (St. Louis Metropolitan Police Department 1992: 21);

- blacks in Memphis were 5.1 times more likely than whites to be shot *fatally* by police during the five years 1969-74, 2.6 times more likely during 1980-84, and 1.6 times more likely over the period 1985-89 (Sparger and Giacopassi 1992: Table 5); and

- considering only *property crime suspects*, blacks in Memphis were 9.4 times more likely than whites to be shot *at* by police during the period 1969-74, 13 times more likely during the period 1980-84, and were the only property crime suspects shot at (in incidents ruled unjustifiable) during the period 1985-89 (Sparger and Giacopassi 1992: Table 4).

However, the enormous reduction in the number of civilians killed by big-city police over a 15-year period (1970-1984) is due almost entirely to reductions in the number of blacks killed (Sherman and Cohn 1986, citing unpublished findings by Mendez 1983).[3] The National Urban League study conducted by Mendez showed that, combining data from 57 large cities (exceeding 250,000 population), the ratio of blacks to whites killed by big-city police dropped from 7:1 in 1971 to 2.5:1 in 1978 before rising somewhat to 2.8:1 in 1979. These ratios compare *numbers* rather than *rates* of people killed by police. One could also compare such rates as the number of blacks and whites shot per 100,000 residing in the jurisdiction, per 1,000 arrested for felonies, per 10,000 living below the poverty line, and so on.

The available data on the percentages of suspects of different races and ethnicities who die when shot by police bring additional insight to studies, such as the Urban League's or Sherman and Cohn's, which focus exclusively on fatalities. The fatality rates of civilians shot by police are not always consistent across racial and ethnic groups. For instance, the variations across different time periods in Chicago, Dallas, and Los Angeles are shown in Table 11.

As we discussed earlier in reviewing the variations in overall fatality rates among jurisdictions, these rates are driven by a number of factors, including number of shots fired, types of ammunition used, location and number of wounds on the body, promptness and quality of first aid administered, and so on. Without being able to review this type of additional data broken down according to the race/ethnicity of the offender who was shot (or the geographic location of the shooting, which in some jurisdictions would correlate highly with the race or ethnicity of the civilian participants), it is not possible to shed much light on

---

[3] The reductions in overall shootings may be driven by the fact that minorities in many jurisdictions account for a substantial percentage of all persons shot by police. But a numerical reduction over time does not, of course, necessarily mean that the racial/ethnic *mix* of persons shot by police has changed appreciably. For instance, Meyer (1980a: 37) revealed that 55 percent of those shot at by Los Angeles City Police from 1974 through 1978 (where race/descent was known) were black. This proportion had changed little since the 1968-71 period, when 57 percent of those shot at by the same agency were black (Meyer 1980a: 37).

variations in fatality rates across these victim groups from city to city and over time.

More recent *national* data on the race/ethnicity of persons killed justifiably by police are not available in *published* studies. We have, however, obtained unpublished FBI tallies of justifiable homicides by peace officers, which shed some light on the racial distribution of police-involved shooting participants in more recent years. These data appear in Figures 62 and 63 and are discussed later in this chapter in the subsection, "Exploring Civilian Race and Other Possible Explanatory Factors."

We also have some data from a few individual cities. In Dallas, for example, Geller (1990), analyzing data furnished by the Dallas Police Department, found that during the decade 1980-89, the ratio of blacks shot (fatally and nonfatally) to whites shot by police was 2.4:1. In contrast to the guess one might have made about Dallas' 1970-79 experience based on the Urban League's study combining all big cities, however, the ratio of blacks shot (fatally and nonfatally) to whites shot during the decade of the 1970s was not markedly different from the current ratio—it was 1.9:1.

Table 10:
Summary of Studies on Racial Distribution of Civilians Shot by Police Versus Racial Distribution of the General Population

Researchers	Location Studied	% Shot by Police/% of General Population		
		Black	White	Hisp.
Alpert (1989b)	Miami, FL	59/25*	11/65*	30/56*
Binder, et al. (1982)	Birmingham, AL Miami Newark Oakland	79/56 51/25 78/58 79/47		
Blumberg (1983)	Atlanta Kansas City, MO	78/51 62/22		
Fyfe (1981a)	New York City	60/25*	-/62*	23/20*
Geller and Karales (1981b) [1974-78 data]	Chicago	70/40*	20/50*	10/14*
Geller (1989) [1974-83 data]	Chicago	69/40*	18/50*	12/14*
Horvath and Donahue (1982);Horvath (1987)	Michigan	72/15**	28/85	---
Kobler (1975a); Sultan and Cooper (1979)	Nationwide	50/11*		
Meyer (1980a)	Los Angeles City	55/17*	22/62*	22/28*
Nat'l Minority Adv. Council (1978)	Philadelphia	71/34*	27/66*	1/1*
N.Y. State Commission on Criminal Justice (1987)	New York State	39/14*	26/80*	34/9*

Researchers	Location Studied	% Shot by Police/% of General Population		
		Black	White	Hisp.
Police Foundation (Milton, et al. 1977)	Birmingham, AL Oakland Portland, OR Kansas City, MO Indianapolis Washington, DC Detroit 　7-city average	80/56* 76/47* 44/ 8* 62/27* 64/22* 89/71* 80/44* 79/39	--- --- --- --- --- --- --- ---	--- --- --- --- --- --- --- ---
Dallas Police Dept. (1990)	Dallas	52/29*	24/62*	24/12*
St. Louis Metro. Police Dept. (1992)	St. Louis†	88/48	12/51	---
Robin (1963)	Nine cities	62/-	38**/-	---

* *Population percentage derived independently of the cited study from U.S. Census information (1970 or 1980, as applicable). Since Hispanics (persons of Spanish origin) may be of any race, in some instances the sum of all racial/ethnic group percentages for a given city will total more than 100 percent (Miami and Dallas are prime examples).*
** *Includes Hispanics.*
† *St. Louis data show the percentages of persons shot at in incidents (i.e., these are counts of incidents rather than people); racial classification is based on the race of the "primary suspect."*

Hence, while the data sets are different between the Urban League study (justifiable homicides by police) and the Dallas data we have analyzed (fatal and nonfatal shootings of civilians by police), our Dallas findings run in the opposite direction from what might have been predicted given national trends. This remains true even when the data sets are made more comparable by comparing the Urban League's justifiable homicide data only to fatal shootings by Dallas officers. The resulting 1970s ratio is 2.4 blacks killed for every white killed by police; the 1980s ratio is 2.9:1.

In Chicago during the mid-1970s, based on population figures, Hispanics were half as likely as blacks but twice as likely as whites to be shot by police. Even so, Hispanics were underrepresented as shooting victims in Chicago based on population figures (Geller and Karales 1981a, 1981b). They were no longer underrepresented by 1991, however. By then, when the racial/ethnic mix of Chicago's residential population was 37.9 percent white, 38.6 percent black, and 19.6 percent Hispanic (with 3.9 percent of residents of other races/ethnicities[4]), whites were 10.6 percent, blacks were 70.2 percent, and Hispanics were 19.2 percent of those shot fatally or nonfatally by Chicago Police (see Table E-57 in this volume).

Computing population-based rates reveals that black persons were 6.2 times more likely than whites and 1.8 times more likely than Hispanic individuals to be shot by Chicago police in 1991. Whereas Hispanics in the mid-1970s were twice as likely as whites to be shot by Chicago officers, in 1991 they were 3.4 times more likely based on 1990 Census population

---

[4] The racial/ethnic population breakdowns were based on the 1990 Census, as reported in Burgos (1991), which reported that, of a total of 2,783,726 residents in Chicago, whites constituted 1,056,048, blacks were 1,074,471, Hispanics were 545,852, and 107,355 persons were of other races or ethnicities.

Table 11:
Variations in Fatality Rates Across Races/Ethnicities
of Civilians Shot by Police in Different Cities

Race/Ethnicity of Person Shot	Degree of Injury and Fatality Rate			
	# Wounded	# Killed	Total Shot	% Killed
CHICAGO (1974-78)				
White	69	31	100	31%
Black	277	83	360	23%
Hispanic	34	16	50	32%
TOTAL	380	130	510	26%
DALLAS (1970-79)				
White	39	19	58	33%
Black	98	45	143	32%
Hispanic	37	6	43	14%
TOTAL	174	70	244	29%
DALLAS (1980-89)				
White	31	18	49	37%
Black	63	53	116	46%
Hispanic	31	20	51	39%
TOTAL	125	91	216	42%
LOS ANGELES (1974-78)				
White	29	42	71	59%
Black	99	64	163	39%
Hispanic	47	21	68	31%
TOTAL	175	127	302	42%

Sources: Chicago data: Geller and Karales (1981a: 123). Dallas data: Dallas Police Department (1990). Los Angeles data: Meyer (1980a: 38).
Note: In all instances, the numbers appearing in the table are those shootings for which the race/ethnicity of the persons shot were identified in the source data provided by the police agencies.

distributions. The Chicago shooting rates we have computed for 1991 are 0.5 whites shot (fatally or nonfatally) per 100,000 white residents; 3.1 blacks shot per 100,000 black residents; and 1.7 Hispanics shot per 100,000 Hispanic residents.

In Dallas, police-furnished data (Dallas Police Department 1990: III-11) reveal that, during 1986, based on their representation in the population, Hispanics stood almost the same chance as blacks of being shot by police: Both minority groups were more than four times as likely as whites to be shot by police.

In St. Louis, over the period January 1, 1986, through September 30, 1990 (see Table E-55), of the 97 persons shot fatally or nonfatally whose races were ascertained, 20 (20.6 percent) were white and 77 (79.4 percent) were black. Persons of Spanish origin are 1.3 percent of the population in St. Louis, according to the 1990 Census, and hence it is not so surprising that Hispanics are not represented among wounded or killed police shooting opponents.

The 1990 Census (Johnson 1991: 781) revealed that whites make up 50.9 percent and blacks 47.5 percent of the St. Louis population of 396,685. The rates of shootings, therefore, may be extrapolated by computing an average annual breakdown of the races of civilians shot by St. Louis police over the 57 months reported in Table E-55: 4.2 whites and 16.2 blacks, on average, were shot fatally or nonfatally during a 12-month period. These numbers produce the following shooting rates: annually 2.1 whites were shot for every 100,000 white residents, and 8.6 blacks were shot for every 100,000 black residents. Thus, blacks during this recent period were approximately four times as likely as whites to be shot by St. Louis officers based on general population distributions of racial groups.

While some researchers (e.g., Takagi 1974 and Clark 1974) believe that such figures from various cities are sufficient evidence of racial bias among police officers, others have continued the search for a more complete understanding of the disproportionate death and injury rates of blacks. Such analyses have generally taken either or both of two approaches: (1) comparing the racial distribution of civilian shooting victims with the racial distribution of persons arrested for serious crimes; or (2) examining the particular reasons the involved officers have given for shooting suspects of different races. Here, we will summarize the research on the first point. Then, following a profile of the race/ethnicity of officers involved in armed encounters and brief discussion of some other characteristics of police-involved shootings, we will turn to an examination of the justifications officers have reported to their agencies for firing at civilians of various races.

The Police Foundation (Milton, et al. 1977), under the leadership of Patrick V. Murphy, was one of the first research institutes to explore the possible relationship between racial shooting disproportion and differential patterns of police encounters with civilians of various races. The Foundation hypothesized that blacks are shot disproportionately because, as a large segment of the unemployed class who spend more time on the streets than the employed, they are involved in confrontations with police more often than whites and not because police are more likely to shoot blacks than whites in similar circumstances (Milton, et al. 1977).

Other researchers theorized that the disproportionate involvement of black and Hispanic civilians in violent crime might explain substantial portions of minorities' overinvolvement as victims of police shootings (Matulia 1985; Fyfe 1978, 1981a; Alpert 1989b), with a small, residual number of shootings being the likely product of police racism and a variety of other factors (Geller 1986). A number of researchers have taken care to distinguish race/ethnicity from poverty as a possible explanation for patterns of participation in violent crime. For example, in an in-house study the Dallas Police Department (1990: III-12) reported data showing disproportionate involvement of blacks and Hispanics in violent crime in Dallas. But the Department cautioned:

"This is not to say that Blacks or Hispanics are more likely to attack police officers or are more criminally inclined because of their race or heritage. On the contrary, violent crime is well recognized as being a lower socio-economic class phenomenon. Blacks and Hispanics comprise a large majority of this lower socio-economic group because of discrimination in education and employment in previous decades. Typically, in large cities, the majority of individuals in these lower socio-economic classes are Black or Hispanic. (In the city of Dallas, the percent of families below the poverty level is 5.2% for Whites, 17.7% for Hispanics, and 21.7% for Blacks.)"

The assurance by Dallas officials that they did not mean to imply that persons of color are more likely than whites to attack police officers raises the question of what is known about the race of those who shoot police officers. Relatively little information is available. At the national level, the FBI's annual report on officers killed and assaulted contains assailant information only concerning the *deaths* of officers. During the period 1981-90, of 1,030 persons "identified in the felonious killing of law enforcement officers," 561 (55 percent) were white, 435 (42 percent) were black, and 34 (3 percent) were of other races. The FBI report does not identify persons of Spanish origin (FBI 1991b: 21). To more fully understand this pattern, one would need to bring to bear such contextual information as the participation of persons of different races/ethnicities in confrontations with police, the distribution of persons of different races/ethnicities in the population, and so forth. City-by-city data would be important for understanding both variations in patterns of officer assailants across geography and possible variations, associated with assailant race/ethnicity, in the motivations of those who shoot police officers. (We discuss motivations of officer assailants later in this chapter.)

Returning to what is known about the race of civilians shot or shot at by police, Table 12 and Figure 48 summarize the findings of various studies comparing the percentages of blacks and Hispanics fired upon with the percentages of blacks and Hispanics arrested for serious crimes. Generally, most studies find a very close match between the percentage of arrestees for serious felonies who are black or Hispanic and the percentage of shooting victims who are black or Hispanic.[5] These findings are informative, and they undercut the notion, held by some, that police shootings of minorities bear no resemblance to arrest patterns. Yet, these findings cannot dispose of questions concerning possible patterns of racial discrimination in police decisionmaking, for if some officers in a department are bigoted enough to shoot a minority group member based at least partly on skin color, surely they would not hesitate to exercise the arrest power improperly.[6]

---

[5] Table 12 and Figure 48 show several potentially meaningful discrepancies between shooting and arrest figures in the cities for which we have data. In some instances, minorities are a higher proportion of persons shot at than of persons arrested. For example, the discrepancy for Hispanics shot at in Dallas is 9 percentage points, and the discrepancy for blacks shot at in St. Louis is 12 points. In other instances, minorities are a *lower* percentage of persons shot at than of persons arrested. Examples include blacks shot at in Birmingham, Alabama (16 points difference) and blacks shot at in Kansas City, Missouri (8 point discrepancy).

[6] Sherman (1980a: 96) asserts:

"The evidence of racial discrimination in arrests undermines any use of arrest rates to show an absence of discrimination in police homicide. * * * The fact that the greater likelihood of police to arrest black suspects can be largely attributed to (a) the greater tendency of blacks to be antagonistic to the police and (b) the greater tendency of black complainants—who do almost all of the accusing of black suspects during street encounters with the police—to demand an arrest does not remove discrimination in a legal sense. Neither suspects' attitudes nor a complainant's preferences constitute proper

Table 12:
Summary of Studies on Percentage of Minorities Shot or Shot at by Police and Percentage of Minorities Arrested for Serious Crimes

Researchers	Location Studied	Findings				
		Race/ Ethnicity	% Shot at	% Shot	% Arrested: All Index Offenses	% Arrested: Violent Crimes*
Binder, et al. (1982)	Birmingham	Black	63		79 (Part I only)	
	Oakland	Black	79		79 (Part I only)	
Blumberg (1983)	Atlanta	Black		76 fatals		83
	Kansas City	Black	63			71
Fyfe (1981a)	New York City	Black Hispanic	60 22			62 15
Geller and Karales (1981a, 1981b)	Chicago	Black Hispanic		70 10		72 11
Horvath (1987)	Michigan (nonurban)	Black	35		36	
Horvath and Donahue (1982)	Michigan (urban)	Black	82		75	
Meyer (1980a)	Los Angeles	Black Hispanic	55 22		56 24	
Milton, et al. (1977) (Police Foundation)	Combined 7 cities (Kansas City, Birmingham, Portland, Oakland, Indianapolis, Washington, DC, Detroit	Black		79	73	

grounds for enforcement decisions."

Indeed, Sherman is utterly unconvinced by research that downplays allegations of police racism based on findings that minority arrest rates closely match minority shooting rates. He argues:

> "In the absence of more conclusive evidence, the demonstrably higher rates of police homicide for blacks strongly suggests racial discrimination on a national basis. Although such patterns are quite likely to vary from one city to the next, such a variation would support the argument that present procedures allow police homicide to be administered in a discriminatory fashion" (1980a: 97).

It should be noted that the "present procedures" to which Sherman referred were pre-*Tennessee v. Garner* (1985), in which the U.S. Supreme Court restricted officer shooting discretion.

Researchers	Location Studied	Findings				
		Race/ Ethnicity	% Shot at	% Shot	% Arrested: All Index Offenses	% Arrested: Violent Crimes*
Alpert (1989b)/Criminal Justice Council (1985)	Miami	Black	59			73**
Dallas Police Dept. (1990)	Dallas	Black Hispanic		52 24		65 15
St. Louis Metro. Police Dept. (1992: 21)	St. Louis	Black	88			76

* Arrests for violent crimes may be better than arrests for all Index offenses as a predictor of shooting levels. Index crimes include typically nonviolent property offenses, such as theft and auto theft, for which police rarely report shooting civilians.

** As reported in Alpert (1989b: 489), the Criminal Justice Council (1985) found that "black offenders committed 73 percent of violent crimes." It is unclear whether these are arrest tallies or offending rates as derived from a local victimization study.

Figure 48 depicts graphically the information contained in Table 12. The studies from which the data in the bar graph are taken are indicated in the table. Alpert (1989b: 489), reflecting on data concerning Miami, Florida, for the period 1980-86, concluded: "These data support the hypotheses which suggest that the over-

"When law enforcement officers fire their guns, the immediate consequences of their decisions are realized at the rate of 1,500 feet per second and are beyond reversal by any level of official review" (McErlain 1992, quoted in Kolts, et al. 1992: 137).

representation [compared with general population distributions] of minorities shot and killed by police correspond closely to the ethnic distribution of violent offenders." Alpert also enters a caution, which cannot be reiterated too often in a book such as this, about the pressing need for better contextual information before one can make penetrating analyses of the meaning of racial disproportions:

> "A meaningful analysis of the ethnicity of officers or subjects must include information concerning the ethnic composition of the department and the community, deployment strategies, the crime rates, geographic correlates, characteristics of the area, housing density, and economic and cultural factors, among others. A study which covers many years must control for changes in these variables.[7] It is also impossible to profile accurately all offenders at whom police officers shoot. Obviously, many are seen only momentarily and others may escape before much is known about them. [T]here is no sophisticated formula which includes all these variables and controls for changes across time..." (Alpert 1989b: 488).

---

[7] Alpert (1989b: 489) points out that a "study of homicide patterns for the period 1979 through 1985 showed black offenders at 50 percent in 1979 but declining to 35 percent by 1985. The number of Hispanic offenders in this study conversely increased from 34 percent to 54 percent by 1985."

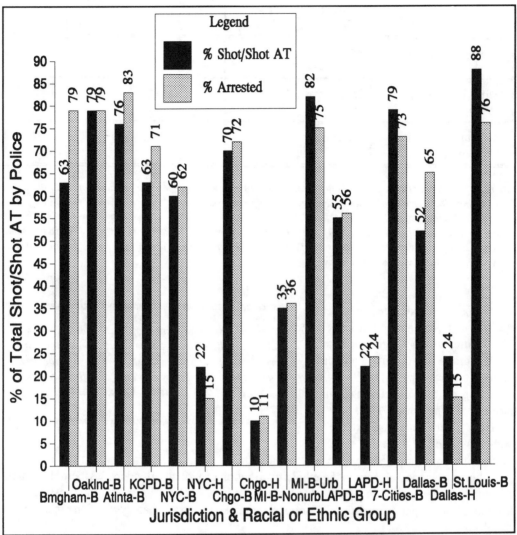

Figure 48: % of Minorities Shot or Shot at by Police & % Arrested for Serious Crimes in Various Jurisdictions & Years
Key: B=Blacks; H=Hispanics

We will examine the *reasons* officers have reported for their use of deadly force against opponents of various races/ethnicities, but first we pause to flesh out the characteristics of officer-involved shooting participants by profiling these officers. We will then briefly provide an overview of what is known about a variety of factors associated with shootings of and by American law enforcement personnel—the duty status and assignment of the involved officers, the time, day, and month of occurrences, the gender, age, and criminal justice experience of shooting participants, location types, and such—before revisiting in more depth the literature focusing on efforts to *explain* shooting patterns.

III. Race/Ethnicity of Officers Involved in Deadly Force Encounters

In several of the big cities that have been studied, black officers are disproportionately shot by civilians (Fyfe 1978; Geller and Karales 1981a, 1982) and are disproportionately likely to shoot civilians (Kobler 1975b; Fyfe 1978, 1979a; Geller and Karales 1981a, 1981b; Nowicki and Stahl 1978: 107). The number of Hispanic police officers in most cities is still so small as to preclude meaningful city-by-city analysis.

Patterns in which officers with certain characteristics (race, ethnicity, experience, age, background, education, and such) appear to have elevated chances of becoming involved in use-of-deadly-force encounters naturally lead to the question whether officers with particular attributes have a special propensity to be violent or to be the victims of violence. In other words, does any one characteristic or combination of attributes seem to play a *causal* role in turning encounters violent? The short answer is that, "there is virtually no empirical support for assertions that individual officer characteristics are measurably related to any type of performance in office" (Fyfe 1989c: 478 n. 3, citing Friedrich 1980: 89 and Sherman 1980b). But insufficient research exists to lay to rest some of the intuitively plausible relationships between officer characteristics and the outcomes of potentially lethal confrontations between police and adversaries (Toch, forthcoming, takes a probing look at the current state of knowledge about "violence-prone" officers). Moreover, we devote space in this book to discussion of individual officer (and civilian) characteristics because we take as our mission not only to reach cautious conclusions about the *reasons* for incident outcomes but also to describe, at least in traditional demographic terms, those who clash with one another and produce the rare events that are police-involved shootings.

Thus, in a nation where few are color-blind—or blind to the volatility of interracial conflict—one of the first questions that arises when police and civilians shoot one another is what the races or ethnicities were of the participants (see the quote from Tony Bouza at the beginning Chapter 1). Over the ten years 1978-87, FBI tallies reveal that, nationally, 87 percent of the officers slain feloniously were white, 12 percent were black, and 1 percent represented "other races" (FBI 1987; see Konstantin 1984 for national data for the years 1978-80). The percentage distribution of officers (municipal, county, state, and federal) killed feloniously nationwide remained identical for the 10-year period 1980-89; of the 801 police victims, 697 were white (87 percent), 97 were black (12 percent), and 7 (1 percent) were of "other races" (FBI 1989b: 21). To place these numbers in some national context, during 1987, 85.4 percent of the police in municipal law enforcement agencies were white, 9.3 percent were black, and 4.5 percent were Hispanic (Bureau of Justice Statistics 1989).

That 12 percent of the officers who gave their lives in the line of duty during the 1980s were black looms somewhat larger when one realizes that through much of this period the national complement of black officers probably was less than the 1987 figure of 9.3 percent. Furthermore, during 1987 black officers were 8.3 percent of sheriff's deputies and just 6.5 percent of state law enforcement personnel throughout the nation—with variations, of course, from jurisdiction to jurisdiction (Bureau of Justice Statistics 1989: 1).

By 1990 the percentages of minorities employed as sworn personnel by the nation's police agencies had increased slightly. Black officers by then constituted 10.5 percent and Hispanic officers 5.2 percent of all local police (Bureau of Justice Statistics 1992a). And in sheriffs' departments, the employment of blacks increased by 1990 to 9.8 percent and the employment of Hispanics edged up from the 1987 level of 4.3 percent to 4.7 percent (Bureau of Justice Statistics 1992b; *Crime Control Digest* 1992b). In 1990 the distribution of American law enforcement personnel slain feloniously was 80 percent white, 18.5 percent black, and 1.5 percent Asian (FBI 1991b: 20).

As an example of differential police victimization rates in a single city, in Chicago, based on their representation on the police force, black officers were nearly three times more likely than their white colleagues to be shot by civilians—1.6 times more likely while on duty and 5 times more likely while off duty (Geller and Karales 1981a, 1982). Ten-year data for Chicago (1974-83) reveal that, of the 156 officers shot (fatally and nonfatally) by civilians, 59 percent were white, 33 percent were black, and 2.6 percent were Hispanic. During this period, black officers were less than 25 percent of Chicago's sworn personnel (Geller 1989). Of the 60 Chicago officers shot by themselves or their colleagues during the period 1974-78, 71 percent were white, 23 percent were black, and none were Hispanic (Geller and Karales 1981a: 93-94, 97).

To date several studies have shown a pattern in which the officers responsible for shooting civilians—particularly *black* civilians (see Figures E-3, E-4, E-6, E-7, and E-10 in this volume)—are disproportionately likely to be black. To say that black officers are overrepresented as *shooters* does not mean that black officers are responsible for a larger total *number* of shootings than their white colleagues, but that the *rate* of shootings is higher for black police based on their numbers among the sworn ranks of some big-city police forces. In New York City in the 1970s, for instance, 11 percent of the force was minority and 19 percent of the firearms discharges were attributed to minority officers (Fyfe 1978). From that finding, Fyfe concluded that black NYPD officers were about twice as likely as white officers to have actually shot or shot at civilians.

More recent New York City data are not as easily interpreted. For instance, it was not until the NYPD's *1990* annual report on firearms discharges by officers and deadly weapon assaults against officers (Cerar 1990: 4, 5) that the NYPD began reporting the races of officers and adversaries involved with one another in violent encounters. But even these reports, when identifying the races or ethnicities of officers, *combine* officers who fired weapons with officers who were shot by adversaries, making it difficult to separately analyze the characteristics of officer shooters and officer victims. Similarly, the NYPD's 1990 report provides the races of perpetrators who assaulted NYPD officers or were shot at by officers, but does not distinguish in which of these two types of incidents the civilians were involved.

> *"Violence in the United States is a public health emergency. * * * The impact of... violence on our nation's youth and minorities is particularly worrisome. Homicide is now the second leading cause of death among 15- to 24-year-olds and the leading cause of death among 15- to 34-year-old black males. It is a tragic reality that the populations of young black American males face a homicide rate that is at least 8 times greater than that of their white counterparts of comparable age"* (Novello, et al. 1992).

With those constraints, we are able to report that, in 1990, of 757 officers involved in firearms discharge/assault incidents, the races/ethnicities of 734 were identified by the NYPD. Of these 734, 70 percent (517) were white, 13 percent (97) were black, 16 percent (118) were Hispanic, and less than 1 percent (2) were Orientals or of other races/ethnicities (Cerar 1990:

4). The latest readily available data on the racial makeup of the NYPD is the Bureau of Justice Statistics' (1989: 6) tally of various big-city departments' employment figures. These data cover the year 1987. In the NYPD during 1987, black officers were 11 percent and Hispanic officers were 10.5 percent of the sworn personnel. Given the incomparability of the two data sets (officers involved in shooting/assault incidents in *1990* versus officers employed in *1987*) there is little we can say with confidence. All we can do is call attention to the fact that the two data sets may imply a more disproportionate involvement of Hispanic than of black officers in dangerous encounters in New York City.

In Chicago during 1974-1978, black officers were 17 percent of the sworn personnel and 25 percent of those who shot civilians (Geller and Karales 1981a, 1981b). In Miami, however, during the period 1980-1986, black officers were 17 percent of the city police force but were responsible for only 14 percent of the firearm discharges at civilians (Alpert 1989b: 489).

As in virtually every other data set of which we are aware, however, minority officers (blacks and Hispanics) in Miami much more frequently shoot persons of color than they shoot Caucasians. With hardly an exception, the only officers who shoot any appreciable number of white suspects are white officers. This has been true from city to city and nationally over the past three decades, during which the vast majority of deadly force studies have been conducted (see Figures E-3, E-4, E-6, E-7, and E-10). Whether this is predominantly a function of officer deployment patterns—in which minority officers are far more likely to encounter violent minorities than violent whites—is difficult to say. Are there other possible explanations for the dominant pattern in which officers of color rarely shoot at white people? One—a proposition for which, we hasten to add, there appears to be no pro or contra evidence in any study—is that many minority officers believe—rightly or wrongly—that if they shoot white suspects, there is a greater chance of generating politically sensitive controversy than there would be if they shot black suspects. Theories along these lines might merely be extensions of arguments that criminal justice systems across the nation judge and penalize more harshly persons of color who injure whites than persons of color who injure others of color. Death penalty opponents, in particular, have pressed hard on the point that capital punishment is disproportionately meted out when the offender is black and the victim was white.

We can imagine still another possible explanation, for which we again readily admit having not a scintilla of empirical evidence. This is that officers of color *do* encounter white suspects more often than the shooting data suggest (a study of arresting officers' and their arrestees' races/ethnicities would shed some light on this question), but for some reason white criminals show a greater propensity to surrender without violent resistance to minority than to white officers. If true, this would suggest that officers of color don't shoot many whites because they don't need to in order to carry out their duties.

It bears repeating that the foregoing are merely speculations unsupported by empirical evidence. Where we *do* have data, the research does *not* universally reveal higher rates of *on*-duty shootings by black officers. Where the phenomenon *has* surfaced, it is typically attributed to the disproportionate assignment of black officers to high-crime districts (Fyfe 1978, 1979a, 1981a, 1981d). Fyfe (1978) noted an irony that arises in this context:

"The *quid pro quo* for assigning minority officers to minority areas in the interests of bettering police-community relations, therefore, involves increasing the chances that minority officers will have to resort to their firearms while working."

An illustration of the important subtleties that unfold when researchers get detailed information about police force deployment and officers' race comes from Geller and Karales' Chicago study (1981a: 132, 150). They found that black officers did not have high on-duty shooting rates, *despite* their disproportionate assignment to high-crime districts, and suggested that this may be because *within* those districts black officers were underrepresented in the elite tactical units, the units most likely to be involved in armed confrontations. (We have cautioned elsewhere in this book, however, about the risks of viewing certain geographical assignments or police missions as *inevitably* violence-laden.)

The higher *off*-duty shooting rates for black officers, which *do* surface consistently in the few studies currently available, have been attributed, in both New York and Chicago, to the fact that black officers generally live and spend their free time in more dangerous neighborhoods than white officers, and hence run higher risks of encountering situations in which they may shoot or be shot (Fyfe 1979a; Geller and Karales 1981a, 1982). In Chicago, 93 percent of the black off-duty officers who shot civilians and 91 percent of such officers who were shot by civilians were in medium- or high-crime areas, whereas 90 percent of the white off-duty officers who shot civilians and 64 percent of those whom civilians shot were in low- or medium-crime districts (Geller and Karales 1981a, 1982). Konstantin (1984: 39), studying all killings of police officers in the United States during the period 1978-80, found that blacks were approximately 6 percent of all police employees and 10.7 percent of those killed overall. Moreover, of those officers killed while off duty, blacks were 28 percent nationwide and 40 percent in cities with more than 100,000 population (*ibid.*: 39). Konstantin concurred with previous findings:

> "[T]he data suggest that [black officers] suffer a fatality rate considerably higher than that of their white colleagues.... * * * These figures bolster the findings of both Fyfe (1981) and Geller and Karales (1981).[8] The assertion that black officers are killed at such high rates because they work and live in high-crime, inner-city areas is further supported when the relationship between the size of city in which an officer was killed and his race is examined. Fifty percent of black officers (n=15) were killed in cities with populations over 100,000, while 37.2 percent of white officers (n=93) were killed in cities in this size category. This pattern is even clearer when only off-duty deaths are examined. Eighty percent of black off-duty officers (n=8) were killed in cities larger than 100,000, in contrast to only 46.2 percent of off-duty white officers (n=12)" (Konstantin 1984: 38-39).

Doerner (1991) analyzed the performance of 56 Tallahassee, Florida, police officers being trained with that agency's "shoot/don't shoot" video simulator. Of these officers, 46 (82 percent) were white and 10 (18 percent) were black (*ibid.*: 4). He explored whether there was an association between officer race and two performance measures: the timeliness of unholstering and of shooting in response to assailants' threats in the video. Although the numbers being studied were small (56 officers, reacting to 363 incidents calling for an unholstering decision and 271 "shoot scenarios"), Doerner discovered that "unholstering was

---

[8] Using the references in our volume, Konstantin was referring to Fyfe (1981d) and Geller and Karales (1981a).

not affected by officer race" (*ibid.*: 6, 7). There were some discrepancies in the shooting decisions, however. Black officers were slightly more likely *both* to shoot "too early" and to shoot "too late." "Too early" was defined as shooting "prior to the shoot stimulus." "Too late" meant "engag[ing] a target after the suspect shoots or...fail[ing] to return fire" (*ibid.*: 6).

Specifically, white officers discharged their weapons (in the simulation exercise) too early in 1 percent of the 224 "shoot scenarios" they encountered and too late in 47 percent. Black officers, by contrast, shot too early in 6 percent of the 47 "shoot scenarios" they were confronted with and too late in 57 percent (*ibid.*: 7). One must be very cautious in interpreting findings based on such small numbers. Still, if the Tallahassee findings *do* in any meaningful way reflect actual street behavior, then the pattern of firing weapons both earlier and later than called for by events could possibly help explain the findings in other cities that black officers are both more likely to shoot adversaries and more likely to be shot by them than are their white colleagues. Why blacks might differ from whites on these shooting decisions we do not know, and it would be prudent, we think, to remain skeptical of this finding until additional evidence becomes available to assess it. Attitudinal differences may not help explain such a pattern (see Maghan 1992, who studied the socialization of black and white recruits and found that they tend to enter basic training with divergent attitudes but come out with a "blue view".

Fyfe (1981d: 381) allows the possibility that blacks officers are, as a general rule, more restrained than their white colleagues in shooting at black suspects. Thus, even though the disproportionate assignment of black officers to black neighborhoods produces elevated levels of shootings by black officers of black suspects, Fyfe suggests that the shooting levels might be still higher if white officers replaced their black colleagues in those assignments. Fyfe does not dispute the logic of overrepresenting black officers in black neighborhoods, but laments the socio-political realities that make this necessary and the human consequences:

> "Until one can no longer intuitively identify...a city's 'high experience' assignments...by the ethnic composition of their populations, minority officers will continue to be rational choices for assignment to those areas; as long as minority officers are assigned to those 'high experience' areas in disproportionate numbers, they will continue to be involved in a disproportionate number of on-duty shootings" (Fyfe 1981d: 377-378).

In those cities where black officers disproportionately suffer the trauma of having to use their weapons, administrators who, admittedly, cannot control the conditions that give rise to this pattern, should at least be sensitive to it. Part of such sensitivity is establishing appropriate training, psychological, and other support systems for officers commensurate with their needs.

IV. Duty and Uniform Status and Assignment of Officers Involved in Shootings

A. Duty and Uniform Status

A number of the studies have described in some detail the differences between on-duty and off-duty shooting rates. Most civilian victims of police shootings are shot by on duty officers, although the percentage of off-duty shootings is considered quite large by several observers. Data on the duty status of officers who have shot suspects present the following illustrative patterns:

- 20 percent of shootings by police in Philadelphia during the early 1970s occurred off duty (Public Interest Law Center of Philadelphia 1975);

- 17 percent of the incidents in which New York City Police Department personnel fired shots at civilians during the early 1970s occurred off duty (Fyfe 1980b);

- 13 percent of the 757 NYPD officers involved in incidents in which they either discharged their firearms or were assaulted with a deadly weapon in 1990 were off duty at the time (Cerar 1990: 5);

- 24 percent of the 307 incidents in which NYPD officers discharged their weapons during 1990 involved off-duty personnel (Cerar 1990: 7);

- 23 percent of the civilians shot fatally or nonfatally in Chicago during the mid-1970s were shot by off-duty officers (Geller and Karales 1981b);

- 16.5 percent of the Chicago officers involved in shots-fired incidents during the period 1975-77 were off duty (Nowicki and Stahl 1978: viii);

> *"Many law enforcement agency policy manuals state the following: 'When off duty and within the corporate limits of the city or county, officers shall take appropriate action to protect life and property, preserve the public peace, prevent crime, and cause the apprehension of violators of criminals laws.'*
>
> *"Okay. That sounds swell. But what does 'appropriate action' really mean? * * * We are, by nature, in the intervention business. It's our job to seek out problems, intervene in their midst, and take some kind of action. This is how we're trained, this is how we're taught to think, and this is how we respond when called upon. Like Pavlov's dog, when the bell rings we come out looking for meat.*
>
> *"As most patrol officers will admit, one of the hardest things to do is 'turn off the switch' after an exciting day or night of police work. It's nearly impossible to change into civilian clothes and leave the station thinking and acting like a 'regular' person. We aren't regular people. Regular people don't break-up bar fights, wrestle with dopers, or chase liquor store robbers in high-speed pursuits.*
>
> *"After seeing the dregs of society pass by your patrol car window for eight or ten hours, it's difficult to turn off your 'natural police curiosity' on the way home. Just because you have a few days off, that doesn't mean you go around with blinders on" (Albrecht 1992: 114-115).*

- 19 percent of the 47 incidents in which Chicago officers shot civilians fatally or nonfatally during 1991 (each incident involved only one person shot by police) involved off-duty officers, whereas 17.5 percent of the 57 officers involved in these 47 incidents were off duty at the time (data collected by Geller for this book);

- 17 percent of the civilians shot by police in the seven cities studied by the Police Foundation during the 1970s were fired upon by off-duty police (Milton et al. 1977: 27); and

- 26 percent of the "deaths by legal intervention" in New York State were caused by off-duty law enforcement personnel (NYSCCJ 1987).

But not all agencies have comparable off-duty shooting experiences. Alpert (1989a) revealed that only two (1 percent) of the 237 incidents in which Metro-Dade police fired their weapons purposefully or accidentally from January 1984 through June 1988 involved off-duty officers.

Like on-duty shootings, off-duty gun discharges by police showed fairly distinct geographical patterns in studies of shots fired in New York City.[9] Whereas Fyfe found the on-duty shootings to be concentrated in high-crime areas, his data showed that quieter areas of the city generally are characterized by relatively high percentages of off-duty shootings (1980b: 108). It is not uncommon for police departments to find a high percentage of off-duty shootings out of policy. In the 1970s departmental disapproval was expressed in 40 percent of the off-duty shootings by NYPD officers (Fyfe 1980b: 73), 18 percent by LAPD members (Meyer 1980a: 53), and 13 percent of Chicago police. To express the Chicago finding differently, 74 percent of all officers whose shootings were disapproved were off duty (Geller and Karales 1981a: 190). Naturally, more current data than from the 1970s would be desirable, but the lack of recent studies on the issue of off-duty firearms use and the absence of a central deadly force data collection system (see Chapter 2) leave the field dependent on decades-old information.

The risk that off-duty officers run of *being* shot is not inconsequential either, although the source of the risk, as discussed more fully elsewhere in this chapter, is often the officer himself or herself, his or her relatives, or friends (Fyfe 1978). Nationwide, more than 10 percent of the officers killed (by *all* weapons) from 1972 through 1978 were off duty (Margarita 1980c). During the 10 years 1980-89, this percentage grew slightly to 12 percent (99 of the 801 officers killed feloniously over this period were off duty when attacked) (FBI 1989b: 19). In 1990, 23 percent (15 officers) of the 66 American police slain feloniously were off duty when attacked (FBI 1991b: 19; Behm 1992). In 1991, 17 percent (12 officers) of the 71 slain were off duty (Behm 1992). The reader should exercise caution in generalizing that lethal attacks on off-duty officers are rising or falling, however, since any one- or two-year change with small numbers of events may not be indicative of a trend.

---

[9] There is reason to expect that rates of off-duty shootings by police will vary considerably from city to city, since surveys (e.g., Matulia 1982, 1985; Heaphy 1978) have indicated that agency policies on whether officers are required to carry their weapons while off duty differ from jurisdiction to jurisdiction. Indeed, Matulia (1985: 75) found that "agencies which make it mandatory to carry an off-duty weapon experience a higher percentage (16.4 percent) of off-duty deaths [caused by police] than do agencies with an optional off-duty weapon policy (9.5 percent)." No recent survey of the off-duty weapons policies of American police agencies has been discovered in the published literature. The IACP's 1982 report on police use of deadly force (Matulia 1982: App. N, p. 8) revealed, that of 53 city departments serving populations exceeding 250,000, 15 (28 percent) mandated that off-duty officers be armed, 21 (40 percent) gave officers an option to choose whether to arm themselves while off duty, and 17 (32 percent) gave officers no guidance in official written policy on this question.

Of course, knowing that an agency permits or encourages (but does not require) its officers to be armed while off duty does not reveal much about the extent to which officers in that jurisdiction and in its different neighborhoods elect to arm themselves while off duty. To be sure, it seems likely that officers fearing retaliation from arrestees will take precautions while off duty. As Matulia (1985: 75) observes, although it is extremely hard to "measure the potential for criminals to strike back at police officers who while off duty are known to be unarmed," it is a safe bet that officers working especially hazardous assignments or cases will think carefully about whether, during their off-duty hours, they need to be armed against possible retaliatory assaults. By contrast, one might hope that officers whose personal relationships suffer from domestic violence will have the presence of mind to try to protect themselves and their loved ones against poor judgments they might make in the heat of an impassioned dispute. For certain officers at certain times the best place for the service weapon may be, as Fyfe (1980b) and others have suggested, in the officer's locker along with the rest of his or her work equipment.

In Chicago, 52 percent of all officers who were shot received their injuries, fatal or nonfatal, while off duty, 51 percent of these coming at the hands of civilians, 44 percent at their own hands, and 5 percent at the hands of fellow officers. Of the self-inflicted shootings, 27 percent were suicides or attempted suicides, and the rest were accidental (Geller and Karales 1981a: 146). We will present more detailed data on officers shot by themselves or their colleagues later in this chapter.

Off-duty and plainclothes police work, in contrast to domestic disturbances, emerge as posing serious risks to officers (see, e.g., Girodo 1985; Cheek and Lesce 1988; and Farkas 1986). In New York, Margarita (1980c) found that 25 percent of the slain officers over 135 years were off duty. In Chicago, 44 percent of the officers shot by civilians were not working police jobs at the time they were shot; there were variations by race: 33 percent of the white officer victims and 61 percent of their black counterparts were off duty at the time (Geller and Karales 1981a: 94, 149).

"[A police officer] was jogging while off duty when he was told by a local citizen that a bank robbery suspect had just left a nearby bank. Although unarmed, [the officer] chased the suspect to a nearby getaway vehicle where the suspect shot him once in the chest. [The officer] was critically wounded but still managed to obtain descriptive information on the suspect and his vehicle, which led to an apprehension a short time later. [The officer] recovered from his injuries and...returned to work" (FBI 1989d: 33).

Two explanations have been offered for the relatively large number of officers who are shot while off duty. First, many police departments require off-duty officers to take appropriate police action when they encounter apparent criminal activity. Police officers traditionally have considered their off-duty responsibility to include aggressive intervention (termination of crimes and arrest of suspects) and not just careful observation and notification of on-duty police (*Law Enforcement News* 1992c). The arming of off-duty police, a practice that has been criticized by a leading commentator (Fyfe 1980b), facilitates such aggressive action. But police frequently are at a tactical disadvantage while off duty, being out of radio communication with other officers, equipped with fewer lethal and less-than-lethal weapons, and typically lacking soft body armor and an extra set of handcuffs (Rutledge 1988: 231). Further, while off duty an officer may see less opportunity than he or she would while on duty to plan a course of action before intervening; the off-duty officer typically is "mobilized" by finding himself or herself in the middle of trouble, whereas the on-duty officer much more often is notified some distance from an apparent crime scene of the need for response (Fyfe 1980b).

Moreover, off-duty officers who happen to be socializing in a tavern when armed robbers enter may be in no condition to outdraw the holdup men, yet the presumed imperative to take police action may prompt an ill-advised confrontation. Off-duty officers who are under the influence of legal drugs may also find that their judgment and reflexes are impaired. As a result, many agencies urge or direct officers to refrain from carrying their guns if they expect to be consuming alcoholic beverages or taking certain types of medication (Fyfe 1980a; Geller 1982b; Geller and Karales 1981a: 189). For example, the Chicago Police Department, in 1980, adopted a policy that provided, in part:

"Police officers, by law, are permitted to carry firearms during non-duty hours. In connection with the exercise of this privilege, police officers are instructed to refrain from carrying firearms during non-duty hours when there is a likelihood that they will be consuming alcoholic beverages or using legally prescribed drugs which may impair their physical or mental ability" (Chicago Police Department 1980; see also Kirby and Gottesman 1992 and Burgos 1992).

Still, many police agencies' policies are silent or ambiguous about the departments' preferences concerning the mixing of guns and intoxicants. An off-duty shooting during a barroom fight in Des Moines, Iowa, in 1992, caused agencies in Iowa to consider their own directives on carrying guns while off duty (*Law Enforcement News* 1992c).

Possible physical impairment is not the only concern about off-duty gun use. Some have argued that off-duty personnel in certain circumstances have impaired legitimacy to intervene and take police action when they are summoned to a disturbance by a civilian complainant. Off-duty officers much more frequently intervene on their own initiative and hence encounter more civilian resistance (see Reiss 1971a).

The second principal explanation for the relatively large number of off-duty officers who are shot is that a certain percentage of police officers—particularly those of minority races—live and spend most of their nonworking hours in relatively high-crime neighborhoods, where they have an elevated risk of encountering and being shot by violent offenders. Fifty-one percent of all off-duty officers shot by civilians in Chicago

> *A big-city chamber of commerce honored an officer "who, while off duty, saw a fellow officer struggling for her weapon with an offender who had broken her leg. [The honoree] shot the offender, who was later arrested" (Anderson 1992).*

were black, and 33 percent of that number were shot in connection with robberies, in which many were the holdup victims (Geller and Karales 1981a: 148).

The presence of a gun in police officers' households also helps explain high off-duty victimization rates for police officers. In Chicago, 20 percent of the off-duty shootings of police by civilians involved officers shot during their own domestic quarrels or other nonpolice situations (Geller and Karales 1981a: 148; also see Fyfe 1978).

> *"Tactical unit officers handle the most hazardous assignments. Their job is to be out in the community going after the worst criminals. * * * The stress of the job is so bad sometimes, [one tac officer] said, that he stays an extra hour at work, just to cool down, before going home. 'A lot of times, I don't tell my wife everything, the most dangerous parts,' he said" (Reardon and O'Connor 1991).*

Officers who fire at civilians or are shot by them while on duty usually are in uniform. For example, during the decade 1980-89, of the 801 American law enforcement personnel feloniously killed, 567 (71 percent) were in uniform at the time (FBI 1989b: 21). In 1990 of the 65 police killed feloniously nationwide, 41 (63 percent) died in uniform (FBI 1991b: 20).

But, as we pointed out in our discussion of car stops in Chapter 2, when calculating the risk that any particular type of activity will result in lethal violence, it is important to understand how often the activity (such as a vehicle stop) occurs. Similarly, the size and missions of different police units (and their resultant likelihood of encountering suspects) must be considered when comparing the risks run by members of each unit (say, the agency's plainclothes personnel and uniformed patrol officers). In Chicago, for instance, Geller and Karales' research (1981a: 132, 150; 1981b; 1982) revealed that, based on their numbers on the force, tactical squad (plainclothes) officers were up to nine times as likely as their uniformed colleagues to become involved in a shooting incident. During the late 1980s and 1990 tactical officers represented less than 6 percent of the sworn Chicago personnel (700 out of 12,500) but accounted for 36 percent of the officers killed in the line of duty (including 5 of the last 14) (Reardon and O'Connor 1991). This pattern of tragedies follows common sense expectations, since the mission of the tactical units, at least in Chicago, is to concentrate on particularly risky situations and offenders (see, e.g., O'Connor 1991; Reardon and O'Connor 1991).

"An officer in plainclothes is difficult to identify as an officer, especially if he's been working vice or narcotics, or has let himself get completely out of shape. Armed citizens, intent on protecting their homes and businesses, don't expect a detective to look scroungy and dirty, to be dressed in old jeans and Budweiser T-shirts, nor to be carrying around a belly that belongs in a Santa Claus suit. When they see such a person with a drawn gun, frightened citizens are likely (understandably) to draw the wrong conclusion" (Rutledge 1988: 232).

Even without calculating *rates*, the *frequency* with which plainclothes police need to resort to their firearms is a reminder to police policymakers and trainers that nonuniformed officer tactics, skills, and safety deserve special attention. There is a high correlation, of course, between an officer's duty status and attire (the vast majority of off-duty officers are likely to be in civilian dress when they become involved in shooting incidents). It is necessary, therefore, for analysts to be clear when exploring the possible nexus between officer attire and likelihood of shooting involvement to know whether or not off-duty incidents are mixed in with on-duty situations in the data being examined. Some studies contain data depicting involvement in shootings by on-duty personnel wearing plainclothes or doing undercover work (the risk that undercover agents will be shot or otherwise seriously assaulted is discussed below). For instance, the percentage of on-duty, plainclothes officers who shot others was:

- 32 percent in Chicago during 1974-78 (Geller and Karales 1981a: 87);

- 33 percent in New York City during the 1970s (Fyfe 1978);

- 40 percent in New York City in 1987 (NYPD 1988); and

- 21 percent in the combined seven-city data collected by the Police Foundation (Milton et al. 1977: 27).

Of the NYPD officers who either were assaulted with deadly weapons or fired shots at others (on or off duty) during 1990, 65 percent were in uniform and the remaining 35 percent were in civilian clothes (Cerar 1990: 5). Of the on-duty officers shot by civilians in Chicago during the 1970s, 44 percent were in plainclothes (Geller and Karales 1981a: 94). In New York City a number of the shootings of plainclothes police officers in the 1970s were mistaken identity shootings by uniformed officers (Fyfe 1978). In 1990 of the 35 NYPD personnel who were shot nonfatally (no NYPD officers were *killed* feloniously that year), 11 percent (four) were shot unintentionally by officers from their own or other agencies. The problem of *mistaken identity* shootings of NYPD personnel seems to have been reduced recently, however. Of the four officers shot nonfatally by other police in 1990, only one incident was classified by the NYPD as a mistaken identity shooting (Cerar 1990: 12).

B. Assignment Type

In the various studies, most of the officers who used their weapons were assigned at the time to their police department's most populous unit, the patrol division. For example:

- 75 percent of the officers who shot civilians in California in the early 1970s were in patrol bureaus (California Department of Justice 1974) and

- 53 percent of the officers who shot civilians fatally or nonfatally in Chicago during the mid-1970s were patrol division personnel (Geller and Karales 1981a: 209).

As noted in the preceding section of this chapter, however, officers in tactical squads, at least in some agencies, are considerably more likely (based on unit size) than patrol officers to become involved as shooters and victims. This experience is likely to vary widely from jurisdiction to jurisdiction based on a host of factors, not the least of which is the nature and aggressiveness of the missions to which special squad officers or patrol division personnel are assigned.

Of the 66 officers killed feloniously during 1989 throughout the nation, 38 (58 percent) were assigned to their departments' patrol units; 19 (29 percent) were on detective or special assignment; and 9 (14 percent) were "off duty but acting in an official capacity when slain" (FBI 1989b: 3, 20; the figures total 101 percent due to rounding). For the ten-year period 1980-89, the distribution of victim officers is similar: 515 (64 percent) were on patrol when killed; 187 (23 percent) were on detective or special assignment; and 99 (12 percent) were off duty (FBI 1989b: 19; the figures total 99 percent due to rounding). In 1990, when 66 American police officers were feloniously killed, 37 (57 percent) were assigned to patrol; 13 (20 percent) were on detective or other special assignment; and 15 (23 percent) were off duty (Behm 1992, correcting FBI 1991b: 19; the assignment of one was not known at press time).

Eliminating from consideration those police feloniously killed while off duty, the splits between patrol and detective/special assignment as reported by the FBI become the following: In 1989 67 percent were in patrol units and 33 percent were in other assignments; over the decade of the 1980s 73 percent were assigned to patrol, with the remaining 27 percent assigned to other field responsibilities; and in 1990 74 percent were on patrol missions, while 26 percent were working more specialized assignments. Considering that in most police agencies less than 26 to 33 percent of the sworn cadre is assigned to detective or other specialized field assignments, the figures of feloniously slain officers underscore the higher risks associated with assignments other than routine uniformed patrol.

A special area of tactical concern is undercover narcotics work. Of the 801 American law enforcement personnel (local, state, and federal) feloniously slain from 1980 through 1989, 67 (8 percent) were killed when attempting arrests in what the FBI characterizes as "drug-related matters" (FBI 1989b: 18). In 1990 and 1991, respectively, 6 and 4 percent of the 66 and 71 officers slain were in the same category of incident.[10] While some of these

---

[10] Interestingly, the annual death toll of law enforcement personnel in "drug-related" arrests has not shown a steady pattern of escalation. Although the numbers are, we are thankful, so small each year that one could not make much statistically of changes, the fact is that no pattern of increasing danger or

involved uniformed officers (15 percent during 1980-89), there is ample basis for concluding, considering both FBI data and the curricula taught at Quantico by the FBI and the Drug Enforcement Administration (DEA), that "buy-bust" and other undercover narcotics operations pose special risks to undercover agents. Of the 67 law enforcement officers feloniously slain during this ten-year period in drug arrest situations, 55 (82 percent) were classified by the FBI as working "detective/special assignment" at the time of their deaths (FBI 1989b: 19). Further, the evidence does not suggest that these deaths come disproportionately in situations where the undercover operative for some reason is working without the assistance of fellow officers. Of the 55 detective/special assignment personnel killed while making or attempting drug-related arrests, 46 (84 percent) were "assisted" at the time of their slaying (FBI 1989b: 19). For the period 1973-82, the comparable figure was 90 percent (FBI 1982: 18).

Even though a slain undercover agent may be classified by the FBI as "assisted," this may not mean that more than one police officer in a buy-bust situation was in the immediate location of the fatal encounter. Rather, it may mean that backup and surveillance personnel were within viewing distance of the drug buy. Hence, one of the most crucial skills of the undercover agent—as with virtually all field personnel engaged in a wide variety of police missions—is the ability to position the situation verbally and physically in such a fashion that the agent achieves maximum possible protection while placing the drug dealer to be arrested at the greatest possible tactical disadvantage. A DEA trainer emphasized the importance of police verbal skills—negotiating expertise—in fostering the success and safety of undercover narcotics buys:

"Countless critical incident reviews have demonstrated that, in the majority of cases in which undercover agents are killed or injured, they themselves have participated in negotiations with their assailant and have agreed to many of the conditions that contributed to their victimization. The negotiation skills of undercover narcotics officers are among the most critical elements contributing

---

increasing safety is readily discernible from the national data. The number of American law enforcement personnel killed each year in drug-related arrests from 1980 through 1991 is:

1980: 9;   1981: 2;   1982: 6;   1983: 7;   1984: 4;   1985: 6;   1986: 7;
1987: 6;   1988: 12;   1989: 8;   1990: 4;   and 1991: 3.

During the ten-year period 1973 through 1982, 56 law enforcement personnel were killed nationally in drug-related situations (FBI 1982: 18). This is an annual average of 5.6 deaths, compared with an annual average for the 1980-89 period of 6.7. During the 1973-82 period, 48 of the police killed were working detective/special assignment missions when slain by drug offenders. The comparable number for 1980 through 1989 is 55 (FBI 1989b: 19).

To assess the risk of undercover work in terms of officer line-of-duty death, one would need data that are not easily obtainable: the number of police personnel engaged during a given time period in undercover narcotics arrest missions. Twice the number of police were killed from 1980 through 1989 in robbery arrest situations (112) as in drug arrest situations (67), but presumably a larger number of American police are engaged in robbery arrests than in narcotics arrests (FBI 1989b: 18).

The U.S. Bureau of Justice Statistics disclosed in 1992 that, during the period from 1987 to 1990, the number of sworn police in the United States grew by 5.4 percent, the number of arrests for all types of offenses grew by 12 percent, and the number of "drug arrests grew by 16 percent" (*Crime Control Digest* 1992b: 1). The 12 percent increase in total arrests may seem surprising, in light of victimization surveys we discuss later showing that most crime is down; but the large gap between the incidence of crime and the number of crimes of which police become aware leaves substantial room for police to increase their arrest activity despite reduced levels of crime.

to their operational success, as well as their personal safety and survival" (Moriarty 1990: 44).

We will return in more detail to a discussion of some of the training that can help reduce the frequency of police-involved shootings in Chapter 5.

C. One- Versus Two-Officer Units and Assisted Versus Unassisted Officers

An issue that has generated considerable discussion about officer safety within the law enforcement community is the one-officer versus two-officer patrol unit. This almost invariably means one- versus two-officer *cars*, but with increasing use of foot patrol in many jurisdictions, data may eventually become available in sufficient quantities to allow analysts to explore whether lone or assisted foot patrol officers' use of force and victimization experiences parallel the experiences of lone or assisted officers assigned principally to motorized patrol.[11]

Some commentators, police executives, and police association leaders have pointed to FBI reports to argue that one-officer cars are unduly hazardous. The ten-year 1981-1990 profile illustrates the pattern: Of the 659 law enforcement personnel feloniously killed nationwide while on duty (another 103 were feloniously slain while off duty), 16 percent (105) were assigned to two-officer vehicles during their fatal encounter; 56 percent (371) were assigned to one-officer vehicles (although slightly more than one-third of these slain officers [126] were assisted by other units); 1 percent (7) were on foot patrol (3 out of these 7 officers were assisted); and 27 percent (176) were on detective or other "special" assignments (nearly three-fourths of these officers were assisted by colleagues) (FBI 1989b, 1991b).

The assumption is widespread that officers are at greater jeopardy of being hurt or killed in the line of duty when working in one-officer units than in two- or multiple-officer units. There is both anecdotal and numerical evidence to support this view. In the early 1970s in an unidentified south-central U.S. jurisdiction, members of two-officer units were approximately 10 percent *less* likely to be injured when assaulted than were officers working alone. But this study of 1,012 officers also found that officers' odds of getting hurt when assaulted rose dramatically if there were *four* officers present and then decreased "as more officers appeared on the scene" (Wilson, et al. 1990). During the period 1981 through 1990, as noted above, 245 of the American police officers feloniously slain were working alone in one-officer vehicles when killed; 231 officers were either assisted while assigned to one-officer vehicles (126) or were assigned to two-officer vehicles to begin with (105).

Thus, the number of officers killed while in the presence of other officers (either their

---

[11] Numbers are starting to become available, but they are still too small for informative analysis. For instance, the FBI reported that, of the 801 American law enforcement personnel feloniously killed during the period 1980-89, ten were working foot patrol at the time of their fatal encounters. Of these ten, seven were alone and three were assisted by other officers when slain (FBI 1989b: 19). Of the 702 police feloniously slain while *on duty* during 1980-89, 370 (53 percent) were assisted by another officer—either a partner or other responding units—at the time they were killed (FBI 1989b: 19). Comparison between the assistance rates of motorized and foot patrol officers who have been killed in the line of duty is premature, given the small number of officers in the data base who were on foot patrol.

partners or officers from other units) over the ten years from 1981 through 1990 was very close to the number of officers killed while on the scene without colleagues (231 versus 245).[12]

Besides the assistance that other police officers may provide in the field, the police call-taker and dispatcher can and should be crucial members of the assistance network for an officer assigned to a potentially dangerous call. Consider a call by an hysterical woman about a family disturbance in progress:

"The person who takes the call should be trained to ask the following questions, at a minimum, and to pass on pertinent information to the assigned officers:

- *What is your name?*
- *What is the address of the disturbance?*
- *Are you there now? (If not, where are you calling from?)*
- *What is your phone number?*
- *Who's causing the disturbance? (Get full name and relationship—whether husband, boyfriend, son, neighbor, etc.)*
- *What is he doing?*
- *Does he have a gun or other weapon?*
- *Is there a gun kept in the house? Where?*
- *Besides yourself and (husband, etc.), how many other people are there?*
- *Does your (husband, etc.) know you're calling the police?*
- *Is your (husband, etc.) wanted by the police for anything? What's his date of birth?*
- *Has he been drinking or using drugs?*

"This may seem like a long list of questions to be asking an hysterical caller; however, if the desk officer firmly cuts in on the caller's hectic, disorganized report and commands the caller to answer these short questions, it will take less time to get more information than by simply letting an upset caller ramble on for several minutes without telling you the things you need to know. A firm desk officer can get all of this information in less than two minutes.

"In assigning the call, the dispatcher should let you know as much as possible about what you're up against: 'Baker-Fourteen, handle a family 415 at 1204 South Walnut. Wife reporting husband is D&D, smashing furniture. He's not reported armed; however, she advises a loaded hunting rifle is kept in the hall closet. Two children in the home. Husband is aware of the call. We're running 28 and 29 and will advise. Baker-Seven will follow from 22d and Main' " (Rutledge 1988: 205-206).

The implication that working in one-officer patrol units creates an elevated risk that an officer will be feloniously killed on duty may or may not be supported by carefully analyzed evidence. Part of the analysis that should be conducted is whether an officer in a single-officer assignment who is assisted by colleagues with whom he or she does not work closely on a regular basis is as effective at successfully and nonviolently resolving dangerous encounters

---

[12] If one examines the FBI-collected data on officers *assaulted*, however, a very different picture emerges, with *accompanied* officers suffering assaults in much larger numbers than *unaccompanied* officers. We will discuss this finding later in this section.

as are partners who have been working together for some time and have established coordinated tactical routines (see Wilson, et al. 1990). The challenges of team work were captured nicely by Danish comedian/pianist Victor Borge in a recent concert in New York City. "The musicians in this orchestra backing me up are all fine musicians," he told the audience. "In fact, each one of them is an artist in his or her own right. It's only when they try to play *together* that we may have some difficulty!"

There is an additional important question concerning the FBI data on assisted officers: How accurately does the classification of an officer as "assisted" actually reflect the number of officers present and engaged in a tactical effort at the moment when the deceased officer was slain? During February 1992 in Chicago, for instance, two officers working in single-officer vehicles responded within moments of each other to the scene of an armed robbery in progress at a currency exchange. Both were shot nonfatally by the culprits, but at the time the first responding officer entered the building, challenged the robbery suspects and was shot, her backup had not yet arrived. And when, a few moments later, her backup officer arrived and engaged the suspects in a gun fight, the first responding officer was no longer able to be of tactical assistance (Recktenwald and Bradbery 1992: 3). We do not know whether the two victim officers will be classified by the Department and, eventually, by the FBI in tallying officers assaulted with deadly weapons, as "alone" or "assisted" while assigned to one-officer vehicles. If the categorization is "assisted" (because multiple officers were assigned to the robbery in progress), the classification could create the false impression that more than one officer was simultaneously engaged in attempting to thwart the robbery and apprehend the suspects.

The only way to answer this classification question with any certainty would be to inquire of the FBI and a sample of police agencies about the definitions employed in making the classification and then to audit police agency narrative reports to see whether they support the classifications ultimately adopted in the FBI's annual reports.

More basically, to interpret properly the risk posed to officers in one- versus two-person assignments in an agency or nationally one must know the mix of officers assigned to single- and double-officer units. For example, let's assume hypothetically that in 1990 the nation's police forces had 300,000 personnel assigned to patrol duty, two-thirds of whom (200,000) were assigned to single-officer units, while the remaining 100,000 were assigned to two-officer units. For instance, patrol officers on the day shift and graveyard shift might generally work alone, while officers on the evening shift might generally work in pairs. During 1990, FBI data (Behm 1992, correcting FBI 1991b) show that 66 officers were killed feloniously, 12 of whom were assigned to two-officer vehicles, 25 of whom were deployed in one-officer vehicles (16 of these 25 were alone when slain; the other 9 were reportedly assisted); one assignment was not ascertained. For simplicity, these data can be repeated as follows:

U.S. Law Enforcement Personnel Feloniously Slain in 1990: Assignment Type			
Two-Officer Vehicle	One-Officer Vehicle		Total Slain (incl. off-duty)
	Alone	Assisted	
12	16	9	66

Applying the FBI data to our hypothetical numbers means that the *rate* at which officers assigned in *two-officer* vehicles were killed (calculated as the number of slain officers working that assignment per 100,000 officers in the nation deployed in that assignment) for 1990 was, hypothetically, 12 (12 divided by 1—the "1" reflecting the 100,000 hypothesized officers using two-officer vehicles). In the same year, the felonious death rate for officers working one-officer vehicles was, hypothetically, 12.5 (25 divided by 2)—almost identical to the death rate for officers in two-officer assignments.

If we exclude from the calculation those officers working one-officer vehicles who were *assisted* during their fatal encounters, then we see that the rate at which personnel working one-officer vehicles (and handling their calls alone) were killed drops to 8 (16 divided by 2—the "2" reflecting, as before, the 200,000 hypothetical officers using single-officer vehicles). Thought of in that way, the death rate for officers truly handling calls alone is lower than the death rate for officers on the crime scene with colleagues. We cannot, without hypothesizing additional data on the national percentage of officers in each assignment who have assistance when handling calls, speculate more precisely on how the rates would change if all officers who were assisted *and* all officers who were initially assigned to two-officer vehicles were grouped together for analysis of their fatality rates.

If our hypothetical numbers made an *opposite* assumption—that most patrol officers in the nation are assigned to *two*-officer vehicles—then note how the officer risk rates would change. Suppose that, out of the 300,000 hypothetical patrol personnel, 100,000 were assigned to one-officer vehicles and the remaining 200,000 were assigned to two-officer cars. To stick with our simplified example of assignment patterns across three patrol shifts, in this instance the general pattern might be single-officer cars on days and two-officer cars on both the evening and midnight shifts. With this assumption, the felonious death rate for officers in *one*-officer units becomes relatively higher. The rate would be 25 (for both assisted and unassisted officers) (16 plus 9 divided by 1); or 16 (for only *unassisted* personnel) (16 divided by 1). These two relatively high death rates would contrast with a rate of 6 for slain officers working in *two*-officer cars (12 divided by 2).

> "[An officer and his colleagues] were attempting to serve a search warrant when the suspect began firing. [The officer] was struck in the head and left forearm. Having exhausted his ammunition, the suspect attempted to escape the scene. Despite his serious injuries, [the officer] chased after the suspect and apprehended him with no further incident. [The officer] required extensive surgery as a result of his injuries, but...recovered sufficiently to return to administrative duties and [was] expected to return to full duty" (FBI 1988a: 34).

Thus, with this second assumption about national deployment patterns (most patrol officers working in *two*-officer cars), the death risks for officers working in one-officer cars would be between 2.7 and 4.2 times as great as the risks for officers assigned with partners (16 divided by 6 and 25 divided by 6, respectively). Thus, it can be seen that additional information beyond that which is readily available in FBI annual reports needs to be brought to bear on the question of whether one-officer cars increase or decrease officers' safety.

A still more insightful examination would also explore deployment patterns (as between one- and two-officer cars) separately for different *shifts*, since we know (as discussed later in this chapter) that police-involved shootings tend to be concentrated on certain shifts. If virtually all officers working the day shift in a given department ride alone but officers working the afternoon and night shifts generally work in pairs, analysts would have to know this to accurately reflect the riskiness of different deployment modes for officers assigned at different times of day.

As noted earlier, another aspect of officer hazard to be considered here, as we have elsewhere in this volume, is the number of officers *assaulted* rather than the number killed. Most of the caveats about interpretation and the need for additional data to put findings in a proper perspective apply also here. But the FBI's numbers on officers assaulted nationwide during 1990 (the most current available as this volume goes to press) paint an interesting portrait of the proportions of officers assaulted, depending on whether they were the only officers present or were accompanied by other police. Figure 49 shows the results of this analysis, displaying the number of officers assaulted (with and without injury), the number of officers present at the time of the assault, and the circumstances at the scene of the assault.[13] The circumstances lump all *disturbance* calls together (despite the undesirability of doing so as we discuss later in this chapter), because the form in which the FBI data were available made separating the various types of disturbances impossible.

Combining all the categories of circumstances at the scene (disturbances, burglaries,

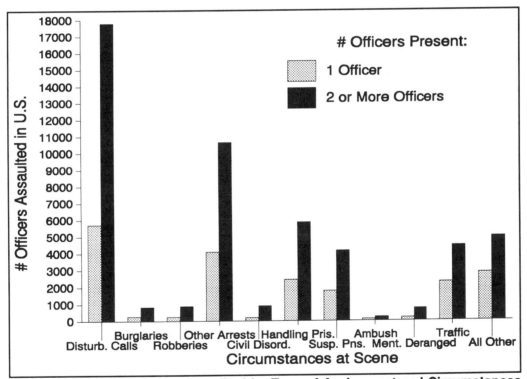

Figure 49: American Police Assaulted by Type of Assignment and Circumstances at Scene, 1990   *Source: FBI (1991b: 45).*

---

[13] The circumstances at the scene of the incident are abbreviated in the graph. The language used by the FBI to label the circumstances is the following: "Disturbance calls (family quarrels, man with gun, etc.); Burglaries in progress/pursuing burglary suspects; Robberies in progress/pursuing robbery suspects; Attempting other arrests; Civil disorders (mass disobedience, riot, etc.); Handling, transporting, custody of prisoners; Investigating suspicious persons/circumstance; Ambush (no warning); Mentally deranged; Traffic pursuits/stops; and All other" (FBI 1991b: 45).

investigating suspicious persons, etc.), we find that, in 1990, 72 percent (51,613) of all the American police who were assaulted were in the company of colleagues at the time; only 28 percent (20,181) of the assaulted officers were the only police personnel on the scene (FBI 1991b). This pattern of more assaults on accompanied than unaccompanied officers holds true for every category of circumstance at the scene, although the size of the discrepancy varies from one category to the next. Thus, in contrast to the seemingly mixed evidence concerning the risk of fatality to officers depending on whether they respond to crime calls alone, the evidence on *assaults* on officers seems much more lopsided: There are fewer officers assaulted when only one officer is present than when two or more are present.

To place this finding in a proper context, we need to know, as with the exploration of officer *fatalities*, what the deployment (dispatching, etc.) patterns are of departments when directing officers to the different types of crime problems. We need such data in order to calculate rates showing the *likelihood* of officers being assaulted given different numbers of police on the scene. As we saw in our hypothetical examples concerning officer fatalities, if most calls in which officers are assaulted are responded to (before the assault) by *multiple* units (either one- or two-officer units), then the *rate* of *lone*-officers being assaulted could be *higher* than the rate of accompanied officers being assaulted, despite the raw numbers cutting in the opposite direction.

The very notion that officers working alone may be safer might seem counterintuitive, given the old adage that there is strength in numbers. But field interviews around the nation with officers working foot beats and other reasonably solitary assignments suggest that police on lone-officer assignments may be protected to some extent by the ancient and honored edict: "Don't let your alligator mouth overload your canary ass." Policymakers need to ascertain carefully whether a cost of single-officer units is that officers too often simply bypass dealing with problems that deserve police attention. That is, one sure-fire way for officers to avoid starting something they cannot finish is not to start anything. But experience suggests that rigorous analysis in most cities will show that conscientious officers in single-officer units *do* aggressively engage problems—but often do so in ways that minimize the necessity for the use of force. Muir (1977) offers an excellent description of the ways in which police negotiate the resolution of potentially violent street encounters.

Still, there are patterns of officer victimization in some jurisdictions that, even though based on relatively small numbers of incidents, powerfully shape the thinking of rank-and-file officers about the relative riskiness of different assignments. For instance, in Chicago during the first 10 weeks of 1992, four officers were shot (one fatally), each of whom was working *alone* in what newspaper accounts characterized as a "dangerous beat" (Recktenwald and Bradbery 1992: 1). Moreover, counter to conventional wisdom (see Figure 51 later in this chapter), three of these four victim officers were shot during daylight hours (*ibid*.: 3).

Nowicki and Stahl (1978), although not explicitly addressing the question of one- and two-officer cars in Chicago, presented interesting related information on the number of Chicago officers involved in shots-fired incidents and the number discharging their weapons. Their findings for the years 1975 through 1977, which provide insight concerning the frequency with which officers discharging their firearms are "assisted" during the incidents, are shown in Table 13.

Table 13:
Officers Involved and Officers Discharging Weapons in
Shots-Fired Incidents in Chicago, 1975-77

# POs Involved and # Firing Weapons	Number of Incidents	% of Total Incidents
1 and 1	366	32.3
2 and 1	463	40.8
2 and 2	143	12.6
3 and 1	37	3.3
3 and 2	13	1.2
3 and 3	9	0.8
4 and 1	30	2.6
4 and 2	18	1.6
4 and 3	7	0.6
4 and 4	8	0.7
5 and 1	6	0.5
5 and 3	3	0.3
5 and 5	3	0.3
6 and 1	6	0.5
6 and 3	6	0.5
6 and 4	1	0.1
6 and 6	2	0.2
7 and 1	1	0.1
7 and 2	1	0.1
7 and 3	1	0.1
8 and 1	2	0.2
8 and 3	1	0.1
8 and 4	2	0.2
8 and 5	1	0.1
8 and 8	1	0.1
9 and 2	1	0.1
9 and 7	1	0.1
10 and 4	1	0.1

# POs Involved and # Firing Weapons	Number of Incidents	% of Total Incidents
12 and 6	1	0.1
TOTAL	1,135	100.3

Source: Nowicki and Stahl (1978: 100-101).
Note: Percentages do not equal 100 due to rounding.

In Chicago in 1991 of the 37 incidents in which on-duty police shot suspects fatally or nonfatally, multiple officers fired their weapons in 8 incidents. In one additional incident, both an on-duty and an off-duty officer participated and fired their weapons (data obtained by Geller for this volume). In New York City in 1990 of 757 incidents in which NYPD officers either discharged their weapons or were assaulted with deadly weapons, other members of the service were present in 617 (82 percent) (Cerar 1990: 5). That same year 344 NYPD personnel were involved in 232 incidents in which on-duty officers fired their guns (*ibid.*: 7). We do not know how many of the 37 shooting incidents in Chicago in 1991 had more than one officer present. But if the 82 percent New York City rate at which multiple officers were on the scene of police-involved shootings applied in Chicago, then these data might suggest that it is common for only some of the officers present to shoot. Applying the 82 percent figure in Chicago, 30 out of the 37 incidents would have had multiple officers present, but more than one officer fired in just 8.

V. Gender, Age, and Criminal Justice Experience of Participants in Police-Involved Shootings

Virtually all the civilians at whom police fire are male (for a recent exception—the killing by Oakland officers of a suspected terrorist—see Gross 1992). For example:

- 100 percent of the Philadelphia fatalities during 1950-1960 (Robin 1963);

- 96 percent of the persons fired at in New York City (Fyfe 1978);

- 95 percent of the victims in Chicago (Geller and Karales 1981a: 86);

- 98 percent of the victims in the seven-city Police Foundation research (Milton, et al. 1977: 17); and

- 98 percent of civilians killed by police in New York State (NYSCCJ 1987) were male.

The same is true for officers victimized. For instance:

- 100 percent of the 187 police shot fatally or nonfatally in Chicago in 1974-1978 (Geller and Karales 1981a: 93, 97);

- 103 of the 104 officers slain nationwide in 1980 (FBI 1981a: 340) and 64 of the 65 slain in 1990 (FBI 1991b: 20);

■ 98 percent of all officers slain feloniously nationwide during the years 1978-89 (FBI 1987, 1989b: 21); and

■ 95 percent of the 40 members of the NYPD who were shot fatally or nonfatally in 1990; excluding suicides and officers shot accidentally, 100 percent were male (Cerar 1990: 22-24).

Female officers are increasingly experiencing all the highs and lows of American police work (see, e.g., Vera Institute of Justice 1977; S. Martin 1990; *Crime Control Digest* 1990c). For the first time, in 1990, the IACP selected a woman as Police Officer of the Year. During the 10 years 1981-90, 18 women officers laid down their lives in the service of their communities (FBI 1991b: 20). On February 11, 1991, for the first time since the Los Angeles Police Department's founding in 1869, a female officer (a rookie with 10 months on the job) was slain in the line of duty.[14] The details of the incident are indistinguishable from hundreds of other senseless tragedies:

> "Tina Kerbrat, 34, was hit in the head by a bullet from a .357 magnum pistol while investigating two men drinking beer on a sidewalk.... Los Angeles Police Chief Daryl Gates told reporters: 'She was shot in an absolutely senseless situation.... She had no chance whatsoever...in a very routine investigation of a drunk.... We have a policewoman, a mother, who is dead because of this (expletive),' Gates said.... [A] 32-year-old Salvadoran, described by police as an illegal alien who killed Kerbrat, was slain in a shoot-out with her partner, Earl Valladares, 45.... After Kerbrat fell dead, Valladares fired 10 rounds, fatally wounding [the assailant]. Kerbrat and her husband, Tim, a firefighter, had two children, Craig, 6, and Nicole, 3" (*Crime Control Digest* 1991: 9-10; see also Berger and Braun 1991).

Chief Gates added that the slain assailant's drinking companion during this incident was "a known member of a San Fernando Valley street gang that was responsible for the death of an officer several years ago" (*New York Times* 1991a).

Women are also represented among the assailants of police. FBI reports show that, of the 1,077 people identified in the felonious killing of 801 police officers during 1980-89, 43 (4 percent) of the offenders were female (FBI 1989b: 22). In 1990 5 (6 percent) of the 80 persons identified as the killers of police nationally were female (FBI 1991b: 21).

Few data are readily available to help assess the frequency (and to predict the likely frequency in coming years) with which female police officers shoot at suspects. For one effort to begin to explore the role of officer gender on the outcome of violent encounters, see Grennan (1987), who explored the frequency with which female officers used deadly force in New York City (also see Bell 1982; Charles 1982; Rubin 1992; Vera Institute of Justice 1977; and Alpert 1989b: 487).

Grennan discovered, as had Blumberg (1983) in studying use of force in Kansas City, that women officers in male-female teams fired their guns less frequently than the male

---

[14] In the Los Angeles Police Department, where women have been assigned to routine patrol duties since the 1970s, 1,118 (13 percent) of the agency's 8,437 sworn officers in 1991 were female (*Crime Control Digest* 1991: 10; see also Berger and Braun 1991: A27).

members of the teams (see also Blumberg 1989: 452). Our own compilation, drawn from the 1989 FBI unpublished supplementary homicide reports, indicates that, of the 362 incidents that year in which American police departments reported to the FBI that their officers justifiably killed a felony suspect, the deadly force was used by female officers in 12 incidents (just over 3 percent). (In 1988 female officers justifiably killed suspects in 10 incidents in the United States.) Alpert (1989b: 487) found that precisely the same percentage of the Miami Police officers who intentionally discharged their firearms from 1980 through 1986 (in 163 incidents) were women (this amounted to four policewomen).

The 3 percent national figure might be considered in light of Susan Martin's finding (1990) that, by 1986 in departments serving populations of 50,000 or more, approximately 9 percent of the sworn police officers were women. The Bureau of Justice Statistics (1992a, 1992b; *Crime Control Digest* 1992b: 1) reported that in 1987 women constituted 7.6 percent of local police officers and 12.6 percent of sheriffs' deputies. By 1990 these percentages had risen to 8.1 percent and 15.4 percent, respectively. When one considers that female officers in many jurisdictions may be disproportionately assigned to police agency units *un*likely to become involved in violent confrontations with suspects,[15] the 3 percent figure is probably within a reasonably predictable range. Still, there are some research findings sug-

"[F]emale officers are not reluctant to use force, but they are not nearly as likely to be involved in use of excessive force. * * * With some exceptions, female officers interviewed believed they were more communicative, more skillful at deescalating potentially violent situations and less confrontational. A suspect's defiance and disrespect of an officer often gives rise to use of force by an officer. Many officers, both male and female, believe female officers are less personally challenged by defiant suspects and feel less need to deal with defiance with immediate force or confrontational language" (Independent Commission on the Los Angeles Police Department 1991: 84).

gesting that, among officers assigned to units where proactive arrest activity is an option, male officers have made more arrests than have their female counterparts (see, e.g., Bloch and Anderson 1974; Sherman 1975). Who made the most arrests in these studies, however, does not, in our view, necessarily answer the question of whether the male or female officers examined were doing more *productive* police work (see, e.g., Goldstein 1990).

As noted earlier in our discussion of the race/ethnicity of officers involved in shootings, Doerner (1991), employed high-tech "shoot/don't shoot" simulation training equipment in the Tallahassee Police Department to explore whether differences in performance could be linked to officer characteristics. As with the race of officers, Doerner explored whether there were any differences between male and female officers on the timing of two decisions: when to unholster their sidearm and when, if at all, to fire it in response to the simulated opposition. Doerner's study involved secondary analysis of the first 56 officers scheduled by the Department for shoot/don't shoot training as part of the Tallahassee Police Department's regular training program. These 56 officers demonstrated "unholstering" behavior in 363 simulated incidents and "shooting" behavior in 271 "shoot scenarios." Of these 56 officers,

---

[15] S. Martin (1990) reports that in five large agencies (Detroit, Chicago, Washington, D.C., Birmingham, and Phoenix) female officers "are more likely to be assigned to administrative and community service units and less likely to be assigned to tactical or patrol support units" than are male officers.

51 (91 percent) were male and 5 (9 percent) were female (whereas 20 percent of the force were female officers) (*ibid.*: 4; see also *Law and Order* 1992c).

Although the results Doerner derived were *not* statistically significant, there were indications that "female officers showed a tendency to stay holstered longer than their male counterparts." Whereas female officers unholstered their weapons "too late" in 23 percent of the 30 simulated incidents they handled, male officers drew "too late" in only 15 percent of the 333 incidents they confronted in the simulation exercise. "Too late" was defined rather conservatively as unholstering "after the assailant has fired the first shot in a high-risk situation" (*ibid.*: 6, 7). Moreover, male officers unholstered "too early" in 29 percent of their incidents, and female officers did so in only 20 percent of theirs ("too early" meant "display[ing] their weapons prior to the draw stimulus" in the video simulation). Doerner also found that male officers discharged their weapons "too late" in 47 percent of the 249 "shoot scenarios," while policewomen shot belatedly in 73 percent of their 22 shoot scenarios. In this instance, "too late" meant "engag[ing] a target after the suspect shoots or...fail[ing] to return fire" (*ibid.*). Among Doerner's tentative conclusions were that, "[c]ontrary to popular belief, female police officers are no more likely to use firearms on patrol than male officers.... In fact...they are more than three times as likely *not* to resort to guns [male officers shot in 60 percent and female officers in 21 percent of the simulation incidents]. But...when female officers do use a gun they are much less likely to hit their target"—78 percent hit rates for male officers compared with 38 percent for females. Doerner speculated that "the average female officer may need to undergo additional training" (*Law and Order* 1992c).

A substantial percentage of civilians shot at by police during the 1970s were between the ages of 17 and 30: 70 percent of the targets in New York City (Fyfe 1978) and 66 percent of those struck by bullets in the Police Foundation's study (Milton, et al. 1977). In Chicago 76 percent of the persons shot by police were 30 or younger (Geller and Karales 1981a: 87). The average age of those killed by police in New York State from 1981 through 1985 was 30, although most were 20 to 24 (New York State Commission on Criminal Justice 1987).

At the same time, among the 1,077 persons identified as having killed American police during the 1980-89 period, 582 (54 percent) were 18 to 29 years of age. Another 85 (8 percent) were under 18 (FBI 1989b: 22). Although many within and outside policing have lamented the seemingly ever younger and more violent cadre of criminals stalking the streets of urban America, it is worth noting that, at least during the 1980s, the under-18-year-old group of police killers has *not* grown markedly as a proportion of assailants. (Marriott [1992b] quotes analysts who report that the crimes young people are committing nowadays are increasingly violent but the *number* of youngsters engaged in such offenses has not grown in the last 10 or 20 years.) In the period 1980-84, police killers under 18 represented 9 percent (56 out of 600) of all assailants; during 1985-89, the same group constituted 6 percent (29 out of 477) of assailants (FBI 1989b: 22). In 1990, 42 (53 percent) of those who killed American police were between the ages of 18 and 29, and 6 (8 percent) were under 18 (FBI 1991b: 21).

To explore these numbers more fully, one would need to compute police assault rates that take into account the likelihood that officers will come in contact with potentially violent suspects of different ages. Thus, police exposure to assault might be expressed as a rate based on the number of young people in the nation or a particular jurisdiction, their participation in crime generally and in homicide specifically (Fingerhut, et al. 1992a, 1992b), their access to firearms (Callahan and Rivara 1992), police patrol patterns that enhance police contact with youth (e.g., special missions at school yards or other places dominated by young people), and other factors. For instance, if in a given year 9 percent of police assailants were under the age of 18, it might be of interest to compare this with the percentages of the general population, persons stopped and questioned by police but not arrested, arrestees, offenders (as identified in victimization surveys), and other groups whose members were younger than 18. If such analysis revealed gross overrepresentation of young people as assailants of police (compared to measures of police intervention with—and potential aggravation of—young people) in a given community, further inquiry might be warranted to explore the motivations of the assailants and possible preventive strategies. Police may gain intelligence that local youth gangs have made attacks on police a symbol of gang loyalty, for example, and members of the force certainly would need to be alerted to this problem. Knowing that "cop fighting" is a right of passage for members of a particular gang could also help social agencies and community leaders respected by the young gang members to develop violence-prevention programs (see Harmon 1992 for a discussion of the role of gangs in youngsters' lives).

On the police side of the equation, 38 percent of the officers feloniously killed nationwide during 1980-1989 were 31 to 40 years of age; in 1990 the figure was 42 percent. In that same decade, 25 percent were between the ages of 25 and 30, and 28 percent were over 40. Only 9 percent were under 25 years old. In 1990 of the officers slain, 14 percent were 25 to 30 years old, 40 percent were over 40, and 5 percent had not yet reached their 25th birthday (FBI 1989b: 21, 1991b: 20). The 801 law enforcement personnel killed feloniously nationwide from 1980 through 1989 averaged nine years of service at the time of their deaths (FBI 1989b: 21). In 1990 the average was 10 years (FBI 1991b: 20).

The career service of the 763 American police slain feloniously from 1981 through 1990 fell into the following patterns: 39 (5 percent) had less than one year on the job; 216 (28 percent) had 1 to 4 years; 235 (31 percent) had 5 to 10 years; and 272 (36 percent) had more than 10 years (FBI 1991b: 20) (one officer's tenure was not ascertained at press time—Behm 1992). Thus, a pattern emerges in which the most experienced officers died in the largest numbers and the least experienced officers accounted for the smallest portion of those slain. To identify whether officers were more *likely* to be killed feloniously as they accumulated more experience, however, we would need data we do not have: the experience distribution of American law enforcement personnel. With such numbers, we could calculate rates showing, for instance, the number of sworn officers with 10 years on the job who were slain compared with the number currently employed by public police agencies. A still more sophisticated analysis might compare the age distribution of officers killed with the age distribution of officers who make higher than average numbers of arrests for violent crimes.

The "criminal justice experience" of those who shot or otherwise killed police (i.e., their arrest histories) is also profiled by annual FBI reports. The criminal records of the 1,077 persons identified as responsible for killing 801 police during 1980-89 are shown in Table 14.

In 1990 of the 80 identified cop killers:

- 62 (78 percent) had a prior criminal arrest
- 54 (68 percent) had been convicted on a prior criminal charge
- 37 (46 percent) had a prior arrest for a crime of violence
- 25 (31 percent) were on parole or probation at the time of the killing
- 5 (6 percent) had previously been arrested for murder
- 26 (33 percent) had a prior arrest for a drug law violation
- 11 (14 percent) had been arrested before for assaulting an officer or resisting arrest
- 39 (49 percent) had a prior arrest for a weapons violation, and

- 18 (23 percent) had no known prior criminal arrests or convictions (FBI 1991b: 21).

Doerner (1991), besides exploring the possible role of officer race and gender in officer unholstering and shooting decisions in shoot/don't shoot simulation training, also tested for differences related to years of police experience. The performance of the 56 officers studied in 363 simulated incidents revealed that "rookies were more likely to display a weapon prematurely than were seasoned officers" (*ibid.*: 6, 7). Rookies displayed their laser guns "too early" in 31 percent of these incidents, while veterans did so in 20 percent (*ibid.*: 7, 10).

Table 14:
Prior Criminal Record of Persons Identified in the Felonious
Killing of American Law Enforcement Officers, 1980-89

Prior Record	# of Assailants	% of Assailants
Prior criminal arrest	763	71%
Convicted on prior criminal charge	518	48%
Prior arrest for crime of violence	334	31%
On parole/probation during incident	257	24%
Prior arrest for murder	52	5%
Prior arrest for drug law violation	238	22%
Prior arrest for assaulting an officer or resisting arrest	96	9%
Prior arrest for weapons violation	308	29%
No prior criminal arrests/convictions	314	29%
TOTAL ASSAILANTS	1,077	*

* Because there is overlap among the categories, the percentages do not add up to 100 percent, and adding the number of assailants in each row would total more than the actual number of assailants (1,077). Source: FBI (1989b).

VI. Time, Lighting Conditions, Day, and Month of Police-Involved Shooting Incidents

The time of day, day of week, and month during which officers were assaulted (by *all* weapons) are depicted in Figures 50, 51, 52, and 53, all drawn from FBI reports (1991b: 14-15). To appraise more fully the riskiness of specific hours of the day, it would be necessary to know the number of officers assigned, the number of felony and perhaps certain types of misdemeanor calls, and other pertinent exposure information pertaining to each block of time shown in the FBI's graph (Figure 50) and our graph (Figure 51).

Unfortunately, such data are not readily available. One would expect less variation in officer deployment by day and by month, although there may well be important variations in other measures of officer exposure (crime patterns, the despondency of those whom the police encounter—such as around Christmas time—and so forth).

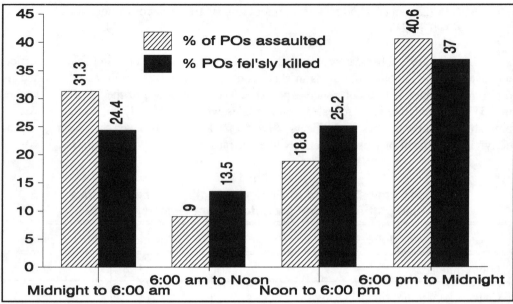

Figure 50: American Police Assaulted or Slain by Time of Day, 1986-90
Source: FBI (1991b: 14).

Figure 50, re-created from an FBI graph, shows, by time of day, both the killing of American law enforcement personnel and assaults on them (some causing injury, some not) over a five-year period. To show the times of day when American police are slain in the line of duty in smaller blocks of time (two-hour segments), we have created Figure 51, based on tabular data in FBI reports (FBI 1989b: 15). The data displayed in Figures 51, 52, and 53 cover the decade of the 1980s.

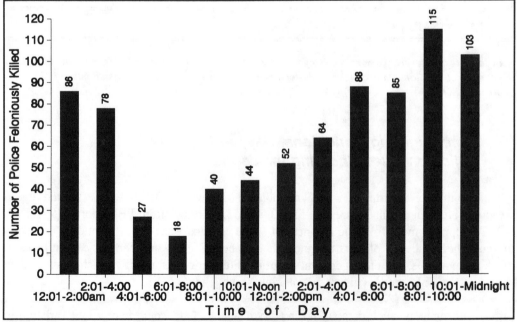

Figure 51: American Police Slain by Time of Day, 1980-89
Source: FBI (1989b).

Comparable data for some individual police departments have also been reported in various studies. To take the time of day, for instance, in Chicago during 1991, of the 47 incidents in which officers shot civilians fatally or nonfatally, 8 (17 percent) occurred between 8:01 am and 4:00 pm, 25 (53 percent) occurred between 4:01 pm and midnight, and the remaining 14 (30 percent) happened between midnight and 8:00 am (data collected by Geller for this book). In New York City during 1990, of 425 incidents in which NYPD members either fired their guns or were assaulted with a deadly weapon, 70 (17 percent) occurred from 8:01 am to 4:00 pm, 192 (45 percent) took place from 4:01 pm to midnight, and 163 (38 percent) transpired between midnight and 8:00 am (Cerar 1990: 3).

Related to the time of day of officer-involved shootings is the lighting conditions at the scene of incidents. A direct relationship between these two factors does not exist, of course, because daytime shooting incidents may occur in dark, indoor locations. Indeed, officers have mentioned to us that the time when they most frequently need—and do not always have—their flashlights is during the day, when they have to enter dark buildings—for instance, in search of burglars or fleeing suspects or to check on the welfare of occupants. During 1991 in New York City out of 440 incidents in which NYPD officers either discharged their weapons or were assaulted with deadly weapons, 79 (18 percent) occurred in "good artificial" light, 8 (2 percent) in "poor artificial" lighting, 99 (22.5 percent) in "daylight," 237 (54 percent) in the "dark," 15 (3 percent) at "dusk," and 2 (0.5 percent) at "dawn" (Cerar 1991: 11). More generally, of these 440 incidents, 178 (40.5 percent) occurred under well-lit conditions, with visibility difficult in the remaining 262 (59.5 percent).

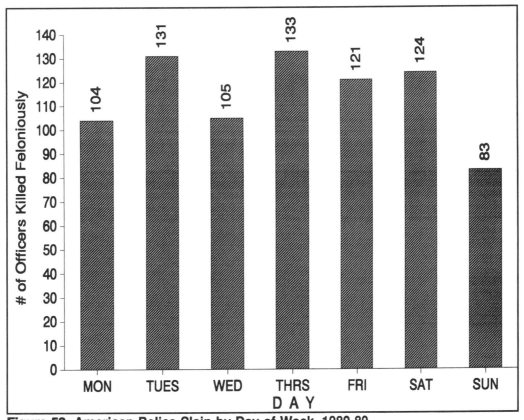

Figure 52: American Police Slain by Day of Week, 1980-89
Source: FBI (1989b).

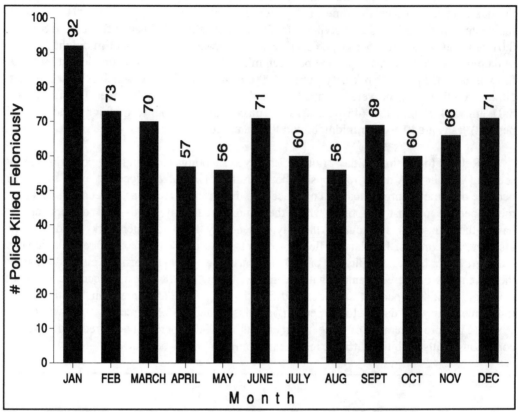

Figure 53: American Police Slain by Month of Occurrence, 1980-89
Source: FBI (1989b).

VII. *Location and Public Visibility of Shootings*

We have already touched on certain aspects of the kind of locations in which police shoot civilians and are shot by them. We did so in attempting to explain certain patterns associated with off-duty shootings and the differential shooting involvement in some cities by officers of different races.

Since the public visibility of police-civilian interactions seems to be an important correlate of police use of *non*deadly force (Friedrich 1980), it is interesting that police shootings of civilians seem to occur predominantly in public locations: 75 percent on the street in Philadelphia several decades ago (Robin 1963: 227), at least 68 percent out-of-doors in Chicago during 1974-78 (Geller and Karales 1981a: 92), and 68 percent out-of-doors in New York City in the late 1980s (NYPD 1988). Seventy-eight percent of the deaths of citizens caused by the police in New York State from 1981 through 1985 occurred in places accessible to the public (NYSCCJ 1987). In New York City in 1990, more than 78 percent of all incidents in which NYPD members fired their weapons or were assaulted with a deadly weapon occurred outside, the overwhelming majority of these on streets (256 out of 333 out-of-doors incidents) (Cerar 1990: 11).

The fact that shootings occur in public locations does not ensure visibility, however. Nowicki and Stahl (1978: viii, 8) found that, of the 1,145 shots-fired incidents in Chicago during 1975-77, 63 percent of which occurred on public streets or public ways, "few [were] reportedly observed by persons other than the officer and offender involved." In Fyfe's examination of New York City shootings, he, too, found that uninvolved witnesses were rarely present at the public locations when deadly force was used, perhaps in part because most of the shootings occur at night (Fyfe 1981b: 381).

However, the New York State study of civilian killings by the police found that in 74 percent of the incidents at least one nonpolice witness was present and in only 13 percent of the incidents was an officer alone (NYSCCJ 1987: 166). In the post-"Rodney King world," in which an amateur video camera operator can alter the national agenda by pointing his or her lens at a police operation, it is just a matter of time before an eyewitness to a shooting of or by police is catapulted from the status of having just "one person's opinion" to being the eyes and ears of the world concerning the event. Already, police car-mounted video cameras and wireless microphones worn by officers have recorded serious altercations between police and suspects.[16]

The Chicago data portray the types of locations where police shot themselves accidentally or intentionally (the most common, 53 percent, being their homes) and where officers were shot by their colleagues (45 percent outside, 28 percent at a residence, 22 percent on police department premises) (Geller and Karales 1981a: 99). Clearly, more data from a wider diversity of jurisdictions are needed before national generalizations can be made about the presence of eyewitnesses during incidents in which police either shoot persons or are themselves shot.

Another aspect of location that deserves mention here (and will be discussed further near the end of this chapter) is that, during several recent years for which FBI data have been published, a disproportionate number of law enforcement personnel have been feloniously slain in the South. The FBI does not explore the reasons for this in its data presentations; they deserve fuller attention by analysts within and outside of police agencies.

VIII. Weaponry in Police-Involved Shootings and Distances Between Officers and Opponents

Discussing the choice of weaponry—both by criminals and police—follows nicely from a summary of the kind of locations in which police-involved shootings historically have occurred. Since one of the prime concerns among police is that innocent bystanders and crime

---

[16] One infamous case from a southern state, broadcast on the Law Enforcement Television Network (LETN), involved three Hispanic suspects in a car stop killing the arresting officer with his own gun. The January 23, 1991, incident, the early stages of which were captured on the squad car-mounted video camera, points out the need for technological improvements in the design or selection of the wireless microphones worn by officers and perhaps in the lenses mounted on the video cameras. The killing of the officer was not visible because when the assailants wrestled the officer's gun from him he was lying on the ground in front of the squad car, and the camera's view was blocked by the hood of the car. Nor was the sound of the fatal shot, fired at close range, audible on the tape, because the decibel level of the blast exceeded the capacity of the microphone. Microphones exist that are capable of recording such loud sounds as close-range gun fire, and their use could well make the difference in such cases between securing a murder conviction of the assailants and other dispositions. Similarly, failure to employ an adequate microphone could allow police who misuse their firearms off-camera to evade justice for their misdeeds.

victims be protected from any violence that results from the police arrest of criminal suspects, the varying capacities of different firearms to inflict injury and to be skillfully aimed and fired are important topics for deadly force analysts. Similarly, officer safety (through use of soft body armor and tactics) may depend importantly on the kind of weaponry likely to be used by offenders.

As we will see later in this chapter, data covering shots-fired incidents in Philadelphia from 1986 through 1990 have been interpreted by some as suggesting that a slight increase in accidental discharges by Philadelphia officers in 1990 may be related to the Department's adoption that year of semi-automatic side arms.

Figure 54 shows the percentages of all 801 American law enforcement personnel who were killed feloniously during the decade 1980-89 according to the type of weapon used against them (FBI 1989b: 13). Clearly, the typical killing of an American police officer is accomplished by means of a firearm, the handgun accounting for more than three-fourths of such deaths.[17] Little and Boylen (1990) report the types of firearms police are likely to face in the line of duty, based on a survey of weapons confiscated by a "major southeastern city" (*ibid.*: 49; see also Bureau of Alcohol, Tobacco, and Firearms 1976; Wright and Rossi 1981, 1985; Kleck 1992).

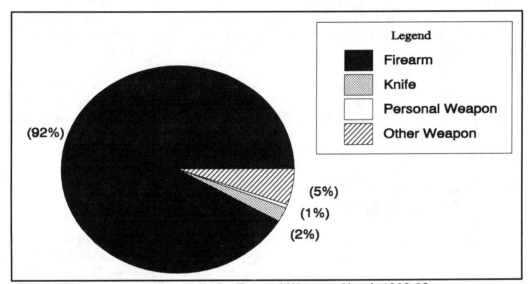

Figure 54: American Police Slain by Type of Weapon Used, 1980-89
Source: FBI (1989b).

Of the 40 American officers killed in 1989 with handguns, 10 (25 percent) were slain with their own weapons (FBI 1989b: 13). In 1990, 3 (6 percent) of the 48 police killed with handguns had their own guns turned on them by assailants (FBI 1991b: 12). In 1991, the comparable number was 8 (16 percent) (Behm 1992). Among many other implications, these

---

[17] Of the 735 law enforcement personnel killed feloniously by firearms during 1980-89, 558 (76 percent) were shot with handguns, 105 (14 percent) with rifles, and 72 (10 percent) with shotguns (FBI 1989b: 13). In 1990 handguns accounted for 86 percent of all the felonious killings of police with firearms (48 out of 56) (FBI 1991b: 12). In 1991 handguns were used in 74 percent of the firearms slayings (50 out of 68) (Behmn 1992). "Assault weapons" are rarely used against police (Kleck 1992).

findings serve as an important reminder of the necessity for high-quality training in weapons retention and the necessity for officers' soft body armor to be sufficient at least to protect against police service weapons. Sufficiency of soft body armor in the context of the burgeoning popularity of large capacity handguns (*Crime Control Digest* 1992b: 7) means armor capable of stopping both high velocity, highly penetrating ammunition and multiple hits (Young 1992). Of the 40 officers slain in 1989 by handguns, 4 were shot by criminals using 9-millimeter weapons. And of the 48 American police personnel killed feloniously with handguns in 1990, 8 were slain with 9-millimeters (FBI 1991b: 12). Kleck (1992) reports that criminals' use of semi-automatics "has been declining since around 1989."

As departments continue to switch to semi-automatic weapons and different ammunition, it is crucial that the soft body armor used by officers in *neighboring* jurisdictions or by officers in joint task forces operating in the locale keep pace with the destructive capacity of this weaponry. These officers could be jeopardized by such weapons stolen from an officer in the newly equipped department or could be shot by an officer accidentally or in a case of mistaken identity. Obviously, powerful firearms are also prevalent among some criminals in various areas of the country, so police need to be protected against them regardless of the service weapon adopted by any particular agency. Police also, of course, need to be trained in the safe handling of any weapons they may confiscate from offenders.

> *"Officers involved in shootings should not be silent with investigators afterwards because there is physical evidence that might support their versions of incidents and that won't be around very long. For instance, the best evidence in a shooting often is the suspect's shirt. It can tell a bullet's trajectory, the distance between the shooter and person shot, the position of the suspect's arms at the time, etc. Everyone thinks the officer's gun is the best evidence. We have that; it's registered. How often is the suspect's shirt thrown away in the hospital emergency room?" (McCarthy 1992).*

Choice of weaponry and tactics may depend to a large extent on the proximity of an officer and his or her assailant in typical high-risk encounters. While descriptive data on *potentially* violent confrontations are extremely difficult to come by (see, e.g., Geller 1985a), the FBI's profile of officers slain feloniously does tally the distance between victim officers and their assailants. Figure 55 shows the number of officers killed feloniously by *firearms* during the 10 years 1980-89, according to the feet between officer and assailant.

In 1990 and 1991, of the 56 and 68 police slain nationally with firearms, respectively, the distributions of distances between the assailants and slain officers were: 0-30 feet—30 (54 percent) in 1990 and 34 (50 percent) in 1991; 6-10 feet—14 (25 percent) in 1990 and 9 (13 percent) in 1991; 11-20 feet—4 (7 percent) in 1990 and 13 (19 percent) in 1991; 21-50 feet—4 (7 percent) in 1990 and 6 (9 percent) in 1991; over 50 feet—4 (7 percent) in 1990 and 6 (9 percent) in 1991 (FBI 1991b: 13; Behm 1992). In 1990, of the 287 incidents in which NYPD members discharged their firearms and in which the distances between officer and perpetrator were identified, 156 (54 percent) occurred within 15 feet, 80 (28 percent) within 15 to 21 feet, 32 (11 percent) within 21 to 45 feet, and 19 (7 percent) within 45 to 75 feet (Cerar 1990: 8).

Alpert's (1989a) compilation of shots-fired incidents by Metro-Dade Police officers revealed that, at the time officers fired their first shot, the distance to the opponent(s) was ten

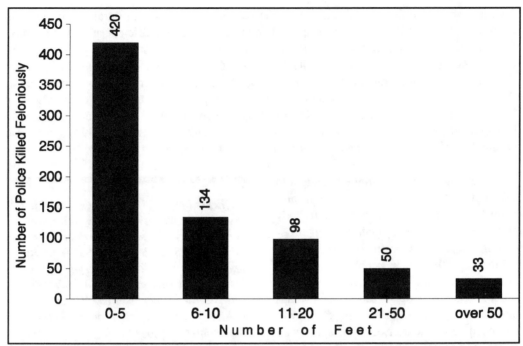

Figure 55: American Police Shot to Death by Distance Between Victim and Assailant, 1980-89 *Source: FBI (1989b).*

feet or less in 61 percent of the incidents, between 11 and 30 feet in 26 percent, and more than 30 feet in the remaining 12 percent (this adds up to 99 percent due to rounding).

The New York City Police Department's firearms and tactics experts in the Police Academy have analyzed officer shooting proficiency when firing in gunfights from varying distances. In 1990, for example, when members of the force engaged in 67 gunfights, the distances between officers and adversaries were identified for 55 incidents. When officers fired from less than 15 feet, they struck their intended target 38 percent of the time (30 strikes out of 79 rounds fired). From greater distances, their hit rate (which the NYPD calls "hit potential") was 11.5 percent (36 hits out of 314 shots fired). In 1990, 48 percent of all gunfights involving NYPD members occurred with 21 feet or less separating officers from opponents; in 1989 54 percent occurred in that range (Cerar 1990: 9).

Including incidents in which distances were not ascertained, the Department's 67 gunfights in 1990 involved 125 officers who fired 548 shots at 74 perpetrators (who in turn fired 190 shots at police). Thirteen officers were injured (all nonfatally) by a total of 12 shots fired by perpetrators, while 37 police opponents were struck (13 fatally) by a total of 105 rounds. Compared with the Department's overall bullet hit rate in these gunfights of 19.2 percent, their opponents struck officers with 6.3 percent of all shots fired. The officers involved in these gunfights in 1990 as a group averaged 4.4 shots per incident, and their adversaries averaged 2.8 (Cerar 1990: 9). The NYPD's annual reports on firearms discharges and lethal weapons assaults against its members are also excellent sources of data on officers' experience with specific types of weapons. For instance, the Glock 19 9-millimeter semi-automatic pistol receives six pages of statistical and anecdotal discussion in the latest available annual report (Cerar 1990: 15-20; for more on the Glock pistols, see Kasler 1992).

IX. Reasons for Shootings

A. Circumstances that Directly Prompted Shootings by Police

In the interest of summarizing the published data on stated police reasons for firing their weapons, this section reports findings from studies spanning the past two decades. The reader should keep in mind, however, that in 1985 the U.S. Supreme Court issued its landmark ruling in *Tennessee v. Garner*, invalidating the practice of using lethal force to capture nonviolent fleeing suspects. Many police departments had already adopted that position through administrative regulation as much as a decade before, but others were required by *Garner* to amend their policies (see Walker and Fridell 1989). Hence, the reasons given by police for firing their weapons at civilians prior to the Supreme Court's ruling on March 27, 1985, in some instances were no longer acceptable after that date.

1. Shooting Typologies

Fyfe (1981c) and other researchers have characterized police firearms discharges on a continuum from "elective" shootings, in which officers, in the judgment of the analyst, could have refrained from shooting without jeopardizing anyone's immediate safety, to "nonelective" shootings, in which shooting is seen (again, by the analyst) as the only feasible way to end an immediate threat to life. In one study, Fyfe (1981c) used a typology that distinguished between various levels of danger that prompted police to shoot civilians. His four types are:

(1) assaults with guns against the police;
(2) assaults with knives or other weapons;
(3) physical assaults on police; and
(4) "unarmed or no assault."

This typology, argues Fyfe, should allow for meaningful comparisons between departments. Departments that exert strong, restrictive control over officers' use of deadly force can be expected to have the higher percentages of their shootings in the more serious assault categories. Less restrictive or less well-controlled departments, he asserts, can be expected to have a broader distribution.

Other researchers (e.g., Geller and Karales 1981a; Meyer 1980a, 1980-b) have used shooting typologies with slightly more categories. For instance, Geller and Karales' shooting types include:

(1) actual or threatened use of gun by opponent

Officers *"on anti-crime patrol...observed male breaking into store window. Inside building, three store employees were waiting for perp. When one PO entered through window, employees thought he was another burglar and fired at PO. PO returned fire, emptying his revolver. Other PO, outside, threw in more speedloaders to first PO. More shots exchanged. Two more [officers] entered through windows and found burglar wounded with two employees. While handcuffing them, [officer] heard sergeant call from another room for assistance. When PO entered office, saw male with gun and fired two more times, killing male. Male was employee of store. Approximately 18 shots fired by [officers], and approximately 5 shots fired by store employees. Burglar shot by employees"* (Cerar 1991: 36).

(2) actual or threatened use of other deadly weapon or physical force by opponent
(3) opponent possessed but did not use or threaten to use some other deadly weapon
(4) flight without other resistance
(5) other reasons for shooting intentionally (e.g., improper shooting)
(6) accidental discharge of weapon
(7) mistaken identity shooting
(8) stray bullet

The "stray bullet" category also includes ricochets (see also Burke, et al. 1988).

The FBI compiles data on "felons killed by peace officers" for its unpublished analyses of the Uniform Crime Reporting program's "supplementary homicide report." These data are filed monthly with the Bureau by participating police agencies nationwide. To display those data, the FBI has adopted the following typology:

(1) felon attacked police officer
(2) felon [a civilian] attacked fellow police officer [the shooter's partner]
(3) felon attacked a civilian
(4) felon attempted flight from a crime
(5) felon killed in commission of a crime
(6) felon resisted arrest
(7) not enough information to determine (FBI 1990c)

Two officers responded to the scene of a flower shop burglary. From their squad car, they noticed a man standing near the shop and gesturing to them. One officer exited the vehicle and talked with the man, discovering that he was the shop owner, who had been called to the location by the burglar alarm company. Learning from the shop owner that a suspect in the burglary was nearby, the officer promptly bolted after the suspect. But the pursuing officer neglected to inform his partner, a rookie in his 17th week of field training, that the man whom the officers saw as they drove up to the scene was the shop owner—the victim of the crime. The rookie partner moments later saw this man draw a weapon and begin heading in the direction of the pursuing officer. Believing that the shop owner might be one of the burglary suspects, the rookie officer ordered the man to halt. When the man did halt and turned in the direction of the rookie with gun still in hand, the rookie officer fired once, inflicting a fatal chest wound. The victim of this mistaken identity shooting was a decorated war hero, and among the tributes paid to him at his funeral was attendance by a police honor guard (Crime Control Digest 1990f: 7-8; Sykes 1991).

This same typology is used to present summary information on justifiable homicides committed by peace officers and justifiable homicides committed by civilians. The Bureau further delineates the number of persons involved in justifiable homicides (whether committed by peace officers or civilians) with the following typology:

(a) single victim/single offender
(b) single victim/unknown offender or offenders

    (c)   single victim/multiple offenders

    (d)   multiple victims/single offender

    (e)   multiple victims/multiple offenders

    (f)   multiple victims/unknown offender or offenders (FBI 1990c)

Bureau UCR staff acknowledge the awkwardness and potential confusion that might result from characterizing the person killed as the "victim" and the person who committed the justifiable homicide as the "offender," but this is done apparently to maintain consistency across all data bases used to record both felonious and justifiable killings by civilians and by peace officers. Although the supplementary homicide report coding guide (FBI 1990c) does not make clear that the police officer, for reporting purposes, is to be listed under the "offender" column (and described in terms of age, sex, and race/ethnicity), apparently the UCR program makes this clear to participating police agencies in other instructional materials.

2. What the Data Reveal About the Circumstances that Led Police to Shoot Civilians Intentionally and About the Prevalence of Accidental Shootings

a. Types of Intentional Shootings

Regardless of the typology used by different researchers, the published (and in the case of FBI analyses, the unpublished) literature makes clear that most shootings by police, regardless of the shooters' or victims' races, are reported to have been in self-defense or in defense of another person's life:

- 72 percent in New York City during the early 1970s (Fyfe 1978); and in 1990, 96 percent if one excludes from the tally of shots-fired incidents animal shootings, suicides, and accidental discharges (198 "self defense"/"defend another" incidents out of 207 shots-fired incidents). If one *includes* in the denominator accidental shots-fired incidents (60 during 1990), then the 198 incidents in which NYPD officers fired to defend themselves or others constitute 74 percent of the relevant 267 incidents (Cerar 1990: 8);

- 67 percent in Chicago in the 1970s (Geller and Karales 1981a, 1982) and 75 percent in 1991 (data collected by Geller for this book) (see Table E-58 and Figure E-8 in Appendix E);

- 73 percent in urban areas of Michigan and 65 percent in that state's less densely populated areas (Horvath 1987; Horvath and Donahue 1982);

- 52 percent of the justifiable homicides committed by American peace officers during the period 1980-89 (at least among those agencies voluntarily reporting the killing of felony suspects to the FBI's UCR program) (see Table E-18 in Appendix E of this volume); and

- of a sample of 223 slayings of civilians by police officers in New York State, 88 percent of the deaths were precipitated by the person killed assaulting or threatening to immediately assault either an officer or another civilian (NYSCCJ 1987, Vol. I).

However, even though *percentages* may be small, substantial *numbers* of shootings have occurred, by the officers' own accounts, in situations in which the victim did not present an imminent threat to anyone's life. Most of the available data come from pre-*Tennessee v. Garner* studies and, indeed, were part of the national pattern that motivated the Supreme Court to reach its conclusion in *Garner*. For instance, in Chicago from 1974 through 1978, 17 percent of all civilians shot by police were fleeing without offering any other resistance at the time they were fired upon (Geller and Karales 1981a, 1981b). Comparable 1970s data reveal rates of shooting nonviolent fleeing suspects of 13 percent in Los Angeles (Meyer 1980a), 39 percent in Boston (Boston Police Department 1974), and 27 percent in Philadelphia (Public Interest Law Center of Philadelphia 1975).

The FBI's national data on justifiable homicides by peace officers show relatively little change over time in the percentage of all such killings precipitated by the suspect attempting "flight from a crime." The annual percentages between 1980 and 1989 ran from a low of 3 percent in 1987 to a high of 10 percent in 1981. Following the low percentage in 1987, the 1988 and 1989 figures were both 5 percent. The 10-year overall averages reveal that 6 percent of all felony suspects slain by American police were attempting to flee at the time (see Table E-18 in Appendix E).

This finding of a fairly stable proportion of justifiable homicides by American police involving fleeing suspects over the entire decade of the 1980s may be surprising to some, given that in the middle of the decade (March 27, 1985) the Supreme Court's *Tennessee v. Garner* decision outlawed the shooting of fleeing suspects unlikely to be violent. Even though the FBI data on justifiable homicides by police are substantial national undercounts, there may be little justification to believe that those agencies that do report and the killings they

> *"[Two supervisors in a university security force] were called to the university's library to calm a disturbance. When they arrived, the man began firing a .25-caliber semi-automatic handgun at them. After warning bystanders away from the area, the two officers returned fire, wounded the suspect in the leg, and safely disarmed him" (FBI 1989c: 33).*

choose to report are skewed in a way that disproportionately undercounts any single type of justification for the killings. Hence, the data suggest that the *Tennessee v. Garner* ruling had little effect on the likelihood that American police would fatally shoot fleeing felony suspects. This is a proposition we hope to explore rigorously in subsequent research.

> *"What the...results [of officer performance in a computerized shoot/don't shoot simulation exercise] show is that officers are reluctant to resort to deadly force. Officers must learn when to shoot as well as when not to shoot. Instead of being a swashbuckling, trigger-happy group of gunslingers, participants kept scanning the scene for more decisive and irrefutable cues that they had no other choice except to fire their weapons" (Doerner 1991: 10).*

In its seven-city study during the 1970s, the Police Foundation found 43 percent of its sample of victims to have been unarmed when shot (Milton, et al. 1977). An unknown number of these persons may have appeared to be armed at the time officers fired their weapons. In a few of these incidents it is even possible that the suspects fired at by police *were* armed—but that their guns were removed from the scene by accomplices or bystanders before being recovered by police. At the same time, the phenomenon of "drop guns" and "throw knives" has been documented in some police departments during certain time periods. (These are weapons carried by an officer and used to frame a suspect for assaulting the officer with a deadly weapon.) Tobar (1992: A18) discusses a case in which a sheriff's deputy was convicted of murdering a suspect after evidence showed the deputy had planted a gun at the crime scene.

All these considerations need to be weighed in interpreting findings about the shooting of armed or unarmed opponents. One such study (Kobler 1975b) discovered that 25 percent of a national sample of persons shot by police (identified through news clippings) were unarmed. So, too, with Meyer's study (1980a), which found 25 percent of the persons fired at by LAPD officers to have been carrying neither a gun nor a knife when fired upon.

Shootings that involve drop guns and other fabricated evidence illustrate that the nature of violent police-civilian encounters sometimes is quite different than might be suggested by outward appearances and official reports. Similarly, occasionally police kill people in situations that have been aptly described in the police vernacular as "suicide by cop"—where a civilian bent on suicide accomplishes his or her objective by threatening an officer's life. While we have not seen police shooting classification systems that identify such incidents from among the group of intentional shootings in defense of an officer's or other persons life, we have little doubt that such cases are a small but identifiable segment of these incidents. Sometimes, these cases surface because heirs of the persons killed challenge the police competence in suicide prevention, as in a New Mexico case where the federal court of appeals, even though reversing the trial court's ruling on other grounds, agreed that the police agency had not adequately prepared its officers to deal with potential suicides:

> "In the early morning hours of December 20, 1986, Deputy Sheriff Martin noticed a car in a parking lot behind a building in Albuquerque, N.M. The sole occupant of the car was Griego. Martin parked in front of the car and saw Griego put her head down on the steering wheel. When Griego did not respond to the deputy's waving spotlight, Martin stepped out of the vehicle and rapped on the car window several times. Griego rolled the window down a few inches but refused to produce her driver's license, telling the deputy, 'I'm not doing anything.'
> "Deputy Sauser then arrived on the scene. Griego still refused to cooperate and tried to roll her window up again. Martin put a flashlight in the window frame to prevent Griego from doing so. Both deputies then saw Griego pick up a pistol. Sauser saw Griego load the weapon. A third deputy, Murphy, arrived. He too saw the gun and witnessed its loading.
> "All three deputies drew their weapons. Martin and Murphy took cover while Sauser moved near the car. Sauser ordered Griego to put down the gun. Griego responded by saying, 'Leave me alone. I want to kill myself.' She placed the gun in her mouth. The deputies became aware Griego had been drinking. Sauser asked Griego to step out of the car so he could talk to her about her problems. Griego put her car in gear and tried to drive away, but she was trapped by the deputies' cars.
> "Griego turned abruptly and, at one point, aimed her gun at Sauser. In response, Sauser fired his weapon at Griego and shot her. As she was pulled from the car, Griego was heard saying, 'I can't believe you shot me.' Griego subsequently died from the gunshot wounds.
> "Griego's estate sued the county, the sheriff, and Deputy Sauser for excessive force and related claims. A jury returned a verdict for the estate on her civil

rights and wrongful death claims, and awarded the estate $1.24 million in damages" (*National Bulletin on Police Misconduct* 1992:1, describing *Quezada v. County of Bernalillo*, 944 F.2d 710 [1991]).

At other times, the manipulation of police by people bent on suicide is discussed in the literature on techniques for averting shootings. For instance, Meyer (1991a: 15) reports that TASERs (discussed in Chapter 5 of this volume) have been used by officers to prevent people from committing suicide (see also *Law and Order* 1992a; Noesner and Dolan 1992: 2).

b. Accidental Firearms Discharges

The data from several studies also show relatively high levels of *accidental* gun discharges or accidental shootings of persons by police officers during different time periods: 9 percent in Chicago from 1974 through 1983 (Geller 1989) and 15 percent in 1991 (data collected by Geller); 27 percent in Boston in the early 1970s (Boston Police Department 1974); almost 13 percent in New York City during 1971-75 (Fyfe 1980b), 24 percent in 1987, and 23 percent in 1990 (Cerar 1987, 1990). Four percent of the deaths of civilians studied in New York *State* were the result of accidental discharges of officers' weapons (NYSCCJ 1987).

In Memphis, Tennessee, a site of special interest because it generated the landmark *Tennessee v. Garner* decision in 1985, *prior* to the *Garner* ruling there was a marked rise in shots-fired incidents reported to have been accidental: During the period 1969-74, 11 incidents involved accidental firings; during 1980-84, 42 incidents were reported as accidentals (Sparger and Giacopassi 1992: Table 3). In the first time period, accidentals accounted for 5 percent of all firearms discharge incidents, while in the second time period accidents represented 20 percent of the total. Moreover, considering accidental discharges as a function of the changing size of the police force over time in Memphis showed that the chances of accidental discharges (or the chances of having them accurately reported) had increased more than 400 percent from the first five-year period to the second (rate of 1.6 per 1,000 sworn personnel employed versus a rate of 7.0) (*ibid.*: 11). Following the *Garner* ruling (examining the period 1985-89), there was virtually no change in the number or rate per 1,000 officers at which Memphis police accidentally fired their weapons. But the percentage that accidentals represented of all shots-fired incidents rose to 25 percent (*ibid.*: Table 3).

The New York City Police Department's Police Academy Firearms and Tactics Section prepares unusually detailed annual data reports on the number and nature of officer-involved firearms incidents. Their characterizations of the circumstances in which NYPD sworn personnel accidentally discharged their weapons in 59 incidents during 1990 (Table 15) provide a good portrait of the myriad but nonetheless often predictable situations in which police guns are fired unintentionally in at least one big city. Besides these 62 accidentally fired rounds, NYPD officers reported accidentally firing some rounds during gunfights or during incidents in which officers also shot at adversaries intentionally. Those rounds are not tallied by the NYPD in its annual report of officer-involved shootings (Cerar 1990: 21).

In the Metro-Dade, Florida, Police Department from 1984 through 1990, 24 percent of all incidents in which police discharged their firearms other than for training purposes involved accidental police gun firings (64 out of 267 shots-fired incidents). Figure 56 shows the mix from year to year of these intentional and accidental gun discharge incidents and adds 1991 to the picture.

Table 15:
Reasons for Accidental Firearms Discharges by NYPD Officers, 1990

Reasons for Accidental Discharges	# Shots Fired Accidentally[1]
Perpetrator grabbing officer's weapon/hitting officer's gun hand	16
Struggling with perpetrator	7
Falling, running, slipping with gun in hand	6
Hitting perpetrator over head with gun	1
Getting bumped, pushed, or hit	6
Grabbing a gun that's falling	3
Unloading a weapon	2
Dryfiring	3
Lowering hammer on live round	1
Cleaning gun	1
Removing gun from holster or holstering gun	3
Removing gun from holster while sitting in chair	1
Gun unholstered in pants pocket	1
Shoving gun in waist area of pants	1
Dropping gun from pants pocket or belt	2
Putting gun on locker shelf	1
Yanking gun from under RMP [radio motor patrol] seat	1
Being dragged by perpetrator's vehicle	1
Exiting RMP [radio motor patrol]	2
Putting car in gear with gun in hand	1
Putting gun in oven for safekeeping—then turning oven on[2]	1
Startled	1
TOTAL	62

[1] *In 2 of the 59 reported incidents of accidental firearms discharges, officers reported discharging 2 shots; hence the total number of shots fired accidentally in 1990 was 62.*
[2] *Does this seem like a once-in-a-blue-moon experience? The very next year, "in one incident PO put gun in oven for safekeeping—forgot about gun—turned oven on—gun discharged six shots" (Cerar 1991: 21). Source: Cerar (1990: 21).*

Figure 56 shows a relatively steady, slight downward trend from 1984 to 1991 in the number of incidents in which officers accidentally discharged their weapons in the Metro-

Dade Police Department, despite the inevitable year-to-year fluctuations. The decrease in accidentals over the six-year period from 1984 through 1990 was 74 percent (from 19 incidents in 1984 to just 5 in 1990).

In considering the Metro-Dade police pattern of intentional and accidental shots-fired incidents, the reader should consider that among the myriad conditions with which the Metro-Dade police have had to contend during these years has been the massive drug trafficking that afflicted much of south Florida. In the face of the gratuitous violence that often accompanies such narcotics trading, any agencies in this region that, like Metro-Dade, have been able to keep police-involved shootings from skyrocketing may take pride in their ability to maintain some semblance of sanity in a frightening environment. As noted earlier, the Metro-Dade Police Department has one of the lowest shooting rates of any agency from which we obtained data (see Figure 28 and Tables 4 and 5 in the text).

"[A] police firearms instructor [was] undergoing transition training [from the revolver] to the [semi-]automatic. The instructor, about to complete the last day of certification, rose early that morning to practice his technique. Standing in front of the bedroom mirror he unleaded the magazine, forgetting that a round was in the chamber. Practicing his stance and trigger pull, the round in the chamber discharged, breaking the mirror, passing through the wall and entering the bathroom where his wife was taking a shower. The bullet struck the officer's wife in the back, inflicting a serious injury" (McCauley and Edwards 1990: 54).

"Two on-duty officers were approached by a woman, who told them of a robbery and beating at a nearby elevated train station. The officers approached the station, drew their guns, and encountered two suspects running down the stairs, being pursued and struck by the victim of the robbery. One of the officers stopped the suspects while the other stopped the robbery victim. The second officer attempted to hold the robbery victim with his left hand, while trying to holster his revolver with his right hand. The robbery victim, attempting to continue striking the suspects, struck the second officer's wrist, which caused his revolver to discharge, hitting a bystander" (Geller and Karales 1981a: 110-111).

Philadelphia data (Figure 57) show the mix of intentional and accidental firearms discharge incidents from 1984 through 1991. During the period 1984 through 1990, Philadelphia officers discharged their weapons accidentally in 23 percent of all incidents in which they fired other than for training purposes (121 accidentals out of 528 shots-fired incidents). In 1991 only 17 percent of the shots-fired incidents in Philadelphia were accidental (see Table E-12 in Appendix E). Although the overall percentage of accidentals is nearly identical to that shown for the Metro-Dade Department during the years 1984-90, in Metro-Dade as of 1990 accidentals seemed to be diminishing as a proportion of all firearms discharges. In Philadelphia, over this time period accidentals increased as a proportion of the total (from 9 percent in 1984 to 27 percent in 1989 to 31 percent in 1990). In Metro-Dade accidental discharges were 38 percent of the shots-fired incidents in 1984, 31 percent in 1989, and 13 percent in 1990.

Conversations with the sergeant who prepared Philadelphia's shooting tallies suggested that one possible explanation for the increased proportion of accidentals in Philadelphia in 1990 might be the Department's adoption that year of semi-automatic weapons. Figure 57 shows that not only accidentals but intentional shots-fired incidents in Philadelphia increased sharply from 1989 to 1990. And in 1991, the Department did better at stemming accidental discharges than at curtailing intentionals. The drop from 38 accidentals in 1990 to 17 in 1991 represents a 55 percent decrease, whereas the drop from 84 intentionals in 1990 to 82 in 1991 amounts to a reduction of just 2 percent (see Table E-12).

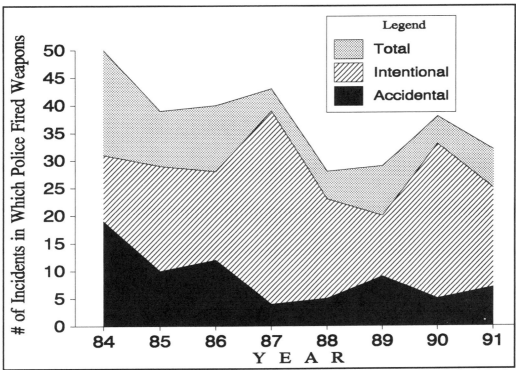

Figure 56: **Intentional Versus Accidental Discharges in Shots-Fired Incidents Involving Metro-Dade Police, 1984-91**
Source: Metro-Dade Police Department.

Conversations with former Metro-Dade Police Department Deputy Director Eduardo Gonzalez (since appointed chief in Tampa) indicated that his agency had an unsatisfactory experience in the earlier years shown in Figure 56 with a particular brand of semi-automatic weapon. The agency believes the vendor misrepresented it as having a heavy trigger pull on the first shot, when, in fact, it had a light trigger pull on every shot. Gonzalez reports that after the problem was identified and addressed by Metro-Dade officials, the Department had a much better record at controlling unintended firearms discharges (Gonzalez 1991).

"In 1986, [New York City's] Harlem Hospital treated 12 children 17 years old or younger for gunshot wounds. In 1991, that number was 52. Lincoln Hospital in the South Bronx treated 13 children for gunshot wounds in 1986, compared with 69 last year. Of all the children who die of an injury north of 110th Street in Manhattan, one-third are shot to death..." (Lee 1992).

Some other agencies believe the safest type of semi-automatic weapon for use by police is one that has a heavy trigger pull on *every* shot fired (a trigger pull of approximately eight pounds, roughly comparable to the pressure required to fire standard police service revolvers—see Spielman 1992, 1992a). Additional discussion of the issues raised by police department adoption of semi-automatic pistols appears near the end of Chapter 5.

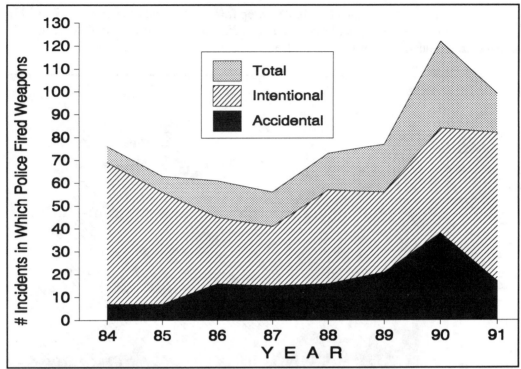

Figure 57: Intentional Versus Accidental Discharges in Shots-Fired Incidents Involving Philadelphia Police, 1984-91 *Source: Philadelphia Police Dept.*

A relatively steady level of accidental firearms discharges over 20 years emerges from Kansas City, Missouri, data, depicted in Figure 58. Despite annual fluctuations, the number of shots-fired incidents in which officers' weapons were discharged unintentionally did not vary by more than five incidents from any one year to the next.

Figure 58 serves as a reminder of the importance of not looking only at total shootings or total shots-fired incidents, for we see that in Kansas City the total number of shots-fired incidents remained almost the same from 1989 to 1990 (a shift from 23 to 25), yet the 1990 result was achieved with a different mix of intentional and accidental incidents than occurred the previous year. One question administrators might want to pursue is whether any changes in officer reporting accuracy were accomplished in 1990 (i.e., whether officers more accurately described off-target shots as intentional shots than as accidental gun discharges).

"Accidental discharges come from poor training and poor disciplinary decisions. An officer can't control where the accidentally fired bullet goes, so discipline should not be determined based on the outcome—whether the bullet hits a squad car and costs $50 in 'Bondo' or hits Mother Teresa. In my view, an officer should be retrained for a first accidental shooting and fired for a second one" (McCarthy 1992).

Although many aspects of officer-involved shootings are subject to definitional variations from department to department and subject to counting error, this is perhaps more true when dealing with accidental firearm discharges. It is the rare department that will even carefully explain how accidental discharges are counted. For instance, the NYPD takes care,

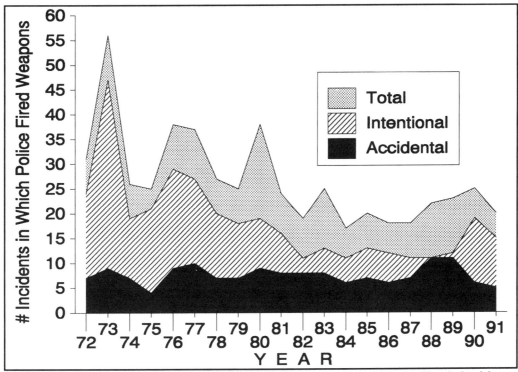

Figure 58: Intentional Versus Accidental Discharges in Shots-Fired Incidents Involving Kansas City (MO) Police, 1972-91
Source: Kansas City Police Dept.

in its annual compilation of reasons for officers' weapon discharges, to indicate that if an accidental discharge occurs during a gunfight or another incident in which the officer fired an additional round or rounds *intentionally*, the incident will *not* be tabulated as an accidental discharge (Cerar 1990: 21).

Another question to be considered by Kansas City officials, assuming the accuracy of officer reporting in both 1989 and 1990 as depicted in Figure 58, is whether any training, equipment, procedural, or policy steps were taken between the two years that helped produce a reduction in accidental firings in 1990 even as intentional incidents increased in number.

Finally, Figure 58 serves as a reminder of another fundamental point. Although it is important for agencies and others to keep track of changes over time in the *number* of police-involved shootings, often a change in

> *An off-duty officer was in his kitchen cleaning his gun with his wife present. When the officer's two children entered the room, the officer gathered up the cleaning implements and reloaded the weapon. As he stood up to leave the room, the weapon began to slip from his hand, reportedly because of oil on the gun's frame. The officer grabbed for the weapon, and it discharged, striking his daughter in the leg (Geller and Karales 1981a:111).*

number alone will not help an outsider predict whether the affected agency and its community experienced tensions surrounding officer-involved shootings. Although Kansas City had a very similar number of shots-fired incidents in 1989 and 1990 (the number increased from 23 to 25), several of the 1990 shootings provoked enormously disruptive controversy. Thus, whenever possible—in operational research, in establishing a reporting system for police-civilian encounters, etc.—it is important to capture information on situational details, not just on the *number* of shootings of or by police.

The experience of the Santa Ana, California, Police Department during the 1980s with accidental firearms discharges is notable compared with data available for other cities, in that there were several years when the number of accidental firearms discharges by officers exceeded the number of intentional firings. The pattern of accidental and intentional shootings for

> *"'A bullet don't have no eyes'—[Chicago Public Housing Authority] resident Johnnie Jones on innocent people getting killed at the [Cabrini-Green] development"* (Chicago Sun-Times *1991*).

Santa Ana is depicted in Figure 59. Overall, combining the years 1981 through 1990, Santa Ana officers discharged their weapons other than for training purposes in 128 incidents, 47 (37 percent) of which involved accidental firings. Of these 47 incidents, suspects were struck in 2 (1 of which was a fatality) and officers were struck in 5 (Santa Ana Police Department 1991).

As Figure 59 shows, the annual number of shots-fired incidents in Santa Ana is not large, and one must be especially careful in suggesting trends on the basis of fluctuations involving relatively small numbers. Nevertheless, one can readily see that since 1984 the Santa Ana police have been gradually bringing the number of accidental firearms discharges under better control while, since 1986, the number of intentional firearms discharges by Department personnel has risen steeply and steadily. Whereas accidentals were 33 percent of all shots-fired incidents in 1981, they were 11 percent of all incidents in 1990. Yet the number of accidentals on which these percentages are calculated were nearly identical (three incidents in 1981, two in 1990. Hence, the dramatic shift in the proportion of incidents involving accidental firings between the two end points on Figure 59 occurs not because of a major change in the number of accidentals but because of growth in the number of intentional shooting incidents.

3. Exploring Civilian Race and Other Possible Explanatory Factors

Some research on the characteristics of officer-involved shootings has examined whether minorities and whites are shot by police in different circumstances. This line of inquiry starts from the assumption that analysis of the *reasons* why persons of different races are shot is more informative than simply tallying numbers without regard to justifications for officer decisions (see Fyfe 1981c; Geller and Karales 1981a, 1981b; Meyer 1980a; Milton, et al. 1977; Blumberg 1986). With a few exceptions (e.g., Fyfe 1982, using data from Memphis; cf. *Crime Control Digest* 1992d), most studies have failed to find evidence that police officers *systematically* discriminate against minorities in their decisions to use deadly force.

Some commentators argue that the research methodologies used thus far to explore questions of racial bias in police-involved shootings make it very difficult to prove—or disprove—that shooting discretion is influenced by bigotry. For instance, Sherman (1980a: 97) argues:

> "[T]he existence of racial discrimination in police homicides can be neither proved nor disproved with the available evidence. Resolution of the issue would require data on the number of blacks and whites who committed acts that made

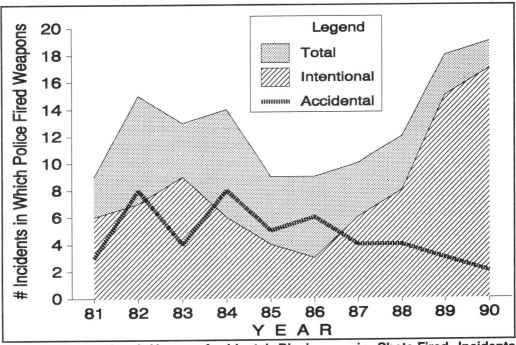

Figure 59: Intentional Versus Accidental Discharges in Shots-Fired Incidents Involving Santa Ana Police, 1981-90 *Source: Santa Ana Police Dept. (1991).*

them legally vulnerable to police homicide: assaulting or threatening to assault police or others, fleeing from arrest for felonies, participating in a riot, or engaging in other specifically covered behavior. Short of a mammoth systematic observation study, costing millions of dollars, there is no reliable way to obtain such data. A sample of the narrative accounts found in arrest reports, somewhat less expensive, would be the next best measure of legal vulnerability of whites and blacks, but no such study has yet been done."

British scholar Reiner (1992), focusing broadly on the exercise of police powers—for instance, decisions to arrest versus to divert juveniles from the criminal justice system—and not specifically on use of deadly force decisions, was even more pessimistic than Sherman: "[E]stablishing beyond doubt that a 'pure' element of discrimination exists, which is not based on legally relevant factors, is methodologically impossible" (*ibid.*: 479). It is true, he concedes, that some studies in the United Kingdom, have shown that "certain social characteristics [including race] are associated with a greater likelihood of being at the receiving end of police powers" (*ibid.*: 478). But "[t]he problem in taking this finding as unequivocal evidence of discrimination is that the 'legally relevant' variables [which would justify different treatment of different persons] are themselves connected to race." Reiner illustrates: "The likelihood of future offending...is taken as indicated by factors such as single-parent families, unemployed fathers, or being a latchkey child, all of which are themselves correlated with ethnic group" (*ibid.*: 479).

Reiner argues that the "artificiality of trying to pursue an element of 'pure' discrimination" lies in the strong correlation between being at the "bottom of the socio-economic hierarchy" and being likely to commit crimes and suffer "police prejudice and discrimination." The "structural location" of people of color disproportionately at the bottom of society's ladder, Reiner concludes, "is the explanation of a vicious cycle of differential pressures leading to offending and differential risk of apprehension, each confirming the other." In other words, "[t]he police are reproducers rather than creators of social injustice, though their prejudices may amplify it" (*ibid.*).

The daunting challenge of using social science techniques to convincingly support or refute charges of systematic police racism notwithstanding, American researchers have devoted considerable effort over the past several decades to exploring patterns of police-involved shootings and the possible influence of racial bias in shaping those patterns. Geller (1985a) called for research on averted shootings as a way of both identifying and "modeling" successful police techniques and exploring differences between police decisions to shoot and decisions to refrain

"While blacks make up only 12 percent of the general population, nearly half the nation's prisoners are black. While the level of drug abuse among blacks is about the same as whites, more than 40 percent of those arrested on drug charges are black, according to a 1990 USA Today study" (Meddis 1992).

"About 80% of [drug] users are white, experts say, but the majority of those arrested are black. Those on the front lines of enforcement wonder whether its strategy has gone awry" (Harris 1990: A1).

"The typical cocaine user is white, male, a high school graduate employed full time and living in a small metropolitan area or suburb." —Drug czar William J. Bennett (quoted in Harris 1990: A1).

when use of lethal force would have been arguably justifiable. Such analysis could provide insight concerning the circumstances under which suspects of different races and ethnicities are shot at by police. Blumberg (1986: 238) has also urged that research to appraise possible racism in police lethal force decisions focus on "whether police are more *likely* to shoot blacks than whites under the same circumstances" (emphasis added).

"For many blacks, particularly the young, the word justice is pronounced 'just us': More likely than whites to be arrested for drugs, or pulled over by a patrol car, or frisked on the street, or denied bail, or thrown into prison. More likely, in short, to be targets" (Meddis 1992).

To explore the *likelihood* of such occurrences, researchers need to know, as Sherman (1980a) noted, "the number of blacks and whites who committed acts that made them legally vulnerable" to being shot (see also Alpert and Fridell 1992: 60). The reasoning behind this recommendation, as we shall discuss again briefly later in this chapter, is that police decisions to engage in confrontations (with or without arrest) with persons of different races may be driven to

some extent by bigotry. As noted by Alpert and Fridell (1992: 49), this view is propounded by Sutherland and Cressey (1970), Forslund (1972), Takagi (1974), and Hinds (1979), based partly on evidence of discriminatory arrest practices or patterns of biased responses to citizen calls for service adduced in such studies as Goldman (1963), Piliavin and Briar (1964), Thornberry (1973), Ferdinand and Luchterhand (1970), and Pope (1979); (also see Smith, et. al. 1984; Gordon 1983; Scraton 1985: chap. 5; Stevens and Willis 1979; Lea and Young 1984: chap. 4; Lea 1986; Reiner 1985: 124-35; Benyon 1986; and Waddington 1983, 1984).[18]

---

[18] Compare the analysis by LaFree, et al. (1992: 157), suggesting the surprising conclusion that indicators of "access to opportunity"—such as employment, income, education, and family stability—during the post-war period in America (1957-88) "have different—usually *opposite*—effects

Powell (1990: 2), on the basis of officers' responses to hypothetical situations involving "middle-level offenses"—traffic, domestic problems, public intoxication, and disorderly conduct—concluded that officers will be inclined to arrest blacks but give a pass to (not arrest) whites in similar crime situations. This finding was consistent with the results of a similar study in a different region of the country a decade earlier (Powell 1981). "The data indicated," Powell wrote, "that the police of the larger urban areas demonstrated the greatest disparity in use of personal discretion throughout the study [i.e., varied the most across departments]." And, he found, police in the larger jurisdictions "were consistently more punitive toward black offenders than whites." As of his 1990 article, Powell hoped to but had not yet examined whether the "racial mix of the cities surveyed and the racial mix of each individual police agency...might have an effect on the findings" (*ibid.*: 5).

Discrimination related to arrest can take at least two forms: a biased decision to make the arrest and the use of harsher arrest tactics than are required based on the arrestee's race, ethnicity, or other characteristics irrelevant to the arrest process. The Christopher Commission addressed concerns about discriminatory arrest tactics:

---

on black and white crime rates during the period" (emphasis added). In other words, these researchers suggest that as whites *advance* in society, crime committed by whites *decreases*. Advancement is measured in terms of "economic well-being, educational attainment, and family stability"; crime is measured using reported arrests for murder, robbery, and burglary (*ibid.*: 159). But as blacks in America make *progress* on these same three socioeconomic dimensions, the number of blacks arrested for serious crimes in the nation *increases*.

The authors acknowledge that they may not be measuring all that needs to be measured or conceptualizing the legacies of American racism in subtle enough terms. For instance, they admit not attempting to appraise the effects of the "breakdown of vertical integration in black communities"—that is, "a growing gap between upper and lower status jobs" within the "black labor force" (*ibid.*: 178). This growing gulf between black "haves" and "have nots" has been portrayed with insight and eloquence by William Julius Wilson (1987) in his landmark study, *The Truly Disadvantaged: The Inner City, the Underclass and Public Policy*. LaFree, et al. (1992: 176) suggest that the effect of growing income and status disparity *among* African Americans may be less crime committed by blacks in the middle and upper classes but more crime committed by "an increasingly polarized black underclass." They argue, further, that as Americans generally have attained higher levels of education since World War II, we as a society have begun assigning lower social status (worth as human beings) than we assigned in earlier decades to persons with little formal education. This might explain the oddity that, as some blacks have risen dramatically in educational accomplishment, those left behind increasingly come to understand that society sees them as second-class citizens.

Moreover, suppose that, as some scholars believe, large disparities in black and white arrest rates are partially the *product* of systematic racism rather than *disproof* of such ugliness (cf. Hindelang 1978). If that were true, then one might hypothesize that it is precisely during a time when at least some black people are making highly visible progress up the ladder toward the American dream (e.g., African-American corporate executives, professionals, government officials, police officers, and managers) that there would be increased pressure to pull other blacks off the ladder and to prevent the most destitute from even getting a foot up on the first rung. Providing minorities with criminal arrest records (or elongating these records) would be a good way of accomplishing such an objective. Pressure of this sort could be generated by people who, out of fear, ignorance, or overt racism, perceive that the best way of preserving their own slice of the American pie is to ensure that others don't get any.

Given the preliminary nature of the line of inquiry LaFree and his colleagues have pursued, it would be irresponsible to rely on their findings at this stage as a basis for altering crime control policy and social safety net structures in the United States. A great deal more study, discussion, and debate concerning their provocative and counterintuitive conclusions is necessary before using them to erode whatever national will and wallet there may be for investing in racial and economic justice as a cornerstone of the quest for ordered liberty.

"Within the minority communities of Los Angeles, there is a widely-held view that police misconduct is commonplace. The King beating refocused public attention on long-standing complaints by African-Americans, Latinos and Asians that LAPD officers frequently treat minorities differently from whites, more often using disrespectful and abusive language, employing unnecessarily intrusive practices such as the 'prone-out'[19] and engaging in use of excessive force when dealing with minorities" (Independent Commission on the Los Angeles Police Dept. 1991: 70; Muwakkil 1992 notes the "crime" of "driving while black").

"There is no copious evidence [in the United Kingdom] that certain social characteristics are associated with a greater likelihood of being at the receiving end of police powers. Being young, male, Afro-Caribbean and/or unemployed or in low paid irregular work are all associated with a greater probability of being stopped and searched, arrested, and charged by the police.... The evidence on policing of women is more fragmentary, but what there is suggests that the police operate with a sharply bifurcated, Madonna/Whore sexual imagery. Usually women as potential suspects will benefit from 'chivalry' if they fit the first image, but if not they are likely to be treated with a heavier hand.... * * *

"What has been hotly debated during the 1980s is the extent to which police differentiation is explicable and justifiable by legally relevant differences between racial groups..., or due to police racism..., or an interaction between the two" (Reiner 1992).

The Christopher Commission also offered striking documentation of the disrespectful language the police in many locales use among themselves and, very likely, with members of the public when referring to persons of color. In its official policy statement, the LAPD's stance on racially offensive communications was clear and exemplary:

"This Memorandum reaffirms the Department policy concerning racially or ethnically oriented remarks, slurs, epithets, terminology, or language of a derogatory nature. These remarks are an inappropriate form of communication which becomes a destructive wedge in relationships with peers and members of the community. The deliberate or casual use of racially or ethnically derogatory language by Department employees is *misconduct* and will not be tolerated under *any* circumstances" (Memorandum No. 1, dated April 24, 1987, "Unacceptable Remarks of a Racial Nature," quoted in Independent Commission on the Los Angeles Police Department 1991: 73; emphasis in original).

But *unofficial* departmental policy, reflected in widespread tolerance by peers and supervisors of electronically recorded and easily monitored communications between officers, differed dramatically. Among the slurs typed by officers to one another using the computer keyboards in their squad cars are the following, which the Christopher Commission observed were "often made in the context of beatings or pursuits" (all spelling errors are the officers'):

---

[19] Officers require a person being arrested or questioned in the field to lie face down on the ground, a tactic that many cities have found especially angers people wearing nice clothing. Sometimes this tactic is required for the safety of officers and others; but when it seems to be employed for harassment, criticism seems justified. For further description and discussion of the "prone-out," see Independent Commission on the Los Angeles Police Department (1991: 75-76).

- "Well...I'm back over here in the projects, pissing off the natives"

  "I would love to drive down Slauson with a flame thrower...we would have a barbecue."

- "Sounds like monkey slapping time."

> *"In proportion to their population, nonwhites are still arrested for nearly all crimes at a much higher rate than are whites. But between 1965 and 1989, for all violent crimes, the arrest rate soared 197 percent for whites and 67 percent for nonwhites"* (Witkin, et al. 1990: 39).

- "Oh always dear...what's happening...we're huntin wabbits"

  "Actually, muslim wabbits"

  "Just over here on this arson/homicide...be careful one of those rabbits don't bite you"

  "Yeah I know.... Huntin wabbits is dangerous."

- "A fem named [C]... I will be careful...we are out to get 211 susp that have been hitting almost twice a night. 2 m/blks...are you busy..."

  "I was for awhile. But now I am going to slooow it down. If you encounter these negroes shoot first and ask questions later."

- "Wees be reedy n about 5"

  "Wees also bees hungry"

- "Don't be flirting with all ur cholo girlfriends"

- "Okay people...pls...don't transfer me any orientals.... I had two already"

> *"It is not the sheer number of cases of killings by police which generates charges of brutality, but rather the circumstances surrounding a handful of cases which symbolize, to numerous minority group members, police attitudes and behavior"* (Mandel [National Council of La Raza] 1981: 45).

- "Just like the word cholo can't be said over the air, I don't make rules"

- "Just clear its buxsy [busy] out hear this hole is picking up. I almost got me a Mexican last nite but he dropped the dam gun to quick, lots of wit"

- "Lt says learn Spanish bone head... Sgt. [A] says tell them to go back to Mexico"

- "Don't cry Buckweat, or is it Willie Lunch Meat" (Independent Commission on the Los Angeles Police Department 1991: 72-73).

The Christopher Commission had little doubt that the department, by its inaction in the face of such communications on officers' mobile digital terminals, implicitly tolerated them, establishing a tone conducive to discriminatory *conduct* as well as conversation. "The officers typing the MDT messages," the commission said,

> "apparently had little concern that they would be disciplined or otherwise sanctioned for making those remarks. Other officers took no steps to prevent this behavior; supervisors made little effort to discipline it or to review the messages. In fact, many of the offensive MDT comments were made from sergeants' field supervisory units" (*ibid.*: 73).

Although we believe it would be unwise to assume that people who talk like racists necessarily *act* like racists,[20] particularly in making such extreme decisions as whether to *kill* someone, there can be little doubt, in our view, that a context of racist remarks lends credibility to those who wish to find discriminatory motivations in otherwise proper conduct. Ideally, police who harbor racist feelings would seek or be offered assistance in trying constructively to overcome them. At the very least, biased cops should have the common sense to avoid uttering slurs in the course of their work. An officer who shoots a suspect *justifiably* but is overheard spewing racist invective before or afterward may well expect to be fired for what triers of fact later interpret as a racially motivated use of deadly force.

To acknowledge that some police hold racist attitudes—distinguishing them little, unfortunately, from the public at large—is not, however, the same as assembling convincing evidence that groups of officers or even entire departments are characterized by *patterns* of racially discriminatory shootings. Such evidence has rarely been adduced by studies of police-civilian violence. Partly, as noted earlier, this is because key *contextual* data are not obtainable. For instance, despite the desirability of data profiling the need for police to intervene in the activities of persons of different races or ethnicities, Blumberg (1986) reported that virtually all research has necessarily employed less satisfactory approaches to studying racial bias questions. Most studies either conduct situational analysis (to portray the danger posed by persons of different races/ethnicities when they were shot by police) or contrast the percentages of minorities shot with the percentages of minorities officially considered to participate in criminal activity (usually represented with arrest data).

Alpert and Fridell (1992: 57-58), too, acknowledge the methodological deficiency of most of the research. And they report on one data set that has been of some use for analysis of "the proportion of incidents (with various characteristics) involving black or white suspects that resulted in a shooting" (*ibid.*: 60).[21] The data were originally collected and analyzed by Binder, et al. (1982). Then Fridell and Binder (1988, 1989) conducted secondary analysis of the data, that comprise a sample of "averted shootings" and all known "purposeful shootings" in four cities. The cities studied were Birmingham, Alabama; Miami, Florida; Newark, New Jersey; and Oakland, California. The "shoot/nonshoot" incidents examined occurred between

---

[20] For discussion of the proposition that "cop humor" is a healthy release valve for officers who must deal constantly with the sordid side of life, see Baum (1991).

[21] Garner and Clemmer (1986) also employed data to attempt to estimate the *likelihood* of police-involved shootings occurring. But they focused on the relative dangers of police being assaulted, injured, or killed in different types of circumstances (domestics, nondomestics, robberies, traffic stops, etc.), rather than on questions of racial equity or discrimination in police shootings. We will return to this study later in this chapter. Bayley and Garofalo (1989), at the behest of the New York State Commission on Criminal Justice and the Use of Force, and Fyfe (1988c, 1989a), on behalf of the Police Foundation, conducted observational studies designed to identify potentially violent encounters in Dade County, Florida, and New York City, respectively.

January 1977 and June 1980.

But even in the original and secondary studies of this data set, methodological considerations precluded appraisal of patterns in each individual city, so instead the researchers combined the data for all four cities and drew conclusions based on the aggregate numbers. After comparing situational factors in shootings and in encounters during which shootings could have occurred justifiably, Fridell and Binder concluded that "racial bias" was not demonstrated by the evidence (see also Alpert and Fridell 1992: 61-62).

Among the factors that Binder, et al. (1982) considered as bearing on shooting decisions were the age of the person shot at by police, whether this person was fleeing or attacking the police when fired upon, and whether the person shot at by officers was armed. It is possible that combining the shooting and averted shooting data for the four cities conceals differing patterns of racial bias or equity within each of the several cities (Fridell and Binder 1989: 9; Alpert and Fridell 1992: 51, 62). Despite the weaknesses of the studies based on this data set, however, Lorie Fridell and her colleagues deserve credit for attempting the very challenging inquiry called for by Sherman (1980a), Geller (1985a), Blumberg (1986) and others.

> *"In a University of Alabama study...white students were asked to administer mild shocks to black students or white students who answered a series of questions, with a shock for each incorrect answer. But before the actual test, all of the students had a pleasant, innocent conversation.*
>
> *"When the white students asked the questions after the friendly talks, there was a tendency to administer the lesser shock to black students than to white students who had answered incorrectly. That result indicated a lack of discrimination or intent to harm on the part of the white students administering the shocks, [Colgate University Professor Jack] Dovidio said.*
>
> *"In a second group, black and white students had hostile conversations, rude and full of insults, before the test was administered. The test results were different this time, and troubling. 'In that case, not only did they shock the person, but they were particularly likely to (give a stronger shock to) the black person who had been rude,' Dovidio said.*
>
> *"'What that shows is that under normal constraints, there isn't much negative response against blacks, but if you give a person an excuse to behave negatively, he will be more discriminatory toward blacks than toward whites'" (Madigan 1992).*

Thus, the state of the art is such that the vast majority of existing studies on race and police shooting discretion have been grounded on less than desirable research data and analytic techniques—a predicament largely dictated by the expense of and, in some instances, by political opposition to, conducting more appropriate studies. In our view, the reader should be aware of the available research on police shooting and race, imperfect as it is, because it contains some insights of importance for police practitioners. And because it has been and will continue to be widely quoted by police, researchers, journalists, and advocates. The tragic riot in Los Angeles in 1992, sparked partly by fury over the unjust acquittal of Rodney King's police assailants and partly by criminal opportunism masquerading as political dissent, substantially heightens the likelihood that all available evidence on race and the American criminal justice system will be sought out and disseminated, often with less critical analysis and with more partisan motives than the public interest requires.

In general, the existing research on deadly force seems to indicate that police officers typically respond more to race-neutral indicators of danger (such as whether the opponent is armed, has used or threatened to use a weapon, the type of crime reportedly committed, etc.) than to such inappropriate considerations as the opponent's race.[22]

> *"If combined with racial and ethnic bias, [a department's] active style of policing creates a potentially grave problem. * * * [The] 'war on crime'…in some cases seems to become an attack on [minority] communities at large. The communities, and all within them, become painted with the brush of latent criminality"* (Independent Commission on the Los Angeles Police Department 1991: 74).

In a study of Shelby County, Tennessee, sheriff's deputies' responses to written scenarios, Dwyer, et al. (1990: 300) concluded that the deputies decisions to shoot were rooted in four factors: the suspect's possession of a weapon, perceived intention to do harm, commission of a felony, and action in leaving a building. The researchers concluded that "static surface properties of the suspect, such as race, do not provide a viable foundation for guiding their decisions to shoot." In other words, the races of the suspect in the vignettes presented to the deputies were not correlated with the deputies' decisions to shoot. Hayden (1981) also found that officers presented with scenarios determined whether to shoot based on the behaviors and intentions of their hypothetical adversaries rather than on their heritage. The respondents in the Dwyer, et al. study were asked to explain briefly in their own words what factors they would weigh in each of 60 scenarios when deciding whether to draw, aim, and/or shoot their firearms. Collectively, the deputies cited the following considerations, from which the four cited above emerged (after multiple regression analysis) as the four best predictors of the most serious decision—the decision to shoot:

"■ *Attributes of Participants*: sex of suspect; suspect is nonwhite; suspect is a minor; suspect is out of control of faculties; partner is present; female partner; partner is a rookie.

■ *Attributes of Setting*: daylight; public versus private location; rainy weather; distance of officer to suspect; officer has cover; officer has clear shot at suspect.

■ *Actions, Intentions, and Resources of Suspect*: suspect is uncooperative; suspect has bad attitude; suspect has weapon; suspect is shooting; suspect is exiting building; suspect is committing felony/serious crime; suspect's weapon is pointed at officer; suspect intends to harm; suspect has superior firepower; officer is outnumbered.

■ *Other*: there are alternatives other than using a gun; officer is threatened; citizen is threatened; partner is threatened; suspects are visible" (Dwyer, et al. 1990: 298).

Such classroom tests of officer deadly force decision making may have considerable

---

[22] See, for example, data and analysis in Fyfe 1981a; Geller and Karales 1981a, 1981b; Brown 1984; Blumberg 1981, 1983, 1986; Binder, et al. 1982; Fridell and Binder 1989; Alpert and Fridell 1992: 51, 59-62; Dwyer, et al. (1990); and New York State Commission on Criminal Justice 1987.

value to policymakers and especially trainers. Still, they are no substitute for examinations of actual shooting decisions. Some of the most important research on actual shootings and race issues has been conducted by former NYPD lieutenant and scholar James Fyfe. Fyfe's early New York City research (1981a) found that "blacks make up a disproportionate share of shooting opponents reportedly armed with guns and a disproportionate share of those reportedly engaged in robberies when police intervened." During the period 1971-75, he found that overall 30 percent of the civilians shot at by police were *not* armed with either a knife or a gun. While 26 percent of the black and 25 percent of the Hispanic suspects fired at were unarmed, *51 percent* of the white victims of police shootings were not armed (1981a: 102). Or, as Alpert and Fridell (1992: 49-50) put it, "a greater proportion of black than white opponents in the New York City shooting incidents [Fyfe] studied were armed. Sixty-one percent of the black opponents in deadly force incidents carried firearms compared to 36 percent of the whites." If Fyfe's data are taken at face value, NYPD officers may have had less justification for shooting at white culprits than at minorities.

If one does *not* take the data at face value, however, one might postulate that, given the impact of the civil rights movement of the late 1960s and early 1970s, police in New York City generally sought more substantial justifications, sometimes exaggerated or fabricated, for shooting at minorities than at Caucasians. The same possibilities exist in Chicago, where Geller (1989) found that, between 1974 and 1978, 39 percent of the white shooting victims, 57 percent of the black victims, and 61 percent of the Hispanic victims struck by police bullets were fired at after reportedly using or threatening to use a gun against the officer or another innocent person (see also Geller and Karales 1981a). The Chicago data, as well as data for the Los Angeles Police Department, are reported for various categories of "precipitating conduct" in Table 16 and are depicted graphically in Figures 60 (Chicago) and 61 (Los Angeles).

In Figures 60 and 61, the types of precipitating conduct shown track those presented in Table 16. Thus, the types are as follows:

Type A = Gun use/threat by civilian
Type B = Other deadly weapon or physical force use/threat
Type C = Other deadly weapon possessed without threat
Type D = Flight without other resistance
Type E = Other reasons for shooting intentionally
Type F = Accidental
Type G = Mistaken Identity
Type H = Stray Bullet

Not all types were represented for both Chicago and Los Angeles in the available data. Thus, in comparing Figures 60 and 61 the reader will observe that the only shooting types that both figures have in common are A, B, D, and F.[23]

---

[23] As noted in connection with the table containing the Chicago and Los Angeles precipitating conduct data, the "not ascertained" category for Los Angeles results from methods used to extrapolate data from the source study (Meyer 1980a: 46, 48). The typology used by Meyer had the following categories of situational characteristics: "using weapon, threatening use of weapon, displaying weapon, assaulting officer or civilian, appearing to reach for weapon, disobeying command to halt, other precipitating action." While there are advantages to Meyer's typology, one disadvantage is that it does not discriminate among the types of weapons the opponent displayed, threatened to use, or used against

One pattern that emerges from visual inspection of Figures 60 and 61 is that in Los Angeles whites and Hispanics are shot at in almost identical numbers in each type of incident. In Chicago, by contrast, there are relatively sizable differences between the numbers of whites and Hispanics shot in several types of incidents (Types B, D, F, and H). In both Chicago and Los Angeles—and many other cities portrayed in the published studies—the number of black suspects shot or shot at is considerably larger than the numbers of whites or Hispanics fired upon and struck (also see Tables E-55 and E-57 and Figures E-3, E-6, and E-7 in Appendix E).

Fyfe's New York City findings led him to argue that "there is little to support the contention that blacks are shot disproportionately in relatively trivial and nonthreatening situations" (1981a). Although opinions differ, a similar conclusion might be reached for Los Angeles, based on Meyer's data (1980a), reported in Table 16. There is no appreciable difference between the races of shooting victims whom Los Angeles police reported firing at because of the use or threatened use of a gun: 49 percent of the whites, 54 percent of the blacks, and 48 percent of the Hispanics.

But one might argue that the data in Table 16 suggest a slight pattern of discrimination by L.A. police in firing at fleeing, unarmed suspects (prior to the Supreme Court's ban on such shootings in the 1985 *Tennessee v. Garner* case). Nine percent of the whites and Hispanics but 15 percent of the blacks shot at by members of the LAPD were fired upon, according to the officers' reports, for fleeing without offering armed resistance. Alpert and Fridell (1992: 50) seem to endorse the view, expressed by Meyer (1980a), that the discrepancy between the rate at which blacks, whites, and Hispanics were shot at for fleeing ("disobeying command to halt" in Meyer's language) evinces discriminatory use of the firearm at fleeing suspects.

A similar conclusion is derived from the fact that, as Meyer classified his data, 12 percent of the black people who were shot at, 9 percent of Anglos, and 6 percent of Hispanics were "appearing to reach for weapons." Further, in Alpert and Fridell's (1992: 50) view of Meyer's data, "the Anglo and Hispanic shootings were more likely to involve the more clearly dangerous situations where the suspect threatens to use, or actually uses, a weapon. Moreover," they note, "28 percent of the black suspects were ultimately found to be unarmed, compared to the figures of 22 percent for Hispanics and 20 percent for Anglos." Still, the differences in these percentages, while in some instances statistically significant, are not pronounced, and one has to be very cautious that sufficient factors have been considered before branding a police agency or any other group as racially insensitive (or free from bigotry).

Less ambiguous were the data Fyfe (1982: 72) studied concerning shootings by the agency—the Memphis Police Department—whose shooting incident was at issue in *Tennessee v. Garner*. Reviewing data for the six years 1969-74, Fyfe (*ibid.*) concluded:

"The data strongly support the assertion that police [in Memphis] did differentiate racially with their trigger fingers, by shooting blacks in circumstances less threat-

---

the shooting officer. It makes little difference, of course, to officers whether a *genuine* risk of great bodily harm comes to them from a brick or a bazooka—dead is dead, however it happens—but the officer's tactical calculus of risk and the prospects for a tactical disengagement (e.g., a withdrawl to safe range) may very well depend on the nature of the opponent's weapon.

ening than those in which they shot whites. * * * [The] black death rate from police shootings while unarmed and non-assaultive (5.4 per 100,000)...is 18 times higher than the comparable white rate (0.3)."

Fyfe's conclusions were based on the data available at the time, which were rather limited (see also Alpert and Fridell 1992: 51; American Civil Liberties Union 1992: 8). More recently, an examination of policy changes in Memphis since Fyfe's study period has been conducted by Sparger and Giacopassi (reported in *Crime Control Digest* [1992d] and in an unpublished paper by the researchers). While we shall discuss this study further in Chapter 5, its relevance to our present purposes is the finding that

"[o]ne of the major effects of the new rules...was a reduction in fatal shootings involving black suspects. During the first study period [1969-74] 76.5 percent of those killed by police were black. During 1985-89, 63.2 percent of those killed were black" (*ibid.*: 7).

Other than Fyfe's 1982 Memphis study, most of the remaining published studies (admittedly, they cover only a few police agencies) depict a relatively even-handed pattern—in which officers'

> *Responding to a call of a man burglarizing a car, an officer encountered a suspect "strolling around the crime scene with a leather jacket hanging over his shoulder.... * * * [T]he patrol officer's sense of danger was heightened when he spotted [the suspect's] sheathed knife. Then the officer saw [that the suspect's] eyes wore the faraway look of a drug abuser, so he pulled out his pistol. The suspect obediently put his hands on the police car as ordered, giving [the officer] a glimpse of some rubber grips sticking out of the suspect's jeans waistband. A gun? It had been drilled into [the three-year veteran officer] at the...Police Academy never to wait to meet the gun face to face—be one jump ahead of the suspect or you're dead. Police cadets learn that when a man has a knife, they need a distance of at least 21 feet between officer and suspect for the officer to squeeze off two shots and still move in time to avoid being stabbed. * * * [The officer told] him several times, 'Don't move, keep your hands on there. I think you're armed. Don't move.' Each time, he would put his hands back but then he would reach in again. This time, he reached in quicker. 'I don't know what he was thinking. He could have easily turned and shot me. I felt for my safety. I felt especially for my partner's safety, because he was on that side. He reached in with his right hand, turning in that direction, and I shot him.' [The officer] fired one bullet to the right lower chest, through the suspect's lung, liver, colon and spleen. [The suspect's] weapon clattered to the ground as he fell: bolt-cutters he had been holding under his armpit. He was listed as a John Doe at Mercy Hospital when he died two hours later" (Petrillo 1990c).*

reported reasons for shooting civilians do not vary substantially with the race/ethnicity of the people shot (cf. Takagi 1974, 1979, 1979a). For instance, Blumberg (1983), like Fyfe, examined New York City. Instead of attempting to specifically identify the race of the civilians shot by NYPD officers, however, Blumberg made statistical estimates of the races based on the geographical areas in which the shootings took place. He concluded that the situational characteristics of police-civilian shooting encounters did not differ in New York City's predominantly black or Hispanic neighborhoods as compared with its predominantly white neighborhoods. Blumberg's analysis also sheds light on another question: Even if police do not discriminate on the basis of race, do they behave differently (perhaps out of fear or communications problems or a sense of different accountability for their actions) depending on the racial makeup or socioeconomic status of the neighborhood involved?

Blumberg earlier (1981) had looked at Kansas City and Atlanta and found no differences in situational characteristics depending on whether the civilian victims were black or white in either city. Among the characteristics that Blumberg examined were whether the shooting victim was armed, whether the victim fired a weapon, the number of officers who fired at the victim, the number of bullets fired by the police, and whether the victim was killed or wounded. He also attempted to provide a context for interpretation by reporting general levels of danger to police as represented by the rates of assault against officers in Kansas City and Atlanta. As a final illustration of research on police shootings and opponent race, the commission studying deaths by legal intervention in New York State found "similar proportions of precipitating actions for each race/ethnicity category of decedent" (NYSCCJ 1987, Vol. I).

Until now, no *national* data have been published on the proportion of white, black, and Hispanic suspects shot by police in response to types of precipitating conduct. We have assembled such data for the years 1989 and 1990, based on unpublished FBI compilations. These compilations, reported elsewhere in this volume, are based on voluntarily reported information, submitted on "supplementary homicide reports" by police agencies around the nation that participate in the UCR program. Many agencies, even those that otherwise fully participate in the UCR program, fail to submit complete and timely information to the FBI concerning the justifiable killing of felony suspects by agency members. Earlier we discussed the reasons why national data derived from this source are unreliable for purposes of *counting* the frequency of justifiable homicides by American peace officers.

However, unless one assumes that patterns of failure to report correlate with either the race/ethnicity or the precipitating conduct of persons killed by police, then it may be cautiously assumed (in the absence of hard evidence either way) that the national FBI data present a reasonably accurate picture of the distribution of slayings among felony suspects of different races and ethnicities. In other words, the actual *numbers* of persons killed, as depicted in Figures 62 and 63, are certainly an undercount, but we have no reason to assume that the *proportions* shown in the bar graphs in Figures 62 and 63 misrepresent the approximate proportions that would be observed if one had complete data for all fatal shootings by all police officers in the nation for the year shown.

> *"There are many fine white officers who are doing their job and do not harbor racist sentiments. However, there is still a significant group of individuals whose old line, deep-seated biases continually manifest themselves on the job"* (an African-American police officer testifying before the Independent Commission on the Los Angeles Police Department 1991: 80).

Whether the distributions would hold true for *other* years is, of course a different question. We have seen throughout this volume that the infrequency of police-involved shootings (and the rarity of police-involved *homicides*) results in quite a bit of variation in patterns of incidents and participants from one time period to another. We will return to the question of how representative the data for 1989 might be.

Table 16:
Precipitating Conduct and Race/Ethnicity of Civilians Shot (Fatally and Nonfatally) by Chicago Police (1974-78) and Shot *at* (Fatally, Nonfatally, Misses) by Los Angeles Police Department Officers (1974-78)

Precipitating Conduct	Department	Race/Ethnicity of Civilians Shot							
		White		Black		Hispanic		Total	
Gun use/threat	Chicago	62	39%	349	57%	63	61%	474	54%
	LAPD	64	49%	173	54%	61	48%	298	52%
Other dw[1] or physical force use/threat	Chicago	38	24%	84	14%	20	19%	142	16%
	LAPD	49	37%	74	23%	49	39%	172	30%
Other dw possessed without threat	Chicago	1	1%	13	2%	0	0%	14	2%
	LAPD	--	--	--	--	--	--	--	--
Flight without other resistance	Chicago	20	13%	95	15%	9	9%	124	14%
	LAPD	12	9%	48	15%	11	9%	71	12%
Other reasons for shooting intentionally	Chicago	3	2%	2	<1%	1	1%	6	2%
	LAPD	--	--	--	--	--	--	--	--
Accidental	Chicago	25	16%	41	7%	9	9%	75	9%
	LAPD[2]	1	1%	3	1%	4	3%	8	1%
Mistaken identity	Chicago	1	1%	5	1%	0	0%	6	1%
	LAPD	--	--	--	--	--	--	--	--
Stray bullet	Chicago	9	6%	23	4%	2	2%	34	4%
	LAPD	--	--	--	--	--	--	--	--
Not ascertained[3]	Chicago	?	?	?	?	?	?	10	1%
	LAPD	5	4%	23	7%	1	1%	29	5%
TOTALS[4]	Chicago	159	100%	612	100%	104	100%	885	100%
	LAPD	131	100%	321	100%	126	100%	578	100%

Sources: Geller (1989), extrapolations from Meyer (1980a: 46, 48).
[1] *Deadly weapons.*
[2] *The "accidental" category for Los Angeles may include one or more persons shot because of "other reasons for shooting intentionally," "mistaken identity," or "stray bullet," as those terms were used in the Chicago study.*
[3] *The "not ascertained" data for Los Angeles result from extrapolation methods; for Chicago the "not ascertained" data result from incomplete file records concerning the civilian victim's precipitating conduct or race/ethnicity.*
[4] *The grand total for Chicago (885) exceeds the sum of the subtotals for each race/ethnicity because the race/ethnicity of 10 persons in the "not ascertained" row was not known.*
Note: The column percentages may not total 100 percent due to rounding.

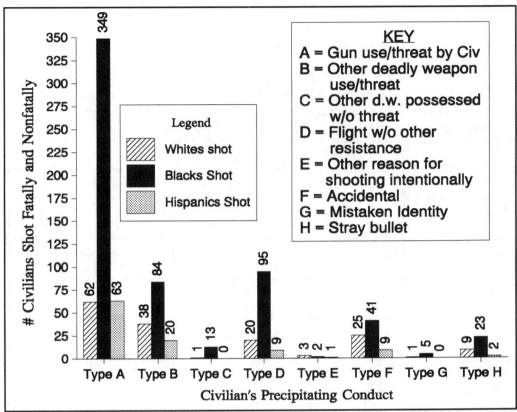

Figure 60: Precipitating Conduct & Race/Ethnicity of Civilians Shot (Fatally & Nonfatally) by Chicago Police, 1974-78 *Source: Geller and Karales (1981a)*

The shooting types represented in Figures 62 and 63 are the following:

Type A =   Felon[24] attacked police officer
Type B =   Felon [a civilian] attacked fellow police officer [the shooter's partner]
Type C =   Felon attacked a civilian
Type D =   Felon attempted flight from a crime
Type E =   Felon killed in commission of a crime
Type F =   Felon resisted arrest

---

[24] The FBI, like some other law enforcement organizations, tends to use the term "felon" rather than "felony suspect," even though, under most circumstances, the latter would probably be more accurate. The so-called "fleeing felon" rule, which American jurisdictions inherited two centuries ago from English common law and that persisted in a few agencies until the Supreme Court outlawed the rule in its 1985 *Tennessee v. Garner* decision, contributed significantly to popularizing the use of the term "felon." The "fleeing felon" rule permitted police to use lethal means to capture a fleeing person who was suspected of committing any felony, regardless of the severity or nature of the felony. Thus, persons suspected of felony-level thefts from unattended automobiles (e.g., a teenager stealing an expensive dashboard stereo system) could legitimately be shot and killed while fleeing from arresting officers, regardless of whether they offered any resistance beyond flight (see Geller and Karales 1981a; Geller 1982b). It is perhaps understandable, although not acceptable, that public relations concerns might encourage law enforcement agencies to gravitate toward terms that enhance the public certainty that the person on the receiving end of police bullets was in fact guilty of a crime, despite the absence of judicial determination of culpability.

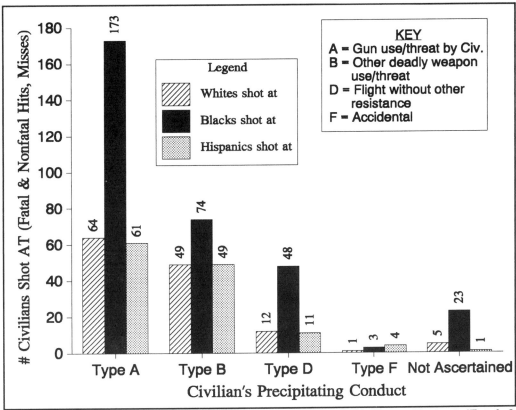

Figure 61: Precipitating Conduct & Race/Ethnicity of Civilians Shot at (Fatal & Nonfatal Hits, Misses) by LAPD Officers, 1974-78 *Source: Meyer (1980a).*

The difference between Figures 62 and 63, both of which contain the same data, are in their presentation. Figure 62 shows the proportions of white, black, and Hispanic suspects killed by police within each type of precipitating conduct (attacking police officer, attacking civilian, etc.). Figure 63 flips this presentation by organizing the types of precipitating conduct within each racial/ethnic group. Thus, it is somewhat easier in Figure 62 to analyze separately each shooting type. And it is somewhat easier in Figure 63 to separately analyze the circumstances in which each racial/ethnic group of suspects is slain by police.

Figure 63 helps show the somewhat different distributions, within each racial/ethnic group, of the reasons given by police for slaying felony suspects. Thus, for example, among the 156 whites killed in 1989 (for whom data on race and precipitating conduct were available), 66 percent were killed collectively for attacking someone, that is, in incident Types A, B, and C (felony suspects slain for attacking a police officer, a "fellow" officer, or a civilian). (In 1990 this percentage was 59 percent—see Table E-62 in Appendix E.) Of the 122 black felony suspects killed in 1989, 51 percent were killed in these three types of situations. (The next year, the percentage was 58 percent—again, documented in Table E-62.) And of the 47 Hispanic felony suspects slain in 1989, 62 percent reportedly engaged in one of these three types of conduct (actually, as the figures show, no Hispanic justifiable homicide victims appear in the FBI data for 1989 as having been killed for attacking a "fellow officer"). (In 1990 exactly the same percentage of Hispanics were shot in these three types of incidents.)

The percentage of persons killed within each racial/ethnic group in 1989 for reportedly

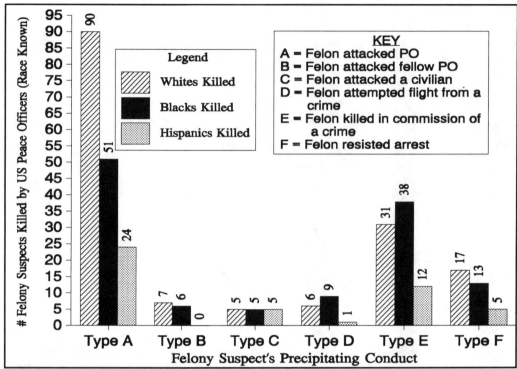

Figure 62: Precipitating Conduct and Race/Ethnicity of Felony Suspects Killed by American Police, 1989
Source: FBI (unpub. supp. homicide reports).

attempting flight from a crime (Type D) were 4 percent for whites, 7 percent for blacks, and 2 percent for Hispanics. (In 1990, 2 percent of whites, 3 percent of blacks, and no Hispanics were slain by police for attempting to flee.)

Concerning Type E ("felon killed in commission of a crime")—the distribution of deaths within each racial/ethnic group for 1989 was 20 percent for white suspects, 31 percent for black suspects, and 26 percent for Hispanic suspects. (The next year, the distribution was 25 percent for white, 25 percent for black, and 26 percent for Hispanic suspects—as shown in Table E-62.)

It is difficult to know what to make of the difference between whites and blacks concerning felony suspects killed in the commission of a crime in 1989. Perhaps 1989 was an aberrant year and 1990's striking consistency across the races in percentage of persons slain while committing a suspected felony is more representative. Obviously, additional years of data would have to be examined to explore this question. Future operational and civil rights research might productively examine it. One preliminary issue worth studying is precisely what the FBI and police agencies participating in the Uniform Crime Reporting program mean by category "E." We have discussed this question with senior staff in the FBI UCR program User Services Section (Major 1992), and have learned that there are no written guidelines instructing either the FBI or local police as to precisely what types of incidents should be classified as "felon killed in commission of a crime." We asked how one would know whether to classify a killing by an officer to protect the victim of an in-progress aggravated battery or rape as a Type E (killed in commission of a crime) or a Type C (felon attacked a civilian). We were told that, although no written guidelines exist, the training of analysts generally suggests that justifiable homicides in this situation by *police officers* be classified as Type E and justifiable homicides in the same situation by *citizens* be classified as Type C.

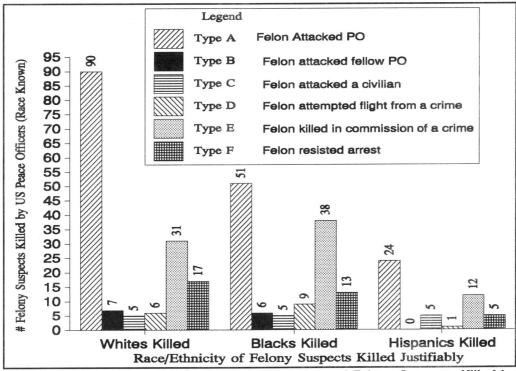

Figure 63: Precipitating Conduct and Race/Ethnicity of Felony Suspects Killed by American Police, 1989

Source: FBI (unpub. supp. homicide repts).

Simply identifying what the FBI means by such terminology—or how it trains police departments or state authorities in making classifications—is almost certainly not sufficient to answer the question of what kinds of justifiable homicides are classified as Type E, given the likelihood of considerable slippage between any FBI definitions and those actually used by local or state personnel in categorizing and forwarding information to the FBI (see, e.g., Sherman and Cohn 1986). Once a clearer understanding emerges of how police Uniform Crime Reporting units around the nation decide to specify the circumstances that justified a justifiable homicide, it will be possible to start asking and answering follow-up questions about what implications data such as those we have discussed for 1989 might hold for police shooting policy and practices around the nation.

In closing this portion of our discussion, we turn to a type of fatal encounter which, in some communities, is likely to produce public skepticism and controversy—persons killed for resisting arrest (Type F). Notably, the percentage of persons within each racial/ethnic group killed for this reason is identical: 11 percent.

As with all other such findings about race and shooting discretion, however, the underlying question that needs to be explored by police and others is whether persons of different races or ethnicities engage in resistance to arrest—or other violent, anti-social behavior—in rough proportion to the extent that police bullets put them in our nation's hospital wards and morgues. There is some evidence, more than a decade old at this point, that the racial distribution of persons arrested for at least some serious felonies matches the racial distribution of those who commit such crimes (as reported in national surveys by crime victims). Hindelang (1978: 100), for instance, discovered that, nationally, blacks were 62 percent of those identified in victimization surveys as robbers and were also 62 percent of those arrested for robbery in the same year.

Suggesting, however, that, "for serious crime, arrest data on race reflect actual offenses" (LaFree, et al. 1992: 167) does not address whether there is a match between offending and official intervention in less serious types of crime.[25] This is important because, as we saw in our discussion of "mobilizing events" early in this chapter, a segment of police-civilian encounters that end with gunfire began over relatively minor infractions (traffic violations, property crimes, etc.).

In any event, no research findings, however demonstrative they might be of police professionalism in the exercise of arrest discretion or the use of force, will ever eliminate all allegations (some sincere, some malicious, some bogus, some meritorious) of police racism and other abuses. By the same token, a box of statistical evidence on virtually any aspect of police-involved shootings will be little match for the weight of personal experiences by police and civilians with the use of lethal force (see Cordner 1985, on the role of *research* generally in shaping policy decisions).

*"Not every white police officer is a bigot and not every police force is a bastion of racism. Some departments have made strides in promoting blacks, teaching tolerance and engaging minority communities in monitoring police work. But the remaining biases are severe.... * * * [I]n Houston, some white Harris County deputy sheriffs observed the Rev. Martin Luther King, Jr.'s birthday this year by promoting the idea of a holiday for his assassin, James Earl Ray. White deputies left a tape of racist songs in an office used by blacks and whites. Ku Klux Klan literature was sent through the department's internal mail to Perry Wooten, who heads the Afro-American Deputies League.*

"Elsewhere, black officers tell of arguments with white colleagues that have occasionally ended with guns drawn; shootings have been prevented only because other officers have stepped in. Subtler prejudice is endemic. A black policeman in Baltimore recalls trying to seal off the scene of a crime as white officers melted away without lending him a hand.

"Even black policemen, off duty, are instant suspects in the eyes of many white officers. Blacks out of uniform have told me of being stopped, searched, interrogated and humiliated before they have a chance to identify themselves as policemen. In two years of interviewing across the country, I have encountered very few black men who have not been hassled by white cops" (Shipler 1992).

Nevertheless, if we did not believe that *some* systematic evidence on *some* issues *some*times makes a difference in real world administrative or operational decisions—no matter how powerful the political and other pressures are in moments of crisis, such as the aftermath of the Los Angeles riot of April and May 1992—we would not have written this book. Credible, systematic evidence—some contained in this volume, much still to be developed in

---

[25] In a sidebar earlier in this chapter we noted that there is evidence that black and white Americans abuse illegal narcotics at similar rates (resulting in many more white than black drug offenders) but that black drug abusers are disproportionately arrested for these crimes (Harris 1990; Meddis 1992).

future research—should help to allay (or bolster) recurrent and nagging concerns about police decisions to use lethal force.

B. Circumstances in Which Police Were Victimized

Many researchers have explored the characteristics of confrontations that result in the serious injury or death of police officers. Among the best sources are the FBI's annual report on *Law Enforcement Officers Killed and Assaulted*, as well as numerous studies of officer victimization in single cities, groups of major cities, or the nation.[26] Throughout the earlier part of this chapter we have profiled many aspects of incidents in which police either shoot civilians or are shot (or killed with other weapons) by civilians. Here, we focus in more detail on the types of calls for service that result in varying levels of jeopardy for American law enforcement personnel and on the extent to which police lives are endangered by other law enforcement personnel. We also summarize the highlights of research exploring factors that may be correlated with patterns of officer victimization across geography and over time.

1. Crime Types and Assailant Characteristics, Motivations, and Dispositions

The FBI's annual statistical reports on *Law Enforcement Officers Killed and Assaulted* generally do not separate officers whose deaths were caused by gunfire from officers who died by other means. Ideally, we would present separate discussions of officers slain by gunfire and officers slain by other means; but given the presentation of data in the published FBI reports, in this section of this chapter we will need for the most part to portray deaths by *all* means. Thus, the reader needs to be aware that both the number of officers slain annually by gunfire and the array of circumstances in which these fatal shootings occur will be slightly different from the composite pictures presented in some instances by the Bureau's published reports and by other portions of this volume.

We do not consider this limitation detrimental for present purposes for two reasons. First, as noted earlier in this chapter, the vast majority (92 percent; 96 percent in 1991—Behm 1992) of slayings of the police are accomplished by use of firearms. Second, in an officer's decision whether to use deadly force against an opponent, it will rarely matter precisely what means of deadly force is being used against the officer so long as the officer reasonably believes that the force being used is capable of producing death or serious bodily injury.[27]

---

[26] See, for example, Fyfe (1978), Geller and Karales (1981a, 1981b), Cardarelli (1968), Chapman (1964), Cramer and Robin (1968), Lester (1978a, 1978b), Little (1984), Meyer, et al. (1978, 1979), Moorman and Wemmer (1983), Morrison and Meyer (1974), Regens, et al. (1974), Vaughn and Kappeler (1986), and Kieselhorst (1974). Summary data on deaths of American law enforcement personnel have been available since 1961 in the FBI's annual publication, *Crime in the United States*. Starting in 1972, such data were also separately published in the Bureau's annual document titled *Law Enforcement Officers Killed*. Starting in 1982, this separate publication was expanded also to cover assaults on officers, and the document since then has been titled *Law Enforcement Officers Killed and Assaulted* (see Garner and Clemmer 1986: 7).

[27] Obviously, as noted earlier, from a tactical point of view, at the outset of an encounter it may make an enormous difference to an officer whether he or she is confronted with a knife, a blunt object, or a firearm. But once an incident has escalated to the point where the offender seems capable, with whatever weapon, of killing the officer, it matters little to the affected officer whether the weapon is

Earlier, we profiled the crime situations in which police have shot civilians fatally and nonfatally over varying time periods. Similar tallies have been published for many years by the FBI to portray the felonious slayings of law enforcement officers nationwide. For instance, Table 17, drawn from FBI data, represents the circumstances at the scene in which officers were killed during the period 1980-90.

Arrest situations predominate in the felonious killing of American police, with deaths related to disturbance calls, investigation of suspicious circumstances, and traffic pursuits or stops following in frequency of occurrence. In Chicago in 1990 police department data portray the circumstances in which officers were assaulted (*nonfatally* and without injury) with firearms: Of the 218 officer victims that year,

- 64 (29 percent) were assaulted in disturbances (both domestic and nondomestic);
- 10 (4.6 percent) were assaulted by burglary suspects;
- 19 (9 percent) by robbery suspects;
- 47 (21.6 percent) when attempting arrests for other offenses;
- 30 (14 percent) while investigating suspicious persons or circumstances;
- 20 (9 percent) without warning (i.e., in ambushes);
- 1 (0.5 percent) by a mentally deranged person;
- 9 (4 percent) when making traffic stops; and
- 21 (9.6 percent) in all other types of circumstances (data collected by Geller from Chicago Police Department for this book).

Of these 218 officers who reported being assaulted in 1990, 45 (21 percent) were injured (*ibid.*). We will return below to a focused discussion of the types of situations in which police are victimized, with a special effort to correct long-standing misimpressions about the danger of domestic disturbances.

We should reiterate in this discussion of police victimization a point made elsewhere in this book concerning shootings *by* police: Planners, operational personnel, risk managers, media assignment editors and reporters, advocacy groups, and Monday morning quarterbacks need to understand clearly the difference between crime situations that eventually escalate into a police-involved shooting and the specific behaviors that immediately precipitate the use of deadly force by or against police. Thus, as we indicated in discussing shootings *by* officers, before one draws conclusions about the danger—or lack of danger—of incidents like traffic stops, shoplifting, and search warrant execution, one needs to carefully analyze at least two factors: the frequency with which the types of persons to be questioned or arrested in these situations jeopardize the lives of police officers; and the frequency with which police in various kinds of situations take professionally prescribed precautions to safeguard themselves from assault. For additional discussion of research findings on the hazards to police in traffic stops, see our discussion in Chapter 2 of the potential for policymakers to be misled by research on police-civilian violence that fails to place data about the prevalence of such violence in the broader context of the number of contacts (prompted by different kinds of

---

a cannon or a badminton racket. At the same time, the police administrator realizes that, in the wake of a shooting by an officer, however justified, the public and political reaction may turn fundamentally on the civilian opponent's choice of weapon, and speculation will center on whether at some point during the confrontation the officer might have found a nonlethal way to prevent the adversary from threatening the officer's life.

crimes or suspected problems) between police and citizens day to day.

**Table 17:
Circumstances at Scene Where Police Were Slain, 1980-90**

Circumstances at Scene	# Officers Killed	% Officers Killed
Disturbance Calls	142	16%
Bar fights, man with gun, etc.	81	9%
Family quarrels	61	7%
Arrest Situations	356	41%
Burglaries in progress/ pursuing burg. suspects	38	4%
Robberies in progress/ pursuing robb. suspects	125	14%
Drug-related matters	71	8%
Attempting other arrests	122	14%
Civil Disorders (Mass Disobedience, riot, etc.)	1	0.1%
Handling, Transporting, Custody of Prisoners	36	4%
Investigating Suspicious Persons/Circumstances	124	14%
Ambush Situations	79	9%
Entrapment/premeditation	41	5%
Unprovoked attack	38	4%
Mentally Deranged	14	2%
Traffic Pursuits/Stops	114	13%
TOTAL	866	99.1%*

Sources: FBI (1989b: 18; 1991b: 17).
* *Does not total 100 percent due to rounding.*

Based on FBI reports, we can describe some of the attributes of persons who have feloniously killed American law enforcement officers over the decade of the 1980s. Nationally, the largest percentage of assailants were male (96 percent), white (56 percent), between the ages of 18 and 29 (54 percent), and had previously been arrested on some type of criminal charge (71 percent) (FBI 1989b: 22). This profile held relatively constant during 1990 (FBI 1991b: 21), with the exception that during that year nearly 78 percent of the assailants had a prior criminal arrest.

In New York City during 1990, of the 631 suspects who either assaulted NYPD officers and/or were shot at by members of the force, 580 (92 percent) were listed in departmental records as male, 22 (4 percent) as female, and 29 (5 percent) as of "unknown" gender—a reflection, we take it, of incomplete record keeping rather than of androgenous police assailants. Of the 573 New York City police assailants/targets of police bullets whose race or ethnicity were identified, 73 (13 percent) were white, 298 (52 percent) were black, 196 (34 percent) were Hispanic, and 6 (1 percent) were of other extractions (Cerar 1990: 5).

The consequences of killing an American law enforcement officer are depicted in Table 18, also drawn from the FBI's annual *Law Enforcement Officers Killed and Assaulted*. The table is interesting not only because of the strong message it sends that "cop killing" is extremely likely to end in apprehension and conviction of murder, but because it provides some limited data on the use of deadly force against these assailants and on their deaths by other means (offenders who were reported to have committed suicide[28] and offenders who died in custody). Moreover, the FBI also points out that 12 of the known assailants "suffered [nonfatal] gunshot wounds" (FBI 1991b: 3).

"A seven-year veteran officer...at approximately 3:30 a.m. on June 7...was on patrol in his vehicle when he noticed a citizen gesturing for him to stop. The complainant pointed out two males and said one had robbed him of $7. Upon seeing the officer, the two fled on foot. One of the males voluntarily stopped and was placed in the patrol unit. The other ran into a wooded area and was followed by the officer. Shortly thereafter, the officer apparently caught up with the suspect and while attempting to handcuff him, lost control of his .38-caliber service handgun. The officer was shot three times in the front upper torso. Later that same day, a 21-year-old male was arrested and charged with the officer's murder" (FBI 1989b: 28).

The sentences of 707 individuals convicted of murdering[29] American police officers during recent years were also reported (FBI 1991b: 4):

- 145 (21 percent) were sentenced to death;
- 347 (49 percent) were sentenced to life imprisonment;
- 213 (30 percent) were sentenced to prison terms ranging from two months to 450 years;
- 1 (0.1 percent) was placed on probation; and
- 2 (0.3 percent) were sentenced to indeterminate terms.

---

[28] Although often hard to prove, some suicidal persons use their violent assaults on police officers as an attempt to provoke a lethal response, thus eliciting police complicity in their own destruction (Noesner and Dolan 1992: 2). Meyer (1991) tells of a man on a front porch holding

"a butcher knife to his [own] neck, the point pressed into the flesh just below his Adam's apple. * * * [A] cop convinced the guy that [responding officers] really wanted to help. The guy stopped crying. Then he quickly reached into his pants pocket with his free hand and pulled out a pack of cigarettes—the infamous 'he reached for a shiny object' routine. Good thing it was daylight. The guy had that gleam in his eye now, the Jack Nicholson look that cops know: 'Hey, I was only testing you. You could have shot me just then and I wouldn't have cared. But since you didn't, now I'm gonna mess with you, since I'm getting all this attention, and my life is worthless anyway, and so is yours, pig'."

[29] An additional 128 defendants were convicted of offenses less serious than murder.

Obviously, the national profile of police assailants and their subsequent fate will not hold true for every jurisdiction; one could expect considerable variation in the characteristics of assailants but probably a reasonably consistent pattern of dire consequences befalling those who slay police. Where the consequences will probably vary most is between states that have and those that do not have a death penalty. Bailey and Peterson (1987) studied the impact of capital punishment on the rates at which police were slain feloniously over the period 1973-84 and concluded, as had prior research, that police were no safer in jurisdictions with the death penalty than in those without it.

Table 18:
Disposition of Persons Identified in the Felonious Killing of American Law Enforcement Officers, 1979-88*

Persons Identified	# of Assailants	% of Assailants
Known Persons		
Fugitives	6	1%
Justifiably killed	152	13%
Committed suicide	45	4%
Identified but not charged	0	0%
Arrested and Charged	976	83%
TOTAL	1,179	100%
Arrested and Charged		
Guilty of murder	707	72%
Guilty of lesser offense related to murder	82	8%
Guilty of crime other than murder	46	5%
Acquitted or otherwise dismissed	99	10%
Committed to mental institution	19	2%
Case pending or disposition unknown	9	1%
Died in custody	14	1%
TOTAL	976	100%

* Current at least as of mid-1991 (the FBI report was published in September 1991).
Source: FBI (1991b: 22).

As one thinks about the array of circumstances in which police lives have been intentionally taken by these assailants—and about potential countermeasures—analysts may tend to assume that police killers' *motivations* for slaying police are obvious. A small number of researchers have not taken this question as one with a simple answer, however, and have drawn on a variety of disciplines to explore it.

One of the most informative studies on the motivations of civilians for shooting police officers has been done by Margarita (1980a). She used departmental records to classify civilians' motivations for slaying New York City officers from 1844 through 1978 into five social-psychological categories previously devised by Toch (1969). She found that police are not generally killed by "senseless madmen or lunatics. Rather, New York [City] police are more likely to be killed by rational robbers fleeing the scene of a crime," whose intention of injuring the

A man charged with murdering two Chicago Police officers claimed he shot them in self-defense. With "bruises and scrapes on his face and body after his arrest for the killings," the defendant "contended that the two officers...were beating [him] in a darkened garage when he picked up [one of the officer's] gun and fatally shot both men" (Chicago Tribune 1991a).

officer is secondary to their attempts to protect themselves from capture or injury (1980a: 63). Thus, violence against the police is far more often "instrumental" than it is "contemptuous" or "expressive" (1980a: 219).[30] Sometimes, the assault on police may even be the product of misguided (or, in rare instances, accurate) perceptions that the suspect must defend himself against summary punishment by police officers (see, e.g., *New York Times* 1992bb, describing defense counsel's claims about the killing of an off-duty New York City Housing officer).

The rarity of planned assassinations of police officers was cited by former LAPD chief Daryl Gates in his memoirs:

"Although 179 [LAPD] officers have died in the line of duty since 1915, when our record-keeping began, almost always they died while trying to prevent a crime. * * * On rare occasions, officers are set up. A call will go out that a police officer is needed, and when the car pulls up, the officers are deliberately ambushed. But [until an incident on Halloween night, 1985] a specific officer had never before been targeted. Criminals are always warning: 'Man, I'm gonna get you.' However, no criminal yet had ever carried out his threat. No officer in LAPD history had ever been killed like this: the stalked target of what appeared to be a painstakingly planned hit. Tom Williams had been assassinated" (Gates and Shah 1992: 258).

Although the 1985 killing about which former Chief Gates wrote may be emblematic of a new style of gratuitous, violent aggression by some criminals toward cops as we enter the last decade of this century, taken together, the research findings from various studies over the past several decades suggest that both police officers and civilians shoot each other more because they feel they must than because they want to.

---

[30] Even when an individual seeks not to elude police but to elicit their assistance in committing suicide (see, e.g., *National Bulletin on Police Misconduct* 1992; Long 1992a; Noesner and Dolan 1992: 2), it would still be accurate to characterize the violence used to provoke police use of deadly force as instrumental rather than contemptuous.

Meyer, et al. (1986) reviewed the 35 ambush-related killings of American police during 1972-82 and concluded that, since 37 percent of the assailants were known to the slain officer, revenge may play a "large role in many [ambush] attacks." That the officer and assailant were not strangers hardly proves that revenge as a motive, however. And 13 such incidents in America over 11 years do not show that contemptuous or expressive violence explains a sizable percentage of the killings of police generally (i.e., in situations other than ambushes). But for a recent clear case of revenge—the mass killing of 17 relatives of police in India to avenge the killing of a militant leader—see *New York Times* (1992t).

2. Tactical Considerations in Incidents with Police Victimizations

Analysts in the FBI during 1990 began work on a potentially important new contribution to the literature on the killing of American police. Agents James Vaugh, Ed Davis, and Tony Pinizzotto conducted detailed interviews with 50 people convicted of slaying police officers and explored intensively a series of tactical questions that may form the basis for improved training and operational procedures. For example, preliminary analysis indicated that in an important percentage of killings of police, the officers encountered multiple civilians at the scene of an intended arrest but guessed wrong about which civilians presented a threat to police and which did not. On the basis of this finding, Bureau trainers began developing specialized instruction on how to approach such ambiguous scenes (FBI 1990f). The FBI expects to release the study (FBI 1992e) in the fall of 1992 (Vaugh 1992).

There is a rather substantial body of literature on officer "survival" and officer safety tactics (some of the leading contributions are cited in the bibliography), and we make no claims to exhaustive treatment of that subject in this chapter or in Chapter 5 (see also empirical data about New York City police gunfights in Cerar 1990). But a few additional findings may be noted here that may be valuable to police tacticians seeking ways to enhance the safety of officers in potentially violent encounters (see also discussion in Chapter 5). For example, in an early, national study of 110 nonrandomly selected police officers who were shot, Bristow (1963) found that 43 percent of officers who were shot during traffic stops were shot after the initial contact, while interrogating, citing, or requesting a radio check on the suspect, rather than during the approach to the suspect's car. In the situations where officers were shot in buildings, 71 percent of the officer victims knew or had good reason to believe that the suspects were armed before the shooting started. Konstantin's (1984) study of officers killed from 1978 through 1980 revealed that, while other studies have shown that three-quarters of all police-citizen contacts are initiated by the citizen, three-quarters of homicides of police officers occur during contacts initiated by the officer.

It seems clear that police today are facing increased hazards (such as the prevalence of automatic weapons among the criminal population in certain areas—see Council on Scientific Affairs 1992). But other presumed hazards to police have to be analyzed more fully. For instance, simply reporting the frequency of shootings that arise out of various types of police-citizen encounters is misleading because it tells us little about the relative riskiness of

> *"At approximately 7:30 p.m. on December 15, a 43-year-old officer...responded to a call from a local department store to investigate a possible shoplifting. Upon arrival at the store, the officer questioned a man who was attempting to return merchandise for a cash refund. In the man's presence, the officer made a telephone call to try and verify his story. Investigation indicates that when the suspect realized he was going to be arrested, he stood up, raised his hands, and suddenly produced a .38 caliber handgun. He shot the victim officer in the front of the head while the officer was still on the telephone, killing him instantly. The suspect fled to a nearby fast food restaurant where he forced two males at gunpoint to drive him to [a nearby city]. A 29-year-old male was arrested four days later and charged with first-degree murder in addition to other related charges. The victim officer was a 17-year veteran of law enforcement"* (FBI 1989b: 32-33).

each type of encounter. To establish relative risk, one must first determine the frequency of each type of encounter, the frequency of armed confrontations during each type of encounter (e.g., traffic stops), and the frequency of shots actually fired during each type of encounter (Scharf and Binder 1983; Sherman 1980a). Very little research has taken all these factors into account (see Alpert and Fridell 1992; Bayley and Garofalo 1989). Acknowledging the limits of their inquiry, Garner and Clemmer compared measures of assaults, injuries, and deaths of police officers with measures of police activity as derived from other studies. They reported that both domestic disturbances and traffic-related encounters are consistently less likely to result in death to an officer than robbery or burglary-related encounters (1986: 5).

3. Myths Surrounding Officer Deaths in Domestic Disturbances

Conventional wisdom within police circles long had held that domestic quarrels were about the most dangerous situations for officers (Auten 1972; Vandall 1976; Bard 1977; Muir 1977; Stephens 1977; Margarita 1980b: 227). In part, the notion that police were more likely to be seriously injured in domestic disturbances than in many other encounters stemmed from the way in which FBI data on injuries to officers often was displayed (Garner and Clemmer 1986: 2; Stanford and Mowry 1990).

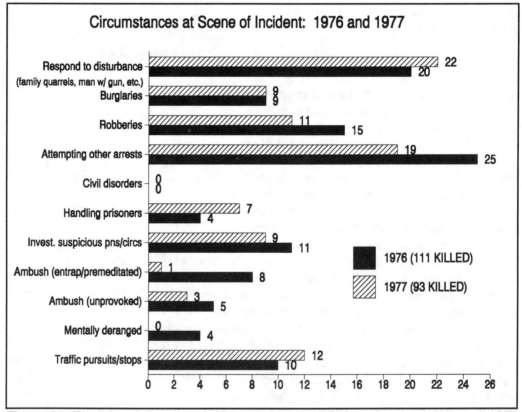

Figure 64: Traditional Display of Circumstances of Officer Deaths, 1976 and 1977 (Number Killed)   *Source: Garner and Clemmer (1986).*

Figure 64, re-created from a 1977 FBI report, illustrates such a traditional display. This graph shows that, in 1976, "responding to disturbances" was the category in which the second largest number of American police were feloniously slain; the following year, it was the leading category. As Garner and Clemmer (1986: 2) observe, "during the period 1960 to 1984, the 'disturbance' category ranked third overall among the FBI categories of police officer deaths."

The percentage of officers killed during domestic disturbances, however, typically is about 5 percent, much lower than has been widely believed (Konstantin 1984; Garner and Clemmer 1986; Swanton 1985). Konstantin (1984: 29) reviewed data on the "type of precipitating incident" for all American officers killed feloniously from 1978 through 1980 and concluded that "the modal [most common] type of...incident is [the general category of] 'attempting other arrests'...and not, as commonly thought, domestic disputes." Garner and

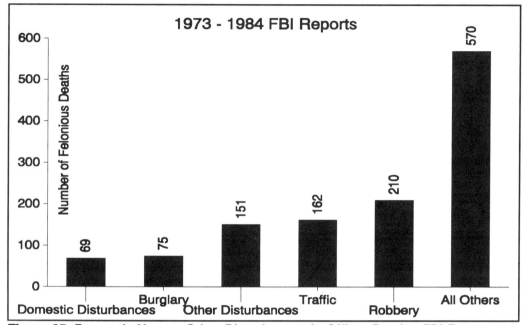

Figure 65: Domestic Versus Other Disturbances in Officer Deaths, FBI Reports, 1973-84   *Source: Garner and Clemmer (1986: 3).*

Clemmer's (1986) display of FBI data on officers feloniously killed during 1976 and 1977 separates domestic from nondomestic disturbances, as shown in Figure 65.

Recent FBI reports include data tables that distinguish between family quarrels and several types of nondomestic disturbances ("bar fights," "man with gun/knife," and other nondomestic "disturbance calls"). But, curiously, these same FBI reports continue to lump all types of disturbances together in *graphic*—and thus far more memorable—displays than the tables present. Only for one year's annual report on officers killed and assaulted[31] did the FBI's *graphic* display of circumstances in which officers were victimized separate domestic from nondomestic disturbances. Then, the following year, the Bureau reverted to lumping all disturbances together in its graphs, and this practice has persisted through at least the 1990 report (the most recent available as this book went to press).

Figure 66, re-created from the FBI's 1990 report on *Law Enforcement Officers Killed*

---

[31] The 1982 report, at page 16.

and Assaulted (FBI 1991b: 16), shows how the casual or busy reader, who fails to study the data *tables*, could overestimate the percentage of officer assaults and deaths that result from domestic disturbances. Even diligent readers, such as those who write officer survival manuals, can be conditioned by the FBI's data format to present the data in ways that mislead others. For instance, Rutledge (1988: 205) declares, based on FBI compilations: "All disturbance calls, including family fights, man with a gun, shots fired, and bar fights, continue to be one of the most dangerous types of assignments for officers, accounting for nearly 16 percent of officer homicides during the last 10 years." This statement is accurate, but the problem is that nowhere in the 15 pages of discussion that follow it does the author clarify the differential fatality rates of officers handling the various types of disturbance calls. While police officers always have to be prepared for potential violence, is it sensible for officers to approach all types of disturbances—bar fights, persons with guns, family quarrels, etc.—in an identical fashion, with identical expectations of potential risk?

Although FBI annual reports on police killed and assaulted disaggregate disturbances into domestics and other types for officer *fatalities*, the same level of detail is *not* provided for assaults (injurious or noninjurious) against police (e.g., FBI 1991b: 44-45). Nor is it clear that current Uniform Crime Reporting program tally sheets would *permit* the FBI to separate *assaults* during disturbances into types of disturbance incidents. In preparing this volume, we reviewed the monthly tally sheets employed during 1990 by the Chicago Police Department under the Illinois UCR program to report assaults and batteries of police officers. Those reporting forms do not divide disturbances resulting in officer victimizations into subcategories of disturbances.[32]

Studying all NYPD officers killed from 1844 through 1978, Margarita (1980a: 69) found that only 2 percent of the fatalities occurred in connection with domestic disturbances, possibly suggesting that these incidents never were as dangerous as had been assumed. In Chicago from 1974 through 1978, 4 percent of the police shot (fatally or nonfatally) by civilians were intervening in domestic disturbances (Geller and Karales 1981a: 95). Fyfe (1978) derived similarly low levels of officer injuries in domestic disturbances in New York City during the period 1971-1975.

The circumstances in which police officers were shot fatally and nonfatally in Chicago in the mid-1970s and slain (with all weapons) nationally during the decade of the 1980s are displayed in Table 19.

Table 20, re-created from Garner and Clemmer (1986: 4), shows the mix of situations in which police officers were slain, assaulted, or injured in various jurisdictions, as reported in eight studies. Data on domestic disturbances appear in the second column from the left in the table.

Stanford and Mowry (1990: 246), studying 143 assaults (threatened, attempted, and actual injuries) against Tampa police officers during 1989 in domestic and "general" disturbances, found that officers were slightly more likely (1.3 times) to be assaulted in general disturbances than in domestic disturbances. Of the 34,839 domestic disturbance calls

---

[32] One way to capture information on the nature of the disturbances in which officers were assaulted is to survey a sample of assaulted officers. McMurray (1990: 47), in such a survey of Washington, D.C., and Newark, New Jersey, police officers in 1986, found that, "[c]ontrary to popular opinion, officers were assaulted more often when investigating suspicious persons...[than] during domestic disputes."

handled that year by the Tampa police, officers were assaulted in 46 (0.13 percent); and of the 58,990 general disturbance calls, officers were assaulted in 97 (0.16 percent).

Using a formula that incorporated data on assaults/injuries and calls/dispatches, Stanford and Mowry estimated "danger rates." They estimated the potential for Tampa officers to be assaulted while handling a domestic disturbance at 2.6 assaults per 1,000 calls; for general disturbances, the danger rate was 3.1 per 1,000 calls—1.2 times higher (*ibid.*). However, when *injury* is considered, the danger rates reverse: "the potential for injury while handling a domestic disturbance is 1.5 per 1,000 calls; the injury...rate for general disturbance calls is 1.3" (*ibid.*: 248). The difference between the *assault* rates is statistically significant,

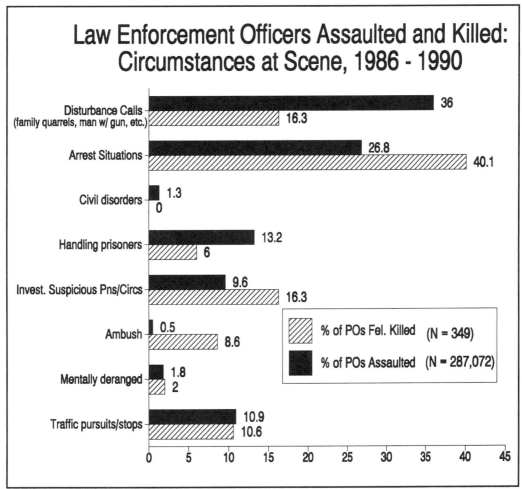

Figure 66: American Police Assaulted or Killed and Circumstances at Scene, 1986-90 (Percentages)   *Source: FBI (1991b).*

but the difference between the *injury* rates is not (*ibid.*). In contrast to most other studies, Uchida, et al. (1988 1990a, 1990b), studying 1,550 assaults during 1984-86 against Baltimore County, Maryland, officers, found that both domestic and general disturbance calls posed relatively significant threats of both injurious and noninjurious assault compared to other categories of incident.

Table 19:
Circumstances in Which Police Were Victimized in Chicago and the Nation

Circumstance at the Scene	% of Police Victimized	
	Chicago: POs Shot Fatally & Nonfatally, 1974-78	POs Killed (all weapons), Nationally, 1980-89
Nondomestic disturbances (man with gun, bar fights, etc.)	37%	10%
Domestic disturbances	4%	7%
Robberies	18%	14%
Burglaries	2%	5%
Personal business	9%	--
Traffic stops or pursuits	4%	14%
Attempting other arrests	12%	22%
Other (including "suspicious activity")	7%	14%
Ambushes/other assaults on officers	7%	9%
Transporting or custody of prisoners	1%	4%
Handling emotionally disturbed persons	--	2%
TOTALS	101%*	101%*

Sources: Geller and Karales (1981a: 147), FBI (1989b: 18).
* Totals more than 100 percent due to rounding.

One other piece of evidence on the likelihood of officers being severely injured or killed in family quarrels comes from the IACP/DuPont Kevlar Survivors' Club. It has tracked the circumstances in which police officers' lives have been saved nationally by soft body armor since such equipment first became generally available in 1972. Tables 27 and 28, near the end of Chapter 5, show the array of circumstances in which officers have been saved by soft body armor over the past 20-plus years. Nine percent (67) of the 760 law enforcement personnel whose lives were saved from *assaults* as of March 15, 1992, were attempting to deal with domestic disturbances at the time they were assaulted (IACP/DuPont Kevlar Survivors' Club 1992).

> *"[V]iolence against Chicago police officers is on the rise. * * * The incidence of officers being targeted by gunfire is up 92 percent for the first eight months of 1992 compared with the same period in 1991. [As of September 8, 1992] police officers have been shot at 83 times; 43 officers had been targets of gunfire at the end of August last year, police records show." Fourteen Chicago officers were struck by gunfire through the end of August 1992, compared with 12 during the first eight months of 1991. " 'It's more dangerous,' Chicago Police Supt. Matt Rodriguez said.... 'If criminals are more bold in their dealings with each other, they're going to be more bold in their dealings with police officers,' he added" (Lenhart 1992).*

Table 20:
Reported Frequency of Harm to Police Officers in Various Studies

Study	Domestic Disturbance	Other Disturbance	Burglary	Robbery	Traffic	All Other	Total
D E A T H S							
FBI	56 5.4%	126 12.2%	65 6.3%	174 16.9%	129 12.5%	481 46.7%	1,031 100%
Konstantin	15 5.2%	17 5.9%	10 3.5%	31 10.8%	55 19.2%	159 55.4%	287 100%
Margarita	4 1.5%	35 13.1%	14 5.2%	60 22.4%	17 6.3%	138 51.5%	268 100%
A S S A U L T S							
Bannon	37 8.5%	68 15.6%	N/A	N/A	83 19.0%	248 56.9%	436 100%
Chapman	168 8.9%	217 11.4%	N/A	N/A	227 12.0%	1,285 67.7%	1,897 100%
Margarita	26 1.5%	400 23.8%	62 3.7%	390 23.2%	90 5.4%	714 42.4%	1,682 100.0%
I N J U R I E S							
IACP	60 4.4%	168 12.3%	N/A	N/A	134 9.8%	1,001 73.4%	1,363 99.9%
Geller/ Karales	4 3.7%	34 31.5%	2 1.9%	19 17.6%	4 3.7%	45 41.7%	108 100.1%

*Source: Garner and Clemmer (1986: 4). Sources used by Garner and Clemmer (1986): **Bannon (1976)** (studied assaults on Detroit police during the period July 1, 1973, through June 30, 1974); **Chapman, et al. (1974)** (studied assaults on police during 1973 in 37 cities in Oklahoma, New Mexico, Arkansas, Louisiana, and Texas); **FBI, Law Enforcement Officers Killed and Assaulted (1975-85)** (studied police felonious deaths nationally during the years 1975-85); **Geller and Karales (1981a)** (studied fatal and nonfatal shootings of Chicago police officers by civilians during the period 1974-78); **International Association of Chiefs of Police (1971)** (studied police injuries and deaths nationally by reviewing 1,800 newspapers monthly from July 1970 through April 1971); **Konstantin (1984)** (studied felonious police deaths nationally during the period 1978-80 by coding narrative descriptions published in the FBI's annual reports on police felonious deaths); and **Margarita (1980a, 1980c)** (studied homicides of New York City police officers during the 128 years from 1851 through 1978 by reviewing NYPD archives).*

4. Police Shot by Themselves or Their Colleagues and Police Who Were Victimized Accidentally

Still another perspective on the incidence of officers' fatal or nonfatal gunshot wounds comes from considering the extent to which they are shot by themselves or their colleagues. In both New York City and Chicago, for example, an alarming proportion of the officers who were shot over the past two decades were shot either by themselves or by colleagues (New York City Police Academy 1971; Fyfe 1978, 1980a; NYPD 1988; Cerar 1990; Geller and Karales 1981a, 1982). The New York and Chicago studies, whose data are reported in Table 21, reveal that anywhere from 25 to 80 percent of all officers shot during the periods studied shot *themselves* (the largest percentages typically come from police *fatalities*).

> On a Friday evening "at approximately 1856 hours, [two] off-duty Police Officers...were present in a bar. At location, [the first] P.O. bent over from the waist to pick up a puck which had fallen from a shuffleboard game. Officer's Glock 29 became loose from his waistband holster and began to fall to floor. The weapon, while falling, glanced against the side of the shuffleboard game when [the] P.O. grabbed for it, causing 1 round to discharge. Round struck [the other] off-duty officer in the thigh causing an injury" (Cerar 1991: 17).

> "Around noon on January 10, a 42-year-old officer...was shot and killed after responding to a man-with-gun call. The 17-year veteran located a man walking along a freeway with a rifle. In his cruiser with the driver's window open, the officer approached the suspect and the two conversed briefly. Investigation indicates the man then stepped back six or seven feet and then shot the officer twice in the face with the .22-caliber semi-automatic rifle. Fleeing the scene, the man allegedly confronted a nearby farmer and wounded him. Later, the 28-year-old suspect was shot in an exchange of gunfire with police. He survived and has been charged in connection with the officer's death" (FBI 1989b:30).

There is reason to believe that, nationally, the percentages of officers shot who are struck by police bullets may have increased in recent years. Although increases or decreases in officer fatalities do not necessarily parallel changes in the number of officers shot nonfatally over time, the data on officer fatalities are often used because they are far easier to acquire. Figure 67 shows the annual changes in the number of American law enforcement officers killed feloniously and who died accidentally in the line of duty from 1960 through 1991 (the numbers associated with this graph appear in Appendix E in Table E-3).

Generally, at least half the officer fatalities in any year are felonious. The reason accidental deaths are a larger proportion of total deaths in the 1980s and 1990s than in earlier years, as Figure 67 shows, is that the number of accidentals rose and the number of felonious killings decreased (see also Table E-3 in Appendix E). Officer use of soft body armor and other protective gear may also help account for their decreasing victimization, despite an apparent escalation of the weaponry used by some criminals.

Though officers have apparently become more skillful at taking precautions against felonious assaults, it remains the case that a substantial portion of police firearm victimizations come from *self-inflicted* wounds. Some departments have openly recognized and begun to search for ways to address this problem. A part of the phenomenon, of course, is officer suicides, which some researchers and commentators have suggested generally exceed national averages for adults.[33]

Table 21:
Persons Who Shot New York City Police Department Officers
and Chicago Police Intentionally and Unintentionally

Study	Year(s) Studied	Injury Level Studied	Number and % of Police Shot by:			
			Civil- ians	Them- selves	Other POs	Total
NEW YORK CITY						
NYC Police Acad. (1971)	1970	fatalities	8 53%	7 47%	0 0%	15 100%
Fyfe (1978, 1980a)	1971-75	fatalities	30 52%	25 43%	3 5%	58 100%
NYPD (1988)	1986	fatalities	2 20%	8 80%	0 0%	10 100%
NYPD (1988)	1987	fatalities	3 25%	9 75%	0 0%	12 100%
NYPD (1988)	1987	woundings	12 46%	9 35%	5 19%	26 100%
NYPD (1989)	1988	wounds/ fatals	?	?	5 9%	53 100
Cerar (1990: 12)	1990	wounds/ fatals	17 43%	19 48%	4 10%	40 101%
Cerar (1991: 15, 21)	1991	wounds/ fatals	22 50%	14 32%	8 18%	44 100%
CHICAGO						
Geller and Karales (1981a, 1982)	1974-78	wounds/ fatals	116 62%	51 27%	20 11%	187 100%
Geller (1988)	1974-83	wounds/ fatals	167 57%	100 34%	27 9%	294 100%

Rutledge (1988: 107) cites an occupational suicide study by the National Center for Health Statistics that "found the law enforcement suicide rate nationally to be 83 percent higher than for the general population. By the most conservative estimates," he concluded, "the law enforcement officer is at least 10 percent more likely to be killed by his own hand

---

[33] For discussions of police officer suicides and stresses within police families see Kroes (1976, 1985); Kroes and Hurrell (1975); Bedian (1982); Wagner and Brzeczek (1983); Lester (1978d); Lester and Mink (1979); Lester and Gallagher (1980); Heiman (1977); Fennell (1981); Russo, et al. (1983); Volanti (1983); Volanti, et al. (1986); Malloy and Mays (1984); Bibbins (1986); Boelte (1989); Madamaba (1986); Stratton and Stratton (1982); Maslach and Jackson (1979); David (1991); Rutledge (1988: 107-120); and *Law Enforcement News* (1991d).

than by a criminal." Rutledge estimated that about two American police officers kill themselves per week; the overall American suicide rate is about one every 15 minutes—or an average of 672 per week (*ibid*.: 108).

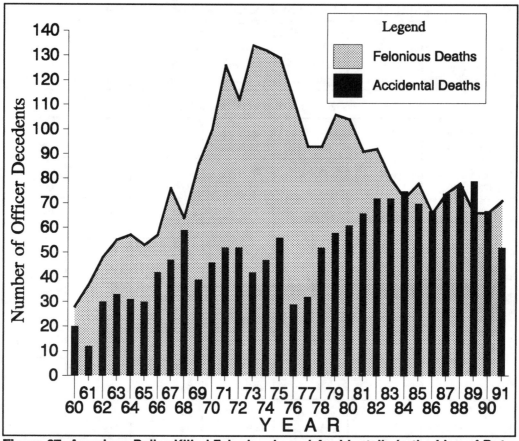

Figure 67: American Police Killed Feloniously and Accidentally in the Line of Duty, 1960-91 *Source: FBI (annual reports).*

The claim that police are 83 percent more likely than the general populace to kill themselves may not square with Rutledge's own estimate that two police suicides occur in the nation per week (104 per year). With a total of about 600,000 publicly employed police in the United States, the annual rate of police suicides is approximately 17 per 100,000 (104 divided by 6). National Center for Health Statistics data reveal that since 1933 the suicide rate for Americans of all ages has ranged between about 10

> *An off-duty officer was installing a trigger guard on his gun, using an allen wrench. The wrench slipped, pulling the trigger back, and the fully loaded gun went off, striking the officer in the abdomen (Geller and Karales 1981a: 144).*

and 15 per 100,000 (Brody 1992: B6). In 1991 the national rate for persons of all ages was 12.6 per 100,000 (*New York Times* 1992u). The difference between 12.6 and 17 per 100,000 suggests that police suicides are approximately 35 percent (not 83 percent) more likely than general population suicides. The general population suicide rate for males between the ages of 18 and 34 in 1991 was 20 per 100,000—18 percent *higher* than the officer suicide rate of 17. To provide a more precise comparison, however, we would need information not readily available at press time: an estimate *for 1991* of the officer suicide rate; and the general population suicide rate for males covering the full spectrum of ages employed as police.

The officer suicide rate reported for the Chicago Police Department over the three years from 1977 through 1979 was five times that for adult male residents of Chicago: 43.8 officer suicides per 100,000 officers versus 8.8 citizen suicides per 100,000 citizens (Wagner and Brzeczek 1983). But the Los Angeles Police Department, studied twice (1970-76 and 1977-88) by Dash and Reiser (1978) and then Josephson and Reiser (1990), presents a counter example. The Los Angeles County suicide rates per 100,000 for adult citizens and police officers are shown in Table 22.

Table 22:
Suicide Rates for Los Angeles County Adults Compared with
Los Angeles Police Department Officers, 1970s and 1980s

Year(s)	Adult Suicides per 100,000 Population	LAPD Member Suicides per 100,000 POs
1970	21.3	---
1970-76	---	8.1
1975	18.2	---
1977-88	---	12.0
1980	14.3	---
1987	13.4	---

Sources: Dash and Reiser (1978), Josephson and Reiser (1990).

The LAPD member suicide rates for the 1970-76 and 1977-88 study periods were both below the general population rates. Although the rise in LAPD officer suicide rates in more recent years is of obvious concern, two points should be emphasized. First, the suicide rate in the late 1980s still remained slightly below the comparable rate for the general population. And second, the numbers on which the LAPD rates—and other departments' rates—are based are small enough to permit substantial fluctuation over time. The total number of suicides in the three-year Chicago study was 20 (including three retirees). The totals for the LAPD studies were far smaller—there were four suicides in the 1970-76 period and 10 in the 1977-88 period.

The New York City police experience is closer to that of Chicago's than of the LAPD's. Research conducted for a training video on suicide awareness and prevention provided the cold statistical evidence of what NYPD members and their families must already have known:

"New York City Police Department [records reveal] that more police officers die by their own hand than are killed in the line of duty. [Between 1986 and late 1991], 37 police officers have taken their own lives, while 17 officers died in the line of duty.... The figures indicate that the suicide rate in the 27,500 officer department is almost twice that of the general population. Approxi-

A New York City Police Foundation staff member, who helped produce a first-ever NYPD training film on officer suicide awareness and prevention, noted the difficulty the film makers had getting law enforcement agencies around the nation to even discuss their own officer suicide problems: There is "a reluctance on the part of police officials to acknowledge suicides. Other departments are not exactly dealing with the problem on the surface. They pretend they don't have a problem. They have hunting accidents, not suicides" (Law Enforcement News 1991d: 9).

mately 30,000 people commit suicide each year nationwide" (*Law Enforcement News* 1991d: 1).

In 1990 the only sworn members of the New York City police killed by a deadly weapon were those (five officers) who committed suicide (Cerar 1990: 12). That year was more extreme than many. In 1989 of the 13 NYPD officers who died from a deadly weapon, 6 were either shot or stabbed by adversaries (an additional officer, not included in this tally, was killed when thrown from a roof), and 7 died by their own hands—6 in what were classified as suicides, another while playing Russian roulette (Cerar 1989: 11). In 1988 five NYPD officers were killed feloniously with deadly weapons; seven committed suicide (Cerar 1988: 11). In 1987 three NYPD officers were killed by perpetrators, and nine took their own lives (NYPD Chief of Department 1988: 3; Cerar 1990: 9). In 1986 two NYPD officers were killed by perpetrators and eight died through suicide (NYPD Chief of Department 1988: 3). In the most recent full year for which data are available as we go to press—1991—two NYPD members were shot and killed by perpetrators, and five were suicides (Cerar 1991: 12).

"A study of 93 police officer suicide cases showed the following statistics:

- *64 percent of the officers were patrol [officers]*
- *83 percent were in the age group of 30 to 45 years*
- *75 percent were married*
- *28 percent were qualified to retire on pension*
- *38 percent had suffered a recent departmental problem*
- *51 percent had suffered a recent marital problem*
- *35 percent were 'aggressive, impulsive' officers*
- *65 percent were 'quiet, reliable, good cops'*
- *90 percent used their service revolvers to kill themselves" (Rutledge 1988: 109).*

Experts suggest that, depending on the study one cites, the suicide rate for police officers is "among either the top three or top five of all professions" (Baltic 1991: 29; Kroes 1976, 1985; Richard and Fell 1975; compare Terry 1985: 403-404; and see *New York Times* 1992u for data on suicide rates in the several branches of the U.S. military). Hill and Clawson (1988) found that, in the state of Washington over the 22-year period 1950-71 white male police officers (the group they chose to study) had a moderately higher suicide rate than the combined average suicide rate for white males in 193 other occupations. Out of 1,586 deaths (from all causes) of white male police officers and detectives during these two decades, 40 were by suicide and 15 were by homicide (*ibid.*: 245). Moreover, they report assertions by police officers that "suicide in their ranks is often covered up by fellow officers. If this speculation is correct," they say, "it may be the case that the police are considerably, and not just moderately, more likely to die in this fashion" (*ibid.*: 244-245). Troubling suicide rates are not limited to the most crime-plagued cities. "Clean, civilized Toronto, of all places, had one cop suicide a month for eight months straight a couple of years ago," according to American police psychologist Bill Lewinski (Baltic 1991: 29).

*"For cops, the risk of being killed in the line of duty, scary though it can be, is dwarfed by the risk of what...Karl Menninger calls 'death by inches': burnout, alcoholism, divorce, suicide. * * * Seventy percent of officers involved in shootings leave police work within five years, mostly because they can't handle the emotional fallout" (Baltic 1991: 29; see New York Times 1992p for discussion of a disability pension case in Teaneck, NJ).*

As indicated, besides *self*-inflicted gunshots, significant numbers of officers are struck by bullets fired by their fellow officers. Typically, this occurs either because of mistaken identity, accidental firearms discharges, or stray bullets during the chaos of a gun battle (see Burke, et al. 1988 on the risk from ricochets). The problem of officers being struck by their colleagues' bullets during operations became a matter of great concern in early 1992 for the Dallas Police Department, which saw two of its officers fall within six weeks to what it termed "friendly fire."[34] The deaths came during narcotics operations (*Crime Control Digest* 1991g, 1992c; *Law Enforcement News* 1992a).

The problem of officers maimed or killed at their own or fellow officers' hands is, of course, not a new one. Nor, unfortunately, are the numbers of such victims always minuscule compared with the number of officers shot by assailants. Nine percent of the Chicago officers shot between 1974 and 1983 were shot by fellow officers, and overall 43 percent were shot either by themselves or their colleagues. During this nine-year period, of the 252 members of the Chicago Police Department who suffered fatal or nonfatal

Two on-duty officers were assigned to a "man with a gun" call on a cold winter day. As the officers exited the squad car, one officer drew his .45 semi-automatic pistol and chambered a round. As he approached the scene of the reported offense with his pistol in the fully cocked position, he slipped on the icy pavement, and his gun discharged, hitting him in the leg (Geller and Karales 1981a: 144).

gunshot wounds, 109 were struck by bullets fired by police officers. Of the 87 officers in this group who shot themselves either accidentally or purposely, 24 percent did so while on duty and 76 percent while off duty. Commenting on the portrait of whose bullets strike police officers painted in an earlier Chicago study (Geller and Karales 1981a), criminologist Norval Morris (1981: iv) articulated the grim conclusion: "It is the armed robber and, paradoxically, the armed policeman who are the threats to the life of the police!"

Fyfe (1978) concluded that during the 1970s police in New York City were "at least as likely to be killed by themselves, their acquaintances or their colleagues as by their professional clientele." As the data above suggest, this situation seems not to have changed appreciably for the New York City Police Department over the past decade. The NYPD's most recent report on firearms discharges and assaults on officers stated the harsh reality: "In 1991, a total of 44 M.O.S. [members of the service] were shot. Of this total, 50 percent either shot themselves or were unintentionally shot by another Police Officer" (Cerar 1991: 15).

---

[34] The military uses both this term and "fratricide" to describe accidental casualties among its ranks during combat (Schmitt 1992).

"The use of concealment not only minimizes the risk of officers, bystanders and suspects, but may also prevent tragic mistakes. I can recount several occasions in which officers responding to such calls [as robberies in progress] have neglected to seek concealment, have encountered armed individuals from positions of total exposure, have—with some justification—perceived imminent danger to themselves, and have shot persons later found to be plainclothes police officers or crime victims who had armed themselves to pursue the actual perpetrators. Many of these tragedies might have been avoided if the officers involved had instead confronted these individuals from positions of physical cover. From such positions, officers make themselves near impossible targets, and are able to give their perceived adversaries opportunities to identify themselves or to drop their weapons without placing themselves in jeopardy" (Fyfe 1989c: 477).

Analysts, among them former NYPD supervisor Jim Fyfe, have been seeking strategies to avert "friendly fire" shootings in New York City since at least the mid-1970s (Fyfe 1989c: 479 n. 8). Among the methods considered useful (on which we'll provide additional information in Chapter 5) are what Fyfe has called "tactical knowledge" and "concealment." The former entails a good working knowledge of the locations—indoor and outdoor—and people that might eventually become the scenes or players in a police-violence drama. The latter, as Fyfe (1989c: 477) described it, involves "disguising one's intent or identity, as well as employing actual physical cover or shelter." Other tacticians find it clearer to distinguish "cover" from "concealment" rather than to subsume "cover" under "concealment," but the salient point is that police experts see considerable promise for averting unintended—as well as unnecessary—uses of deadly force by police.

While not diminishing any of the dangers of police work imposed by criminals, data such as we have provided above on the *sources* of police gunshot injuries can help police administrators invest wisely in a multi-faceted program for protecting officers against the various hazards they face (also see Robin 1963; Margarita 1980b). Most of these hazards arise out of confrontations between individual officers and individual or small numbers of adversaries. Insofar as violence control efforts are also to focus on crowd control methods—especially the control of hostile crowds in which officers may be jeopardized by "friendly fire," police analysts would do well to

"With the recent 'friendly fire' deaths of two of its narcotics officers, the Dallas Police Department...introduced a panel of five outside experts who will study the agency's drug raid tactics. On December 11, [a detective] was mistakenly shot by fellow officers during a drug sting in which two suspects were also killed. [O]n January 22, [an officer] died when he was struck by pellets from a shotgun held by another detective during a struggle with a suspect" (Crime Control Digest 1992c; see also Crime Control Digest 1991g and Law Enforcement News 1992a).

stay abreast of developments in military research attempting to minimize the extent to which our troops or allies are victimized by American weaponry (see, e.g., Schmitt 1991, 1992).

5. Efforts to Explain Variations Across Jurisdictions and Over Time

Just as researchers have examined whether rates of justifiable homicide by police

> *Fifteen years ago, "severe headaches, double vision, dizziness, a persistent fever and the inability of doctors to relieve the pain in his face had forced [Officer Jones—not his real name] into severe depression. He had separated from his wife and two children. Two operations had done nothing to ease his torment. He was drinking and taking anti-depressant drugs, and he decided he wanted to die. Armed with his service revolver, [Jones] telephoned his best friend, police Sgt. [Stevens—also a pseudonym], and told him: 'My time is up, I'm really going to do it.'*
>
> *"Stevens rushed over to Jones' home and for the next 2-1/2 hours Jones, holding a .38-calibre pistol in one hand and a Scotch and water in the other, alternately pointed the gun at himself, at Stevens and at his wife—all the time constantly cocking and uncocking the weapon. Finally, Jones' wife tried to pass a pack of cigarettes to Stevens, but they fell to the floor. Nerves. All three bent to pick up the cigarettes. Jones switched his drink to his gun hand, and the weapon discharged. Stevens was hit in the face.*
>
> *"Stevens was hospitalized for eight days. He survived with only a slight loss of hearing. Jones dropped all thoughts of self-destruction, checked himself into a psychiatric hospital for 20 days, and reunited with his wife. Although everyone agreed that the shooting was an accident, the...Police and Fire Board fired Jones. The disability payments stopped, and Jones' wife was forced to work at three jobs. Jones fought his firing.*
>
> *"[Fourteen years after the shooting incident], a new operation...relieved Jones of his pain for the first time in at least 15 years. [Over the objections of the employing village, nearly two years after his successful surgery, Officer Jones won his litigation and was reinstated] at his old rank and [paid] $99,142 in back pay. * * * Stevens, now a police commander, is...uncertain about how things will work out [with Jones returning to the force after 15 years' absence]. 'Time will tell,' he said. 'They say that time heals all wounds' " (Skolnik 1992).*

officers from different jurisdictions correlate with any identifiable community variables or social conditions, they have explored the possible correlates of police line-of-duty deaths. Analyzing the felonious slayings of police in all 50 states for the period 1977-1984, Peterson and Bailey (1988) concluded that a positive correlation existed between the officer death rate and rates of poverty and divorce in the community at large. Among their most interesting findings, however, are those reporting factors that are *not* correlated with killings of law enforcement personnel:

> "[H]omicides of police [are not] associated significantly with region or with racial income inequality.... [P]olice killings are not tied to the level of serious crime, and thus are not simply an expected cost of doing police work."

Peterson and Bailey argued that police performance characteristics—"lack of competence, errors in judgment, and negative attitudes and prejudice"—might play a role in explaining variations in the rate at which police are feloniously killed, but such factors constitute at best a partial explanation.

Peterson and Bailey's finding that region is not an explanatory factor for police line-of-duty deaths is consistent with Vaughn and Kappeler's earlier (1986) study. The 1986 study argued that, although Uniform Crime Reports data on police killed feloniously typically show substantial differences in the number of personnel slain in each region of the country, these differences mainly reflect different population sizes rather than varying risks by region. It would probably be wise to conduct such appraisals on a recurring basis to examine whether emerging patterns of gun use and violent crime alter the strength of the correlation between geographic region and killings of police.

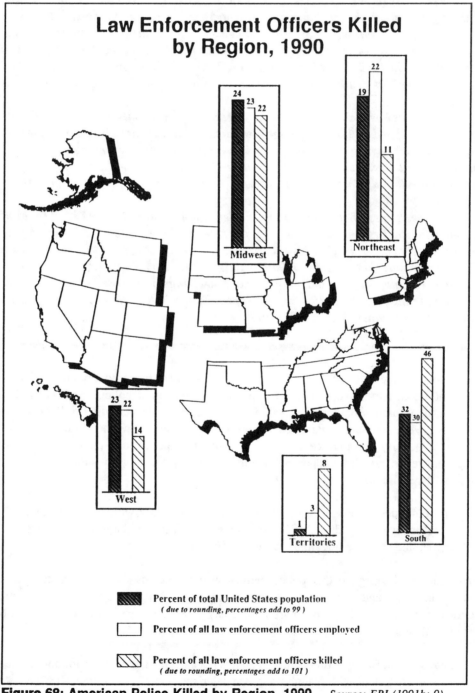

Figure 68: American Police Killed by Region, 1990   *Source: FBI (1991b: 9).*

Some of the data required for this continuing analysis are contained in the FBI's annual report, *Law Enforcement Officers Killed and Assaulted*. The report shows for each of the regions the percent of law enforcement officers killed, the percent of U.S. general population, and the percent of law enforcement officers employed. An illustrative graphic appears in Figure 68.

Visual inspection of this figure shows that the relationship between percent of officers employed in a region and percent of officers who die in that region is hardly a consistent one. In the Midwest, Northeast, and West, a smaller percentage of all officer deaths occur than one might expect from the employment information. But in the South and the Territories, a larger percentage of officer deaths occurs than one might predict based on the employment distribution.

Tables E-47 through E-50 and E-63 in Appendix E report FBI compiled data on the percentages of American law enforcement personnel employed and slain in the different regions of the country and on rates at which officers are feloniously slain per region. In 1987 through 1990 a higher percentage of police were slain than were employed in the South, with the discrepancy ranging from 5 percent in 1987 to 21 percent in 1989. In 1989 28 percent of American police worked in the South while 49 percent of those slain were based in the South (FBI annual reports).

Using the FBI's 1990 figures on the distribution of police employees across the nation's five regions (FBI 1991b: 9) and FBI data on total police employees in the nation (FBI 1991c) in 1990, we can roughly calculate the *likelihood* of officers being feloniously slain in the regions. The calculations for this and other rates we will discuss below are shown in Table E-63 in Appendix E. Officers in the Northeast were slain in 1990 at the rate of 5.4 per 100,000 officers employed in that region. Employment-based rates in the other regions were 10.4 in the Midwest, 17.0 in the South, 7.0 in the West, and 28.3 in the Territories. Thus, in 1990, officers in the South were 3.2 times more likely (based on national employment distributions) to be killed than were police in the Northeast, 1.6 times more likely than midwestern police, and 2.4 times more likely than police in the West. In the Territories, where in 1990 five officers were killed feloniously, they were considerably more likely based on employment levels to die in the line of duty than were their counterparts in the other regions. The greatest discrepancy in rates—fivefold—was between the Territories and the Northeast.

Rates based on other demographics besides police employment levels are also illuminating. Table E-63 shows that, if one considers the levels of police felonious deaths against the backdrop of reported violent felonies (murder, forcible rape, robbery, and aggravated assault), the likelihood of police dying in the regions in 1990 was the following: In the Northeast, 1.8 police were killed feloniously for every 100,000 violent felonies reported; in the Midwest, police were slain at the rate of 4.0 per 100,000 such crimes; in the South, the rate was 4.6; and in the West the rate was 2.1. Overall, the national rate was 3.6 police slain for every 100,000 violent felonies reported. (The Territories are omitted from this analysis, because data on the number of violent felonies reported in the Territories are not available in the FBI documents used for this analysis.)

Thus, using reported violent felonies to estimate the differences in danger among the four regions, we see that the region in which police are most likely to die feloniously is still the South, with a rate of 4.6 per 100,000 offenses. But the Midwest is now a very close second, with a rate of 4.0. The safest region by this calculus is the Northeast (1.8), and the

West is close behind (2.1). Put another way, using reported violent felonies as the basis for calculating risk, police in the South are 1.2 times more likely than police in the Midwest, 2.2 times more likely than police in the West, and 2.6 times more likely than police in the Northeast to meet a felonious death. The Midwest also is approximately twice the risk for officer felonious death (based on reported violent felonies) as are the Northeast and West.

The last way in which we have examined the relative riskiness of the four major geographic regions for officer felonious killings is by calculating rates based on the number of arrests officers made collectively in each region for violent felonies (again, murder, forcible rape, robbery, and aggravated assault). We have readily conceded before in this volume that arrests are, of course, the product of officers exercising their discretion (a discretion which could be abused just as could an officer's discretion to employ deadly force). Nevertheless, the patterns and frequency of police arrest decisions may be the best available reflection of varying degrees of police exposure to violent encounters. As Table E-63 reveals, the South again emerges as the most lethal environment for police to perform their duties. In that region, during 1990 police were killed feloniously at the rate of 17.5 per 100,000 arrests for violent felonies. This compares with rates of 15.8 for the Midwest, 5.9 for the Northeast, and 4.9 for the West. The implication is that southern police are slightly more likely (1.1 times more likely) than midwestern officers to be feloniously slain, 3.0 times more likely than northeastern law enforcement personnel, and 3.6 times more likely than their western colleagues to die felonious deaths based on arrests for violent felonies.

As we saw with the calculations based on *reported* violent felonies, midwestern and southern police have by far the highest risks of dying feloniously. The *arrest*-based rates show midwestern police 2.8 times more likely than northeastern officers and 3.2 times more likely than their counterparts in the West to be killed in criminal attacks. Thus, if, as has been true historically, geographic region today remains a poor predictor of levels of police slayings, researchers and tacticians may wish to examine the factors that may account for higher proportions of killings of law enforcement personnel in the South and the Midwest than in the Northeast and West.

The FBI, in the annual data report, *Law Enforcement Officers Killed and Assaulted*, offers no speculation on the *reasons* for disproportions in police felonious deaths across the regions. As we have talked generally with officers around the country about the regional pattern, two of the most commonly suggested factors to account for higher victimization levels in the South are: (1) the warmer climate, which leads to more contact between police and others; and (2) the greater concentration of guns in the South than in other regions (Jacobs and Britt [1979] discuss the history of lethal violence in the South). A third possibility, not suggested as frequently by our police colleagues, is that the warmer climate in the South results in a lower rate of officers wearing soft body armor. A study commissioned by the Justice Department's National Institute of Justice in 1991 concerning the slaying of police officers may lead to more insight concerning different police victimization rates across geographic areas (NIJ 1991).

Still other reasons, perhaps insightful but possibly just reflections of northern prejudice toward southerners, have been offered by police officials for the overrepresentation of southern police among the cadre of slain officers. One Wisconsin police chief, who owns property in the South and spends a great deal of time there, suggested to us recently that there are two additional explanations for the high death rate of southern police: first, a different culture of confrontation and engagement in the South (at least in all but the biggest cities), according to which officers are less likely than their colleagues in other regions to back down from avoidable violent confrontations; and second, a lower caliber of recruit in southern police agencies, owing primarily to a lower pay scale (relative to other occupations). We simply do not have the first-hand experience, nor have we had the opportunity to conduct the necessary research, that would equip us to express an opinion concerning such unflattering explanations for disproportionate line-of-duty deaths for peace officers in the American South.

Just as research has explored the question of whether the felonious killing of law enforcement personnel is significantly correlated with region of the nation, some studies have touched on the possible relationship between police victimization and the characteristics of *neighborhoods* within particular cities (e.g., Geller and Karales 1981a). The NYPD's annual report on firearms discharges and assaults on officers contains data on the distribution of shots-fired and officer assault incidents across the city's five boroughs and its several dozen precincts (e.g., Cerar 1990: 4, 6). But data would need to be compiled from other sources concerning the concentration of NYPD personnel across geographic areas and the hazard levels of these boroughs and precincts before meaningful analysis could be conducted of the likelihood of dangerous encounters occurring in different locales in New York City. When such research is conducted, and findings point to a correlation between officer victimization patterns and other geographically varied factors, a useful next step for the analyst trying to identify the correlates of police risk is to explore whether the same factors hold up as strong correlates *over time*.

While few strong *geographical* correlates of officer victimization have been identified in the published literature, it is possible that, *over time*, changing officer victimization levels might be linked to various police organizational and societal factors. Although the available research has not statistically demonstrated a connection between changing levels of violence in the community and officer endangerment, the logical connection seems powerful.

It may be noteworthy that, as killings of and by police officers have been slowly declining during the past 15 to 20 years, crimes of personal violence (other than homicide) committed against the general population also slowly declined (or at least failed to increase) for much of this period. The nonhomicide violent crime reduction is measured not by Uniform Crime Reports' tabulations of crimes *reported* to police but by national surveys of American households conducted for the Justice Department by the Census Bureau (Bureau of Justice Statistics 1990; *Crime Control Digest* 1990b: 2).

Although there are gaps in coverage of these national "victimization" surveys,[35] for many types of offenses they may offer a more complete snapshot of the level of crime in the United States than do the UCR data, which are affected by the failure of crime victims to report offenses to authorities. Thus, for example, in the fall of 1990 the National Crime Survey results, released by the Justice Department's Bureau of Justice Statistics, showed that "the number of violent crimes [in 1989] was 11 percent lower than the 1981 number" (*Crime Control Digest* 1990b: 1). Moreover, "[c]ompared to 1973, the first year for which complete data was available, the rates of crime in 1989 per 1,000 persons or per 1,000 households declined in all major crime categories other than motor vehicle thefts" (*Crime Control Digest*

---

[35] For example, homicides and commercial crime are not counted. Moreover, all victimization data are statistical estimates for the United States based on representative national surveys. In these surveys, U.S. Census Bureau staff interview approximately 97,000 persons age 12 or over about crimes they may have experienced during the prior six months (Bureau of Justice Statistics 1990). Moreover, there is research suggesting that, at least with respect to the crime of forcible rape, the national victimization studies substantially undercount the prevalence of criminal offending (Johnston 1992).

1990b: 2). In 1990 the number of violent crime victimizations in the United States rose slightly, to 6,009,000 from 5,861,000 the previous year (Bureau of Justice Statistics 1992: 4).

But if one takes into account the growth over time in the national population, then violent crimes against Americans (as reflected in the victimization studies) have taken a path since 1973 that is virtually never reported by the media, politicians, or other major public opinion shapers: the violent crime victimization rates have been *decreasing* or remaining stable over time (see Geller 1991). In 1973, for every 1,000 persons age 12 or older in the nation, 32.6 Americans were the victims of crimes of violence (rape, robbery, assault—victimization surveys exclude homicides) (Bureau of Justice Statistics 1992: 6). These annual rates varied little through 1985 (running from a high of 35.3 in 1981 to a low of 30.0 in 1985). Then, in 1986 the annual rate dipped below 30 per 1,000 to 28.1. Since that time the rate did not again rise above 30 until 1991. The 1987 rate was 29.3, the 1988 rate was 29.6, the 1989 rate was 29.1, and the 1990 rate was 29.6 (*ibid.*). The 1991 preliminary rate, the most recent available at press time, was 31.3 crimes of violence per 1,000 Americans age 12 or older (*Crime Control Digest* 1992f: 3).

National victimization surveys have been conducted each year by the U.S. Census Bureau since 1973. The percentage changes in violent crime victimization *rates* in the United States between the peak year of 1981 and the year for which the most recent *final*[36] data are available (1990) are shown in Table 23, as are changes in victimization rates for other categories of crime.

It becomes apparent that, with the exception of motor vehicle theft, which increased nearly 20 percent over this nine-year period, the *likelihood* of Americans suffering a personal or household victimization was considerably less in 1990 than it was at the beginning of the 1980s. Does this mean that, contrary to public alarm over crime and violence, the nation is *not* suffering from serious crime? Obviously not, for several reasons. One is that, as noted earlier, the national victimization surveys exclude homicides, which have been breaking records in recent years.

Another reason is that, while national victimization rates reveal a rosier picture than one might take from the news media or others, the patterns may differ from one jurisdiction to another. Certain areas, especially large metropolitan areas, may have victimization rates higher than in previous years (unfortunately, we do not know this to be true or false, because victimization surveys, for cost reasons, normally are not conducted at the level of individual cities). Moreover, it is almost certainly the case that, *within* jurisdictions, the patterns of victimization rates over time differ from one locale to another.

The often-repeated commentary that, in some inner-city neighborhoods in America, a generation of youth are being lost as productive members of society is an unhappily accurate

---

[36] In releasing the preliminary results of the 1991 National Crime Survey, the federal Bureau of Justice Statistics cautioned: "If trends that occurred during the first part of 1991 were to be reversed during the latter half, especially during the final three months, then it is likely that none of the changes in the preliminary estimates would be statistically significant in the final data" (*Crime Control Digest* 1992f: 3). That is, the 5.9 percent rise in national victimization rates from 29.6 violent crimes per thousand in 1990 to 31.3 per thousand in 1991, which, based on the households sampled, represented a statistically significant national change in the preliminary analysis, could, with the addition of new data later in the year, cease to be a reliable basis for concluding that there had been an increase in the national victimization rate.

portrait. As Reverend Joseph Lowery of the Southern Christian Leadership Conference observed in an address to the National Organization of Black Law Enforcement Executives in 1990, "Our youth have despair for breakfast, futility for lunch, hopelessness for dinner, and sleep on a pillow of desperation" (Geller 1991: xi).

Table 23:
Percentage Change in Criminal *Victimization Rates* in the United States, 1981-90

Type of Victimization	Percentage Change (+ or -) in Victimization Rate[1]
PERSONAL CRIMES	***-22.5%***
Crimes of violence	-16.2%
Rape[2]	-40.0%
Robbery	-23.0%
Assault	-13.7%
Crimes of theft	-25.0%
HOUSEHOLD CRIMES	***-28.8%***
Burglary	-38.8%
Household larceny	-28.4%
Motor vehicle theft	+19.9%

[1] *The victimization rate is the number of victimizations per 1,000 persons age 12 or older in America (for personal crimes) or per 1,000 households in the United States (for property crimes) (Bureau of Justice Statistics 1992: 6).*
[2] *Johnston (1992) describes a federally funded survey by a rape-victim support organization that suggests the national victimization surveys substantially undercount the prevalence of forcible rape.*
Source: National Crime Survey data released by the Bureau of Justice Statistics (1992: 6).

Thus, despite the generally good news about steady or decreasing national victimization rates, there is plenty of bad news to go around for police in many jurisdictions—as they know without our telling them. The soaring murder rates garner so much news media coverage not only because of their magnitude but also because of the murders' link with drug and youth-gang problems. The apparent increase in random stranger-killings in some cities (e.g., drive-by shootings in Los Angeles, Chicago, and other cities and "wilding" among youth gangs in New York City) has elevated fear levels, both within the general population and among police. The live television images of rioting Angelenos dragging perfect strangers from their vehicles and attempting to beat them to death during the height of the April-May 1992 south central Los Angeles riot will linger long as testament to the danger confronting urban dwellers who are in the wrong place at the wrong time.[37] People may disagree whether the public's and the

---

[37] On a far more optimistic note, so, too, will the images of heroism during the L.A. riot stand as shining examples of the greatness of the American spirit. An inspired nation joined with officials in Los Angeles in honoring such men as Gregory Alan Williams, an African American actor and writer who, animated by the golden rule, went out of his way to enter a mob scene at an intersection and, forsaking his own safety, rescued Japanese American Takao Hirata from his Ford Bronco, where he was being

police community's levels of fear are excessive in light of the actual number of offenses, but there can be little dispute that the 1990s have brought many communities a different level and type of aggravated assault and murder problem than they had previously known.

Data suggesting that the country's murder rate would jump 8 percent in 1990 compared with 1989 led the U.S. Senate Judiciary Committee to comment that if that pace continued, 1990 would be the bloodiest year in American history (Zeichner 1990). Unfortunately, the prediction was correct. The number of murders (not the rate), rose 10 percent between 1989 and 1990 (*Crime Control Digest* 1991c: 5). If this rise reflects an increasingly violent work environment for America's police offices, then continuing progress in safeguarding officers and the persons whom they arrest would stand as a remarkable accomplishment.[38]

It is also noteworthy that officers' national line-of-duty death rate continued declining during a period (since about 1984)[39] when many jurisdictions around the nation suffered the violent effects of the crack cocaine epidemic. Many have commented that both the physiological effects of crack use and competition among dealers have produced increasing levels of violence directed against the police, rival dealers, and the citizens at large (see, e.g., Horrock 1992: 1; Witkin, et al. 1990: 36; Marriott 1992b). The increasingly reckless and brazen nature of violence in drug turf battles fills the daily news in many locales with horrifying examples of innocent bystanders caught in the crossfire (Witkin, et al. 1990).

This has not been the first time in recent history, of course, that the nation seemed to be passing through a cycle of violence directed at police. Looking back on the 1960s and 1970s, an FBI agent suggested to a newspaper reporter that those were years when "radical groups often targeted police for violence, and cop killings rose quickly. Officers were caught in ambushes, and booby-trapped bombs were left at crime scenes" (quoted in McMillin 1992). One of the more frightening prospects as the smoke cleared over south central Los Angeles following five days of rioting in 1992 was the intelligence coming to the LAPD that leaders of the notorious Crips and Bloods street gangs were proposing a truce among their members for the purpose of turning their joint energies instead to the killing of LAPD officers (*Crime Control Digest* 1992g: 4-5). Thus, unhappily, as the nation moves through the last decade of the 20th century, there is ample reason to expect that the use of deadly force by and against police officers will persist—as a public health problem and a public policy dilemma.

"pummeled with bricks" (Pauly 1992: 8). Mr. Williams, as well as Titus Murphy, Terri Barnett and Lei Yuille (who aided 36-year-old white gravel truck driver Reginald Denny), were aptly characterized by civic leaders as "sunbursts" in the city's darkest hour (*ibid.*: 1; see also C. Hall 1992; *USA Today* 1992).

[38] Earlier in this book, we noted that deadly weapon assaults against police officers have risen in recent years. To an important extent, decreases in the number of officers feloniously killed are the product of officer safety precautions, especially the wearing of soft body armor, as we also discussed. We recounted as well the experience of a New York City undercover narcotics investigator whom we had the pleasure of riding with. He had worked in Spanish Harlem for many years without being shot at by arrestees and without having to shoot at his myriad criminal adversaries. Without presuming that it is a common experience across police forces or cities, we view this one officer's perhaps remarkable experience as an illustration that one cannot always use geography to predict jeopardy (Palermo 1990). This does not mean, of course, that an officer working in his or her city's high-crime areas need not take extraordinary precautions in the line of duty. Rather, it suggests that those precautions, artfully employed, can produce positive results even in the face of prolonged exposure to hazards.

[39] Crack cocaine hit different regions at different times. For instance, Wisconsin Attorney General James Doyle reported that crack hit cities in his state only in 1991 (Doyle 1992).

Chapter 5:

SHOOTING CONTROL STRATEGIES

T he shooting reduction strategies advocated in the empirical literature generally concern initiatives that police administrators or legislatures can take in such areas as policy development, policy enforcement, personnel practices, training, weapons and other equipment changes, and research to identify other control strategies (Geller and Karales 1981a: 180-206).

The empirical literature has been relatively pessimistic about the use of criminal prosecutions to control shootings, noting their scarcity,[1] and has not devoted much attention to the role of civil court proceedings, although there is a substantial nonempirical, legal literature tracking the evolution of municipal and police civil liability. Formally studying the effects of civil liability on police deadly force policy and practice may well be a fruitful area for empirical inquiry.[2] The control strategies discussed on the following pages are by no means the only reasonable steps that could be taken to stem unnecessary or unwarranted shootings, but they have been thought by the empirical researchers (and by many police agencies that have been studied) to be among the best ways to work toward this goal. As intimated above, a common feature of these various control mechanisms is that they concern factors over which police administrators potentially can have some control (e.g., police decisions to shoot nonviolent opponents, police reward structures, supervisory systems, and deployment patterns), rather than variables that, although possibly correlated with shootings,

---

[1] Criminal prosecutions are discussed later in this chapter.

[2] Informal conversations with police administrators around the nation suggest a reasonably widespread perception that the prospect of civil liability is indeed a significant consideration in framing deadly force policy and in individual officers' decisions whether to use deadly force in "elective shooting" situations (i.e., shootings not necessitated by an immediate threat to someone's life).

are relatively immune to administrative alteration (such as crime rates and poverty) (see Fyfe 1981b: 148).

I. *Policy Development*

A. *The Long March Toward the "Defense-of-Life" Standard and Other Restrictive Provisions in Departmental Shooting Policies*

For more than six decades after the American colonists' declaration of independence from England, they were policed by English-style constables, armed only with clubs. When the American urban constabularies began to be organized during the 1840s into bureaucratic police departments,[3] many of the organizational structures, procedures, and practices continued to be inspired by British models (the London Metropolitan Police Department, founded in 1829, being the greatest influence). But an important departure from the British practice began just a few years after the consolidation of urban constables into formal, public police agencies. While the British bobbies (and their criminal adversaries) rarely carried firearms, American city policemen started taking firearms with them on routine patrol. Historian Wilbur Miller (1975, 1983: 75) notes the emergence of the armed policeman in New York City:

> "New York's locally-controlled Municipal Police carried only clubs, but when the state government took over the force in 1857—prompted by a mixture of reform and partisan motives—many New Yorkers violently expressed their hostility to the new Metropolitan force and the police replied in kind. Individual Captains encouraged their men to carry revolvers for self-protection against a heavily armed underworld. By the end of the 1860s, revolvers were standard equipment, although they were never formally authorized."

Not only were revolvers not formally authorized by the New York City and other municipal police departments for many years, there were senior police officials who openly opposed the use of firearms by police. George W. Matsell, chief of the New York City Municipal Police, was said by a city police captain in 1857 to have "made it a standing rule to look upon every man as a coward and unfit to be put a second time on duty, where he had descended to the use of a pistol" (Miller, 1975, 1983: 83 n. 26).

Although the carrying of firearms represented a sharp break with the British tradition of unarmed police, the inherited British common law[4] governing police use of force in making arrests was not altered in most American jurisdictions. It allowed police to use lethal force to prevent the escape of a person wanted for *any* felony, regardless of whether that felony may have entailed violence or threats of violence. For short hand, this deadly force rule

---

[3] New York City's police force, organized in 1845, is generally credited as being the nation's first full-time police force (Miller 1975, 1983: 72). Compare Williams and Murphy's view (1990) that, in a meaningful sense, the southern "slave patrols" may be thought of as the earliest full-time, organized police forces.

[4] Common law is the body of law developed by courts through a succession of decisions that fills the void where legislatures have not enacted statutes on a particular subject. Common law is just as binding on public officials and private citizens as statutory pronouncements—within the deciding courts' jurisdiction.

has come to be known as the common law rule or the "any felony rule" (see Geller and Karales 1981a; Alpert and Fridell 1992). Thus, operating under very similar rules governing the situations in which deadly force could be used, the American police and their British counterparts had vastly different technologies available for the infliction of death.

It is generally assumed in discussions among police policymakers that the common law "any felony" rule was the rule of the day almost everywhere in England and the United States until very recent times. But commanders in both the London Metropolitan Police in the 1830s and the New York City Municipal Police in the 1840s "warned their men to use lethal violence only for self-defense and prescribed punishments for violators of this essential principle."[5] Reportedly, however, in America the "policeman's use of force was much less carefully monitored than in London" (Miller 1975, 1983: 75).

Despite uneven supervision of police use of deadly force in American cities, public expectations had been created early on that police should exercise great restraint in their efforts to halt the flight of unarmed suspects. Thus, hot on the heels of American police becoming armed came public controversy over police use of deadly force. For instance, when a New York City officer in 1858 shot and killed a fleeing suspect (within a few days of the murder of a fellow officer in an unrelated confrontation), the *New York Times* challenged the right of the police to slay the fleeing suspect: "If a policeman needs to defend his life, the use of force is permissible, but if he is chasing a suspect he has no right to shoot the man." The *Times* further asserted that lethal capture was becoming the first rather than the last resort in apprehension methods, turning the lone patrolman into "an absolute monarch, within his beat, with complete power of life and death over all within his range...without the forms of trial or legal inquiry of any kind" (Miller 1975, 1983: 75).

As American criminals and American law enforcers matched one another's escalating use of violence over the decades, the early police administrative insistence on great restraint with firearms could easily be dismissed by police leaders as a relic of simpler times. Even though many in the public were more than willing to condone police "streetcorner justice," concerns about police decisions to employ force would surface again and again throughout the nation's turbulent history.

In the 134 years since the *New York Times* decried the killing of an unarmed fleeing suspect, police deadly force policy has been widely discussed and debated, usually in the aftermath of tragic and bloody confrontations involving the police. Their adversaries have varied—common criminals, labor union activists, racial or ethnic minorities and others advocating civil rights reform or economic justice, students protesting wars, and others.

A series of early complaints about excessive and racially biased use of force (and biased provision of police services) came in the aftermath of the first World War. As black veterans returned in triumph to the United States, they discovered that, although enemy bullets had not discriminated on the basis of soldiers' skin color, American police, employers, schools, hospitals, and myriad other public and private institutions did. These and other frustrations quickly found expression in a series of bloody urban riots in several American cities (see, e.g., the report of the Chicago Commission on Race Relations [1922], which examined the so-called "Chicago Race Riot of 1919"). A number of the riot study commissions of the 1920s

---

[5] Miller (1975, 1983: 75), citing, among other sources, *Rules and Regulations for Day and Night Police of the City of New York with Instructions as to the Legal Powers and Duties of Policemen*, 1846.

cited police hostility to persons of color as crucial contributing causes of the riots and called for restraint and good judgment in the exercise of police force when dealing with criminal suspects (see generally Williams and Murphy 1990 and our discussion of riots in Chapter 1).

The riot post-mortems were being written at about the same time that more broadly focused examinations of police missions, methods, and accomplishments were being undertaken by an assortment of state and local "blue ribbon commissions." It was not uncommon for these commissions to recommend steps designed to temper what was seen as a police inclination to overstep proper bounds in exercising physical authority.[6]

Continuing concern (shared by a few within policing) over the techniques used by police found expression in one of the 15 reports issued in 1930 and 1931 by President Herbert Hoover's crime study commission, known popularly as the Wickersham Commission after Attorney General George W. Wickersham. The Commission's central mission was to identify ways to stem the rising tide of public disobedience to lawful authority during Prohibition, but its contradictory and ambiguous findings about the wisdom and enforceability of the 18th Amendment produced such widespread (and bipartisan) ridicule, even from President Hoover himself, that most of the Commission's sensible insights into crime control and police control went largely unnoticed (Zimring and Hawkins 1983: 354).

But oblivion was hardly the fate of the findings and recommendations contained in the Commission's volume entitled *Report on Lawlessness in Law Enforcement*, dog-eared copies of which could be found in the libraries of every major police reformer of the past six decades. The long-term impact of that volume of the Wickersham report cannot be denied. Its exposé and condemnation of the "third degree" and other inappropriate exercises of police power have influenced generations of police executives, mayors, judges, and legislators as they have reshaped the contours of legitimate police discretion and altered public expectations about appropriate police use of force (see National Commission on Law Observance 1931; Pearson 1930; Kelling and Stewart 1991: 8, 12; Walker 1985a).

One of the few powerful national bodies that undertook to refine the rules for police use of force in making arrests in the wake of the Wickersham Commission's reports was the American Law Institute (ALI), a legal group that summarizes and comments on trends in the nation's laws and court decisions. The ALI's publications are often relied on by lawyers and judges in litigation and thus have profoundly shaped the direction of American legal policy in every aspect of civil and criminal law during the 20th century. In a 1934 publication, the ALI advised that, although the prevailing rule in most states and most police agencies was that officers could shoot fleeing suspects wanted for *any* type of felony, the wiser policy was to limit authority to "cases of so-called dangerous felonies" (ALI 1934, discussed in LaFave 1965: 212). This visionary view, which would not be made the law of the land until 51 years later by the U.S. Supreme Court, was short-lived. By 1949 the ALI realized its recommendation had fallen on deaf ears in state legislatures and courts and revised its position to reflect the prevailing "any felony" rule (ALI 1949; LaFave 1965: 212).

After the Wickersham Commission disbanded, decades passed before other presidential crime commissions turned serious attention to police use of force in making arrests. When they finally did, in the late 1950s, 1960s, and 1970s, their studies and recommendations often

---

[6] See, for example, Cleveland Foundation (1922), Missouri Association for Criminal Justice (1926), and Illinois Association for Criminal Justice (1929).

included criticism of the common law rule on police firearms use, incorporated in many state criminal codes and followed by many local police agencies.

The state of the art of police deadly force policies was such that, in a 1965 report in the American Bar Foundation's[7] series of studies of the administration of criminal justice, the Milwaukee Police Department's "any felony" rule was cited as a model—not because of its content but because it had been committed to writing and because it *explicitly* prohibited shootings to apprehend fleeing *misdemeanor* suspects (LaFave 1965: 210). Similarly, departmental policies were cited as exemplary by the American Bar Foundation's 1965 study if they prohibited shooting unless "all other methods [of apprehension] have proved ineffectual" (a 1950 Milwaukee policy) and if officers were authorized to shoot only if they knew as a virtual *certainty* rather

> *"Officers in a patrol car saw a man slumped over the steering wheel of a car stopped in the middle of the street. The officers thought the man was intoxicated. When they approached the car and opened the door the man lunged toward them. The police thought the man was resisting arrest and used the force they thought necessary to subdue him. After the man had been taken to the station it was learned that his violent movements were due to an epileptic seizure"* (LaFave 1965: 212).

than as a reasonable belief that the fleeing suspect had committed a felony (a 1956 Kansas City, Kansas, policy) (LaFave 1965: 210, 217). By contrast, the Detroit Police Department's 1955 policy was sufficiently ambiguous that officers might find in it authority to shoot any and all fleers, felony and misdemeanor suspects alike. It read, in part:

> "No amount of force is too great in making an arrest if it is necessary to overcome an obstinate and dangerous resistance; no measure of severity is justified where there is no reason to fear an escape. * * * While the officer is required to be as gentle and considerate in making an arrest as the circumstances will permit, he must always remember that he is the representative of the law, to whose lawful demands all must submit. The officer is charged with the duty and armed with the power to compel submission" (Detroit Police Department, *Revised Police Manual*, chap. 16, sec. 28 [1955], quoted in LaFave 1965: 210).

During the 1950s and 1960s, some police policy manuals still made no mention whatsoever of the criteria governing when officers could properly use deadly force (LaFave 1965: 209), leaving the task of guiding these decisions solely to state statute, common law, or police organizational culture. Many other police manuals or training materials of the day discussed shooting criteria but "failed to draw the common law distinction between felony and misdemeanor arrests" (LaFave 1965: 210).

Although the FBI's "defense-of-life" shooting policy, in force since the 1940s, would often be cited during the 1970s and 1980s as the exemplar for all local police agencies to follow in revising their use-of-force policies, for the first several decades of its use by the FBI it was not generally viewed as a relevant model.

Some police agencies had written policies that could hardly be considered more useful than no policy whatsoever. The Police Foundation noted that, until 1968, a large southwestern police agency's use of deadly force policy consisted entirely of the admonition, "Never take

---

[7] The American Bar Foundation is a research affiliate of the American Bar Association.

me out in anger; never put me back in disgrace." Similarly vague guidance was offered in two other policies cited by the Foundation: "Leave the gun in the holster until you intend to use it" and "It is left to the discretion of each individual officer when and how to shoot" (Milton, et al. 1977: 47-48; see also Sherman 1980a: 94).[8]

As recently as the early 1980s, surveys disclosed many agencies without written deadly force policies. Nielsen (1983: 106) surveyed all sheriffs' departments and all police agencies serving populations of 20,000 or more in five states and concluded that "an alarming number of law enforcement organizations do not have written policies regarding the use of deadly force." He found that rural departments were even less likely to have policies than were urban departments.

Most of the national commission and professional organization studies of police practices that began to emerge in the late 1950s and 1960s were undertaken at least partly in response to the American civil rights movement's agitation for racial equity in the application of government benefits and the imposition of government controls over the lives of citizens. As had occurred after World War I, black war veterans returned to America in the late 1940s and found that, when the ticker tape blizzards subsided, all too often they were not treated like heroes by American police,[9] employers, school systems, and others. Their frustration and many others' outrage over the continuing shame of American racial bigotry began to alter the nation's constitutional landscape. In 1954 the U.S. Supreme Court announced the landmark ruling in *Brown v. Board of Education*, prohibiting the forced separation of the races in public schools. In 1961 the Justices imposed on local and state police procedural penalties for improperly seizing property (*Mapp v. Ohio*, 367 U.S. 643). Some years later in *Miranda v. Arizona* and related decisions the Court fashioned procedural safeguards designed to prevent the "third degree" and other oppressive interrogation techniques condemned more than three decades earlier by the Wickersham Commission.

It was within the context of this civil rights and civil liberties revolution of the 1950s, 1960s, and 1970s that well-funded national commissions, determined advocacy groups, and an eclectic assortment of policy researchers in both academic and police circles began to press for further restrictions on police shooting policies—restrictions that would reject the broad license to kill embodied in the "any felony" rule.

---

[8] Some police departments had detailed policies on use of deadly force but kept those policies secret from the public—and, in some locales, even secret from city council members serving on the public safety committee. In August 1988, for example, the Dallas Police Department for the first time released the contents of its deadly force policy to the media and to the city council, in conjunction with the adoption of several policy changes (Brumley 1988; Iannello 1988; see also Dallas Police Department 1990; Alpert 1987b). A Department spokesman explained that the agency's previous reluctance to disclose the use of deadly force policy was based on the view that "releasing the policy would harm police security and allow criminals to know what acts they could commit without fear of being fired upon" (Brumley 1988: 1). The change in attitude toward public disclosure of public policy was explained by another senior official: "Although police agencies have a continuing concern about officer safety, many have abandoned the practice of keeping their shooting policies secret in an attempt to combat stereotypes of police indifference" (Iannello 1988: A-1, A-9).

[9] Although police still often mistreated black persons whom they encountered in the line of duty, the post-war employment opportunities opened to black war veterans in American police departments, while modest, were often more substantial than job opportunities afforded to blacks by many other public and private employers.

The recommendations for tighter controls on police use of deadly force came from many sources:

- the American Bar Foundation's landmark series of studies on the administration of criminal justice in America, begun during the late 1950s and early 1960s (e.g., LaFave 1965: 208-217);

- the American Law Institute's *Model Penal Code*, tentative drafts of which began to be published and widely discussed in legal circles in the late 1950s (see, e.g., Model Penal Code section 3.07, Comments, Tentative Draft no. 8, 1958);

- the President's Commission on Law Enforcement and Administration of Justice, whose relevant final reports (especially the Task Force Report on the police) were published in 1967;

- the National Advisory Commission on Civil Disorders (report published in 1968);

- the American Bar Association's "Urban Police Function" Standards, under development since 1963, approved by the ABA House of Delegates in 1968 (American Bar Association 1982: vol. 1, pp. 260-262);

"An officer on foot signaled a speeding driver [suspected only of the misdemeanor speeding violation] to stop. The driver ignored the officer, who drew his revolver and fired five shots at the speeding car. [In the 1950s and 1960s] some provisions are found in the statutes and police materials which authorize the police to employ deadly force in order to arrest a fleeing misdemeanant. Because of this or because they are unaware of any rule to the contrary, officers occasionally use firearms in attempting to arrest a misdemeanant. Courts have generally held that it is 'better to allow one guilty only of a misdemeanor to escape altogether than to take his life'.... In cases similar to the one above, officers have been found guilty of murder for shooting the driver [1931 Kentucky case] and guilty of manslaughter when death followed a disabling of the vehicle by gunfire [1922 Illinois case]" (LaFave 1965: 213).

- the National Commission on the Causes and Prevention of Violence (final report in 1970) and several of the separately published book-length "task force" reports prepared for this commission;[10]

- reports by civil liberties and civil rights groups (e.g., ACLU of Southern California 1967; National Minority Advisory Council on Criminal Justice to the Law Enforcement

---

[10] These task force reports, which either directly or obliquely present materials on the need for police to exercise suitable restraint in the use of physical and deadly force, include Jerome Skolnick's *The Politics of Protest: Violent Aspects of Protest and Confrontation* (1969); Donald J. Mulvihill and Melvin Tumin's *Crimes of Violence* (1970); George D. Newton and Franklin E. Zimring's *Firearms and Violence in American Life* (1969); Robert K. Baker and Sandra J. Ball's *Mass Media and Violence* (1969); Paul L. Briand, Jr.'s edited *Hearings on Mass Media and Violence* (1969); James S. Campbell, Joseph R. Sahid, and David P. Stang's *Law and Order Reconsidered* (1969); Daniel Walker's *Rights in Conflict: The Violent Confrontation of Demonstrators and Police in the Parks and Streets of Chicago During the Week of the Democratic National Convention of 1968* (1968); Louis J. Hector and Paul L. E. Helliwell's *Miami Report: Civil Disturbances in Miami, Florida, During the Week of August 5, 1968* (1969); and Louis Masotti and Jerome R. Corsi's *Shoot-out in Cleveland: Black Militants and the Police, July 23, 1968* (1969). Full citations for these reports, not provided in our bibliography, can be found in the final report of the National Commission on the Causes and Prevention of Violence (1970).

Assistance Administration [LEAA] 1978);

- police policy researchers (e.g., Moreland 1954; Note 1955; Chapman and Crockett 1963; Griffen 1969; Bittner 1973; Fyfe 1978, 1979b; Sherman 1980a; Meyer 1980a, 1980b; Geller and Karales 1981a; Matulia 1982, 1985; Alpert 1987b.) An extensive list of legal and empirical research advocating tighter shooting policies is provided in Geller and Karales 1981a: iv-v, 39-41, 183-184, and Matulia 1985: 57-62; and

- police-run organizations founded to help professionalize the police through the adoption of what they viewed as more humane and more effective policies and practices than those embraced at the time by traditional organizations of police leaders. Examples include the Police Foundation's multi-city study of police use of deadly force published in 1977 (Milton, et al.) and the National Organization of Black Law Enforcement Executives' (NOBLE's) public call for deadly force policy reform in 1979 (see Geller and Karales 1981a and Matulia 1985: 61).

During the 1960s cutting-edge reform advocates pressed state legislatures and police to restrict authority to employ lethal force to those instances in which the police find "there is a substantial risk that the person to be arrested will cause death or serious bodily harm if his apprehension is delayed" (American Law Institute 1962). Although it would be more than two decades before the U.S. Supreme Court adopted this stance as a mandatory national minimum, a number of police agencies began to examine the efficacy of this position during the 1960s, and a few began to adopt it as policy.

Many of the calls for police policy reform in the 1970s and 1980s expressly urged the adoption of a defense-of-life shooting policy such as that adopted decades earlier by the FBI. Such a policy permits shooting only to defeat an immediate threat to life. As noted above, NOBLE in 1979 was one of the first national police executive groups to take a strong position favoring a defense-of-life rule (Matulia 1985: 61). NOBLE's voice in these days hardly represented an establishment perspective. Indeed, at the 1980 IACP annual convention, a NOBLE-sponsored resolution calling for police agency adoption of a defense-of-life policy was defeated by the delegates (Adams 1980, cited in Sherman 1983: 108). Less than three years later, the Commission on Accreditation for Law Enforcement Agencies (1983), co-founded by NOBLE, the IACP, the National Sheriffs' Association, and the Police Executive Research Forum, required that an agency adopt such a policy in order to become nationally accredited. Many agencies have done so.

A variant of the defense-of-life policy, which the Chicago Police Department in 1985 called a "protection-of-life" policy, allows police to shoot to apprehend suspects whom police believe have violent propensities, even if those propensities are not being displayed at the moment when the police employ lethal force. Based on our role in deliberating the policy eventually adopted by the Chicago Police Department, we can report that the suspects the Department had in mind with its protection-of-life policy are those who have shown their dangerous proclivities by committing a violent crime *in the presence* of police officers. Sherman (1983: 108-109) observes that different departments require different evidentiary foundations before an officer concludes that a fleeing suspect has violent propensities (e.g., an officer's reasonable belief versus his or her "direct personal knowledge" that the suspect has used or threatened violence against another person).

The Chicago requirement of direct officer knowledge that the suspect is dangerous was also reflected in shooting policies adopted in Kansas City, MO in 1973 and in Atlanta in 1976

(Sherman 1983: 108). Compare with these policies the provision that an officer have "probable cause" to believe in the suspect's propensity for endangering others, contained in the IACP's 1985 model policy (Matulia 1985: 69) and in the 1989 revision of that model policy (see Appendix B in this volume). The NYPD's 1972 policy, a model in many ways for other agencies, nevertheless contained the same evidentiary basis as that favored by the IACP (Sherman 1983: 108). In a "concepts-and-issues" paper prepared in conjunction with its 1989 model use of force policy, the IACP suggested that it would be very "difficult" to justify officers' shooting at escaping felony suspects unless the officers "had positively identified [the suspect] as one who had just committed a violent crime" (IACP 1989: 3). But nothing in the language of the policy would lead a court or others to conclude that such a positive identification is strongly preferred over second-hand information. In any event, in the Chicago, New York, IACP, and many other policies, shootings are considered permissible only when less lethal means of capture are unavailable or inappropriate.

Despite the IACP's assertion (IACP 1989: 7) that the 1989 version of its model deadly force policy meets Standard Number 1.3.2 of the Commission on Accreditation for Law Enforcement Agencies (CALEA) (see the text of this standard in Appendix A), we disagree. The CALEA standard incorporates the notion that a fleeing felony suspect, if allowed to escape, will pose an *"immediate"* danger of seriously injuring someone. The IACP policy is looser, permitting shots at escaping suspects whom the officer reasonably believes "will pose a significant threat to human life should escape occur." While the IACP policy sounds on its face like eminently reasonable public policy, the problem with its dropping the concept of immediacy is that, as is well known within the criminal justice policy community, nobody—forensic psychologists, psychiatrists, parole boards, seasoned police officers—has yet demonstrated an ability to predict a given individual's *future* dangerousness with anything approaching even 50 percent accuracy.[11]

Predicting dangerousness in the *immediate*

"Police officers were summoned to a neighborhood where a door-to-door magazine salesman had been so persistent in attempting to sell his wares that he had committed a criminal assault in the process. When the officers arrived on the scene, they found a group of local residents pursuing the salesman. One of the officers fired a few shots in the direction of the salesman. He observed later that he felt such action was justified because the salesman was trying to escape from the custody of those residents, which was a felony. * * * [I]n Kansas, where [this] incident...occurred, the crime of escape is a felony even if the offense for which the arrest was made is only a misdemeanor" (LaFave 1965: 215).

"Officers were pursuing a car thief. The squad car was unable to gain on the stolen car without traveling at an unsafe speed. The thief, in attempting to avoid arrest, was creating a considerable risk of harm to others. The officers, knowing that the thief was a minor, decided to refrain from use of firearms in order to avoid unfavorable publicity about the department should the youth be killed by their fire. * * * [E]ven if the police generally are uncertain of the limits on their authority to use force, they are apt to limit their use of deadly force to those instances where they believe such action would receive public approval" (LaFave 1965: 215-216).

---

[11] On clinical efforts to predict potential parolees' violent recidivism, see Monahan (1981a, 1981b) and Petersilia, et al. (1985).

future, such as while a suspect is running down the street with gun drawn looking for some house to break into so he can take a hostage, almost certainly poses less difficult challenges of prediction. The IACP's "concepts-and-issues" paper (IACP 1989: 3) explains that "*imminent* risk to the public or the officer" (emphasis added) is an important element of the model policy's authorization to shoot at an escaping suspect. And the IACP acknowledges that "even in the case of repetitive violent offenders, one cannot accurately predict the offenders' future behavior" (*ibid.*) But, as we noted above concerning the required evidentiary basis of an officer's conclusion that the fleer has a propensity for violence, there is nothing in the language of the IACP's model policy that suggests "imminence" or "immediacy" of risk as a substantial factor in weighing the propriety of lethal force.

In March 1985 the approach taken by the Chicago Police Department and a good number of other agencies throughout the nation over the preceding two decades (see Fyfe 1979b; Geller and Karales 1981a; Sherman 1983) was adopted as a mandatory national standard by the U.S. Supreme Court in *Tennessee v. Garner*, 471 U.S. 1, 105 S. Ct. 1694, 85 L. Ed. 1. Specifically, the Court ruled that state laws (and departmental policies) that authorized police officers to use deadly force to apprehend unarmed, nonviolent criminal suspects were unconstitutional under the 4th Amendment's prohibition of unreasonable seizures of persons (as that prohibition had been applied to the states by the 14th Amendment). While the decision did not mandate a strict defense-of-life standard, it set a new outer limit for deadly force laws and policies that has forced many jurisdictions to reevaluate their police regulations (see Hall 1988a, 1988b, 1992). The IACP's 1989 model policy conforms to the *Garner* rule, but, in our view, is no more restrictive—in contrast to the more demanding CALEA standards.

The Supreme Court's 6-3 decision in *Garner* is considered a landmark, because for the first time it established a *national* minimum standard governing police use of deadly force. While ambiguities remain, the ruling closed the door on certain arguments that had long troubled lower courts and policymakers in many jurisdictions. For instance, among the contentions the Court considered but rejected was the notion that a criminal suspect forfeits his or her right to live by committing a crime and disobeying a lawful police order to surrender. The Court reasoned that there must be proportionality—reasonable balance—between the alleged criminal conduct and the governmental response.

Although, as indicated, prior to 1985 many police agencies had adopted policies as strict or stricter than the standard the Supreme Court adopted in *Garner*, there can be little question that a substantial number of police agencies across the nation were required by this ruling to change their policies and practices. Walker and Fridell (1989: 6) surveyed the 100 largest police departments in the nation and found that, of the 96 responding, nearly one-third

> *"It is not better that all felony suspects die than that they escape"—U.S. Supreme Court opinion in* Tennessee v. Garner, *471 U.S. 1, 11 (1985).*

(29 departments) considered themselves bound to amend their departmental shooting policy because of the *Garner* ruling. Given the belief of some experts that hardly any departments serving challenging urban communities were still permitting officers to fire at nonviolent fleeing suspects as of the mid-1980s, this finding underscores the significance of the Supreme Court's decision. Moreover, the *Garner* ruling had a confirming power—an effect in bolstering the direction of deadly force policy and practice reform in most jurisdictions in the nation. While this effect is difficult to quantify, it nonetheless presents a historically important force in the evolution of efforts to control official uses of deadly force. Many policies adopted

in the wake of the *Garner* ruling closely track the "protection of life" language that the Chicago Police Department and others developed before the Court decision.

B. The Experience with Restrictive Deadly Force Policies

There have been several studies, both before and after the *Garner* decision, of police policies and their effects on the use of deadly force. Uelman (1973), studying 50 Los Angeles County police departments, was one of the first empirical researchers to suggest that departments with restrictive shooting policies experienced lower levels of shooting by officers than departments with more permissive policies. Specifically, he concluded that the departments with the least restrictive policies reported more than twice as many incidents per 1,000 felony arrests as did the departments with the most restrictive policies. "The difference is accounted for largely in shooting incidents involving fleeing felons," he reported (1973: 48). As were his successors, Uelman could not be certain, however, whether a strict policy helps *produce* a low shooting rate or rather *results* from factors (such as community and media pressure stemming from an especially questionable shooting) that also prompt shooting restraint by officers (see also Friedrich 1980: 84; Sherman 1980b: 86; Scharf and Binder 1983: 200).

In 1971 the Oakland Police Department issued an internal research report on all gun discharges by Oakland officers from 1968 through 1970 (Gain 1971). Then-Chief Charles Gain found a substantial drop in the number of shooting incidents per month after the July 1968 imposition of a departmental policy prohibiting shooting burglary and theft suspects. The report also condemned the practice, which an increasing number of police departments have since prohibited (Geller and Karales 1981a: 36; Matulia 1982, 1985: 71-72), of firing at or from moving vehicles. Data were presented showing that when shots were fired at a moving vehicle, "seldom was [it] hit, although the likelihood of hitting a building or other car was substantial" (Gain 1971: 18; see also Matulia 1985: 72). Traffic law enforcement expert Larry Thompson (former head of the Arizona Highway Patrol) observed the continuing trend toward prohibiting shots at moving vehicles:

> "Our policies have changed over the years. Not too long ago we specified that 12-gauge rifle slugs could be used to disable fleeing vehicles. Our officers would attempt to puncture the radiator of the vehicle and cause it to stop (eventually). This policy was changed for two reasons: the inaccuracy of the slug and the eventuality of more rear-engined vehicles. We also found this to be ineffective in concluding pursuits—it didn't work so it was eliminated" (Thompson 1990: 78).

Similarly, the Nassau County, New York, Police Department policy against firing at fleeing vehicles is based on a determination that the potential costs outweigh the possible benefits:

> "Firearms should not be used in an attempt to stop a pursued vehicle. This applies to officers at roadblocks, as well as to pursuing officers. Fortunately, such action is rarely taken, because most officers realize it is extremely dangerous and ineffective. A car traveling at high speed with a wounded or dead person at the controls would be far more dangerous than the pursuit, and a danger that none of us can justify" (Nassau County Police Department 1982; see also Milton, et

al. 1977: 52; Nugent, et al. 1989: 13; Alpert and Fridell 1992).

Former Kansas City, MO and former San Jose Chief Joseph McNamara, in debates about deadly force policy during the 1970s and 1980s liked to chide those who advocated license for police to shoot at moving vehicles. "I've never seen a cop," he'd say, "who killed a car by shooting it." McNamara's home agency, the NYPD, under Commissioner Patrick V. Murphy's leadership banned shooting at automobiles in 1972 (unless an occupant was shooting at officers) following an in-house study documenting the prevalence and problematic nature of shots fired at cars (Burnham 1971, cited in Sherman 1983: 110). Sullivan (1992a) reports on the recent experience in Newark. Concern about the accuracy of shots fired *from* a moving vehicle also is long standing (see Walker 1977: 161).

Another early experience with the effects of policy change came in Omaha, where the department abandoned its policy permitting the shooting of persons suspected of any felony in the wake of a federal court decision invalidating that policy (*Landrum v. Moats* 1978). Walker and Fridell (1989: 19) report that

> "following the revision of the Omaha deadly force policy, the number of firearms discharges involving citizens (i.e., excluding accidental discharges and destruction of dangerous animals) dropped substantially, from an [annual] average of 13.2 between 1975 and 1979 to 5 between 1980 and 1984."

The Police Foundation, too, led by former NYPD Commissioner Patrick V. Murphy, saw hope for administrative control of shootings in the Kansas City, MO experience: a marked drop in police use of deadly force against young people after then-Chief Clarence Kelley issued a rule restricting shootings of juveniles, except in defense of life (Milton, et al. 1977).

More recently, Sherman (1983) more fully analyzed the Kansas City experience under former Chief Joseph McNamara, who succeeded Kelley. In 1973 McNamara instituted an even more restrictive shooting policy. Sherman found that, controlling for changes in the levels of reported crimes and arrests, Kansas City police shot substantially fewer people[12] and that a larger proportion of those who were shot or shot *at* had posed serious threats to police or others after the 1973 policy took effect. The percentage of incidents in which police fired at fleeing suspects declined from 46 percent of all civilians fired at to 22 percent after the rule change (*ibid.*: 118). Similarly, before 1973, 64 percent of the civilians shot at by Kansas City police were unarmed, compared to 43 percent afterward (*ibid.*: 119).

Importantly, there was little evidence in Kansas City that officers were subverting the new policy restrictions by altering their reporting of shootings to exaggerate the danger posed by their opponents. The percentage of civilians fired upon who were reported as "unarmed but appeared to be armed" actually declined from 7 to 4 percent after adoption of the new shooting guidelines (*ibid.*: 119). But, in the same study, Sherman did find evidence that police in Atlanta may have provided "a classic example of bureaucratic subversion of policy through reporting practices" (*ibid.*: 118). In that jurisdiction, the percentage of shooting incidents in which the civilians struck by police bullets "appeared to be armed" but in fact were not

---

[12] Sherman noted that Kansas City did not have enough cases to employ a test of the statistical significance of the change, but that visual inspection of the trend leaves little doubt that the policy change was followed by a substantial drop in the quarterly frequency of all police firearms discharges (1983: 112).

increased from 6 percent before a July 1976 policy change to 22 percent afterward (*ibid.*: 119).

A similar change surfaced in a related category of justification given by officers for shooting suspects in Atlanta—that their adversaries "made a motion [a 'furtive gesture'] as if to reach for a weapon," a weapon that further investigation disclosed did not exist. Before the policy change, Atlanta police reported this explanation in 5 percent of their fatal and nonfatal shootings of civilians; after the change, this excuse was given in 18 percent (*ibid.*: 118).

Sometimes, the numbers involved in studies of the effects of policy interventions are relatively small, requiring analysts to exercise caution about overclaiming the likely observability and influence of changes in shooting levels.

In New York City, the adoption under Commissioner Patrick V. Murphy in 1972 of a policy that, as enforced, prohibited all but defense-of-life shootings (coupled with a rigorous review of each police gun firing by a departmental Firearms Discharge Review Board, greater accountability of supervisors for shootings by their subordinates, and officer-survival training) was followed by a significant reduction in shootings and a change in the types of shootings (Fyfe 1978, 1979b; Sherman 1983). Firearms

> *"For some time now I have noticed an increase in the use of deadly force by police in arrest situations and have observed conditions which contribute to this trend. A number of television programs depicting 'authentic' police operations have raised questions in my mind as to the manner by which arrests and raids are made. Media accounts of apparently needless shooting incidents by police in the apprehension of suspects have become more frequent. I also find the reporting of accidental shootings by fellow officers in arrest or raid situations reprehensible, and tragic in the extreme. * * **
>
> *"There are many examples of the questionable or clearly improper use of deadly force. Shooting a fleeing suspect not known to be a felon posing a threat to the community, interpreting an innocent movement by a suspect to be a threat to the officer's life, a refusal by a suspect to comply with an officer's request or command, and continuing to fire at an obviously incapacitated suspect are all matters of great concern"* (John Warner, former director of foreign operations, Drug Enforcement Administration, 1992: 1, 2).

discharges decreased by 31 percent overall; *non*-defense-of-life shootings by police decreased by more than 80 percent. As in Kansas City, these changes were not simply the result of shifts in crime or arrest rates or in the size of the police force.

Reported accidental shootings, however, increased in New York City from 4 percent to 9 percent of all firearms discharges, suggesting possible officer subversion of the new ban on warning shots. Officers might have preferred to risk discipline or retraining for an accidental discharge rather than admit to superiors that they willfully violated the prohibition of warning shots. By contrast, when the Kansas City Police force banned warning shots in 1973, such firearms discharges dropped from 31 percent of all cases to just 5 percent (Sherman 1983: 120).

The IACP has recommended that departments prohibit warning shots (see Matulia 1985: 71 and Appendix B in this volume). There is reasonably wide concurrence with this recommendation, on the ground that warning shots may strike innocent bystanders or other officers and that officers could attempt to conceal unjustified shootings by reporting that warning shots "accidentally went astray" (Sherman 1983: 110; see also Milton, et al. 1977: 52). Police executives have also observed that allowing warning shots creates a loophole for officers who violate a ban on intentional shootings (say, at nonviolent fleeing suspects). Chief McNamara, while serving in San Jose, commented, "If the bullet misses, the officer may hide behind the 'warning shot policy.' In other words, the officer would simply state that he/she was firing a warning shot at the fleeing suspect, thereby relieving the officer from departmental liability charges (assuming all other conditions for the discharge of the weapon were valid)" (Burke 1990).

In recent years, policy restrictions in the NYPD again have been credited with achieving favorable reductions in shootings. A blue-ribbon committee, including former Commissioner Patrick V. Murphy and appointed by then-Commissioner Lee P. Brown "after a spate of police-involved shootings in January and February [1990] claimed at least 14 lives" (*Law Enforcement News* 1990a: 3), found there had been a reduction in shootings by police over the decade of the 1980s. This was attributed to a set of factors that included strong policy:

> "[T]he 12.6 percent decrease in police-involved shootings—from 377, involving
> 491 officers, in 1980, to 329 incidents and 415 officers in 1989—was attributable
> to the department's increased use of non-lethal weapons, its comprehensive
> training in the use of force, and guidelines...that [encompass] 'one of the nation's
> most restrictive firearms policies' " (*ibid.*).

Empirical research on Los Angeles police-involved shootings in the 1970s yielded results similar to the findings of early research on New York City. Meyer (1980a: 12) found a significant decline in the number of incidents in which Los Angeles police fired shots after September 1977, when the LAPD adopted a policy permitting shooting only to apprehend a person considered dangerous. The number of persons shot at declined from a yearly average of 128 before the policy change to 102 after. Paralleling earlier experiences, Los Angeles saw a change not only in the quantity but in the "quality" of shootings. Meyer (1980a: 23) reported:

> "Shootings precipitated by suspects' disobeying orders to halt or appearing to
> reach for weapons, and shootings of suspects ultimately determined to be
> unarmed decreased in both number and in proportion to total shooting incidents."

The Dallas Police Department (1990) has appraised the effects of various of its own policy and other administrative interventions on officer-involved shooting rates during the 1980s. The policy interventions studied were the release of new agency shooting guidelines on October 15, 1984, and August 19, 1988. The 1984 policy prohibited use of deadly force to protect property interests, inserted a statement about the agency's "reverence for life," advised officers not to "place themselves in front of oncoming vehicles where deadly force may be a likely outcome," clearly separated criminal and administrative investigations, and established a Firearms Discharge Review Board (Dallas Police Department 1990: III-5). The study compared the 12-month periods before and after this new policy and found that intentional discharges of police firearms at individuals or their vehicles dropped by 37 percent (from 43 to 27).

Similarly, there was a 39 percent decrease in shootings after the second revised Dallas policy was adopted in August of 1988 (a drop from 31 intentional shots-fired incidents in the 12 months before the policy adoption to 19 in the next 12 months) (Dallas Police Department 1990: 2). The 1988 policy, according to agency officials quoted in a Dallas newspaper story, made "few substantive changes," but "the revisions and the document's public release symbolize an emphasis on the 'ultimate value of human life' and a new attitude of openness" (Iannello 1988: 1).

The 1988 Dallas policy emphasized shooting in defense of the officer's or another innocent person's life and aimed to express the imperative of appropriate officer restraint in language that was simple and easy to apply on the street. As we shall explore in more detail later in this chapter, the policy change was not the only important administrative intervention around this time in the Dallas Police Department. Indeed, the 1988 policy became effective on the same day that Chief Mack Vines took the helm in Dallas, arriving from out of town with what was widely understood in the community and the police department to be a mandate for reducing police-civilian violence (Iannello 1990: 1). Ironically, Vines eventually left Dallas in the wake of a controversy fomented by Dallas officers opposed to his crackdown on officers' unnecessary use of deadly force.

A recent study focused on the effects of shooting policy changes in Memphis—the city whose fatal shooting by police of unarmed youthful burglary suspect Edward Garner resulted in the Supreme Court's landmark decision in *Tennessee v. Garner* (1985). Sparger and Giacopassi (1992 and *Crime Control Digest* 1992d) picked up where Fyfe (1982), who had characterized the Department's pattern of using deadly force in the 1970s as racially discriminatory, left off. Studying incidents in which Memphis officers discharged their weapons (hits as well as misses) over a 21-year period (1969-89, with data missing for the years 1975-79), the researchers concluded that positive effects were realized by the Department's abandonment in 1979 of

> *"'Sorry Son, A Policeman Has to Play for Keeps'*
>
> *"Dear Ann Landers: I don't want to go into too much detail, and I'm not signing my name, but if you use your imagination you can figure out what happened.*
>
> *"With so many guns loose these days, this letter could have come from Chicago, Memphis, Florida or New York. Actually, I live in Los Angeles. Please, Ann, print this message:*
>
> *"Dear Teenager: I didn't mean to break your mother's heart or bring your family grief.*
>
> *"If you were my son, I would have told you, 'Son, if a policeman says "Stop!"—stop. Don't move. Drop whatever you're carrying and put your hands where he can see them. Treat him with respect. If you don't, you could make a lot more trouble for yourself, and you already have plenty.'*
>
> *"I also would tell my own kid, if you're driving a car and you see flashing red lights or hear a siren, stop. Pull over to the side of the road and put your hands where the officer can see them. Someone may have just been murdered, a child may have been raped or a bank robbed.*
>
> *"I don't know if you're carrying a Bible or a sawed-off shotgun, but I'm not taking any chances. You may think I'm scared, and you're right. I am scared to death. I'm scared that I might never see my family again. I'm scared that my little kids are going to grow up without a father. I've been to too many of my buddies' funerals to think it couldn't happen to me.*
>
> *"You may think life is just a game, so you play the game for fun. I'm sorry, son, but I'm a policeman and I have to play for keeps. Those are the rules and nobody can change them.*
>
> *—Law Officer in California" (Landers 1991).*

its "fleeing felon" deadly force policy in favor of a rule permitting officers to shoot only to stop fleeing suspects believed to have committed enumerated "dangerous felonies." As in some other locales at the time (e.g., Chicago), however, these dangerous felonies still included "burglary in the first, second, or third degree" (Sparger and Giacopassi 1992: 19 n. 1). The new policy also prohibited officers from shooting "to apprehend a juvenile unless the use of deadly force 'is immediately necessary in the defense of the officer's life or of another person's life'" (*ibid.*: 19 n. 3).

Besides these policy changes, the Memphis Police Department also took initiatives in training and post-shooting investigations to help curtail unnecessary shootings. Both of these steps had been recommended in a report released in 1978 by the Tennessee Advisory Committee to the U.S. Commission on Civil Rights (Tennessee Advisory Committee 1978; see also Sparger and Giacopassi 1992: 3-4). The Sparger-Giacopassi study could not sort out the separate effects on Memphis shooting practices of the advisory panel's public report criticizing the department and the policy and training changes the report had urged. Nevertheless, it is of interest to see what changes may have occurred in shootings of and by Memphis officers and in other activities in the wake of these various community, policy, and training influences.

In August 1985, five months after the Department's loss of the *Tennessee v. Garner* case in the Supreme Court, the Memphis police adopted additional policy changes, generally adhering to the language of the Supreme Court's decision and otherwise making clear that deadly force was to be used only as a last resort to protect people whose lives might be endangered if the subject were not immediately apprehended (Sparger and Giacopassi 1992: 5; *Crime Control Digest* 1992d: 7). These 1985 policy developments were again accompanied by training changes, principally attempting "to provide officers with realistic simulations of potential shooting situations and examples of when deadly force was permitted" (*ibid.*).

Measuring the number of firearms discharge incidents involving Memphis police during three five-year periods—before the first set of changes, in between the two sets of changes, and following the 1985 changes—Sparger and Giacopassi found continued reductions. There were 225 shots-fired incidents[13] during the period 1969-74, followed by 213 (a 5 percent drop) during 1980-84, followed by 172 during 1985-89 (a 19 percent drop from the second period and a 24 percent drop from the first period) (*Crime Control Digest* 1992d: 7). "That amounted to a reduction in the annual police shooting *rate* from 33.5 in the first five-year period to 27.9 per 1,000 officers in 1985-89" (*ibid.*; emphasis added to distinguish the drop in *rate* from the decreases in *number* of shooting incidents).

Arrest levels were not adversely affected by the Memphis changes: "[A]rrests for violent felonies increased from 587 during 1969-74 to 1,348 per 1,000 officers during 1985-89" (*ibid.*), which means that members of the force in the most recent study period were 2.3 times more likely than Memphis officers in the late 1960s and early 1970s to make an arrest for a violent felony. Measured against violent felony arrests as an indication of potential officer hazards, it is noteworthy that the rate of shots-fired incidents by Memphis officers per 1,000 arrests for violent felonies dropped from 57 in the 1969-74 period to 21 in the 1985-89 period (a 63 percent decline). By this yardstick, Memphis officers in the 1969-74 period were nearly three times more likely than their present-day counterparts to resort to lethal force in the performance of their duties. Considerable reductions in fatal shootings of black suspects were also realized by the Memphis police.

---

[13] As Table E-65 in Appendix E of this volume shows, Sparger and Giacopassi's data included all shots fired, intentionally and accidentally, on and off duty, and at persons as well as animals.

Moreover, "[s]ince 1976 [two years after burglary suspect Garner was killed], no *fleeing* property crime suspect has been fired on by Memphis officers," according to reports filed with the Department by its officers (*Crime Control Digest* 1992d: 7). In 1985 two incidents occurred in which black property crime suspects were fired upon (apparently not during flight) by Memphis officers, resulting in penalties for unjustified shootings (Sparger and Giacopassi 1992: 13). Since 1985, according to reports on file with the Department, no property crime suspect (fleeing or otherwise) has been shot at by Memphis officers (*ibid.*). During the period 1969-74, 96 black persons and 16 whites suspected of property offenses (primarily burglary) were shot at by Memphis police. During the five-year period 1980-84, the numbers of blacks and whites suspected of property offenses who were shot at (but not, apparently while in flight) dropped to 37 and 3, respectively. In the 1985-89 period, two black suspects were shot at in these circumstances (the two shootings noted above that were ruled unjustified), and no whites (Sparger and Giacopassi 1992: Table 4) (see Figure E-9).

Several studies have explored the effects of restrictive shooting policies on shootings *of* police and on other "outcome measures." The administrative initiatives in the NYPD were followed not only by reductions in shootings *by* police but by reductions in shootings *of* police. Moreover, no adverse impact on crime or arrest rates was registered following the more stringent control of shootings (Fyfe 1979b, 1978: 293; also see Tsimbinos 1968). Fyfe (1981b: 379) suggested that shootings by police might actually be criminogenic (i.e., capable of causing crime) insofar as they have been identified by presidential commissions as the catalysts for a number of riots (see also Matulia 1985: vii).

Sherman (1983) addressed these issues as well. In addition to concurring with Fyfe that officer safety seemed to improve following the NYPD's new stance on shootings in 1972, he looked at the experience in Atlanta. In July 1976 the Atlanta Police Department restricted officers to shooting dangerous suspects and then only when the officer had personal knowledge of the alleged criminal events. Moreover, the new policy prohibited warning shots and shots at moving vehicles and forbade shootings that might endanger bystanders (see Matulia [1985: 71] and Appendix B in this book for the IACP's recommendation on risk to bystanders). Like New York City and Kansas City, Atlanta also began subjecting every police firearm discharge to departmental scrutiny.

Following the institution of the new policy, a 64 percent decrease was registered in shootings by Atlanta police. This dramatic decrease was not accompanied by as impressive results in terms of reported crime levels and officer safety as had followed reforms in New York City. The number of officers injured in Atlanta after the policy change declined slightly, although when reductions in the size of Atlanta's police force are taken into account, officers were slightly more likely to be injured after the 1976 policy shift. This development may be attributable to a variety of factors. It could have been a chance occurrence, since the numbers involved are small and the increase was slight. Or, as Sherman (1983) suggests, an increase in reported violent crime might have enlarged officers' risks. Sherman cautions, however, against attributing the crime increase to the shooting policy shift. He argues that the increase occurred more than a year after the promulgation of the new policy and that although violent crimes increased, burglary (an offense whose suspects typically could no longer be shot under the new deadly force policy) actually decreased substantially following the change. Blumberg (1989: 461 n. 12) adds the observation that "because...restrictive [shooting] policies in no way inhibit the officer from using deadly force in self-defense, it is not surprising that they do not adversely impact on officer safety."

Sherman also reasoned that decreases in the number of arrests by Atlanta police following the policy amendment may have been due to other factors. He pointed out that a demoralized police force is likely to reduce its arrest activity and conceded that officers may have been demoralized to some extent by changes in the department's shooting policy. However, he suggested that it is much more likely that Atlanta officers were demoralized during this period by the combined impact of three other factors: (1) an extended pitched battle (with racial overtones) between the mayor and the Department over who would be the police chief; (2) a scandal in which the Atlanta public safety director was fired for helping police cheat on a promotion test; and (3) a steady decline in the size of the police force.

Officers in Los Angeles and Oakland, like their counterparts in New York City and other jurisdictions, experienced no greater danger after the adoption of stricter policies. Indeed, in Los Angeles 15 percent fewer officers were assaulted per year after the late 1977 policy change (Meyer 1980a: 43). In Oakland, Chief Gain's report (1971: 18) took issue with the frequently heard assertion that "a restriction against shooting nondangerous felons... allows more felons to escape." The report indicated that in the 29 months studied, only two officers believed that the ban on burglary suspect shootings permitted a burglar to escape. And whether or not the burglary suspects who did escape were successful because of the officers having to hold their fire, Gain (1971: 15) pointed out that 60 percent of these escaped suspects eventually "were apprehended by means that were entirely unrelated to the initial firearms discharge." Whether these suspects committed any further crimes while they were at large—and by what yardstick one should compare that social harm to the harm of slaying the suspect—was not addressed by Chief Gain's statement.[14] Nor have these difficult questions been addressed by other published studies, even though they have taken on perhaps even greater weight in the wake of the *Tennessee v. Garner* decision's prohibition of shooting nonviolent fleeing suspects.

Thus far in considering the impact of policy changes, we have touched on a variety of policy interventions that various practitioners and analysts believe have a salutary effect on police-involved shootings without producing offsetting problems. It is worth pausing to attempt to summarize. There are four basic sets of inquiries that need to be conducted, if possible, before making declarations (as politically enticing as they may be) about the *effects* of policy shifts (or other efforts to influence the prevalence and nature of police-civilian violence):[15]

1. What changes might be expected? Some of the possibilities include changes in:

    -   number of firearms discharges (including warning shots and accidental firings)
    -   number of persons shot (fatally and nonfatally)
    -   distribution of pre-intervention situations ("mobilizing" events—those that eventually escalated into shootings)
    -   distribution of police mobilization methods (police initiated, citizen request either on-site or through a dispatcher, and attacks on officers)
    -   distribution of civilians' precipitating conduct (actions that immediately preceded officers' decisions to shoot, including the extreme provocation of citizen attacks on officers with deadly weapons)

---

[14] See our discussion in Chapter 2 under the heading "How Much Shooting Is Too Much Shooting?"

[15] This summary draws on Sherman (1983) and other sources.

- percentage of persons shot or shot at by police who were armed (by type of weapon)
- percentage of persons shot or shot at by police who appeared to be armed but were not, or who appeared to be reaching for a weapon (making furtive gestures) but who subsequent investigation revealed had no weapon readily accessible
- percentage of officers assaulted or injured
- police-community rapport and collaboration
- public support for police
- racial/ethnic distribution of persons shot at and persons struck by police bullets

2.   Did any of these anticipated changes occur?

3.   If so, are there factors *other than* the new policy that may have produced these changes? This is an effort to seek to eliminate "rival hypotheses" about the reasons for change. The kinds of factors that could possibly have had as great or even greater impact than any policy changes on shooting outcomes include changes during the period in question in:

- reported crime levels
- actual crime levels (victimizations, whether reported to police or not)
- mobilizing events (e.g., changes in styles of gang warfare and propensity of criminals to fight with arresting officers)
- mode of mobilization (e.g., more or fewer police intervened on their own initiative in potentially violent encounters)
- the frequency of high-risk police activities (e.g., buy-bust, stakeouts, decoys, warrant service, raids)
- police morale
- police disciplinary patterns (even a single well-known disciplinary case can sometimes have an important effect)
- police leadership (chief or other senior officials)
- other governmental leaders (mayor, city manager, et al.)
- population size
- daytime and/or evening population composition (socioeconomic, racial/ethnic, etc.) due to changing residential, employment, recreational, business, or other factors
- police-community rapport (based on either a wide array of individually unnoticeable events or one or more dramatic and highly visible occurrences)

4.   If policy can be *presumed* to have had some desirable effects, were there any unintended consequences of the policy change(s)? Such consequences might include changes in:

- public safety (criminal victimizations, reported crimes)
- police safety (assaults, injuries of police)
- arrest productivity
- productivity, regardless of arrest levels, in solving or ameliorating crime and disorder problems
- officer work load considerations
- officer morale
- public/governmental confidence in police professionalism and capacity to protect the community

This line of inquiry is appropriate for exploring cause-effect relationships[16] concerning police-civilian violence, regardless of whether those introducing a change *intended* thereby to produce an effect on violence levels. For instance, a variety of changes are made from time to time in police incident-handling and problem-solving tactics without any particular expectation that they will influence police-civilian violence. In contrast, sometimes enforcement tactics are rejected or abandoned out of concern that their riskiness outweighs their benefits. For instance, Fyfe (1978: xi) discovered that a switch in New York City from "buy and bust" street-level narcotics enforcement to pursuit of higher-echelon dealers was accompanied, as hoped, by fewer narcotics arrest-related shootings both by and of police. Policies and procedures for police handling of the mentally ill are also considered relevant in efforts to control officer-involved shootings (New York State Commission on Criminal Justice 1987, vol. I: 369). In 1992 the New York City Police Department, after intra-agency debate, decided not to follow the recommendation by the Citizens Crime Commission, a private advocacy group, that the Department establish "gun squads" intended to "make frequent, visible arrests of people carrying guns in high-crime neighborhoods, thus fighting the perception that guns can be packed with impunity." Among the considerations for the Department's decision was "fear that such searches could provoke deadly shootouts" (Eckholm 1992).

In the early 1970s other evidence began to surface in New York City that policy decisions can help *protect officers*. At that time, adoption of an order prohibiting New York officers from carrying unapproved handguns was followed by a sharp reduction in accidental, self-inflicted woundings of officers (Fyfe 1978: 293; see also Leslie 1992). In Chicago Geller and Karales (1981a: 98) found that semi-automatic weapons were involved in a disproportionate number of accidental, self-inflicted shootings of officers. There is reason to believe, moreover, that single-action firing of revolvers by officers also presents heightened risks of accidental shootings of both civilians and police (Matulia 1985: 74). The IACP (Matulia 1985: 73) also noted an apparent positive correlation between police department weapon caliber and rates of justifiable homicide by police. They cautioned, however, that the reason for this correlation was uncertain. Moreover, the IACP raised the question whether policy on the types of service weapons authorized might affect the risk of officers being killed, reporting that there is no evidence to suggest that "more officers who are using a .38 caliber weapon [are] murdered as a result of their weapon's inability to stop a suspect."

Fyfe (1980a) urged police departments to reconsider completely the routine arming of off-duty police (also see Lester 1981: 56). Fyfe (1980a: 81) suggested more than a decade ago that further research may well demonstrate that both officers and the community will be safer if we "require off-duty police to leave their guns in their lockers with the rest of their uniforms" (1980a: 81). Fyfe's data showed, for example, that off-duty officers who remained passive during tavern robberies survived unhurt, while many officers who tried to intervene were wounded or killed (1980a: 80). The IACP's policy recommendation on off-duty weapons in 1985 (Matulia 1985: 75) was that

"officers are encouraged, but not mandated, to carry a handgun when off duty.

---

[16] It is a premise of scientific inquiry that experimental tests of hypotheses can produce conclusions about the *likelihood* of causation but that firm conclusions cannot be derived that one factor definitely *causes* another to occur or change. Possible causal factors *can*, however, be *eliminated* from consideration based on evidence that changes in "independent variable" (the possible cause) do not produce changes in the "dependent variable" (the outcome under consideration) (see generally Cook and Campbell 1979).

An officer who elects *not* to carry a handgun while off duty shall not be subjected to disciplinary action if an occasion should arise in which he could have taken police action if he were armed. Exception: Off-duty officers while operating a department vehicle shall be armed with an approved weapon."

In its 1989 revision of the model deadly force policy (see Appendix B of this volume), the IACP dropped the guidance it had provided in 1985 on police use of firearms while off duty.

In sum, the empirical research suggests with remarkable unanimity, but, admittedly, with less data and weaker research techniques than are desirable, that restrictive policies seem to have worked well where they have been tried. Although establishing causation always is a difficult task, the pattern seems clear: Adoption of restrictive policies usually has been followed by marked decreases in shootings by police, increases in the proportion of the shootings that are responses to serious criminal activity, greater or unchanged officer safety, and no adverse impact on crime levels or arrest aggressiveness.

This conclusion does not imply that policy changes are the *only* viable means of controlling the use of deadly force or even the most effective means. Scharf and Binder caution that the process of policy "socialization" is less complete than police administrators like to believe and that the attitudes of officers' peers and supervisors about the use of deadly force weigh more heavily than written rules (1983: 234). Waegel (1984a, 1984b) concluded in his study of police shootings in Philadelphia that subcultural norms of police officers minimize the effects of restrictive shooting policies.[17] Nonetheless, the hope among many, is that, the ice having been broken by the departments that have adopted restrictive policies, many other departments—including those, if any, that have not even taken the initial step of committing their shooting policies to writing (Milton, et al. 1977)—will adopt tighter shooting guidelines. If nothing else, continued interest of many departments in becoming accredited by the Commission on Accreditation for Law Enforcement Agencies should reasonably well ensure continuation of the current trend toward adoption of restrictive deadly force policies (see the CALEA deadly force policy in Appendix A).

C. An Emerging Counter-Trend Away from the Defense-of-Life Policy: The FBI Initiative and Other Moves to Alter Standards

There is, however, an emerging counter-trend that deserves note. This trend is to pull back from a defense-of-life posture to one that adheres strictly to only those obligations imposed by *Tennessee v. Garner*. According to police in St. Petersburg, the Florida state legislature in 1990 made an unsuccessful attempt to adopt legislation that would have required all municipal police agencies in the state to have shooting policies no more restrictive than state law (which reportedly mirrored the *Garner* rule). In this context, it is important to understand clearly the outer limits of discretion found permissible by the U.S. Supreme Court in *Garner*. At the permissive extreme, the Court's language would support as legitimate a shooting of a *currently non*violent, *fleeing* suspect whom the officer reasonably believes

---

[17] Gary Sykes, director of the Southwestern Law Enforcement Institute, argues that the emergence of "administrative culture" as a source of guidance for police conduct is a phenomenon only of the past 20 years in many jurisdictions. Earlier, in many departments, he asserts, "street culture" governed most matters, including use of deadly force. This might be true historically even in agencies that had a written deadly force policy issued by the chief's office, but it would almost certainly be true in agencies that had not developed an administrative position on firearms use and committed that position to writing (Sykes 1990; see also Reuss-Ianni 1983).

committed a felony involving the *threat* but *not* the *use* of force. Thus, presumably, an unarmed, fleeing person suspected of attempted (but unsuccessful) strong-arm robbery could be shot by police within the guidelines articulated in *Garner*. If such a shooting would violate the *spirit* of the *Garner* ruling, it would not seem to violate the *letter* of the decision.

At its November 1990 meeting in St. Paul, Minnesota, the Commission on Accreditation for Law Enforcement Agencies heard testimony from a chief in a small town in Georgia asking that the Commission relax or clarify its use of deadly force standard (sections 1.3.1 and 1.3.2—see Appendix A in this volume). The chief said that the Georgia legislature had recently adopted a state use-of-force law conforming to the language of *Tennessee v. Garner* (1985) and argued that CALEA's standard is generally perceived to be a defense-of-life standard and, therefore, more restrictive than *Garner*.

We agree with this interpretation of the relative restrictiveness of the CALEA and *Garner* requirements. For example, as noted above, the Supreme Court's rule in *Garner* permits police to shoot at fleeing felony suspects currently known to be unarmed if they previously demonstrated their violent propensity by committing a crime of violence (e.g., armed robbery).

The Georgia chief asked the CALEA board of commissioners—made up principally of current and former police officials—to "reinterpret the standards or grant a blanket waiver to all Georgia agencies." Presumably, the chief thought it unfair that CALEA should hold accredited agencies to a higher standard than that mandated by state law, a curious argument if it indeed represents the chief's view. The purpose of CALEA, as we understand it, was to provide a new, independently derived set of benchmarks to inspire professional law enforcement agencies to a higher level of proficiency and legitimacy than that which already was provided by state law and other sources of authority. The commissioners reportedly held "lengthy discussion" on the requested softening of the Commission's use of deadly force standard and decided to incorporate the matter "into an ongoing study" of the use-of-force provisions (Bentley 1990: 3-4). As this book goes to press, no changes have been made that relax the CALEA rule on use of lethal force.

The most significant initiative thus far in the 1990s to pull back from the strict defense-of-life standards was undertaken by the FBI in 1990. The Bureau at that time indicated, in response to media inquiries, that it sought to amend its long-standing defense-of-life shooting policy. The potentially far-reaching effect of an FBI policy shift on the policies and practices of thousands of police agencies across the United States justifies an extended discussion of what the FBI leadership seems to have in mind and what various leaders in the law enforcement world believe might be the impact of the FBI's initiative.

The logical starting point is a statement of current FBI policy. Burke (1990) quotes it:

"Agents are not to utilize deadly force against any person except as necessary in self-defense or the defense of another, where they have reason to believe they or another are in danger of death or grievous bodily harm. Emphasis must be placed on planning arrests so that maximum pressure is placed on the individual being sought and they [*sic*] have no opportunity to either resist or flee.... Where the lawless person initiates action to cause physical harm, there should be no hesitancy in using such force as is necessary to effectively and expeditiously bring such a person under control.... There are many situations in which an Agent may draw their [*sic*] weapons when making an apprehension and without being confronted with existing deadly force.... No warning shots are to be fired by Agents or other Bureau employees authorized to carry firearms in an effort to stop a fleeing person or for any other purpose."

Portions of this policy are also quoted in *Law Enforcement News* (1990: 5). FBI internal memorandum No. 31-72, dated November 21, 1972, which was quoted by the U.S. Court of Appeals for the 8th Circuit in *Mattis v. Schnarr* (1976), provides that "an agent is not to shoot any person except, when necessary, in self-defense, that is, when he reasonably believes that he or another is in danger of death or grievous bodily harm." Sherman (1980a: 92) reports that in an interview in 1979 a Justice Department official indicated ambiguity in other portions of the FBI's guidelines on use of deadly force by suggesting that agents were authorized to use "any force necessary to effect an arrest."

Matulia (1985: 62) amplifies our understanding of how ambiguous FBI use of force policy has been at times (at least to those outside the Bureau). He quotes five sources: an April 14, 1966, letter from Director J. Edgar Hoover to Attorney General Nicholas B. Katzenbach; the November 21, 1972, FBI memorandum quoted in *Mattis v. Schnarr* and excerpted above; an *unsigned* November 23, 1979, letter from the FBI to Ronald L. Gainer, acting deputy assistant attorney general; a September 1980 statement by Director William H. Webster in a National League of Cities publication; and a 1981 FBI manual titled *The Legal Handbook for Special Agents*. No two of the statements of Bureau deadly force policy are identical word for word, although the *Legal Handbook* language conforms very closely the language quoted years earlier in *Mattis v. Schnarr*. The handbook provides: "Agents are not to shoot any person except as necessary in self-defense or the defense of another, when they have reason to believe they or another are in danger of death or grievous bodily harm" (FBI 1981b: 32).

Thus, although it seems that FBI policy may have been somewhat vague—to outsiders, if not to agents—at some points over the past several decades, FBI spokespersons have never disputed the characterization of the FBI's policy as one prohibiting all but defense-of-life shootings. The Supreme Court's representation of the FBI policy in *Tennessee v. Garner* (1985) stands as an authoritative interpretation of the current policy. The Court said: "The Federal Bureau of Investigation and the New York City Police Department, for example, both forbid the use of firearms except when necessary to prevent death or grievous bodily harm."

How does the Bureau seek to change this policy? In June 1990 reports began to surface (e.g., Ostrow 1990) that the FBI intended to amend its deadly force policy to permit agents to fire warning shots and to fire at fleeing suspects who were not, at the moment of decision, attempting to harm an agent or any other person. Officials criticized press depictions of the thrust of the policy initiative but were not particularly forthcoming in clarifying what the Bureau might have in mind and exactly what the status of the policy initiative was—a mere "trial balloon" launched to explore public and official reaction to such a change, a formal plan, or a *fait accompli*.

As a result of this confusion, speculation ran rampant throughout the law enforcement community and the various watchdog communities that maintain a continuing interest in police practices around the nation. NOBLE, at its July 1990 annual conference in Houston, adopted a resolution that, although not explicitly mentioning the FBI, was intended to decry the prospect of a change in the Bureau's long-standing policy and to urge all other law enforcement agencies to employ a defense-of-life standard, consistent with the requirement of the Commission on Accreditation for Law Enforcement Agencies.[18] The NOBLE resolution is quoted in its entirety in Appendix G of this book. It may not be only NOBLE's pattern of progressiveness that prompted it to take the leadership among police organizations in challenging the wisdom of the proposed FBI policy change. In addition, African-American police executives generally may be even more sensitive than other police executive groups to historic patterns in which police liberty to shoot at fleeing suspects perceived to be dangerous translated disproportionately into police shootings of minorities (W. Williams 1991).

Among other prompt, public, and negative reactions to the FBI policy change was that of researcher, expert witness, and former police manager James Fyfe. He voiced objections to the Bureau's plan to permit warning shots, even though the Bureau insisted that emphasis would be placed on being sure that such shots would not endanger bystanders. Warning shots, Fyfe contended, typically are useless (Burke 1990; Ostrow 1990). He also observed that allowing warning shots provides a cover for officers who missed their intended targets and do not want to report truthfully to superiors their intention to shoot the subject (Ostrow 1990; Burke 1990).

In seeking to authorize explicitly warning shots when they are considered useful and nonthreatening to innocent persons, the FBI's policy development is moving in exactly the opposite direction as that of the Commission on Accreditation for Law Enforcement Agencies. At its November 1990 meeting CALEA's board of commissioners gave preliminary approval to and sent to all accredited agencies for comment an addition to the commentary on Standard 1.3.5. Previously, agencies were not guided in how substantively to comply with Standard 1.3.5: "[The accredited agency has] a written directive [that] governs the discharge of 'warning' shots." The addition advises adoption of a policy on warning shots which provides that "warning shots should not be used" (Bentley 1990: 4).

> *The pursuit of "officer safety" affects many aspects of police work. Few have been as eloquent or incisive in proposing ways to enhance officer safety without impeding good, humane police work as tactics expert Ronald McCarthy of the IACP and formerly of the Los Angeles Police Department. Accordingly, McCarthy's comments (1992) about officer safety are especially provocative:*
>
> *"Philosophically, officer safety is not of paramount importance even to police. They put the safety of children and women ahead of their own. They risk their lives all the time to protect citizens. If officer safety was the most important thing, officers would not run to robbery-in-progress calls; they'd wait until the robber was gone. We should quit saying that officer safety is paramount. We should expect courage on the part of our officers.*
>
> *"USA Today conducted a study, based on the Titanic sinking. Eighty percent of the people who died on the Titanic were men, because they gave up their lifeboat positions to women or children. In USA Today's national survey, they found that 63 percent of men said they would not give up their position in a lifeboat to women or children. Fifty percent said they wouldn't give up their position in a lifeboat to their mother! I'm worried that we're hiring some of those men as police officers in America. We want officers who will be courageous, who will put the safety of citizens first."*

---

[18] We can speak with confidence about the origin and intent of the NOBLE resolution because the lead author of this volume was present at the NOBLE meeting while the resolution was discussed and voted upon on July 18, 1990.

The September 1991 update of the CALEA standards included the proposed language in the commentary to Standard 1.3.5.

Some who advocate the return to a pro-warning shot policy cite the Supreme Court's *Tennessee v. Garner* ruling as support. Burke (1990) points out that the ruling stated:

> "If a suspect threatens the officer with a weapon or there is probable cause to believe that he has committed a crime involving the infliction or threatened infliction of serious physical harm, deadly force may be used if necessary to prevent escape and if, where feasible, *some warning* has been given (emphasis added)."

Burke argues that the language we have italicized "provides the justification for warning shots." Among other possible problems with this logic is that practitioners have generally come to recognize that, in most settings, warning shots should not be used unless deadly force is already justified by the circumstances because, as James Fyfe puts it, "What comes up, must come down." It is difficult, therefore, to make the case that one can use a form of deadly force (warning shots) in order to create the justification for employing deadly force in the first instance.[19]

Amidst the immediate and intense objections to the FBI policy change, then-Attorney General Richard Thornburgh reportedly took the matter under advisement, although it was not precisely clear at the time whether as a matter of law the FBI really needed the Attorney General's approval for such a policy initiative. Few doubted, however, that once the Attorney General expressed interest in the matter it was the better part of wisdom for the Bureau to

---

[19] An ominous legal theory lurking on the horizon may be used some day to suggest that warning shots are in fact *not* a form of deadly force subject to the scrutiny of courts under the 4th and 14th Amendments, despite the assumption that they would be after the 1985 ruling in *Tennessee v. Garner*. Ruling in an Oakland, California, crack cocaine possession case, the U.S. Supreme Court on April 23, 1991, narrowed the definition of a "seizure" in the context of police pursuits. Juveniles fled when they saw an approaching unmarked squad car, and the police, without any basis for suspicion other than the flight, gave pursuit. Police confiscated a small rock of crack that one of the youths discarded during the foot chase. The state court held that the juvenile had been "seized"—implicating the constitutional right to be free from unreasonable seizure—"when he saw the officer running toward him" (*Crime Control Digest* 1991p: 1, 3). "The State of California, supported by the Bush administration, appealed to the Supreme Court, arguing that a seizure does not occur until the fleeing suspect has been physically restrained. The Supreme Court [by a 7 to 2 vote, in an opinion by Justice Antonin Scalia] agreed (*ibid.*: 3). The Court held that the constitutional protections against illegal searches and seizures "take effect only after the use of physical force against a suspect or when the suspect submits to the officer's show of authority" (*ibid.*: 1).

Justice John Paul Stevens, in a "sharply worded dissent," accused the Court of breaking with established precedent and worried about the line of rulings that might be expected to flow from the Court majority's reasoning. "In its decision," Justice Stevens wrote, "the court assumes, without acknowledging, that a police officer may now fire his weapon at an innocent citizen and not implicate the 4th Amendment as long as he misses his target" (*ibid.*: 4). If Justice Stevens is correct, then another assumption that might fit the Court's decision is that, in firing warning shots at suspects who do not stop upon hearing the gunfire, officers are similarly beyond the scrutiny of the Constitution since they neither intended to use physical force nor succeeded in using it against the fleeing person. Such reasoning might also exempt officers and municipalities from liability under the Constitution for the unintended shooting of a bystander struck by a warning shot. See *Cameron v. City of Pontiac* (1985) and Santos (1991: 14).

place the policy adoption on hold pending his reactions. For more than eight months following the June 1990 news reports of the FBI's intended policy change, the status of the change remained ambiguous to sources outside the Justice Department.

In March 1991 knowledgeable persons reported that the Attorney General had approved the change sought by the FBI but had insisted on uniformity of policy among all Justice Department law enforcement agencies (the Drug Enforcement Agency, FBI, Immigration and Naturalization Service's Border Patrol and Special Agent Investigators, the U.S. Marshals Service, and others). Reportedly, the demand for consistency with the FBI's new policy had encountered strenuous resistance in the Marshals Service and thus delayed announcement of the FBI's new standard pending resolution of the matter by the Attorney General's office.

Although official clarification of the precise nature of the proposed changes in the FBI's deadly force policy *still* had not been issued by the end of July 1992, we earlier gleaned some insight about the nature of the changes sought from conversations with Department of Justice personnel in 1991. Knowledgeable sources stated unequivocally that the policy would authorize the shooting of fleeing suspects whom an agent reasonably believed posed an immediate and continuing threat of death or great bodily harm to innocent persons. This threat could be demonstrated, for example, by the suspect's prior commission of a violent crime and possession during flight of a deadly weapon. To be fired upon by agents while fleeing, suspects would no longer need to be jeopardizing anyone's life at the moment when agents decided to fire. It would be sufficient that the firing agent reasonably conclude that deadly force was the only effective means of defeating the suspect's escape and that failure to employ this means might lead to the suspect's injuring or killing an innocent person.

Sources also explained that for the past five decades agents have at times committed what could be considered violations of the FBI policy by firing at fleeing suspects who had previously threatened someone's life but were not doing so at the time the agent shot. A simple example would be an agent shooting at a fleeing bank robber who, during the course of the robbery, murdered a bank teller and, when confronted by FBI personnel, turned and ran while still in possession of a firearm but without attempting to use it against the agents.

Further motivation for the change in policy reportedly came from a small number of incidents over the past decades in which agents, fearing they would run afoul of the Bureau's shooting policy, hesitated to fire at suspects whom FBI officials believed *should* have been fired at to prevent their inflicting further harm (see our discussion later in this chapter of "unreasonable restraint"). A highly publicized example was a shoot-out involving agents near Miami on April 11, 1986. In that incident,

> "two FBI agents were slain and five were wounded, along with two heavily armed bank robbery suspects.... FBI agent Edmundo Mireles, Jr., despite serious wounds, dragged himself to an automobile and killed both suspects. Mireles, who took a year to recover from his wounds, received a Justice Department award and in April became the first recipient of the FBI's medal of valor. But sources familiar with the incident said that Mireles may have technically violated the FBI's policy that shots are to be fired only in self-defense. By the time Mireles reached the suspects' car, they had stopped shooting" (Ostrow 1990).

FBI officials noted that, although no longer shooting, the suspects in the Miami shoot-out were still armed at the time Agent Mireles fired at them; this, they believe, clearly justified shooting. Thus, the purpose of the impending FBI policy change, officials indicate, is to clarify to agents that they may shoot at fleeing violent crime suspects who, in the reasonable judgment of the agents, present a continuing threat of violence to the community regardless of whether or not that violence is being exhibited at the moment agents discharge their weapons.

Incidents like the Miami shoot-out in 1986, involving heavily armed assailants, also prompted the Bureau, after lengthy research and development, to change its issued sidearm from a .38-caliber revolver to a 10-millimeter semi-automatic pistol (Ostrow 1990).

Most of the critics of the FBI's new policy stance have not suggested that the agency's highly trained and disciplined agents are likely to abuse their right to employ deadly force. Nor have the critics intimated that FBI personnel will file false reports about agent-involved shootings. Rather detractors worry that other federal, state, and local police agencies, which look to the FBI for policy leadership, will take the Bureau's example as license to relax their own policies and practices (Ostrow 1990)—and that in some of these other departments officers will not continue, after such a policy change, to exercise the same level of restraint in the application of force as one might reasonably expect FBI agents to persist in using.

No responsible friend or foe of the police today suggests that local police agencies would, as a matter of *policy*, encourage shootings that violated the constitutional requirements of *Tennessee v. Garner*, which FBI sources believe are still less stringent than the Bureau's proposed policy in some ways. Rather, the concern, as noted above, is that, *in practice*, ill-trained, incompetent, or malevolent officers will make more mistakes or hide more of their misdeeds in the aftermath of a departmental policy relaxation than would be possible under a defense-of-life standard. Police Foundation President Hubert Williams' reaction to the FBI's intention to modify its policy exemplified the perceptions of many in the police profession: "If you provide that level of discretion in police departments, I think there will be more abuses and more instances of people shot by police" (*Law Enforcement News* 1990: 5).

There is also a concern that a shift in FBI policy, when echoed at the local level, will provide a scope of discretion within which local police may more easily discriminate racially in their decisions to shoot at fleeing suspects. A policy requiring an unambiguous perception by the shooting officer that his own or someone else's life is in jeopardy *right now* leaves far less room for racial bias or other inappropriate considerations to affect the officer's shoot/don't shoot decision than a policy that invites police to speculate on what the criminal suspect might or might not do in the near future if not gunned down promptly.

Racial discrimination in this situation might not even be intentional; it might simply be the product of ill-founded presumptions by officers about the future danger posed by suspects of different races or ethnicities. Or racially discriminatory shooting at fleeing suspects might reflect an officers' misconceptions—or even accurate beliefs—about the relative prospects for apprehending escaped suspects of different races or ethnicities. A common dilemma in some urban ghetto neighborhoods—especially those with high-rise slum housing projects—is that suspects of the same race as the dominant occupant group in the housing project seem able to "disappear" while being pursued by police.

Even if there was a demonstrable difference in the apprehension rate of suspects of different colors and ethnic heritages, such patterns could well be attributed to deficiencies in some officers' skill at precisely describing suspects of different races or ethnicities. Vague descriptions of facial characteristics and complexion will inhibit other officers from identifying the wanted persons. Or perhaps such patterns might result from differential cooperation with police by residents in the neighborhoods to which suspects with different characteristics might flee. Neither an officer's inability to describe adequately a suspect of a race different from his or her own nor a department's weakness in cultivating a cooperative relationship with its service population, in our view, should serve as a legitimate basis for licensing expanded use of lethal force against fleeing offenders.

Still another concern about departments that have already adopted a less restrictive rule than the defense-of-life standard is that the change could send an unintended message to local criminals. Intuitively, one's first assumption might be that putting offenders on notice that they may more readily be shot by police will result in greater compliance with police demands and less need for police to use deadly force. But, notwithstanding our data on officers who would have died in recent years except for the protection afforded by their soft body armor, there is also another possible explanation for long-term

"[T]he apprehension of felons is one area where the police can create a favorable public impression, and therefore one from which they derive considerable gratification.... Each man obtains prestige and a greater chance for promotion by the publicity which attends the apprehension of the felon. The force as a whole is justified as an existing body. What public judgment of the police does occur is seldom in regard to the extensive time and activity they devote to their mundane service activities...but rather in terms of how they behave in more dramatic and newsworthy areas, of which the apprehension of the felon is the outstanding" (Westley 1951: 125-126).

downward trends in shootings *of* police by those they attempt to stop or arrest. It is the possibility that at least some potential police assailants have been made less afraid over the years that the police will administer "street justice" with a nightstick or lethal weapons and hence are less likely to shoot an officer to protect themselves. Reasonable or not, there can be little doubt that some of those who assault police do so in the belief that the officers are looking for an excuse to harm them and will do so unless prevented. A change in deadly force policy perceived in the community as "taking off the gloves" could well exacerbate such unwarranted[20] but highly consequential fear.

If, as critics of the FBI's policy change claim, there is relatively little concern about FBI agent decisions to use deadly force under the new rules but great concern about the message that will be sent to local police, then an empirical question arises: Is a switch in FBI written policy in fact likely to stimulate a switch in local police agency policies or practices? One aspect of this question is how many agencies currently have a written policy stricter than the one the Bureau proposes adopting. This amounts to asking how many police departments currently have strict defense-of-life policies. Regrettably, no current survey of the nation's more than 15,000 police departments sheds light on this issue. Another aspect of this question is how much latitude for officer shooting decisions is allowed, in light of each agency's disciplinary and training practices, regardless of what each department's written policy technically requires. If the previous question is *difficult* to answer, this one may be nearly *impossible*.

---

[20] Among the many tragic consequences of the LAPD's videotaped beating of Rodney King in March 1991 is the legitimacy the incident granted to the view—held by criminals, by jurors, and by ordinary citizens—that at least some police engage in horrible abuses of their discretion to employ force.

Perhaps all that one can do at this point is to think critically about the impact that FBI policy has had on local agency standards in the past and about some of the factors that might affect the ability of the Bureau's proposed policy to alter local preferences. It can hardly be claimed that the FBI's adoption of a defense-of-life policy approximately 50 years ago prompted a rapid and pervasive switch in local police policies. Indeed, during the legal and political battles to reform local police agency policies on use of force, proponents of the status quo were quick to explain the inapplicability of FBI rules and procedures to local policing due to dramatic differences in the kind of work performed by local police and FBI agents.

Nevertheless, there can be little doubt that the FBI's long-standing operation under a defense-of-life deadly force policy helped bolster the protracted campaign for local agency adoption of this strict policy. The campaign achieved substantial success in 1982 with publication by the IACP of its report, *A Balance of Forces* (Matulia 1982). This book recommended a defense-of-life policy for local agencies. Nor can the FBI's model be said to have been unimportant in the Commission on Accreditation for Law Enforcement Agencies' decision in 1983 to mandate a defense-of-life policy for any agency wishing to be accredited (CALEA 1983: standard 1.3.2, p. 1-2).

Nor is there any doubt that the long-term commitment of the FBI to a defense-of-life standard influenced the Supreme Court's 1985 decision in *Tennessee v. Garner*. The Court explicitly cited the FBI's rule, the New York City Police Department's strict deadly force policy, and the CALEA standards as evidence that highly respected law enforcement organizations did not consider their performance of duty to be impeded by strict limits on the use of lethal force to arrest.

Moreover, for decades the FBI has built up a fund of goodwill and interchange with the local police world by offering free mid- and upper-management training on policy and other matters at the FBI Academy in Quantico. The opportunity in this environment and in the social and professional interchange afforded by gatherings of FBI Academy alumni for new FBI standards to "rub off" on local agencies is substantial (see Geller and Morris 1992). As we go to press with this book, it is just over two years since reporters first disclosed the FBI's interest in amending its deadly force policy (e.g., Ostrow 1990). According to the FBI's press office (Markardt 1992, 1992a), the planned policy change remains in limbo, still awaiting approval by higher authorities in the Department of Justice.

II. *Policy Enforcement and Personnel Practices*

A restrictive shooting policy is no better than its enforcement. Discussing analogous considerations in the context of pursuit driving control, Alpert and Anderson (1986: 5) urge: "[A] strong, clearly defined policy can be undermined if no one enforces it, or if those who violate it are not properly disciplined." A policy can be enforced—or given an effective implementation—by many and varied means, some punitive, some in the nature of rewards, others entailing inspirational leadership, and still others involving support of officers through training or assistance in dealing with personal stresses or relief from counterproductive agency requirements or processes (see generally Skolnick and Fyfe, forthcoming).[21]

---

[21] Relief from agency requirements might involve, for instance, administrators accepting the fact that they cannot hope to get an officer to admit candidly his or her good faith mistakes in use of force if they respond by punishing the slightest, inconsequential errors. A positive response, including retraining and expressions of gratitude for officers' candor, would be far more likely to accomplish the objective

Fyfe (1978, 1979b) suggested that the marked decrease in the rate of "*non*-defense-of-life" shootings in New York City during his 1971-75 study period was in large part due to two initiatives: (1) the creation of the Firearms Discharge Review Board, which put teeth into the new restrictive policy, and (2) an administration that used the supervisory structure to hold officers accountable for their actions (also see Geller and Karales 1981a: 58-59).

A. The Effects of "Administrative Climate"

Sherman (1983) echoed Fyfe's conclusion regarding Kansas City and Atlanta, where he found that continuing administrative pressure is an essential supplement to a restrictive written policy. Sherman concluded after analysis of Department-furnished data that when Chief Joseph McNamara left Kansas City, shootings by Kansas City officers reverted to what Sherman characterized as the high level they had attained before McNamara's adoption of a strict policy (Sherman 1983: 123). Sherman attributed this development to a change in administrative climate, since Chief McNamara's written policy remained in effect, saying, "One might infer that the impact of a restrictive written policy is limited in the absence of a strong perceived message from the police executive to use restraint in shootings" (*ibid.*).

The numbers on which this conclusion is based were too small to provide statistically significant findings. Moreover, as shown in Figure 69, over the 20-year period of 1972 through 1991, the number of persons intentionally shot at (missed or struck fatally or nonfatally) by Kansas City police officers each quarter actually reached its high point during the twilight of Chief McNamara's tenure (in the third quarter of 1976). Whereas the data in Figure 69 (which we collected) show *intentional* firearms discharges, the data on which Sherman relied presumably included shots accidentally fired as well (he says the data include "all" firearms discharges).

Figure 69 extends well beyond Chief McNamara's tenure and that of his immediate successor. In the graph, the letters "a" through "f" refer to the times at which the Kansas City Police Department experienced a transition from one chief to another:

"a" =   On July 9, 1973, Chief Clarence M. Kelley left to become director of the FBI. He was succeeded by Acting Chief James R. Newman.

"b" =   On November 1, 1973, Acting Chief Newman was succeeded by Chief Joseph D. McNamara.

"c" =   On October 4, 1976, Chief McNamara left to become chief in San Jose. He was succeeded by Acting Chief Marvin L. VanKirk, who was named chief of police on January 1, 1977.

"d" =   On February 7, 1978, Chief VanKirk was succeeded by Chief Norman A. Caron.

"e" =   On March 31, 1984, Chief Caron was succeeded by Chief Larry J. Joiner.

"f" =   On March 14, 1990, Chief Joiner was succeeded by Chief Steven Bishop.

---

of gaining insight from the field concerning how to improve deadly force decision making.

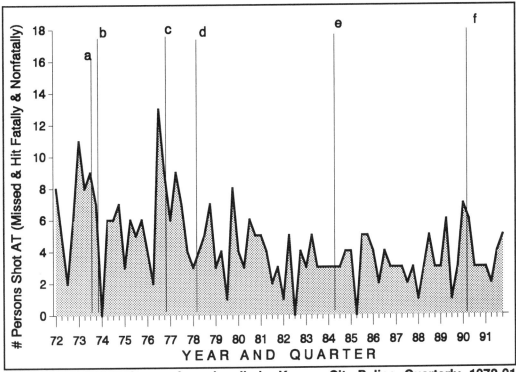

Figure 69: Persons Shot at Intentionally by Kansas City Police, Quarterly, 1972-91
Source: Kansas City Police Department.

Figure 70, which we will discuss below, shows the number of persons shot at and hit and shot at but missed over the same 20-year period.

As Figure 69 and Table E-4 in Appendix E show, the number of intentional shots-fired incidents *increased somewhat* when one compares the 12 month periods before and after Chief McNamara left Kansas City (25 versus 31 incidents). Moreover, the *monthly* average number of *intentional* shots-fired incidents in Kansas City during the administration prior to Chief McNamara's was 2.4. During McNamara's tenure the monthly average was 1.8; in the 15 months thereafter the monthly average was 2.3 (see Table E-67 in Appendix E).

Sherman (1983) also examined New York City and Atlanta to explore the proposition that policy changes plus changes in administrative climate can produce officer restraint in the use of deadly force. In New York City, following an array of NYPD policy and other administrative changes in 1972, the average monthly number of firearms discharge incidents declined to 37.1, compared with a monthly average of 52.4 prior to the changes (Sherman 1983: 112). And in Atlanta "the number of incidents in which a citizen was hit dropped from a quarterly mean [average] of 7.6 before the formal policy change [in 1974] to 2.7 after the change" (*ibid.*).

Sherman (1983) and others showed that Chief McNamara's *arrival* in Kansas City marked the beginning of a change in the number of times police weapons were used. In the 12 months before his arrival, Kansas City officers intentionally fired their weapons 34 times; in the first 12 months of Chief McNamara's tenure, that number dropped to 17 (based on monthly shooting data furnished to us by the Kansas City Police Department). The reader should keep in mind, however, that the numbers used for this analysis are relatively small.

It seems to us to be intuitively plausible that a written policy must have "teeth" put into it through various administrative initiatives. The reduction in shots-fired incidents during the early months of Chief Steven Bishop's tenure in the latter half of 1990, although still based on very small numbers, may be a further indication that a variety of strong and clear messages from the chief's office, coupled with consistent training, discipline, and reward decisions, can help produce a desirable change in the frequency of officer-involved shootings.

In Chief Bishop's case, shortly after he became Kansas City Chief on March 14, 1990, he made several major disciplinary decisions in brutality cases that did not involve shootings—cases in which the police conduct at issue occurred before Bishop's appointment as chief. In the first two of these cases he decided early in his tenure, he imposed stiffer penalties than might have been expected by the rank and file, given prior disciplinary patterns. Such decisions often send police employees powerful messages about the importance of restraint in the use of force, and insiders believe these discipline cases help explain the drop in use of deadly force during the second half of 1990 and the first half of 1991 compared with the first six months of 1990 (Zacharias 1991).

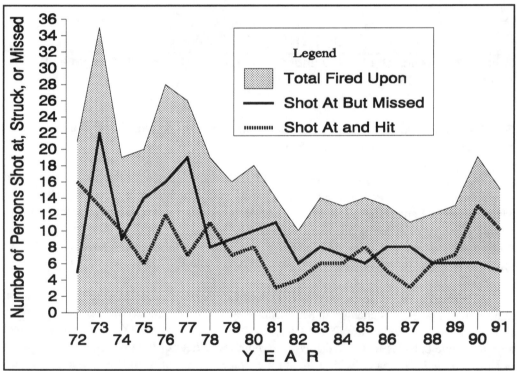

Figure 70: Persons Shot at Intentionally by Kansas City Police, Annually, 1972-91
Source: Kansas City Police Department.

It is true, of course, as Figure 69 shows, that the third and fourth quarters of 1991 saw an increase in intentional shots-fired incidents in Kansas City. But to more fully understand whether the most recent period in that jurisdiction represents a problematic development it is useful to consider Figure 70, which adds information about the *outcome* of shots-fired incidents on an annual basis. In 1990, the number of persons struck by police bullets (13) rose to a level exceeded only at the outset of the 20-year period 1972 through 1991. Then, as indicated, Chief Bishop's multi-faceted approach to controlling violence between his officers and the citizenry was followed by the promising mid-1990 reductions shown in Figure 69 and the 1991 reductions in hits and the slight decline in off-target shots shown in Figure 70.

One should, of course, be cautious about attributing desirable outcomes to any particular initiatives before exploring and eliminating rival explanations (crime and arrest rate changes, etc.) (Sherman 1983). One might even argue that the relatively higher levels of people struck by police bullets during 1990 resulted not so much from less restraint in shooting as from superior aim. Thus, in 1990, 68 percent of the persons shot at intentionally were struck by police bullets (13 out of 19), compared to 58 percent in 1989 (7 out of 12) (see Table E-46 in Appendix E).

In any event, these numbers must all be considered against the backdrop of violent crime, arrests, and other measures of the potential for dangerous police-civilian encounters in order to be more meaningful. Sherman (1983: 12) found that relevant data to conduct this analysis for Kansas City were unavailable at the time of his inquiry. Earlier in this volume and in tables in Appendix E we presented, for a number of major cities, the kind of data on violent crime arrests, general population homicides, and other environmental factors that Sherman urged subsequent researchers to employ in deadly force research. Researchers may wish to use these data to explore rival hypotheses—those that conflict with the notion that administrative interventions shaped the shooting patterns depicted in the various graphs. In addition, it is important to remember that, without denigrating the human and other costs associated with any particular shooting incident, the numbers of incidents in many sizable jurisdictions (Kansas City being a prime illustration) are relatively small and, therefore, subject to large percentage fluctuations from year to year based on relatively small actual number changes.

B. Internal Shooting Review Systems

As indicated, we place confidence in the capacity of effective police leadership to influence the safety of officers and to minimize their career risks by discouraging unnecessary shootings. In this regard, the deadly force review system established in the New York City Police Department by Commissioner Murphy in August 1972 (NYPD Chief of Department 1988: 2) merits a few comments. Two of the most promising features of the Firearms Discharge Review Board in New York (and of Los Angeles' shooting review system—see Meyer 1980a: 54) are that its jurisdiction includes all shots fired, not just persons struck, and that its dispositional options are not limited to finding shootings justified or unjustified.

These features were—and remain—absent in the review systems in many other cities, where the dispositional options include only finding a complaint against an officer "sustained," "not sustained," or "unfounded," or "exonerating" the officer (Geller and Karales 1981a; Geller 1992). Indeed, 18 percent of the 2,155 Firearms Discharge Review Board adjudications Fyfe reviewed held that, although the shootings were technically within policy guidelines, the officers should be given additional training in the use of firearms or in relevant law and policy. The NYPD Board also has the option to recommend transferring the officer to a less sensitive assignment, psychological testing, or alcoholism counseling (Fyfe 1979b: 322; see Matulia 1985: 72-87 concerning shooting investigation processes nationwide). For discussion of a recent appraisal of the NYPD use of force investigative apparatus, see *Law Enforcement News* (1990a).

In the interest of fairness and effectiveness, it seems to us that departments would want to expand the repertoire of conclusions that post-shooting debriefings or investigations can reach. At present, the common practice seems to be to examine principally whether the subject *officer(s)* did anything wrong. But due consideration seems not to be given to whether the employing *agency* created unreasonable policy, procedural, supervisory, training, equipment, or other restrictions or circumstances of ambiguity that made any undesirable conduct by the officer more likely. Thus, we believe, a post-shooting review board should be able to render findings pertaining not only to the individual employee's culpability but also to contributory administrative deficiencies.

At times, such a panel will need to conclude that key agency officials or other powerful government officials have sent mixed messages that weakened officers' resolve to comply with professional obligations (see Geller 1992). For the most part, the clear message sent to officers by the review systems established in police departments with restrictive shooting policies has

"We would urge persons who review use of force situations to be very cognizant of the fact that persons reviewing the incident are in a far different position from the officer involved in the incident. The most obvious differences are as follows:

a. the reviewer has a great deal of time to carefully evaluate the situation and make decisions. By contrast the officer may have to evaluate, make a decision and take action in a split second; and

b. the reviewer is not placed in any jeopardy during the review process. By contrast the officer may be placed in extreme jeopardy while he or she is trying to evaluate and make decisions; and

c. there are many factors which can affect a situation (lighting, weather, fatigue, etc.) that [reviewers] may be unaware of unless they ensure that their investigation is thorough" (Jamieson, et al. 1990: 12).

been that the administration will not countenance shootings outside policy guidelines. Whether such systems speak with equal credibility to the public at large—particularly segments of the public suspicious of the police—is a difficult question. It is part of the larger question of designing effective and credible systems to review allegations of police misconduct (see Kerstetter 1985; Perez 1992).

Some practitioners and observers believe that the credibility of shooting review systems depends to a considerable extent on whether the review is conducted by sworn officers within the involved officers' chain of command or by police and others outside that chain. For instance, researcher Arnold Binder saw the fact that police departments in Chicago, Detroit, Los Angeles, New York, Orange County (CA), Philadelphia, Phoenix, and San Francisco use officers from internal affairs or other special units or civilian investigators employed by the police agencies as providing far greater credibility to the general public than the use of homicide investigators alone (Petrillo 1990a: A-10). Community leaders and others familiar with the same cities might not draw the same distinctions or derive the same inferences, however (e.g., see the Christopher Commission's findings concerning the LAPD—Independent Commission on the LAPD 1991).

In a matter so subjective as *credibility*, it is important to remember that people will interpret practices through a complex filter of prior knowledge, presumption, and prejudice. Binder, for instance, without specifying the agencies he had in mind, voiced strong objection to the use of homicide detectives to investigate police-involved shootings. "There is such biased reporting by homicide detectives that it's hard to imagine they're even seriously calling that independent" (Petrillo 1990a: A-10). Our view is that the matter is far more subtle and complex within any given agency over time; in part, it depends on the personnel—first-line and supervisory—assigned to units and across agencies. With Kerstetter (1985), we consider it crucial that a department's chain of command play a strong role in conducting post-shooting inquiries. But like Kerstetter (1985) and Perez (1992), we also consider it crucial that additional mechanisms be established to assure all concerned parties, including the public at large, that the investigations conducted were complete, accurate, fair, and as expeditious as feasible. In any event, we see little basis for the kind of gross generalizations Binder was quoted as making about the quality and integrity of homicide investigations. Almost certainly, homicide and other investigations around the nation are both far better and, perhaps in some ways, even worse, than Binder suggested depending on when and where one looks.

Table 24 shows the percentage of police shootings found *un*justified by police agencies in three cities. All had a significant deadly force or investigative policy changes, and the before-after experience with investigative outcomes is displayed where the data are available. The early 1970s dispositional pattern of firearms discharge investigations in the New York City Police Department (in which 29.2 percent of the firearms discharges were ruled unjustified) may be supplemented with late 1980s data from New York City. In 1987 the NYPD's Firearms Discharge Review Board reviewed 200 incidents in which members of the force fired their weapons (with varying effect). Of those 200 cases, the Department found that 26 intentional firings (11.8 percent) violated Department policy and that an additional 25 *accidental* discharges (11.4 percent) fell outside policy restrictions. Thus, 23.2 percent of the reviewed discharge incidents were found to have involved unjustified conduct by the involved officers (in 1985 the total found unjustified was 18.5 percent and in 1986 the total found unjustified was 25 percent—NYPD Chief of Department 1988: 6). Of the balance of the 200 incidents investigated during 1987, 140 intentional firings (63.6 percent) were found to be consistent with Departmental policy, and 29 accidental firings (13.2 percent) were found not to violate policy (NYPD Chief of Department 1988: 1).

Nowicki and Stahl (1978: viii, 12, 103), studying shots-fired incidents involving Chicago police during 1975-77, found that following internal investigations of 319 incidents in which a person was wounded or killed by police bullets, 5 percent (16) of the shootings were found to have violated state law or Department policy. They found (1978: 11) that an additional 5.6 percent (18) of the woundings or killings were ruled to be accidental (officers displayed their weapons legally but discharged them accidentally). The remaining 89.3 percent were ruled justified by the Department's civilian-staffed Office of Professional Standards.

These Chicago data represent both on- and off-duty uses of firearms by police. Fyfe (1988a), examining *on-duty* shootings during an early period in Philadelphia, characterized the Philadelphia Police Department as having a notoriously poor record of disciplining officers for shootings that violated even a permissive departmental policy. Between 1970 and 1978, Fyfe could only find two instances in which officers who fired their weapons on duty were disciplined (1988a: 182). Fyfe concluded that when Frank Rizzo, an outspoken defender of police use of deadly force, was in power (whether as police commissioner or mayor), the rates at which Philadelphia police officers resorted to deadly force went up (1988a: 184; see also Waegel 1984a, 1984b).

As noted earlier, we and others (see Geller and Karales 1981a: 190-194) see promise not only for a process that adjudicates officer liability but for a departmental panel whose mission would be to review shootings to identify *preventive* strategies, whether in the area of policy development, training, weapons or other equipment modifications, or supervisory changes. Such inquiries often have their greatest success if commenced as reviews of "averted" shootings (incidents in which an officer would have been legally and administratively justified in shooting but found another way to resolve the situation) or as reviews of shots-fired incidents that involved minimal or no personal injury and minimal potential for officer liability. Getting candid information from incident participants is much easier when the information is unlikely to be used for disciplinary purposes (see Geller 1985a).

Table 24:
Percentage of Shootings Found Unjustified in Three Police Departments
Before and After New Policy and/or New Internal Review Panel

		Shooting Type	
City	Time Period	Persons struck	All firearms discharges
Atlanta	Before ('71-76)	5.5% (n=162)	---
	After ('76-78)	15.4% (n=26)	---
Kansas City	Before ('72-73)	3.7% (n=27)	34.4%
	After ('73-78)	20.7% (n=58)	40.2%
New York City	Before ---	---	---
	After ('72-75)	---	29.2%

Sources: Sherman (1983), Geller and Karales (1981a).

The NYPD and other departments have for some years assigned officers to study shootings and consider how department policies, training, weaponry, and other elements might be improved. The Phoenix Police Department's objectives in conducting management review of high-speed pursuits provide another illustration of an appropriately broad scope of inquiry in the wake of a critical incident. That agency's purposes are to determine whether:

"1. The Pursuit was necessary and within departmental policy.
2. Training needs should be considered.
3. Policy changes need to be considered" (Phoenix Police Department 1986; Nugent, et al. 1989: 15).

It takes administrative courage for a department to determine that the principal reason for an unnecessary shooting was not officer dereliction but policy failure or improper training.[22] Some agencies have begun to display such courage. The IACP model policy on

---

[22] Delattre (1989: 220) observes:

"Some deaths, especially in high-speed pursuits and in shootings, occur because departmental training standards are not good enough. If officers are not well-taught how to work together in dangerous raids, levels of competence and expectation vary. A sudden and unpredictable movement by a suspect, bystander, or officer can cost a life. A department may find such factors hard, perhaps impossible, to admit, and so may a victim's family. An officer whose action directly caused the death may believe that considering such facts is only a cowardly search for excuses. Those who feel guilty may be unable to give themselves the benefit of an honest appraisal of the facts. Their friends and colleagues may have to press such an appraisal upon them."

police use of force (contained in Appendix B of this volume) encourages departments to consider these factors in "administrative review of critical incidents"—see sections III.E.2.a.(2) and (3). In order to provide "early warnings" of unsatisfactory performance or policy—and to curtail unacceptable practices—the Charleston (SC) Police Department, under Chief Reuben Greenberg, for years has required officer reporting not only of shots fired but of pointing their firearms at another person.[23] As an example of the dynamic interaction of progressive policy and strict but thoughtful enforcement, officers in Charleston have been separated from the force for failing to *report* weapons activity that was *within* policy, while officers who have candidly reported mistakes have been retrained and returned to productive duty.[24]

Enlightened approaches such as Charleston's send several important messages to field personnel. One is that officers will be treated with understanding when they have made an honest, reasonable appraisal of facts and acted decisively based on that appraisal. In too many agencies, officers are made to "walk a plank" because an after-the-fact review establishes not that their judgments at the time of an incident were unreasonable but that the consequences of their decisions have proven politically controversial. If an officer is not taught how to skillfully manage street conflict—and not given administrative support when he or she puts that training into practice—we may field dangerously indecisive police officers. As author William Ker Muir (1977) has observed, officers who are not capable—or permitted—to take professional, responsible risks in a sincere effort to establish moral and, where appropriate, physical authority in difficult, complex street situations, may have to resort to the use of deadly force more often than their colleagues. That an officer is prepared to settle a situation forcefully, if necessary, in a manner consistent with professional and community standards, must be clear to those who might otherwise misinterpret the officer's commendable restraint.[25]

To be sure, just as police agencies must not err in the direction of excessive controls

---

The American Bar Association's "Urban Police Function" standards, first released in 1968, call attention to the need for reviews of police work to explore agency influences as well as individual officer decisions:

> "[L]ittle attention has been paid to analyses of individual police officers' behavior in the
> context of departmental policy. Most of the controls [on officer conduct] have been in the
> form of sanctions of a particular police officer, leaving departmental policies and practices
> unaffected" (ABA 1982: vol. 1, p. 150).

[23] There have been a small number of studies, all involving *simulations* of officer decision making or written questionnaires posing *hypothetical* scenarios, that have explored the question of when and why officers (of differing characteristics—racial and gender) choose to unholster their weapons (see Holzworth and Pipping 1985; Holzworth and Brown 1990; and Doerner 1991).

[24] It is, of course, important that agencies have the determination and skill to separate officers who misuse deadly force from the department when that is warranted. Such separations can send powerful messages to officers. In 1991 and 1992 the 7,988-member Los Angeles Sheriff's Department, facing what some characterized as a spate of problematic shootings, separated four deputies from the force for improper shootings and demoted a fifth (Kolts, et al. 1992: 15, 138; Merina 1992: A20).

[25] Compare the discussions in the Christopher Commission report (Independent Commission on the LAPD 1991) and Rubin (1992) of how some officers—particularly some female officers—seem to approach certain conflict situations with less of a propensity than others to resort precipitously to coercion.

on officers, they must not forsake the obligations of leadership and supervision. To appraise the quality of any given agency's administrative climate concerning the latitude that officers have in making decisions to use deadly force, one obviously would need to know much more than merely its record of imposing discipline after officer use of deadly force. Nevertheless, setting forth what little information the published literature contains on agency discipline records may assist those who wish to bring additional relevant data to the study of different types and qualities of departmental shooting control strategies.

As one would expect, and as Table 24 suggests, police departments vary in the proportions of shootings by officers ruled in violation of departmental policies and procedures. For example, departmental *disapproval* was expressed in:

- 7 percent of all shootings by police in Chicago during the mid-1970s (Geller and Karales 1981a: 169) and 27 percent (30) of the 112 shootings of civilians by Chicago officers during 1989 and 1990 (Shines 1992);
- 29 percent in New York City during the mid-1970s (Fyfe 1979b: 322);
- 23 percent in New York City in 1987 (NYPD 1988);
- 18 percent in Los Angeles during the mid-1970s (Meyer 1980a: 53); and
- 12 percent of the shootings by police nationwide in 1970 and 1971 that were identified through a newsclipping analysis (Uelman 1973: 40).

Just as we argued earlier that studying questions of police racism in the use of firearms *begins*, rather than *ends* with the realization that in some jurisdictions blacks and Hispanics are shot out of proportion to their representation in the general population, an analogous point can be made here: Identifying varying discipline rates across police agencies is but the first step on a long analytic journey. It will have to explore the types of cases in which discipline was and was not imposed; the quality of investigations conducted; the political, administrative, labor-management, and other contexts in which the shooting and post-shooting investigations and adjudications occurred; whether patterns of favoritism or prejudice emerge in who gets punished for doing what to whom; and so on.

It is also important to realize that, in certain contexts, a single, high-profile disciplinary decision can send powerful messages throughout a police organization and a community that might not be reflected in the two-dimensional internal affairs division data published in a police department's annual report. As discussed briefly elsewhere in this book, there is evidence that in Dallas the Department's decision to fire a sergeant in August 1984 for the shooting death of a fleeing, unarmed robbery suspect helped send a powerful message about shooting restraint to his colleagues. Comparing the 12 months preceding the officer's termination with the 12 months afterward, intentional firearms discharges by Dallas police (fatal and nonfatal hits as well as off-target shots) dropped by 48 percent (Dallas Police Department 1990). This Dallas report also contains additional discussion of policy enforcement and personnel terminations in the Department.

C. Commendations, Recruitment and Screening Strategies, Employee Assistance Programs, and Other Personnel Practices

The types of personnel policies and practices that complement other policy enforcement measures and can have an effect on the use of deadly force by police are varied. They include both clearly punitive measures and positive rewards. Among the punitive steps are reassignment, demotion, suspension (with or without pay), and discharge from the force. At the other extreme are such rewards as commendation, favorable reassignment, and promotion.

Potentially more neutral (depending on how a department characterizes these responses) would be retraining and psychological counseling for officers experiencing difficulties (see Matulia 1985: 87-88). (Training is discussed later in this book.)

Some researchers have suggested that departmental awards be given for "commendable restraint" by police officers, in recognition that such conduct often involves bravery of equal stature to that involved in shooting (see, e.g., Geller 1983, 1986). We hasten to add, however, that not all restraint by officers in the use of deadly force is *commendable* restraint—and not all commendations for such restraint are deserved—Kolts, et al. (1992: 152). Table 25 shows in the simplest terms the possible combinations of positive and negative outcomes that come from officer restraint or use of deadly force.

Table 25:
Reasonableness of Officer Decisions to Shoot or Refrain from Shooting

Conduct of Officer	Reasonableness of Officer's Conduct	
	Reasonable	Unreasonable
Shot Fired by Officer	Praiseworthy or Acceptable Shooting	Improper Shooting
No Shot Fired by Officer (Officer Restraint)	Commendable Restraint	Unreasonable Restraint[1]

Source: Geller (1985a).
[1] *The assumption reflected in this cell is that, by failing to shoot, the officer was unduly restrained; that is, greater force than the officer used was called for. One could readily imagine a set of facts in which an officer declined to fire a shot but nevertheless used excessive (nondeadly) force. The point of this table, however, is to illustrate that there are times when deadly force is the necessary and proper police response, just as there are times when restraint in the use of physical force is the professional way to accomplish the police purpose.*

In keeping with the notion that commendable restraint is a relatively "soft," hard-to-quantify phenomenon (one would be trying, in a sense, to count "nonevents" or the *absence* of uses of deadly force), Fyfe (1981b: 388) recommended that

> "police internal reward systems should be structured in such a manner that quantitative measures of police work (such as the number of arrests) and involvement in violent activities are not the predominant or exclusive means of obtaining recognition for outstanding performance."

Improper shootings (or improper uses of nonlethal force) by police can helpfully be classified in two basic categories: "willful and wrongful use of force by officers" (brutality) and "police violence emanating from simple incompetence" (Fyfe 1989c: 465, 467), which, it is suggested, may be called simply "unnecessary" force (*ibid.*). The distinction is offered on the ground that officers' motivations for engaging in each type of improper force are decidedly different. So, too, should the corrective methods be different for officers who *intentionally* use more force than is warranted and officers who, although well-meaning, use unwarranted force out of ignorance or ineptness (Fyfe 1989c: 467).

Just as administrators must employ creative and effective means to identify and redress *misuses* of deadly force, they should also find methods that help to make positive role models of officers who show sound judgment about when to use and not use varying levels of force. Indeed, although the details of exactly how to identify and organizationally praise prudent officer restraint can be vexing, doing so is arguably one of the most important initiatives a police administration can take to communicate its values to the rank and file without having to make a negative example of officers. The message that needs to be communicated is that proper restraint is smart and bold behavior and not the conduct of "spineless desk jockeys." Referring to military strength, President Dwight Eisenhower once made a similar point when he referred to "the courage of patience."

"Officers [must] diagnose the most critical problems they face—those that may require the use of extreme force—BEFORE they occur, and...attempt to apply to their resolution techniques of tactical knowledge and concealment. We demand that from the military and from the fire service, both of which spend considerable time diagnosing and planning for exigencies that we are someday likely to ask them to resolve. We do not tolerate it when their actions in emergency situations demonstrate that they have been taken by surprise and forced to react on the basis of instinct rather than of careful advance diagnosis and planning. But, when police resort to forcible means to resolve readily foreseeable problems that could have been peacefully resolved with advance diagnosis and planning, we not only tolerate but also often reward their behavior" (Fyfe 1989c: 477).

As to the relationship between recruit characteristics and police-involved shooting patterns, Blumberg (1989) reported that no clear relationships have emerged between demographic characteristics of officers and their propensity to use deadly force. (This parallels the point we made in Chapter 4 about in-service personnel: that virtually none of the empirical research to date establishes a strong correlation between individual officer characteristics and the outcome of potentially lethal police-civilian encounters.) For administrators wishing to continue the examination of whether recruitment strategies can help control officer-involved shootings, the research suggests that it may be worth studying more closely whether younger officers have a greater propensity to use both lethal and nonlethal force (Sherman and Blumberg 1981; Croft 1986; but see Binder, et al. 1982) and whether female officers have less proclivity to use force (Sherman and Blumberg 1981; Grennan 1987; Blumberg 1983; see also S. Martin 1990; Independent Commission on the LAPD 1991: 83-84).

The Police Foundation has urged the use of psychological tests to screen out potentially violent police candidates, but conceded that the reliability of such predictive tools is low (Milton, et al. 1977: 90-91). This view of the state of the art was shared by the Christopher Commission, which examined use-of-force issues in the LAPD (Independent Commission on the LAPD 1991: 110), but not by another investigative panel, which studied the Los Angeles *Sheriff's* Department and seemed to place considerable faith in psychological testing to weed out violence-prone applicants (Kolts, et al. 1992: 211-216; for other critiques of the Kolts report, see Stolberg 1992a; Reich 1992a, 1992b;). Nowicki and Stahl (1978: 39-53) encountered the deficiencies of psychological screening during the 1970s, when they explored whether slightly different types of psychological screening batteries administered to different entering classes of Chicago police recruits were correlated with differential shooting involvement and career success. Unable to control for a host of personal characteristics of the officers due to the unavailability of data, lack of sophisticated analytic tools, and relatively small sample sizes, Nowicki and Stahl tentatively concluded (1978: 46) that they could observe no meaningful correlation between "variations in the psychological screening processes" and "the likelihood of the screened officers' involvement in use of a firearm."

The soundest thinking about psychological screening as a predictive tool for police applicants' propensity to use inappropriate force (too much or too little) if hired seems to be that only the most obviously maladjusted personalities will be screened out by written tests or interviews by psychologists. The best guide to future conduct seems to be, as it has long been, *past* conduct (Independent Commission on the LAPD 1991: 111-112). Earlier discussions of the limited capacity of psychological screening tools to ferret out violence-prone police candidates can be found in Eisenberg and Kent (1972), Saxe and Fabricatore (1982), Hargrave and Kohls (1984), and Benner (1986).

Sherman and Blumberg (1981) have conducted one of the few assessments to date of the possible impact of officer higher education on police use of force (see also Carter, et al. 1989). They explored the association between appropriate and inappropriate use of deadly force, as dependent

"While [intentionally excessive] police violence is egregious, it probably occurs far less frequently...than does police violence emanating from simple incompetence. Such violence occurs when police lack the eloquence to persuade temporarily disturbed persons to give up their weapons, but shoot them instead. It occurs when, instead of pausing to consider and apply less drastic alternatives, officers blindly confront armed criminals in the midst of groups of innocent people. It occurs when officers called to quell noisy but non-violent disputes act in a way that provokes disputants to violence to which the police must respond in kind. In short, it occurs when well-meaning police officers lack—or fail to apply—the expertise required to resolve as bloodlessly as possible the problems their work requires them to confront" (Fyfe 1989c: 467).

variables, and, as independent variables, the officers' level of education, age, length of service, and father's occupation. Control variables included the civilian adversary's precipitating conduct and variations across officer assignments in arrest/encounter rates. Their analysis did not reveal any significant relationships between education level and shooting involvement, a finding which they theorize might be different with a sample of officers containing *older* college graduates; the effects of "youth and inexperience" were considered as counteracting any substantial influence of higher education.

For in-service personnel, early warning systems have been recommended to monitor officer conduct and alert administrators to inappropriately forceful members of the department (see Geller and Karales 1981a: 196; Independent Commission on the LAPD 1991; Nowicki, et al. 1991: 297; Alpert 1989b: 485). Factors considered relevant in assessing an officer's propensity to misuse force—factors that can be used to assess an officer's career risks—are:

- civilian complaints against the officer;
- rates of charges filed by an officer against arrestees for resisting or assaulting the officer and rates of disorderly conduct charges filed by the officer against arrestees (in Miami, "control-of-persons" incidents are tracked—Alpert 1989b: 485);
- the officer's involvement in prior shooting incidents or incidents resulting in injury, including K-9 bites and in-custody injuries or death "where the deceased was under direct control" of the officer (International City Management Association 1991: 297);
- the officer's record of assignments, including partners and supervisors;
- the officer's record of discipline; and
- the officer's prior commendations and evaluations (Geller and Karales 1981a: 196).

As the Christopher Commission (Independent Commission on the LAPD 1991) discovered in Los Angeles, of course, an officer experiencing difficulties with use-of-force decisions may have glowing performance appraisals by his or her supervisors. This may be, as the Christopher Commission suggested for Los Angeles, a consequence of irresponsible supervision—which serves as an important reminder that, generally, no single indicator in an early warning system should be taken as sufficient by itself to allay concerns about substandard conduct. Similarly, before an officer is subjected to interventions designed to correct problematic behavior, sometimes (although not always) it will be sensible to wait until more than one sign of trouble appears. The existence of *multiple* indicators that an officer needs assistance with his or her use-of-force decisions can help clarify an otherwise ambiguous warning signal.

> "*A Puerto Rican falls to his death from a tenement roof and two cops are suspected of throwing him down. In the heat and frustration, and under the anonymous cover of night, the temptation to dispense justice often proves irresistible. The cops in question are not indicted, but they are fired from the force.*
>
> "*Almost exactly one year later the frustration of the officers can be seen in an exchange of gunfire with a fellow who had held up a dice game. In the streets delay may mean death. A well-intentioned impulse by the cop—to see what the other guy will do— seems to accompany every cop's death. The simple rule becomes to shoot first. In this case the cop does and the shotgun wielding holdup man falls dead. The ghetto elements who flock to troubled waters immediately call for a rally to protest this 'cold blooded murder.' The deceased was 'shot in the heart,' by a 'trigger-happy pig,' 'after surrendering.' The shot he'd aimed at the cop, which missed, is now conveniently forgotten.*
>
> "*These two events reflect the chasm between ghetto residents and the police and help explain why the police so frequently have to fight onlookers to retain their prisoners, no matter how awful the original charge may have been nor who may have lodged it. The prisoner will shout 'Brothers, save me. The pigs are taking me in for playing the numbers.' The message is believable to onlookers, who can draw on real and fancied tales of police arrogance, brutality or criminality. The police, sensing the uselessness of it all, never respond—even when a Spanish-speaking officer may be in a position to immediately refute the prisoner's cries. The chasm widens. The police don't even seem to realize that they are battling for the minds and hearts of the onlookers. The endless rounds of violence and response proceed despite a mother's wails of anguish or the stricken cries of the wounded*" (Bouza 1990: 59).

Employee assistance programs that help officers deal both preventively and, after a shooting, recuperatively, with a wide variety of personal and job-related circumstances can also have a beneficial effect on officer fitness for duty and morale (Paradise 1991). Problems with alcohol or substance abuse (including such drugs as steroids, which can induce abnormally violent behavior) obviously need prompt attention by the employing agency—hopefully, before the troubled employee becomes a problem employee (Nowicki, et al. 1991: 297).[26]

Similarly, officers having family, financial, or other personal problems that may make them unduly impatient or cloud their thinking in tense, rapidly developing street situations

[26] A pioneering, highly acclaimed initiative to help police officers with alcohol and substance abuse problems and stress produced by various factors is the Davie, Florida-based Seafield 911 program, founded in July 1989 by former Boston police officer Ed Donovan and former deputy sheriff and New York City firefighter Ed Benedict (Witkin, et al. 1990: 43-44). Said one Seafield staff member: "This place is saving cops' lives from the most common cop-killer. It's not the gun-wielding maniac. It's the bottle" (*ibid.*: 44). Some surveys bear out this sad diagnosis, suggesting that "as many as one in four police officers may be alcoholic." Relatedly, other studies suggest that "the divorce rate among police officers may be as much as twice that of the general population" (*ibid.*).

must be identified and helped through their difficulties.[27] Often such help will be better received if provided outside the physical setting of a police agency. The police department's approach to encouraging employees to come forward and seek needed support and counseling often will have a determinative effect on whether such employees willingly participate. A police executive whose words or deeds make it clear that employees who admit any weakness will be considered unfit for duty and penalized in subtle or not so subtle ways should not be surprised when few employees step forward to seek help.

Police psychologists and psychiatrists have identified a variety of post-shooting traumatic responses that police officers around the nation have experienced. For example, Russell and Beigel (1990: 368-373) have identified the following stressful reactions among officers who have shot someone:

"1. *Sensory distortion.* Time slows down; everything happens in slow motion.

2. *Flashbacks.* Many things subsequently occur that instantly remind you of the shooting—another shooting, the sight of a body in the street. You live it over and over.

3. *Fear of insanity.* Officers may have this fear because of symptoms in (1) and (2) above.

4. *Sorrow over depriving a person of life.* It is very difficult to break the cultural and religious prohibition against killing. Even police officers who have previously killed in military combat state that a police shooting is entirely different. [As one officer put it], 'In a war, that's what you're there for...to wipe them out. Police work isn't like that. You are certainly not on a search and destroy mission' (Cohen 1980).

5. *Crying.* This usually happens outside the police environment because the macho image does not permit tears.

6. *Grasping for life.* Officers become very concerned about their families, their home life, being loved and accepted by others—a sort of guilt reaction to the shooting.

7. *Nightmares.* One officer reported frequent nightmares in which the suspect kept coming at him, looming ever larger and ever nearer while the officer frantically pumps bullets into the apparition.

> *"An American law enforcement officer encounters more human tragedy in the first three years of his career than most of us see in a lifetime" (Scrivner 1985).*

8. *A heightened sense of danger.* A shooting brings officers face to face with their own mortality. No longer can they maintain the idea that 'It won't happen to me.' For some officers, this has resulted in their leaving law enforcement [see, e.g., *New York Times* (1992p); Ford and Malnic (1992)]. Although exact statistics are not available, it has been reported that between 50 and 80 percent of officers involved in shootings have left police work (Baruth 1986: 307).

---

[27] On alcohol and substance abuse problems as they may affect police-involved shootings, see Pendergrass and Ostrove (1986) and Stratton and Wroe (1980). On officer marital tensions and their possible effects on line-of-duty conduct, see Bibbins (1986); Boelte (1989); Madamaba (1986); Stratton and Stratton (1982); and Maslach and Jackson (1979).

9. *Anger and hate toward the victim/suspect.* Solomon and Horn (1986) state that this is the second most frequent and severe post-shooting reaction. Officers curse the victim/suspect for 'making them do it,' but this anger may mask the feelings of fear and vulnerability that the incident aroused in officers so that the curse more properly may be expressed as 'goddamn you for making me feel so vulnerable.'

10. *Isolation/withdrawl.* Officers may think that no one will understand what they are going through. They don't want to risk being ridiculed or put down. Peer support from another officer who has gone through a shooting experience can be most helpful at this time.

11. *Fear and anxiety about the next time it happens.* One officer who shot a suspect who he thought was armed (but wasn't) expressed fears that the 'next time maybe I'll hesitate to shoot and this time the asshole will have a gun and he'll blow my f—— head off.'

12. *Fear that they will be fired, criminally charged, or sued in civil court.* These are frequent reactions. Police policies and procedures may add unnecessary stresses to officers involved in a shooting. Delays in completing the investigation, a negative attitude, or lack of support from supervisors and/or administration can compound the psychological damage. [Investigations that last several months, even if they clear the involved officer of any wrongdoing, have disrupted families, producing stresses that led to divorce. Civil and criminal court proceedings against officers for shootings] make psychological intervention more difficult because officers become preoccupied with the legal ramifications of what they say to the psychologist rather than trying to express feelings about the shoot-ing.... Even if [the confidentiality of the officer's interview with a psychologist is legally assured], an attorney [representing the officer] may decide that it is not in the best legal interests of his or her client to participate in such sessions."

Solomon and Horn (1986) prepared a similar list of 18 distinct types of reactions that officers they interviewed had to the trauma of shooting someone. As summarized by Ayers and Flanagan (1990: 7-8), these reactions included:

"heightened sense of danger, anger, nightmares, isolation/withdrawl, fear and anxiety about future situations, sleep difficulties, flashbacks/intruding thoughts, emotional numbing, depression, alienation, guilt/sorrow/remorse, the 'Mark of Cain' (an assumption that others blame or shame them), problems with authority figures/rules/regulations, family problems, feelings of insecurity/loss of control, sexual difficulties, alcohol/drug abuse, and suicidal thoughts" [see also McMains 1986; McCafferty, et al. 1989; and the discussion of post-traumatic stress syndrome in Paradise 1991].

Among the most promising of all approaches to employee assistance—certainly on a recuperative basis and perhaps even preventively—is one pioneered over two decades ago by the Oakland, California, Police Department with technical assistance from State University of New York-Albany Professor of Criminal Justice Hans Toch. The initiative, a version of which was being implemented by the Kansas City, Missouri, Police Department in 1991,[28] in Oak-

---

[28] The effort undertaken recently in Kansas City stands as an endorsement of this agency's belief in the potential for peer assistance to modify the conduct of overly aggressive officers because the Kansas City police in the mid-1970s had an unsuccessful experience attempting to transplant the Oakland program to Kansas City (Pate, et al. 1976; Sherman 1983: 98). Among the possible reasons for

land was called a peer review panel. Essentially, this was a guided group self-retraining effort, in which officers who themselves had problems with controlling their use of force helped one another, with the expert assistance of Toch and his co-workers, to reorient their thinking so they could more successfully pursue their police careers. Toch and colleagues have written about the approach in some detail, including in 1991 a book-length treatment that casts the conceptual approach used in Oakland in the more modern framework of thinking entailed in "problem-oriented" strategies for improving policing (see, e.g., Toch 1969, 1970a; Toch, et al. 1975; Toch and Grant 1991).

> *"Some officers involved in shoot-outs state that they hated all the adulation they received from their fellow officers afterward. One officer says, 'You can't really talk to someone who hasn't been there. They want to hear the gory details, not about your problems handling it, because it's heavy and it reminds them that it could happen to them' (Cohen 1980)" (Russell and Beigel 1990: 368-369).*

Other peer support programs are also available to assist officers (or, in the event of a death, an officers' survivors) suffering in the aftermath of traumatic experiences. One, formed in 1983 by 10 young widows of police officers, is Concerns of Police Survivors (COPS), which "focuses on the emotional and other support needs of law enforcement families, friends, and co-workers who have lost a loved one in the line of duty." A grant from the National Institute of Justice in 1985 helped the group become more firmly established and helped it develop written materials outlining the needs of police survivors (Sawyer 1989; Concerns of Police Survivors 1988; see also FBI 1992f).

Another peer support group, founded the same year in New York City by a detective who was blinded and maimed while trying to disarm a terrorist bomb, is the Police Self-Support Group (PSSG). Said PSSG founder Richard Pastorella of his initial trauma and how he chose to deal with it:

> " 'It's a tragedy initially, but the trick is to take a tragedy and turn it into something worthwhile so you can now help not only yourself but somebody else. That's the healing process. The psychological dynamic is that I still have value because obviously I'm helping someone else who is less fortunate than me. So how bad off can I be?' * * * When an officer has been hurt, the PSSG waits five to seven days before making an approach. Then a member who has suffered a similar injury will visit. 'If he's an amputee, I'll send an amputee,' said Pastorella. 'If he's been shot, a shooting victim will go. If he's blind, I may go.' Sometimes, the newly injured officer gets a shock. Pastorella recalled an incident in which a member visited an officer who had suffered an amputation and was suicidal. 'Our member walked in and sat down,' said Pastorella, 'and the guy said, "How do you know what I'm going through? Get out of here and leave me alone." And our member took his leg off and said, "Now can we talk?" The message is simple: If this guy can do it, I can do it' " (Burden 1990a; see also *Law and Order* 1991).

Perhaps the most basic step in assisting employees involved in shootings is to relieve

---

the earlier lack of success was the failure of those who sought to test peer assistance in Kansas City to tailor the programmatic elements to this department's particular needs, opportunities, and preferences (Toch and Grant 1991: 270, 286 n. 1).

officers for a reasonable period of time from the full obligations associated with their field assignments. McMurray (1990: 46), studying the Washington, DC, and Newark, New Jersey, police departments, noted that in a sample of officers he surveyed who had been shot at, "all but one...reported staying on the job or reporting to work the next day." Even if, as may have been the case, these officers were given the choice of taking some time off and opted not to, administrators and supervisors still need to consider the best interests of the employees and the public. "It is conceivable," McMurray suggested, "that...officers [who have been shot at] might overreact and use unnecessary force, or underreact [i.e., avoid proper and necessary police engagement in incidents reminiscent of the one in which they were assaulted], which can be a threat to themselves as well as to fellow officers. In either case, neither the needs of the officer nor of the police department are fully met" (*ibid.*; see also McMurray 1988).

D. Criminal Prosecutions, Civil Suits, and External Review Board Sanctions for Wrongful Shootings by Police

Uelman (1973: 40) found, as others have,[29] that compared to the use of departmental discipline for improper shootings, local or federal criminal prosecution of officers was rare. In 50 departments in Los Angeles County, he found that criminal charges were filed against 6 percent of the officers who violated departmental shooting policies. Petrillo (1990a: A-1) reports that the San Diego County District Attorney's office absolved San Diego police officers of any criminal liability in all of the 190 officer-involved shootings that occurred from January 1, 1985, through December 20, 1990. Out of 477 shootings, 174 of them fatal, by deputies of the 7,998-member Los Angeles County Sheriff's Department from 1979 through September 7, 1991, criminal charges were filed against only one deputy (Katz 1991: A22).[30] That deputy served eight months in jail "after falsely reporting a disturbance at a...home in 1982 to justify a raid there. After kicking the door down, he shot Delois Young, 22, who was

---

[29] Fyfe and Blumberg (1985); Blumberg (1989: 458-59); Waegel (1984a); Knoohuizen, et al. (1972).

[30] Commenting on these figures, Los Angeles County Deputy District Attorney John Spillane, whose responsibilities include the review of police misconduct allegations, said: "We're not saying there aren't some questions about some of these cases. But our gut feelings and hunches can't be proved beyond a reasonable doubt. That's the law we face" (Katz 1991: A23). Defending his agency's use of deadly force, L.A. County Sheriff Sherman Block reported that he had fired 146 deputies for brutality and other misconduct between 1988 and September 1991 (*Crime Control Digest* 1991m: 8). The Sheriff did not say how many of these officers were fired for violating departmental shooting policy; but Kolts, et al. (1992: 138, 147) reported that between 1980 and July 1992, only five were—four of them in 1991-92.

The L.A. District Attorney's rate of prosecuting LASD deputies for shootings was blasted by the "Kolts Commission," in a report issued July 20, 1992. This commission was convened by the L.A. County Board of Supervisors to look into alleged abuse of deadly force in the L.A. Sheriff's Department and was chaired by former L.A. County Superior Court Judge James G. Kolts. Several of the panel members had served the previous year on the Christopher Commission, which criticized policies and practices in the Los Angeles Police Department (Kolts, et al. 1992; Tobar and Reich 1992; Merina 1992; Reich and Muir 1992). The Kolts report identified 382 shootings by officers that were reviewed by the DA's Office during the 1980s. As noted in the text, these resulted in only one prosecution (Kolts, et al. 1992; Tobar and Reich 1992: A18). At a July 20 news conference releasing the Kolts report, Merrick J. Bobb, general counsel to the panel, called the DA's failure to prosecute more of these cases "incomprehensible" (Reich and Muir 1992: A20). The DA's Office retorted that it would have explained its declination decisions if the Kolts panel had taken the time to interview officials in the DA's office (Stolberg 1992a: A16; Reich 1992a). Kolts, et al. (1992: 143-146) said the DA's Office was not entirely to blame, charging that Sheriff's deputies frequently thwarted the DA's investigations. Two-term L.A. District Attorney Ira Reiner announced on September 18, 1992 that he would not pursue his bid for re-election in November of that year (Mydans 1992d).

pregnant and holding an unloaded rifle. Young survived, but her 8-month-old fetus was killed" (*ibid.*: A23).

Kobler (1975a: 163) found that criminal prosecutions were begun nationally in only one of every 500 cases of fatal shootings by police during the 1970s. (The prosecution of the one Los Angeles Sheriff's Department deputy out of 174 fatal shootings noted above produces a prosecution rate nearly three times as high as Kobler discovered.) He reasoned that the prosecution rate of one per 500 cases might be due to the more stringent standards typically imposed by departmental policy than by state criminal law,[31] to prosecutor-police interdependence (see Hubler 1991: B1; Levitt 1991), and to prosecutors' realization that juries are unlikely to convict law enforcement officers of misconduct against criminal suspects (see also Blumberg 1989: 458-59).

> "*A rookie...City police officer was charged with murder...in the fatal shooting of a man trying to steal his car...as the officer was getting ready to go to work.... The officer...told investigators that he had surprised the man...inside his car in front of his...house, and then shot him three times in the chest because [the car thief] was menacing him with a screwdriver. But...the Medical Examiner's office determined that [the thief] had been shot three times in the back. * * * [The officer] was arrested by Internal Affairs officers on order from the...District Attorney's office and suspended without pay. He was arraigned...on second-degree murder charges and released on his own recognizance*" (New York Times *1991: 14*).

There can and will be exceptions to this pattern of declining to use the criminal law as a tool for controlling unwarranted police use of force. In 1979 four white Metro-Dade, Florida, police officers beat black traffic violator Arthur McDuffie to death and were indicted for their actions. They were acquitted in May 1980, resulting in a costly and bloody riot in the Liberty City section of Miami (Grogan 1992), a frightful forewarning of the sequence of events that would occur more than a decade later in Los Angeles.

Dade County (FL) has been the site of other efforts to use the criminal law to remedy police abuse of force. During a six- month period (November 1982-March 1983), four officers were indicted by the Dade County grand jury for manslaughter. Three worked for the Metro-Dade Police Department, the fourth for the City of Miami Department (Alpert 1989b: 481-482). Of these four, only one, a 29-year-old Metro-Dade rookie with six months' experience on this force, was convicted. He was sentenced to five years in the penitentiary (*ibid.*: 484).

In keeping with the pattern in 1980, one of the acquittals, that of the Miami City officer charged (a Hispanic), sparked several days of rioting in March 1984 in the predominantly black Overtown neighborhood of Miami. This 1984 insurrection was not the first civil unrest caused by the accused officer's conduct (fatally shooting a 20-year-old black man under ambiguous circumstances). There was collective violence during December 1982 and January 1983 in the immediate aftermath of the killing (*ibid.*: 483). From March 1983, when the fourth of these errant officers was indicted, through January 1987, "all shootings by police officers

---

[31] In this regard, a failed legislative effort in Florida during 1990 to require that no local agency have a deadly force policy more restrictive than state law, if it had succeeded, might have placed a larger burden on prosecutors than they currently have to prosecute errant police officers. Fyfe and Blumberg (1985) and Blumberg (1989: 458-59) see little prospect for enactment of state statutes embodying a strict defense-of-life standard for police use of deadly force, despite recommendations by others (e.g., Griswold 1985) that this be done.

An officer was prosecuted by the County District Attorney for killing "a hostage being held by a bank robber. [The officer] fired the bullet that killed [the] 22-year-old [hostage] after she had just escaped from her abductor,...who himself died in a hail of police bullets.... [The following year, the] jury [considering the case against the officer] stayed out less than six hours and in a single vote acquitted [the officer] of involuntary manslaughter. The shooting and criminal trial so unhinged [the officer], then 25, that he was granted permanent disability retirement" (Petrillo 1990a: A10).

in Dade County [were] ruled justified without the need for a grand jury investigation" (Alpert 1989b: 481). In December 1989, however, Hispanic Miami officer William Lozano was convicted of manslaughter by a multiracial jury in Miami for the fatal shooting of a black motorcyclist (whose passenger also perished when the vehicle crashed). Three days of rioting followed the incident, the fourth "race riot" in Miami of the decade. The conviction was overturned on appeal in the summer of 1991, the court ruling that "jurors had been influenced by their fear of more rioting" (*Crime Control Digest* 1992m: 1). By August 1992, judges in several Florida cities had spent months issuing change-of-venue orders, each seeking to avoid holding the controversial retrial of the officer in his own locale (*ibid.*; Rohter 1992, 1992a).

In April and May 1992 the nation had another powerful illustration that acquittals of officers charged with assaulting suspects can have a criminogenic (i.e., crime-generating) effect. Reflecting on the Los Angeles riot, perhaps it is not surprising that the County District Attorney began scrambling even before the smoke had dissipated to consider retrying the one LAPD officer whose actions caused a hung jury on one charge. At press time, it looked like that retrial would be cancelled or at least postponed until the outcome of a federal prosecution of the four officers tried initially in state court (*New York Times* 1992l). Perhaps less predictable, given the difficulties of proof (Stolberg 1992b; Mydans 1992c), was the Justice Department's decision to prosecute these officers on federal civil rights charges, a decision revealed on August 5, 1992 with announcement of grand jury indictments (Newton and Berger 1992; Reinhold 1992a; Nasser and Lovitt 1992).[32] County and federal officials presumably

---

[32] Prosecuting police officers in federal court for civil rights violations after their acquittals or lenient sentences in state courts is uncommon and controversial. Sherman (1980a: 93) reported that "from 1970 through 1976, the average number of federal civil rights prosecutions for police homicide was four per year; in 1977 and 1978 [during the Carter administration] it was only two per year" (see also American Bar Association 1982: vol. 1, p. 145). Warren (1992: 23-24) discusses the use of "follow-up" criminal prosecutions of police officers by the Justice Department's Civil Rights Division:

"Two 1977 Texas cases, involving police officers accused of murder, eased the way for follow-up federal prosecutions, which had been rare until then even though the civil rights statutes had been on the books for a century. In a San Antonio case, a city marshal accused of shooting to death his prisoner was convicted of the lesser offense of aggravated assault and sentenced to only 10 years in prison. In a Houston case, a jury came up with negligent homicide for six police officers accused of beating and then pushing a prisoner into a bayou, where he drowned. They were sentenced to one year of probation. * * * Political pressure [was] the catalyst for a decision by then-U.S. Attorney General Griffin Bell to loosen the government policy restricting dual prosecutions.... Federal convictions were subsequently won in both Texas cases and the precedent was set. * * *

"A divided U.S. Supreme Court ruled in the late 1950s that conducting separate state and federal trials does not constitute double jeopardy for the defendant. [But legal opinion remains divided. This division] is typified by that within the American Civil Liberties Union. The ACLU championed the right to a federal follow-up trial in the turbulent 1960s

sought to restore public confidence that the justice system is not a tool of injustice; some charged the federal indictments were politically motivated (Newton 1992; O'Connell 1992).

> *"It's better to be judged by 12 than carried by six."*

It is odd that the media and public place so much emphasis on the outcome of *criminal* cases to settle the question of whether the officers who beat Rodney King to within inches of his life behaved properly. Doing so is somewhat like any of us, faced with the necessity of having medical surgery, interviewing possible surgeons and accepting as evidence of their bona fides the doctors' assurances, "Don't worry, dear patient, we have never once been convicted of aggravated battery as a result of our work in the operating room." We expect doctors to adhere to a higher standard than avoiding criminal conviction for malpractice. We want doctors not only to comply with minimal standards of human decency, but to strive for excellence, certainly including the avoidance of needless harm. Similarly, in the police world consumers have a right to expect—and should look to evaluation mechanisms that are designed to assess—police efforts to carry out their responsibilities with minimal harm and maximal efficiency and effectiveness. The criminal law is far too crude a measuring instrument to tell us most of what we need to know about the professionalism of any given instance of police work (see Klockars, forthcoming).[33]

Civil suits take one step closer to asking the right questions about officer competence, for here the inquiry typically is whether the police conduct at issue suffered from recklessness, sloppiness, or neglect (negligence) on the part of individuals or organizations. But even civil suits fall short of asking the questions capable of being addressed in police administrative reviews about whether the conduct at issue exemplifies the kind of work that the police agency finds most effective, efficient, and consistent with organizational values and goals.

Asking which arena of review focuses on the most important questions is slightly different, however, from asking what the deterrent or remedial capacity of criminal

---

and '70s, but in 1990 its national office approved a policy that branded the practice double jeopardy. But the new policy was never endorsed by the Southern California ACLU office, which [as of May 1992 was] urgently calling for federal charges in the King case.

"In practice, federal civil rights charges are often threatened, but seldom actually pressed. [Between] October 1988 [and May 1992], there have been only five federal civil rights cases involving police officers who were prosecuted following state trial acquittals, three in the South and two in Puerto Rico. * * * [F]ederal prosecutors are...careful to take only cases that they believe they can win. * * * [T]hey know it can be as difficult to prove an officer's intent to deprive a person of his civil rights as it is to prove an intent to kill" (see also *New York Times* 1992q; Stolberg 1992b).

[33] Because criminal prosecution is a poor tool for making the sometimes subtle distinctions between desirable (even exemplary) police work and undesirable conduct, it provides little guidance to police officers and society about how police might best perform their difficult assignments. But when officers act beyond the scope of their duties and commit common crimes, the criminal law seeks to play the same roles—public education about impermissible behavior, incapacitation of the offender, etc.—as with any other law breakers. Although we do not have data on the subject, we suspect that the rate at which police officers who commit common crimes outside the scope of their employment are prosecuted criminally is much higher than the rate at which police are prosecuted for line-of-duty actions. As one instance of an officer being prosecuted for actions unconnected with his job, in July 1992 a Brooklyn, New York, grand jury indicted an officer for murder, accusing him of "fatally shooting a liquor store owner during an attempted robbery while the officer was off duty" (*New York Times* 1992h).

prosecutions or civil litigation is. Sometimes the outcomes of *civil* suits may *directly* affect the nature and extent of police-involved shootings, as many believe happened with the *Tennessee v. Garner* case. But whether or not a direct connection can be shown between particular judicial rulings and future police policies and practices, experienced practitioners and risk managers generally agree that the prospect of civil liability has an important impact on police agency shooting control efforts (see, e.g., Blumberg 1989: 459) and a deterrent effect on officers' "elective shootings." (Elective shootings—like elective surgeries—are those *not* necessitated by a

> *"Lawsuits challenging the professionalism of police work are filed every year at the rate of about one suit for every 30 officers in the U.S. About 40 to 45 percent of these suits allege police abuse of force. At one time in the 1980s, the City of Los Angeles had more police-related suits pending than police officers on the job. In 1962 the going rate for police professional liability insurance was $12 per year per officer on the force; today that rate has jumped to about $900" (Schmidt 1992).*

present threat to a person's life.[34]) Risk management seminars presented by most management training institutes address the development of deadly force policy and policy enforcement mechanisms and discuss the risks of civil liability for both municipalities and individual employees. For discussions of the prevalence and effects of civil liability on police administrative initiatives, see McCoy (1985); Schmidt (1976, 1976a, 1985); Lant, et al. (1979); Barrineau (1987); Avery and Rudovsky (1992); Littlejohn (1981); Meadows and Trostle (1988); Americans for Effective Law Enforcement (monthly newsletter and 1974); *National Bulletin on Police Misconduct* (monthly newsletter); Stafford (1986); del Carmen (1981, 1991); American Bar Association (1982: vol. 1, pp. 142-145); Independent Commission on the LAPD (1991); Kappeller (1988); and Kappeler and Kappeler (1992).

Fueled in no small measure by the visibility given to police abuses by the Rodney King beating in Los Angeles in March 1991 and the riot it spawned in 1992, there has been a resurgence recently of interest in civilian review boards and other civilian-based accountability mechanisms.[35] Drawing on a study by Walker and Bumphus (1991), one long-time institutional advocate of civilian review of police work reported: "By the end of 1991, more than 60 percent of the nation's 50 largest cities had civilian review systems, half of which were established between 1986 and 1991" (American Civil Liberties Union 1992: 15; see also *Law*

---

[34] One would not expect to find concerns about civil liability weighing heavily on an officer who believes he must shoot to save a life (a *nonelective*—or essential—shooting). In the Portland (OR) Police Bureau, a survey of officers about potentially violent encounters revealed that the vast majority had been in situations where they believed they "could have shot someone, with full justification, but chose not to" (Snell and Long 1992a). Among the explanations given for declining to shoot were: "took a risk to spare the subject" (23 percent), "threat not as first perceived" (24 percent), "feared hitting bystander" (17 percent), "was able to use alternative" (11 percent), "just couldn't pull the trigger" (1.4 percent), and "other" reasons (17 percent). The remainder of the explanations pertain to the deterrent power—or lack thereof—of civil, administrative, and criminal review processes and penalties. Thus, 4 percent of the officers said they chose not to shoot because they "dreaded going through investigation/grand jury" and only 1.7 percent said the "fear of a lawsuit" motivated their decisions (*ibid.*).

[35] For discussion of the early experiments with civilian review of police work and their general lack of success, see American Bar Association (1982: 1-148 through 1-150); President's Commission on Law Enforcement and Administration of Justice (1967: 200-202); Note (1964); and Comment (1962). For a more optimistic view of the accomplishments of civilian oversight bodies, see American Civil Liberties Union (1992); but compare Kerstetter (1985) and Perez (1992).

Enforcement News 1991a). These civilian-involved review systems are not all of the sort in which civilians receive, investigate, and adjudicate allegations of police improprieties. A clear description of the variety of police oversight mechanisms in which civilians typically participate is provided by Kerstetter (1985) (see also Perez 1978, 1992; Terrill 1990; and American Civil Liberties Union 1992: 16).

III. Training, Weapons, and Equipment

A. Training

The empirical literature has recommended training in four basic areas: (1) policy interpretation; (2) human relations and "cultural awareness" skills; (3) conflict management techniques (training in physical, verbal, and judgmental "violence-reduction" tactics); and (4) tactics for the proficient use of weapons when shooting is required.

1. Policy Interpretation

The drafting and adoption of written policy on permissible use of deadly force are, as we discussed in the previous section of this chapter, hardly sufficient to influence officers' conduct on the streets. Policy enforcement (through rewards, punishment, and appropriate refresher training) is also crucial. But leaving officers guessing as to the meaning of possibly ambiguous organizational policy until such time as they receive "object lessons" in the form of penalties to officers for out-of-policy performance is an ill-advised management approach.

New policy should be framed and adopted with sufficient input from the rank and file to ensure policymakers that all crucial points of view and representative experiences in the use and avoidance of deadly force have been considered. Then, before the enforcement of new policy, all affected members of the police force should be given adequate training in its meaning. Some departments have experienced intense labor-management strife in the wake of the firing of an officer for violation of a new deadly force policy. In some instances the meaning of the policy was clear to all affected parties, and the strife simply reflected entrenched points of view concerning appropriate policy, officer safety, the popularity of a particular police administration, or other local circumstances. But in other instances (some of which have embroiled the agencies and their city administrations in lingering and highly costly internal and external conflicts), the extreme labor-management difficulties (and the attendant morale and other problems) could have been avoided if the police administration had realized that policy introduction needs to include detailed training, not just the circulation of a training bulletin.

Detailed training to supplement the adoption of written policy becomes more essential to the extent that the new policy is complicated or represents a radical departure from the previous rules. Thus, classroom (and, probably simulation) training would be advisable when a department shifts from a policy that permits firing at unarmed, fleeing, violent crime suspects[36] to a policy that emphasizes shooting only in response to an immediate threat to

---

[36] *Tennessee v. Garner* (1985) permits shooting at unarmed fleeing suspects so long as the shooting officer(s) reasonably believes that the suspect fired upon has committed a violent crime and, therefore, may commit further violence against innocent persons if not apprehended promptly. Many police agencies have adopted policies that are more restrictive than this, but most authorities agree that this is an accurate interpretation of the minimal standard announced by the Supreme Court in *Garner*.

human life. Such training would also be highly recommended to help introduce a new policy that attempts to communicate the concept that a shooting decision sometimes results from a series of smaller tactical decisions (about entry into scenes, approaches to suspects, information exchange between officer and suspect, etc.)—decisions that will now become the subject of performance appraisal and disciplinary review (see Scharf and Binder 1983; Alpert and Fridell 1992).

However complicated or simple a training program may be, there is no doubt that police departments are required to provide training in the constitutional standards governing police use of deadly force. In *City of Canton v. Harris* (1989), the U.S. Supreme Court, addressing a question concerning high-speed pursuits, noted in passing:

> "[C]ity policymakers know to a moral certainty that their police officers will be required to arrest fleeing felons. The city has armed its officers with firearms, in part to allow them to accomplish this task. Thus, the need to train officers in the constitutional limitations on the use of deadly force (see *Tennessee v. Garner*...) can be said to be 'so obvious' that failure to do so could properly be character- ized as 'deliberate indifference' to constitutional rights" (*City of Canton v. Harris* at 1205 fn. 10).

In contrast to the notion of basic classroom training in constitutional standards, a number of departments have mounted extensive in-service training programs to help officers understand the nature and importance of a newly adopted use-of-deadly-force policy. One example with which we are familiar is the Chicago Police Department, which undertook an agencywide training intervention in 1985 that extended into 1986, in the wake of an 18-month policy development process that culminated in the adoption of a "protection of life policy." This policy essentially paralleled the rule (announced during the tail end of the Department's policy development process) in the U.S. Supreme Court's March 1985 *Tennessee v. Garner* decision. As part of the lengthy policy development process, the Department, with the aid of an outside research consultant, generated a number of recommendations that went well beyond the written policy eventually adopted by the agency. Some of these recommendations addressed the need for training modifications and were incorporated in the Department's training program, begun in 1985. This training, administered to all 12,500 sworn personnel in the agency (earlier officer survival training had been administered on a priority basis, mainly to officers in high-risk assignments), introduced the new protection-of-life policy and provided guidance about techniques for averting shootings. Work done by researchers to examine critically what Fyfe (1986b, 1989c) has more recently called the "split-second syndrome" became a centerpiece of the training.

Thus, officers were asked to think about the shooting decision not only as an instantaneous "Should I pull the trigger?" question, but as part of a series of decisions spanning space and time. These decisions would encompass such issues as: "Should I engage this suspect? Should I engage him *alone*? Should I engage him *now*? What is the best way to enter the scene? What do I need to know about the suspect, the scene, any possible third parties who might be present, and so forth to improve my chances of controlling this encounter and having it come out in a proper fashion?" These and other such questions discussed at greater length elsewhere in this volume were addressed.

Numerous other police agencies, at all levels of government,[37] have provided varying levels and qualities of training on tactical engagement (and disengagement) techniques, conflict management, and other skills relevant to the control of police-involved shootings. We believe in the utility of such training, although, as the Chicago example suggests, depending on the yardstick one uses to appraise the administrative interventions, progress may or may not be evident.

The most basic question, of course, is whether after a policy or training initiative there was more or less bloodshed than before. Using that criterion, the Chicago experience was a good one. Some background is necessary: When Chicago Mayor Harold Washington, the first black elected to that post, named Fred Rice, Jr. as the Department's first black Superintendent in 1983, Rice was called upon to allay the notion, prevalent in some segments of the community, that Chicago police used deadly force too freely, especially against minorities. He took steps promptly to convey the message both within and outside the Department that, although he strongly supported his officers in their difficult jobs, they would need to redouble their efforts to ensure they used lethal force only when it was a justifiable last resort. He did so through informal and formal policy statements and through the more formal training noted above. By the yardstick of reducing bloodshed, Fred Rice's early experience was impressive (recognizing, of course, that many variables can and probably do affect the frequency of shootings and other police-civilian encounters). After a year on the job, Superintendent Rice enjoyed a decrease from 84 shootings (in 1983) to 68 (in 1984), a decline of 27 percent (see Tables E-2 and E-35 in Appendix E). In 1985, 50 civilians were shot fatally or nonfatally. The annual tally was 46 for each of the next two years.

If, however, one attempts to compare the number of shootings to the number of arrests for forcible (violent) felonies, one gets the pattern depicted in Figure 71 (which is identical to Figure 29 and is reproduced for the reader's convenience). Due to fluctuations, some quite large, in the levels of arrests from year to year, the shooting *rates* in Figure 71 present a slightly less clear picture of reform than do the *numbers* above. The substantial decline in shooting *rate* under Superintendent Rice (from 1983 to 1984—a decline from 9.1 to 4.9 persons shot per 1,000 persons arrested for forcible felonies), came during a time when the Superintendent and his team were informally urging use-of-force restraint and developing the agencywide training that would be administered in 1985 and 1986. Except for the shooting *rate* increase from 1984 to 1985 (during a time when the *number* of persons shot actually dropped from 68 to 50), Superintendent Rice's tenure was marked by decline and maintenance of a lower shooting rate than had been the norm before he took office.

Under Rice's successor, LeRoy Martin, who served from November 18, 1987 until April 1992, the annual *number* of persons shot rose initially, the fell (see Tables E-2 and E-35). While the shooting *rate* decline shown in Figure 71 during the Martin years at first glance seems quite impressive, as we noted in discussing Figure 29 in Chapter 3, the decreases in 1988 and 1989 followed a somewhat artificial change in the forcible (violent) felony arrest rates due to a changing definition of assaults used to calculate the rates.

Just as police in Chicago during the mid-1980s were trained to reflect on whether, when, how, and with whom they should enter potentially dangerous situations, officers in New York City, beginning some years earlier, received similar training. Although we do not have

---

[37] Citing, among other factors, a series of confrontations in which smugglers' weapons overpowered agents' firearms, the U.S. Border Patrol recently developed a 16-hour officer survival training program; it focuses on various techniques for controlling potentially dangerous encounters (P. Smith 1990).

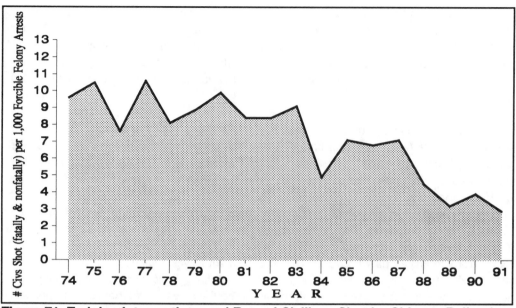

Figure 71: Training Interventions and Rate of Civilians Shot by Chicago Police (per 1,000 Forcible Felony Arrests), 1974-90 *Source: Chicago PD.*

specific data to support the proposition, a New York City police captain who served for years on the NYPD's team that handled hostage/barricade situations made a telling observation. During his tenure on the emergency response team in the 1970s and 1980s, the number of hostage/barricade incidents in New York City increased tenfold (Gorman 1991). Why was this? Was it because there was a 1,000 percent increase in the activity of hostage takers and persons barricading themselves? That is doubtful. It is much more likely that this tenfold increase stands as evidence that, following their training, first-responding NYPD officers were "converting" into incidents meriting the response of the Department's highly regarded emergency squad situations that in previous years would have been handled with immediate interventions by whichever officers happened to be present. By containing situations and seeking expert assistance, first-responding NYPD officers were investing the Department's resources in an effort to produce outcomes that were less bloody for offenders, victims, and officers alike (compare the exceptional incident described by Fried 1992 and Marriott 1992a).

2.   Human Relations and Cultural Awareness Training

Human relations and "cultural awareness" training have been urged so as to sensitize officers to individuals' motivations, fears, and needs to be treated with basic respect, and to familiarize officers with cultural differences between racial and ethnic groups (and between *subgroups within* racial and ethnic groups).

Human relations training has been recommended specifically to help officers develop problem-solving skills for responding to domestic disputes (Bard and Zacker 1976; Eck and Spelman 1987) and more generally to assist them in handling other frequent calls for police service (see Goldstein 1990). Education about human relations and cultural diversity are recommended to strengthen officers' communication skills generally so that they may provide more effective police services to diverse populations.

But in the context of preventing extreme police-civilian violence, there is a more particular purpose, especially for cultural awareness training. The purpose is to help officers avoid misreading the degree of danger in their encounters with potential opponents (Geller and Karales 1981a: 196-197; Geller 1986).

Moreover, if any given police officer does not already show a suitable level of respect to the civilians—of all races and ethnicities—whom he or she encounters in the line of duty, then improvements in this area might result in the officer receiving more respect for his or her authority and humanity in return. Just as poet e.e. cummings once observed that "hatred bounces,"[38] so too does respect.

While the tangible benefits of improved rapport between police and community may not always be demonstrably *tactical* (e.g., greater officer safety, efficiency, and effectiveness in dealing with potentially violent street situations), there are at least two good reasons to invest administrative energy and political capital in progress in this domain.

> *"Sensitivity programs can evoke negative reactions as they are introduced into a department. For instance, what is the first thought that comes to the mind of an officer who is ordered to attend a sensitivity training session? For many officers, the title of the training alone sends a message that they are viewed as insensitive. The notion that police are insensitive is repugnant to many officers who have been involved in pulling victims from car crashes, talking people out of suicide, and helping to deliver babies. And when this type of training follows an incident involving alleged use of excessive force that stirs up the community, it is often viewed by officers and supervisors alike as punishment that officers will have to endure to appease the community"* (St. George 1991: 8; see also Torres 1992).

First, there is likely to be a much better flow of useful information—the lifeblood of any police organization—from communities. People who feel the police disrespect them understandably are reluctant to "help the police." Second, the police in an organized society are an important instrument of government policy. If American policy is equal rights under the law, then police work, in its overt and more subtle aspects, must exemplify equal respect for the basic humanity of all people. This does not mean a police officer can't shoot and kill someone. But it does mean that the justification for a shooting must be rooted in the otherwise uncontrollable misbehavior of the offender, rather than his or her heritage.

It is also important, we believe, to deal with the fact that many members of the public do not show proper respect for police officers. Rather than merely accepting disrespect as an occupational hazard, police might find creative and effective ways to encourage members of the public to come to grips with the fact that respect is a two-way street. Naturally, police cannot afford to behave unprofessionally just because members of the public treat them uncivilly. But the public needs to police itself—parents, teachers, and other adult role models guiding children, adults applying peer pressure and self-restraint—to create an atmosphere in which police are respected and in turn show respect for civilians they encounter in trying

---

[38] As good ball players who are familiar with their playing fields know, some bounces are more predictable than others. This is true as well in the arena of racism and retaliatory hatred. In this regard, see a brave Op-Ed piece by Henry Louis Gates, Jr., professor of English and chair of the Afro-American Studies Department at Harvard University, criticizing black anti-Semitism. Suggesting that this hatred is the product in modern times of a conspiratorial effort by Afro-American separatists, Gates makes a strong case for police to be watchful in the years to come for hate crimes and retaliatory offenses by black and Jewish hate mongers (Gates 1992). (Incidentally, our failure in the text to capitalize poet e.e. cummings' name is not a typo—the bard insisted on lower case letters for his name!)

circumstances.[39] We do not naively assume that marketing and other public relations techniques—or even dramatically different styles employed by police on the streets—will eliminate all disrespectful behavior or lethal violence directed at officers. It is in the nature of police work that officers are summoned when people lose their self-restraint and will not listen to reason. Nevertheless, we do believe that disrespect is a vicious cycle and that police initiatives, taken day by day and beat by beat across the nation, can influence whether mutual recriminations and hostility rise or fall.

Although American policymakers and police leaders from time to time have taken strong initiatives to struggle against institutional racism in various aspects of public and private life,[40] British government and police officials in the past decade or so have had the issue of institutional racism thrust on to their agendas in much the same fashion that it recurs in the United States—as a result of street rioting in multi-ethnic communities (Scarman 1981).

---

[39] Part of such community "self-policing" is presenting programs to help the public—especially young people—develop skills for dealing with other people at least nonviolently if not respectfully. The Washington, D.C.-based Center to Prevent Handgun Violence has developed a comprehensive school curriculum, geared for children from prekindergarten through 12th grade, to help youngsters learn to "resolve conflicts without violence and to control their anger." The curriculum was being tested with students in various cities as this book went to press (Rudd and Bradbery 1992: 8). Miedzian (1991: 133-144), in a book with numerous insights for police violence-reduction trainers and policymakers, praises the Resolving Conflict Creatively Program, administered since 1985 to hundreds of New York City elementary school teachers so that they might in turn help their students become better nonviolent problem solvers.

[40] See, for example, Williams and Murphy (1990). Hubert Williams and Patrick V. Murphy angered a great many police leaders in their 1990 essay, which suggested that the first *organized* police agencies in the United States were not the large Northern agencies generally cited as the pioneering bodies but rather were the Southern "slave patrols." If their argument is overstated for emphasis, they nevertheless point to a sordid legacy of American enslavement of black people that cannot be ignored by modern public officials. Indeed, to this day as we travel the country working with police managers, we occasionally hear about middle- and upper-level managers in police departments who are members of such groups as the Ku Klux Klan (on the origins of the Klan in Pulaski, Tennessee, in 1865, see Andrist 1987: 50, 54). A colleague who shared the podium with our lead author at a law enforcement conference on police brutality in Texas in 1992 reported that, after he made some remarks about the ACLU's consistency in defending civil liberties, including the First Amendment rights of Nazis and KKK members, two police executives from the audience approached him during a break and identified themselves as members of the Klan who appreciated the ACLU's support.

When matters reach such extremes that agencies discover they are employing individuals who belong to groups that perpetrate hate crimes and other atrocities, measures well beyond sensitivity training may be warranted. Although citizens have a right to peaceably assemble for any nonviolent obnoxious purpose they chose, creative police administrators should be able find ways to make it clear that the values espoused by hate groups have no place in an agency whose highest mission is to enforce the letter and the spirit of the Constitution. People on police payrolls whose views conflict with the basic tenets of a free society should be weeded out of the organization lawfully but hastily.

Two police executive organizations have taken steps to begin to address less obvious problems of racism and racial tension afflicting American policing. In September 1991, the Police Executive Research Forum and NOBLE held the first national conference on "Racial Issues Facing Policing." Titled "Unfinished Business—A Conference for Police Executives on Reducing Racial and Ethnic Tension, Building Bridges and Preventing Conflict," the conference overflowed with black, white, and Hispanic police leaders from coast to coast. NOBLE and PERF have planned a September 1992 sequel to this conference, again focusing on problems of both police-civilian racial tension and racial problems *within* police agencies. These issues were also addressed in July 1992 at the NOBLE annual conference in New Orleans, in a panel discussion for which our lead author was a speaker.

After a decade of research and developmental work, British authorities have fashioned a program for training that nation's police on "ethnic relations." The "key lessons that can be learned from the British experience" thus far were summarized by Oakley (1990: 55-56) and have direct application throughout America despite the many years' head start that our nation has had:

"(1) Training on ethnic relations (except for specialist training) is most effective when conducted not in distinct, free-standing courses, but when integrated into existing professional training curricula.

(2) Training on ethnic relations should not address knowledge or attitudinal objectives in isolation from behavioural objectives but should address all three together, with ultimate emphasis on skills and performance.

(3) The rationale of conducting training on ethnic relations should not be to criticise or condemn personal attitudes, but to enhance *professionalism* in working in multi-cultural situations.

(4) Methods used in training on ethnic relations should be diverse and capable of attaining different levels of objectives, but in all cases an essential requirement is to acknowledge and then work with course participants' own experience.

A NEWSPAPER EDITORIALIZES ON POLICE UNION DISRESPECT FOR KIDS AND POOR FOLKS:

"Whether it was the Patrolmen's Benevolent Association president Phil Caruso or a PBA attorney who urged—in official arbitration papers—that pay raises for cops come from cuts in youth sports and benefits for 'shiftless and lazy' people 'flocking to New York City to take advantage' of welfare, the statement is yet another example of PBA demagoguery that hurts both cops and the city. Add PBA attorney Richard Hartman's claim that failure to raise cops' pay could leave the city with a force of 'cowboys, thieves and psychos,' and you have a union fanning fear and hate.

"Don't officers realize that such tactics don't make their jobs easier? When will they tell Caruso that he's making them look like the antagonists of those they're sworn to serve? The PBA's use of the code words of bigotry is ignorant as well as self-defeating. Since Caruso doesn't live in the city, maybe he's unaware that no group is 'flocking' here these days; welfare rolls are up because jobs are down. Maybe he doesn't know that hundreds of child-welfare workers have been laid off in the budget crunch. Or that a leaner welfare system now knocks more than 30,000 people off the rolls monthly, some entitled to benefits. Sure, cops deserve more pay, even if not the 30-percent raise the PBA wants. And, sure, welfare needs reform. But not at the price of mindless, polarizing rhetoric. Phil Caruso's PBA, fat and sassy thanks to hard-pressed New Yorkers' generosity to the NYPD in tight times, should know when to can it" (New York Newsday 1991).

(5) Training on ethnic relations should balance the need to address issues of racism and ethnicity directly with the need to subsume these issues within a broader understanding of community relations and equal opportunity issues generally.

(6) Outside contributors should be involved in both the design and delivery of training on ethnic relations, and training design should provide maximum

opportunity for controlled learning on ethnic relations from first-hand experience.

(7) Training on ethnic relations requires firm management and should form part of an explicit strategy to implement organisational (and, where appropriate, government) policy on ethnic relations and equal opportunities."

If training and personnel decisions can help reduce any racial and ethnic bigotry that police officers may harbor or practice, then in addition to other tangible and intangible benefits, one might indeed expect a reduction in shootings. The reduction might be expected both because some shootings are probably motivated in part by disregard for the humanity of members of different racial groups and because improved relations between police and civilians of different races might help reduce violence by civilians against police.[41]

However, the results of Brown's (1984: 140) study of police officers' responses to hypothetical scenarios involving the potential for deadly force suggest that race is *not* a controlling factor in officers' decisions to shoot. Putting aside possible methodological concerns, this finding does not indicate, of course, whether race or ethnicity is a contributing factor in *preliminary* decisions made by officers in earlier "phases" of a potentially violent encounter. As both empirical work (e.g., Scharf and Binder 1983) and common sense suggest, such officer decisions may set in motion a sequence of escalating actions and reactions culminating in an officer's perception that shooting is essential to protect life.

One of the important contributions that cultural awareness training may make to the skill with which police handle street confrontations is sharpening officers' ability to distinguish harmless verbal sparring from what the courts in free speech cases have termed "fighting words." Fighting words, as that term has been used in First Amendment rulings, essentially are words that, for most reasonable people, would be an almost inevitable prelude

---

[41] Former Deputy Chief James Griffin of the St. Paul Police Department, the highest ranking black officer in that agency's history, has offered the opinion that, throughout the nation, a fair number of the shootings of police by minorities can be attributed to fear on the part of the assailants—that, during and after apprehension, they will be physically mistreated by the arresting officer(s). Sometimes this fear may be justified, in which case administrators have to address the employees responsible for such intimidation and abuse. Much more often, however, fear of mistreatment upon arrest is misplaced, so police agencies might gain from focusing research and development resources on the question of how arresting officers can ease suspects' fear during apprehension (Griffin 1990). A publication that addresses the question of fear by police when dealing with certain types of adversaries is *Fear: It Kills!* (International Association of Chiefs of Police 1990a), sponsored by the U.S. Justice Department's Bureau of Justice Assistance (BJA) (see also Snell 1992a, containing an interview with John Campbell of the FBI's Behavioral Sciences Unit about officer fear). The profession might also benefit from BJA or other government sponsorship of a parallel examination of the tactical benefits of reducing fear on the part of arrestees and other police "opponents."

Officers everywhere are walking encyclopedias of tactical "tricks of the trade" for de-escalating potentially violent encounters. For instance, former Oklahoma State Bureau of Investigation agent James Pratt recounted how, during arrests of potentially resistant suspects, he tried to calm the arrestees by anticipating and trying to address their immediate fears and concerns about being arrested and transported to jail. Pratt would ask whether the suspect needed to notify anyone to care for children, wished to bring cigarettes, wished to lock any doors in his or her home, etc. In part, such questions showed the suspect that he or she would be treated like a person deserving basic respect but, equally as important, such questions helped the officer maintain control over the situation. For one thing, such conversation occupied the suspect's mind and thus helped the arresting officer efficiently take the suspect into custody and examine the immediate surroundings for contraband, weapons, etc., while maintaining a mental (tactical) edge (Pratt 1990).

to physical conflict. But what police—and, perhaps, the courts—need to understand is that what constitutes fighting words differs in different cultures. For instance, as Kochman (1981) and others have discussed, in many black communities it is common for people to verbally spar without any reasonable likelihood of a physical fight resulting. Such playful combat ("woofing") or slightly more serious verbal encounters ("signifying") *could* lead to a physical fight, but typically do not. Weaver (1992: 4-5) notes a similar Mexican-American tradition with death threats. However, the same words used in a different cultural group may have a far

To excel in police work in the community, police need "a multi-cultural focus that transcends sex, race, nationality, and ethnicity. Too often, cultures tend to be lumped into races or nationalities. [Ours] is a society that likes nice, neat categories. For example, an officer may be responsible for a specific area within the 'black' community. The question needs to be asked, what constitutes the 'black' community? Within the race, there are many and diverse cultures. Within a particular community, there may be blacks of Hispanic, African-Caribbean, American, European, or Asian descent. Each culture (as opposed to race) within a community brings a uniqueness that has different, while at the same time similar, needs that require serious consideration and must be addressed if police agencies are truly to 'serve and protect' " (Stewart and Fisher-Stewart 1990: 2).

greater chance of producing a steady escalation of emotions and actions until a physical fight results.

"Each culture presents arguments differently. For example, Anglo-Americans tend to assume that there is a short distance between an emotional, verbal expression of disagreement and a full-blown conflict. African-Americans think otherwise. For black Americans, stating a position with feeling shows sincerity. However, white Americans might interpret this as an indication of uncontrollable anger or instability, and even, worse, an impending confrontation. For most blacks, threatening movements, not angry words, indicate the start of a fight. In fact, some would argue that fights don't begin when people are talking or arguing, but rather, when they stop talking" (Weaver 1992: 5).

Still, the way in which police approach such verbal encounters and decide to intervene in them can alter the nature of the event. For example, an officer who misunderstands the ritualistic, strictly verbal character of an insult-trading episode between two black men on a crowded street corner may make an ill-advised effort to flaunt his authority and, by so doing, attack the verbal combatants' manhood. When that happens, the need to preserve dignity may result in a physical fight, one precipitated by the poor judgment of the intervening officer (Littleton 1990; on Nation of Islam practices that police need to understand, see Katz 1992: A20). The same problem of police precipitating violence when it might not otherwise have occurred has often been described in our conversations with Hispanic police and community leaders. The word that immediately leaps from their lips when they are asked what Anglo police fail to understand about how to de-escalate the violence in street encounters with Hispanic men is "respect"—the officer failed to show proper respect for the suspect and, for instance, insulted or shamed him needlessly in front of his woman or children.

Like the misreading of harmless verbal sparring in some black communities, police may also misread the meaning of certain other culturally-connected behaviors or may miscalculate

*"No longer are police departments homogeneous entities unto themselves and composed of people who are similar in appearance, backgrounds, and goals, ready to impose [a uniform set of] values upon the community. * * * Prior to being able to handle cultural diversity in the community, police agencies must get their own houses in order. The first step is to look within, because if differences cannot be accepted as an organizational way of life within the police agency, it is unrealistic to believe that those in the community who are different will be accepted"* (Stewart and Fisher-Stewart 1990: 4-5).

the ways that certain standard police techniques might be interpreted across different cultures. For instance, as Philadelphia Police Commissioner Richard Neal observed, in some Hispanic and Asian cultures, it is a sign of *respect* for a youth to avert his or her eyes when conversing with an elder or a person in a position of authority (*New York Times* 1992n; see also United Way 1992). Weaver (1992: 3-4) reports a similar custom among Nigerians. An officer unaware of this may read the lack of eye contact not as politeness and deference to authority but as rudeness, deception, or guilt in the face of the officer's inquiries or accusations. The meaning of eye contact in the dominant American culture is reflected clearly in a popular recent booklet titled

Life's Little Instruction Book, whose "instruction 7" reads simply: "Look people in the eye" (H. Brown 1991). An illustration with even clearer *tactical* relevance is that, in certain Southeast Asian cultures, for a person to be ordered by police to kneel on the ground and clasp his hands behind his head would be taken as a *prelude to assassination*. An American police officer unaware of this could suddenly find himself or herself in a life-and-death struggle with a suspect whom the officer matter-of-factly instructed to assume this position to be handcuffed.[42]

Obviously, there are no off-the-shelf formulas that police can use to understand when a verbal confrontation is likely to escalate to physical violence, whether a suspect's behaviors are intended to convey respect or disrespect for the officer's authority, or how discretion needs to accommodate a suspect's idiosyncratic fears in deciding what arrest and custodial techniques to employ. But the hope is that, through high-quality, tactically-oriented cultural awareness training, police will improve their chances of making the proper judgments during encounters with people of different cultural traditions.

We may suggest still another example of how greater familiarity with other cultures may have immediate tactical significance (putting aside entirely for the moment the likelihood that appreciation of cultural diversity will strengthen officers' talents in working collaboratively with community members to prevent and redress crime problems). The more familiar

---

[42] Many other examples could be developed collaboratively by police and representatives of different cultural groups of how certain police standard operating procedures may unwittingly impede police work because they show disrespect for cultural or subcultural norms. Commenting on an issue not directly related to police use of force, Stewart and Fisher-Stewart (1990: 8) provide another illustration of a clash of police and minority community cultures:

"Most agencies have strict policies prohibiting the acceptance of gifts.... However, failure to understand the implications of blindly accepting rules [may cause] the rules and regulations of a police agency [to] work against its acceptance by minority communities. It is a custom among certain Asian cultures to exchange gifts at initial meetings. Upon such a meeting with members of this community, the...officer can be placed in the uncomfortable and unfortunate position of having to offend those he/she is there to serve...by not exchanging gifts."

officers are with persons of different races and ethnicities, the more likely they are to pick up skills of observation and communication that will help them describe with some precision wanted persons whose races or ethnicities differ from the officers'. Goldstein (1991) and others have noted the pervasive problem of white police employees (officers, "911" call takers, and dispatchers) accepting and disseminating overly general descriptions of minorities who are wanted by the police: "Be on the look out for a black male, about six feet tall, between the ages of 25 and 40, wearing a red jacket and high-top sneakers. Suspected of armed robbery and pistol whipping the victim." In many cities, such a description, in the absence of details (if possible) about the suspect's complexion, facial features, obvious scars, hair style and length, style of walking, and other distinctions that two

One of the ways cultural awareness training may help police reduce the potential for police-civilian violence is by helping police understand and possibly prevent certain types of violence in the community. Hate crimes may be an illustration. "[M]any police agencies are instituting training on hate crime violence without understanding the nature of hate crime violence and the conditions that give rise to the violence. Hate crimes are the result of a conflict in values; a conflict of cultures. Just as the police agency is slow to accept change because of fear of what change will bring, when a people's cultural way of life is threatened, it should not be surprising that they will strike out" (Stewart and Fisher-Stewart 1990: 3).

African Americans—police or nonpolice—would use to describe another black person, could fit a fair number of the men police would see when cruising through a black neighborhood. Use of such vague descriptions often results in field personnel making unwarranted stops and needlessly engendering resentment among those stopped and questioned (*New York Times* 1992v; Blackwell 1992: 20; but Klockars argues that some unwarranted police intrusion is inevitable in high-crime neighborhoods). Sometimes, the consequence may be more dire: an injury or death arising out of a mistaken-identity confrontation. Goldstein (*ibid.*) suggests the preparation of training films and other materials and exercises to help police learn to describe with greater precision suspects of various races and ethnicities.

One of the largely unexplored potential resources for helping police develop a comprehensive approach to fostering respect for cultural diversity is the American military. Although this may seem an ironic suggestion in light of the thrust toward policing strategies and styles that are less militaristic (e.g., community-oriented policing), many astute observers have noted that the military is one public institution that has made exemplary strides in combating institutional racism toward its own personnel. Pulitzer Prize winning author David Shipler (1992), in an Op-Ed piece in the *New York Times*, wrote that the military uses four basic approaches to preventing and remediating racism within its ranks:

■ *"Command Commitment."* Annual performance appraisals "include a judgment of the officer's or noncom's support for equal opportunity" and personnel have "gradually come to understand that a record of racial slurs and discrimination can derail a career."

■ *"Training."* The Defense Equal Opportunity Management Institute (DEOMI), located at Patrick Air Force Base in Cocoa Beach, Florida, puts personnel from all branches of the armed forces through intensive multi-week encounter groups and workshops to prepare them to serve as Equal Opportunity Advisors in their respective units. From what we have learned about this program, it is one of the best efforts in the nation to constructively cut through the veneer of interpersonal interaction so as to identify and help ameliorate the fear, ignorance, and bigotry that virtually everyone harbors toward one or more groups in our society (on

Hispanic subgroup rivalries, for example, see Gonzalez 1992).[43] In addition, every military recruit gets at least one hour of training on "race relations," a reduction from the training time devoted to this subject several years ago but, as Shipler observes, more than many police officers get. Although we are not sure to what extent DEOMI has already been tapped for training police trainers or police equal opportunity specialists, we know of at least one police executive, former Chicago Deputy Police Superintendent Dennis Nowicki, who in the early 1980s was foresighted enough to send several sergeants to DEOMI so that they might pick up pointers for designing the Chicago Police Department's cultural awareness training.

■ *"Complaints and Monitoring."* Equal Opportunity Advisors, after training at DEOMI, both serve as passive recipients of complaints about racial and gender bias, but also proactively visit units throughout the armed services and inquire about the quality of race and gender relations in the work group. Shipler reports: "Surveys are done and informal discussions are held to take the temperature of racial tensions. This is practically unknown in police departments."

■ *"Promotions and Assignments."* According to Shipler, "Although test scores tend to steer blacks toward some specialties like food service and supply, military promotion boards are under orders to strive for representative numbers of people from minority groups and women. The result has been uneven, but it has often meant that whites are supervised by blacks, which breaks down stereotypes" (1992: A15).

3. Conflict Management Training

Suggesting that training in conflict management is merely a component of a broader police training curriculum, while technically accurate, in a sense denigrates its central importance. After all, one might argue convincingly that managing conflict lies at the very core of police work. As Baltimore County Police Chief and former senior NYPD official Cornelius Behan has long been fond of saying, in the constellation of interpersonal contacts, where police operate is at "the point of discontent." Bittner (1973, 1974, 1975) added the enormously influential observation that what uniquely positions police as workers in society is their capacity, if necessary, to resolve conflict when and where it arises through physical force. Departments and regional training academies across the country offer several types of training (with varying intensity and quality, of course) to help officers make sound judgments about the techniques to employ in managing interpersonal conflict and safeguarding themselves in the process. Some of the most important types of training are discussed next.

---

[43] While DEOMI focuses on understanding and overcoming racial, cultural, and gender biases, presumably this unit does not have any authority to address sexual preference bias. The Pentagon's 49-year-old policy that homosexuality (whether overt "acts" or merely "inclinations") is "incompatible with discipline and morale among uniformed members of the armed forces" received recent reiteration and enforcement in the dismissal of a highly regarded colonel with 26 years of service in the Washington State National Guard on the basis of her admission that for three years she has been a lesbian (*New York Times* 1992c; Egan 1992). Thus, with its official approval of sexual preference discrimination (Schmitt 1992a), the military is hardly a model for American police agencies, several of which have been fighting gay-bashing within their communities and within their own ranks as part of their efforts to stem hate crimes and intolerance. Lorch (1992a) discusses gay and lesbian officers in the NYPD.

a. The Continuum of Force and Unarmed Control Tactics

Entire books (e.g., Clede and Parsons 1987 and Schultz 1990, among numerous others) have been written about the "force continuum" and unarmed control tactics. And entire schools are devoted to the teaching of martial arts and related maneuvers. So it is well beyond our capacity in this volume to attempt to provide anything more than a small window into that arena of knowledge. It is clear, however, that a wide variety of verbal (both oral and written) communication skills and unarmed physical control tactics must be a core part of any professional basic training curriculum for police.

The "force continuum" connotes a spectrum of control tactics from body language and oral communication to weaponless physical control to nonlethal weapons to lethal measures. It has been written about with clarity and helpfulness by such nationally regarded experts as Kevin Parsons, executive director of the Appleton, Wisconsin-based Justice System Training Association; John Desmedt, of the U.S. Secret Service's Office of Training (e.g., Desmedt 1984); and Gregory Connor, an associate professor at the University of Illinois Police Training Institute (Champaign, IL) and career police officer and trainer. Connor's expertise led to his service during 1990 and 1991 as a resident use-of-force expert at the multi-agency Federal Law Enforcement Training Center in Glynco, Georgia (see Graves and Connor 1992).

Writing with firearms and tactics expert Bill Clede, Parsons (Clede and Parsons 1987: 6-8) outlines what have become widely accepted as the key categories of normally nonlethal "tools" in the police officer's repertoire of control techniques. (The equipment and other devices they mention are discussed more fully in the "Weapons and Equipment" section of this chapter, below.) We can summarize the categories that Clede and Parsons discuss:

- Body language as a control method (including such elements as personal stance/posture and eye contact).

- Oral control (including use of a command voice and the issuance of clear instructions that should be readily understandable by the particular individuals with whom the officer is dealing).

- Unarmed restraints and "come-along" holds (including blanket holds, the escort position, pressure-point control, thumb and forefinger hold, bent wrist hold, fingerlock, bar hammerlock, and other forms of pain compliance). Come-along holds normally are used to "escort individuals for short distances. The handcuffs should be used to control the subject for long distances" (Schultz 1990: 27-34).

- Neck restraints (including bar arm holds, carotid restraint, and lateral vascular neck restraints).

- Short sticks and batons (including such martial arts sticks as the Yawara, Nunchaku, and Kubotan and an array of longer batons and break-resistant flashlights). Such devices can be used as impact weapons (e.g., for clubbing a subject on the head, as with the billy club of Old English notoriety or the sap), but in most modern police training they are used in more restrained ways, such as for jabbing or applying pressure to various pressure points and for striking below the shoulders (Clede and Parsons 1987: 82, 86).

- Handcuffing techniques.

- Knife fighting techniques. Clede and Parsons (1987: 103) observe that sometimes an officer's rescue knife is the only weapon available in a violent encounter and that proper knife fighting skills are critical to comprehensive officer survival training).

> *"The 1992 California legislature considered but rejected a law that would have made it a misdemeanor for an officer to use pain compliance against a passive demonstrator [in an unruly crowd]. If passed, this certainly would have led to more use of stretchers by police"* (Beene 1992: 67).

- Mechanical devices (including capture nets; physical impact weapons that launch such nonlethal projectiles as rubber rounds, bean bags, and stun grenades [which distract a subject with the noise and flash of their explosion but do not disperse dangerous shrapnel]; pneumatic piston impact weapons that deliver baton-like body blows over a distance of up to seven feet; etc.).

- Electronic devices (such as stun guns and TASERs).

- Chemical devices (including such materials as Mace, tear gas, smoke, and capsicum—known under the brand name Cap-Stun.

In 1980 Parsons published "The Confrontational Continuum," a copyrighted graphic depicting three crucial dimensions of encounters between police and adversaries: "assailant action," "force options" available to the officer, and "officer reaction" (the force options selected by the officer). Republished by Americans for Effective Law Enforcement in 1988 (AELE 1988: 7), Parson's model presents six escalating levels of force option available, in varying combinations, in the diverse encounters police officers have with potential or actual adversaries. These six options (expressed by Parsons as tactical objectives), and illustrative activities or instruments for attaining them, are (AELE: 1988: 7):

> "1. Persuade: Dialogue
> 2. Compliance: Escort
> 3. Compliance: Pain
> 4. Compliance: Mechanical
> 5. Impede: Baton
> 6. Stop: Weapon"

Parsons emphasizes the importance of officers striving throughout a developing incident to maintain the "ability to disengage *or* escalate" (AELE 1988: 7). Tactical disengagement may simply be a fancy term for "retreat," an objectionable concept to many police officers. But prudence (and survival) dictate that there are times to rush onward into the jaws of conflict, times to maintain the status quo of a stand-off between officer and suspect, and times to draw back to a safer and more tactically advantageous position (see Albrecht 1992: 194-197). "Keep in mind," Albrecht (1992: 196, 197) suggests,

> "that a tactical retreat has many forms. In one set of circumstances it may call for [the officer] to leave the scene altogether and in others it may just call for [the officer] to stop fighting with the suspect and loosely contain him until more help

arrives. * * * Consider [also when deciding whether a retreat is advisable that] something worse may happen if you continue [without disengagement]."

Knowing when to "cut your losses" in an encounter that is rapidly getting out of control and that may be quelled by the officer's temporary tactical retreat is a central part of the "judgment" training that must accompany use-of-force proficiency training for new and seasoned police personnel.[44]

Before his most recent work in collaboration with staff at the Federal Law Enforcement Training Center on a multicolor graphic depicting officer use-of-force options in relation to adversaries' challenging behavior (Graves and Connor 1992), Greg Connor continued during the 1980s to refine his widely used force continuum. In its latest version, introduced by Connor and Summers in their 1988 volume *Tactical Neutralization Techniques*, the use-of-force model envisions a range of appropriate police responses to varying levels of challenge. The challenges vary from no challenge (a "cooperative" subject) to what Connor (1991: 30; see also Connor and

> *"Police training must focus on the fact that physical conflict is a rare event. Despite the emphasis placed during training on the dangers of policing and the consequences of thoughtless action, officers soon learn that every tour is not a war and every call is not a crisis. There is a paradox here. Police officers must be trained for war but prepared for peace. Inattention may be more serious than not being able to shoot straight"* (Bayley and Garofalo 1989: 20-21).

Summers 1988: viii-4) characterizes as "Resistant Level I, Resistant Level II, Assaultive Level I and Assaultive Level II." Within each category of escalating resistance, Connor suggests that, as a generalization, various of 16 different levels of police force might be appropriate. He groups these 16 levels of force into three categories: "no force, ordinary force, and extraordinary force." Ordinary force he defines as "physical force not likely or intended to cause death or great bodily harm," and extraordinary force is "force likely or intended to cause great bodily harm" (Connor and Summers 1988: 1). The levels of police force he specifies (Connor 1991: 30) are, from least to most injurious:

---

[44] There is a story about knowing when to cut your losses that our police management trainees around the nation have enjoyed. A man driving in a rural area with which he is unfamiliar finds he needs to use the bathroom but sees no facilities other than a farm house. He knocks on the door and asks if he might use the farmer's rest room. The farmer says he may but the only facility they have is an outhouse in the backyard. The traveller, upon entering the outhouse, is surprised to find it's a two-seater. And in fact, the other seat is occupied by a local fellow. Our friend sits down and is doing his business when he sees the gentlemen next to him finish and start to pull up his pants. As the trousers are pulled up, some change falls out of the man's pocket—and goes right down the hole! At this point, the man who has lost the change becomes very distraught and starts patting around for his wallet. Our friend watches as the guy finds his wallet, opens it, takes out a $20 bill, and throws the bill down the hole. At this point, the traveller can't contain his curiosity any longer and says, "Excuse me, but I just had to ask you. How come you threw that twenty down the hole?" Whereupon the stranger looks at him incredulously and asks, "You didn't think I was going down there for *thirty-five cents*, did you?"

Colorful Texas newspaper reporter Molly Ivans captured the plight of those who don't know when to stop compounding their mistakes in a recent speech broadcast on National Public Radio. Speaking of politicians who cling with mindless consistency to bankrupt social policies, she counseled: "We should all recognize the 'first rule of holes,' which is that when you are *in* one you should stop digging" (Ivans 1992).

No Force
1. controlled confrontation
2. body language
3. verbal persuasion

Ordinary Force
4. contact controls
5. joint restraints
6. weapon-assisted leverage techniques
7. nerve center controls
8. weapon-assisted pain compliance techniques
9. chemical irritants
10. electrical devices
11. intimate impact weapons

Extraordinary Force
12. extended impact weapons
13. weaponless techniques with debilitating potential
14. weapon techniques with debilitating potential
15. service firearm
16. supplemental firearm

Although classifying options 4 through 11 as ordinary force, Connor and Summers (1988: 1) observe that these are

> "weapon/tactic areas that have proper application in the realm of ordinary force but if abused could become extraordinary force. For instance, a joint lock technique is normally used to secure a resisting subject and diffuse aggressiveness well within the parameters of ordinary force. However, if the officer decides to intentionally apply pressure on the joint in order to dislocate it, such action would fall into extraordinary force."

Connor's model (1991: 31-32) envisions the following allocation of justifiable force to respond to the indicated levels of threat:

Cooperative Subject (said to represent 95 to 97 percent of the typical police officer's contact with the general population): **Force levels 1-3** (controlled confrontation through verbal persuasion).

Resistant Level I (preliminary "cues of resistance," such as verbally challenging the officer's instructions or authority or going limp and thereby "negating the officer's appropriate directions"—both behaviors within the legal definition of resisting an officer): **Force levels 2-7** (body language through nerve center controls).

Resistant Level II (resistance or defiance of the officer's orders is expressed physically—"the subject may turn away from the officer and attempt to leave the scene; or pull out of the officer's grasp; or attempt to hold on to the steering wheel and refuse to exit. Critical to the categorization of Resistant Level II is that no physical force or violence has been directed toward the officer."): **Force levels 2-11** (body language through intimate impact weapons).

Assaultive Level I ("active, hostile resistance" to the officer, expressed as "an actual physical attack upon the officer." To be an Assaultive Level I rather than resistant level II, a battery must hold a reasonable potential to "harm...the officer. For example, in a domestic dispute, an officer would be hard pressed to classify a woman in the Assaultive Level I category if she throws a pillow at the officer....[but would reach the opposite conclusion] if the same women were to throw a frying pan at the officer."): **Force levels 2-12** (body language through extended impact weapons).

Assaultive Level II ("This category includes the least frequently encountered individuals, but obviously the subject of most concern to all officers." The adversary conduct classified in this assault level "has the potential to cause the officer great bodily harm or even death."): **Force levels 2-16** (body language through supplemental firearm).

One of the great virtues of Connor's important work in developing this force continuum and the range of appropriate responses to varying levels of threat is his insistence that, at every level of threat, even the least coercive, least injurious types of police responses may be appropriate and sufficient. Thus, in the summary above, Connor allows that, under actual field conditions, it may be justifiable for an officer to respond to a life-threatening assault by using verbal or other weaponless responses. Connor's approach may be contrasted to what might be thought of as a "superhighway" model of escalating force, in which few off-ramps exist for officers to turn away from a rapid progression toward extreme violence in a developing incident. Connor, in contrast, presents a sort of local street model, in which many side streets and alleys are available for digressing from the path toward extreme violence.

Recommending, among other things, the funding of a full-time position in the Province of British Columbia (Canada) Police Academy specializing in use of force training and conflict resolution, a government advisory panel observed:

"There will be costs associated with our recommendations. We would respectfully suggest that spending the money now will save an enormous amount of suffering and cost later. The effect of crippling or disabling injury that may have been unnecessary is a life sentence to a police officer or a citizen alike. Such cost is incalculable" (Jamieson, et al. 1990: 35).

Connor's work and the work of some other strategists and tacticians emerge from the martial arts and reflect much of the essential Oriental philosophy in which the martial arts are rooted. For example, Connor and Summers (1988: iv) selected as an emblem for their system of "tactical neutralization" a fist covered with the palm of a second hand. They explain their choice and the principles it represents in their training approach:

"The symbolism of the covered fist...is common to those familiar with Far Eastern philosophical disciplines and directions in the martial arts. Traditionally representative of the endeavor to achieve harmonization of mind, spirit, and body it has come to dignify more contemporary applications and, hopefully, the institutionalized aspirations of law enforcement. We perceive the symbol as indicative of the attitudes, perspectives, and orientations of which the Tactical Neutralization Techniques paradigm consists. * * * [T]he symbol was approached with desired and designed ambiguity: force yet discretion; power yet restraint; control yet tempered compassion; and aggression potential, yet the power of passivity, are but a few representations of the conceptual meaning of our selected symbol."

Connor and Summers (1988: 1) also acknowledge that an officer may, by *abusing* body language or verbal tactics in an encounter not initially involving physical force by either an officer or the subject, unjustifiably provoke a violent incident through intimidation or threats to the subject. This—as well as actions by officers that, perhaps unwittingly, induce the subject to fear for his or her personal safety—are areas that have not received sufficient exploration in the training- and policy-oriented literature. The federal Bureau of Justice Assistance sponsored a pioneering treatment of the role of officer fear in escalating and de-escalating officer hazards (IACP 1990). The "dynamics of fear" model developed by police psychologist Roger Solomon for the IACP/BJA publication is discussed later in this chapter (see also Trojan-owicz and Banas 1985). While the series of important essays commissioned by the IACP helps to bring officer fear "out of the closet" as a subject of professional discussion, however, not one of the essays says a single word about the way in which officers may unwittingly (or purposely) induce unnecessary fear in civilian *subjects* and thus precipitate an assault on the officer, in turn requiring police use of force.

The Oakland Police Department's Peer Review Panel, in which officers helped colleagues who were having problems with use of force, knew that the "problem" officers had to be allowed to come to their OWN conclusions, through discussion with an officer "interviewer," that there was room for improvement. One officer described the typical—and counterproductive—approach taken by many departments to confronting officers about their abuse of force:

"You're never going to get to the crux of the problem by pointing to the problem. Because this is the M.O. (modus operandi) that this department has always used. When there was a big purge in patrol division, all these guys were called into the DC's office and told if they have any more 148s they're going to be fired. That's what happened. 'Killer' Baridon went to (a neighboring department) and 'Killer' was a pretty sharp guy. He could have worked out a lot of his hang-ups on the street—he has. But my point is this. The M.O. has always been, 'Look, Louie, you've got a problem. And you'd better stop whatever you're doing, although you don't know what it is, or you're going to be fired.' And the guy walks out of the room saying 'son of a bitch.' I did when I was called in by a captain several weeks ago. I really thought that I was doing a good job. I'm a hell of a cop. I get involved, I get out there and I fight crime, and I'm running into nothing but assholes—bad luck. You know, right, we all do good police work and it's the citizen's fault. Resistances. And I thought, "F——— them. I'm not going to do nothing" (Toch and Grant 1991: 135).

Another area requiring more discussion and analysis is the possibility that, like some civilians, certain police officers again and again engage in violent encounters with suspects because they are poor at communicating through nonphysical means—and hence, knowingly or unconsciously, escalate adversarial situations to the level at which they are proficient in "communicating" (see Toch 1969; Toch and Grant 1991). A popular training program has been developed and administered to several hundred police departments bearing the unhappily ambivalent title of "verbal judo." The program description sounds laudatory: "It teaches officers, dispatchers, and other police employees how to stay calm and professional under verbal assault, and how to generate voluntary compliance from the most difficult people" (*Crime Control Digest* 1992k; see also Jamieson, et al. 1990: 24; Krier 1990; Thompson 1983; Verbal Judo Institute, no date; Reyes 1992). We, along with many police leaders with whom we have conferred, find the concept of this training appealing but dislike the mixed message sent by its title.[45] In our view, communication skills that help avert violence need not be dressed up as aggression in order to appeal to working police officers, who understand only too well the jeopardy in which they needlessly place themselves, their colleagues, and their loved ones when they fail to minimize the physical dangers in their daily work.

Experienced law enforcement officials with whom we have conferred over the years suggest that a large but unknown number of serious injuries and slayings of police officers in the United States might have been averted if officers were more aware of the way their actions during an incident frightened a subject into believing that an assault on the officer was needed for self-defense (e.g., Griffin 1990). The civilian subject in such incidents might or might not have been accurate in believing he or she was facing an imminent *illegal assault* by the police officer. (After the Rodney King beating in Los Angeles and the April 1992 state court jury verdict declaring their conduct to have been legal, would it be surprising if more suspects throughout the nation come to believe, accurately or inaccurately, that their arresting officers may wish to administer life-threatening "street justice"?) Regardless of the reasonableness of a suspect's perception that arresting officers intend him or her harm, officers injured or slain by such suspects might have suffered less harm if they had been more sensitive to the way in which their actions helped feed rational or irrational fears in their adversaries. For self-protective reasons alone—putting aside considerations of legality and professionalism—many officers need to more proactively communicate during potentially violent encounters in a way that reassures suspects that they can avoid being injured by nonviolently complying with police instructions. In studying these important questions in the future, analysts would do well to consider, among other learning, the literature on victim-precipitated homicides, which explores in the context of civilian-on-civilian killings the ways in which conduct by the deceased might have provoked the killing.

A subset of "victim-precipitated homicides" of special interest to police and conflict-management trainers is what some call "suicide by cop." As noted in Chapter 4, these are instances in which a civilian carries out his or her suicidal mission by threatening the life of an officer until the officer shoots in self-defense. Usually, these cases are difficult to discover in official records because there is little or no documentation of the victim's suicidal intent, and departments rarely classify intentional shootings in such detail. Sometimes, however, these cases surface as a result of adverse civil judgments (e.g., *Quezada v. County of Bernalillo*, described in *National Bulletin on Police Misconduct* 1992), which demonstrate that the failure of departments to train officers sufficiently in suicide prevention techniques can be financially costly, not to mention the human suffering of the suicide's survivors, the officer, and others (DiVasto, et al. 1992). For additional discussion of civilian manipulation of police officers to commit suicide, see Kindrick (1992); Long (1992a); Noesner and Dolan (1992: 2).

We will return later in this chapter to a discussion of assorted nonlethal weapons and other items of equipment used by varying numbers of police agencies in the United States. Before leaving this brief overview of weaponless tactics, however, it is worth noting that the

---

[45] In fairness, the creators of the Verbal Judo training program use as a synonym "Tactical Communication," but they still place emphasis in marketing on the verbal judo term (Verbal Judo Institute, no date).

public and the police profession have had widely different reactions to different weaponless control techniques.

The unarmed police control tactics that have received the widest and most adverse publicity in recent years are the "neck restraints." They are of basically three types and should not all be lumped together: the arm bar, carotid restraint, and lateral vascular neck restraint. The three were described succinctly by a Kansas City Police Department (KCPD) internal task force assigned by Chief Steven Bishop to review comprehensively the agency's capabilities and needs for using force with proper restraint (KCPD 1991: 36):

> "The arm bar technique applies pressure with the forearm across the [front of the] neck which cuts off the subject's air supply and may damage the throat. For these reasons the arm bar has been widely rejected by police agencies. The carotid restraint technique is taught by many agencies and involves the application of the forearm to one side of a subject's neck and the bicep area of the upper arm to the opposite side of the neck. The crux of the elbow is placed at the front of the subject's throat with particular care so as not to apply pressure to the esophagus. The lateral vascular neck restraint, used by officers of [the Kansas City Police Department], permits officers to subdue a subject by controlling his or her balance and provides an officer with the ability to increase pressure on the subject proportionate to resistance.[46] The lateral vascular neck restraint can give a smaller, weaker officer an advantage over a larger or stronger belligerent opponent and allow the officer to control that person without having to resort to using a baton.... The only disadvantage noted for the use of this neck restraint technique is that in violent struggles, it may be difficult to apply correctly" (KCPD 1991: 36).

Of these three, only the first—the arm bar—could properly be called by the slang term used by critics of neck restraints: chokehold.[47] While inability to administer properly the carotid restraint or the lateral vascular restraint may result in an officer unwittingly—and harmfully—choking a struggling adversary, only the arm bar is actually *intended* to choke the subject, thus cutting off his or her air supply and inducing unconsciousness. Indeed, the arm bar technique is "a variation of a U.S. army killing technique" (Rohrlich 1991: A28). As with any less-than-lethal or lethal police conflict management techniques and devices, proper training is crucial. Untrained or poorly trained officers will almost certainly be a danger to themselves, their colleagues, those they are trying to control, and those they are trying to protect. If an officer, because of deficient training, applies pressure to the *front* of a subject's

---

[46] The Kansas City Police Department report from which this quote was taken did not describe precisely how the lateral vascular neck restraint is applied. But others have reported that the "Kansas City" hold was developed by physical training supervisor Jim Lindell in the Kansas City Police Department and that it is "a subtle variation on the carotid [hold] which...makes it mechanically more difficult for the officer to slip into the bar-arm" (Rohrlich 1991: A28). Lindell reported that Kansas City officers apply the lateral vascular neck restraint "safely about 20 times a day" (*ibid.*).

[47] Many people and sometimes even state legislatures refer to all types of neck restraints as "chokeholds." The state of Nevada adopted a statute, effective July 1991, regulating police training on and use of chokeholds, defining all neck restraints as such holds (Americans for Effective Law Enforcement 1991a).

neck, cutting off the subject's air supply, instead of to the *sides* of the neck,[48] inducing fainting, the results can be personally, organizationally, and publicly devastating. Koiwai (1987) conducts a forensic review of 14 cases in which death was allegedly caused by officers' use of chokeholds.

Fyfe (1991), lambasting the Los Angeles Police Department's leadership after the brutal beating of Rodney King in March 1991, asserted: "[F]or encouraging and tolerating brutality and excessive force, the Los Angeles Police Department has for several years been the outlaw among big American police departments." Although some argue that such sweeping generalizations are unreasonable ways to characterize entire complex organizations and their command cadres, nevertheless one of the specifics Fyfe offers as evidence is pertinent here: "During one five-year stretch," he reports, "twice as many Angelenos died after suffering police chokeholds as in the 20 other largest American cities combined." Department and medical officials on other occasions have observed that the causes of death were in dispute in many of the cases that Fyfe and others criticized (Rohrlich 1991: A28).[49]

Despite disagreement about causation, however, the pattern of neck restraint injuries and fatalities and the resulting civil litigation and public relations problems[50] led the LAPD in 1982 to ban use of neck restraints. Chief Daryl Gates had banned the arm bar hold during litigation over its harmful effects, and the civilian Police Commission banned the carotid re-

---

[48] It is commonly believed that application of force to the sides of the neck constricts the carotid arteries on both sides of the neck (hence the term "carotid" hold). In theory, this would reduce the blood supply to the brain, depriving the brain of oxygen and inducing unconsciousness. But medical experts say this is not the way this hold accomplishes its purpose. The carotid arteries, they report, are too well protected to be squeezed with the arm hold commonly used by police. Instead, the so-called carotid artery hold actually accomplishes its purpose by compressing veins on the sides of the neck. "[C]onstricting the veins, which carry blood back to the heart, makes the heart pump faster and with more force. This result[s] in lightheadedness..." (Rohrlich 1991: A28).

[49] It may be largely academic to those directly affected *why* a person dies after being subjected to a neck restraint, but for a host of obvious reasons it is important that medical experts be able to specify precisely what factors led to the demise of a subject involved in a police encounter. A St. Louis forensic medical expert, Dr. James Cooper, believes,

> "that most of those whose deaths have been attributed to chokeholds by coroners have actually succumbed to what doctors call 'sudden death syndrome,' in which death occurs unexpectedly in a person who previously seemed healthy. 'The extent of our present knowledge is that discharge of the adrenal glands excites them so much that they develop cardiac arrhythmia and die from that and the heart appears normal,' he said" (Rohrlich 1991: A28).

Further discussion of "sudden death syndrome" appears in IACP (1990: 59-60).

[50] Much as the LAPD mobile digital terminal communications that the Christopher Commission discovered (Independent Commission on the LAPD 1991) removed most doubt among police professionals that the LAPD had a pervasive attitudinal and behavioral problem (beyond the single instance of Rodney King's pummeling), comments by LAPD officers following their use of neck restraints colored interpretations of officer intent in using those tactics. Thus, the *Los Angeles Times* reported that "officers used to joke about suspects they subdued with the hold, saying, 'You choke them out until they do the chicken.' This was a reference to the involuntary flapping of a subject's arms and legs as he was being choked" (Rohrlich 1991: A28).

straint—except in situations where deadly force was justified (*ibid.*). Yet, on the rebound from criticism of its use of batons against Rodney King, departmental officials announced that they were reevaluating their earlier decision to prohibit neck restraints, in the belief that officers need to have a variety of options to select from when confronted with resistant subjects and that, properly applied, neck restraints are extremely unlikely to produce serious injury (*ibid.*: A1). The Department's announcement that it would consider reauthorizing use of neck restraints met with mixed reviews, along predictable lines. The head of the L.A. chapter of the Urban League ob-

Specifying which neck restraints are and which are not officially authorized will not necessarily relieve a police department from liability when an unauthorized technique is used: "A Chicago family accepted a $500,000 settlement for the death of a man who died from an arm-bar hold. The city offered the settlement despite the fact it did not authorize the hold and instead teaches the carotid restraint method" (Americans for Effective Law Enforcement 1988: 5).

jected vehemently, asserting that the chokehold had been used as a tactic of racial aggression. The rank and file was pleased, having earlier revealed in a departmental survey that 92 percent of their membership believed they should have the option to employ neck restraints instead of batons (*ibid.*: A28).

Written materials distributed to the Kansas City Police Department and others in 1990 as part of an IACP training program for police departments on stemming use of excessive force advocated the use of the carotid neck restraint or "sleeper hold":

"The truth is that the neck restraint...is the only method that can be applied to a violent subject that will not cause injury the majority of the time it is used. It is probably the single most humane method of controlling a violent subject. In some of these deaths [attributed to chokeholds], injuries to the trachea area have occurred, causing death. These cases are rare. Literally tens of thousands of violent, combative subjects have been subdued by the neck restraint with only a few, probably less than one percent, suffering serious injury or death. Compare this figure with the number of deaths that can occur with the use of a baton, TASER, firearm, tear gas, and other forms of restraint" (IACP 1990: 59).

The IACP argued, further, that many deaths blamed on misuse of chokeholds are in fact examples of what doctors call "sudden death syndrome" (discussed earlier in a footnote).

b. Violence-Reduction and Officer-Survival Training Programs and the "Split-Second Decision"

"Better than being able to win a fight is being able to prevent one" (Rutledge 1988: 259).

Training in unarmed or nonlethal control tactics is a *foundation* for violence-reduction training but is not in itself violence-reduction training. Tactics short of deadly force are the *skills* needed for violence reduction, whereas violence-reduction training is a *point of view* by the employing department about the priority that officers should (or must) give to using the least injurious control techniques available in any given situation. Similarly, officer survival training—if done well—provides guidance to officers in making *judgments* about the right tactics to use in various field situations, beyond simply teaching proficiency in the use of assorted tactics and weaponry. Moreover, in recent years officer survival training has broadened to include "tactics for avoiding alcoholism, divorce, and suicide, which have ruined more cops than gunfights have" (Baltic 1991: 18). Officer survival, conceived expansively to address the full range of human needs of officers, is about far more than physical survival; it also includes legal, psychological, and emotional survival (*ibid.*: 26).

Tactical conflict management or "violence reduction" exercises have been developed in New York City, Chicago, Dade County (Florida), and many other jurisdictions.[51] These teach officers through role playing how to control a potentially violent encounter and how to de-escalate rather than exacerbate tensions between themselves and their "clientele." The noncontroversial premise of such training, of course, is that officers have at least some capacity to influence the outcome of at least some of the situations they handle. As one police academy instructor put it:

> "We all know both police officers who are capable of turning a parking ticket into a riot and other officers who can deal with some of the toughest offenders and, more often than not, leave them thanking the officer for the way in which he handled the arrest. The object of violence-reduction training is to identify and, as much as possible, impart to police in general what the most successful officers do instinctively."

These tactical exercises allow officers safely to experiment with a variety of techniques to reduce the risk of violence in dangerous encounters (see Fyfe 1978, 1989a; Margarita 1980a: 71, 1980b: 229; Geller 1986). Not all officers will attain the same level of proficiency in violence reduction, just as officers' talents differ in general. But through opportunities to safely explore their strengths and weaknesses, officers will gain a "working knowledge of their skill limitations" (Schofield 1990: 77) and will learn to overcome some deficiencies and to compensate for those they cannot change.

Before describing violence reduction training, it is important to be clear that the police executive and other public opinion makers and liability managers must create reasonable expectations for what such training can accomplish. What the police administrator—and the public—must come to grips with so as not to place officers in an untenable situation is that police officers, no matter what level of screening, training, and supervision they are given, will operate within a professional range of proficiency in the field. That is, not every officer will handle—or will be capable of handling—identical situations in identical ways.

This does not mean, of course, that officers at the low end of the proficiency scale should be allowed to practice their trade below tolerable bounds of performance. Nor does it mean that the vast majority of officers operating within a solid middle ground of proficiency should be made to feel inadequate for not emulating what the truly gifted members of the force are able to do. Incompetent or venal officers should be separated from the force if their conduct cannot be corrected. But the immutable—and, sometimes, politically unpalat-

---

[51] The "Kolts Report," issued on July 20, 1992, criticized the Los Angeles Sheriff's Department for allowing "some deputies [to] shoot or beat innocent bystanders with predictable frequency, allowing routine traffic stops and domestic disputes to escalate into violent confrontations where the use of force becomes inevitable" (Tobar and Reich 1992: A1-A18; Kolts, et al. 1992). For discussions of the need for and reviews of experiments with violence-reduction or "officer survival" training, see Geller and Karales (1981a: 197-199, 251-252); Geller (1985a); Police Foundation (1988); and Fyfe (1988c, 1989a).

able—fact is that different police officers, like different workers in most other occupations, will exhibit different strengths and weaknesses as they attempt to perform the tasks assigned to them. The better the match between assignment and talent, the happier all will be—the officer, the public, the administrator, the risk manager. This variance in officer skill may be modified to some extent by really excellent tactical and violence-reduction training, but it is only reasonable to expect that, even after their training, some officers still will be better than others at defusing potentially violent situations.

A number of police training academies have developed fairly sophisticated simulation training programs that can be used for violence-reduction and officer survival training. Some of these programs involve mock city blocks and buildings (see, e.g., Korzeniowski's [1990] description of the Tampa Police Training Academy's "Survival City," which was slated for completion in 1992, Katz's [1991] discussion of the Los Angeles County Sheriff's Department's "Laser Village," and Geller and Karales' [1981a] description of "The Apartment," constructed at the NYPD's outdoor firing range in the late 1970s). The FBI's famous "Hogan's Alley" at the Bureau's academy in Quantico, Virginia, has kept pace with developments elsewhere and has blossomed into a sort of Hoganville—complete with

"I once worked with a partner who was a master at getting cooperation from even the biggest, meanest, drunkest men in town. Although this officer was in excellent physical condition and was a martial arts expert, he never came on like he was anxious to prove his superiority. He always offered the other guy a peaceful, face-saving way out, and the other guy usually took it.

"For example, we once went into a bar in the roughest neighborhood in town on a 'keep the peace' call, and found a guy who looked like the Incredible Hulk creating a disturbance. Instead of running up and grabbing this big guy, my partner just took out his traffic whistle and blew it to get everyone's attention. When he asked the Hulk what the problem was, the Hulk said: 'None of your business, Cop! You think I can't whip your ass?'

"My partner said: 'Oh, I don't suppose I'd even be any contest for you. But I go off duty in an hour and I've got a date with a hot little mama who's expecting me to come over in good shape, and if you do anything to mess me up, she'll come over here and turn you every which way but loose.' The Hulk and everybody else in the bar started laughing. The trouble was over" (Rutledge 1988: 260-61).

"a bank, post office, drug store, rooming house, bar/deli, pawn shop (actually a front for a clandestine casino), pool hall, motel, movie theatre, trailer park, warehouse area, and a residential street with townhouses and apartments. The fronts and backs of the buildings often have different uses. For instance, the rear of the row of buildings which includes the bar/deli, pawn shop/casino, and pool hall is part of the motel 'set'. This facade is actually a false front for part of the motel, but these motel rooms are only 24 inches deep. The use of angles and contrasts in 'Hollywood set' technology gives the illusion of depth and space" (Pledger 1988: 6-7; see also Slahor 1992).

Other agencies have developed somewhat simpler but still realistic simulations. Examples include the Provo, Utah, Police Department's "replicative" (i.e., replicating actual street circumstances) outdoor training range (see Nielsen 1990); and the Anaheim, California, Police Department's firing range (Schrader 1988).

The pedagogical assumption behind these and numerous other exercises that allow officers to simulate making use-of-force decisions is that officers generally will gain deeper and more lasting lessons from role playing than from classroom lectures (Goddard 1988). As the Tampa Police Department's director of training said of the rationale behind his agency's planned Survival City, "There's an old adage that goes, 'If I hear it, I'll forget it. If I see it, I'll remember it. But if I do it, I'll understand it.' [R]ealism in training is the wave of the future." (Korzeniowski 1990: 31). The Anaheim Police Department and other agencies have taken this adage full circle; after the officer "does it," he or she has an opportunity to sit down with trainers and review videotape of the officer's strengths and weaknesses in carrying out the assigned exercise. In Anaheim the video has been shot from four different camera angles to attempt to capture all important tactical information (Schrader 1988: 3).[52]

Most training programs that use live "opponents" in role playing sessions have police personnel assume the roles of the offenders and bystanders. The Tampa police have found that enlisting local actors and other civilian volunteers to play the bystander and suspect roles in police tactical training adds an additional element of realism, without, apparently, creating offsetting liabilities or other problems. Trainers with the Minneapolis Police Department and the FBI who co-authored an article echoed the concern in other quarters about using experienced police to play offenders, victims, and bystanders in simulation training. Writing about hostage negotiation training, the trainers argued:

> "The negotiation exercises offered to many hostage negotiators often involve the use of fellow officers in the roles of suspects and hostages. For example, an officer may be instructed to play the role of an armed robbery suspect trapped in

After six hours of "plodd[ing] through minor fender benders, stolen-car reports, false burglar alarms and disturbance calls in which little was disturbed...at 10 p.m. the radio crackles with reports of a drive-by shooting, the by-product of bad blood between [two street gangs]. As [the two officers] pull up and begin coaxing information from a wailing Hispanic woman and angry bystanders, the red truck from which the shots were fired zooms by. The chase is on. [The officer driving] throws the patrol car into a transmission-shattering reverse. Tires spin and smoke. Within seconds, [the pair of officers] rocket down a side street, slam on the brakes at a stop sign and lay down rubber as they catapult onto a crowded thoroughfare. Moments later, they are careening in and out of traffic at 80 miles per hour, before the chase skids to a halt in a parking lot. As two other police cars converge, [the officers who began the chase] dive from their car, throwing open doors for protection while they draw and aim their guns in a single fluid motion. Meanwhile, to their surprise, other officers run right up to the truck—that 'old John Wayne BS,' [one of the officers who remained behind cover] will say later—and yank a chunky youth from the cab, hurling him to the pavement, their guns at his head" (Witkin, et al. 1990:33).

"Fools rush in where angels fear to tread" (18th Century English poet Alexander Pope).

---

[52] The Anaheim Police Department keeps a video library showing precisely what type of range training officers have been given at particular times in the event this is needed in court to bolster the agency's argument that its officers were professionally prepared for combat shooting situations they might encounter on the streets (Schrader 1988).

322 DEADLY FORCE: WHAT WE KNOW

a convenience store. This is not particularly desirable for a number of reasons. An officer in this role often will overact his part, thus contributing to a less-than-realistic training experience. The officer also has more knowledge of what to expect than most actual suspects would have. Further problems are created when the role-playing officer personally knows the negotiator, because it is hard to predict how the negotiations will be affected by the personal knowledge each has of the other's negotiation style. Finally, the practice may take place 'in house' [i.e., among trusted colleagues], a setting far removed from those encountered in authentic situations. The end result is a training exercise lacking much of the stress, complexity and unpredictability of an actual hostage-taking event" (Geiger, et al. 1990).

Having studied a wide variety of simulation firearms and tactics training programs before settling on their planned Survival City, Tampa police officials warn that an unrealistic simulation can be worse than none at all, because it can teach trainees tactics that are unlikely to be effective in actual street encounters (Korzeniowski 1990: 31, 34).

Some police trainers also have expressed concern that police will learn habits that could endanger them in actual combat circum-

> *"[An officer] volunteered to pose as the owner of a service station which, as intelligence reports indicated, would be robbed by an organized group on a specific date. When [the officer], disguised as the owner, began to walk the morning deposit out of the office, he was approached by two armed suspects. They forced him to the ground at gun point and took the money bag he was carrying. While the assailants fled on foot, [the officer] calmly directed members of the apprehension team via radio. All members of the ring were arrested a short time later" (FBI 1990a).*

stances. While perhaps an extreme example, Nielsen (1990: 37), citing Adams, et al. (1980: 222), suggests:

> "On the traditional firing range, the shooter is constantly indoctrinated to keep his weapon 'down range'. In the real world, however, the officer may find himself in a 360° arena where there is no 'down range'. On the traditional firing range, the officer always knows where the target will be; in the real world, this is obviously not the case. On the traditional firing range, the officer is told when to load and unload, when to holster and unholster by a coach or rangemaster. In the real world, there are no coaches or rangemasters present during an actual combat shooting. The outcome of such training is often that the shooter adapts to the range, rather than to the conditions he will encounter on the street. As the authors of *Street Survival: Tactics for Armed Encounters* have noted, 'Some officers have been killed because they took extra time to catch the ejected cases and put them in their pockets, as they'd done when shooting targets on the range'."

Rutledge (1988: 278-279) disputes the meaning ascribed to the infamous incident in which a California Highway Patrol officer put his empty shells

> "into his pocket during a firefight, as he had been trained to do on the firing range. From this incident, theorists draw the conclusion that the officer was reacting unconsciously, under stress. I doubt that that was actually the case (we'll

never know, since the officer didn't survive). In fact, three other CHP officers who were killed in the same battle did not pocket their brass, even though they had the same training. Hundreds of officers in other shootings over the years who had similar training did not pocket their brass. This isolated incident hardly proves a general proposition that you will revert to trained conduct under stress. The more likely explanation for the fact that this one officer bothered to put empty shell casings into his pocket in the midst of a heavy firefight is either that he didn't want the enemy to see or hear the brass dropping onto the street, thereby revealing that he was in a vulnerable, reload situation, or else the officer was seeking normalcy."

A common theme in many of the violence-reduction and officer survival training programs is to help officers devise safe ways of *approaching* the scenes of possible confrontations, making maximum possible use of cover, concealment, communication skills, and other tactics.[53] Fyfe (1989a) has hypothesized that reductions in violence between the police and civilians will come primarily from improvements in officers' *approaches to* (i.e., *entry* into) potentially violent encounters, rather than from any changes in the officers' actions *during* the encounter (see also Hayden 1981; Scharf and Binder 1983; Bayley and Garofalo 1989: 20). This suggestion is in line with observations made more than two decades earlier by Bristow (1963), after examining officer injuries during vehicle stops.

By focusing on officer decisions made prior to arrival in the immediate presence of the subject, trainers and analysts have begun over recent years helpfully to debunk the myth of the "split-second

"Some policemen have developed ways of restraining certain persons, notably, the mentally ill and women, that result in a minimum of pain and injury. They do this, even though they occasionally encounter formidable resistance, because they do not define such cases as contests. At present the choice of these methods is based mainly on feelings of compassion or chivalry. But there are no reasons why these techniques of achieving restraint could not be adapted to all situations on the basis of their technical superiority to ordinary brawling" (Bittner 1973: 61).

decision." This myth or, as Fyfe has called it, the "split-second syndrome," holds that the only key decisions within the control of most police officers in most potentially violent confrontations will be those that can be made in an instant, such as whether to pull the trigger or make some other rapid last-ditch maneuver. The split-second syndrome is also associated with other fallacious assumptions, as Fyfe (1989c: 474-475) observes:

"The split-second syndrome...assumes that, since no two police problems are alike, there are no principles that may be applied to the diagnosis of specific situations. Thus, no more can be asked of officers than that they respond as quickly as possible to problems, devising the best solutions they can on the spur of the moment. * * * Second, because of [the] stresses and time constraints [of

---

[53] A survival course compiled by the U.S. Border Patrol with assistance from Police Executive Research Forum staff and other training experts is premised on strengthening officer skills in utilizing "the five C's—cover, concealment, control, containment, communications" (P. Smith 1990: 111). Albrecht (1989) has written insightfully about the "contact and cover" method of approaching a potentially dangerous person or scene, in which one officer makes initial contact while the second officer provides cover to protect his or her partner (see also Albrecht and Morrison [1992]).

most police encounters], a high percentage of inappropriate decisions should be expected, but any subsequent criticism of officers' decisions...is an unwarranted attempt to be wise after the event. * * * Finally,...assessments of the justifiability of police conduct are most appropriately made on the exclusive basis of the perceived exigencies of the moment when a decision had to be taken. So long as a citizen has, intentionally or otherwise, provoked the police at that instant, he, rather than the police, should be viewed as the cause of any resulting injuries or damage, no matter how excessive the police reaction and no matter how directly police decisions molded the situation that caused those injuries or damages."

Unfortunately, what the concept of the split-second decision overlooks is the string of decisions that an officer can and typically does make (albeit often unconsciously) minutes or much longer in advance of any decision to use deadly (or nondeadly) force. To say that decisions may be made "unconsciously" reflects at least two phenomena. First, officers may genuinely be unaware of choices they are making by instinct, as a product of training, or for other reasons. Second, officers may not be accustomed to *conceptualizing* a "deadly force incident" as beginning at the moment when it was only a *potentially* violent encounter.

The notion of the time frame within which a critical incident is conceptualized as having started and concluded deserves a few more words. Alpert (1989b: 488), studying incidents in which Miami police officers discharged their weapons during the period 1980 through 1986, reported that surveyed officers who had participated in these violent encounters said that "90 percent of the shooting incidents ended in a matter of seconds." The IACP, in a paper issued in explanation of the IACP's 1989 model policy on police use of force (IACP 1989: 4), repeated the 90 percent finding (without citation, but perhaps drawing on the Alpert study), stating:

"[S]tatistics reveal that about 90 percent of shooting incidents take place within a three-second time frame. Within this time frame a police officer takes appropriate steps to stop the threat and rarely, if ever, engages in a decision-making process about his intent or the degree of injury that will be inflicted. The realistic motivation is primarily reactive and designed to stop the threat or the aggressive behavior."

IACP training manager, Ronald McCarthy, whose influence on the profession's thinking about police use of force has been widespread, has repeated the three-second concept of police-involved shootings to thousands of police trainees across the United States, and reiterated the point not long ago to the *Washington Post*: "Police shootings usually are over within three seconds" (Jennings 1991a: A9).[54]

While no detail is presented concerning the wording of the Miami survey question discussed by Alpert or the context in which Ron McCarthy's training or the IACP's 1989 paper was talking about the speed with which lethal force encounters transpire, it is probably safe to assume that the Miami officers, the IACP paper, and McCarthy all were estimating the time period from officers' first awareness of a *need to shoot* through the moment they *stopped firing*. This segment of an encounter—from the need to shoot until the smoke clears—can be contrasted with the duration of an officer's entire visual and physical contact with the person

---

[54] In a widely read officer-survival manual, Rutledge (1988: 269) suggests that slayings of officers also occur very rapidly: "Most fatal officer shootings...[consume] less than 5 seconds."

at whom he or she ended up shooting, including any emergency first aid the officer might have administered to the assailants.

To be sure, there are some important points to be made in support of a split-second notion of shootings. First, some incidents genuinely do occur in split-seconds, and there is little that the involved officers could have done differently to alter the encounters.[55] Second, once a potentially violent encounter has turned lethally violent—once shooting has commenced—if in fact it is true that the vast majority of incidents are over in just seconds, that requires post-incident investigators and commentators to come to grips with certain psychological and physiological realties. Experts such as the IACP's Ron McCarthy, formerly head of the Los Angeles Police Department's Special Weapons and Tactics (SWAT) team, quite rightly observe that an officer engaged in a life-and-death fight will experience a variety of perceptual alterations. Tunnel vision may set in, meaning that the officer's peripheral vision—needed to see other dangers, innocent bystanders, and the like—is effectively nullified. San Diego Police experts (Hall 1991: recommendation 86) have cited "time distortions" and "*increased* auditory and visual acuity" among the other physiological effects of high-stress confrontations. Thus, internal affairs investigators and external reviewers must understand that it may be unrealistic and unfair to expect an officer facing a threat to his or her own life to notice that employing deadly force might endanger an innocent bystander across the block or in a nearby playground.

> *A state trooper "responded to a high school where a youth brandishing a shotgun was terrorizing students and teachers. After being escorted to the assailant by school officials, [the trooper] attempted to calm and reassure the youth, as he walked closer to him. When he was within five feet, the youth pointed the weapon point blank at the trooper's chest. When the young man was momentarily distracted, [the trooper] wrestled away control of the gun, and with the assistance of other troopers now on the scene, subdued the assailant without incident" (FBI 1990d).*

> *For decades, firearms experts have been emphasizing the split-second nature of shooting encounters. For instance, 50 years ago Fairbairn and Sykes (1987 reprint: 5) said: "The average shooting affray is a matter of split seconds. If you take much longer than a third of a second to fire your first shot, you will not be the one to tell the newspapers about it."*

But to acknowledge that officers typically cannot notice and accommodate such important elements as risk to bystanders once a short, chaotic struggle has commenced is *not* to say that officers should therefore be relieved of the obligation to check for such factors as they approach the scene of a potentially violent encounter. Training in violence reduction should give officers practice, in safe settings, in sizing up the total scene they have arrived upon before deciding whether, how, and when to enter it and what precautions to take. As

---

[55] Dwyer, et al. (1990: 295) make the questionable argument that an effect of the *Tennessee v. Garner* decision (1985), prohibiting shooting at nonviolent fleeing suspects, was to "force [officers] into [more] split-second decision[s] as to whether their lives were in jeopardy." What they really seem to be saying is that, under the pre-*Garner* rules, officers could shoot at people with less certainty about their dangerousness: "When officers operated under [the pre-*Garner*] standards and they used their firearms...[i]f they were not quite certain that they were faced with imminent harm..., their actions were still consistent with the 'fleeing felon' alternative" (*ibid.*).

Ron McCarthy has pointed out, police officers should, and can, develop habits of checking in-progress crime scenes for dangers and bystanders just as all of us automatically survey the sidewalk ahead of us for holes and other dangers (McCarthy 1992). Failing to distinguish the difficulties of surveillance and analysis *in the heat of battle* from the opportunities for such information gathering and tactical decision making *prior* to the onset of extreme violence does officers and the public a disservice. Officers may be unfairly criticized for actions that they could not possibly have been expected to take in the midst of a deadly force encounter. At the same time, if officers are not clearly told and trained how to try to minimize the risk of hurting innocent people in the course of their duty to engage and apprehend violent suspects, everyone loses—the public, the officers whose careers may be ruined, the police agencies whose reputations may be diminished, and the bystanders who lives may be sacrificed.

Besides clouding the possibility of better officer decision making in the moments preceding—and sometimes even during and immediately after—a potentially violent encounter, there are other problems created by the split-second decision mythology. Consider the way in which the split-second syndrome may influence administrative review of shooting decisions. What post-hoc justifications of officer shooting decisions premised solely on the opponent's conduct that *immediately* precipitated the shooting overlook is the possibility that police tactical choices needlessly and tragically helped force a confrontational impasse requiring instant resolution. Kolts, et al. (1992: 150), having studied the Los Angeles Sheriff's Department's internal investigations of shootings by deputies, reported: "Our staff reviewed many cases in which officers unnecessarily walked into or created situations which ultimately required the use of deadly force. * * * [T]he question of whether the confrontation could have been avoided in the first place...is the key question...in each instance." The reader may wish to reflect on this line of analysis in reconsidering the data presented in Chapter 4 concerning two phenomena: (1) the types of situations (e.g., traffic stops, armed robberies in progress, shop lifting) that initially required police intervention and ultimately escalated into deadly force encounters; and (2) the adversaries' actions (e.g., furtive gestures, such as reaching quickly for one's belt as if to draw a weapon; fleeing; and attacking the officer with a lethal weapon) that immediately prompted police to fire their weapons.

> " 'It's unbelievable how they Monday-morning quarterback you,' says [a Dallas officer] who underwent a vigorous internal investigation last spring after he fired at, but missed, a man who pointed a gun at him. 'I'm out there sweating bullets, my heart's going 95 miles per hour and some guy is sitting in an air-conditioned office telling me what I should have done' " (Witkin, et al. 1990: 38-39).

Among the most important work done in debunking the myth of the split-second decision is that by Scharf and Binder (1983). They characterized five key decision phases in a potential or actual deadly force encounter: anticipation; entry and initial confrontation; dialogue and information exchange; final frame decision; and aftermath (see also Geller 1985a: 157-158). Curiously, the Scharf-Binder model omits what seems to us to be a crucial and distinct phase—nonlethal tactics—in between the dialogue/information exchange and final frame decision points.

We may summarize as follows the five Scharf-Binder stages, supplemented with our suggestion that officers consider nonlethal tactics, if feasible, prior to pulling the trigger:

1. ***Anticipation***, defined as the period from the officer's first awareness of the need

for intervention to his or her arrival on the scene where the encounter occurs (or at least begins) with the opponent. A critical element of this phase is the substance, amount, and accuracy of information that the officer receives and may use in forming expectations of and preparations for the upcoming encounter.

2. *Entry and initial confrontation*. This is the period in which the officer physically enters the scene or first approaches the citizen. It is theorized that tactical decisions made in this phase can significantly influence the officer's later options. These decisions would include whether to seek cover (behind an object, protective ballistic shield, or the like) or concealment (which may be achieved through the use of physical barriers or deceit as to identity—see Police Foundation [1984] and Fyfe [1989c]) and whether to enlist the aid of individuals whom the suspect may trust.

3. *Dialogue and information exchange*. This is a "definitional" phase in which, through oral or other communication, the officer(s) and civilian(s) "size up" the situation and each other. Included in this phase are orders to "halt," "drop the gun," and so on issued by the police, threats or signs of contempt by the civilian toward the officer, and brief attempts to reason with the opponent or extended negotiations, as in hostage-barricade situations.

4. *Nonlethal (or less-than-lethal) physical control tactics*. The possible armed and unarmed tactics that might be employed are numerous and varied. They could include weaponless controls without debilitating potential, weapon-assisted leverage techniques, weapon-assisted pain compliance, chemical irritants, electrical devices, impact weapons, weaponless controls with debilitating potential, nonfirearm weapon techniques with debilitating potential, and so forth (see Connor and Summers [1988], whose work was discussed earlier in this chapter).

> *"Imagine that you have been on routine patrol for several hours when the dispatcher reports a silent alarm indicating a robbery in progress at a savings and loan association. Since you are only two blocks away, you respond to the call. As you cautiously stop about a half block from the front entrance, watching for signs of unusual activity, a lone male carrying a shotgun runs from the building. He starts in your direction, then freezes, wide-eyed, as he spots your patrol car. Looking around, you realize the old clunker next to you is probably his get-away car. You draw your weapon and assume a position of cover; he turns and runs back into the savings and loan. When the screams of panic from inside die down, you hear a raspy male voice yell out, 'Hey, you out there! Any stupid moves on your part and these people in here will get it! Do you hear me?' While reaching for the radio mike, you can't help but think, 'What would Dirty Harry do now?' " (Dolan and Fuselier 1989: 10).*

5. *Final frame decision* to shoot or not shoot. The officer's actual determination about firing the weapon.

6. *Aftermath*. This final phase includes both on-site events immediately following a decision to shoot or not shoot and activities, such as departmental review and future contact between the officer and his or her opponent, that may occur days, weeks, or months later. Among the consequential actions or decisions that may follow in the

immediate aftermath of the shooting are the provision or absence of emergency medical assistance to wounded persons; tactics used for taking custodial control of the police opponent(s); decisions about whether and how to pursue an escaping subject(s); the way in which any crowd that has gathered around the confrontation is handled; and efforts made to recover weapons, if any, used by the opponent(s). Events that will follow less immediately but that still have a profound impact on the way a shooting or non-shooting incident may shape departmental image, officers' careers, and various public concerns include the way in which the encounter is documented; the nature and quality of administrative and/or criminal investigations of the participating officer(s)' decisions; and handling of public information by police officials in the immediate aftermath of the incident and during and after the post-incident investigation (see discussion in Chapter 6 of the post-shooting public information function).

The "aftermath" phase described by Scharf and Binder does not actually encompass decisions affecting whether or not deadly force is *employed* in the scenario at hand. Still, certain judgments noted above, such as those concerning the administration of first aid and the transportation of wounded persons to trauma units, made in the immediate aftermath of a decision to employ deadly force may well affect whether in fact that force proves *deadly*.

Just as we saw earlier in this volume that different analysts employ typologies with varying levels of generality to portray the factors that immediately precipitated officer-involved shootings, so, too, do we encounter different numbers of "decision phases" in the literature on potentially violent encounters. In contrast to Scharf and Binder's five stages (to which we have added the sixth), Bayley and Garofalo (1989:

Some of the tools of conflict management: time, collaboration, and respect for a suspect's privacy and dignity.

"If urgency and time constraints sometimes lead to violence, it follows that police should slow the pace of their encounters with citizens so that cooled tempers and the restoration of reason may eventually lead to non-violent outcomes. If involuntariness [the civilian's lack of choice about complying with police instructions] sometimes leads to violence, it follows that police should attempt to diminish their clients' feelings that something is being done TO them, by trying to win their confidence and devising problem solutions that at least appear to be collaborative rather than exclusively coercive. If the public settings of police-citizen encounters sometimes lead to violence [because on-lookers judge how tough the civilian and officer are in the face of mutual challenges and challenges from third parties], it follows that police should inject as much privacy as possible into these encounters" (Fyfe 1989c: 473).

12) devised a three-part model. They suggest that there are sets of crucial decisions to be made at the "contact, processing, and exit stages of encounters." By not focusing attention on what Scharf and Binder have termed the "anticipation" phase, however, Bayley and Garofalo may be overlooking an important set of officer choices that can, and often do, constrain or create further options as an incident evolves.

Regardless of the level of specificity contained in different decision models, however, virtually all analysts who have considered the topic of potentially violent police encounters concur that through *early* decisions concerning how, when, and whether to engage a suspect in a confrontation, police often can influence the eventual outcome of confrontations (see also

Alpert 1989b).[56] The tactics employed by highly skilled hostage-barricade team members in containing, controlling, and resolving these dramatic events is perhaps the most obvious illustration of how police need not simply passively accept all situations as they present themselves but can shape events and outcomes in desirable directions (see Schlossberg and Freeman 1974).

Without meaning to undermine the praise justly deserved by hostage negotiation and SWAT teams in police agencies nationwide, it is perhaps worth pausing to observe that, typically, the *unsung hero* of most successfully handled hostage-barricade incidents is the first patrol officer on the scene, who had the presence of mind to recognize the potential of safely and successfully resolving the incident by calling for expert backup instead of forcing a premature confrontation. Dolan and Fuselier (1989: 10) observe:

"The first 15 to 45 minutes are the most dangerous time in a hostage crisis (excluding a rescue attempt). According to Spaulding [1987: 26], the average crisis management team response time is 45 minutes to one hour. Therefore, the most crucial moments of this situation are in your hands, the first officer on the scene."

The observations made by Bristow (1963), Clede and Parsons (1987), Connor and Summers (1988), Fyfe (1989a, 1989c), Bayley and Garofalo (1989), and others about the overriding importance for officer safety of how police *enter* street situations may have more application to typical police patrol work than to certain specialized missions, such as undercover work. DEA training experts emphasize the importance of undercover police negotiating tactically favorable terms concerning the location of any meetings—which does, of course, influence the capacity of police to *enter* the "buy" scene safely. But the tactical experts also suggest that buy-bust outcomes will often turn primarily on how officers show

---

[56] Whether police will be held *legally* responsible for having made tactical errors or debatably sound decisions at early stages of encounters is an entirely separate question from whether there are real gains to be made—in reducing officer career risks and stemming bloodshed—from attention to lethal force decision models. A leading manual on civil litigation against police misconduct (Avery and Rudovsky 1992: 2/36-2/37) terms "rather harsh" (from the plaintiff's perspective in suits against the police) a recent decision by one U.S. Court of Appeals. In *Greenidge v. Ruffin* (1991), the Court of Appeals for the Fourth Circuit held that the lower federal court "had properly excluded evidence of matters prior to the immediate moment when the decision to use deadly force was made" (Avery and Rudovsky 1992: 2/37). This was a case in which

"an officer shot the plaintiff during a prostitution arrest, causing a serious spinal cord injury. Plaintiff alleged that the officers recklessly created a dangerous situation by improperly approaching his car, without flashlights. Plaintiff alleged that the shooting would have been avoided had proper police procedure been followed. * * * [Rejecting this line of argument, the] court ruled that the officer's behavior must be judged by examining the situation immediately prior to and at the very moment she fired her weapon, and that the events which occurred before she opened the auto door were not relevant" (also see Americans for Effective Law Enforcement 1991b).

Even if courts will not mandate police department attention to the sequence of decisions by which officers sometimes paint themselves into dangerous corners, there is some indication that police administrators increasingly are recognizing the wisdom of exploring this area. Witkin, et al. (1990: 38) report that, "in determining whether a shooting is justified, many departments today consider not only the split-second decision to fire but just how the officer got into a situation that left him no choice."

drugs or "buy money" to those targeted for arrest and on other tactical decisions they make following entry on the scene. Both Moriarty (1990) and Wade (1990) stress the importance of negotiating skills to the successful conduct of such dangerous activities as "buy-bust." For instance, Wade argues:

> "When an undercover narcotics officer is injured or killed in the line of duty, it is typically because the flashroll was mismanaged. The object of any drug trafficker's affection is the buyer's money. If he can acquire that money through negotiation, fine. However, if the buyer makes it easy to simply rip off that money, he is exposing himself to tremendous danger. Narcotics officers realize that 'buy-bust' scenarios are among the most dangerous in drug

> *Members of the Chicago Police Department's "Hostage/Barricade/Terrorist (HBT) Unit" highlight the way in which such teams use time as a weapon to foster the successful resolution of critical incidents without undue jeopardy to officers:*

> *" 'Time is on our side.... We've got nothing but time. We might have 50 police officers at a scene. There are 11,500 Chicago coppers altogether. We can always send this 50 home and get another 50, endlessly.' * * * 'Before HBT,' says [Lt. John] Kennedy [head of the Chicago HBT team], 'some nut would grab a kid or a stickup guy would grab a liquor store clerk if the robbery went sour; shots might be fired, the guy barricades himself in the house or goes in the back room of the liquor store and the police arrive. The supervising officer would show up and everybody would look at him expectantly and he'd say, "Follow me, men." and they'd go into the back room and get killed. Now, they have an option' " (Fletcher 1991: 204-205).*

law enforcement; there is no such thing as a 'simple' buy/bust. The most dangerous time during the scenario is when the drugs and money are in the same place. * * * One thing is certain: An undercover officer who continues to operate without regard to the length of time a subject has access—or thinks he has access—to the flashroll is likely to die for a few kilograms of powder (Wade 1990: 48, 49)."

At least in some types of undercover work, officer decisions and conduct *during* the encounters may be at least as important to the officer's safety as the decisions and conduct *prior to* or *during entry into* the encounter.

Wade (1990: 49, 51) also observes that, in missions, such as narcotics buy-busts, that involve highly skilled teamwork, the *supervisor* plays a crucial role in making decisions that may avert or necessitate the use of deadly force. Focusing particularly on "flashroll management," he explains:

> "Undercover officers sometimes develop a false sense of security, possibly disregarding danger signals and the basic tenets of undercover safety. When deeply involved in an investigation, it is easy for a UC [undercover agent] to develop tunnel vision and lose sight of the importance of employing sound undercover tactics. The supervisor cannot fall prey to the same tunnel vision, sacrificing safety for the success of the case. He must be prepared to take any steps necessary to enforce his policies regarding flashroll management. * * * [For example,] there is clearly no purpose in pursuing an undercover investigation when every sign points to a rip-off. It is incumbent upon the manager, case agent and street

supervisor to accurately assess these signs rather than ignore them for the sake of a seizure."

"THE HOLLYWOOD TEN: TV COPS' TACTICAL ERRORS:
As much as we like to criticize the cookie cutter plots and the 'shots fired, back to work in ten minutes' mentality, the tactical errors from Hollywood often mirror our own mistakes. * * * This list represents the major tactical flaws you might see during an average prime-time cop show. * * *

1. Gun pointed straight up while moving.... If your gun needs to be out of your holster, keep it horizontal and on target. It takes too much time to pull it level, find your target, and fire.

2. Gun too far away from body during building search.... What usually happens when [the cops] cross a doorway? The crooks chop at their wrist, and the struggle is on....

3. Standing too close to suspect....the 'in your face' interrogation technique, [which] violate[s] your suspect's 'space' [and often results in] you on the ground and him screaming curses in your ear....

4. Finger pointing.... Waving your digit at a crook just encourages a smart remark, a fistfight, or a complaint.

5. Barehanded fistfights. God loves police officers. Why else did He give us so many 'impact instruments' to use instead of our brittle hand bones?....

6. Bad or no cover during shootout....

7. Losing sight of the suspect during foot pursuit.

8. Not watching behind you for other suspects. This is known in Hollywood as the 'Final Insult.' Our hero is just getting ready to save the day when—out of nowhere—another crook puts a gun in his ear and takes him hostage....

9. No cover units.

10. Nonexistent reports.... Our hero saves the city after a 75-car pileup, a 5,000 round shootout, and a 15 minute wrestling match with Godzilla's brother-in-law. Wiping the sweat from his sturdy brow, he heads home for a cold one" (Albrecht 1992: 80-82; see also Wilson 1970; Fogelson 1977: 141-268).

Reiss (1980) a decade ago began to lay a groundwork for restructuring police decision making in a wide array of potentially violent encounters so as to involve the supervisor as a key player. He recommended involving supervisors in critical decisions that would shape police responses, so that decisions to shoot need not be made in "split seconds" (also see Binder and Scharf 1980: 116-119; Fyfe 1986b). Parallel developments concerning the control of high-speed pursuits have been occurring in many departments, which have required that supervisors participate, via radio communication, in the decision whether to continue or cease an in-progress high-speed chase (see Alpert 1987a; Alpert and Anderson 1986; Fyfe 1989b; Alpert and Fridell 1992). Still another area in which there may be potential for violence reduction through supervisory involvement is on stake-outs. Some agencies have been criticized for allegedly lying in wait for armed offenders, allowing them to menace or even injure their crime victims, and then engaging the culprits in gunfights as they attempt to flee the scene (see, e.g., Freed 1989; Stolberg 1990; Connelly 1992).[57] Still another area in which

---

[57] The LAPD's Special Investigations Section, "an elite surveillance squad that gathers evidence against dangerous criminals by watching them commit crimes and attempts to arrest them afterward (Stolberg 1990: A1), has been a target of considerable criticism. A *Los Angeles Times* exposé reported

supervisory attention may help reduce police-civilian violence is in the handling of emotionally disturbed persons. The NYPD took an initiative in this regard in 1988, adopting a policy that instructs officers to summon a supervisor and establish a flexible zone of safety around potentially violent, emotionally disturbed persons to lower risks of shootings.

Whether dealing with highly volatile emotionally disturbed persons or other potential adversaries, police officers must increasingly understand and harness the *positive aspects* of the fear that they, as human beings—despite any training and machismo organizational culture—will inevitably feel in dangerous encounters. And officers must better learn to understand and control the *counterproductive aspects* of their own fear in tense situations. Some of the most important insights on the problem of officer fear and the ways it can shape officer safety come from Washington State Patrol departmental psychologist Roger Solomon. Solomon (1990) presents a graphic, reproduced below as Figure 72, depicting the onset, management, and effects of officer fear in potentially dangerous encounters.

Solomon suggests six critical stages to be understood by officers so that they can better control themselves and others[58] with whom they must deal in potentially violent situations.

---

that

> "teams of well-armed SIS detectives had, for years, tailed career criminals but often ignored opportunities to prevent armed robberies and burglaries by legitimately arresting suspects beforehand on lesser crimes or outstanding warrants. Instead, records showed, the officers routinely stood by until the suspects they were watching had committed violent crimes. Many suspects were shot when they returned to their getaway cars" (Freed 1989: B1).

Between 1967 and June 1990, the SIS reportedly killed more than 25 suspects and wounded another 24 (Stolberg 1990: A1; see also Meyer and Connelly 1992).

Planning confrontations with suspects in ways designed to maximize the opportunity for the police to find justification for killing them—and thus to short-circuit the adjudicatory role of the criminal justice system—is the opposite of another, undoubtedly more pervasive practice, in which police fail to avert preventable crimes in the hope of catching suspects in the act and thus acquiring the evidence needed to prosecute them on serious charges. Kelling (1991) has criticized the latter approach on the ground that it uses crime victims as "bait to feed the criminal justice system."

[58] Among the "others" officers may be able to help control are their colleagues. In the wake of the Rodney King beating in Los Angeles during March 1991, a number of police agencies and training experts have begun to develop what some call "intervention" training. This is training to help officers intervene to calm down their colleagues when tempers are flaring and one or more officers seem inclined to employ a level or type of force not warranted by legitimate police tactical needs. San Diego Police Department training academy head David Hall, working at the California Police Officers Standards and Training (POST) program during 1992, was helping to develop such training, as was his counterpart, David James, in the Dallas Police Department. The Sacramento Police Department reportedly during late 1991 had developed simulation training in which the Rodney King incident was replicated and officers were guided on how to intervene to stop the swinging batons and gratuitous kicks. On August 27, 1991, the Los Angeles Police Commission amended the Department manual to clarify that officers are required "to report and intercede if a colleague is involved in misconduct" (*Crime Control Digest* 1991l: 9), but such mandates, to be effective, must be supported with the kind of "how to" training being developed by the other agencies noted above.

The activity of departments in offering "intervention training" has the dual virtues of being both helpful to officers and a fulfillment of agencies' constitutional obligation. "It is now well settled law," a police legal advisor wrote, "that a police officer who fails to intervene to prevent a constitutional

The stages are:

1. Awareness of danger or trouble (which Solomon labels "Here Comes Trouble");
2. Vulnerability Awareness (represented in myriad human experiences by the nearly universal exclamation "OH SHIT!");
3. Threat Acknowledgment and Shift of Focus from Personal Risk to the Conditions Producing the Threat (which Solomon captures in the phrase "I've Got to Do Something");
4. Selecting a Tactic or Tactics for Survival;
5. Making a Mental Commitment to the Survival Plan and Summoning 'Survival Resources' (which Solomon places under the heading "Here Goes!"); and
6. Response (the attempted physical implementation of the survival plan).

These "stages" may, of course, be compressed into seconds, and in many circumstances officers will not consciously or even unconsciously progress in a linear way from one stage to the next. At any point from stage 3 (acknowledgment of the threat and focus on the details of the incident producing the threat) through 6 (attempted response by the officer), an officer's inability to accomplish the desired objective may "loop" him or her back, as shown in Figure 72, to an earlier point in the effort to resolve the problem at hand.

---

violation may be held liable under 42 U.S.C. section 1983. The leading case followed by every circuit hearing this issue is *Byrd v. Brishke*, 466 F.2d 6 (7th Cir. 1972)" (Spector 1992). Since the resurgence in administrative interest in intervention training was stimulated by the Rodney King beating, the facts of *Byrd v. Brishke* are noteworthy. Taken as accurate for purposes of the decision, the plaintiff's allegations were

> "that he was surrounded by approximately a dozen Chicago police officers and struck repeatedly. Because he could not identify the individual officers who struck him, the plaintiff's theory of liability was that even if the officers didn't participate in the beating, they should be held liable for 'negligently or intentionally failing to protect the plaintiff from others who did violate his rights by beating him in their presence' " (Spector 1992, citing the ruling at p. 10).

The court concurred. Later case law has clarified that

> "an officer's mere presence at the scene of a constitutional violation will not be sufficient to prove liability. The officer must have knowledge of or deliberate indifference to the action that violates constitutional rights. *Masel v. Barrett*, 707 F.Supp. 4 (D.D.C. 1989); *Wilson v. City of Chicago*, 707 F.Supp. 379 (N.D.Ill. 1989). In an excessive force case, an officer will be held liable if he was present when the plaintiff was beaten or knew that such force was being used and failed to stop the officers from using such force. *Peterson v. Dept. of Navy*, 687 F.Supp. 713 (D.N.H. 1988). A plaintiff must also prove that the officer had a realistic opportunity to prevent the use of force" (Spector 1992).

Not only is *civil* liability a possibility, but "an officer may be arrested under 18 U.S.C. sections 241 and 242 for failure to prevent a constitutional violation. *United States v. McKenzie*, 798 F.2d 602 (5th Cir. 1985)" (*ibid.*). This is the basis for the federal prosecution of the LAPD sergeant who let his subordinates allegedly violate Rodney King's civil rights in the March 1991 beating (Reinhold 1992a).

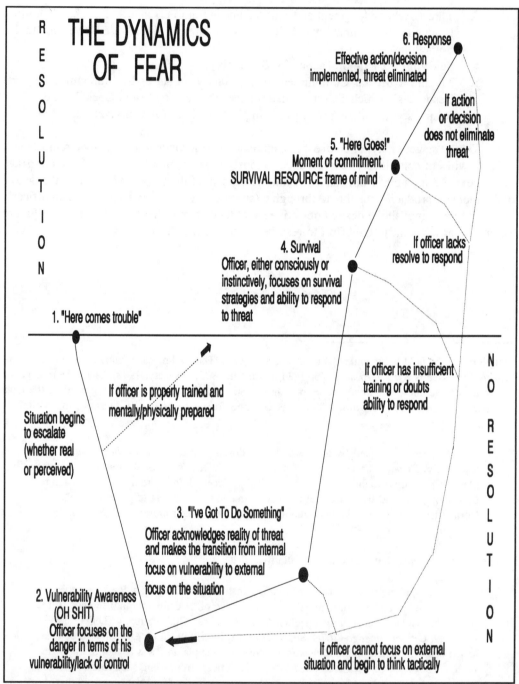

Figure 72: The Dynamics of Fear
Source: Solomon (1990: 15).

*"Way back in the academy, we all learned about the ten deadly errors for police officer survival from Pierce R. Brooks, the author of...*Officer Down, Code Three *[Brooks 1975]. The list is a good one, and it bears repeating" (Albrecht 1992: 199).*

*"Obviously, many good officers are killed each year, and sometimes there is no way the tragedy could have been avoided. The ambush slaying by the sniper is the best example. The cases cited in this book, however, fall into another category: the avoidable tragedies. * * * The...deadly errors [include]:*

1. Failure to maintain proficiency and care of weapon, vehicle and equipment [and, Albrecht (1992: 201) adds, "your handcuffs, Mace, speedloaders, ammo, Buck knife, flashlight, and assorted leather gear"].

2. Improper search and use of handcuffs.

3. Sleepy or asleep.

4. Relaxing too soon [what Albrecht (1992: 200) calls "complacency—'routine' calls or stops. That simple traffic ticket may turn into the fight of your career"].

5. Missing the danger signs [trust your intuition about situations and people that just don't look right, about people who "don't belong" on your beat, etc. "Three guys wearing overcoats in a summertime supermarket are nothing to ignore" (Albrecht 1992: 119)].

6. Taking a bad position—[don't have] your back turned to the subject...or, while confronting the barricaded gunman, be casual or curious from your place of concealment rather than careful and cautious from a place of cover.

7. Failure to watch their hands—where else can the subject hold a gun, or a knife, or a club?

8. Tombstone courage—why wait for backup? [Albrecht (1992: 199) argues "sometimes bravery is just a mask for stupidity." Fyfe (1986b) talks about this under the rubric of the "split-second syndrome"].

9. Preoccupation [which Albrecht (1992: 199) calls "improper attitude," saying "you can't perform effectively if you're distracted or preoccupied by personal problems. As hard as it is to do, you must put your problems on the...'back-burner' so you can fully concentrate on your work"].

10. Apathy—a deadly disease for the cynical veteran police officer" (Brooks 1975: 6-7).

c. Researching the Effectiveness of Violence-Reduction and Officer-Survival Training

Relatively little empirical evidence is available on the effects of police violence-reduction and officer-survival training programs on use of deadly force practices. Common sense suggests that one might expect the same sort of favorable effects as have been found in the wake of thoughtfully and seriously implemented policy changes (see Fyfe 1979b; Alpert 1989b: 492; Sparger and Giacopassi 1992; and the Chicago example, discussed above). Moreover, police have developed experience and gut reactions concerning the utility of violence-reduction and officer-survival training in numerous jurisdictions in recent years. According to practitioners and analysts familiar with the Metro-Dade Police Department's violence-reduction efforts, they have been very successful in reducing shootings by police, enhancing officer safety, and improving police-civilian rapport (e.g., Torres 1992). A detailed description and appraisal of this experience would be an important contribution to the field.

Chicago presents one illustration of officer survival training with which we have first hand experience. There, in 1984, a role-playing program was initiated. A mock city block, including store fronts and streets and a two-story apartment building (used for building entry and control exercises), was constructed inside the Police Department's large gymnasium. Police squad cars and other equipment were on site and usable in connection with car stops, building approaches, and such. The point of the survival training was, as with many such programs developed more recently in other agencies, to help officers hone tactical skills that allow them to use deadly force effectively when necessary and to use nonlethal force or verbal commands, where possible, as an alternative to deadly force.

It is possible with this and other officer survival training programs that officers will take different messages from the training than were intended. Careful research is warranted concerning the impact on officers' attitudes and incident outcomes of various approaches to tactical and judgment training. One concern expressed by many police executives with whom we have talked nationwide is that an officer survival course, by emphasizing hazards that might be confronted out of proportion to the need for prudence and restraint, can make officers excessively nervous. This conditioning could then induce officers to shoot precipitously in potentially violent street encounters.

> *"The decline in deaths of officers is being attributed by experts to the growing use of body armor, now mandatory in many departments, and to a growing sophistication in training. 'Cops today are trained differently,' said Patrick V. Murphy, former head of the New York City and Washington [D.C.] police departments. 'They're trained to be cautious, not macho. Don't rush in. Size up every situation before moving. Get backup. Don't treat everybody like a bad guy. Most progressive chiefs won't discipline a cop if someone gets away—"We'll catch him tomorrow"—but they will be tough if an officer is too aggressive' " (Malcolm 1990a).*

San Diego Police Chief Robert Burgreen publicly suggested in May of 1991 that a widely used, award-winning officer training video on "surviving [attacks with] edged weapons" induced "a sense of paranoia" among his officers and may have contributed to a surge in unnecessary shootings by San Diego police. Chief Burgreen said two of his officers told him that their shooting conduct (which was found within legal limits by the county prosecutor) was guided by the training video. Burgreen indicated that the alarmist effects of the film were produced by "overly graphic" segments and also suggested that parts of the video were "out-and-out racist" (*Crime Control Digest* 1991d). A deputy chief in the San Diego Police Department, whose son had been involved in one of the shootings that Chief Burgreen found regrettable, said he was not necessarily convinced that the training video "triggered the spate of shootings" but did say the video "didn't give you a whole lot of options to deadly force." Reportedly, "the key message to the officers is that there is a minimum distance of 21 feet that will give an officer enough time to pull his gun and shoot an onrushing attacker," so that once an assailant with an edged weapon approaches closer, he or she has closed the "reactionary gap" (Albrecht 1992: 45) and entered a kill zone, requiring that the assailant must be taken out (*Crime Control Digest* 1991d: 2).

Not unexpectedly, the creators of the video, which has been available since early 1989, vehemently denied Chief Burgreen's assertions about its harmful effects (Anderson and Remsberg 1991: 1). They went on the attack, suggesting the chief "has displayed a regrettable lack of support for officers under his command who have been forced to defend themselves against threats to their safety" (see also Albrecht 1992: 43-45 and Baltic 1991: 24). They also challenged the assertion by the deputy chief that the video fails to cover the range of tactical options available to officers, suggesting that the video "demonstrates and discusses the full range of the force continuum. Information is given on when and how to use tactical deployment, verbal challenges, empty-hand techniques, and a baton, as well as deadly force, in dealing with edged weapon offenders" (Anderson and Remsberg 1991: 3). As to the accusations about the video being overly graphic, its makers assert:

> "In truth, the film is realistic. Confrontations depicted are based on actual incidents, and evidence photos from medical examiners are included to accurately reinforce the nature and seriousness of edged weapon injuries. The research behind 'Surviving Edged Weapons' indicates that officers often dismiss knives as being dangerous because they are so commonplace" (*ibid.*).

Anderson and Remsberg also reject the notion that the film is racist or feeds racist predispositions among certain officers. They say the video "is believed to have become the best-selling law enforcement training film ever released" (*ibid.*: 4).

Still, Burgreen's is not the only voice of concern. Other police executives with whom we discussed the controversy in private conversations indicated some misgivings about certain portions of the video, suggesting, as Burgreen had, that the message is an overly mechanistic one. That is, while the force continuum is indeed discussed and demonstrated, the message that officer trainees are left with is that once an assailant with an edged weapon approaches within seven yards, there are rarely any options available to threatened officers other than lethal force. At least one chief indicated his response to such concerns was not to scrap the video entirely, as Chief Burgreen did (*Crime Control Digest* 1991d: 1) but instead to "heavily edit" it to remove the parts he found objectionable.

> *"The creation of a violence-reduction training program is based on the observation that police officers [in Miami] encounter approximately eight situations per shift which are potentially violent. Police are obliged to confront irrational individuals or offenders whose actions leave even the most restrained and best trained officers little choice but to use force to protect themselves or others. Attempts to modify police behavior through training cannot be expected to eliminate violence in those situations, but it is likely that the degree of violence can be reduced. Despite the large number of situations which are potentially violent, a police shooting is, indeed, a rare occurrence"* (Alpert 1989b: 492).

Our point in reviewing both sides of the argument on this video is not to weigh in with our own opinion on its possible merits or drawbacks. Instead, we aim to highlight the fact that, whether Chief Burgreen is correct or not, he, along with Anderson and Remsberg's response, have provided a professional service by publicly beginning the discussion of two crucially important questions: (1) Do police executives responsible for setting policy and shaping organizational "culture" on use of lethal force *know* what messages are being sent to their personnel by training materials, whether developed in-house or by outside vendors? and (2) What are some of the principles and considerations by which line officers, trainers, police leaders, public policymakers, and the public should evaluate the appropriateness of training messages? More particularly, how should training programs attempt to strike the essential, delicate balance between adequately preparing officers to protect themselves and the public, on the one hand, and, on the other hand, alarming officers to the point where their emotions overcome their cool tactical reasoning, leading them to make ill-advised, bloody, career-threatening peremptory strikes against adversaries?

The San Diego debate is not, of course, the first and won't be the last time concerns have been raised about whether an officer survival training program backfired, leading officers to be "judged by 12" in circumstances where they would not otherwise have been "carried by six." Indeed, there is limited evidence from another jurisdiction that officers themselves sometimes find that shoot/don't shoot-type officer survival training sends an unbalanced message. For instance, Alpert (1987b: 31) surveyed Dallas police officers who had discharged their weapons in the line of duty and discovered that, while 65 percent of the respondents indicated that such training was "helpful," only 40 percent found it "helpful in training officers when *not* to shoot" (emphasis added; see *Law Enforcement News* [1992a] on training to prevent "friendly fire" injuries and Schmitt 1992 for discussion of the military's efforts to prevent inadvertent friendly casualties after concern over the problem was prompted by instances of "fratricide" during the Persian Gulf War).

Does the experience in Chicago with officer survival training during the 1980s provide limited empirical evidence of a situation in which officers may have taken an unintended message from the training? This is conceivable, though not likely. The letter "a" on Figure 71 (presented earlier—see Contents for the page) shows the 1984 shooting rate (number of civilians shot fatally or nonfatally per 1,000 forcible felony arrests over the course of the entire year). Because the officer survival training was administered throughout 1984, it is conceivable that the year's overall shooting rate might have been influenced to a certain extent by the training program. But a potential flaw in such an interpretation is that the survival training was administered to a relatively small percentage of the Department's field personnel (several hundred out of a total of several thousand). If, however, it is true that the survival training had a demonstrable impact on the agency's overall shooting practices, then the increase in shooting rate from 1983 (10.4 shootings by police per 1,000 forcible felony arrests) to 1984 (12.8 per 1,000) suggests that officers to a certain extent may have misinterpreted what the police administration was trying to tell them. In effect, while the training message about shooting was a balanced one (shoot when necessary, avoid violence when possible), officers may have come away from the dramatic exercises with an undesirably heightened propensity to fire their weapons when confronting dangerous suspects.

> *A "don't shoot" scenario in a Calibre Press training video that promotes helpful caution about racially oriented assumptions:*
> The "scenario opens with the officer walking down a sidewalk. A bystander runs up and says excitedly that he's just seen a black man accost a white man in a nearby parking lot and take him into an adjacent alley. The cop cautiously approaches and peers around a corner into the alley. A black man in a jumpsuit is holding a semi-automatic pistol on a white guy, whose hands are in the air. In the next instant, the white guy takes off running down the alley and the black man whirls toward the camera. It turns out he's an undercover cop, but in the instant it takes him to hold up his badge, he's been 'shot' many, many times" (Baltic 1991: 28).

We hasten to add, however, that we do not know nearly enough about other developments going on at the time in Chicago to suggest *firmly* that the survival training in any sense backfired as far as controlling the use of deadly force by police. Earlier in this chapter we cited the package of Chicago training and policy initiatives as having a salutary effect on officer shooting patterns and perhaps on officer safety. We stand by that positive view of the overall impact of the administrative interventions. Here, we have merely called attention to the possibility—however remote—that *early* in the approximately 18-month set of initiatives some officers may have reacted in a way unintended by the survival course trainers.

The reader should keep in mind that, by representing the shooting data in Figure 71 as a *rate* based on arrests of potentially violent individuals, we have already controlled to an important extent for possible variations in the frequency with which Chicago officers confronted dangerous people from year to year. Thus, the figure shows that, based on this measure of danger (forcible felony arrests), officers were more likely in 1984 to shoot civilians than was the case in 1983. At the same time, as we saw earlier in our discussion of the effects of training to familiarize officers with newly adopted policy, officers were less likely to shoot suspects in 1985 (the annual rate dropped to 7.1 from the 1984 rate of 12.8). The numbers used to calculate these rates appear in Table E-1 in Appendix E.

Optimism about the effects of officer survival training and violence-reduction training comes from many quarters. Most recently, Sparger and Giacopassi (1992), although unable to differentiate the effect of policy changes from the impact of officer survival training, credited these dual initiatives for producing a decrease in shootings by police in Memphis. Encouragingly, the shooting reductions were obtained in the midst of increasing levels (and rates) of arrests for violent crimes.

As suggested above, the seminal field experiment with violence reduction training, however, comes from the Metro-Dade Police Department in the Miami area. While at the Police Foundation, deadly force researcher and former New York City police lieutenant James Fyfe designed and helped implement an ambitious program to provide officers with enhanced violence-reduction skills. The planning and implementation processes have been written about in Fyfe (1988c, 1989a; see also 1986b), Police Foundation (1988), and Alpert (1989b). Fyfe, who plans to continue writing about the mid- and long-term benefits of the violence-reduction training in Metro-Dade, has indicated in personal conversations with us that these effects are substantial and positive. Officers credit the violence-reduction training for a decrease in bloodshed on both sides of the police-adversary equation and suggest their training has helped them be more effective in crime control and more popular among those who used to criticize the Department for excessive use of force.

Before closing this discussion of violence-reduction and officer survival training, it is important to make two points. First, training of either type may be remedial as well as preventive. Many police trainers and analysts (e.g., Brown 1984) have urged that, in addition to routine, agencywide, in-service firearms training, specialized training be provided for officers who have been involved in violent situations to help prevent overreactions to violence in the future. Brown also suggested that officers (particularly those who will patrol alone) be continually retrained in nonlethal defensive tactics to bolster their confidence in their abilities to resolve violent encounters without resorting to deadly force (also see Geller and Karales 1981a).[59] Post-shooting trauma counseling for officers has also come to be accepted as a

---

[59] Incidentally, it is not at all clear from the limited available research that officers responding alone to potentially violent situations are more likely than officers accompanied by partners or other responding units to use deadly force. Indeed, interviews with police officers around the nation suggest that officers working alone readily perceive that they will have to use their wits and verbal skills to deal

workable and important method for reducing the career risks confronting police officers (Geller 1985a, 1986; Matulia 1985: 87-88).

The second point is that one should have reasonable but not exaggerated expectations for what officer survival training, violence-reduction training, or any other type of preparation can accomplish. Sometimes, commentators seem, perhaps unwittingly, to leave the impression that life's twists and turns are more within human control than may be the case. For instance, Alpert (1989b: 493) declared:

> "Training can improve police officers' responses to potentially violent situations. Other than those situations which place officers or civilians in imminent danger of death or serious injury, through the actions of the offender, confrontations can be classified in terms of the following categories:
>
> 1. confrontations which are skillfully defused;
> 2. confrontations in which an error leads to escalation with no violence; or
> 3. confrontations in which an error precipitates a violent outcome.
>
> "The second category includes cases in which officers deal less skillfully and less sensitively with potentially violent situations and people. Usually, these errors or provocations do not lead to violence because the civilian acquiesces to police authority. In the third category, the officers' lack of skill or sensitivity in dealing with situations and/or people triggers violence or fails to prevent it."

But surely this typology doesn't cover the universe of explanations for outcomes. What about confrontations that are defused through "dumb luck"? There is much truth in the adage, "I'd rather be lucky than good." The implication of fortune for post-shooting tactical debriefings is crucial. Analysts would make a profound mistake if they concluded that whatever techniques preceded a successful incident outcome deserve replication. Sometimes things turn out well *despite* our efforts, not because of them, as implied in Alpert's category number 2. Police officer-writer Steve Albrecht (1992: 202) captured the point nicely in writing a chapter titled "Tombstone Courage: Tactical Errors During High-Risk Calls." The chapter began, "The story you are about to read is true. The names have been changed to protect the lucky."

Further, what about confrontations that, despite all reasonable and even heroically skillful efforts by officers, nevertheless end in a wholly undesirable use of lethal force by police? There is a Spanish phrase, popular among American police in its English translation, that captures the harsh reality: caca pasa.

4. *Shooting Proficiency Training*

To better prepare officers for the occasions when they will have to shoot, trainers and researchers have urged the development of more realistic firing range simulation of street

---

with many situations where a show of force by several officers might otherwise accomplish a similar objective. And sometimes when a department attempts to use a show of force (through the presence of several officers) as a nonlethal control technique, that becomes a provocation to the subject—and perhaps even to officers—and the encounter escalates uncontrollably into a use of deadly force. This may be even more likely when there are partisan bystanders on the scene.

conditions. This includes firing at night with dim or variable lighting, after running several blocks, with multiple opponents to think about, with other officers and bystanders on the scene, and while wearing on-duty clothing (see, e.g., Morgan 1992). More frequent range practice than the annual or semiannual sessions that are common in some departments has also been recommended so officers can develop better gun handling habits and increase their proficiency in using weapons (Geller and Karales 1981a: 199-200; see also Matulia 1985: 76-79). Some smaller agencies currently have range practice every *week*. Frequent in-service training is far from inexpensive; but the liability consequences of failure to administer such training could be far more expensive. One tactics expert endorsed the notion of weekly shooting practice:

Recommendations that police practice shooting under circumstances that resemble field conditions are not new. In 1942, Fairbairn and Sykes (1987 reprint: 2) wrote:

"[B]eyond helping to teach care in the handling of firearms, target shooting is of no value whatever in learning the use of the pistol as a weapon of combat. The two things are as different from each other as chalk from cheese, and what has been learned from target shooting is best unlearned if proficiency is desired in the use of the pistol under actual fighting conditions."

"No matter how often your department requires you to qualify [with a firearm], you should be shooting once a week. Half of this shooting should be done at night. All of it should be done at ranges of 2 to 20 feet. * * * Few officer gunfights are of a sustained duration—in most, only 1 or 2 shots will be fired. Therefore, it's better for you to shoot 6 rounds, 4 times per month, than to shoot 24 rounds at one session" (Rutledge 1988: 269, 272-273).

Infrequent practice shooting is hard to understand (except in terms of its financial cost), given the importance of officer proficiency with weapons and the challenges of mastering the weapon. If a concert violinist knew she would have an opportunity once every few years to perform with the world-renowned Chicago Symphony Orchestra, would she practice her instrument just a few times per year? We accept that the analogy is not perfect; a concert violinist will often practice for hours every day, and this is hardly feasible for police weapons practice. Nevertheless, police administrators and government risk managers need to rethink the priorities that prevent officers in many agencies from firing their weapons often enough to feel confident in their proficiency.

Range firing and simulation exercises designed to maximize firing accuracy and self-confidence in officers that they can use deadly force decisively and skillfully when it is required are, of course, closely related to the violence-reduction training and conflict management training discussed immediately above. But besides helping officers improve their judgment concerning whether and when to use their firearms, there is an independent need to ensure that officers understand the proper functioning of their service weapons—and all weapons they are likely to encounter and potentially have to handle on the street.[60] Maximizing officer skill in firing their weapons accurately under the stress of combat

[60] Officers also need to be trained in distinguishing, to the extent possible, toy and replica guns from real guns. For a thorough discussion of the issues surrounding toy guns and officers' encounters with persons armed with them, see Carter, et al. (1990).

situations is no small part of an overall strategy for officer safety, crime reduction, and violence reduction. Particularly in recent years, when the vast majority of police recruits lack military experience, it has become imperative that police agencies devote as much attention as each rookie requires to developing proficiency in firearms use and safe handling.

There is a substantial body of literature on weapons proficiency training that, like the weaponless tactics literature, cannot adequately be summarized in this volume, given our primary focus on empirical information about shootings of and by police. Among the primary institutional sources of state-of-the art information about shooting proficiency training are the firearms and tactics units at most state and major city police departments, the FBI's academy in Quantico, Virginia, and the Treasury Department's Federal Law Enforcement Training Center, headquartered in Glynco, Georgia.

Although much of the attention in the shooting-control literature understandably focuses on the need to ensure that officers have the self-restraint to avoid shooting unless shooting is imperative, it is no less important to ensure that officers have the courage and self-discipline to draw, point, and fire their weapons at another human being without freezing from fright when the use of deadly force is dictated by the circumstances. Fear of firing is not a small problem among recent police recruits in some jurisdictions, according to police trainers with whom we have spoken around the nation. It is not a problem to be celebrated by those who wish to reduce police-civilian violence. For the lessons of history make clear that, whether one is

> *"Most fatal officer shootings take place at night, on the street or highway, at distances of less than 3 yards, consuming less than 5 seconds. That's the threat you should be training to meet—not the prospect of a paper silhouette popping out at you from 25 yards away and waiting for you to draw a sight picture. Target shooting has only one beneficial use, and that's to promote your familiarity with your weapon. It has nothing whatever to do with teaching you to win a gunfight. Don't depend on it for that"* (Rutledge 1988: 269).

considering relations between nations or the outcome of a one-on-one encounter in a dark alley, a credible threat to use force sometimes can facilitate the peaceful resolution of conflict. Al Capone put the point simply: "You can get further with a kind word and a gun than you can with a kind word alone."

Improving officer proficiency in "bullet placement" is seen by many firearms and training experts as essential to officer safety and the reduction of unintended injuries to bystanders and fellow officers. NYPD firearms expert Inspector John Cerar, along with colleagues from the Dallas, Houston, and Los Angeles Police Departments, the IACP, and others, argues that "stopping power" does not come from larger, faster, harder types of bullets. What stops suspects in their tracks, they say, is proper placement of the rounds. Competence in bullet placement comes only from frequent, realistic training and rejection of what some firearms experts derisively call the "spray and pray" theory of shooting—firing as many bullets as possible in the general direction of the opponent and hoping for a hit (Pilant 1992: 39; McCarthy 1992).

Officers are pretty quick to detect problems among their colleagues in use-of-force decision making. (*Detecting* is not the same as *disclosing*, of course; and the *quality* of those appraisals is likely to vary widely among the officers who make them.) An opinion poll of the Portland, Oregon, Police Bureau conducted by a local newspaper revealed that 84 percent of the responding officers said they "have...worked with at least one officer within the past year or thereabouts whose judgment [they] would deem questionable in a deadly force situation" (Snell and Long 1992a). Pressed for more detail, 18 percent of the officers responded (in *unpublished* data that were provided to us) that they believed their co-workers would have been "too ready to shoot." But the concerns that most animated the respondents ran in the opposite direction. Thus, with officers allowed to pick more than one category of answer (resulting in percentages that total more than 100), 52 percent of the 90 officers who answered this survey question worried that co-workers would be "too hesitant to shoot," 39 percent worried about shooting proficiency ("so lacking in marksmanship or other skills that he/she would be a menace"), and 22 percent cited "other" reasons for questioning their colleagues' deadly force judgment and/or tactical competence (*ibid.*).

B. Weapons and Equipment

1. Revolvers Versus Semi-automatics and Other Weapons Issues

In Chapter 3 we summarized some of the literature describing and attempting to offer explanations for patterns of police-involved shootings as they relate to the weapons used by police and by police assailants. Here, we explore a bit further some of the policy and operational considerations pertaining to police firearms.

Perhaps the highest profile weapons issue facing police administrators in the 1980s[61] was whether to authorize a switch from the revolver to a semi-automatic pistol as a standard service handgun. While every region of the country undoubtedly had well known tragic cases in which officers were at a tactical disadvantage because of their weaponry compared to that of their

> "[T]his weapons transition [from revolvers to semi-automatics] represents the first time in the history of American law enforcement that there has been a technical rearming" (Edwards 1991b).

adversaries in gunfights, three particular shoot-outs became particularly infamous throughout the law enforcement community. These three cases—along with the U.S. military's switch in 1985 from its traditional single-action .45 caliber pistol to a 9-millimeter double-action semi-automatic (Malcolm 1990; McClain 1989: 30)—had much to do with driving the determination of police in many jurisdictions during the 1980s to increase their "firepower." These cases, as summarized by McCauley and Edwards (1990: 35), were the following:

- "In December 1977 Maryland State Police Trooper G. A. Presbury was shot and killed during a traffic stop. Trooper Presbury emptied his service revolver and struck the assailant twice, however, he was not incapacitated. While [the trooper was] attempting to reload the service revolver the assailant, who was armed with a semi-automatic, approached the trooper and killed him.

---

[61] The debate about the relative merits of revolvers and semi-automatics dates at least from the early 1940s and has not raged only in the United States. Fairbairn and Sykes (1987 reprint of 1942 edition: 11-16) strongly advocate what were then called *automatic* rather than *semi-automatic* pistols for use by the uniformed officers of armed police forces (e.g., in the Shanghai Police Department, where they served in senior posts for a number of years).

■ The...murder in 1981 of New Jersey State Trooper Philip Lamonaco, who was shot eight times with a high capacity 9-millimeter after making a routine traffic stop. Next to Trooper Lamonaco was found his empty service revolver.

■ The...FBI shoot-out that took place in Miami in 1986, where two FBI agents died and five agents were seriously injured in a gun battle with two armed bank robbery suspects."[62]

This FBI shootout in particular "became a symbol in law enforcement of under-armed officers coming out the poorer against well-armed criminals" (Malcolm 1990; see also McClain 1989: 30). By the end of the 1980s, the FBI was a leading advocate of conversion from revolvers to semi-automatic pistols (McClain 1989: 30; National Teleconference on the 9-millimeter Semi-Automatic Pistol 1988). The Bureau's support differentiated among types of semi-automatics, however. Five years ago, the FBI decided not to authorize use of

> *"Officers must...moderate the temptations of available firepower.... [P]olice must understand and practice regulating fire based on necessity and not availability" (McCauley and Edwards 1990: 41).*

Glock semi-automatics, a brand used by many other agencies, on the ground that "the gun's light trigger pull and short trigger travel made it 'too easy for someone to have an accidental discharge,' " according to James Pledger, chief of the FBI's Firearms Training Unit (Fritsch 1992a). Pledger also pointed out that, in a more recent series of "drop tests," in which guns are dropped to the floor from waist height to see if the impact causes them to fire, "the Glock was the only semiautomatic to fail" (*ibid.*). Instead of the Glock, which is popular with many other law enforcement agencies, the Bureau authorized its agents to use both SIG-Sauer and Smith and Wesson semi-automatic pistols (*ibid.*).

Through the 1980s and into the early 1990s, some agencies considered the matter of converting from revolvers to pistols at length and reached a firm decision to either make the change agencywide or, at least for the immediate future, forgo it. Other agencies are still wrestling with the issues involved. In its survey of the nation's 57 largest city police departments in the early 1980s, when the determination to adopt pistols was just beginning to crystallize, the IACP found that 16 percent of the departments by that time had policies expressly authorizing personnel to use semi-automatic weaponry (Matulia 1985: 73).[63] In 1989, one expert estimated that "85 percent of the U.S. law enforcement agencies are still armed with the double-action revolver" (McCauley and Edwards 1990: 35). More recently, police groups, scholars, weapons manufacturers and news media outlets have suggested that as many as half the nation's police agencies have authorized officers to use semi-automatic pistols in lieu of revolvers (Bratton 1990a, 1991a: 3; Krajick 1990: 58; Edwards 1991a, 1991b; Malcolm 1990). The Justice Department's Bureau of Justice Statistics, in its 1990

---

[62] The FBI shoot-out not only fueled the movement for widespread adoption of high-capacity pistols, it also prompted a reconsideration of the FBI's long-standing defense-of-life shooting policy. We discussed this contemplated change of policy at some length earlier in this chapter.

[63] The agencies whose policies explicitly permitted use of 9-millimeter pistols as of the 1980 survey included those in Albuquerque, Birmingham (AL), Detroit, Houston, Long Beach, Louisville, New Orleans, San Antonio, and San Diego. Of the 57 big-city departments surveyed, 11 had policies that were silent on whether officers could or could not use 9-millimeter pistols. Another 33 (58 percent) prohibited officers from using 9-millimeter pistols (Matulia 1982: Appendix N, p. 8).

"Law Enforcement Management and Administrative Statistics" survey of a nationally representative sample of police and sheriffs' departments, concluded:

> "About 73 percent of all local police departments, which employed 91 percent of all local police officers, authorized the use of one or more types of semiautomatic weapons, as did 80 percent of the state police departments and 74 percent of the sheriffs' departments" [*Crime Control Digest* (1992b: 7); Fountain (1991) describes the shift to semi-automatics among suburban departments in the Chicago area].

Hence, in the early 1990s the issue confronting most police administrators is no longer *whether* to authorize semi-automatic weapons, but which weapons to allow, what training needs to be provided to officers, and what the consequences are of the decisions made.

In our discussion of fatality rates and hit rates in Chapter 3, we reported some of the data currently available in published and unpublished studies considering the implications of changing the police service weapon from a revolver to a semi-automatic handgun (usually, a 9-millimeter pistol). Here, we focus somewhat more on the policy dimensions of this question, presenting some additional data and referring to certain data introduced earlier.

In favor of semi-automatics some in the profession argue that they will give police both a psychological and a tactical advantage as they increasingly face offenders armed with semi- or even fully automatic weapons.[64] More specifically, experts suggest that many semi-automatics can provide greater accuracy; and, of course, they make more rounds available to officers without reloading (typically between 15 and 20, compared with the six rounds available in most revolvers) (Matulia 1985; Pagano 1984; Krajick 1990). The head of the Atlanta Police Department's training academy expressed the view that a semi-automatic pistol's principal benefit to officers who carry it is in the area of confidence-building rather than life saving. "Most of our officers who have been killed," he declared, "never got off a round" (Maj. Jimmy Hall, quoted in Krajick 1990: 59).

Some leaders in the profession, notably former Police Commissioner Lee P. Brown of the NYPD (*New York Times* 1992b; Verhovek 1992, 1992a; Fritsch 1992, 1992a), and some scholars (e.g., Edwards 1991a, 1991b; McCauley and Edwards 1990, James Fyfe—interviewed in Malcolm 1990) are not at all sanguine about allowing officers assigned to routine patrol duties to switch from revolvers to semi-automatics. They point to experiences since the 1970s in which semi-automatics were disproportionately involved in accidental police firearm discharges, injuring police and civilians (not infrequently bystanders) alike (e.g., Geller and Karales 1981a; Fritsch 1992, 1992a; Brown 1992: 3). They suggest, moreover, that greater gains in officer safety could be accomplished by making the wearing of soft body armor mandatory and by providing better and more training (Malcolm 1990).

In the Chicago Police Department, where, like other agencies, prior research documented the way in which semi-automatics present career risks to police officers, former Superintendent LeRoy Martin took a strong stand *against* an agency-wide switch from

---

[64] To illustrate the presence of semi-automatic and fully automatic weapons in the criminal population, Bratton (1990a), citing data furnished by the NYPD's Planning and Management Unit, reports that, in the first six months of 1990, the NYPD confiscated 9,794 weapons, of which 3,562 (36 percent) were semi- or fully automatic weapons.

revolvers to semi-automatics as his officers' *primary* weapons until all officers had been instructed and demonstrated range proficiency with semi-automatics (L. Martin 1990; Fritsch 1992, 1992a; see also Matulia 1985: 69, 73).[65] This meant that new recruits, whose basic training included instruction and certification in the use of semi-automatics, could carry pistols as their primary weapons, but veteran officers could carry semi-automatics only as a secondary weapon until they received training and were found qualified in the use of semi-automatics (and paid for the weapons themselves) (Spielman 1992). On the eve of his retirement as chief, Martin finally yielded to continuing rank-and-file pressure and, in February 1992, said he would issue an order authorizing semi-automatics as the *primary* weapon for all Chicago police officers (*ibid.*).

Although data from the 1980s are only starting to become available in published reports, Alpert (1989a), in an unpublished consulting study, discovered that, in the Metro-Dade, Florida, Police Department, "most of the purposeful and accidental shootings [from 1984 through mid-1988] involved revolvers. However, accidental discharges involving semi-automatic weapons and shotguns were disproportionate" (Alpert 1989a: 5). Out of 226 incidents from 1984 through June 1988 in which Metro-Dade police officers

"Noting that nearly half of the 39 [NYPD] officers shot last year had either wounded themselves or were accidentally shot by fellow officers [New York City Mayor David] Dinkins warned that the number would surely rise if semi-automatics became standard issue for the department" (Law Enforcement News 1992e).

discharged their weapons, in 140 (62 percent) the involved officers used revolvers. In 36 (16 percent), the officers used either semi-automatics (35 incidents) or fully automatic handguns (1 incident). The officers using revolvers fired purposefully in 81 percent of their shots-fired incidents. By contrast, the officers using semi-automatics fired purposefully in only 46 percent of their incidents. Figure 73 displays the Metro-Dade data graphically.

Although we do not know from these data (or from the study from which they were drawn) what percentage of Metro-Dade officers carried revolvers and what percentage carried semi-automatic weapons as their weapon of first choice in a combat situation, we do see from Figure 73 that semi-automatics represent a much larger percentage of accidental shootings than they do of purposeful shootings. Of the 46 accidental shootings shown in this figure (an additional 15 entailed use of shotguns and another 4 use of assault rifles), 19 (41 percent) involved officers using semi-automatic weaponry. By contrast, 16 of the 129 displayed

---

[65] Martin, noting that Chicago officers who had demonstrated suitable weapons proficiency had long had the option to carry a semi-automatic pistol as a secondary weapon, argued that it is important to have a high degree of standardization among police service weapons (and among ammunition) so that officers can use one another's weapons and ammunition when needed during combat situations (L. Martin 1990; see also Matulia 1985: 73; Bratton 1990a). It is also important that on- and off-duty pistols be similar in operation so that officers keep the chances of confusion to a minimum (Leslie 1992).

Former Superintendent Martin's and other police administrators' reservations about semi-automatic weaponry stemmed at least in part from historical patterns in which pistols malfunctioned or were mishandled more often than revolvers. For example, Geller and Karales (1981a: 98) reported that in 32.5 percent (13) of the instances in which Chicago officers accidentally shot themselves during the period 1974 through 1978, the weapon was a semi-automatic. Bratton (1990a) and others have argued that more recent design improvements have remedied the problems with pistols so that they now are no more likely than revolvers to jam or discharge accidentally.

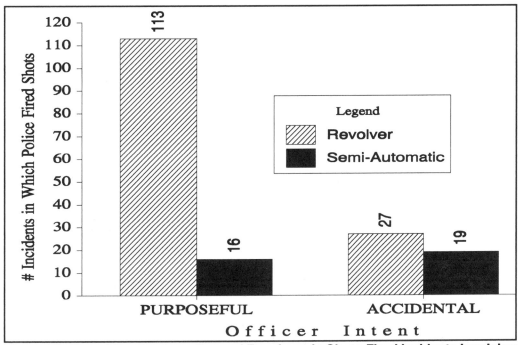

Figure 73: Use of Semi-automatics and Revolvers in Shots-Fired Incidents Involving Metro-Dade Police, 1/84-6/88   *Source: Alpert (1989a).*

purposeful shots-fired incidents entailed use of semi-automatic weapons—just 12 percent of the total.

The NYPD's experience between mid-1989 and mid-1992 showed "that there are nearly 14 accidental discharges per 1,000 semi-automatic pistols compared to .75 (less than 1) [for] .38 calibre revolvers" (Brown 1992: 3). Former Commissioner Brown explained one of the reasons why semi-automatics are prone to unintentional firing: There is a

> "two-step process to unload a semi-automatic pistol. The first action is to drop the magazine; the second action is to clear the chamber by pulling back the slide and ejecting a remaining round of ammunition. If the order is reversed, with the slide pulled back first followed by dropping the magazine, a bullet will be left in the chamber. This one bullet in an 'unloaded' gun poses a threat to police officers on the job, their families at home, and innocent bystanders in the street" (Brown 1992: 3).

A quite different pattern of the involvement of semi-automatics in intentional and accidental police firearms discharges emerges from a look at the experience over ten years in Santa Ana, California. There, as Figure 74 shows, although semi-automatics dominate among accidental discharge incidents, they also dominate among intentional discharge incidents. This suggests two things: that the semi-automatic was the most prevalent weapon in the Department during this period (a fact confirmed by correspondence with the agency (Santa Ana Police Department 1991), and that semi-automatics did not figure more prominently in accidental discharge than in intentional discharge incidents. Combining the ten-year data, semi-automatic pistols were used in 52 percent of the 81 *intentional* discharge incidents; revolvers were used in 47 percent; and shotguns in 21 percent (the three percentages total

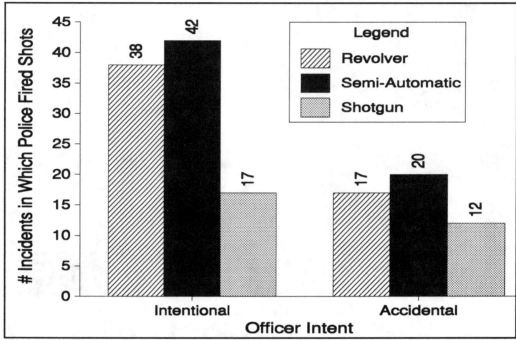

Figure 74: Type of Gun Used in Shots-Fired Incidents Involving Santa Ana Police, 1981-90   *Source: Santa Ana Police Department (1991).*

more than 100 percent because officers in some incidents used more than one type of firearm). By comparison, in the 49 *accidental* discharge incidents from 1981 through 1990, Santa Ana officers used semi-automatic pistols in 41 percent, revolvers in 35 percent, and shotguns in 25 percent (Santa Ana Police Department 1991) (the numbers exceed 100 percent due to rounding). Thus, accounting for all weapons used in all incidents, the semi-automatic is actually more prevalent in intentional than in accidental firearms discharges over the period studied.

Concerns about *accidental* discharges are not the only reason some police executives are ambivalent about semi-automatic pistols. The argument also is offered that, despite the limited available evidence (e.g., the LAPD study and the study conducted by the New York City Transit Police, both discussed in Chapter 3) officers using semi-automatics will, with troublesome frequency, fire an excessive number of rounds, at least in certain types of incidents (Fritsch 1992). Still, the risk of unintended shootings seems to be a predominant concern. It is suggested that, like most of the semi-automatics on the market during the

> *"In 1986 [an] officer responded to a man-with-a-gun call and a gun battle ensued. The officer, wearing his protective vest, was reloading his service revolver when the assailant walked up and shot him in the head with a 9 mm semi-automatic handgun"* (New York State Police 1989: 7).

1970s, many of today's offerings also have a dangerously light trigger pull—at least after the first round is fired—which makes unintended discharges more likely.

Although the Chicago Police Department had already approved officers' use of 45 different models of semi-automatic pistols, former Chicago Police Superintendent LeRoy Martin opposed adoption of the "Glock 17," asserting that it has a "hair trigger" and consequently is prone to "accidental discharges." A leading opponent of the Glock semi-automatics is Chicago Police Department firearms examiner Richard W. Chenow. After three years of evaluation of the Glock, Chenow said that the weapon's

> "short trigger travel 'is what makes the gun dangerous'.... The standard revolver and the newest generation of semi-automatics can be fired only by exerting a constant heavy pressure on the trigger for the entire distance that the trigger moves, Mr. Chenow said. The Glock trigger, however, has a substantial amount of slack before it reaches a point of resistance" (Fritsch 1992a).

Department officials and city aldermen, who were pushing introduction of this 46th model of semi-automatic,[66] indicated an intent to meet with the manufacturer to see whether modifications could be made to the pistol (the addition of a safety and a stronger trigger pull) to allay concerns. A Glock spokesperson said the trigger pull had been increased for other big-city departments, but said addition of a safety would not be considered, since other pistols approved by the Chicago Police Department also lacked a safety (Spielman 1992a; Kass 1992; see also Fritsch 1992a). The former Chicago chief was not alone, however, in favoring an external, manually operated ("active") safety on semi-automatic pistols (see McClain 1989: 36).

Other proponents of the semi-automatic (e.g., Sweeney 1990, Bratton 1990, New York City Transit Police 1991: 31-32), suggest that some of the semi-automatics currently on the market have a trigger tension much closer to that associated with most service revolvers. For instance, two models of Smith and Wesson 9-millimeter pistols have approximately an 8-pound trigger pull, entailing double-action firing on *every* shot. Similarly, the Colt model 2000 pistol, introduced in 1991, has an 8-pound trigger pull on every shot, which Colt technicians claim "is virtually identical to that of a double action revolver" (Clede 1991: 8). This was also the case, however, with the Glock to which the Chicago police chief objected—on the ground that his personnel were accustomed to their service revolvers' 12-pound trigger pull.[67] By contrast, the semi-automatic pistols adopted by the New York City Transit Police have a trigger pull of 11 pounds instead of a 10-pound pull on the agency's service revolvers and a 2.5-pound

> *"Clearly the decision [to convert from revolver to semi-automatic] is far more complicated than just the desire for increased firepower. A department's firearms policy probably needs revision; transitional training—including the training of the trainers—definitely needs to be considered. Factors individual to the agency and the community deserve to be deliberated" (Edwards 1991b).*

---

[66] The three aldermen pushing the adoption of the Glock 17 all were themselves former Chicago police officers (Spielman 1992a; Kass 1992). The talk among the local press was that at least one of them had a business relationship in which he stood to profit from a departmental decision to adopt the Glock pistol. In Chicago it has long been standard operating procedure for the pundits (and prosecutors) to look for corruption in every alderman and for aldermen in every corruption scandal.

[67] The disparity between the trigger pressure required for some revolvers and some semi-automatics is even larger. Some revolvers require approximately 14 pounds of pressure (about the pressure required to push a thumbtack into a piece of wood), while many automatics require between 8 and 10 pounds of trigger pressure (about the effort needed to push a tack into a piece of cardboard) (Zane 1992).

trigger pull when the revolvers are cocked (New York City Transit Police 1991: 32). As indicated, some semi-automatics have a heavy, long trigger pull on the first shot but a much lighter and shorter pull for subsequent shots (Matulia 1985: 73; Sweeney 1990)—a result of the slide drawing back into the cocked position after each shot fired. A common configuration of trigger pressure and pull is 10 to 12 pounds and a long, smooth pull on the first shot and 4-6 pounds and a short pull on subsequent shots (McClain 1989: 36). As noted above, however, it is possible for pistols to have double-action on every shot, as well as a trigger pull comparable to that of revolvers (*ibid.*: 37; Clede 1991: 8).

Supporters of semi-automatics also contend that the early experience with such pistols has *not* shown an inclination on the part of officers to fire a significantly greater number of rounds per incident. As noted in Chapter 3 and in this chapter, the early evidence seemed to support this contention; more recently, the experience has been mixed. In Chapter 3 we saw that a study by the LAPD found that the average number of shots fired by officers per incident increased by one round after use of 9-millimeter semi-automatics became widespread within the agency (Krajick 1990). And an informal survey of 17 police agencies in New York State during 1990 by the New York City Transit Police revealed an increase in average number of shots fired per incident

The president of a Fraternal Order of Police chapter "has waged a four-year campaign for [adoption by his police department of] semiautomatics [and] said the [recent] shooting of two police officers at a...currency exchange underscores the need for more police firepower. He noted that [the female officer on the scene] 'ran out of ammunition in a shootout with three guys carrying fully automatic weapons.... She got one of them. If she had a semiautomatic, she may have been able to shoot all three. She was holding her own until she ran out of ammunition' " (Spielman 1992).

following a switch from revolvers to semi-automatics of less than one round (Bratton 1990). But the NYPD in mid-1992 reported experiences with both its own officers and those in the New York City Transit Police Department in which officers using semi-automatics fired twice the number of rounds as their colleagues using revolvers (Brown 1992: 3).

As we observed earlier in this book, whether an increase of just one round per incident is important or not will depend on a vigorous appraisal of what seems to be happening with that round: Are suspects struck more often? Killed more often? Are bystanders struck more often? Are fellow officers struck more often? Are officers', victims', and bystanders' lives saved because of the additional shots fired or because of the knowledge on the part of offenders that police have enhanced firepower?

"The National Rifle Association...takes no position on the 9-millimeter guns. 'However, it's an unassailable fact that almost all gunfights are over in three shots or less,' said James Baker, the association's director of Federal affairs. 'And a large clip of ammunition is no substitute for intensive training' " (Malcolm 1990).

The IACP made a preliminary study of the relationship between officer safety and service weapon type. Its research question and answer, as of 1985, was: "[A]re more officers who are using a .38 calibre weapon murdered as a result of their weapon's inability to stop a suspect? We find no evidence to this theory" (Matulia 1985: 73). James Fyfe and other researchers argue that the drop in the number of police murdered nationwide (down to 65 in 1990 and a March 1992 preliminary count of 69 in 1991) is attributable to "beefed-up officer training and the increased use of bullet-resistant vests—not heavier weaponry" (Krajick 1990: 59). Moreover, a NYPD study,[68] summarized by Matulia (1985: 73), "indicated that it was not the size, shape, configuration, composition, calibre or velocity of the bullet which performed the task [of effectively and quickly stopping a violent offender]. It was the placement which stopped the assailant."

Despite the rapid and widespread adoption of semi-automatics by officers coast to coast, there is no consensus among police weapons experts at this point on many issues pertaining to handgun and ammunition selection (see generally, Pilant 1992). Many police professionals disagree that the results of the LAPD study and the informal New York State survey are representative of the experience nationwide. Range instructors also question whether such research findings are a fair indication of the shooting experience that can reasonably be predicted as more and more semi-automatics find their way into police holsters. The Police Executive Research Forum in 1991 surveyed the nation's largest police departments to explore their policy stance and track record with revolvers and semi-automatics (Carter, et al. 1991). Other such surveys will be conducted periodically by other professional police organizations and, undoubtedly, by weapons manufacturers.

> *The Metropolitan Police Department in Washington, D.C., converted from revolvers to 9-millimeter semi-automatic pistols as the primary weapon for several reasons. One cited by former Chief Maurice Turner was that "there had developed an apparent new willingness by the criminal element to fire on the police with little provocation. Without a doubt, we were being challenged for control of our streets by criminals who were well armed and not at all hesitant to use their weapons against the police and innocent citizens of our community" (Turner 1989).*

Attempting to pull together a wide array of assertions made about the relative advantages of revolvers and semi-automatics, Matulia (1985: 73) during the mid-1980s summarized key arguments offered on both sides.[69] Combining his contribution with arguments advanced by Bratton (1991a: 3), Glock company spokespersons (quoted in Malcolm 1990), police executives (e.g., Turner 1989), the FBI (McClain 1989: 30, 32), and a Police Executive Research Forum national survey of police departments serving populations of 50,000 or larger, we may summarize these various arguments as follows:[70]

---

[68] Matulia (1985: 91) does not provide a full citation to the study, entitled "Analysis of Police Combat Situations, 1854-79."

[69] Some of these arguments will assume greater or lesser importance as technological developments lead to modifications in weapon features. For instance, Krajick (1990: 58), having interviewed weapons experts around the nation, reported that "recent advances in design have made pistols less likely to jam."

[70] Some readers may feel like reviewing at length the arguments for and against adoption of semi-automatics is a largely academic exercise, given that the vast majority of American police agencies have already authorized their officers to use semi-automatics. But it takes little imagination to surmise that there will come days in various cities when tragic uses of police guns will be attributed to the adoption of semi-automatics in the escalating arms race with criminals. At such times, public officials who must issue reasonably informative statements explaining the issues surrounding the revolver to semi-automatic transition may appreciate a summary such as the one which follows in the text.

Arguments in favor of the revolver include:

(1) the revolver can be more safely carried and loaded;

(2) it is less subject to malfunction (misfires, feeding, extraction and ejection problems) because it has fewer moving parts than a pistol;[71]

(3) the revolver will not jam when a cartridge misfires;[72]

(4) dropping a partially full magazine from a semi-automatic on a hard surface can result in the remaining rounds moving so that the magazine will not fire;

(5) the long double-action trigger movement and heavy trigger pull minimize the possibility of an unintentional shot;

(6) lack of a safety permits firing with either hand;

(7) revolvers are easier to lock at home using a lock or handcuffs;

(8) the automatic must be cleaned more frequently;[73] and

(9) the ammunition typically used in semi-automatics has a greater tendency than ammunition suitable for use in revolvers to ricochet and penetrate targets beyond what

---

[71] Special problems with semi-automatics can arise when shooting next to barricades or other hard objects because "contact of the slide against a hard surface may cause resistance and result in the pistol not cycling." Further, "when firing a semi-automatic from the left side of a barricade...ejected casings [could] bounce off a wall and back into the ejection port of the weapon" since the spent cartridges eject to the right in most pistols (McClain 1989: 37). And "officers should be aware that if the slide of a semi-automatic is pressed back about one-fourth of an inch (such as against someone during a struggle, etc.), the weapon may be taken out of 'battery' and may not fire." Finally, "semi-automatic pistols are designed to be fired with a very firm 'locked-in-place' grip. 'Limp-wristing' may cause the pistol to malfunction" (*ibid.*; but on specifications for "limp-wrist firing capability, see Castricone [1989: 42]). A reported design-flaw in one model of 10-millimeter semi-automatic pistol used by some police agencies in Virginia and Oklahoma is discussed in *Crime Control Digest* (1991f). The Edmond, Oklahoma, Police Department alerted police agencies nationwide in April 1991 that two of its 10-millimeter pistols "had fired...without an officer pulling the trigger." The next month, the FBI announced a recall from its agents of 750 10-millimeter pistols because, on several occasions, the weapons "jammed or the trigger would not work" (*ibid.*).

[72] The NYPD, skeptical of claims that 1992 models of semi-automatics have overcome problems of jamming, reported (Brown 1992: 2):

"In [a] recent incident [involving a NYPD officer in the pilot program with Glock semi-automatics], after the officer fired one round, the shell casing did not eject from his 9mm weapon. A semi-automatic pistol is inoperable if the expended round is not cleared from the chamber. In this case the officer was rendered defenseless. The Albany and Buffalo Police Departments have also discovered that the semi-automatics have a tendency to jam. Interestingly, semi-automatics cause problems for suspects as well as law enforcement officers. During 1991, there were 12 incidents in which semi-automatic weapons used by armed felons misfired. This finding alone justifies extreme caution in considering a move to replace a revolver with a semi-automatic as the authorized service weapon for *all* New York City police officers."

[73] Cleaning certain brands of semi-automatic pistols can be a dangerous process unless officers are well trained. The Glock comes in for particular criticism by some experts:

"One of the Glock's most troubling features, in the view of some, is the necessity of pulling the trigger in order to dismantle the weapon for cleaning. No other brand of semi-automatic requires a trigger pull for cleaning. That feature can lead to unintentional firing, as it apparently did in [a] 1990 incident in New York" (Fritsch 1992a).

is tactically desirable.[74]

Arguments in favor of the 9-millimeter semi-automatic include:

(1) a larger magazine capacity (more rounds of ammunition);

(2) faster reloading ("the insertion of a magazine is faster than a revolver 'speedloader,' which requires much more precision to align properly, especially under stressful conditions" (McClain 1989: 30);

(3) extra ammunition magazines are less bulky to carry than ammunition for revolvers (especially when stored in "speedloaders");

(4) greater accuracy—partly because of the lighter trigger pull and partly due to less recoil than revolvers produce;

(5) can be aimed while reloading—or at least "while reloading a semi-automatic, an officer's vision can remain focused on the target," which is "impossible when reloading a revolver" (McClain 1989: 30);

> *Loud (1990: 51), quoting two firearms experts, challenges the advantages of larger magazine capacity. It's "not that important," they argue. "These tactical problems are over very quickly...you will run out of time before you will run out of bullets. You don't want 'firepower.' You want to be able to hit your target with the first shot'. * * * 'Firepower' is an appropriate concept in military situations, not in domestic defensive shooting. Main Street is not a battlefield...you have to be concerned where each and every bullet goes."*

(6) greater dependability (e.g., "most auto-loader malfunctions can usually be 'cleared' almost instantaneously by the shooter, while revolver malfunctions often require repair by a gunsmith"—McClain 1989: 30; and problems with "certain older model semi-automatic pistols 'jamming' because they were overly 'ammunition sensitive'...have [been] overcome"—*ibid.*: 37);

(7) simpler to use;

(8) easier to clean and require cleaning less frequently (cleaning required after firing approximately 1,500-2,000 rounds, whereas revolvers must be cleaned after firing 200-300 rounds);[75]

(9) if automatic is taken from the officer, unfamiliarity with safety may gain valuable time;

(10) can easily transfer a full magazine to a downed officer;

(11) less expensive: although most semi-automatic pistols cost twice as much as most revolvers, in the long-run pistols may be more economical because they are more

---

[74] Brown (1992: 3) explained:

> "Semi-automatic ammunition is often jacketed to improve the cycling of each round through the magazine into the chamber. Jacketed ammunition has a greater propensity to penetrate targets and ricochet upon impact.... [T]hese bullets threaten the safety of police officers and civilians. Some police departments reduce this danger by using lower velocity ammunition. However, this reduces the cycling efficiency of the gun and could cause the weapon to jam."

[75] Obviously, the experts and proponents of different types of handguns disagree on whether revolvers or semi-automatics need to be cleaned more often (see item number 8 under the list above in the text of arguments in favor of revolvers). See footnote 73 on a danger in cleaning certain pistols.

durable. The life expectancy of the all-steel pistol and, reportedly, of the lighter-weight polymer-frame pistol is 10 to 25 years, whereas the life expectancy of a revolver may be as short as five years. But the service life of the *alloy* pistol, which, like the polymer-frame weapon, weighs less than the all-steel, will be shorter than that of either the all-steel or the polymer version (McClain 1989: 32, 34);

(12) safer than a revolver;

(13) less muzzle flash than a revolver;

(14) no more likely than a revolver to discharge accidentally, in part because the first shot is double-action[76] and hence requires a long trigger pull and a reasonably heavy pressure on the trigger (McClain 1989: 32);

(15) less "training fatigue" because the recoil is "cushioned" by the functioning of the weapon instead of being transmitted to the trainee;

(16) has the stopping power of a .45;

(17) no more destructive than a .38 revolver, when comparable ammunition is used; and

(18) more comparable to criminals' weapons than the revolver (Matulia 1985: 73; Carter, et al. 1991: 11; Bratton 1991a: 3; McClain 1989; Turner 1989).

An undercover narcotics detective opened the trunk of his car, the pre-arranged signal to fellow officers stationed a block away to move in for the arrest. But the heavy fog prevented them from seeing the opened trunk lid, and the drug dealer soon panicked, assaulting the officer. During the assault, the officer's semi-automatic changed hands several times, but neither the officer nor the offender was able to fire it since the safety had not been released. It was the closest this officer came to being shot on the job during his 12-year assignment to undercover narcotics enforcement (Palermo 1990).

An officer "fought off three heavily armed opponents in a wild, 60-round gunfight with his revolver in 1988. His backup—who was carrying a 9-mm—was killed before he got a chance to draw. [The officer] survived by emptying his gun repeatedly, then diving for cover where he reloaded. Now he carries a 16-shot Sig-Sauer 9-mm semiautomatic and two extra magazines. 'Things might have happened very differently that day,' he says. 'I'm more comfortable having 16 to start with' " (Krajick 1990: 59).

There are not only operational but public relations considerations in the adoption of a service weapon. In some instances, the public may see police switching to a higher-powered,

---

[76] McClain (1989: 32) notes that most police agencies seem to favor a semi-automatic pistol that has "double action" on the first shot:

> "While world class-level combat pistol competition shooters continue to tout the assets of the single-action semi-automatic, most police agencies favor the double-action pistol. The long first-shot trigger pull of the double-action is seen as a safety feature and transition is simplified by its similarity to the traditionally carried double-action revolver. Single-action 'cocked and locked' semi-automatics are usually reserved for specialized units (SWAT, etc.), whose needs may be unique and whose training is more frequent and intensive."

As with other comparisons between revolvers and semi-automatics, experts differ concerning the likelihood of unintended discharges. NYPD Deputy Inspector John C. Cerar, commanding officer of the Department's Firearms and Tactics Section, said that all brands of semi-automatic pistols "have features that will lead to more accidental discharges than revolvers" (Fritsch 1992a).

larger capacity handgun as a positive way of controlling crime and violence; yet others may see police participation in the "arms race"[77] as contributing to hostilities and bloodshed. To bring insight to the continuing debate over the relative operational and public relations advantages of revolvers and semi-automatic pistols (and different types of ammunition), Alpert (1989a), Matulia (1985: 73-74), and others suggest the collection of the following kinds of data within police agencies:[78]

> *"[T]he 9 mm represents more than just a change in equipment. Whether we like it or not, the 9 mm has become a symbol of management's willingness to do what is necessary to assist and protect our officers as they carry out their dangerous tasks. Failure to respond to our officers' concerns about safety and their ability to meet the challenge of the well-armed criminal can only court skepticism about management's dedication to those who risk their lives to make our cities a safer place to live and work" (Turner 1989).*

- The types of weapons and ammunition used by offenders whom police have shot at.

- The types of weapons and ammunition used by officers who have purposefully shot at criminal suspects.

- The types of weapons and ammunition used by officers who have accidentally discharged their weapons.

- The types of weapons and ammunition used by offenders to shoot at police.

- The types of weapons used by officers and suspects in "incidents when police were justified to shoot but selected other means to resolve the situation" (Alpert 1989a: 2)—what we have referred to in this book as "averted shootings" or "potentially violent encounters." These incidents would include encounters in which police were fired on but did not shoot back.

- The number and types of weapons confiscated from arrestees.

- The shooting proficiency (hit rate, stopping power, speed of using the weapon, speed and ease of reloading, etc.) of officers with different types of weapons and ammunition

---

[77] New York City Police Inspector John Cerar, commanding officer of the Firearms and Tactics Section, has been particularly skeptical of police participation in an arms race with criminals:

> "[Y]ou have to define 'out-gunned.' If a criminal out there has an AK-47, does that mean we have to have AK-47s with at least the same capacity of rounds? Is that how we out-gun? If someone throws a hand grenade at an officer, does that mean we throw two back? Where do you stop? Are we protectors of life and property, or are we military units?" (Pilant 1992: 35).

As noted earlier in this chapter in our discussion of shooting proficiency training, police firearms experts concur that "stopping power"—the ability to immobilize instantly an opponent—comes not from bigger bullets but from better bullet *placement* (*ibid.*; McCarthy 1992).

[78] Few agencies could or would collect *all* of this information and tabulate it. But practitioners should consider this variety of potentially important issues and determine for themselves which pieces they are able to compile most efficiently and usefully.

(both at the range and in combat situations).

- The comparative reliability of different types of handguns (risk of jamming, misfiring, accidentally discharging during weapon maintenance operations, etc.).

- The comparative ease of maintaining different types of handguns in peak working order.

- The number of shots fired at police by criminal suspects using different types of weapons.

- The number of rounds fired by police in combat situations using different types of weapons and ammunition.

- The difficulties in adequately training and controlling police who will be using semi-automatic weapons as their standard service weapon.

> *"In a 1986 shoot-out, FBI agents with 9-mms fatally wounded a Miami gunman armed with an assault rifle—but he lived long enough to kill two of them and wound five. So this year [1990] the FBI began issuing pistols that shoot 10-mm rounds, designed to create greater 'tissue displacement'—4.11 cubic inches per shot, measured in ballistic gelatin, versus 2.82 for a 9-mm. The FBI is a trendsetter; already at least three state agencies have bought new 10-mms" (Krajick 1990:59).*

- Any special "environmental" conditions likely to be encountered by the subject police agency that would make semi-automatics particularly suitable or unsuitable in certain types of situations. For instance, in late 1990 the New York City Transit Police Department mounted a marketing campaign to shift the opinions of relevant authorities and the public away from the presumption that use of 9-millimeter pistols by police in subway cars and subway stations would be inherently risky to innocent bystanders.[79] Police professionals debated the issue hotly, in an exchange of views likely to be replayed many times in many locales over the next several years.

---

[79] Then-Chief Bill Bratton of the New York City Transit Police, interviewed by *Newsweek* magazine at the time, argued: "If you have to shoot more than once or twice, you could hit a bystander. The pistol is safer." An FBI trainer echoed the point: "The primary thing is that [semi-automatics are] easy for most people to shoot well." Others observed that "some smaller officers have trouble gripping and aiming the .38" (Krajick 1990: 58). As shown in Table E-66 in Appendix E, the limited experience of the NYPD since mid-1989 with the several hundred semi-automatic pistols (Glock 19s) the agency has issued on an experimental basis has been that officers firing at other persons intentionally have hit them with 33 percent of the rounds fired (Cerar 1989, 1990, 1991). This is not a dramatic departure from *bullet* hit rates obtained by NYPD members with other weapons (see discussion in Chapter 3 under the subheadings related to "hit rates").

On June 15, 1992, it was announced that the experiment with semi-automatics in the NYPD will expand from 613 officers, who carried Glocks during the past several years, to a total of more than 1,600 officers. The 1,000 additional officers will carry various brands of semi-automatics so that the strengths and weaknesses of each may be assessed. The Department's decision to expand field testing of semi-automatics resulted from an agreement reached by then-Police Commissioner Lee Brown and the Patrolmen's Benevolent Association and other lobbying groups that pushed the New York State Legislature in 1992 to pass a law requiring the City police force to issue semi-automatics to its officers over the objections of the police leadership. In exchange, the legislation was killed (Lyall 1992; Fritsch 1992, 1992a; Verhovek 1992).

Among other sources, the NYPD's annual report on firearms discharges by its personnel and armed assaults against them provides very helpful statistical summaries of gunfights, including information about the weapons used, hit rates, and the like. Studies of the slaying of police officers being conducted as this book goes to press by the FBI and the Police Foundation, under National Institute of Justice sponsorship, might also be good sources of information on some of the topics listed above (see also FBI 1992e).

"Traditionally, police have been armed to the same degree as...the criminals or the populace they serve. In 19th century cities of Eastern America, the civilian population was not widely armed and neither were the police. In the wild west, firearms were a necessary tool because most of the population was armed with firearms" (Rivetti 1987: 1).

Whether or not a department changes from one type of sidearm to another, there is the separate question, touched on above, of whether a department might want to customize its sidearms in the interests of officer safety and the protection of innocent persons. Some departments have physically modified police service *revolvers* (in 1983, the Miami Police Department, which in 1987 switched to semi-automatics, changed all service revolvers from "single/double action to double action only"—Alpert 1989b: 486; see also Nilson 1990). Some agencies have purchased "spurless hammer" revolvers to preclude the intentional or accidental cocking of the weapon. Cocked weapons have led to many accidental shootings by police without, in the view of many experts, affording offsetting safety benefits (see data and expert opinions reported in Geller and Karales 1981a: 199-200, 246, 256-261; Matulia 1985: 87-88). In its model deadly force policy, the IACP takes the position: "The authorized revolvers will be modified to ensure double action capability only" (Matulia 1985: 73). The IACP explains:

"In the event that the policymaker chooses the revolver [over a semi-automatic pistol], there is a demonstrated need to modify the weapons to ensure double-action capability only [citing Geller and Karales 1981a]. This modification is recommended to reduce accidental discharges and possible injury to officers and others. There is no tactical advantage to be gained by using a single action mode" (Matulia 1985: 74).

As noted earlier concerning the debate in early 1992 over adoption of Glock pistols in Chicago, it is also possible for departments—at least large ones—to order certain custom modifications of semi-automatic pistols. We saw earlier that some of the proponents of the move to semi-automatics insist that the way to avoid the potential dangers of misfiring or accidental discharges when officers use pistols is to mandate that the pistols fire in the double-action mode on *all* shots, not just on the first shot, as some semi-automatics do (see, e.g., Sweeney 1990).

"With the growing sense that they are outgunned by the criminal element, police officers no longer feel the confidence of a seldom-used but always reliable .38 revolver. Indeed, on the first day of semi-automatic availability in [the] Corpus Christi [Police Department], over 10 percent of department personnel singed up to purchase the more expensive firearm, and there was a noticeable rise in morale" (Sullivan 1989: 49).

Optimism has long been expressed that *training* can help enormously in averting unwanted discharges of semi-automatic pistols and revolvers. For instance, in the late 1970s, Yount and O'Rourke (1978: 76), both police trainers, estimated, based on empirical research on Illinois police accidental gun discharges, that it is possible to prevent more than 91 percent of all such firings. McClain (1989: 34) concurs: "It is the *training*, not the weapon selected, that will be the most important factor in the success (or failure)" of a department's program to convert from one type of sidearm to another.

2.   *Less-than-Lethal Weapons: Considerations in Their Adoption and Continued Use*

In 1969 the National Commission on the Causes and Prevention of Violence (National Commission 1969, 1970: 155) called on the "federal government [to] join with private industry to speed the development of an effective non-lethal weapon," adding that the Commission "consider[s] this recommendation to be of the utmost importance." It was tempting then and remains so now to hope for technological and scientific solutions to human problems, whether hunger, poverty, disease, or violence. Technology and science may eventually provide police with a tool that nonviolently and instantly immobilizes

> *"The ideal nonlethal weapon would be hand-held, operated by one officer who would carry it on the equipment belt, allowing appropriate distance to be maintained between the officer and the suspect, temporarily yet harmlessly incapacitating to only the intended target, and easy to use and maintain" (Meyer 1992: 4; see also Meyer 1992a).*

adversaries—like the "phasers" or ray guns of science fiction fame. In the near term, however, less-than-lethal devices clearly have been conceived as *supplements* to, rather than substitutes for, firearms (see, e.g., Geller 1986). The hope is that, in the "force continuum" of options considered during any potentially violent encounter (the force continuum was discussed earlier in this chapter), less-than-lethal tools (and tactics) will suffice to accomplish the police objective.[80] At the same time, all who advocate the merits of less-than-lethal weapons readily acknowledge that some encounters are life-and-death-struggles calling for the prompt and decisive use of deadly force.

Before going further, definitional issues should be addressed with more precision: What is a less-than-lethal weapon? As Meyer (1991a: 10) observes, it is possible to define such weapons in terms of their effects, the tactics and situations for which they are suitable, and their objectives (e.g., shooting avoidance). He cites Peak's (1990: 9) definition of the desired effects of a successful less-than-lethal weapon:

> "...there is only a temporary effect and minimal medical implications to normally healthy subjects; there is a high probability of instantaneous control over a highly motivated suspect; and there are observable effects, with a high probability of affecting only the intended targets."

There are no guarantees that death will not occur in field confrontations with less-than-lethal weapons (see, e.g., Kansas City Police Department 1991: 31), but if used as designed these devices should not produce serious or permanent injuries except possibly to persons with

---

[80] It is because less-than-lethal weapons may be properly thought of as tools for averting shootings that they deserve discussion in a book on the causes and prevention of police-involved shootings.

unusual susceptibility (stemming, for instance, from heart problems or nervous system disorders). The general rule of thumb used by federal officials in classifying weapons at a national conference in 1986 was that a weapon qualified as less than lethal if it failed to kill 95 percent of the time (Sweetman 1987; Rivetti 1987). The question of how often a weapon meeting this requirement succeeded in effectively controlling suspects is a separate and crucial one. And even if a device fails to kill 95 percent of the time, police would still need to make decisions about its utility based on how often it produces nonlethal but moderate or serious injuries to suspects (Meyer 1991a).

Meyer (1981: 127) earlier offered a definition describing appropriate situations for using less-than-lethal weapons. These are

> "[d]evices which may be used to aggressively take control of a deteriorating tactical situation prior to that point in time when control holds, batons, or deadly force may become necessary;...when it is unsafe for an officer to move to within contact range of the suspect; and when attempts by the officer to control the suspect by conventional means will likely result in serious injury to officers, suspects, or both."

A number of agencies have experimented with nonlethal devices and are excellent sources of information based on both simulation and field testing. Two of the leading sources of innovation and expertise have long been the Los Angeles County Sheriff's Department (see Geller and Karales 1981a: 253) and the NYPD. For instance, the NYPD developed "blanket restraints," used to wrap extremely volatile prisoners for transportation to a detention facility; and when occasional problems arose with suspects overheating, the Department experimented successfully with putting more holes in the blankets (McCarthy 1992).[81] The Kansas City, Missouri, Police Department, too, has done careful appraisals of the utility of less-than-lethal devices. And the Justice Department's National Institute of Justice has built a knowledge base on less-than-lethal weaponry through its underwriting of military-based research and development over the past several years and, more recently, through its support of national surveys to discover issues and practices concerning police and corrections uses of such devices. One of the grantees working on unclassified less-than-lethal weapons research as this volume goes to press is the Institute for Law and Justice (ILJ), based in Alexandria, Virginia. ILJ was funded in the summer of 1991 to produce a summary of the state of the art and current and intended agency practices concerning less-than-lethal weaponry for dissemination to the field in 1993 (see also *Journal of Contemporary Criminal Justice* 1990).[82]

---

[81] Sometimes, individual police officers of necessity have devised ingenious, low-cost, highly effective nonlethal methods for protecting themselves and minimizing the risk of injuring their prisoners. For instance, tactics expert Ron McCarthy, when he was an officer in the LAPD, found he could minimize concerns about contracting diseases from a prisoner who tried to spit at officers by placing a common, full-face ski mask over the prisoner's head and turning it backward so the mouth hole was at the back of the head. The prisoner could breathe but could not spit through the knit cap (McCarthy 1992).

[82] The ILJ study was one of four described by the National Institute of Justice in congressional testimony on May 7, 1992, as responsive to the pressing national need for knowledge about the control of police abuse of force. The other three studies were an assessment of key issues facing the police profession and the nation (by the Police Executive Research Forum), a national survey of police agencies (to be conducted jointly by the Police Foundation and the IACP), and a study by Prince Georges County, Maryland, police psychologist Ellen Scrivner of the contribution that police

The LAPD, too, has undertaken a fair amount of in-house research on the feasibility of less-than-lethal weapons. Perhaps its most ambitious work has been done by Sergeant Greg Meyer when he served as the Department's "nonlethal weapons researcher" in 1979 and 1980 (Meyer 1991a: x) and, more recently, when he conducted an empirical analysis of the use of various less-than-lethal tools and techniques (Meyer, 1991, 1991a, 1992, 1992a). During his 1979-80 research, Meyer explored the possible utility of

"more than a dozen innovative devices. Some of the devices were eliminated from consideration after preliminary research disclosed that they failed to be reasonably safe and/or failed to effectively address the need to keep the factors of time and distance on the side of the officer. Eliminated were the following: animal 'come-alongs' (used by zoos and rely on the choking force of a wire around the neck); beanbag guns (deadly at close range); rubber bullets (apparently valuable only in riot control, deadly at close range); tranquilizing guns (used in animal control, but frequently lethal even when the drug dosage is adjusted for the particular animal's weight and dietary habits); and various close-range electrical shock devices (which require direct physical contact between the officers and subjects)" (Meyer 1991a: 11-12).

Before adopting a less-than-lethal weapon, or in evaluating the continued suitability of one for a particular police agency or unit, a variety of issues should be considered. Among these are the agency's or unit's specific needs (what kinds of situations does it handle for which such a device might be useful?), the utility of the device for meeting the identified needs, safety and operational efficiency questions, political and legal liability considerations, infrastructure considerations (training, policy, procedural support required, maintenance issues, etc.), and cost-benefit calculations. A brief overview of each of these follows.

■ **Needs Assessment.** What kinds of situations does the agency handle routinely (e.g., traffic stops, high-risk raids, and search warrant service) and on an extraordinary basis (e.g. hostage-barricade, civil unrest) where officers might benefit from the availability of the less-than-lethal weapon? Has the department's ability to safeguard officers using conventional weapons diminished with the advent of crack cocaine, PCP, steroids, and other drugs that enhance hostility and proclivity to violence? Has the department's ability to apprehend fleeing suspects suffered with the ruling in *Tennessee v. Garner* (1985) that police may not use deadly force to stop nonviolent fleeing suspects who pose no imminent threat of violence? As the Rodney King-related riots in Los Angeles and lesser civil unrest in other cities during April and May 1992 have made vividly clear, police confront the possibility of collective violence in the 1990s with crowd and riot control tactics and technologies that have changed little since the 1960s (see Serrano 1992a; L. Berger 1992a). Are there one or more nonlethal weapons that would enhance the ability of police to deal with collective violence in a more effective and humane fashion than occurred in the past three decades? Which devices are intended for use with large numbers of people, which ones are effective against small groups, and which ones are personal weapons (useful against only one person at a time)?

Besides types of incidents, departments must consider the practicality of any given less-than-lethal weapon in light of deployment options. Does a device have to be transported to the scene or can it be worn on officers' utility belts without adding so much weight that they

---

psychologists are making and could make to the prevention and remediation of police abuse of force (Civil Rights Subcommittee Hearings 1992).

can't maneuver freely and may incur hip injuries? How many officers does it take to use a device efficiently and effectively?

Does the device's utility depend on environmental conditions (weather, temperature, humidity, wind velocity, lighting, terrain, etc.)? If it rains frequently in the area, an electrical device that can produce unintended injuries under moist conditions would be a poor choice. If most of the needs for physical control tactics come during the evening shift, a device which works best in daylight could be of little value. By the same token, such weapons as flashbangs (discussed in the next section) work best in the dark because they depend partly on the abrupt transition from darkness to extreme brightness for their shock power.

Finally, at what kinds of locations do the officers most often have need for the less-than-lethal weapon under consideration? Some weapons work best (and with least risk of affecting untargeted persons, including the officers) in open spaces, others may work best indoors. Are the "hot spot" addresses at which police frequently need to handle potentially combative adversaries located in congested areas or in areas where innocent bystanders are unlikely to be endangered by the use of device?

 ▪ **Effectiveness.** How quickly does the weapon take full effect? How long does its effect last (enough time to take the individual into custody)? Does the device work consistently? How many times out of 1,000 uses will it fail to function as intended? What circumstances will produce the failure (e.g., design limitations, operator error, product failure, external conditions)? Among the external considerations are whether the device is variably effective against persons in different states of physical fitness, persons of varying body mass, persons with short-term or chronic health problems or conditions (e.g., epilepsy; heart condition, including persons equipped with heart pacemakers; psychotic individuals; pregnant women); persons under the influence of stimulant or depressant drugs or alcohol; and persons who take protective measures (e.g., covering skin, wearing gas masks, wearing soft body armor). Finally, over what range is the weapon effective: arm's length only, as with the hand-held impact weapons and stun guns; within a few yards, as with Mace and capsicum propelled by hand-held aerosol sprays and the TASER; or over longer distances, as with projectiles and tear gas, Mace, or capsicum launched in a canister or other delivery system?

 ▪ **Safety and Operational Efficiency.** Is the device at least as reliable and easy to use as a firearm? How controllable are the effects of the device? What is the risk that its effects will permeate an area (as with an airborne chemical), afflicting officers and other persons not targeted? Are there other, less obvious, risks to officers and bystanders (e.g., health hazards to officers who repeatedly use devices over a period of time)? How quickly can officers safely approach the subject against whom the weapon has been used without suffering some of its effects? For example, officers using some chemical weapons have a relatively small window of opportunity to move in and take custody of a subject; they need to wait long enough not to be affected by direct contact with the subject but to move quickly enough that the subject is still feeling the effects of the substance and not able to counterattack.

What are the risks of significant temporary injury, permanent injury, or death? (This is also a liability concern.) Meyer (1991a: 32), studying the injury patterns for TASERs, Mace, and several more conventional less-than-lethal tactics and weapons used by the LAPD, developed a five-part typology of injury that other analysts may find useful in future research (see also Meyer 1992a).[83] What are the weapon retention issues? Is it easy for the officer to maintain control of the device? Is it easier for an assailant to grab the device than it would be to grab the officer's sidearm? If an officer now has to be concerned about retention of multiple weapons (holstered firearm, baton hanging from a utility belt, and whatever additional nonlethal weapon the officer may have in hand), what tactics and grip design considerations arise? Since a fairly sizable percentage of officers in various jurisdictions have been slain with their own weapon after they lose a struggle to retain it, it is not fanciful to worry that a chemical spray canister, a TASER, stun gun, or impact weapon might be grabbed and turned on the officer.

If tactical considerations call for repeat applications of a device, is that feasible? For instance, how efficiently can a TASER, which is a single-shot device, be reloaded with electrodes to be fired a second time at a combative suspect? How would officers safely retrieve a capture net tossed off-target and how rapidly could they restore the net to its throwing position? How easy is it for officers to learn to use and remember how to use the device when they go long periods between field uses?

A special concern in evaluating the possible impact of any less-than-lethal weapon on officer safety is whether the weapon is likely to draw blood from suspects and to require officers, who themselves may be bleeding, to come into close contact with these suspects. Since suspects and officers may be bleeding from other causes than the use of a less-than-lethal weapon (e.g., either may have fallen during a foot chase), weapons that do not require direct contact between officer and suspect are desirable. As Meyer (1991a: 53) observes, "the AIDS virus presents a relatively new but compelling reason for police officers to adopt weapons and tactics which allow them to maintain distance between themselves and combative suspects."

- **Political and Legal Liability**. These two concepts are distinct but related. Given a sufficient political outrage over a device, courts or juries could determine that civil or criminal liability should be imposed against a department for using a particular weapon. For instance, stun guns or water cannons may be too reminiscent of the cattle prods and crowd dispersal tactics used to quell civil rights demonstrations to find political acceptance among those who remember those domestic struggles (compare the discussion of police dogs in Chapman [1990: 82-86]). It may be possible, through a creative public marketing campaign, in which the public has a fair opportunity to voice its concerns and learn about the advantages and drawbacks of various police weapons, to overcome initial resistance to a given less-than-lethal implement.

Even if a majority of the public, frightened of crime and willing to trade civil liberties for greater security, finds a particular weapon politically acceptable, departments may incur legal liability for using or abusing the weapons. Substantial damage awards have resulted from civil suits or settlements of suits over such tactics and tools as chokeholds and electrical or chemical devices that have proved more incendiary than anticipated. Even short of litigation,

---

[83] His injury categories and their definitions are as follows: "None=no injury"; "TASER/Gas=effects from TASER or chemical irritant spray only"; "Minor=complained of pain, minor scratches, skin redness"; "Moderate=small lacerations, welts, contusions, bruises"; and "Major=breaks, concussions, large lacerations or contusions, sprains, strains." This typology was used to portray injuries both to suspects and officers employing the weapons or tactics. Meyer explained the major injury category: "To qualify...officers had to have been placed off duty or on 'light' (non-field) duty; suspects were usually hospitalized" (Meyer 1991a: 32).

what has been the experience of other jurisdictions with civilian complaints of excessive force with a less-than-lethal weapon to internal affairs or other administrative investigators?

Far from least important, what is or can be expected to be the popularity of the device with working police officers? If there are general concerns among American police officers about the device or concerns specific to the history of a given police force or special unit, it may be unwise to attempt to force acceptance of an unwanted weapon. Still, a savvy marketing program that works for the public may overcome officer reluctance as well. What the public wants and what officers want may sometimes be quite different. The goal in any such marketing campaign should be a win-win situation, where no key constituency feels like it is worse off after adoption of the new weapon.

A prime source of legal (and political) liability would be a weapon that, used *properly*, caused more harm than it was designed to, either because of design problems or because the victim proved to be unusually susceptible. Another common cause for liability would be improper or excessive use of the device (such as the use of a stun gun to coerce a confession or the use of a baton for an overhead strike under circumstances where deadly force was not justified).

Liability might also arise from (1) the near certainty that less-than-lethal weapons will be used much more often than *lethal* weapons, resulting in more frequent, lower-level damage awards, which in the aggregate could total nearly as much as larger judgments in fewer cases of improper use of *deadly* force; (2) the possibility that serious, *permanent* injuries produced by a less-than-lethal weapon will obligate the department and/or the officer to pay disability compensation that rivals or even exceeds what might be awarded in the case of an improper *fatal* use of force; and (3) workers' compensation suits by officers who were injured because of the failure of a less-than-lethal weapon to function in accordance with their agency's representations.

■ **Infrastructure Considerations**. These include training, policy, procedural, logistical support, maintenance issues, and so forth. What initial training in use of the device is needed and how often is refresher training required? What level of proficiency in use of the weapon should be required before officers are certified in its operation? If the weapon is not to be a general-issue item, which personnel should be trained in its use? Is it necessary for personnel who are not expected to operate the device but in whose presence it might be used to have some briefer (at least roll call) training, so that they are aware of the power and potential of the weapon to accomplish both its intended purposes and unintended consequences?

What training is required for the administration of first aid to persons intentionally or unintentionally exposed to the less-than-lethal device? Are there environmental impacts of the weapon (e.g., chemical weapons) that must be attended to as promptly as feasible after the police action concludes? Do environmental safeguarding and first aid require the training and equipping of special personnel in the police department or another public agency, or can the officers involved in the incident do what is required?

What type of weapons retention training and weapons retention equipment are needed? How often does the less-than-lethal weapon (the round and/or delivery system, if the device has these elements) need testing and maintenance to ensure it is at peak operating efficiency and effectiveness? Does the device have to be periodically recharged, as with a fire extinguisher or rechargeable battery in a flashlight or radio? What is the shelf-life of the weapon (ammunition and delivery system, if applicable)? Under what kinds of storage conditions (both in supply facilities and in such field locations as squad car trunks) will the device remain in optimal operating condition the longest?

■ **Cost.** What are the start-up costs? What are the on-going maintenance costs? How often must ammunition be replaced if unused? Who bears the initial and replacement costs—the agency or individual officers? This question has arisen, for instance, in connection with issuance of soft body armor. What are the infrastructural costs (e.g., training, evaluation of field experiences

> *"If we have the technology to put a man on the moon and return him safely to Earth, why don't we have the technology to put a man on the ground and take him safely to jail?" (Meyer 1992: 4).*

to ensure the device performs satisfactorily when used as intended and that it is used as intended by officers)? Will vendors provide training? If so, is this desirable from the department's point of view in terms of controlling not only messages about how well the weapon works and what its drawbacks might be but also in controlling messages about the *judgments* that officers have to make concerning when and how to use the weapon? What is the potential for these weapons to pay for themselves by averting liability for more serious injury and improving the department's reputation for professionalism and restraint? What is the potential for officers to misuse the weapon intentionally or accidentally, thus incurring liability for the jurisdiction and themselves and impairing the agency's public image? What are the potential gains in rank-and-file satisfaction? What are the potential losses in rank-and-file morale that might have fiscal and other costs in labor-management negotiations?

The foregoing are among the questions a department's research and development and weapons and tactics experts ideally would address in evaluating the advantages and disadvantages of adopting or continuing to use any given less-than-lethal implement. While exploring every one of these questions could be a monumental task for a department, many of them will be important enough for individual agencies to study prior to authorizing the use of particular weapons. In the case of some less-than-lethal weapons, individual departments need not conduct this elaborate battery of inquiries in-house, because government testing agencies, such as the Justice Department's National Institute of Justice or standards and testing agencies at the state or regional levels, have done so. Still, departments will want to ensure that issues of particular concern to them have been addressed by externally conducted evaluations. Without attempting to review each of these criteria for each device, let us now turn to an overview of the less-than-lethal weaponry in field use around the United States during the early 1990s.

3. Current Less-than-Lethal Weapons

Besides garden variety less-than-lethal devices, such as the straight baton, some of the more exotic implements that have been used by various departments around the nation are electric stunning devices, capture nets, chemical agents, tripping devices such as long-reach grappling poles, and water cannons and other long-distance impact weapons. These weapons have shown some promise in safely subduing violent individuals or groups, but concerns about reliability and abusive uses persist (abusive uses are those not intended by the manufacturers or by the police agencies that authorized the weaponry) (see Americans for Effective Law Enforcement 1988; Sweetman 1987; Hull and Frisbie 1987; New York State Commission on Criminal Justice 1987, vol. I: 230-238).

The Kansas City Police Department (KCPD) in 1990, as part of a comprehensive task force study of police use of force and its control, evaluated 11 types of less-than-lethal weapons (KCPD 1991: 31-43):

- straight baton
- "PR-24" baton
- expandable baton
- "Handler 12" baton
- heavy metal flashlights
- saps and slappers
- Mace
- capsicum
- electronic stun devices
- capture nets
- 37-millimeter projectile launchers

The following year, the San Diego Police Department completed its own rigorous appraisal of training, policy, and equipment relevant to use-of-force options for its personnel (Hall 1991). Most of the devices evaluated by the Kansas City Police Department were at the time authorized for use by the San Diego Police Department, which also includes in its less-than-lethal arsenal the nunchaku, an ancient Oriental weapon not employed in Kansas City.[84] Moreover, the San Diego police report raises the question whether canines should most appropriately be classified as less-than-lethal "weapons" for purposes of policy and analysis (Hall 1991: recommendations 60, 81; see also International Association of Chiefs of Police 1991a, 1992; Blaricom 1992: 14).

The Kansas City list serves as a convenient starting place for organizing our discussion of these tools, and we will briefly mention some additional devices as well. Much of the analysis and text found in the Kansas City study is derived from a study released the previous year by the British Columbia Police Commission in Northwestern Canada (Jamieson, et al. 1990).

a. Straight Baton

One of the oldest police tools of the trade, the wooden baton is still widely used for less-than-lethal control of subjects. A 1987 survey by the IACP (IACP 1988: 39) revealed that 75 percent approved officer use of night sticks. The Kansas City police baton, a typical one, is made of wood and measures 26 inches long by 1½ inches in diameter at the handle, tapering to 1 inch at the tip. Advantages of the straight baton as a standard less-than-lethal weapon are its low cost, its effectiveness as a "blocking" instrument, and the relative ease of training officers to use it properly (KCPD 1991: 37). Further, batons are lightweight, inexpensive, familiar to the public (and generally accepted as standard, professional police gear), have longer reach than short close-combat implements such as blackjacks, saps, or flashlights (if flashlights can be properly thought of as weapons—a question that we will address below), can be used effectively to "immobilize a combative person" and to disarm a person carrying "an offensive weapon," can serve as a "come-along [pain compliance] device in some situations," and are recommended by manufacturers "as impact weapons" (Americans for Effective Law Enforcement 1988: 3).

---

[84] The nunchaku is discussed below in this section.

The Kansas City police caution that "a baton can be used as an overhead striking device" (*ibid.*), which violates training and policy in most jurisdictions. And, as the LAPD readily conceded after the baton beating of Rodney King, Jr., "any time a baton is used, some injury results, even if it is only a bruise. * * * [Moreover], the baton can break bones, sever blood vessels, rupture internal organs and cause heart attacks" (Rohrlich 1991: A28). The Kolts Commission in L.A. also cited the destructive capacity of batons, criticizing the way in which some deputies had employed them (Kolts, et al. 1992; *New York Times* 1992j). L.A. Sheriff Sherman Block, agreeing, announced a change in the Department manual prohibiting head strikes with batons, heavy flashlights and other such weapons "unless circumstances justify the use of deadly force" (Reich (1992b: A1). ("Yawara" sticks and "Kubotans" are short sticks useful for come-alongs but not for such strikes—Steele 1992: 39.)

Some tactical and risk management experts argue that, to limit potential departmental liability, "a good argument can be made for NOT TRAINING officers in the use of baton-assisted come-along holds, if batons are not routinely used for such purposes in field confrontations. [M]any officers avoid using their batons for come-along holds, because the dynamics of a hostile confrontation make it difficult, if not impossible, to successfully apply these holds to a resisting person. Moreover, many trainers believe that hand-applied pain compliance techniques are tactically superior to baton-applied come-along techniques" (Americans for Effective Law Enforcement 1988: 4).

Other potential drawbacks to the common straight baton include:

- "They are cumbersome and, therefore, are often left in the car.

- They are not concealable, and are not well suited for plainclothes officers.

- They are often in the way when an officer is running.

- They can be lost if they fall from a belt ring and create a hazard.

- It is difficult or impossible to avoid head strikes in all cases, particularly in combat situations. Although intensive training minimizes this risk, it cannot entirely eliminate it. Paralysis or death may result, even days later, caused by subdural or bilateral hematoma.

- Facial strikes often cause lacerations and substantial blood loss. This impairs the department's public image, when citizens have blood-splattered injuries on TV news programs, or at the scene of arrest, or while visiting a hospital emergency room.

- Departments must periodically retrain officers to maintain baton proficiency" (Americans for Effective Law Enforcement 1988: 3).

Amid the public alarm over police abuse of force generated by the Rodney King incident, some politicians and community leaders suggested that police batons should be prohibited. "This would be a serious mistake," responded Americans for Effective Law Enforcement Executive Director Wayne Schmidt. "It would create a vacuum between the whistle and the pistol. The baton, when properly used, is a invaluable intermediate use-of-force technique" (*Crime Control Digest* 1991e: 10). Sometimes, calls for elimination of a misused tool are based on basic misunderstanding of the capacity of the tool to be used effectively. For instance, in a letter to the editor of the *New York Times*, a citizen wrote:

> "We can understand that the police should have the means to defend themselves against armed felons. The absence of gun control legislation in vast areas of the country makes that necessary. However, you have to be very close to somebody to strike him or her with a baton. A baton cannot be presented as a valid means of defense. Nor is it a valid offensive weapon. The police officer's club can only be used as a punishing instrument. Officers are there to protect law and order, not to judge and punish" (Clesca 1992).

Aside from the extreme posture that the simple baton should be banned as a police tool, there remains the question whether it should be classified as a deadly weapon—a weapon reasonably capable of causing death or serious bodily injury when used as intended. Most police tactics experts and, we presume, most courts and legislatures, would agree that proper use of the baton classifies it as a less-than-lethal weapon. Most police agencies train officers that they are not to make overhand strikes with a baton or to strike the subject about the head area. Typically, the baton is intended for jabbing the torso area or striking limbs. There seems to be widespread concurrence among police leaders that in the Rodney King incident, batons were used to

"*Patrolman Jones was working the housing project district when dispatch advised him of a domestic disturbance occurring at the north apartment complex. Backup was summoned knowing that the area has violent incidents on a daily basis.*

"*Upon arrival at the scene, Patrolman Jones observed an emotional female in a rage, screaming and hitting a young man with a broom handle. The officer saw the severity of the situation and drew his police baton for protection. The large crowd that had gathered in the apartment complex started taunting the officer, 'What are you going to do, hit the woman with that stick?' Patrolman Jones ordered the woman to stop striking the young man and to put down the instrument. The woman, totally out of control, started screaming at the officer saying she would hit her son if she wanted to. She approached the officer in a violent manner with the broom handle high over her head. The officer reacted by striking the woman in the leg with the baton without successfully stopping her advance. Patrolman Jones panicked and struck the woman on the weapon-held arm, and by accident, also hit her in the face. She went down and after a short struggle the officer was able to handcuff her and place her under arrest.*

"*Immediately after she was handcuffed, her son attacked the officer and during the struggle removed the officer's baton. He struck the officer several times and broke the officer's jaw. During this time, backup arrived, and the crowd of bystanders told the arriving officer that Patrolman Jones was using his nightstick to hit the female in the face and that is why her son jumped in to help save her.*

"*When the backup officers tried to remove the handcuffed, 200-pound female, she resisted the officers who were trying to move her, causing all of them to fall on the entrance stairway to the apartment. This caused a muscle tear injury to her shoulder and fractured one of her handcuffed wrists. Two of the four officers got back injuries when they fell. One officer got kicked in the face. And the entire incident almost turned into a riot.*

"*Three officers including Patrolman Jones were out on extended injury leave. The arrested female sued the city, department and officers for use of excessive force. The local newspaper took pictures of the woman's face and has launched its own anti-police media campaign with front page coverage of the incident. The District Attorney has ordered an investigation related to departmental use of force*" (*Personal Protection Consultants 1991*).

inflict serious bodily harm and to nearly kill Mr. King. Thus, some have argued that the King beating should be properly thought of as a deadly force incident with a nonfatal outcome. Certainly, there will be others in the police business who would argue vehemently that this is not a deadly force case and that all the baton strikes were best (if not uniformly successful) efforts to comply with LAPD training and policy concerning where and how to use a baton against a subject.

Regardless of how one comes down on the classification of the Rodney King beating as a deadly or nondeadly force incident, the fact remains that the baton is capable of being used as an implement of deadly force (so is a fountain pen, a clipboard, and a heavy box of "give peace a chance" bumper stickers). What is wrong with employing the baton as a deadly weapon on those occasions when deadly force by the officer is justified and called for? Perhaps the simplest answer is that other tools (primarily the firearm) are likely to be far more effective than a baton or club. But although an officer might be ill-advised to select a baton with which to defend his or

> *"British Police have shelved plans to replace some of their traditional truncheons with U.S.-style batons in view of the violent furor caused by the beating of a black motorist in Los Angeles and the jury's acquittal of four white officers. 'After discussion with the Home Office, the view was taken that there should be a pause, given the sensitivity that is obvious following the disturbances,' Brian Johnson, president of the Association of Chief Police Officers, said in London"* (Chicago Sun-Times 1992; see also Steele 1992: 38).

another's life from imminent peril, suppose for some reason the baton is the only weapon available to the officer under these conditions. His or her weapon may be out of ammunition or may have been taken away during a struggle or ambush.

We realize that public perceptions may be clouded by the use of a baton to defend a life, but we see no reason in principle why an officer who uses a baton—or other less-than-lethal weapon—to inflict death or serious bodily harm should not be judged administratively and in other arenas on the same terms that he or she would be judged if a firearm or other unquestionably deadly weapon had been used. That is, among the questions that should be asked on review is whether the officer was justified in using deadly force at the time he or she employed a normally nonlethal weapon as a tool of deadly force.

b. "PR-24" Side-Handled Baton

A brand name for a "side-handled" baton which first hit the market in 1974 and was adopted by the Los Angeles Sheriff's Department the next year (Steele 1992: 39), the PR-24, manufactured by the Monadnock Company, is made of a break-resistant plastic, runs either 24 or 26 inches long, and is three-quarters of an inch in diameter. Its distinctive feature is an 8-inch side handle that protrudes at a right angle from the main shaft. A shorter version (PR-18) is available for use by plainclothes personnel (Jamieson, et al. 1990: 25). In recommending evaluation and probable adoption of the PR-24 baton, the Kansas City Police Department task

> *"Responding to a domestic disturbance...police officers used a baton to apply pressure to the back of a man's neck, while he lay face-down on the floor, causing death by asphyxiation. Although PCP, marijuana and hashish were found in his system, the jury awarded $950,000 to his estate, widow and daughter (Americans for Effective Law Enforcement 1988: 5).*

force summarized the advantages and disadvantages cited in the internal evaluations conducted by nine different law enforcement agencies (KCPD 1991: 37). The advantages include:

- "When carrying the PR-24 in a 'ready position' the major portion of the baton is concealed, and therefore is less likely to antagonize citizens.

- The PR-24 provided officers greater protection (especially from overhead or downward strikes) than the conventional straight baton.

- It is believed that use of the PR-24 reduces injuries to both subjects and officers [and thereby helps avert civil liability].

- The public associated the PR-24 with Karate-type training, thus giving officers a psychological advantage.

- The PR-24 is easier to retain than the conventional baton.

- Jabs, chops, and blocks can be utilized faster and with more force than with a conventional baton.

- The PR-24 has good strength to prevent breaking and it will not warp under intense heat or break upon impact in extreme cold. The finish keeps a professional appearance, even after long periods of use.

- One hundred percent of test officers positively accepted the PR-24 after being trained."

Still, the Kansas City officers noted some disadvantages to be considered in adopting or using a side-arm baton (KCPD 1991: 38):

- "Any baton can be used as an overhead striking device, when used improperly *and* in violation of department policy.

- Sixteen hours of training are needed to become proficient in the use of this baton.

- More hours of in-service training are needed to remain proficient than with the straight baton. The recommendation is made that eight hours of training be held every six months. This translates to a minimum of three days of training within the first year of issue and two days of training each year afterwards.

- The initial price per unit [$42.50 in 1990] and the purchase of a belt carrying ring for each issued baton would result in high start-up costs.

- Because of the 'unbreakable' nature of this baton, in those instances where it is being used excessively, the body and/or bones of the target subject are subjected to greater damage."

Other experts cite additional reasons for preferring the traditional straight baton to the side-handled version:

- "[The straight baton] generates greater *fluid shock waves* (which inflict more trauma but cause less damage to tissue);

- is superior when used in confined locations;

- is easier, quicker and more economical to train officers [with] to a satisfactory level of competency;

- is no more likely to result in unintended head strikes than the side-handled baton;

- has a shorter recovery time (for additional strikes); and

- is more effective when used by shorter and smaller officers, particularly the new small-diameter light-weight models" (Americans for Effective Law Enforcement 1988: 4).

In its 1987 survey, the IACP (1988: 39) discovered that 54 percent of the responding law enforcement agencies approved use of PR-24 batons for their personnel. Some less-than-lethal weapons designers have considered developing a break-away baton, intended to snap when used with a force that generally would be associated with misuse of the tool. There are several possible concerns with this notion. Perhaps the most obvious is that the breakaway point may be different in field applications than in laboratory demonstrations. Moreover, a baton occasionally may be needed to defend the officer's or someone else's life (i.e., for strikes likely to produce serious injury or death, such as when an officer's firearm is taken away in a struggle), and it may be too high a price to pay in officer—and others'—safety to craft a baton that could be expected to fail under such circumstances.

Another possible drawback to the PR-24 is that officers may catch their legs on it when running and trip. PR-24 designers have responded to this concern by developing a version that collapses to 12 inches and can be expanded to full size with a flip of the wrist.

c. Expandable Baton

The side-handled PR-24 is not the only expandable baton. One expandable *straight* baton is the Extend-a-Ton, which was evaluated by the Kansas City Police Department in 1990. It is a "ten-inch stainless steel rod that, with a snap of the wrist, expands to 24 inches. It tapers from one-half inch at the handle to one-quarter inch at the tip" (KCPD 1991: 39). Although reporting that the telescoping baton holds the attractions of being small and easily carried out of sight and permitting officers to refrain from a "show of force" until needed (see also Steele 1992: 40), the Kansas City study team concluded that the weapon's advantages are outweighed by three drawbacks:

- "The telescoping batons have a smaller diameter than the normal 1.25 inch batons. When this thinner baton strikes a subject, the force generated is focused on a smaller area, which increases the risk of injury.

- Telescoping or spring loaded batons require servicing to ensure their mechanical components are functional (straight or side handled batons require no servicing).

- There are occasional failures to telescope or spring which can have serious operational consequences" (KCPD 1991: 39; see also Jamieson, et al. 1990:

25).

A variation on the theme of "expandable" batons is a pneumatic piston impact weapon that delivers baton-like body blows over a distance of up to seven feet (Clede and Parsons 1987: 6-8).

d. "Handler 12" Baton

A 14-inch metal bar coated with rubber, this device has a "rounded handle on one end and a modified shepherd's hook on the other" (KCPD 1991: 39; see also Steele 1992: 39-40). Opposing adoption of this implement, which costs in the vicinity of $60 plus the holster, the Kansas City task force saw it as intended to serve the same purposes as "open hand" control tactics (come-along holds, wrist and arm locks, and so forth) (see Clede and Parsons 1987: 44-51) but not performing as well or as predictably as those unarmed maneuvers. Admitting that its size makes it easily concealable and that "its new and strange look may cause possible confusion to subjects," affording an officer a psychological advantage, the study team said these benefits were outweighed by the following difficulties:

- "It is too small to be used for blocks.

- An officer using this device may risk wrist or hand damage if used for blocking.

- It has a limited use as an impact weapon.

- The flat end is hard to hold onto when making strikes.

- A subject on whom the device may be used may suffer arm or bone damage when the device is applied" (KCPD 1991: 40).

e. Heavy Metal Flashlights

Some experts recommend forbidding the use of heavy flashlights as an impact weapon under all circumstances. This is the recommendation, for instance, of the study group convened to advise the British Columbia Police Commission in Canada (Jamieson, et al. 1990: 33). Others contend that such a sweeping prohibition is unrealistic and inadvisable. For instance, Clede and Parsons (1987: 80-81) take the position that a police flashlight, besides its obvious use for illuminating dark areas that could contain dangers, should be thought of as a form of police baton. They do not advocate using the flashlight as a makeshift baton when a dedicated baton is available, but they observe that, sometimes, in a sudden assault on an officer, the flashlight in his or her hand is the most accessible defensive tool:

"If you have a flashlight in your hand when someone jumps you, you've got no choice. Are you going to drop your only light source to grab your baton? Of course not. You'll smash that plastic two-cell, or whatever else is in your hand, into the guy praying to buy time so you can grab a better weapon. That's the way life is" (*ibid.*).

As of 1988, one flashlight manufacturer parted company with the Clede/Parson's recommendation that a flashlight should be thought of as a baton, declaring: "It would be irresponsible to use a flashlight for striking, jabbing or other offensive moves.... Our company has never advocated the use of the flashlight as a weapon, nor to our knowledge has any responsible flashlight manufacturer" (Americans for Effective Law Enforcement 1988: 2).

Insofar as departments might approve the use of flashlights as baton substitutes, however, their potential advantages and drawbacks in this regard should be understood. Among the advantages of the flashlight:

> *Misuse of flashlights has generated fairly large damage awards in a number of jurisdictions, according to Americans for Effective Law Enforcement (1988: 2): $1.25 million to a Los Angeles man who was struck on the head during a tussle, following a routine traffic stop for a loud muffler; $1.5 million to a Virginian who suffered a speech impairment and paralysis when struck by a flashlight during a driving-under-the-influence (DUI) traffic stop; and $450,000 to a Michigan man whose nose was broken when struck by a police flashlight during a bar fight.*

- "It is usually available, especially at night; it is considered standard equipment.

- It does not give the outward appearance of an offensive weapon.

- It can be used with minimal reaction time, if held in one's hand. * * *

- It is 'effective' as an impact weapon, in that it will deliver a heavy blow" (Americans for Effective Law Enforcement 1988: 2).

And the disadvantages are said to include:

- "Manufacturers are reluctant to approve or endorse the use of their flashlights as impact weapons. * * *

- Flashlights have too short a reach for effective use as a tactical weapon.

- Flashlights provide a slower response than batons; the recovery time is not rapid enough.

- Flashlights have sharp edges that will cut a person.[85]

- Multi-cell lights are very heavy; a blow to the head can be fatal or cause permanent paralysis.[86]

- An officer who carries a weighted flashlight and a baton will be reluctant to drop his light and pull the baton. If the officer does discard the light, it could be used as a weapon against him. He may therefore strike the offender with the light

---

[85] As noted earlier in this chapter, with the proliferation of the AIDS virus, any police weapon that has a high likelihood of causing bleeding of suspects and, because it is used at close range, may also bring a bleeding officer into contact with the suspect's blood, raises serious concerns about officer safety (Meyer 1991a: 53).

[86] The Kolts Commission report on the L.A. Sheriff's Department condemned, as had Amnesty International (Murphy 1992; Mydans 1992b), use of flashlights to strike suspects in custody or after high-speed chases, also chiding the Department for having "no clear policy on deputies' use of 'head strikes' with flashlights and batons" (Tobar and Reich 1992: A18; see also Kolts, et al. 1992; Merina 1992: A20). As noted earlier, the Department concurred and amended its policy (Reich 1992b: A1).

(which is already in hand) instead of using the baton, as he was trained" (Americans for Effective Law Enforcement 1988: 2; see also *New York Times* 1992j; Cox, et al. 1985).

Meyer's (1991a: 36, 44) study of the effectiveness and injuries produced by various less-than-lethal weapons in the LAPD revealed that flashlights, though used as striking or jabbing weapons relatively infrequently compared to batons (batons were used about six times as often as were flashlights), were highly effective in controlling suspects. But flashlights were also likely to cause injury (80 percent of those struck with flashlights versus 61 percent of those struck with batons suffered either moderate or major injuries). Examining only those cases in which the flashlights were effective in controlling suspects, 83 percent of those suspects suffered moderate or major injuries) (*ibid.*: 36; see also Meyer 1992a). Cox, et al. (1985) observe that a flashlight weighing 750 grams can inflict blows with 425 pounds of force, sufficient to fracture the skull.

Another use of flashlights is to momentarily blind a subject, distracting or disorienting him or her long enough for an officer to make a needed maneuver. Similar use can be made of lights mounted on police cars, especially during nighttime vehicle stops. The combination of headlights (set on bright), the adjustable spotlight (mounted on the side of the car), and "take down" lights and strobe lights mounted on the roof light bar can be blinding. Said one Chicago officer: "If the person being stopped turns around, all he sees is white" (Baltic 1991: 32). "Flashbangs," discussed below, also function to momentarily blind and disorient a suspect so police can make needed maneuvers.

Police, however, must also be trained that, while flashlights can provide great tactical advantages, they can also pinpoint an officer's location in a dark place. Training must emphasize the importance of holding a flashlight away from the officer's body so the light does not provide a target for the subject to aim at.[87] Experienced officers also observe the

---

[87] An "officer survival" specialist cautions that holding the flashlight away from the body may give police a false sense of safety:

> "I know that some survival instructors teach you to hold your flashlight in your extended weak arm, away from your body, and high and slightly forward. If there's sometime when you absolutely have to use a flashlight in a building search, that's the best way to use it.... But most officers use it unnecessarily, and in their attempts to make things easy for themselves, they also make target identification easy for a concealed, armed burglar. It doesn't take a really bright felon to know that a flashlight doesn't float in mid-air. If you think the average burglar can't figure out that the flashlight he sees coming in his direction has got to be at the end of somebody's non-gun arm, you're underestimating your enemy. And if you think you're going to escape the scatter pattern when that burglar pumps off a round or two of double-ought buck at the general vicinity of your flashlight, you're overestimating the length of your arm" (Rutledge 1988: 202).

It is possible that in some encounters the blinding power of flashlights or flashbangs would be used not to create a window of opportunity for officers to safely move but to scan the suspect's location to determine how to approach. Other devices might also help officers safely examine a dangerous scene from a protected position. On the high-tech end is a robot equipped with two-way audio and video (Quinn 1990); on the low-tech end is a common, pocket-size, unbreakable mirror that officers can use to peer around corners. Mirrors are available that snap onto the end of expandable batons to facilitate looking around objects (*Law and Order* 1992b). Another simple device that can be used to afford officers cover, if not concealment, during raids when the setting does not provide objects useful for

importance of carrying flashlights during the daylight hours, when some officers would not expect to need them but when they will be needed in basements and other dark places. Heavy flashlights (containing three to six batteries) were authorized for police use by 89 percent of the police departments that responded to the IACP's 1987 administrative survey (IACP 1988: 39).

f. Saps (Slappers)

Clede and Parsons (1987: 87) place saps (also known as slappers), the old British bobby's billy club, blackjacks, and such in the category of "historical" weapons, "because that's where they belong—in history" (also see Steele 1992: 38-40). But such devices were not confined to police museums in all departments, according to the IACP's 1987 national survey: 16 percent of the responding agencies still formally authorized the use by officers of "saps, blackjacks or sap gloves" (IACP 1988: 39; see also Murphy 1992: B1). The sap is

> "a lump of lead between two layers of leather. It is more rigid than a blackjack and, theoretically, is less likely to crush a skull. Its effectiveness is in striking bones, such as ankles, shins or wrists. It's handy for close-in fighting" (Clede and Parsons 1987: 86-87; see also Steele 1992: 39-40).

Despite their potential value for close combat, Clede and Parsons conclude that the liability risks outweigh the tactical benefits:

> "They are bound to be construed as weapons of aggression...because society sees them as serving no other purpose than to hit with. After all, the object of...non-lethal force is to gain compliance, to control a combative subject, not to knock him senseless" (Clede and Parsons 1987: 87-88).

Blackjacks, saps, and billies are readily concealed, inexpensive, easily carried, and lightweight. Still, there are negatives from a purely tactical point of view (putting aside entirely the temptation to use such weapons for facial and head blows). Among the negatives are that they are considered by many too short to be a useful weapon, too flexible to "generate enough shock waves to be effective," dangerous in that they have sharp edges, and inhibiting to officers because many of the devices have loops that "constrict an officer's hands" (Americans for Effective Law Enforcement 1988: 39; see also Steele 1992: 39-40).

g. Nunchakus

The nunchaku, employed by a number of southern California police agencies, the largest being the San Diego Police Department[88] (Serrano 1990: E1), is based on an ancient martial arts weapon and consists of

> "two cylindrical polycarbonate cylinders joined by a four-inch nylon rope. The nunchaku is primarily utilized as a pain compliance tool and not as a striking

---

cover is the "body bunker," a bullet-resistant shield that officers can crouch behind as they move closer to a dangerous suspect (Federal Law Enforcement Training Center 1989: 5).

[88] As of January 1990, the LAPD had begun testing the nunchaku, and Sergeant Fred Nichols, the Department's supervisor for physical training and self-defense, expressed hope that the weapon would become standard issue for LAPD officers. "They're great, just great," he said. "They're the best thing that ever happened.... We have heard nothing but accolades for this tool" (Serrano 1990: E2).

weapon. * * * The nunchaku sticks are placed on the wrist, arm or ankle. When brought together the sticks exert pressure and cause intense pain which leads to compliance" (Jamieson, et al. 1990: 27; also see Albrecht 1992: 122-125; Serrano 1990).

In the version employed by police agencies in southern California in 1990, the two plastic rods were 12 inches long.

Generations ago, Asian peasants began using the nunchaku as a farm tool, twisting the cord around stalks to harvest rice (Serrano 1990: E1). As the tool migrated from mainland China to Japan, eventually, about 300-400 years ago, farmers began using the implement also as a defen-

> An officer *"believes the nunchaku helped her stop a 'very intoxicated and hostile' woman from attempting to leap off the 250-foot-high San Diego-Coronado Bay Bridge.... 'I put a control hold on her right wrist and she got in the patrol car,' the officer said (Serrano 1990: E1).*

sive weapon (Serrano 1990: E2). When American street gang members began using nunchakus in imitation of Bruce Lee martial arts movies in the 1970s, police faced with this challenge in Colorado Springs sought advice from Kevin Orcutt, a sergeant in the Thornton, Colorado, Police Department, a "part-time bank security guard * * * [and] black belt in Kukado karate" (*ibid.*). Orcutt and his family began assembling "slimmed down," 12-ounce nunchakus for use by police and have built a substantial business selling what they market as the "Orcutt Police Nunchaku" (*ibid.*).

Because the nunchaku allows officers to exert much more leverage with less effort on wrist holds than is possible with unarmed techniques, the device gained considerable popularity among San Diego officers, especially female officers. A single officer can generally inflict enough pain on a suspect's wrist to hold him or her "immobile until help arrives" (*ibid.*: E1). Police have found the device "particularly useful against people who are under the influence of drugs" (*ibid.*: E2).

Still, the San Diego experience with nunchakus has been mixed. Use of the weapon generated "a new round of police brutality complaints from the public, mostly resulting from extensive police use of the nunchaku in mass arrests of antiabortion demonstrators" (*ibid.*: E1). Complaints from such demonstrators have included sprained wrists and hands and even nerve damage to thumbs and fingers (*ibid.*). Tactical expert Kevin Parsons, interviewed by a newspaper, expressed a preference for the expandable baton over the nunchaku: "There are a lot of things that work and we want to find what works the best.... If you're talking about thrashing rice, then that's when [nunchakus, used in a flailing motion] work the best" (*ibid.*: E2; see also Steele 1992: 40, on the "nutcracker" technique). Proponents of the nunchaku respond that other police less-than-lethal weapons, including the baton and flashlight, can produce much more harm (Serrano 1990: E2). Moreover, officer safety can be enhanced through use of the nunchaku, according to the San Diego Police-Community Advisory Board (*ibid.*):

> "Andrea Skorepa, chairwoman of the advisory panel, said she sympathized with the [antiabortion] protesters [who demanded that the police stop using the nunchakus], noting that she engaged in the Vietnam War demonstrations of the 1960s and '70s. But she also worries about potential back sprains and other injuries to police officers forced to drag, lift and carry protesters who go limp in front of abortion clinics."

Although the nunchaku typically is wrapped around a limb as a pain control device, San Diego Police have also been permitted to "swing [it] in the air as a martial arts weapon. When it is [used this way], the nunchaku can extend from 14 inches to 28 inches in a flash, strike around corners and send disabling blows to a thigh or knee" (*ibid.*; see also Steele 1992: 40).

h. Mace

A brand name for tear gas (CS or CN types), Mace is sprayed from an aerosol container and is used widely by the public and some police agencies (as of 1987, 50 percent of the departments in the U.S. authorized its use by sworn personnel—IACP 1988: 39). Tear gas is not literally a *gas* but a fine powder usually transported by "smoke in a grenade or liquid in an aerosol container" (Clede and Parsons 1987: 110). There are two types of tear gas, which differ both in their potency and in the speed of their effectiveness. The form first developed was CN (chloroacetophenone). It makes the subject's "tear ducts flow, his eyes smart and his eyelids try to close. A burning sensation is felt on moist skin" (Clede and Parsons 1987: 110). CS (ortho-clorobenzalmalonontrile), adopted by the U.S. Army in 1960, is

> "more effective than CN against a large mob. The effects of CS include extreme burning sensation of the eyes, flowing tears, involuntary closing of the eyes, coughing and chest tightening, sinus and nasal drip, extreme burning sensation on areas of moist skin, such as the face, armpits, and groin. If you use it indoors, it's more difficult to clean up than CN" (Clede and Parsons 1987: 110).

By "clean-up," Clede and Parsons mean not only decontamination of the area, but also administration of first aid to all persons (officers, bystanders, and adversaries) affected by the chemical agent—a key responsibility of officers who use chemical agents (Clede and Parsons 1987: 110-111).

Although CS is considered a more potent agent against a large group, CN (the milder of the two chemicals), when delivered as part of an aerosol spray (as with a hand-held canister) and sprayed in a stream directly into a subject's face, takes effect more rapidly. This is because CN vaporizes more quickly than CS (Clede and Parsons 1987: 110). An agent newer than CN and CS is CH, a liquid that, once vaporized, produces effects similar to the other two chemicals: eyes water, skin itches, normal breathing is impaired.

Among the agencies that have used Mace (first marketed by the Smith and Wesson Chemical Company in 1965 [Clark 1990: 6]), the NYPD has compiled data on its effectiveness and has made those findings available to the profession. Cerar (1990, 1991) reports on Mace's usefulness in immobilizing NYPD adversaries, examining the five years 1987 through 1991. Figure 75 shows these annual variations in effectiveness of Mace (effective against from 60 to 82 percent of the adversaries[89] against whom it was employed). The five-year average rate of effectiveness for Mace in the NYPD was very similar to the long-term effectiveness rate obtained by the NYPD for the TASER (see discussion below in

---

[89] In both Figures 75 and 76, the term "perpetrators" is used to describe those persons sprayed with Mace or shot with a TASER. Though this term may incorrectly imply legal certainty about the guilt of the individuals, we use it because it is the word employed by the NYPD in their data compilation. The issue is identical to the one we have raised elsewhere in this volume when we criticized the police and legal professions' pervasive use of the term "fleeing *felon*" to describe an escaping person whose guilt typically has not been legally adjudicated. An exception would be the convicted felon escaping from prison or from police or court officials transporting him or her to or from prison.

this chapter).

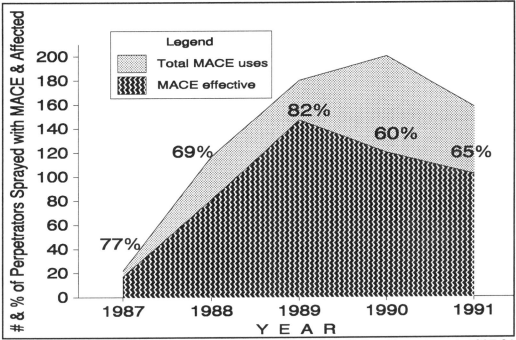

Figure 75: Use of Chemical Mace by the New York City Police Department, 1987-91
Sources: Cerar (1990: 41, 1991: 45).

A popular nonlethal weapon for police in the 1970s, police interest in Mace (as delivered by small aerosol spray canisters) has been falling off in recent years in a number of agencies (KCPD 1991: 41). Although Mace carries the advantages of being relatively inexpensive, small, and lightweight (thus easily carried on an officer's utility belt), the Kansas City police task force recommended against use of Mace by its own officers, citing four concerns:

- "Mace is not effective against all suspects and can have no effect at all on crazed or extremely intoxicated persons;

- Mace presents serious contamination problems for police, health care and custodial workers who have subsequent dealings with a 'Mace' subject;[90]

- Mace has no effect on vicious dogs; and

- there are documented instances of Mace causing severe eye damage"[91] (KCPD 1991: 42).

---

[90] Even though Mace had a 90 percent effectiveness rate when used by LAPD officers, those officers rarely used it, mostly out of concern for their own contamination and the contamination of squad cars used to transport prisoners. Officers reported being unable to use a squad car contaminated with Mace for several days after the exposure (Meyer 1991a: 44, 48, 52-53).

[91] See, e.g., Levine and Stahl (1968), cited in Jamieson, et al. (1990): 37.

Three other concerns have been expressed: "There is a time lag between application and effect" and therefore it might "not stop aggressive behavior rapidly enough" (Americans for Effective Law Enforcement 1988: 5); Mace can and has caused second-degree burns; and "officers may object to transporting prisoners who have clothing saturated with a chemical irritant" (*ibid.*). When Mace or tear gas-type chemicals are used for crowd control, innocent people in the vicinity may be affected by the weaponry, especially under windy conditions. As we go to press, a famous innocent victim of tear gas deployed on a windy day was President George Bush. His scheduled speech in Panama on June 11 (during a stopover on the President's trip to Brazil to discuss *environmental pollution* with world leaders at the "Earth Summit"!) was disrupted when local officials fired chemical weapons to disperse a crowd of violent anti-American protesters (Wines 1992). Front-page newspaper photos of the president and Mrs. Bush dabbing their eyes because of the effects of the wafting chemical graphically illustrated both the utility of such less-than-lethal weapons and the ease with which they can inadvertently afflict innocent parties.

While there are numerous reservations within the American law enforcement community about tear gas and Mace, especially as a tool for one-on-one or small group confrontations, the Kansas City study team, FBI tactical experts, and other police analysts have not viewed all chemical agents in the same light. Capsicum is considered more suitable as a police nonlethal weapon.

i. Oleoresin Capsicum

Oleoresin capsicum (OC) is an "organic extract of cayenne pepper,...[which] is quite pungent and is an inflammatory agent to the eyes and mucous membranes" (KCPD 1991: 34). As is Mace, capsicum (marketed in this country under such brand names as "Cap-Stun", "Nebulizer," and "Punch" [Clede 1992: 57])[92] typically is sprayed from a small aerosol canister (approximately 5 inches high and 1.25 inches in diameter), which can be easily carried on an officer's utility belt. This size canister is said to be good for 150 one-second sprays (Jamieson, et al. 1990: 26). The chemical can also be employed in a grenade (KCPD 1991: 34; Jamieson, et al. 1990: 29). Compared with Mace, however, capsicum is said to be far more effective, quicker acting, and less hazardous to police who spray it and to police or medical personnel who must subsequently handle the person sprayed.

Most of the interest expressed by the Kansas City police task force in experimenting with capsicum is based on prior favorable reviews of the substance by the FBI's Firearms Training Unit in 1989 (followed by issuance of capsicum to bureau field agents and tactical weapons teams) (KCPD 1991: 35) and by the British Columbia Police Commission (Jamieson, et al. 1990: 26-27). Capsicum has been used for over 20 years by U.S. Postal Service mail

---

[92] During 1991 the Cap-Stun brand name was sold by Aerko International, a Fort Lauderdale company that first manufactured it, to a new company, Zarc International, which began selling the spray under a new formula but with the original brand name, Cap-Stun. The original *formula* was then sold under the new brand name "Punch." The change in names resulted in some operational confusion in at least one police agency. A diluted version of the capsicum formula is sold for use by civilians in self-defense, and mislabeled canisters found their way into the hands of Isle of Wright, Virginia, Sheriff's deputies, who discovered the hard way that the product did not perform as effectively as the more potent formula. The difference is a 1-percent cayenne pepper solution for civilian use versus a 5-percent solution for police use. (The stronger solution typically is 5 percent capsicum and 95 percent propellant—isopropanol, etc.) Manufacturers said, however, that even the 1-percent mixture should have accomplished the tactical objective and suggested that "windy conditions may have been the reason why [the] suspect did not succumb" (*Crime Control Digest* 1991i; Clede 1992: 57).

carriers (Clede 1990a: 60), whose aerosol canisters, issued by the service and typically clipped onto the mailbag, bear the brand name "HALT."

Among the advantages to capsicum cited by the Kansas City police study group, based on earlier work by the FBI and the British Columbia Police Commission, are:

- "the incapacitation effect is immediate and works on all suspects, including those who may be deranged, high on drugs, or intoxicated;

- there are no decontamination problems (the isopropanol propellant evaporates);

- there are no documented instances of death or serious injury occurring from usage of capsicum;

- it is effective on vicious animals;

- it is effective up to 10 feet [but should not be used closer than 3 feet to ensure adequate misting—Clede 1992: 58];

- practical considerations (shelf life, accuracy of the spray, size of the canister, amount of training needed, etc.) are all positive [for capsicum]; and

- reasonable cost" (KCPD 1991: 35).

The reason capsicum is more effective than Mace or tear gas on some subjects, particularly those under the influence of intoxicants, is that CS and CN gases

> "are irritants while capsicum is an inflammatory agent. Since irritants cause pain by activating receptor cells within the nervous system, when a subject's neural transmitters are blocked by drugs or high levels of endorphins, they might not work.[93] This is why mace has lost some of its acceptability. Capsicum, however, as an inflammatory causes swelling. If a subject has eyes and breathes, he or she is susceptible to OC [oleoresin capsicum]. When a person's eyes and airways swell, vision is limited and breathing is difficult even if [the person is] high on drugs. Adding to this debilitating situation is the burning sensation on skin which has been exposed to OC" (Morgan 1992: 2; 1992a).

In addition, police officials familiar with the effects of capsicum report that, after being sprayed with the chemical, "the subject reflexively bends forward at the waist and covers his eyes" (Rohrlich 1991: A29). While impairing vision is obviously a central reason why capsicum works well, tacticians caution officers to beware that any substance which hinders the vision of a violent adversary in possession of a knife or blunt object may cause the person

---

[93] Commentators have suggested that chemical less-than-lethal weapons fall into two broad classes: those that work on the central nervous system and those that act "peripherally" (Rivetti 1987: 8)—for instance, on the circulatory or respiratory systems (Shubin 1984: 35). Most of those that affect the central nervous system (e.g., nerve gas and other potent substances sometimes used during wars) are not available for use by local American police and would not be deemed appropriate by them. Sometimes chemical devices intended for other purposes than controlling resistant people may prove useful as less-than-lethal weapons. An example is fire extinguishers (Rivetti 1987: 15).

to "lash out in an indiscriminate manner" (Americans for Effective Law Enforcement 1988: 5).

There are a few other concerns as well. The principal cautions expressed by the Kansas City Police Department about capsicum were the cost of initial purchase for an entire agency as well as "reports that Cap-Stun may be flammable" (KCPD 1991: 35). On August 9, 1990, NYPD Emergency Services Unit personnel, confronting an emotionally disturbed 14-year-old boy armed with knives and a hammer, sprayed him with Cap-Stun. When this did not have the desired effect, the officers, apparently unaware that the chemical's propellant was alcohol, "shot" the youth with a TASER. "The charge from the darts apparently ignited the substance, engulfing the boy in flames [and producing] first- and second-degree burns" (*Law Enforcement News* 1990d: 9; see also Clark 1990; Clede 1992: 59).[94]

The Goldsboro, North Carolina, Police Department trained its officers in the use of capsicum. "Based on previous experiences in [lawsuits] where training content was challenged, we videotaped the entire course each day it was repeated. In addition, we chose to have each officer who would be carrying OC...experience an actual one to two second burst of the chemical. That way they could personally assure anyone they sprayed that although they might be suffering, they would survive. It also teaches officers to wait about ten seconds before moving in on someone who has been sprayed so that they don't get any fallout effects. Reruns of the videotaping of the officers getting their dose of OC were very popular as everyone wanted to see just how they reacted" (Morgan 1992: 4-5; 1992a).

If the liability implications of this incident are not enough to suggest the importance of investigating the flammability of any supposedly less-than-lethal weapon, one need only recall the extraordinarily damaging fire set unwittingly by the Philadelphia Police Department when it sought to dislodge the radical group MOVE by dropping a grenade containing a chemical agent on the group's stronghold. That tragic error on May 13, 1985, led to 61 neighborhood houses being engulfed in flames, leaving 253 people homeless. As of May 1992 the City of Philadelphia had incurred liability judgments or had settled suits over the MOVE bombing totaling $27.3 million. This included a $2.5 million settlement of suits brought by MOVE over the wrongful deaths of five children who perished in the blaze (*New York Times* 1992a; Nemeth 1991; see also Hinds 1992). In a less publicized but still costly incident, Minneapolis was rocked in 1989 when "an elderly couple died in a fire caused by a diversionary grenade ignited by police during a botched drug raid. Police said they didn't know the couple were in the apartment" (Harrison 1991: A14).

It is not the capsicum that may burn, but the isopropyl alcohol used as a delivery system. Alternate delivery systems are available, but they have drawbacks as well. As Morgan (1992: 3; 1992a) notes, the nonflammable alternatives to alcohol

"normally are either ozone depleting, toxic, or carcinogenic since Freon (CFCs), Dymel (HCFCs) or Methylene Chloride are used as their carrier. If everything else is acceptable in the delivery systems, it comes down to a choice among the potential for a fire under very limited circumstances, some environmental

---

[94] Gardner L. Whitcomb, president of Luckey Police Products, which manufactured and supplied Cap-Stun to a large number of agencies at the time, caused quite a stir by charging publicly that this "incident was orchestrated by the New York City Police Department and a competitor, the Def-Tech Corp., to discredit his product" (*Law Enforcement News* 1990d: 1; see also Clark 1990).

deterioration, or exposure to possible cancer causing ingredients. Each 'danger' is very slight and the only one that is controllable by the user is flammability and that can be achieved through policy. The Freon concern, however, will disappear in 1995 or sooner when it no longer will be allowed as an aerosol carrier [if inhaled, Freon can induce heart attacks—Clede 1992: 59]. In the near future companies should be able to produce sprays that eliminate all these...dangers."

Moreover, the alcohol used in the delivery system is only mildly combustible. According to Morgan, chief of the Goldsboro (NC) Police Department, "[a]lcohol is not combustible like gasoline; however, if you spray it directly on a flame at close range, it should ignite" (1992: 2-3; 1992a). The same is true, he observes, for hair and deodorant sprays. Morgan concludes:

"Using the same precautions as used for household aerosol units, isopropyl alcohol can be used as a carrier for OC. * * * The decision as to what type of unit to buy...should be made by considering how and when OC will be used. [Our department] felt our primary use would be in individual behavior modifications rather than in crowd dispersement. Thus we chose isopropyl alcohol as our carrier for routine patrol use, but prefer a nonflammable for rare tactical/SWAT-type incidents where saturation might be necessary" (ibid.: 3; 1992a).

Other concerns have been raised about capsicum: "Sometimes, it can give a false sense of security as evidenced by an officer's response to the offer of a back up: 'I don't need one, I got my OC.' " (ibid.: 7). Also, "over-spraying" is cited as the most common tactical error by officers. This can prevent misting, impairing OC's intended effects (Clede 1992: 57-58).

Since the Kansas City Police Department completed its work in 1990, the Department, along with others, has begun field use of Cap-Stun, prompted in part by the heightened concern over police use of excessive force brought on by the March 1991 Rodney King beating. The initial reports on Cap-Stun's performance have been quite favorable. Anecdotes abound of violent, drug-crazed adversaries being safely apprehended with use of this chemical agent.

> "[O]nce [capsicum's] effects become known on the street, it becomes more of a deterrent to violent behavior because it could and would be used to subdue any violent suspect. It is not meant to be an absolute last resort weapon as is a firearm, and that is what makes it so good" (Morgan 1992: 7; 1992a).

Kansas City Chief Steven Bishop told a local newspaper: "This stuff'll drop you like a rock" (North 1992: B1; see also Meyer 1991, 1991a; 1992a).

Department records showed that between June 3, 1991 and January 31, 1992, Kansas City officers sprayed Cap-Stun in 211 incidents—out of approximately 50,000 arrests. Department officials indicated that, as of February 1992, nobody had yet filed a complaint with the Office of Citizen Complaints over the use of Cap-Stun, and nobody had been reported as suffering any physical effects beyond the momentary disablement (North 1992: B1, B6). The Goldsboro, North Carolina, Police Department, which has prepared a very clear and informative report on capsicum as a law enforcement tactical tool (Morgan 1992, 1992a), attempted to conduct an evaluation of field experiences with capsicum by issuing the weapon to some officers but maintaining a group of "have nots" as a control group. But the experiment was abandoned after several weeks because "the control group voiced so much concern about their 'have not' status [that the Department] had to scrap our 'pure' research model" (Morgan 1992: 7; 1992a). Police in a number of California agencies have expressed a strong desire to add capsicum to their relatively limited arsenal of nonlethal weapons, but both the state Departments of Justice and Environmental Protection have banned OC "until all the chemicals in it are proven safe" (Rohrlich 1991: A29).

j. Electronic Stun Devices

The Kansas City task force recommended *against* the use of electric shock weapons by their police department (KCPD 1991: 40). Other departments take a different view. Two basic types of devices are on the market for domestic police use in America: so-called "stun guns" and TASERs.[95] The "stun gun" is "a hand-held device with two short metal prongs that must be touched to the suspect's body while the current is turned on" (*ibid.*).

The TASER (a brand name acronym for "Thomas A. Swift Electric Rifle"—Johnston 1981b: 26) is, in fact, not a rifle but a relatively small "hand-held device which shoots two barbed hooks to a distance of approximately 15 feet" (KCPD 1991: 40; see also Meyer 1991, 1992, 1992a) or, as other experts report, a distance of up to 30 feet (Clede and Parsons 1987: 109).[96] Not only does the TASER not need to be used at close range, it may not function effectively if fired too close to the target. The reason is, according to manufacturer's specifications, that the TASER darts need space after being fired to spread out to about 18 to 24 inches apart "in order to deliver the most effective, incapacitating shock to the suspect" (Meyer 1991a: 101-102). "The lower dart drops about one foot for each five feet of range, and for full effectiveness it is necessary to have a dart separation of eight inches or more. Less separation may provide only a stunning effect" (*Law and Order* 1992a).

The "wire-trailing darts [are fired] from cassettes by means of smokeless gunpowder" (Uchida, et al., 1981: 37 n. 18). Because gunpowder is used as a propellant, TASERs are subject to regulation by the federal Bureau of Alcohol, Tobacco, and Firearms under Title I of the Gun Control Act of 1968 (*Law and Order* 1992a). "The hooks affix to the suspect's skin or clothing and are attached on the other end to the hand-held unit by thin wires. The current is transmitted to the suspect through the wires and can be controlled from the hand-held portion of the device" (KCPD 1991: 40).

The TASER was seen by hundreds of millions of people around the world on broadcasts of the videotaped beating in Los Angeles of Rodney King. In the video, an LAPD sergeant is seen holding the TASER, whose darts had already affixed to King, and attempting to keep the wires from tangling or tearing as fellow LAPD members beat the suspect. The technical requirements of using the TASER properly (e.g., needing to keep the wires from tearing) may produce scenes such as the LAPD sergeant apparently being preoccupied with his weapon rather than controlling the actions of his officers, that make for bad public relations. Similarly, manufacturers suggest that the TASER will be most effective if the subject is shot "in the back." This is both to reduce the risk of hitting the subject in the eyes and also because, "since the clothing is usually tighter across the back, [the back] makes for a better target"

---

[95] Other electrical weapons include such brand name implements as "The Source" and "The Talon." The former is a flashlight equipped with electrodes on the tail end; the latter is a glove equipped with electrodes designed to be worn by an officer during close control tactical efforts.

[96] It is not clear whether the reference in the literature to a 30-foot range is a mistake or is based on a model of TASER that has 30-foot wires attached to the darts. All TASERs of which we are aware have 15-foot wires that connect the darts to the main portion of the weapon (see, e.g., *Law and Order* 1992a). The most effective range for TASERs is said to be between 5 and 12 feet (*ibid.*).

(*Law and Order* 1992a). A crowd of onlookers, unaware of such reasons why officers might "shoot a subject in the back" with a TASER, could well reach an erroneous—and infuriating—conclusion that the police were engaged in gratuitous use of force.

Both stun guns and TASERs operate by "generat[ing] a high voltage/low amperage current into a suspect and thereby caus[ing] incapacitation" (KCPD 1991: 40). The jolt delivered by the TASER typically is 50,000 volts. With both stun guns and TASERs, it is essential that both probes or darts touch the subject or his or her clothing, since the devices work by generating an electric arc. TASERs reportedly will work through as much as two inches of

> *"At close range, the TASER is more effective than a .38 pistol in stopping an attacker. Unlike a conventional firearm, the TASER does not require a hit in a critical area, such as heart, brain, or spine to immobilize. Any hit with both darts over eight inches apart will do the job quickly—and the subject will live"* (Law and Order *1992a*).

clothing (Meyer 1991a: 65; 1992a: 12; a manufacturer's description says that the TASER's charge will only penetrate between 1.25 and 1.5 inches of clothing [*Law and Order* 1992a]). The incapacitation results because the "pain-producing shock cause[s] a retractive reflex..., inducing [involuntary] muscle spasms..., causing loss of muscular control, leaving the subject dazed but conscious" (Clede and Parsons 1987: 108; Uchida, et al. 1981: 37 n. 18).

The KCPD task force conceded that electronic stunning implements, when officers are able to use them according to manufacturers' instructions, immobilize "about 75 percent of the individuals they are used on" (KCPD 1991: 41). This finding is consistent with the experience of the NYPD, which has employed both stun guns and TASERs. Although the stun gun is no longer favored by the NYPD (or in many other locales),[97] the NYPD continues to use the TASER. One advantage of a stun gun over the TASER is that it is possible to employ it as a tool of *psychological* rather than *physical* intimidation. A "demonstration arc" with the stun gun (displaying the spark zapping noisily between the electrodes without applying the electrodes to the potential subject) can convince some police adversaries to comply quietly with police instructions.[98] Because electricity does not flow between the TASER's electrodes until the weapon is fired and the body of the person struck closes the circuit between the electrodes, displays of this weapon's incapacitating potential are not as easily conducted. The stun gun is also less expensive, smaller, and more easily concealed than the TASER.

---

[97] In 1987, only 15 percent of the nation's police forces reported authorizing the weapon's use (IACP 1988: 39), although a single-state survey a year earlier in Nebraska revealed that 36 percent of the 205 responding police and sheriffs' departments used stun guns (Overton 1986).

The Chicago Police Department has banned use of stun guns (Nelson 1992a: 26), but in the summer of 1992 a 13-year old suspected of a gang-related murder charged that his confession in September 1991 had been coerced through use of a stun gun or functionally similar device (Nelson 1992b). A detective with the unfortunate name of Michael Kill, who had participated in the youth's interrogation, denied any improprieties in the questioning (Nelson 1992a: 26). Some departments have reduced the frequency of allegations that they coerced confessions by videotaping all or at least portions of station house interrogations and confessions (Geller 1991b).

[98] Laser sights on firearms can have a similarly salutary effect as harmless demonstrations of police capacity to escalate their coercive power if necessary. Laser light generators mounted on either handguns or long-guns allow police to place a visible dot of light on their adversary as an aid in aiming. In some instances, simply placing the dot of light on the opponent is sufficient to induce his or her surrender since it is very likely that any shots fired at that point will be on target.

The NYPD (Cerar 1990, 1991) compiled data (shown in Figure 76) on the effectiveness rate of the TASER over the five years 1987 through 1991. The device's effectiveness ranged from a low of 55 percent to a high of 75 percent of subjects immobilized. An LAPD expert on the TASER reported effectiveness rates in the LAPD of about 86 percent (Meyer 1991, 1991a: 44; 1992, 1992a). Previous reports indicated that, as of early 1987, the LAPD had 550 TASERs and had employed them (since May 1980) 775 times (Americans for Effective Law Enforcement 1988: 6). Between 1981 and 1991, the LAPD amassed experience with the TASER in between 2,000 and 3,000 field confrontations (Meyer 1991, 1991a, 1992, 1992a). When TASERs (or stun guns) do *not* function as intended, typically the reasons for the ineffectiveness include:

- the officer's inability to strike the subject properly with the darts or to apply the stun gun's electrodes properly (Sweetman 1987: 4; Peak 1990: 17);

- the officer's failure, with a TASER, "to hold down the switch (trigger) after firing: letting go turns off the voltage, making the shot ineffective unless you...trigger it again. Voltage can be applied anytime as long as the darts are in place" (*Law and Order* 1992a). A stun gun also will be ineffective if the officer fails to press the switch—or has his weapon wrestled away (see *Law and Order* 1992d on a "safety disconnect pin");

- weak batteries (*Law and Order* 1992a); and

- some subjects' abnormal physiological resistance to the electric shock, which sometimes is drug-induced (Sweetman 1987: 4; Peak 1990: 17).[99]

Other experts add that TASERs and stun guns may fail not only against persons under the influence of narcotics but also against emotionally disturbed individuals.

Although conceding an effectiveness rate in the 75 percent range, nevertheless the Kansas City study team advised against use of stun guns and TASERs, making the following arguments:

- "the close contact device [the stun gun] is not an effective weapon against any armed suspect since the officer is required to touch the suspect with it. Getting this close to a knife-wielding suspect is grossly unsafe;[100]

- there have been documented applications of electronic stun devices where

---

[99] Meyer (1991a: 15, 18; 1992a) argues that, among the most "enduring myths" about the TASER is "the oft published assertion that the TASER does not work well on violent PCP suspects." PCP (phencyclidine), also known as "Angel Dust," is a drug that produces extraordinary strength and extremely violent behavior in users (*ibid.*). Many police departments have experiences in which four or more officers have been unable to control a lone, unarmed adversary high on PCP. Meyer (1991a: 19) reports that a Los Angeles Police Department Planning and Research Division study in 1980 concluded that the "TASER completely and immediately incapacitated violent PCP suspects, who were then arrested without injury to themselves or the officers."

[100] Perhaps to counter this drawback and perhaps partly to impede misuse of stun guns (see brief discussion later in the text), the NYPD during the 1980s required that stun guns be "mounted on a six-foot pole." An NYPD advisory commission on use of force in late 1990 suggested repealing this rule so that stun guns could be hand held "depending on the circumstance" (*Law Enforcement News* 1990a: 9).

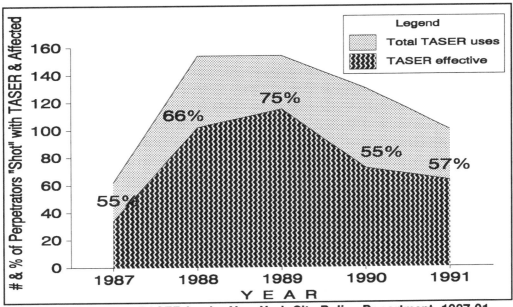

Figure 76: Use of the TASER by the New York City Police Department, 1987-91
Source: Cerar (1990: 42, 1991: 45).

fatalities have occurred [particularly when used in proximity to water or when used against persons with heart pacemakers];[101]

■ both devices are not 100 percent effective [nor, one might observe, are any other weapons, including firearms]. A tactical instructor cited empirical statistics which would indicate that 25 percent of the time the suspect is able to resist the current and is not incapacitated (e.g., a Prince George's County, MD, woman was hit twice with a TASER with no effect—H.I. Smith 1992);

■ there have been storage/shelf life battery problems with these devices, leading to operational failures;[102] and

---

[101] A manufacturer disagrees, asserting that the weapons "will not induce ventricular fibrillation (heart attack) in 'normally healthy adults.' They will not stimulate a heart pacemaker and have been successfully used on a pregnant woman (in prison)" (*Law and Order* 1992a). A medical study revealed in 1986 that, of 218 persons stunned with TASERs in California, 3 had died, but there was evidence that the causes of death may have been PCP rather than electrical shock (Americans for Effective Law Enforcement 1988: 6, citing *Los Angeles Times* 1986). Further, Meyer (1991a: 19; 1992a) argues that, while there have been published articles attributing seven deaths to TASERs, "medical authorities do not believe the TASER was the cause of death in six of these cases, and the authorities argue over whether it was a contributing factor in the seventh." The Los Angeles County Coroner's Office reported in 1987 that, of the seven people in question who had died between 1983 and the end of 1986, "[i]n all cases, the victims were on drugs and died of cardiac arrest," with the TASER contributing to death in only one of these incidents. Meyer cites a local doctor who researched the same cases and concluded that even in the one case the TASER was not very likely to be the cause of death (1991a: 19). At press time, the most recent publicized death connected with a TASER in the L.A. area was that of a County Jail inmate, whom fellow inmates alleged was beaten severely before being shot twice with a TASER by Los Angeles Sheriff's Department deputies on July 19, 1992 (Ford and Rae-Dupree 1992).

[102] It is recommended that TASERs not be stored in car trunks "since long term exposure to temperature extremes could cause damage to the gun" (*Law and Order* 1992a).

■ these devices can be ineffective against a person wearing several layers of clothing"[103] (KCPD 1991: 41).

A manufacturer also warns that the TASER darts are "dangerous to eyes" (*Law and Order* 1992a). Moreover, TASERs must be reloaded to be used more than once or twice (at least some models contain two cartridges, allowing a second shot if the darts miss or do not make proper contact on the first try [*Law and Order* 1992a]), and this may impose unacceptable tactical disadvantages for officers. Stun guns, in particular, have been criticized for being less effective against larger persons than against persons of smaller stature. And the sparks from electrical weaponry can ignite flammable or explosive substances (*Law and Order* 1992a). Thus, as noted in our prior discussion of capsicum, even if a less-than-lethal implement is reliably nonlethal when used as intended and *on its own*, it can become a deadly weapon if used under environmentally hazardous circumstances (e.g., around explosive gases or flammable substances) or if used in conjunction with another normally nonlethal weapon (e.g., an alcohol-propelled chemical followed by an electrical device).

Clede and Parsons (1987: 108) summarize various reasons why the public often has adverse reactions to the use of electricity to control human subjects:

"The electric chair is hardly a nonlethal compliance device, but people think of it when you mention electricity. * * * During World War II, the 'telephone' was used by the Gestapo to aid interrogations. A military field telephone has a hand-cranked magneto to provide ringing power. When interrogators applied electrodes to sensitive parts of the body and turned the crank, intense pain was induced. During the Algerian War, the French used an adaptation of the telephone technique taught at the 'St. Joan of Arc Interrogation School' run by French intelligence agents. During the disorders of the 1960s, some officers used cattle prods against the demonstrators. In psychiatry today, electroshock therapy has fallen into disfavor after a few fatalities showed it was not as safe a treatment as first thought. Then you have the mad scientist movies, with Tesla coils and spark gaps lighting the laboratory where Dr. Frankenstein's monster was made. All this reinforces the negative image of electricity. * * * [Moreover,] electricity can be unpredictable when [the area in which it is used is] wet. Sparking can ignite combustible vapors. And it's too easy to misuse or abuse it."

Meyer (1991, 1992a), an LAPD sergeant who served as the Department's primary researcher on nonlethal weapons before and during the agency's field tests with the TASER (which began in 1981) defended the weapon in the wake of public condemnation after the Rodney King incident. "The TASER," he said, in LAPD field use has been

"largely successful in temporarily but harmlessly incapacitating violent people. No nightsticks. No hospitals [but medical personnel generally are needed to remove the darts—Reich 1992c: B8]. No torn uniforms. Quick resolution to the types of incidents that previously sent a lot of folks (suspects and officers alike) to the hospital and, occasionally, to the grave" (Meyer 1991).

During 1981-91, when LAPD officers used TASERs a few thousand times, they made about 3.5 million arrests (Meyer 1991, 1991a, 1992a). This track record, with barely any post-

---

[103] As noted above, Meyer (1991a: 65; 1992a: 12) says that TASER darts can penetrate up to two inches of clothing.

incident effects of the TASER on its targets other than "two small Band-aids covering the bee sting-like punctures, where the TASER darts hit," led Meyer (1991) to conclude:

> "The TASER has saved lives. Major injuries have been averted. There should be a TASER in every squad car in this country, and they should be used as the weapon of choice over more injurious tactics such as batons and kicks. For the future, the nation that built the Patriot missile and put astronauts on the moon ought to be able to develop an even better nonlethal weapon...."

The L.A. Sheriff's Department has also supported TASERs, insisting that it would continue using the weapons despite criticism by a grand jury (*Crime Control Digest* 1992l; Reich 1992c) and Amnesty International (Murphy 1992: B1; Mydans 1992b), both in June 1992.

Meyer's study of the injuries produced by TASERs and other less-than-lethal weapons or tactics used by LAPD officers bolsters his enthusiasm. Meyer (1991a: 44) compared TASERs with batons, karate kicks, punches, flashlights (used as batons), Mace, the "swarm" tactic (an "organized tackle," in which several officers move in on a suspect, each having responsibility for grabbing and immobilizing a different part of the suspect's body), and "miscellaneous" less-than-lethal tactics. He found that every tactic had a high success rate—effectively achieving the control officers sought in the encounters—ranging from a low of 75 percent effective with punches to 96 percent with flashlights (*ibid.*). But there were marked differences in the likelihood that officers and/or suspects would sustain moderate or major injuries as a result of the effective or ineffective use of the weapons and tactics. TASERs and Mace stood out from the group in that not one officer or suspect in Los Angeles was injured as a result of these weapons. These injury rates compare with effectiveness rates of 86 and 90 percent, respectively (*Law and Order* 1992a reports an "85 percent effectiveness rate in the field"). The injuries Meyer captured were those in which suspects were hurt by the weapon or tactic used and those in which officers were hurt in several situations: in an attack by the suspect while the officer was using the weapon; "from lack of proficiency or physical conditioning; and/or from being struck by another officer who was also confronting the suspect" (Meyer 1991a: 100-101; see also Meyer 1992a).

Summarizing the success and injury rates for some of the other weapons and tactics he studied may help the reader draw comparisons with TASERs. The rates of effectiveness and of moderate/major injuries were: batons (85 percent effective; 16 percent of officers and 61 percent of suspects injured); kicks (87 percent effective; 11 percent of officers and 26 percent of suspects injured); punches (75 percent effective; 36 percent of officers and 64 percent of suspects injured); miscellaneous (94 percent effective; 15 percent of officers and 46 percent of suspects injured); flashlights (96 percent effective; 4 percent of officers and 80 percent of suspects injured); and the swarm technique (92 percent effective; 16 percent of officers and 24 percent of suspects injured) (Meyer 1991a: 44; see also Meyer 1992a).

For Meyer (1991a: 47; 1992a), the bottom line of his analysis was that "the Los Angeles Police Department's nonlethal weapons (TASER and [Mace]) cause fewer and less severe injuries than conventional force types (baton, karate kick, punch, flashlight, swarm, and miscellaneous bodily force)."

Different agencies will reach different conclusions about using electronic weapons based on the available evidence and the evocative imagery of electricity as an instrument of human control. It is a continuing irony of the less-than-lethal weapons field that sometimes the devices that hold the greatest potential for controlling police adversaries with minimum injury are so rooted in Western society's imagery of evil that they become politically untenable. A related point can be made about less-than-lethal *tactics*. Although it is tempting to write the argument off to the necessary partisanship of a courtroom, an LAPD tactics expert, testifying for the defense in the trial of the four officers indicted for beating Rodney King, made an interesting assertion: The LAPD's ban in the early 1980s of the chokehold made officers' use of batons more prevalent. Indeed, the expert, Sergeant Charles L. Duke, Jr., asserted that "King could have been taken into custody within seconds if officers had not been restricted in its [the chokehold's] use" (Serrano 1992).

k. Capture Nets and Extended-Reach Grabbing Devices

Borrowing an idea from the fishing industry, some agencies have used large nets that two officers can throw to ensnare suspects. These devices have proven their worth when officers have had stand-offs with emotionally disturbed or drug-sodden individuals and circumstances permitted fetching the net from a car trunk (Clede and Parsons 1987: 107-108).[104] The L.A. Sheriff's Department has amassed considerable experience with nets and would be a good source of information (Johnston 1981b). Los Angeles *Police* Department nonlethal tactics specialists also favor use of nets (and a related implement, the "leg grabber" or grapple pole),[105] although as of early 1992 budget constraints precluded making these devices available to officers (Serrano 1992). According to Canadian criminal justice policymakers, the Los Angeles *Sheriff*'s Department was dissatisfied with its field experience with capture poles. These are telescoping poles with a noose or net on the end that are used to try to snare a suspect. Reportedly, they proved ineffective for the Sheriff's Department because "the long stand-off distance and slowness of deployment result in a suspect being able to elude the noose or net end of the police; and it takes time to deploy and put together the telescoping sections of the pole" (Jamieson, et al. 1990: 22; see also Steele 1992: 38).

Somewhat similar to nets are restraint blankets. These are not designed to be flung at suspects but are used to wrap around a suspect once apprehended whom authorities believe will continue to struggle violently if simply handcuffed. In a sense, such blankets are an inexpensive form of full body straight jacket (Serrano 1990 : E2). While these have and can be used advantageously, officers have to be careful to avoid having subjects' bodies overheat, which in extreme cases can be fatal. Related to restraint blankets is a product called the "Emergency Response Belt." A cloth belt about six inches wide, it can be used to block an opponent's attempt to strike the officer and to restrain a resisting adversary temporarily (*Law and Order* 1990a).

l. Canines

Police dogs, like other tools of the trade discussed above in this section, can be used to safely and humanely control adversaries or they can be unleashed to maim or even kill. The leading academic authority on historical and current uses of dogs in police work writes:

---

[104] In 1992 the National Institute of Justice was planning to research the acceptability of a variety of new less-than-lethal weapons, some not yet fully developed. One was a capture net capable of being shot from a projectile launcher, which would open as it flew through the air and would be large enough to entangle two people standing close together.

[105] New York City police have experimented with a similar device, a shepherd's hook, which can be hooked around a person's foot to bring him or her down (Serrano 1990: E2). Meyer (1991a: 12) refers to the LAPD's and Los Angeles Sheriff's Department's "intense evaluation" of, among other implements, the "Immobilizer (a combination of poles and chains)" (see also Johnston 1981b: 28).

"Without question, a trained police service dog can inflict serious, even fatal, injuries on a suspect.... However, police service dogs are considered neither as deadly or excessive force nor are they trained to rip, tear, and decimate people. Just the opposite: the dogs are trained to make apprehensions and await the instructions of their handlers. The dogs are considered a tool, much as is a baton, liquid tear gas, a firearm, a flashlight, handcuffs, or keys and whistles. The dog is under the control of the handler, as are any of the tools listed above, and are used as necessary, if at all, within the context of circumstances facing the handler" (Chapman 1990: 126).

At least one federal court of appeals has concurred that use of police dogs does not per se constitute deadly force, even though the dog in question killed a burglary suspect by biting him in the neck (*Robinette v. Barnes* 1988; IACP 1992: 8). But, the court noted, the officer's intent and the training of the dog in question are factors to be weighed in deciding whether a particular dog bite constitutes deadly force (*ibid.*). To be sure, it is widely acknowledged that a canine is an instrument of nonlethal force and, as such, must be used only to the extent that the situation justifies "a real or implied use of force" (IACP 1991a: 1, sec. IV.C.; IACP 1992: 4, 7; see also Blaricom 1992).

In late 1991, the LAPD, already under intense criticism because of the misuse of batons against Rodney King in March of that year, was again assailed—this time for the participation of one of its K-9 officers in a video, intended for broadcast on a local cable station but picked up and aired on CBS network news. The criticism came against the backdrop of community reports that "officers allegedly had dogs attack minority youths already in custody or failed to call off the dogs after the suspect was under control" (Independent Commission on the LAPD 1991: 77-78).[106] The video implied that "dogs are allowed to bite suspects as a reward for having completed a successful search" (Ford 1991a: B1). Specifically, the K-9 officer was interviewed in a video titled "Why Be a Cop?"—which some contend, but LAPD spokespersons deny, was intended for police recruiting. The officer's words were "A patrol dog—his reward, of course, is to bite the suspect" (*ibid.*: B11; Blaricom 1992: 14 concurs that reward bites are common). Besieged departmental officials responded that the K-9 officer was misunderstood and that he was referring not to proper use of *LAPD* dogs but to how *military airport security personnel* use *their* canines (*ibid.*). If the rejoinder was sincere, it provided less than complete reassurance about standards in the profession for use of canines.[107]

---

[106] In July 1992 a panel, headed by former Los Angeles County Superior Court Judge James G. Kolts, and convened by the L.A. County Board of Supervisors, issued a report criticizing the L.A. County Sheriff's Department for, among other things, "the unnecessary use of police dogs in arrests" (*New York Times* 1992j; Kolts, et al. 1992: 75-87).

[107] Even the earliest recorded training of American police dogs did not involve granting bites as rewards. When police dogs were first deployed by American police (the New York City Police Department first experimented in 1907 with dogs imported from Belgium, where the Ghent police had begun using canines in the 1890s), training reportedly included teaching the animals that "any person in uniform was friendly and that all others were potential enemies. [T]he dogs were taught to wrap their legs around one of the suspect's legs and to hold tightly in order to throw the person to the ground. Thereupon the dog was instructed to pounce upon the suspect and bark until the officer arrived" (IACP 1992: 1). Today, there are two principal schools of thought in police dog training: "find and bark" and "find and bite," the latter meaning that the dog holds onto any body part it can get until called off. In the first approach, the canine barks to alert its handler that the suspect has been found and to intimidate the suspect until the officer arrives. But a suspect who resists or attempts to flee will typically then be bitten (Kolts, et al. 1992: 77-79).

Regardless of who meant what in this debate, the flap gave visibility to the question how best to use man's best friend as a constructive, violence-*reducing* part of the police repertoire for securing compliance with lawful instructions. Comparative statistics cited by news reports may lend credence to those who criticized the Department for allowing its dogs to bite suspects too freely. For instance, the Philadelphia Police Department was said to have twice as many dogs as the LAPD. Yet, during 1989-91 in Philadelphia there were 20 reported bites by canines while LAPD dogs, according to departmental statistics, bit people 900 times (*ibid.*). One cannot infer too much from this alone, however, since to compute what police dog specialists call a "bite-ratio"—the ratio of bites to canine deployments or apprehensions without bites—one must have information not only on the number of dogs available in each department but on how frequently each agency fielded its canine teams (Kolts, et al. 1992: 79). One also needs tactical details on how handlers instructed their dogs in various types of encounters, since an unacceptably high "bite ratio"—said by experts to be bites in more than 30 percent of encounters (*ibid.*)—could stem from a problem with the animals, a problem with their handlers, or policy or training decisions (IACP 1992: 4). For instance, the Philadelphia (and Chicago) Police Departments reportedly train their canines in a "find and bark" approach, whereas the L.A. Sheriff's Department reports that about 70 percent of all the agencies it surveyed nationwide follow its own practice of training in the "find and bite" tactic (Kolts, et al. 1992: 78; see also Murphy 1992: B1; Blaricom 1992: 14).

In August 1992, a committee of the LAPD's citizens' police commission praised the Department's recent decision to switch from a find-and-hold to a find-and-bark canine tactic (*New York Times* 1992r). The committee also urged officers in Los Angeles adopt the practice in San Diego, San Francisco, Philadelphia, Indianapolis and other locales, in which officers "routinely issue warnings before the dogs are deployed" (*ibid.*; *Crime Control Digest* 1992r).

The IACP has called upon agencies to thoroughly document each canine incident, regardless of whether an injury occurs, including such details as "whether the canine was immediately called off when the officer could determine that the suspect was under control or not dangerous...and if the dog was leashed immediately thereafter" (*ibid.*; see also *Kerr v. City of West Palm Beach* 1989, discussed in IACP 1992: 8). In addition, the IACP's discussion paper concerning its model policy on police canines recommends that prevailing practice be changed so that dogs are trained "to detect and bark rather than to detect and hold. A canine hold," the report observes, "will almost assuredly result in some degree of injury to a suspect, particularly if the suspect resists" (*ibid.*: 7).

In a more measured response than that made by some critics of police batons (who call for their removal from the police tool kit), critics of the LAPD's use of canines suggested a moratorium on their use until it could be learned whether "the animals have been trained to bite people without provocation" (Ford 1991b). At about the same time, other agencies (e.g., the San Diego Police Department—Hall 1991), recognizing the potential of properly trained dogs for less-than-lethal control of suspects, were expanding their canine units. Nieves (1992) reports an effort to ban use of dogs for *crowd control* in Linden, NJ; on canines generally, see Rivetti (1987): 8, 12, 67-68; Revering (1974); and Chapman (1990). If one is inclined to think of police controlled animals as "less-than-lethal *weapons*," then it would probably be sensible to include police horses and their riders in considerations of the various tools available to police officers for handling different types of situations (especially crowd control).

m. Projectile Launchers

Some less-than-lethal weapons are suitable for general duty officers in that the devices can be worn comfortably on a utility belt. Others are limited to use by special weapons and tactics or emergency response teams. Projectile launchers generally will be of use only for the special squads. The 37-millimeter launchers, manufactured under the brand name "Arwen 37," propel a variety of "low lethality projectiles," including rubber cylindrical batons, tear gas canisters, and stun grenades.[108] Other projectile launchers propel bean bags (typically filled with metal pellets) and water balloons. A double-barrelled weapon called "Flash-Ball," distributed by a Canadian company, shoots rubber, putty-like, and ink-marker balls (*Crime Control Digest* 1992o). Arwen 37s, which contain a five-shot rotary magazine, are used by a number of tactical teams across the United States (Jamieson, et al. 1990: 28). For example:

> "In a circumstance where a suspect is armed with a knife, axe or similar weapon, a tactical team contains the area and deploys the Arwen gun approximately 30 yards away from the suspect. The 'baton' round knocks the suspect over and generally incapacitates him for a period of time. The arrest team can then move in and secure the suspect" (KCPD 1991: 32; see also Jamieson, et al. 1990: 28).

Citing an effective range of 100 yards (rather than the more conservative Kansas City estimate of 30 yards) for the Arwen 37, an advisory team of police policy experts appointed by then-NYPD Commissioner Lee Brown in 1990 recommended that the NYPD add this nonlethal projectile launcher to its arsenal (*Law Enforcement News* 1990a: 9).

Although expensive (in 1990 the launchers sold for $1,500 to $4,000, with each round costing about $20), such weapons (when purchased in small quantities for tactical or SWAT teams) may be cheap compared to the human and financial costs of an officer's or suspect's death. A virtue of the projectile launcher, besides its customary nonlethality, is effectiveness over distances well beyond the immediate striking range of a suspect armed with a contact weapon such as a knife, club, or shovel (see Reich 1992c: B8 for a grand jury's suggestion that the L.A. Sheriff's Department adopt Arwens). Arwen 37s come in different models; some are single-shot; others hold up to six rounds of projectiles. Agencies with field experience using projectile launchers reported to the Kansas City police task force (KCPD 1991: 33) that the device has proven effective against suspects who are mentally deranged or high on drugs and that the typical result of a hit with these projectiles is "bruising with occasional fractures." A possible drawback to firing ballistic projectiles such as rubber batons, bean bags, and such is that until they have travelled a certain distance (some experts estimate at least 20 yards), the projectiles may produce unacceptable injuries (*Crime Control Digest* [1992p] and H.I. Smith [1992] report a close-range death in Prince George's County, Maryland). Moreover, some of the projectiles cannot be fired with what is considered acceptable accuracy.

Besides the Arwen 37-millimeter projectile launchers, some projectiles can be launched

---

[108] Stun grenades (also called "flashbangs") produce a loud bang and bright flash but do not emit shrapnel (some early devices on the market *did* injure people with flying metal pieces, but these fragmentation problems have been largely overcome—Jamieson, et al. 1990: 29). They are typically used to distract and disorient momentarily barricaded suspects so that officers can rush them during the confusion (Clede and Parsons 1987: 108; Heal 1990). Flash-sound diversionary devices generally produce effective disorientation for approximately five seconds. They have become increasingly familiar parts of the arsenal in the "war on drugs," in which police raid teams sometimes engage in highly coordinated assaults on drug houses to execute search and arrest warrants. The Los Angeles Sheriff's Department has long experience with flashbangs, reporting that they were deployed hundreds of times over the 1980s without producing any serious injuries (Heal 1990). Still, there are drawbacks to these devices, including the risk of sparking a fire, causing hearing loss, propelling loose objects that they are touching when detonated, and inducing heart problems in particularly vulnerable persons. Strobe lights have also been studied for their disorienting effects, and they can induce seizures in epileptics.

from specially equipped M-16 rifles. One such projectile, which can be fired with more accuracy than some other ballistic projectiles and is considered nonlethal at all ranges,[109] is known as the sting-RAG (ring airfoil grenade) (Sweetman 1987). Developed by the U.S. Army (Shubin 1984: 35), this is not cloth (as the RAG acronym might suggest) but a small, pliable, cylindrical rubber ring about 2½ inches long and 1½ inches in circumference (Rivetti 1987: 14). A variant on this impact weapon is the "soft-RAG," a similarly shaped soft rubber cylinder that contains tear gas or mace powder, which is released upon impact (*ibid.*). Thus, the soft-RAG is a hybrid impact/chemical weapon. The softness of the rubber used in both the sting- and soft-RAGs is said to prevent them from causing injury upon impact, unless the subject is struck in an especially vulnerable location, such as the eyes. Designers say they are effective at nearly 200 feet. Among the disadvantages of RAGs are all those associated with tear gas and mace (see discussion above), as well as the possibility that wind could take the projectile off course or impede the effectiveness of the small cloud of tear gas (approximately 4 feet in diameter) that is released on impact. Heavy clothing can also reduce the effects of the RAGs. They also need to be fired from an M-16 launcher (*ibid.*).

One of the oldest nonlethal "projectiles" is water, sprayed under high pressure from water "cannons." Sometimes used for crowd control (especially in prison riots), pressurized water has the virtue of being very unlikely to produce death or serious injury (although panicked crowds could trample some of their members in the process of retreating). A number of police experts find water cannons undesirable on the grounds that they are expensive and unwieldy pieces of equipment (Jamieson, et al. 1990: 23). As with several other less-than-lethal weapons, water cannons may also be unacceptable not for technical but for political reasons. They may be associated with state repression of political demonstrators around the world.

Thus when police departments contemplate using various nonlethal weapons (especially electric stunning weapons), they must be mindful not only of effectiveness and potential lethality but of the way at least some segments of the public may (accurately or inaccurately) perceive use of these weapons. Some nonlethal weaponry evokes powerful emotional reactions because it is reminiscent of implements of oppression used in other times and places. For instance, part of the national horror over the brutal beating of Rodney King by LAPD officers was that the specter of agents of the state clubbing and kicking a downed black man evoked images of overt racial oppression in American history and of modern day abuses in South Africa and elsewhere.

Similarly, when two New York City police officers on April 22, 1985, misused a stun gun to torture incriminating information out of a criminal suspect, at least part of the reason then-Commissioner Benjamin Ward responded by demoting or otherwise punishing virtually everyone in the officer's chain of command, up through the NYPD's chief of patrol (*New York Times* 1991: 14; Clede and Parsons 1987: 108), was the symbolism attached to the stun gun. The device evoked images of torture techniques under totalitarian regimes and of the use of cattle prods to control political dissidents.

Sometimes a police department expects that its use of nonlethal weapons in lieu of firearms will win it greater support in sectors of the community where the department traditionally has not enjoyed strong support (see, e.g., Meyer 1991). Sometimes this will be

---

[109] In appraising whether it is likely to be nonlethal at all ranges, the reader might consider estimates that the impact of being struck by the sting-RAG is like taking a "sharp jab" from "a professional boxer" (Rivetti 1987: 14).

the case. But often the department's "reward" for breaking a suspect's leg or zapping him with a TASER rather than shooting him will be cries of police brutality. What may make the difference between expressions of gratitude and calls for the chief's head in the wake of high-visibility violent encounters are two factors: (1) the department's prior reputation for professionalism and restraint in the use of force; and (2) the department's prior success in educating the public and shaping its expectations about what is possible—and what is not possible—for police to do, given the state of the art of lethal and nonlethal weaponry.

The public, the media, politicians, and other public opinion makers need to understand that, typically, it is *not* possible for police to shoot a gun out of a suspect's hand ala Wyatt Earp or to "wing" a fleeing dangerous suspect. That is why police almost universally are trained to shoot for the largest portion of an adversary's body (the torso)—in the hope of hitting him at all. There needs to be widespread understanding, too, that the alternative to using various nonlethal weapons and to inflicting a variety of nonlethal wounds (such as broken bones) may well be a fatal encounter, in which the victims may be not only suspected offenders but police officers, crime victims, and bystanders.

Police departments are not unaccustomed to a violent suspect's family thanking the police for having found a nonlethal (even if somewhat injurious) way to subdue their relative, rather than resorting to deadly force. But these situations are hardly the norm. Perhaps with more concerted attention to enhancing police skills with nonlethal weapons and providing officers with these devices, as well as improved efforts to educate the public about the myths and realities of police tactical options,[110] departments can reduce bloodshed and reap the rewards of a better public image.

Still, there appears to be no technological breakthrough on the horizon that will relegate the revolver and the pistol to police museums. As our discussions earlier in this volume of the move to semi-automatics as officers' primary sidearms suggest, changes in the firearm itself, if any, are more likely to continue in the direction of greater rather than less lethality to meet the "arms escalation" by at least some segments of the criminal population. Nevertheless, lightweight, readily accessible *ancillary* nonlethal devices may continue to gain favor with police departments that recognize that different tasks require different tools.

4. The Quest for Effective, Practical, Less-Lethal Weapons: On the Drawing Board

As policing evolves during the final decade of this century, the quest for a supplement to the police firearm that would allow for nonlethal capture of individuals continues. "Practical" is the key word here. In the early days of experimentation with less-than-lethal devices, brainstorming led to all kinds of options, some of which were amusingly *impractical.* One of our favorites has long been the electronic instrument that generates a low frequency tone, which causes loss of bowel control. Reddin (1967), writing in *Police Chief* magazine, enthused about this device's "fantastic potential for suppressing riots." The only problem, he conceded, was that as yet nobody had figured out how to make the device *directional.*

In recent times, the principal governmental initiative to stimulate the needed research and development began with former Attorney General Edwin Meese III's "Attorney General's Conference on Less-than-Lethal Weapons," held at the FBI Academy in Quantico, Virginia,

---

[110] Some information about police capabilities and tactics obviously should not be publicized lest police work be made even more dangerous than it is already.

in 1986 with support from the National Institute of Justice (see Sweetman 1987; for earlier work on less-than-lethal weaponry, see research cited and discussed in Geller and Karales [1981a: 200, 253-55]). This was a follow-up to a U.S. Attorney General's Conference on "The Future of Less Lethal Weapons" held in 1972 (Rivetti 1987: 15). The 1986 conference and subsequent government initiatives were prompted by the U.S. Supreme Court's March 1985 decision in *Tennessee v. Garner*,

> "which held that use of deadly force to apprehend an apparently unarmed, nonviolent fleeing felon is unreasonable seizure under the fourth amendment. This highlighted law enforcement officers' need for nonlethal weapons to avoid killing or inflicting serious injury to fleeing suspects" (National Institute of Justice 1992a: 135).

The 1986 Attorney General's conference heard presentations from a wide variety of researchers (military scientists and engineers, police agency-based policy analysts, social science scholars, civil rights experts, and others), including the lead author of this volume.

It was not always easy during the deliberations at this conference to determine how close the research and development efforts being conducted by military researchers were to developing a substantially more effective less-lethal weapon. Nor was it at all clear that the military's objectives for such a weapon (e.g., for riot control purposes or the nonlethal control of civilian populations during times of military conflict) would necessarily have a direct bearing on the typical hostile police-civilian encounter in the United States. Nevertheless, there was a general consensus among the conferees that if a breakthrough came in the military arena there might be important opportunities for adaptation to civilian policing.

One got the impression from presentations by military researchers at this conference that there already existed both rapidly (perhaps instantly) incapacitating nonlethal chemicals and some promising ideas for instruments that would deliver these chemicals over a relatively long distance (perhaps 10-30 yards).

One line of research apparently was exploring the utility of chemical agents and delivery devices. If such a device had an instantaneous effect on all people (at least those unequipped with gas masks) within a predictable range of the place where the chemical was released, it would be of obvious value in hostage situations. For instance, in a bank robbery-turned hostage situation, police would greatly benefit if they could envelop the entire bank with a chemical that would "freeze" or put to sleep everyone within the building so that police could safely approach and remove the victims and offenders. As the American public learned

> *"Non-lethal weapons offer an opportunity to save life and to avoid the uncomfortable and sometimes devastating consequences that can accompany police shootings. We currently appear to be on the threshold of the discovery of weapons and chemicals that will provide safe and functional substitutes for death-dealing guns" (Geis and Binder 1990).*

during the Persian Gulf War, however, when there was much discussion about Iraq's possible use of chemical weaponry, exactly how broad an area is affected by chemicals delivered by an exploding projectile depends on a number of factors. Some of these factors can be controlled by those in control of the weaponry; others are weather and other environmental conditions well beyond the tactician's and field operative's control.

Another line of research and development presumably being pursued is the development of less-than-lethal weapons with a discrete impact on a targeted individual rather than on all persons within a given area. Close-combat examples of such less-than-lethal weapons currently in use are the TASER, stun gun, and hand-held capsicum spray cans, all discussed above. But the objective of most of the research described at the Attorney General's Conference was the development of a device useful over greater distances.

In pursuit of a breakthrough in less-than-lethal weaponry, the challenge remains to identify containers or other projectiles that can be fired accurately and at high speed, that can penetrate clothing (including heavy layers of outerwear)—or that do not depend for effectiveness on direct contact with skin—but that will not produce lethal harm on impact. One possibility discussed at the 1986 conference that generated considerable interest was the sting-RAG, a soft rubber impact projectile capable of carrying tear gas-type chemicals. We discussed it above.

The federal Office of Justice Programs (OJP) (which comprises the National Institute of Justice [NIJ], Bureau of Justice Assistance [BJA], Bureau of Justice Statistics [BJS], and other funding and technical assistance agencies) in January 1991 announced its intention to continue funding research on less-than-lethal weapons: "This project...supports research on a field prototype of a less than lethal weapon" (Office of Justice Programs 1991: 1694). The OJP announced its intention to commit $1.7 million to this area of technology development, with the NIJ retaining sponsorship and oversight of the research.

In NIJ's 1992 *Research and Evaluation Plan*, the agency again included "research to develop less-than-lethal weaponry for use by law enforcement" in its Technology Research and Development Program. Also in 1992 the NIJ enlisted the assistance of federal Department of Energy scientists in researching less-than-lethal control technology (*Crime Control Digest* 1992p: 6). Summarizing recent work, NIJ reported that "[l]ess-than-lethal weapons development has concentrated on the identification and development of prototype delivery systems for alternatives that include chemical agents and laser light" (NIJ 1992a: 134). After holding a small conference of law enforcement practitioners and academics in July 1991 to receive input from a variety of interested parties concerning less-than-lethal weaponry (Nulton 1991), the NIJ also detailed its plans for research and development in this area during 1992 and beyond (*ibid.*: 135):

> "Law enforcement officials have...cited a need for nonlethal or less-than-lethal weapons for use in [apprehending fleeing suspects], hostage situations, domestic disturbances, barricade/tactical assault, search warrant/raid, and prison/jail disturbances.

> "It has been recognized that no one technology can meet the needs of all law enforcement situations. Less-than-lethal technologies can take many forms. In 1992, NIJ will investigate recent developments in such technologies as visible light, laser beams, microwaves, sound waves (acoustics), entanglement, impact weapons, electromagnetic fields, and electric fields.[111] Issues to be investigated in these technical assessments will include delivery systems for a range of existing and future less-than-lethal weapons, safety margins for the operational

---

[111] As early as 1984, an NIJ scientist predicted that military research on "human sensory perceptions...may produce non-lethal weapons based on the use of sound, light, or odorants" (Shubin 1984: 35).

use of proposed methods such as chemical and laser systems,[112] and quantifying other issues such as cleaning up hazardous materials employed in less-than-lethal technologies.

"To clearly define user needs and requirements, NIJ will sponsor a survey to be conducted through working groups of law enforcement and criminal justice officials and representatives from other government agencies. The working groups will explore the kinds of weapons currently being used, the policies and procedures that agencies have developed for the use of nonlethal force, and the relative effectiveness of the types of less-than-lethal weapons currently employed by State and local law enforcement agencies. The survey is designed to provide information on the extent of current less-than-lethal weapon use and to serve as a foundation for the development of a long-term research agenda featuring development of multiple technologies for NIJ."

Shortly after the 1986 Attorney General's Conference on Less-than-Lethal Weapons, a police manager studying at the Command College sponsored by the California Commission on Police Officer Standards and Training (POST) in Sacramento, California, conducted a "Delphi" study[113] in which a panel of experts was convened to forecast possible future scenarios concerning the development of less-than-lethal weaponry for American police. Two of their alternative future scenarios—the "worst case" and case "most likely to occur"—struck us as worth sharing with a wider readership than the unpublished paper might have received (Rivetti 1987). Thus, from the vantage point of 1987, here is how these lines of development were envisioned by a panel that included "one police officer, two police chiefs, one lieutenant colonel with the United States Air Force, one doctor, and two [staff] members of the National Institute of Justice" (*ibid.*: 21):

"*Scenario 1: Worst Case*

"It is the year 2000. The world continues in the worst recession/depression since the 1930s. The banking collapse due to Third World loan defaults in the early 1990s has yet to be repaired. The huge United States Federal deficit kept the United States from being able to absorb the shock of the defaults, and the United States economy reached record lows, with the Dow Jones Industrial Average returning to below 1000.

"With the price of oil returning to $40+ per barrel, the United States foreign trade deficit continues to grow. As the cost of electricity soars, the United States moves to increasing use of nuclear power as a means to reduce dependence on foreign crude oil suppliers.

"The financial crash affected the Soviet Union terribly, destroying its ability

---

[112] Laser technology obviously has provided wonderfully useful breakthroughs in many fields, particularly medicine and communications. Yet, some of the devices studied for police use have been rejected as less-than-lethal weapons because they are too likely to cause burns and blindness. Among the existing—and contemplated—less-than-lethal devices to which the NIJ sought to explore practitioner receptivity in 1992 were a "sticky foam," which would inhibit a suspect's movement or flight, a projectile entanglement net (to be shot out of a launcher rather than thrown by hand, which would also thwart escape and resistance), and a strobe-type light that disorients viewers.

[113] A Delphi study is a set of methods that can be used to forge agreement among a number of experts convened as a group to explore the likelihood of various events occurring.

to purchase food from producing nations.[114] The United States continues to use food as a weapon of diplomacy.

"The only sector of the economy that continues to boom is the aerospace/defense industry. With most world economies in shambles, localized civil wars are common. At the present time, the United States is involved in three major 'police actions': Egypt/Middle East, Indonesia, and Central America. Only the wrecked Soviet economy keeps that country from expansionist adventurism.

"In the United States, food and race riots have become common. In more than one city, marshal law has been ordered with shoot to kill orders for looters.

"Community support for police is high, as it is the last defense against barbarism. But judicial and community attitudes have changed towards suspects and criminals. Judges nominated and confirmed during the Reagan Presidency are likely to side with police in lethal force situations, and are much harder on violent criminals. The public, afraid of the lawless streets, continue to push for more [and] tougher police, but in lean monetary times, police budgets are extremely tight. Any money available is spent on officers.

"The less lethal weapons that made a strong showing in the mid-1980s have for the most part disappeared. The cost of such weapons in terms of training, maintenance, support, replacement and upgrade became more than most police departments could afford."

"Scenario 2: Most Likely to Occur

"The year is 2000. Following the 1993 invasion of Nicaragua by the United States Marines in retaliation for Sandinista forays into Costa Rica and Guatemala, anti-United States demonstrations at major universities became common. The hot spot, as usual, was Berkeley, where sit-ins regularly led to violent confrontations with local police. At one such violent demonstration, a mentally disturbed young man opened fire with a semi-automatic 'assault' type weapon. Three police officers were killed before their colleagues could return fire. By the time the smoke cleared, the three police officers were dead, but so were 17 innocent protestors. Although police shooting teams and coroners' juries absolved the police of blame, civil liability awards nearly bankrupted the City of Berkeley, California.

"Fearing a similar situation in the south, Los Angeles Mayor Michael Woo ordered the Los Angeles Police Department to train a special squad to deal with potentially dangerous demonstrators. The squad was armed only with an array of various less lethal weapons. This squad was backed up by conventionally armed officers. During a major demonstration at the University of California at Los Angeles (UCLA), the Los Angeles Police Department's Less Lethal Weapon SWAT Team disabled 43 rock and bottle throwing demonstrators. One demonstrator, shooting a .22 caliber pistol, wounded one officer in the arm but was disabled and arrested without further incident.

"After several more roll-outs for the Less Lethal Weapon SWAT Team, the Los Angeles Police Department began teaching seminars in less lethal weapon tactics to police departments nationwide. By 1995, 370 local and major metropolitan law enforcement agencies had initiated Less Lethal Weapon SWAT Teams. Unfortunately, the less lethal weapons available could only be considered

---

[114] The experts may be forgiven for not having the clairvoyance in 1987 to anticipate the complete dissolution of the Soviet Union.

improvements over the weapons available in the late 1980s. Aspiring to be the Governor, Mayor Woo organized a national Ad-Hoc committee in 1996 to promote the development of less lethal weapons. Mayor Woo's committee consisted of police chiefs of both large and small police departments, mayors, city managers, parents and businessmen.

"Using the Freedom of Information Act, the Committee for less lethal weapons obtained records of all military less lethal weapons research and development. In testimony before Congress, Mayor Woo charged that the military was refusing to release non-sensitive less lethal weapon technology on the false pretext of national security concerns. Small and medium sized businesses charged that the military was keeping the technology secret in order to keep large defense contractors from having to compete with smaller, more efficient companies in less lethal weapon manufacturing.

"With the continued success of less lethal weapons in the field, the public, and therefore the media, became interested in less lethal weapons. And, under pressure from the White House, the Department of Defense declassified several mature less lethal weapon technologies in late 1997. Many firms entered the less lethal weapon business, but both the technologies and the less lethal weapons produced continued to be expensive. The military continued less lethal weapon research and declassified technology when appropriate. Large metropolitan police departments pooled resources to research less lethal weapons peculiar to large urban police situations. Federal funds through the Federal Bureau of Investigation, the Justice Department, and the National Institute of Justice trickled down to contractors who continued to develop improved systems. Smaller law enforcement agencies benefited from the efforts of large police departments and federal expenditures.

"By 2000, 89 percent of all police departments had officers trained in state-of-the-art less lethal weapon tactics and technology. The number of less lethal weapons in the field continued to be small when compared to firearms, but their number was increasing yearly. The number of firearms issued declined in relation to the number of officers in the field. Slowly, as costs were reduced, less lethal weapons entered service. The Department of Justice forecast predicts near complete saturation of effective less lethal weapons by 2030" (Rivetti 1987: 40-45).

5.   *Soft Body Armor and Other Protective Gear*

One type of supplementary protective equipment—soft body armor—is gaining acceptance among police. It has demonstrated its ability to save police lives, and eventually it may also be shown to bear a constructive relationship to officer arrest effectiveness and violence reduction. The best evidence that such devices have demonstrated their worth in protecting officers are the 1,448 "saves" documented by the IACP and the DuPont Corporation (which manufactures the "kevlar" fabric used in soft body armor) between 1972, when the products went on the market,[115] and September 21, 1992. Of the 1,448 officers, 795 were saved from assaults and 653 from accidents (Slavin 1992a). Experts estimate that at least 200 additional

---

[115] The development and field testing of soft body armor, as an alternative to heavy flack jackets of earlier vintage, was prompted by NIJ, which had commissioned research to invent a better way to make tires for police squad cars—so that tires would not so readily blow out during high-speed pursuits. Out of this line of inquiry came the invention of the fabric kevlar, which NIJ scientist and technology assessment program staff member Lester D. Shubin had the insight to experiment with not only for belting tires but for placing in protective apparel (Shubin 1984: 33; compare IACP 1990c: 3).

officers have had their lives saved during this nearly 21-year period.

Tables 26, 27, and 28 show the weapons, types of accidents, and underlying circumstances involved in the documented 1,381 "saves" that occurred as of March 15, 1992 (IACP/DuPont Kevlar Survivors' Club 1992).[116]

During the years 1972 through 1991, FBI annual reports on law enforcement officers killed and assaulted document the *felonious* slaying of 1,845 officers (see Table E-3 in Appendix E). Thus, adding the 760 officers saved from assaults as of March 15, 1992, it becomes clear that, without soft body armor, the death toll of American police who were slain *feloniously* over this more than 20-year period would have been more than 2,600.

This is not to say that officers wearing vests never suffer fatal wounds. They do, as Table 29, based on FBI data, shows. But police officials, FBI analysts, and soft body armor industry professionals generally agree that it is extremely rare for a bullet-resistant vest to be defeated in field combat by a round it is designed to stop. Where the fatal injuries, reflected in Table 29, have occurred, generally they result from a bullet entering an unprotected area on the officer or from use of a round with a higher penetrating potential than the soft body armor was designed to stop (see IACP 1990c: 4).

*It began as a routine investigation of a car without plates parked by the edge of a wooded area. Two squad cars responded. The driver of the parked vehicle, whom police would later learn was a fugitive from a neighboring state, "walked quickly to the side of [one of the squad cars] and fired twice.... The officer [still seated in his squad] was wearing a wrap-around bullet-proof vest, but one shot went through his unprotected shoulder. A second bullet slammed underneath his armpit and severed his heart, killing him instantly police said. After [the offender shot the first officer, he] apparently wheeled to his left and fired three quick shots at [the second officer, then standing beside the front of his squad car], who was also wearing a protective vest. The officer, who was hit once on the right side and once in the lower abdomen, fell to the ground, bleeding. * * * But as [the culprit] jumped behind the wheel of his car to make his getaway, [the wounded officer] managed to lift himself up and fired two shots through the windshield, hitting [the assailant] in the face [and killing him]" (Koziol and Donato 1992).*

"It was a routine traffic stop.... Officer Harrison Speakes ordered the motorist out of the car. Apparently high on drugs, the man pointed a handgun at Speakes. Speakes grabbed him, and they fell into the street together. The motorist shot Speakes twice in the abdomen, knocking the officer back. Then he shot Speakes two more times, point-blank. Speakes was wearing a bulletproof vest. He had some nasty bruises, which lasted a year, but was otherwise OK. It was November 27, 1987. Thanksgiving Day" (Ritter 1992).

"The first soft body armor was made of silk fibers and worn in medieval Japan. Later, silk vests provided limited protection against handgun bullets fired at low velocity. Austrian Archduke Francis Ferdinand was believed to be wearing a vest when an assassin shot him, setting off World War I" (Ritter 1992).

---

[116] Such detailed data were not available as of September 21, 1992, when we received an updated tally of total saves to date, and therefore were not available as we went to press.

"The U.S. Army developed nylon vests during World War II and the Korean War. They gave greater protection [than silk vests] but were bulky. The major breakthrough came in the early 1970s, with the introduction of Kevlar, a strong plastic fiber made by DuPont. Kevlar fibers are woven into fabric; most vests contain about 20 layers.

"Early Kevlar vests were heavy and bulky. But DuPont has developed lighter, stronger fibers, and manufacturers have become more adept at using the material. A typical vest now is just a quarter-inch thick and weighs 2 to 4 pounds. Kevlar is five times stronger than steel, and DuPont is working to develop even stronger fibers. Meanwhile, some manufacturers are beginning to use a competing high-strength plastic fiber made by Allied Signal, called Spectra. And genetic engineers are trying to make a material with the same properties as spider silk, which is stronger than Kevlar. But making a cool vest will be the biggest challenge. Plastic fabric doesn't breathe, so it feels like a raincoat. A few manufacturers are using a liner made of Coolmax. This DuPont fabric, originally designed for athletes, cools the body by whisking sweat away from the skin so it evaporates more quickly" (Ritter 1992).

Table 26:
"Saves" of American Officers by Soft Body Armor: Weapons Used in Assaults and Types of Accidents, as of March 15, 1992 (n=1,381)

Incident Type	Weapon/Type of Accident	# of POs Saved	% of All POs Saved by SBA
Assaults	Handguns	414	30%
	Shotguns	55	4%
	Rifles	14	1%
	Unknown Calibers	42	3%
	TOTAL FIREARMS	(525)	(38%)
	Knives/Cutting Instruments	166	12%
	Clubs/Blunt Instruments	42	3%
	Other (dogs, beatings, etc.)	28	2%
Accidents	Automobiles	524	38%
	Motorcycles	42	3%
	Other Vehicles	14	1%
	ALL VEHICLES	(580)	(42%)
	Falls	13	1%
	Firearms	13	1%
	Other (fires, explosions, etc.)	14	1%

Source: IACP/Dupont Kevlar Survivors' Club (1992).

**Table 27:
Circumstances of Assault in "Saves" of American Officers by
Soft Body Armor, as of March 15, 1992 (n=760)**

Circumstances During Assault	Number of Officers Saved	% of All POs Saved in Assaults
Traffic Pursuits/Stops	122	16%
Invest. Suspicious Persons	114	15%
Drug-related matters	91	12%
Attempting arrests *other than* robbery, burglary, and drug-related	84	11%
Domestic Disturbance	67	9%
*Non*domestic Disturbance	61	8%
Mentally Deranged	46	6%
Robbery in Progress/Pursuit	46	6%
Burglary in Progress/Pursuit	46	6%
Ambush (entrapment, pre-meditated & unprovoked)	38	5%
Handling of Prisoners	15	2%
Civil Disorders	15	2%
All Others	15	2%
TOTAL	760	100%

Source: IACP/DuPont Kevlar Survivors' Club (1992).

When one understands that the data provided in Table 29 generally do not imply any deficiency in the soft body armor worn by these officers and that, to the contrary, soft body armor is a proven life-saver for law enforcement personnel, it is readily apparent why the IACP recommends in its model policies on deadly

"Police [in suburban Chicago] have reacted to the increased violence by improving training and by wearing the bullet-proof vests they once left hanging in their lockers. 'In the last year or two, there's been a tremendous increase in the number of...officers who are wearing them,' said [a suburban police chief]. 'We went from about 40 or 50 percent who wore them on a daily basis—now it's 97 percent' " (Goering and McRoberts 1992: 20).

force and body armor that departments mandate the wearing of department-authorized soft body armor at all times by on-duty officers assigned to "field operations" (Matulia 1985: 79; IACP 1989a, 1990c; see also Appendix B). This recommendation would exempt detectives while working indoors and other personnel on an as-needed basis (e.g., during undercover

Table 28:
Circumstances of Accidents in "Saves" of American Officers by
Soft Body Armor, as of March 15, 1992 (n=621)

Circumstances during Accident	Number of Officers Saved	% of All POs Saved in Accidents
Resp. to Emergency Calls	149	24%
Routine Patrols	106	17%
High Speed Pursuit	75	12%
Pursuing Suspects	62	10%
Directing Traffic	50	8%
Traffic Stops	37	6%
Enroute to/from Work	31	5%
Firearms/Bombings	31	5%
Responding to Non-Emergency Calls	25	4%
Assisting Motorists	19	3%
All Others	36	6%
TOTAL	621	100%

Source: IACP/DuPont Kevlar Survivors' Club (1992).

work when the protective apparel might give the agent away or when an officer has a medical problem that precludes wearing the vest) (IACP 1990c: 7). While not mandating the wearing of soft body armor, the standards of the Commission on Accreditation for Law Enforcement Agencies provide that "a bulletproof vest or jacket [should be] available to officers assigned to routine field duty" (CALEA 1988: Standard 41.2.16). This is important because, as John Jay College of Criminal Justice found in a

"A vest protects by catching the bullet in a 'netlike web of fibers,' explains a recent study by Congress' Office of Technology Assessment. 'As in any net, the key to success is that many fibers, even those not actually touching the bullet, elongate in response to the collision and so absorb the energy of the bullet' " (Ritter 1992).

national survey of 3,500 police officers, officers are more likely to wear soft body armor if it is provided to them by their employers (*Law Enforcement News* 1991; *Crime Control Digest* 1991o; see also our discussion of soft body armor in Chapter 3).

Those who urge mandatory wear policies might increase their persuasiveness by pointing out that, just as police labor to keep pace with the increasingly powerful and high-capacity weapons in the hands of criminals, they should keep pace with those criminals who place bullet-resistant vests on their own backs. In a shoot-out that made national headlines in June 1992, a gunman wearing soft body armor entered an office building in Phoenix and began shooting people, killing a woman and injuring two others before police shot him to death (*New York Times* 1992e).

The NYPD is an example of a big-city agency that has taken the initiative in the past several years to mandate that at least specified groups of field personnel wear soft body armor. The reasons are not difficult to fathom: Between February 1978 and the end of 1991, 35 of New York's finest had their lives saved by bullet-resistant vests; all but three were saved from gun assaults (Cerar 1990: 29-30, 1991: 31).

Table 29:
Location of Fatal Firearm Wounds for All American Officers Killed and
Officers Killed While Wearing Soft Body Armor, 1985-91

Year	Head Wounds		Upper Torso		Lower Torso		All Wounds	
	Total POs Killed	POs Killed While in Armor	Total POs Killed	POs Killed While in Armor	Total POs Killed	POs Killed While in Armor	Total POs Killed	POs Killed While in Armor
1985	27	8	43	5	0	0	70	13
1986	26	6	33	6	3	2	62	14
1987	31	13	32	3	4	0	67	16
1988	37	15	36	3	3	2	76	20
1989	27	10	24	6	6	3	57	19
1990	31	11	22	2	3	2	56	15
1991	36	N/A[1]	28	N/A[1]	4	N/A[1]	68[2]	24
Total #	215	63[1]	218	25[1]	23	9[1]	456	121[1]
Total %	47	66	48	26	5	9	100	101[3]

Sources: FBI (1989b, 1991b), Behm (1992).
[1] *The subtotals of officers killed in 1991 while in armor were not available at press time (Behm 1992).*
[2] *The number of officers killed with all weapons in 1991 was 71; 68 were killed with firearms (Behm 1992).*
[3] *Does not total 100 percent due to rounding. All the percentages in this row for officers wearing soft body armor when slain were calculated on a total of 97 deaths (i.e., excluding from 121 the 1991 tally of 24).*

In Chicago, the Police Department for several years tried to mandate the wearing of soft body armor by *all* sworn personnel (L. Martin 1990; Kass 1992a). The Department and the Fraternal Order of Police went to arbitration over whether the costs of the equipment (about $300 per vest), would be borne by the agency or individual officers. The arbitrator ruled in 1991 that only officers whose vests' five-year warranties had not expired could be ordered to wear them, which obligated only about 20 percent of the force to wear the protective gear. While the parties continued their dickering, several Chicago officers who were not wearing soft body armor were shot while on duty, among them a young policewoman (who lived) and a veteran policeman (who was buried on March 12, 1992) (Recktenwald and Bradbery 1992; Stein and Wiltz 1992; Stein 1992; Seibel 1992). On August 4, 1992, the City administration announced it would spend $2.6 million in drug asset forfeiture funds to buy vests for all Department members, in return for which it would expand the mandatory wear order agencywide. Union officials acknowledged the increasing dangers faced by its members—"83 [Chicago] officers were shot at while on duty during the six months that ended June 30, [1992] compared with 43 during the first half of 1991" (Brown 1992: 1)—but still groused about a mandatory-wear policy (*ibid.*; Kass 1992a; O'Connor 1992a).

In its 1990 Law Enforcement Management and Administrative Statistics survey, the federal Bureau of Justice Statistics found that approximately 24 percent of America's "local police departments required all regular field and patrol officers to wear body armor while on duty." The prevalence of mandatory wear policies was about the same among sheriffs' departments (21 percent), but only 12 percent of state police departments imposed a similar obligation (Bureau of Justice Statistics 1992a, 1992b; *Crime Control Digest* 1992b: 7). Agencies have been reluctant to mandate the wear of soft body armor because of rank-and-file opposition to having their choices foreclosed and the concern that violations of a mandatory-wear policy would deprive injured officers of workers' compensation benefits and the survivors of slain officers of insurance benefits (IACP 1990c: 7). Neither of these considerations outweigh the importance of mandatory-wear regulations, according to the IACP (*ibid.*).

> "A Wood Street District patrolman said Friday that 'I thought someone had thrown a brick at me' when a .22-caliber bullet hit his bulletproof vest—instead of his heart. 'It went just to the left of my star, directly to my heart,' said [the officer], 24. 'The doctor told my mother it would've been non-survivable if it hadn't hit my vest.' Instead, 'It knocked the wind out of me, like someone had punched me in the chest,' [he] said. [The officer], who had been on the force about a year, was patrolling with his partner outside the...public housing complex on the West Side about 7 p.m. on Thursday.
> " 'They noticed two boys fighting and pulled over to break up the dispute,' he said. 'They were two brothers, aged 10 and 12,' [the officer saved by his vest] said. 'They were fighting on the street because the little guy wouldn't go home and the older one was trying to make him go home.' The officers escorted the boys to their apartment in the...high-rise...and then returned to their squad car. 'We never heard a sound' when the bullet was fired, he said.
> "He felt it hit and yelled, 'Get down! Get down!' to his partner.... We were on our hands and knees, hiding behind the car....' [His partner] looked over and said, 'There's a hole in your vest. You've been shot....' Police believe the shot came from a .22-caliber long rifle fired from the upper floors of the...high-rise.... * * * [The victim officer] said he didn't know whether the shot was meant for him or was random fire. * * * [A] sergeant checked [the] vest to see whether the bullet had penetrated and found a bullet between the layers of his vest, right over his heart. [It had first penetrated his leather jacket.] * * *
> "[The police chief] has been urging use of the bulletproof vests and [the saved officer], a third-generation police officer who follows the tradition of his grandfather, his father and his mother, said he hopes his close call will help persuade other officers to wear them. That includes his mother, [a] Foster Avenue District Officer..., and his partner..., who wasn't wearing a vest when the shot rang out Thursday night. 'Thank God it was in my vest,' [the saved officer] said, 'and not in his chest'" (Myers 1991; also see Casey 1991).

Often composed of or lined with the same material as soft body armor are other items of protective gear. These include jackets, raincoats, sportcoats, overcoats, ballistic helmets, shields, clipboards, and various other pieces of police equipment that might stop a bullet or other life-threatening objects (Rutledge 1988: 131-132; IACP 1990c: 5). Except in special circumstances, they are not substitutes for but may be useful supplements to the wearing of soft body armor by police.

Chapter 6:

SOME FINAL THOUGHTS

I. Setting Agency Standards of Conduct by Managing Organizational Values

Generally, the two most promising types of strategies for controlling the use of deadly force by police officers are:

- shrinking the outer limits of discretion to use deadly force (through laws, policies, training, equitable disciplinary systems, the shaping of peer pressure, and other methods for managing a police department's "organizational culture"); and

- strengthening officers' capacities to exercise self-restraint in using deadly force.

We have seen in Chapter 5 that officers' capacities for self-restraint may be enhanced through many approaches: personnel selection (i.e., seeking officers with suitable self-control—by no means an exact science at this time); counseling; "coaching" by supervisors (see Kelling, et al. 1988); violence-reduction training (see, e.g., Geller 1985a: 154; Fyfe 1989a) and other skill building; ancillary equipment (mobile communications, less-than-lethal weaponry, soft body armor, etc.); procedural modifications (e.g., concerning methods for high-risk warrant service [see McCarthy 1990]); and by providing officers with timely, tactically useful information (any history of police problems at a location to which officers have been summoned, the criminal background of suspects whom police are about to stop and question or attempt to arrest, and so forth).

Ultimately, to minimize or, more accurately, to "optimize"[1] the use of deadly force by police, the values of the police culture need to be purposefully shaped (see Wasserman and Moore 1988; Kelling, et al. 1988). The aims would be to encourage a high respect for human

---

[1] By the somewhat awkward but nevertheless precise concept of "optimize" we mean attaining a proper combination of prudent restraint and prudent use of force. By contrast, in our view, those who claim their goal is to "minimize" police use of deadly force have either abandoned hope of police safety and effectiveness or have not come to grips with the implications of what they are saying.

life among officers and encourage responsible (but not foolhardy) restraint in the use of force—what we earlier referred to as commendable restraint (see Table 25 and accompanying discussion in Chapter 5).

This type of proactive values development has occurred and is continuing to occur in many agencies across the nation (see Delattre and Behan 1991; they prefer the term "principles" to "values," on the ground that the latter can reflect either admirable or reprehensible beliefs). In a considerable number of smaller police agencies, where the necessity to use deadly force typically arises less frequently than in large, urban departments, formal and informal indicators of organizational culture also attest to a reverence for human life and prudent restraint in the use of force. This is so even though annual shooting tallies are consistently so small as to be of little use in demonstrating the effects over time of administrative control strategies. Through policies, rhetoric, leadership by example, training, supervision, personnel practices, and the development of alternative tactics and tools, police administrators in agencies of all sizes can stimulate and support such an orientation in the organizational values of the police (see, e.g., Delattre 1989).

One of the many ways administrators can attempt to shape organizational culture for optimal restraint in police use of deadly force is clear and consistent policy statements. The Houston Police Department's deadly force policy, adopted under former Chief Lee Brown and maintained under his successor, former Chief Elizabeth Watson (recently named chief in Austin), has been widely considered an exemplary statement of police values concerning the protection of human life. The full policy appears in Appendix I of this book. It states, in part:

"The Houston Police Department places its highest value on the life and safety of its officers and the public. The department's policies, rules and procedures are designed to ensure that this value guides police officers' use of firearms.

"The citizens of Houston have vested in their police officers the power to carry and use firearms in the exercise of their service to society. This power is based on trust and, therefore, must be balanced by a system of accountability. The serious consequences of the use of firearms by police officers necessitate the specification of limits for officers' discretion; there is often no appeal from an officer's decision to use a firearm. Therefore it is imperative that every effort be made to ensure that such use is not only legally warranted but also rational and humane.

"The basic responsibility of police officers to protect life also requires that they exhaust all other reasonable means for apprehension and control before resorting to the use of firearms. Police officers are equipped with firearms as a means of last resort to protect themselves and others from the immediate threat of death or serious bodily injury. * * *

"[N]o officer will be disciplined for not discharging a firearm if that discharge might threaten the life or safety of an innocent person, or if the discharge is not clearly warranted by the policy and rules of the department.

"Above all, this department values the safety of its employees and the public. Likewise it believes that police officers should use firearms with a high degree of restraint. Officers' use of firearms, therefore, shall never be considered routine and is permissible only in defense of life and then only after all alternative means have been exhausted."

Besides formal policy statements, police administrators have numerous other opportunities to provide guidance and leadership on the values they believe their department's badge symbolizes. For instance, former New York City Transit Police Chief William Bratton (more recently the superintendent-in-chief of the Boston Police Department) made creative and effective use of marketing experts to help him prepare frequent video messages from the chief to be played at roll calls. These videos became an important source of clear, consistent messages about the root values that the agency stood for—in its strategic choices for providing police service and in employee performance appraisal.

The *consistency* of messages—whether in words or deeds—is of paramount importance. Mixed messages are the bane of many a working police officer's existence. The bosses say one thing, the politicians another, the community groups tug in a different direction, and the media make a circus of it all. Such conflict and divergence of opinions are inevitable in an open society on a matter as important as policing. Still, it is not too much for officers to ask that their own supervisors and their own senior administrators strive for consistency in *internal* police department decisions and statements on important issues.

The most familiar set of mixed messages about policing arises in the clash between "go get 'em" demands for crime control and stern pronouncements of an administration's "zero tolerance for brutality." We do not mean to imply that improper force—whether intentional brutality or merely the inept use of unnecessary force—inevitably will be a common side effect of an effective policing regime. But to fail to recognize the occasional trade-offs between aggressive crime control and the amount of force used by officers is unrealistic. Moreover, denying this tension hardly helps officers who are struggling both to do the right things and to do things right.

Finally, those who would shape organizational culture in the hope of thereby affecting officer use-of-force decisions must understand that there usually is not a *single* culture in a police organization. Despite the appearance sometimes of an "us versus them" dichotomy when the police feel besieged by their critics in the community, there are multiple police cultures—or, if you will, subcultures. There are very likely value differences *among* rank-and-file officers who have different backgrounds and other dissimilarities. And there is almost certainly a sharp cultural divide in most departments between what Reuss-Ianni (1983) has called "street cops" and "management cops." Any second-year sociology or social psychology student worth his or her salt could wander through a police organization and quickly discover that, while management preferences have an effect on shaping organizational culture, what working cops believe has at least as powerful an influence. To fail to appreciate and try to harness the power of peer pressure to shape police operating values when one attempts to control abuse of force—and to foster officer safety—is to miss the mark by a country mile.

In contemplating the capacity of peer opinion to reinforce *positive* conduct within a police organization, a survey conducted by the Portland *Oregonian* (a daily newspaper) provides intriguing data. More than 200 Portland Police Bureau personnel answered the question, "Do you feel that you get enough recognition from supervisors/fellow officers/the media when you skillfully defuse dangerous situations without using deadly force?" Of these officers, only 28 percent said they get enough recognition after such activity from supervisors and only 3 percent said they get sufficient recognition from the media. Yet 72 percent of these Portland police said they *do* get proper recognition from fellow officers for these acts of commendable restraint (Snell and Long 1992a). Lines of inquiry such as the one pursued in the Portland study might be very informative for those prone to assume that rank-and-file officers automatically frown on or belittle acts of restraint and compassion and applaud acts of needless aggression by their peers.

That officers may disapprove or approve of a colleague's use-of-force decisions does not always help one anticipate whether they will step forward—particularly when they *disapprove*—and alert supervisors or others who need to know about the conduct. The "blue curtain," or code of silence among police rank-and-file officers can be an extraordinarily firm barrier against administrative knowledge. A values-oriented approach to guiding use-of-force decisions would, we believe, benefit from finding ways to appeal to the best instincts in police officers, ways to harness their pride in their badge. The object is not to get officers to "rat" on their colleagues but to encourage them to strive for continuous improvement in the way officers perform and supervisors and administrators help them work more effectively. By drawing back the blue curtain, officers will expose to a generally uninformed public not only the few miscreants whose behavior needs stern rebuke but the majority of officers who are struggling hard to do their challenging jobs safely, effectively, and lawfully. In persuading officers of the virtue of stepping forward when they see procedures or behaviors that need correcting, managers have the law as a prod. As noted in Chapter 5, officers who fail to identify and, when feasible, try to intervene to stop their colleagues from violating others' rights are subject to both civil liability and criminal prosecution (Spector 1992; Strum 1992 discusses a Newark officer who agreed to testify against colleagues about a shooting).

II.   A Delicate Balance: Supporting Officers While Holding Them to High Standards of Conduct

In devising control strategies for shootings, the police administrator must be careful to strike an appropriate balance between accountability and support for officers. Many years ago, former St. Louis Police Chief Robert Scheetz captured this delicate balance with elegant but deceptive simplicity. He was explaining what he typically said to any of his officers who, with the best of motivations, used unnecessary force or cut constitutional corners in pursuit of laudable efforts to keep the community safe. "I appreciate what you're trying to do," Scheetz would say, "but you'll have to find another way to do it."

> "*To Joseph McNamara, police chief in San Jose, California, and a former New York City patrolman, the key [to violence reduction between police and civilians] is a chief's ability to convey and enforce a firm firearms policy without crippling the ability of officers to protect themselves. 'It ain't easy out there,' said Chief McNamara. 'You don't want an officer getting killed because he's afraid of the chief and hesitated too long, and you don't want jumpy officers shooting someone when they go to scratch themselves'*" (Malcolm 1990a).

While we have learned in the ensuing years that police departments bear a major responsibility for helping officers find the "other way" (see, e.g., Toch and Grant 1991), the salient point about Scheetz's statement is its balance: All too often, police managers convey only *half* of this message (either support or criticism), with undesirable consequences for officer effectiveness, community safety, and police morale. Lax supervision and weak internal accountability can be catastrophic for both the police and the public they serve, as the nation learned from the Christopher Commission's critique of the LAPD following the Rodney King beating (Independent Commission on the LAPD 1991). So too, excessive or unfair scrutiny and mistrust of officers (by their superiors, other government officials, or the public) can undermine efforts to strengthen the best of police values (see Geller 1991a).

III. Managing the Public Information Function in the Aftermath of a Controversial Police-Involved Shooting

One of the most important aspects of any public information effort is to disseminate accurate information in such a way that an agency's work is not tarnished through undeserved criticism. Thus, the release of public information is an exercise in managing perceptions and influencing public opinion. Although this may sound manipulative, it is only inappropriate if the information is provided in a deceitful or disingenuous way.[2] Given

> *"How do I feel about the media?" asked a colorful police chief from a medium-sized town in Texas. "I'll tell you. If you have to die, nobody minds getting eaten by the tiger—because the tiger is a worthy adversary. But the media!—what I can't abide is getting nibbled to death by ducks!"*

the crucial importance to the public of life-threatening acts of violence, it would be odd if public information about the use of deadly force by and against police did *not* have an effect on the way the citizenry views the police and police work.

> *"In the interest of enhancing our image as professionals, we need to regard the media as the mongoose regards the cobra—very carefully"* (Albrecht 1992: 149).

One of the best "friends" a police agency can have in the aftermath of a controversial police-involved shooting is a widely credible independent investigation. We discussed internal and external review of police-involved shootings earlier in Chapter 5 in connection with our overview of deadly force policy enforcement and personnel practices. How an investigation achieves the status of "independent" and fair in the minds of police personnel generally, the public, and those more directly involved in a violent encounter is a complex matter. This involves balancing a quality investigation, conducted by those with the skill to understand police work and how police think and might tend to cover up any deficiencies in their performance, with an audit of the quality of that investigation. The audit needs to be conducted by a body, internal or external to the police agency depending on each jurisdiction's history and current needs, that will have credibility to all significant constituencies. As Kerstetter (1985) explains, the audit need not entail a complete re-investigation of each or even very many police-involved shootings. The objective is to examine the integrity and strength of the investigation sufficiently that the auditor can periodically place a seal of approval on the investigative *process* (see also Perez 1992).

During the height of post-shooting media coverage and at any subsequent important moments of public concern, it is crucial that the police chief and, depending on local circumstances, the local prosecutor or other officials outside the police agency communicate clearly and convincingly that a high quality investigation is being conducted. Moreover, it must be clear that the investigation will be completed as expeditiously as possible, consistent

---

[2] An expert advisory panel to the NYPD in 1990 made several recommendations for administrative steps to bolster the Department's performance and to communicate more effectively its accomplishments concerning restraint in the use of deadly force. Among the recommendations was that the leadership of the agency "[d]evise for the Police Department's public information and community affairs divisions a more proactive, goal-oriented approach to disclosing information to the public about firearms discharges" (*Law Enforcement News* 1990a: 3).

with the need to uncover and weigh all relevant facts. Police executives who decline to comment at all on an officer-involved shooting until the agency's investigation is completed often cause trouble for themselves. In these cities, the chief, confronted with a flurry of media inquiries, tends to say only, "I cannot comment on a pending investigation." This leaves an information vacuum that all too often is filled with rumor and partisan speculation about the professionalism of the police.

A chief or other public spokesperson for the police obviously should not compromise the integrity or quality of an investigation by revealing facts or stating opinions prematurely.[3] Nor should provisions in police labor-management contracts that govern the confidentiality of investigations be violated. But there is much that can be said about the nature of the investigation to be conducted that will reassure the public that the police department takes officer-involved shootings very seriously. For starters, if a department has a deadly force policy of which it is proud, a spokesperson can make copies of the policy available to the media so they can disseminate the standards by which the officer(s) will be judged. Moreover, one way to provide reassurance to officers and the public alike about how policy will be interpreted is for the chief or some other senior official to explain the dispositions that would result from different sets of hypothetical facts—facts bearing *some* but not complete resemblance to the apparent circumstances in the case under investigation. Suggesting how different hypothetical cases would be decided may sound like a risky proposition, but done with care this is simply one way of explaining, with some specificity, what the department stands for—what "goes" and what "doesn't go" under the incumbent administration in terms of use of deadly force.

> *If ever there was a case calling for proactive management of the public information function...*
>
> *"A...man who has used a wheelchair since a 1990 shooting involving a police officer was shot and wounded again Sunday on the same street...by a different officer.... [The wheelchair-bound suspect] was shot twice by a...patrol officer.... He allegedly had made a threatening gesture while being questioned about reported drug dealing.... * * * [He] suddenly reached toward his waistband after being told repeatedly to put his hands behind his head. [The arrestee] was holding a black bag in his lap containing a pellet pistol that resembled a 9mm semi-automatic when [three] officers first approached him.... The gun was confiscated before the shooting, and [the suspect] did not use it to threaten the officers," a police spokesperson said (Duggan 1992).*

In the aftermath of a shooting investigation, information should be made available to

---

[3] Minneapolis Police Chief John Laux said he learned a lesson the hard way in his public comments on a pending investigation of a fatal shooting of a black youth by one of his white officers on December 1, 1990. Upon completion of a preliminary forensic investigation, the chief announced that the youth, suspected of unlawful use of a weapon, had been shot in the chest. But when the forensic investigation was completed it turned out that "investigators initially mistook exit wounds in [the youth's] chest for entry wounds." The department had to retract its earlier statement and admit that the young man had been shot in the back. This provided ammunition for community activists, who had long criticized the police, to use in charging a cover-up. "'I erred,' [Laux admitted] in hastily announcing that [the officer] acted properly...and that the youth had been shot in the chest." The mixed messages inordinately complicated an already difficult situation. Eventually, the city took the unusual step of appointing a special, independent investigator for the case (Harrison 1991).

the public concerning the nature of the incident and official determinations concerning the justifiability of the use of deadly force or other police practices at issue.[4] An exemplary practice, followed in Denver for many years, is release of a post-investigation report by the county prosecutor's office detailing the facts of the case, the conclusions of official agencies concerning the use of deadly force by police, and the reasons for those conclusions. This report is widely circulated by the prosecutor's office to the media, key political officials, community groups, the police, and other interested parties. Police executives we interviewed in Denver said this practice has done much to reduce the circulation of unfounded rumors and to bring credibility to police decisions to use deadly force. The Los Angeles County District Attorney's Office, at least during the late 1970s and early 1980s, also made publicly available its "decision letter" stating the outcome of its investigation of police-involved shootings and the reasons supporting the conclusion (Uchida, et al. 1981: 27-28). In New York City, while a grand jury deliberated whether to indict an officer in a controversial shooting of a Hispanic suspect, city officials hastily conducted educational sessions in the affected Hispanic community concerning American criminal justice procedures, in the hope of forestalling violent protests if an indictment was not handed down (Gonzalez 1992; see also Giuliani 1992).

By contrast, the criminal justice leadership in some communities seems oddly callous to the need to make police shooting decisions and post-shooting investigations credible—even to those traditionally suspicious of police. A veteran elected prosecutor in one large city was quoted in the local press as rebuffing the suggestion that his office examine autopsy results before concurring with police agency decisions that officers' fatal shootings were justified. "The idea of reinvestigation is a waste of time," he declared. "What kind of difference will an autopsy make?" (Petrillo 1990a: A-10). Whether or not examination of the autopsy would actually be likely to alter a prosecutor's conclusions in any given case is, of course, only part of the point. Equally important is that such a statement tends needlessly to breed distrust in the community. If this public official was quoted accurately by his community's newspaper, his statement might be offered as a model of how to *worsen* police-community trust.

IV. The "Next Frontiers" of Operational Research on Controlling Police-Civilian Violence

Unfortunately, researching and trying to prevent extreme police-civilian violence is a growth industry in the 1990s. A strong argument could be made that the long-term downward trend in felonious slayings of police officers in the United States is substantially the result of conscious efforts to brainstorm the problem and devise technological and tactical countermeasures. Such efforts will need to be redoubled as the "arms race" between police assailants and police continues to escalate.

An equally strong argument could be advanced that, where they have occurred, decreases in use of deadly force *by* police—and even *stable* levels of shootings in the face of rising challenges to officer safety—have been largely the products of administrative, legal, and community pressures to make police practices conform to deep-rooted democratic values. These efforts, too, will need to be redoubled. The objective is not only averting needless killings and maiming of police (including their "friendly fire" victims), nor curtailing

---

[4] The NYPD's advisory Firearms Policy Review Committee in 1990 noted: "Public confidence in the police could be greatly enhanced by publicly disclosing the final administrative determination of police-involved shooting incidents" (*Law Enforcement News* 1990a: 9).

bloodshed by their adversaries, their colleagues, and innocent bystanders. Divisive shootings by police officers must be prevented, if possible, because, as history amply demonstrates, they can impede the forging of police-community collaborative arrangements that are crucial to achieving a modicum of security in an increasingly insecure society. For these and other reasons, we believe the issues discussed briefly in the balance of this chapter deserve priority attention by government policymakers and police leaders. Success in addressing most of these needs will come more easily, we believe, if a national reporting system is established for police use of deadly force (we discuss such a system in Chapter 2).

A. Advancing the State of the Art in Police Conflict Management and Other Violence-Reduction Tactics

As discussed in Chapter 5, a number of researchers, operating on one of the "next frontiers" of deadly force research, have begun to explore the value of operational inquiries to better understand averted shootings (Fyfe 1978, 1989a; Binder and Scharf 1980; Scharf and Binder 1983; Fridell and Binder 1988; Geller 1985a; Bayley and Garofalo 1989; see also Milton, et al. 1977; *Law Enforcement News* 1990a: 3; Nicoletti (1990); Alpert and Fridell 1992). More broadly, these studies also have begun to explore what Fyfe (1989a) and others have termed "potentially violent" police-civilian encounters. As such, these studies have aspired to help police develop techniques not only to avert *deadly* force but to minimize (or "optimize") the use of *non*deadly force and even verbal aggression.

A modest effort to identify officers who exercise restraint and who help to teach other officers safe approaches to averting the use of deadly force was undertaken by the New York State Commission on Criminal Justice and the Use of Force (1987; see also Bayley and Garofalo 1989 for additional discussion of this research). From a limited sample of officers who reported averted shootings, researchers concluded (in contrast with Fyfe's 1989 study—1989a) that the actions of the opponents, more than any other situational or personal variables, dictated whether officers shot. Specifically, opponent actions were highly correlated with incident outcomes but particular officer tactics were not (NYSCCJ 1987, vol. I: 226; compare Fyfe 1989a). Other such research almost certainly will add complexity and perhaps contradictory evidence on this crucially important subject.

The profession would be well served if police agencies, operational researchers, and funding sources combined to mount the sort of ambitious and promising field experiments in violence-reduction training that Fyfe directed for the Police Foundation in the Metro-Dade Police Department (Police Foundation 1984, 1988; Fyfe 1989a).[5] A hallmark of the training in Metro-Dade was its realism in terms of the conditions officers had encountered and would continue to face on the streets (see Nicoletti 1990: 39 on the importance of conducting such training at "arousal levels similar to what the officer will be experiencing on the street").

---

[5] Violence-reduction efforts might attempt to train not only officers but the public. Creating citizens' police academies like those in Houston, Orlando and other locales, in which, among other topics, police procedures and their necessity are explained, is one direction such efforts might take. Among the important subjects that might be addressed in such training is the enhanced risk of police-civilian violence that citizens produce unwittingly when, in the hope of prompting more rapid police response, they exaggerate the seriousness of an incident, including falsely reporting in their "911" that a culprit at the scene has a gun. As J. Berger (1992) puts it: "Lying to 911 about a gun is a cunning trick for gaining something more than a languid police response, but it runs the risk of making the officers approaching an encounter far more on edge than they need to be." Seeking merely a *rapid* response, citizens may also prompt a *rabid* one.

Unfortunately, as sometimes happens with pioneering efforts, the formal *evaluation* of the Metro-Dade project was at least partially thwarted by implementation problems (Fyfe 1989a: 21), and the research thus far has failed to identify statistically significant differences between the "experimental" (specially trained) and "control" (normally trained) groups of officers in levels of violence experienced (*ibid*.: 22-23).

Much more important than the inability to write a first-class social science article, however, is the fact that all reports from Metro-Dade (by practitioners and researchers alike) suggest that the violence-reduction training had a beneficial and long-term *practical* effect on officer and civilian safety. Future research can stand on the shoulders of Fyfe's ground-breaking efforts for the Police Foundation in Metro-Dade and, hopefully, replicate that study's strengths while overcoming its methodological limitations.

If what Fyfe (1986b) has called the "split-second syndrome" is to loosen its choke hold on the patrol forces of America's police agencies, there needs to be a great deal of research, development, field experimentation, demonstration projects, and conferences to disseminate findings about the feasibility of defusing potentially "explosive" encounters.

B. Developing a Departmental "Infrastructure" that Supports the New Balance Between Discretion and Restriction

As we noted earlier in this chapter and near the beginning of Chapter 5, the evolution of deadly force control strategy in the United States over the past several decades has been a story about shifting the balance between discretion and restriction. That is, there has been a movement away from leaving most shoot/don't shoot decisions to individual officers in the field and toward greater restrictions on officers. These restrictions have come primarily from policy and procedural directives. In the context of high-speed vehicle pursuits, however, which some characterize as a form of deadly force, these restrictions have also come from supervisory personnel "patched into" the chase via police radio (see, e.g., Alpert 1987a; Alpert and Anderson 1986; Alpert and Fridell 1992; Fyfe 1989b). Whether there are analogous opportunities for supervisory support and control in police firearms encounters, as Reiss (1980) suggested, is a question that remains to be considered by police and their students.

As Herman Goldstein (1963) and others argued 30 years ago, however, efforts to eliminate completely individual officer discretion in most field situations are both hopeless and misguided. As principal draftsman of the American Bar Association's *Urban Police Function Standards*, first developed in 1963, Herman Goldstein put the point with what, at the time, was unusual candor:

> "The nature of the responsibilities currently placed upon the police requires that the police exercise a great deal of discretion—a situation that has long existed but is not always recognized" (American Bar Association 1982: 1-97; see also Goldstein 1977).

One might add that, with the "problem-solving" responsibilities that Goldstein and other advocates of problem-oriented policing have prompted many police to add to their strategic repertoire, the need for individual police officer discretion has become even more pronounced (see, e.g., Goldstein 1979, 1987, 1990; Eck and Spelman 1987; Eck and Williams 1991; Spelman and Eck 1989; Bieck, et al. 1991; Moore and Stephens 1991a, 1991b; Toch and Grant 1991).

The parameters within which police make use-of-deadly-force decisions have been narrowed by rules prohibiting shooting at nonviolent suspects, policies against firing warning shots, and the like. Still, there can be little doubt that American police officers still do and must exercise a wide discretion to decide which tactics (lethal and less-than-lethal) are called for by the circumstances confronting them. Much of the challenge that lies ahead for those interested in the control of police-civilian violence lies in developing a departmental "infrastructure" that supports sound officer decision making.

Just as officers' problem-solving efforts necessitate the enhancement of many organizational systems—information management, supervisory support and control approaches, performance appraisal, and training—so too with deadly force decision making. Increasingly, officers are being asked to avert violence even where its use would be legally justifiable. As we have discussed, this requires the enhancement of analytic and tactical skills on the part of individual officers. They need to learn how better to spot the potential for nonviolent conflicts to escalate and how to manage these encounters in the direction of de-escalation by marshalling the resources available to them both on the scene and through others who might be summoned. But it would be unfair in the extreme to hold officers individually responsible for all the research and development work that needs to be done in the violence-reduction area. Some departments have recognized this, but most have yet to do much about it.

Departments asking their officers to avert shootings when possible need to help develop new tactical knowledge about what currently works and does not work in bringing officer-suspect conflicts to a successful resolution. The most talented people in these departments and in the criminal

Some agencies are starting to explore the nexus that community policing may generate between officer safety, officer effectiveness, officer use of force, and officer accountability to the citizenry:

"The community policing philosophy and police use-of-force issues are dovetailing in Portland, Ore., where police officials have announced a one-day, public symposium at which force policies will be explained and anti-violence strategies will be discussed. * * *

"Proposed by Chief Tom Potter..., the meeting is an outgrowth of several violent incidents involving both police and civilians.... Included among the incidents...was the fatal shooting of a suspected car thief by a homeowner.... [Also to be discussed is an incident in which] a five-year-old was shot in the back of the head and killed by a suspected teenage member of the Bloods gang who aimlessly fired a .357 caliber Magnum handgun out the window of a nearby home. [And the meeting will also focus on a recent case, in which] police shot and killed [a] prowler and his 12-year-old hostage ...during a standoff at the youth's home. * * *

"In keeping with the Police Bureau's commitment to community policing, neighborhood residents are directly involved in the planning of the meeting, working side-by-side with police organizers.... [T]he session will aim not only to educate citizens about police deadly force policies, but also to give them the opportunity to comment on those policies" (Law Enforcement News *1992b: 1, 9*).

justice policy community also need to devise better personnel selection, training, and assignment systems (see, e.g., Nowicki, et al. 1991); better discipline and reward structures; and better post-incident assessment methods (that honestly identify *administratively* imposed conditions that contributed to unwarranted shootings and not only officer culpability or mistakes). In short, while efforts proceed to help *officers* more intelligently use their discretion, *departments* need to continually and more rigorously assess and fine-tune the efficacy, efficiency, and equity of *organizational* restrictions on officer discretion.

It is possible that the enhancement and qualitative improvement of officer discretion implied by community policing and problem-oriented policing strategies may have a long-term bearing on the nature and prevalence of officer-involved shootings. Some police executives who have been leaders of the movement toward these new strategic thrusts (e.g., former Tulsa Police Chief Drew Diamond) believe these methods will pay fringe benefits in greater officer safety and fewer injuries to police adversaries. Some proponents of community policing believe these benefits have already been realized in some locales (Trojanowicz 1991; see also Trojanowicz and Bucqueroux 1990, 1991; Trojanowicz and Banas 1985; S. Trojanowicz 1992). Hard data as yet are hard to find. The most specific information (e.g., Trojanowicz and Banas 1985; S. Trojanowicz 1992) focuses on officer's attitudes—their *perceptions* of safety—rather than on actual frequencies of assaults on officers. Obviously, officers' own feelings of security or insecurity are a major piece of the puzzle, and the limited empirical evidence thus far is encouraging. It may well be useful in the next several years for police researchers to explore systematically what the track record for officer-civilian violence (lethal and nonlethal) has been in departments that have embraced community problem solving rather than more traditional strategies.

The possible connection between community problem solving and officer-civilian violence highlights the fact that American policing, in the months and years ahead, needs to seek a *more comprehensive approach* to police safety and police effectiveness. Thus far, the two often have been addressed as if they were barely related phenomena. In part this may be because of specialization on the part of the expert practitioners and scholars who are looked to for leadership in these spheres. But any working cop can readily feel the need for some synthesis and reconciliation of inconsistent approaches, expectations, and demands.

Frequently, when officers sense any conflict between the requirements of community policing and officer safety, they quite understandably resolve all doubts in favor of officer protection. But sometimes the intuitive reaction is not the right one, not the one presenting the greatest long-term benefits in terms of officer welfare.

For instance, Albrecht (1992: 118), in a manual on officer safety and survival, discusses some of the safety precautions officers should take while off duty. He offers several pieces of advice, but says one is of paramount importance: "Avoid living on or near your beat at all costs." How can this advice be reconciled with the strategic experiments in some locales in which officers do precisely what Albrecht cautions against in the interest of building a better rapport with those who live and work on their beats? If Albrecht is correct, then in a community policing regime, officers living in proximity to or in the midst of their work areas are "sitting ducks." And no sensible advocate of this innovative policing strategy would favor a residency requirement for police officers. But we hardly have enough information to make anything but seat-of-the-pants appraisals at this point. A sensible starting place would be to talk with officers who have *chosen* to live on their work beats, and see what they think about this question.

Another illustration of the need for more "holistic" thinking about officer safety, violence reduction, and community policing comes from the Christopher Commission's report on the LAPD (Independent Commission on the LAPD 1991). A centerpiece of its sweeping recommendations for reforming abuse-of-force problems in the LAPD, announced after 100 days of deliberations, was adoption of community policing as the dominant modus operandi of the Department. Another suggestion, intended to avert racial discrimination in assignment practices and to break up cliques of officers who were bad influences on one another, was to rotate periodically officers from one unit and geographical area to another (see Geller 1991a). If members of the Christopher Commission were aware of the tension between urging implementation of community policing and recommending stepped up rotation of beat officers, they showed no indication of it. A cornerstone of community policing, of course, is leaving officers in their units and beats for long periods so that they and their service populations can get to know and trust one another (Trojanowicz and Bucqueroux 1990; R. Trojanowicz 1992). Officers can be forgiven if they are left confused, concerned, and even resentful by recommendations that appear to be sending mixed messages.

On most of these subjects, the field has hardly begun to scratch the surface of the accomplishments that may be possible before this century draws to a close. But these accomplishments will only come through a dedication of what President George Bush once referred to as "the will and the wallet." Police departments cannot, of course, sit back and await federal initiatives. Such a passive role would be neither humane policy nor responsible liability management. But the efforts of police agencies and police executive organizations to build *genuine* research and development capacities (see, e.g., Reiss 1991) will not succeed without an infusion of knowledge and resources from a wide variety of external sources, including private industry and public funding agencies (see, e.g., H. Williams 1991).

C. The Special Needs and Opportunities of Small Police Agencies

To date, most of the published analyses of police-involved shootings have drawn data only from large jurisdictions, with the principal exception of the FBI's annual reports on *Law Enforcement Officers Killed and Assaulted*; it captures data from nearly every jurisdiction in the nation. The few other exceptions are some statewide studies (e.g., Horvath and Donahue 1982; Horvath 1987; New York State Commission on Criminal Justice 1987; Moorman and Wemmer 1983), metropolitan-area studies (e.g., Uelman 1973; Uchida, et al. 1981), and those early national studies drawing data principally from newspaper stories or coroners' records (e.g., Kobler 1975a, 1975b). The reason for this focus on big cities in most of the literature is relatively straightforward: Any analysis of events is strengthened by considering large enough numbers of incidents that any identified patterns are unlikely to be the product of chance. Thus, researchers naturally gravitate toward the bigger cities, which typically experience more police-involved shootings in any given time period than do small agencies. The *rates* of shootings may or may not be higher in the big cities, but the *numbers* almost always are.

But the need to develop tailored guidance for police administrators, officers, and nonpolice government leaders in small and medium-size jurisdictions remains. The IACP's recent book *Operational Issues in the Small Law Enforcement Agency* (IACP 1990b), advertised in prepublication announcements when we began writing this volume, looked like it would be a useful first contribution to the profession's thinking about the causes and prevention of police-involved shootings in the special environments confronted by small-town police. When the book arrived in December 1990, however, we were chagrined to find that the three chapters on police use of deadly force were simply reprints of materials written years before without any special consideration of the unusual challenges faced by administrators in small jurisdictions. Indeed, with a mixture of pride and alarm, we noticed that the chapter titled "Controlling the Use of Deadly Force" in small law enforcement agencies was a reprint of a piece that one of *us* had written for *Police Chief* magazine years ago. Although there is nothing in that piece that seems likely to *mislead* administrators in small towns, neither was it (or the other two chapters in the IACP book) written with any intention of providing insights that would be especially helpful to decision makers in *small* departments.

Hence, the need remains great for studies on policy, procedure, tactics, training, supervision, discipline, equipment, employee assistance, post-shooting investigation, and other matters that take special account of the small town law enforcement agency. One of the few published writings we have found that genuinely addresses the idiosyncratic needs of small police departments is that by Snow (1990: 34), exploring the planning that such agencies need to do to deal with the rare cases of officers killed in the line of duty. "[B]ecause [large departments] have more line-of-duty deaths," he observes,

> "they consequently know, often through painful mistakes, what should and should not be done [following an officer's slaying]. Many small departments, on the other hand, have never experienced a line-of-duty death and have no idea what to do if one does occur. A recent National Institute of Justice study[6] found that 67 percent of the police departments surveyed had no formal, written policy concerning what to do if an officer dies in the line-of-duty" (see also FBI 1992f).

The National Institute of Justice in the early 1990s developed and began funding a research agenda on policing strategies in small and rural jurisdictions, working with police administrators and city managers to devise and disseminate appropriate assistance (NIJ 1992a: 49, 50, 56-60). Around the same time, Lesce (1991) wrote about the special hazards faced by rural officers. NIJ's attentiveness to the needs of these neglected jurisdictions may bode well for future research on controlling police-civilian violence in these locales.

One of the greatest challenges confronting the leadership of smaller police departments in terms of officer protection and officer proficiency in conflict management is how to keep officers from either becoming complacent or overreacting to provocations. Officers in smaller departments are apt to have less frequent exposure to potentially violent situations than their counterparts in larger jurisdictions. As noted and depicted graphically in Chapter 4, FBI tallies of officers assaulted and injured nonfatally show a reasonably distinct pattern in which the rate of officer injury per 100 officers on the force decreases steadily as the size of the police agency decreases (see, e.g., FBI 1989b: 51).

Another possible line of inquiry is whether, as a generalization, big-city police and small-town police have important differences in rapport with their service populations, with consequences for the likelihood that potentially violent encounters will escalate or de-escalate. This issue is related to the one we noted earlier in this chapter concerning the possible nexus between community problem solving and officer safety.

Many other questions with potential relevance for deadly force training and procedure could be suggested. Just as we should address gaps in our knowledge concerning the needs and experiences of mid-size and small police agencies, we need to learn more about the differing needs and capacities, relevant for deadly force policy and procedures, of agencies serving densely populated areas and less congested regions. America's big cities differ substantially, of course, in population density. Contrast New York City, with an average of 23,268 people crammed into each of its 314.7 square miles; San Francisco—15,704 residents

---

[6] The study was conducted in 1985 for Concerns of Police Survivors (COPS) by Frances A. Stillman (National Institute of Justice Grant 85-IJ-CX-0012) (see Sawyer 1989: 15).

per square mile; Chicago—12,184 per square mile; Philadelphia—11,659 per square mile; Los Angeles—7,457 per square mile; Minneapolis—6,686 per square mile; Houston—2,804 per square mile; Dallas—2,664 per square mile; New Orleans—2,492 per square mile; Indianapolis—2,116 per square mile; and Tulsa—1,909 per square mile (Johnson 1991).

D. The Wisdom to Study Successes and the Courage to Study "Failures"

In studying officer-civilian violence, one way to explore preventive strategies is to look at situations in which officers have, in retrospect, unnecessarily used their weapons and ask, "How could this situation have been resolved less violently?" This is a much needed line of inquiry, and it should be pursued far more often than it has been inside and outside police agencies. But equally as promising, perhaps, would be looking at situations in which officers *did* prevent things from escalating to the point where deadly force was used and asking them, "How'd you do that?"

We have noted earlier (Geller 1985a: 161-162) the potential benefits of researchers focusing (at least initially) in police field studies on successes in averting shootings. A leading benefit is that the respondents may then develop greater trust in the interviewers and be more inclined to share candid information about what they did well and not so well on those occasions when they did have to fire their weapons. Studying the causes of success rather than the causes of failure is not only diplomatically useful but substantively important. It is *easier* than studying inappropriate uses of deadly force because those with accurate information are more likely to share it. But it is also *harder* in the sense that there will inevitably be complex threshold questions about whether an incident really qualifies as an averted shooting; that is, how one *knows* that but for tactical acumen or other factors the incident probably would have resulted in a use of deadly force. Still, if one tried to focus narrowly in police shooting research on *unnecessary* uses of lethal force, there would be similar—and much more politically sensitive—questions to tackle about inclusion or exclusion of cases in the study.

An examination of successful *avoidance* of shootings by police looks not at "cops who shoot when they shouldn't" but at "cops who don't when they could" (Geller 1985a: 161). Such a study also has potential to provide insight concerning "cops who don't when they *should*" (*ibid.*). To their credit, some police agencies have begun the challenging process of trying routinely to capture information on incidents in which officers have avoided lethal force "with a less violent option" (Jamieson, et al. 1990: 30).

As we have noted earlier in this volume (see Table 25) and in other writings, both decisions to shoot and decisions to exercise restraint ought to be assessed for their reasonableness, because unreasonable police decisions of either type create dilemmas for the police and the community. Moreover, it is important to remember that "good" incident outcomes (whether these involved use of deadly force or not) are not necessarily evidence of good police *handling* of the incidents. Sometimes good things happen because we do the right things, and sometimes, as noted earlier, they happen despite our seeming determination to screw up. And a happy ending to a police-civilian conflict, of course, is not a reason to ignore any errors in tactics or judgment that might have been made during the encounter. This is so for three principal reasons: (1) the mistakes could be repeated in a future incident, when they might not prove to be so harmless; (2) administrative passivity in the face of tactical mistakes could be construed, in subsequent litigation, as implicit *approval* of the erroneous conduct, thus expanding the government's potential monetary and political liability; and (3) subpar police techniques can, incrementally, "aggravate citizens' dissatisfaction, distrust, or resentment" of the police, leading to further problems for *all* members of the department (Police Foundation 1984).

Still, it is predictable that it will be easier to elicit candor from officers by studying their successes than by examining incidents in which their decisions to use force have been criticized. In this regard, Goldstein and Susmilch (1982: 139), writing about problem-oriented policing, observed that police officers

> "at times ... welcome the opportunity to share ... accounts of the way in which they used their ingenuity and resourcefulness to achieve common sense solutions for the endless variety of troublesome situations they confront."

Research efforts looking for *what works* rather than what does not work might take a cue from a series of case studies of labor-management relations in America published in the late 1940s and early 1950s by the National Planning Association under the title "The Causes of Industrial *Peace*" (Golden and Parker 1955—emphasis added; see Geller 1985a: 162). This pioneering effort very likely still stands out amid the mountains of studies of industrial *strife*. For much too long, as Sherman (1980c) noted, empirical research on police performance was principally an account of what does *not* work. That has begun to change in studies of strategic policing (Sherman 1992), in studies of police administration generally (Cordner and Hale 1992), and in studies of violence-reduction (see our discussions above in this chapter and in Chapter 5).

Pierce Brooks, "a legendary former Los Angeles homicide detective," later chief of the Lakewood, Colorado, Police Department, and author of a leading book on officer survival tactics, began his pioneering work on officer survival techniques after his investigation of the infamous "Onion Field" murder of a police officer in 1963.

"The onion-field murder had reinforced something that had been nagging at Brooks for years: whenever a cop was killed in the line of duty, the gritty details never seemed to come out. 'You'd get ten different stories,' he says. 'I remember as a young police officer going to a police funeral and wondering why we weren't being told the whole story' (Baltic 1991: 18).

*"Stanley Morris became director of the [U.S.] Marshals Service a few months after the Kahl shoot-out [a 1983 gunfight in North Dakota with white supremacist tax-resister Gordon Kahl, in which two federal marshals were killed, another suffered permanent brain damage, two local officers were wounded, and Kahl escaped from the scene; four months later, he was cornered in Arkansas by dozens of local, state and federal officers, and he and a county sheriff shot each other to death—Baltic 1991: 24, 26. [Morris] saw a dispassionate postmortem of the shooting—and training based on it—as a way to both purge the inevitable rumors and prevent more of his people from getting killed. The easy way, he says, would have been to 'just bury them in flags, as heroes. That's horseshit. The fact is, some mistakes get made. * * * The best memorial to Cheshire and Muir [the two federal agents killed by Kahl] is a better-trained, more alert agency....' People felt the training made them better, smarter, and safer" (Baltic 1991: 26; but compare O'Connor and O'Brien 1992; James 1992; and Burleigh 1992).*

But what do we mean when we urge studying "failures"? For one thing, we mean studying situations in which police shot when they would have done well to hold their fire. We mean also that there needs to be more examination of the equally difficult topic of avoidable police deaths and injuries—losses that might have been averted if the officers had employed more suitable tactics.

"The LASD [Los Angeles Sheriff's Department] keeps careful and abundant statistics about itself. Each year, for example, it produces an inches-thick compilation of data entitled 'Year in Review.' In it, one can find out almost anything: the percentage of female, Hispanic civilians in the LASD, the number of blood/urine alcohol tests performed, the number of juveniles arrested by the Temple Station for gambling and the number of females, age 22, arrested for disorderly conduct.

"In sharp contrast, however, the LASD keeps surprisingly little information in useable form pertaining to the use of force. Although the Department is making advances in terms of its computerization of force-related data, and may in a few years have a reliable system, it does not have one today. To a large extent, this is a result of a previous policy of self-imposed ignorance. Driven by fears that data on use of force and citizen complaints would be used against it in civil litigation, the LASD followed advice from County Counsel to avoid creating 'paper trails' when it could. When it could not, the information was scattered throughout the LASD and kept haphazardly. * * *

"This lack of concrete and specific information cripples management in several ways.... [I]t disables the LASD, its training bureaus and its task forces from adequately reviewing and evaluating weaknesses in current training and policy. * * * [T]he Department is placed in the uncomfortable position of being reactive, waiting until a 'headline incident' occurs before poor training receives Department-wide attention.

"[T]he lack of useful information prevents the Department from identifying individual problem officers, or cliques of problem officers, until after the damage has been done, possibly subjecting the County to millions of dollars in civil exposure. * * *

"[T]he absence of a uniform, Department-wide force tracking system gives rise to an inference that the LASD puts a low priority on identifying and rooting out those who resort to excessive force. * * * As one lieutenant put it, 'Deputies try to read the bosses to figure out what they can and cannot do.'

"[F]ailure to document and track all uses of force disables the LASD from countering and putting to rest allegations by citizens' groups that either outright misconduct or questionable force is widespread within the LASD. * * * Sheriff Block and his executive staff have made it clear that the LASD is now fully-committed to a state-of-the-art force tracking system" (Kolts, et al. 1992: 169-171).

We have noted earlier that the desire to honor the dead and the grievers makes difficult candid appraisals of what officers might have done to contribute to their own demise. A situation requiring much better analysis than has yet been conducted by police tacticians is that in which officers are injured by apprehended suspects with weapons that went undiscovered in the officers' search of the prisoners. In November 1989 two New York City police detectives were killed by a prisoner in the back seat of their car during his transport to jail from a police squad room. Apparently, the assailant, while cuffed on one hand only to a metal bar in the police station, was left unattended and was able to reach with his uncuffed hand into a locker with a defective lock and to steal a pistol from it (Fried 1990). After the killing of the officers, then-New York City Police Commissioner Richard Condon courageously discussed the mistakes made that cost two of his men their lives: "...not frisking the prisoner before taking him from the squad room, ...cuffing his hands in front rather than behind him for the car ride and...placing him alone in the back seat, rather than having one detective with him in the back" (Fried 1990). The Detectives Endowment Association cited still other contributing factors, preferring to downplay its members' contribution to their own deaths: "[T]he cause of the killings was inadequate detention rooms, forcing use of the locker area to hold prisoners" (*ibid.*).

In Chicago in January 1991 two officers were shot in the back of the head, one fatally, under related circumstances. They and colleagues failed to find in their field search and more than one station-house search a gun possessed by a narcotics dealer. After booking, while the officers were driving the suspect, with his hands cuffed in front, to a location where he promised they would find a more prominent dealer, the two officers were shot with a revolver the culprit apparently had concealed in his crotch under several layers of clothing. Then-Superintendent LeRoy Martin raised questions about agency handcuffing procedure. And senior Department members Raymond Risley and Matt Rodriguez critiqued the officers' conduct, suggesting that the inadequate searches may have resulted from one or more factors: complacency or incompetence; fear of getting stuck with concealed hypodermic needle that might be infected with AIDS or some other disease; and reluctance to search a suspect's crotch area (Petacque and Casey 1991; Kupcinet 1991; Rodriguez 1991a; see also Stein 1992b: 2; Blumberg 1989a: 210-212).[7]

On July 20, 1992, two federal agents—one a deputy U.S. Marshal and the other an armed security guard (and retired Chicago policeman) employed part-time by the Marshals Service, were killed by a federal bank robbery defendant, Jeffrey Erickson, who had often bragged to federal and other authorities about his expertise with weapons and knowledge of police procedure. Also accused of attempting to murder a suburban Chicago police officer during a high-speed pursuit, ex-Marine marksman Erickson was in the parking garage of the Dirksen Federal Building in Chicago, enroute from his trial to the federal detention center. His hands were cuffed in front of his body, and the cuffs were connected to a "belly chain" around his waist, in apparent conformity with Marshals Service procedures (O'Connor and O'Brien 1992a: 12).

During the elevator ride down from the courtroom, the prisoner, who either fabricated or obtained a handcuff key from a source not yet identified as this book went to press (Stein 1992c), was able to unlock his cuffs, put a choke hold on and wrestle a revolver away from a part-time, 23-year-old rookie employee of the Marshals Service (technically not a full-fledged deputy but what Marshals Service officials called an "intermittent deputy") who was escorting him and other federal defendants to a waiting prisoner van. Erickson promptly used the gun to kill her partner, shooting him twice, once at point-blank range after the victim (a full-fledged but inexperienced deputy U.S. Marshal) had fallen to the ground from the first shot. Erickson then exchanged shots with the security officer. Both suffered fatal wounds and, apparently realizing the seriousness of his injury, within seconds Erickson shot himself in the head, ending the chaotic confrontation (O'Connor and O'Brien 1992, 1992a; Burleigh 1992; James 1992; Rossi 1992; Stein 1992c; O'Brien and O'Connor 1992).

Although the handcuffing procedure used during the transfer of this prisoner apparently was consistent with Marshals Service procedures, experts questioned both the wisdom of those procedures and the decision that allowed this very dangerous prisoner to be transported, along with eight other prisoners, in the custody only of inexperienced personnel, and apparently without being searched for contraband prior to leaving the courtroom area (Rossi 1992; Stein 1992c; Cohen and Blau 1992). At the moment when Erickson grabbed the part-time employee's weapon, she was guarding the nine prisoners alone, her partner having stepped away to prepare the prisoner van. The Marshals Service, a month later, disciplined four Chicago-based supervisors (*Crime Control Digest* 1992n) in connection with the incident but continued to defend the two deputies' actions. A spokesperson confirmed earlier that the intermittent deputy, who had been hired nine months prior to the incident, had no formal pre-service training and only on-the-job instruction that included "searching and escorting prisoners,

---

[7] We also discussed this incident in section I of Chapter 4.

serving court papers,...a short course on women's self-defense," and a shorter period of firearms instruction than is provided to full-time deputies in their basic training (O'Brien and O'Connor 1992). She had recently received passing scores at the firing range with both her .357 magnum revolver and with an AR-15 assault rifle. Her deceased partner, also hired nine months earlier, had completed a 23-week training program at the Federal Law Enforcement Training Center in Glynco, Georgia (*ibid.*).

Years before the tragic death of these two federal agents and before Commissioner Condon, the Chicago officials, and former U.S. Marshals Service director Stanley Morris (quoted in a sidebar in this section) bravely and constructively spoke out about deficiencies in police work that needlessly endangered officers, a number of determined tacticians began studying a wide variety of officer mistakes and poor judgments that contributed to their injuries or deaths. Indeed, candidly identifying fatal errors is what the best—the *empirically grounded* portions—of the "officer survival" literature are all about (see, e.g., Clede and

"A Federal marshall was shot to death today while trying to arrest a fugitive white supremacist holed up in a remote mountaintop cabin near [Naples, Idaho], 40 miles south of the Canadian border.... Marshals and the police evacuated about 30 residents from the area near Ruby Ridge.... That ridge is where the 44-year-old white supremacist, Randy Weaver, [a former Special Forces soldier in Vietnam,] has lived in self-imposed exile with his wife and four children since February 1991, when he failed to appear for trial on a Federal weapons charge. It was not immediately clear that Mr. Weaver had killed the marshal.... But Mr. Weaver had said that his exile would end only with the death of himself and his family or an admission by the authorities that the weapons charges against him were untrue" (The New York Times 1992m). "[S]ix deputy marshals were checking on Mr. Weaver..., just as they had been doing periodically for many months, when they came under fire. The slain deputy was identified as William F. Degan, 42, who was based in Boston" (The New York Times 1992o; see also Egan 1992a, 1992b).

Parsons 1987; Rutledge 1988; Albrecht 1992; Baltic 1991). The FBI and, more recently, tactical experts at the Treasury Department's Federal Law Enforcement Training Center, as well as trainers in various police academies[8] have had the courage and sensitivity to prudently but honestly scrutinize what might have "gone wrong" in officers' defensive efforts against assaults. The National Institute of Justice, as we noted earlier, in 1991 and 1992 advanced the effort by awarding grants to the FBI and the Police Foundation to examine in some depth the circumstances that led to killings and serious injuries of American police.

We applaud those who would look for ways to strengthen officers' defensive capabilities. We trust and hope that their work will bring the field closer to a helpful synthesis of answers to two daunting questions: How can police more effectively pursue their highest goal—the protection of life? And how can they simultaneously increase their own odds of coming home safely when their tours of duty end?

---

[8] Houston Police Department tactical experts James Connelley and Terry Bratton have conducted background research for their officer-survival training by videotaping interviews with imprisoned, convicted cop killers (Connelley and Bratton 1991). This unusual but potentially important source of information on why and how people slay police has also been tapped by FBI analysts to explore ways to improve officer survival tactics.

REFERENCES AND BIBLIOGRAPHY

Abbott, Les (1988) "Pursuit Driving." *FBI Law Enforcement Bulletin* (November): 7-11.

Adams, J.P. (1978) "Finding Alternatives to the Use of Force." *Engage/Social Action* (November/December): 18-24.

Adams, J.E. (1980) "Police Chiefs Again Back Firing at Fleeing Felons." *St. Louis Post-Dispatch* (September 18).

Adams, Ronald J., Thomas M. McTernan, and Charles Remsberg (1980) *Street Survival: Tactics for Armed Encounters*. Northbrook, IL: Calibre Press.

Alderete, A.M. (1981) "Use of Physical Force by Police: A Perennial Chicano Community Dilemma." In *Report from the National Hispanic Conference on Law Enforcement and Criminal Justice*. Rosslyn, VA: Interamerica Research Associates.

Albrecht, Steven (1989) "Contact and Cover: One Common-sense Procedure Can Make All the Difference to An Officer's Survival." *Police* (April): 33-36, 69.

_____ (1992) *Street Work: The Way to Officer Safety and Survival*. Boulder, CO: Paladin Press.

Albrecht, Steven, and John Morrison (1992) *Contact and Cover: Two-Officer Suspect Control*. Springfield, IL: Charles C. Thomas.

Alexander, Fritz W., 2d (1992) "Peace and Provocation in New York City." *New York Times* (August 12): A19.

Alpert, Geoffrey P. (1987a) "Questioning Police Pursuits in Urban Areas." *Journal of Police Science and Administration* 15: 298-306. Reprinted in Roger G. Dunham and Geoffrey P. Alpert (eds.), *Critical Issues in Policing: Contemporary Readings*. Prospect Heights, IL: Waveland Press, 1989.

_____ (1987b) "Review of Deadly Force Training and Policies of the Dallas Police Department." Unpublished consulting report (September).

_____ (1989a) "Metro-Dade Police Department Discharge of Firearm Study: 1984-1988." Unpublished consulting report to the Metro-Dade Police Department (January).

_____ (1989b) "Police Use of Deadly Force: The Miami Experience." In Roger G. Dunham and Geoffrey P. Alpert (eds.), *Critical Issues in Policing: Contemporary Readings*. Prospect Heights, IL: Waveland Press.

Alpert, Geoffrey P., and Patrick Anderson (1986) "The Most Deadly Force: Police Pursuits." *Justice Quarterly* 3: 1-13.

Alpert, Geoffrey P., and Lorie A. Fridell (1992) *Police Vehicles and Firearms: Instruments of Deadly Force*. Prospect Heights, IL: Waveland.

American Bar Association (1982) "The Urban Police Function." In ABA, *Standards for Criminal Justice*. Boston: Little, Brown and Co. (pp. 1-5 through 1-266).

American Civil Liberties Union (1992) *Fighting Police Abuse: A Community Action Manual*. New York: ACLU.

American Civil Liberties Union of Southern California (1967). *Day of Protest, Night of Violence*. Los Angeles: Sawyer Press.

American Law Institute (1934) *Restatement of Torts* sec. 131.

_____ (1949) *Restatement of the Law*, 1948 Supplement 628.

_____ (1958) *Model Penal Code*, section 3.07, Comments (Tent. Draft No. 8).

_____ (1962) *Model Penal Code*, sec. 3.07 (Proposed Official Draft).

Americans for Effective Law Enforcement (1974) *Survey of Police Misconduct Litigation, 1967-1971*. Chicago: Americans for Effective Law Enforcement.

_____ (1988) "Use-of-Force Tactics and Non-Lethal Weaponry." Chicago, IL: Americans for

Effective Law Enforcement.

_____ (periodical) *AELE Liability Reporter*. Chicago, IL: Americans for Effective Law Enforcement.

_____ (1991) "Two Officers Awarded $275,000 for Libel Against Man Who Accused Them of Using Excessive Force During Arrest." *AELE Liability Reporter* No. 219 (March): 43.

_____ (1991a) "Choke Holds: Nevada Passes Statute Regulating 'Choke Holds' and Establishing Training and Supervision Requirements." *AELE Liability Reporter* No. 227 (November): 166.

_____ (1991b) "Officer's Shooting of Suspect in the Jaw Was Objectively Reasonable Despite Her Alleged Failure to Follow Standard Police Procedures for Making a Night Time Prostitution Arrest; Reasonableness is Measured by What the Officer Knew Immediately Prior to and at the Moment She Fired the Shot." *AELE Liability Reporter* No. 223 (July): 105.

_____ (1991c) "Officer Awarded $2 Million Against Woman Who Falsely Accused Her of Shooting at a Suspect." *AELE Liability Reporter* No. 224 (August): 122.

Anderson, David C. (1992) "Editorial Notebook: The Good Cops in Los Angeles—Community Patrol, Alive and Well." *New York Times* (May 29): A14.

_____ (1992a) "The Television Time Bomb: Violence on the Tube, a Public Health Issue." *New York Times* (July 27): A12.

Anderson, Dennis, and Charles Remsberg (1991) "Letter to the Publisher: Responding to Chief Burgreen's Attack on 'Edged Weapons'." *Crime Control Digest* (June 24): 1, 3-4.

Anderson, Rhonda (1992). "Honors Go to Those Who Made City a Safer Place." *Chicago Tribune* (March 27): section 2, p. 3.

Andrist, Ralph K. (1987) *The American Heritage History of the Confident Years*. New York: American Heritage/Bonanza Books.

Apple, R.W., Jr. (1991) "Washington Talk: In Clashes, a Hispanic Agenda Enters." *New York Times* (May 9): A10.

Applebaum, D. (1983) "Looking Down the Wrong Side of the Gun: The Problems of the Police Use of Lethal Force." *Police Chief* (May): 55-59.

Applebome, Peter (1992) "Black Officers: An Agonizing View for Those Who Are Both Police Officers and Black." *New York Times* (May 1): A12.

Associated Press (1991) "Fewer Police Killed in '90." *Chicago Tribune* (January 2): 13.

Association of Chief Police Officers (1990) *Manual of Guidance on Police Use of Firearms*. London, England: Assoc. of Chief Police Officers.

Auten, J. (1972) "Domestic Disturbance: A Policeman's Dilemma." *Police Chief* 39 (10): 16-22.

Avery, Michael, and David Rudovsky (1992) *Police Misconduct: Law and Litigation*. New York: Clark Boardman Callaghan.

Ayers, Richard M., in collaboration with George S. Flanagan (1990) *Preventing Law Enforcement Stress: The Organization's Role*. Washington, DC: Bureau of Justice Assistance, U.S. Department of Justice.

Ayoob, Massad F. (1980) "Killing Experience." *Police Product News* 4 (7, July): 26, 28, 30, 69.

_____ (1984) *Stress Fire*. Concord, NH: Police Bookshelf.

Ayres, B. Drummond, Jr. (1991) "Second Day of Violence Is Reported In Capital's Hispanic Neighborhood." *New York Times* (May 7): A10.

Bailey, William C., and Ruth D. Peterson (1987) "Police Killings and Capital Punishment: The Post-*Furman* Period." *Criminology* 25 (1): 1-25.

Baker, James N. (1989) "The 'You Fly, You Die' Debate: Should the Customs Service Shoot Down Drug Planes?" *Newsweek* (October 2): 26.

Baltic, Scott (1991) "Be Careful Out There: Calibre Press Teaches Cops the Delicate Art of Staying Alive." *Reader: Chicago's Free Weekly* (November 22): 1, 18 and passim.

Bannon, James D. (1976) "Assaults Upon Police Officers: A Sociological Study of the Definition of the Situation." (Unpublished Ph.D. dissertation. Available through University Microfilms, Ann Arbor, MI—# AAD76-26108).

Bard, Morton (1977) "Family Crisis Intervention: From Concept to Implementation." In M. Roy (ed.), *Battered Women*. New York: Van Nostrand Rhienhold (pp. 172-192).

Bard, Morton, and Joseph Zacker (1976) *The Police and Interpersonal Conflict*. Washington, DC: Police Foundation.

Barrineau, H. (1987) *Civil Liability in Criminal Justice*. Cincinnati: Anderson.

Baruth, C.L. (1986) "Pre-Critical Incident Involvement by Psychologists." In James T. Reese and Harvey A. Goldstein (eds.), *Psychological Services for Law Enforcement*. Washington, DC: Federal Bureau of Investigation (pp. 305-309).

Bassiouni, M.C. (1971) "Use of Force in Riots." In M.C. Bassiouni (ed.), *The Law of Dissent and Riots*. Springfield, IL: Charles C. Thomas.

Baum, Geraldine (1991) "What Does Cop Talk Really Say: Some in Law Enforcement Contend That 'Blue Humor' Helps Police Face a Grim, Dangerous Job; Critics Argue That it Predisposes Officers to Violence and Must be Toned Down." *Los Angeles Times* (Sept. 11): A1, A14-A15.

Bay State Film Productions (1980) "Police Civil Liability: Limits of Physical Force, Part 3." (22-minute film available through Harper and Row Media, Hagerstown, MD).

Bayley, David H. (1986) "The Tactical Choices of Police Patrol Officers." *Journal of Criminal Justice* 14: 329-348.

Bayley, David H., and James Garofalo (1989) "The Management of Police Patrol Officers." *Criminology* 27 (1): 1-23.

Bedian, A.G. (1982) "Suicide and Occupation: A Review." *Jnl. of Vocational Behavior* 21: 206-222.

Beene, Charles (1992) *Police Crowd Control: Risk-Reduction Strategies for Law Enforcement*. Boulder, CO: Paladin Press.

Behar, Richard (1992) "Thugs in Uniform: Underscreened, Underpaid and Undertrained, Private Security Guards Are Too Often Victimizing Those They Are Hired to Protect." *Time Magazine* (March 9): 44-47.]

Behm, Loretta (1992) Personal communication between the FBI Uniform Crime Reporting program Research Analyst responsible for writing the *Law Enforcement Officers Killed and Assaulted, 1991* report, and William A. Geller (September 18).

Bell, D.J. (1982) "Policewomen: Myths and Reality." *Journal of Police Science and Administration* 10: 112-120.

Benner, Alan W. (1986) "Psychological Screening of Police Applicants." In James T. Reese and Harvey A. Goldstein (eds.), *Psychological Services for Law Enforcement*. Washington, DC: Federal Bureau of Investigation (pp. 11-19); reprinted in Roger G. Dunham and Geoffrey P. Alpert (eds.), *Critical Issues in Policing: Contemporary Readings*. Prospect Heights, IL: Waveland Press, 1989.

Bentley, S. Woodruff, Sr. (1990) "CALEA Enters New Era of Tougher Policies." *Crime Control Digest* (December 3): 1-4.

Benyon, John (1986) *A Tale of Failure: Race and Policing*. England: University of Warwick, Centre for Research in Ethnic Relations.

Berger, Joseph (1992) "Metro Matters: Family Feud No Game for Police or Neighborhood." *New York Times* (August 17): B3.

Berger, Leslie (1992) "Services for Slain Maywood Officer Evoke Tears and Bittersweet Smiles." *Los Angeles Times* (June 5): B8.

———— (1992a) "Racial Tensions, Economics Cited in Riots: Poll by Independent Commission Also Shows That 75% Said the Slow Police Response Was Because of Poor Planning and a Lack of Leadership in the LAPD." *Los Angeles Times* (August 28): B1, B8.

Berger, Leslie, and Stephen Braun (1991) "Rookie Becomes First L.A. Policewoman Slain on Job: Her Partner Shoots to Death Gunman, An Illegal Immigrant; Gates Lashes out at the INS." *Los Angeles Times* (February 12): A1, A27-A28.

Bergesen, A. (1980) "Official Violence During the Watts, Newark, and Detroit Race Riots of the 1960's." In Pat Lauderdale (ed.), *Political Analysis of Deviance*. Minneapolis: Univ. of Minnesota Press.

Berke, R. (1977) "Pitchess Motions and the Destruction of Records" (audiocassette, from "Criminal Law Seminar, 1977, Tape 2," available from California Attorneys for Criminal Justice, Los Angeles) (defense attorney strategies for obtaining police Internal Affairs records on citizens' complaints of police misconduct, or, if such records have been destroyed, for obtaining sanctions).

Berman, J., H. Jones, and R. Rickman (1979) *Providence (RI) Human Relations Commission Report to the Citizens on Police Use of Deadly Force*. Providence, RI: Providence Human Relations Commission.

Bibbins, V.E. (1986) "The Quality of Family and Married Life of Police Personnel." In James T. Reese and Harvey A. Goldstein (eds.), *Psychological Services for Law Enforcement*. Washington, DC: Federal Bureau of Investigation (pp. 421-426).

Bieck, William, William Spelman, and Thomas J. Sweeney (1991) "The Patrol Function." In William A. Geller (ed.), *Local Government Police Management* (3d rev. ed.). Washington, DC: International City Management Association.

Binder, Arnold, and Lorie Fridell (1984) "Lethal Force as a Police Response." *Criminal Justice Abstracts* 16 (2, June): 250-280.

Binder, Arnold, and Peter Scharf (1980) "The Violent Police-Citizen Encounter." *Annals of the American Academy of Political and Social Science* 452 (November): 111-121.

_____ (1982) "Deadly Force in Law Enforcement." *Crime and Delinquency* 28: 1-23.

Binder, Arnold, Peter Scharf, and Raymond Galvin (1982) "Use of Deadly Force by Police Officers: Final Report." Washington, DC: National Institute of Justice (Grant no. 79-NI-AX-0134).

Bishop, Steven (1991) Conversation between the chief of the Kansas City (MO) Police Department and William A. Geller (April 4).

_____ (1991a) "So Much Asked of Police." *The Kansas City Star* (March 24): J-1, J-4.

Bittner, Egon (1973) *The Functions of the Police in Modern Society*. Washington, DC: Center for Studies of Crime and Delinquency, Department of Health, Education and Welfare (publication no. [HSM] 73-9072.

_____ (1974) "Florence Nightingale in Pursuit of Willie Sutton: A Theory of The Police." In Herbert Jacob (ed.), *The Potential for Reform of Criminal Justice*. Newbury Park, CA: Sage.

_____ (1975) "Capacity to Use Force as the Core of the Police Role." In Jerome H. Skolnick and Thomas C. Gray (eds.), *Police in America*. Boston: Little, Brown & Co.

Bixler, T. (1978) "An Exploratory Analysis of Assaults On Police Officers." (Unpublished Ph.D. dissertation. Available through University Microfilms, Ann Arbor, MI).

Black, Donald J. (1971) "The Social Organization of Arrest." *Stanford Law Review* 23 (June): 1087-1111.

Black, Donald J., and Albert J. Reiss, Jr. (1967) *Field Studies III. Studies in Crime and Law Enforcement in Major Metropolitan Areas*, vol. 2. Washington, DC: President's Commission on Law Enforcement and Administration of Justice.

Blackwell, James E. (1992) "Social and Criminal Justice: The Temperature of the Nation." *ACJS [Academy of Criminal Justice Sciences] Today* 11 (2, September/October): 1 and *passim*.

Blak, R.A. (1986) "A Department Psychologist Responds to Traumatic Incidents." In James T. Reese and Harvey A. Goldstein (eds.), *Psychological Services for Law Enforcement*. Washington, DC: Federal Bureau of Investigation (pp. 311-314).

Blaricom, D.P. Van (1992) "K-9 Use of Force: A Biting Example of Questionable Policy." *Law Enforcement News* (July/August): 11, 14.

Blau, Robert (1991) "Cop Death Resurrects Guns as Issue." *Chicago Tribune* (January 11): 1.

Blau, Robert, and Linnet Myers (1990) "One Week's Roll Call of Slaughter." *Chicago Tribune* (June 17): sec. 2, pp. 1, 5.

Blau, T.H. (1986) "Deadly Force: Psychosocial Factors and Objective Evaluation—A Preliminary Effort." In James T. Reese and Harvey A. Goldstein (eds.), *Psychological Services for Law Enforcement*. Washington, DC: Federal Bureau of Investigation (pp. 315-318).

Bloch, Peter B., and Deborah Anderson (1974) *Policewomen on Patrol: Final Report*. Washington, DC: Police Foundation.

Blumberg, Mark (1981) "Race and Police Shootings: An Analysis in Two Cities," in James J. Fyfe (ed.), *Contemporary Issues in Law Enforcement*. Beverly Hills, CA: Sage.

_____ (1983) "The Use of Firearms by Police Officers: The Impact of Individuals, Communities, and Race." (Unpublished Ph.D. dissertation, School of Criminal Justice, SUNY at Albany. Available through University Microfilms, Ann Arbor, MI).

_____ (1986) "Issues and Controversies with Respect to the Use of Deadly Force by Police," in Thomas Barker and David L. Carter (eds.), *Police Deviance*. Cincinnati: Pilgrimage.

_____ (1989) "Controlling Police Use of Deadly Force: Assessing Two Decades of Progress." In Roger G. Dunham and Geoffrey P. Alpert (eds.), *Critical Issues in Policing: Contemporary Readings*. Prospect Heights, IL: Waveland Press.

_____ (1989a) "The AIDS Epidemic and the Police." In Roger G. Dunham and Geoffrey P. Alpert (eds.), *Critical Issues in Policing: Contemporary Readings.* Prospect Heights, IL: Waveland Press.

Boelte, E.R. (1989) "Marriage Survival" A Proactive Approach to Improving the Law Enforcement Marriage." *Police Stress* 9 (1): 13-15.

Boscopoulos, G. (1979) "Police Use of Deadly Force: Trends are Changing." *Trooper* 14 (4, October): 64-68.

Boston Globe (1986) "Study Shows Drop in Killings by Policemen." *Boston Globe* (Oct. 20), p. 4.

Boston Police Department (1974) "The Use of Deadly Force by the Boston Police." Boston: Boston Police Department.

Boutwell, J. Paul (1977a) "Use of Deadly Force to Arrest a Fleeing Felon—A Constitutional Challenge, Part I." *FBI Law Enforcement Bulletin* 46 (September): 27-31. Reprinted in James J. Fyfe (ed.), *Readings on Police Use of Deadly Force.* Wash., DC: Police Foundation, 1982.

_____ (1977b) "Use of Deadly Force to Arrest a Fleeing Felon: A Constitutional Challenge, Part 2." *FBI Law Enforcement Bulletin* 46 (10, October): 27-31.

_____ (1977c) "Use of Deadly Force to Arrest a Fleeing Felon: A Constitutional Challenge, Part 3." *FBI Law Enforcement Bulletin* 46 (11, November): 9-14.

Bouza, Anthony V. (1990) *Bronx Beat: Reflections of a Police Commander.* Chicago: Office of International Criminal Justice, University of Illinois at Chicago.

_____ (1992) Interview on WBEZ-FM Radio, Chicago, Illinois (May 28).

Bowman, Jim (1984) "1933: The Year Chicago's Criminals Declared Open Season on Policemen." *Chicago Tribune Magazine* (February 5).

Boxall, Bettina (1992) "Gays Praise Kolts Report as Accurate Portrayal of Bias." *Los Angeles Times* (July 22): B12.

Boylen, Max, and Robert Little (1990) "Fatal Assaults on United States Law Enforcement Officers." *Police Journal* 63 (1): 61-77.

Bratton, William J. (1990) Communication between the chief of the New York City Transit Police and William A. Geller (October 26).

_____ (ed.) (1990a) *Police Use of Force and the 9 mm Semi-Automatic Weapon: Background Materials for New York City Transit Police Chief William J. Bratton's Presentation to the Board of Directors, Metropolitan Transportation Authority of New York.* (Unpublished reports compiled by the New York City Transit Police) (November 1).

_____ (1991) Communication between the chief of the New York City Transit Police Department and William A. Geller (April 23).

_____ (1991a) "Semi-Automatic Handguns: Opposing Views on Police Firearms—A Clear Choice, The 9mm Handgun." *Police Union News* 1 (4): 1, 3 (newsletter of the International Union of Police Associations, AFL-CIO, published in Washington, DC).

Brill, Steven (1977) *Firearm Abuse: A Research and Policy Report.* Washington, DC: Police Foundation.

Brinkley, Joel (1991) "Israel Judge Says Police Provoked Al Aksa Violence That Killed 17." *New York Times* (July 19): A1, A6.

Bristow, Allen (1963) "Police Officer Shootings—A Tactical Evaluation." *Journal of Criminal Law, Criminology, and Police Science* 54: 93-95.

British Columbia Police Commission (1990) *Recommendations of the Committee on the Use of Less Than Lethal Force by Police Officers in British Columbia.* Vancouver, B.C., Canada (July).

Brody, Jane E. (1992) "Suicide Myths Cloud Efforts to Save Children." *New York Times* (June 16): B5, B6.

Brooke, James (1990) "Brazil Police Accused of Torture and Killing in Rights Report." *New York Times* (June 19): A3.

Brooks, Pierce R. (1975) *Officer Down: Code Three.* Northbrook, IL: MTI.

Brower v. County of Inyo (1989) 109 S.Ct. 1378 (U.S. Supreme Court).

Brown, H. Jackson, Jr. (1991) *Life's Little Instruction Book.* Nashville, TN :Rutledge Hill Press.

Brown, Lee P. (1978) "Appropriate Firearms Policies." *Engage/Social Action* (Nov./Dec.): 35-37.

_____ (1990) "It's Time to Create a Crime Panel." *New York Times* (November 24): 15.

_____ (1991) "Foreword." In William A. Geller (ed.), *Local Government Police Management* (3d rev. ed.). Washington, DC: International City Management Association.

_____ (1992) "The Choice of Handguns for Police Officers: Revolvers or Semi-Automatics." New York: New York City Police Department (May).

Brown, Mark (1992) "No Ironclad Accord on Vests for Police: City Will Pay for Bulletproof Gear, But Cop Union Hedging." *Chicago Sun-Times* (August 5): 1, 36.

Brown, Michael F. (1983) "Shooting Policies: What Patrolmen Think." *Police Chief* (May): 35-37.

_____ (1984) "Use of Deadly Force by Patrol Officers—Training Implications." *Journal of Police Science and Administration* 12 (2, June): 133-140.

Brumley, Al (1988) "Deadly-Force Policy Unveiled for First Time: Dallas Officials Praise Police for Openness." *Dallas Morning News* (August 19): 1, 14A.

_____ (1977b) "Use of Deadly Force to Arrest a Fleeing Felon—A Constitutional Challenge, Part II." *FBI Law Enforcement Bulletin* 46 (10, October): 27-31. Reprinted in James J. Fyfe (ed.), *Readings on Police Use of Deadly Force*. Washington, DC: Police Foundation, 1982.

_____ (1977c) "Use of Deadly Force to Arrest a Fleeing Felon—A Constitutional Challenge, Part III." *FBI Law Enforcement Bulletin* 46 (11, October): 9-14. Reprinted in James J. Fyfe (ed.), *Readings on Police Use of Deadly Force*. Washington, DC: Police Foundation, 1982.

Burden, Ordway P. (1990) "New Technologies Make Their Presence Felt." *Law Enforcement News* (November 30): 5.

_____ (1990a) "Those Who Help, Help Themselves." *Law Enforcement News* (December 15): 5.

Bureau of Alcohol, Tobacco, and Firearms, U.S. Department of the Treasury (1976) *Project Identification: A Study of Handguns Used in Crime*. Washington, DC: Bureau of Alcohol, Tobacco, and Firearms.

Bureau of Justice Statistics, U.S. Department of Justice (1988) *Report to the Nation on Crime and Justice* (2d rev. ed.) Washington, DC: Bureau of Justice Statistics.

_____ (1989) "Bulletin: Profile of State and Local Law Enforcement Agencies, 1987" (March). Washington, DC: Bureau of Justice Statistics.

_____ (1990) "Criminal Victimization 1989: Bulletin" (October). Washington, DC: Bureau of Justice Statistics.

_____ (1992) *Criminal Victimization in the United States, 1990* (February). Washington, DC: Bureau of Justice Statistics.

_____ (1992a) "State and Local Police Departments, 1990." (NCJ-133284). Washington, DC: Bureau of Justice Statistics.

_____ (1992b) "Sheriffs' Departments, 1990." (NCJ-133283). Washington, DC: Bureau of Justice Statistics.

Burg, K.K. (1979) *Womanly Art of Self-Defense: A Commonsense Approach*. New York: A. and W.

Burge, J.H. (1984) *Occupational Stress in Policing*. La Canada, CA: American Educators Publishing.

Burgos, Frank (1991) "Two Versions of Census Breakdown for Chicago." *Chicago Sun-Times* (February 17): 40.

_____ (1992) "Off-Duty Cop, Second Man Slain in Bar Fight." *Chicago Sun-Times* (July 26): 4.

Burke, Tod W. (1990) "Warning Shots: A Change in Perspective." *Law and Order* (October): 51.

Burke, Tod W., Ray Griffin, and Walter F. Rowe (1988) "Bullet Ricochet from Concrete Surfaces: Implication for Officer Survival." *Jnl. of Police Science and Administration* 16 (4): 264-267.

Burleigh, Nina (1992) "Ex-Police Trainee Boasted of Escape." *Chicago Tribune* (July 21): sec. 1, p. 4.

Burnham, David (1971) "Police Killed 54 in the City in 1970." *New York Times* (July 25): 1.

_____ (1973) "3 of 5 Slain by Police Here are Black, Same as the Arrest Rate." *New York Times* (August 26).

Byrd v. Brishke (1972) 466 F.2d 6 (U.S. Court of Appeals, 7th Circuit).

Byrne, James, and Robert Sampson (eds.) (1986) *The Social Ecology of Crime: Theory, Research, and Public Policy*. New York: Springer-Verlag.

California Department of Justice (1974) *Peace Officer-Involved Homicides in California, 1971-1972*. Sacramento, CA: California Department of Justice.

California Highway Patrol (1983) *Pursuit Study*. Sacramento, CA: California Highway Patrol.

Callahan, Charles M, and Frederick P. Rivara (1992) "Urban High School Youth and Handguns: A School-Based Survey." *Journal of the American Medical Association* 267 (22, June 10: 3038-

3042.

Cameron v. City of Pontiac (1985) 623 F.Supp. 1238 (U.S. District Court, Michigan).

Campbell, D. (1978) *Police: The Exercise of Power.* Plymouth, England: MacDonald and Evans, Ltd.

Canadian Civil Liberties Association (1973) "Canadian Civil Liberties Association Submissions to the Task Force on Policing in Ontario." Toronto: Canadian Civil Liberties Association.

Cannon, Lou, and Leef Smith (1992) "L.A. Curfew Lifted; Troops Stay on Patrol: Death Toll Reaches 58 as Attention Turns to Re-building Economy in Riot-Torn Areas." *Washington Post* (May 5): A13.

Cardarelli, Albert P. (1968) "An Analysis of Police Killed by Criminal Action, 1961 1963." *Journal of Criminal Law, Criminology, and Police Science* 59: 447-453.

Carr, Rebecca (1992) "Suburbs Losing Image as Safe Haven for Cops." *Chicago Sun-Times* (August 11): 3.

Carro, J. (1981) "Impact of the Criminal Justice System on Hispanics." In *Report from the National Hispanic Conference on Law Enforcement and Criminal Justice.* Rosslyn, VA: Interamerica Research Associates.

Carter, David L., Allen D. Sapp, and Darrel W. Stephens (1989) *The State of Police Education: Policy Direction for the 21st Century.* Washington, DC: Police Executive Research Forum.

_____ (1990) *Toy Guns: Involvement in Crime and Encounters with the Police.* Washington, DC: Police Executive Research Forum.

_____ (1991) "Survey of Contemporary Police Issues: Critical Findings—A Summary of Findings from a National Study of Policing Issues." (Prepublication copy distributed at the May 1991 annual meeting of the Police Executive Research Forum, Washington, DC). Washington, DC: Police Executive Research Forum.

Casey, Jim (1991) "Officer Safe After Shooting: Vest Credited." *Chicago Sun-Times* (Feb. 9): 13.

Casey, Joe D. (1988) "Research and Development Needed for Less-than-Lethal Weapons." *Police Chief* (February): 7.

Castricone, Rick (1989) "Firearms Selection Procedures: The Semi-Automatic Pistol Transition." *Police Chief* (May): 40-42.

Center for the Environment and Man, Inc. (1970) *A Study of the Problem of Hot Pursuits by the Police.* Washington, DC: U.S. Department of Transportation.

Cerar, John C. (1987) "Firearms Discharge Assault Report, 1987: New York City Police Department Academy Firearms and Tactics Section." (unpublished annual report by NYPD).

_____ (1988) "Firearms Discharge Assault Report, 1988: New York City Police Department Academy Firearms and Tactics Section." (Unpublished annual report by NYPD).

_____ (1989) "Firearms Discharge Assault Report, 1989: New York City Police Department Academy Firearms and Tactics Section." (Unpublished annual report by NYPD).

_____ (1990) "Firearms Discharge Assault Report, 1990: New York City Police Department Academy Firearms and Tactics Section." (Unpublished annual report by NYPD).

_____ (1991) "Firearms Discharge Assault Report, 1991: New York City Police Department Academy Firearms and Tactics Section." (Unpublished annual report by NYPD).

Chamlin, Mitchell B. (1989) "Conflict Theory and Police Killings." *Deviant Behavior* 10 (4): 353-368.

Chaney, Rodney (1990) "Judgment Training in the Use of Deadly Force." *Police Chief* (July): 40-44.

Chapman, Samuel G. (1964) "Killings of Officers in Problems Facing Police and Public." In Samuel G. Chapman (ed.), *Police Patrol Readings.* Springfield, IL: Charles C. Thomas.

_____ (1967) "Police Policy on the Use of Firearms." *Police Chief* (July). Reprinted in James J. Fyfe (ed.), *Readings on Police Use of Deadly Force.* Washington, DC: Police Foundation, 1982.

_____ (1970) "Justifiable Homicides by Police Officers." In Samuel G. Chapman (ed.), *Police Patrol Readings* (2d rev. ed.) Springfield, IL: Charles C. Thomas.

_____ (1976) *Police Murders and Effective Countermeasures.* Santa Cruz, CA: Davis.

_____ (1979) *Police Dogs in America.* Norman, OK: Bureau of Government Research, University of Oklahoma.

_____ (1990) *Police Dogs in North America.* Springfield, IL: Charles C. Thomas.

Chapman, Samuel G., and Thomas S. Crockett (1963) "Gunsight Dilemma: Police Firearms Policy." *Police* 6: 40-45.

Chapman, Samuel G., C.G. Swanson, and C.K. Meyer (1974) *Descriptive Profile of the Assault Incident.* Norman, OK: Bureau of Government Research, University of Oklahoma.

Chappell, Duncan, and Linda P. Graham (1985) *Police Use of Deadly Force: Canadian Perspectives.* Toronto, Canada: Center of Criminology, University of Toronto.

Charles, M.T. (1982) "Women in Policing: The Physical Aspect." *Journal of Police Science and Administration* 10: 194-205.

Chavez, Stephanie (1992) "FBI Inquiry Focuses on Fatal LAPD Shooting at Watts Housing Project." *Los Angeles Times* (February 1): B1, B14.

Cheek, J.C., and T. Lesce (1988) *Plainclothes and Off-Duty Officer Survival.* Springfield, IL: Charles C. Thomas.

Chevigny, Paul G. (1969) *Police Power: Police Abuse in New York City.* New York: Pantheon Books.

_____ (1990) "Police Deadly Force as Social Control: Jamaica, Argentina, and Brazil." *Criminal Law Forum: An International Journal* 1 (3, Spring): 389-425 (published by Rutgers University, Camden, NJ).

Chicago Commission on Race Relations (1922) *The Negro in Chicago: A Study of Race Relations and a Race Riot.* Chicago: University of Chicago Press.

Chicago Police Department (1980) "General Order 80-20: Weapons Policy—Department and Personal." Chicago: Chicago Police Department. Reprinted in William A. Geller and Kevin J. Karales, *Split-Second Decisions: Shootings of and by Chicago Police*, p. 231. Chicago: Chicago Law Enforcement Study Group.

_____ (1990) "News Release from Office of the Superintendent" (concerning number of Chicago police officers shot in the line of duty during 1990 to date) (November 28).

_____ (1990a) Correspondence to William A. Geller from Commander Nelson S. Barreto, Public and Internal Information Division, Chicago Police Department (April 26).

_____ (1992) Personal communication between Ms. Pat Williams, Research and Development Division, Chicago Police Department and William A. Geller (March 25).

Chicago Public Library Information Center (1984) Personal communication between Information Center staff and William A. Geller (February 14).

Chicago Sun-Times (1991) "1991: The Year That Was—Notable Quotables." *Chicago Sun-Times* (December 29): 5.

_____ (1992) "L.A. Lesson To Britain." *Chicago Sun-Times* (May 20): 6.

Chicago Tribune (1991) "Suspect Didn't Face Return to Prison." *Chicago Tribune* (January 11): sec. 2, p. 3.

_____ (1991a) "Cop Killings Suspect Bruised, Defense Says." *Chicago Tribune* (May 7): sec. 2, p. 3.

_____ (1991b) "DC Imposes Curfew in Second Violent Night." *Chicago Tribune* (May 7): sec. 1, p. 3.

_____ (1992) "A Bloody History: Civil Unrest in America." *Chicago Tribune* (May 10): sec. 4, p. 1).

_____ (1992a) "Last Federal Troops Withdraw from L.A." *Chicago Tribune* (May 11): sec. 1, p. 12.

_____ (1992b) "Poll: Whites, Blacks See Riots as 'Warning'." *Chicago Tribune* (May 11): sec. 1, p. 13.

_____ (1992c) "Editorial: L.A.'s Tragedy in Many Acts." *Chicago Tribune* (August 7): sec. 1, p. 12.

Christian, Sue Ellen, and Robert Becker (1992) "Suburb Shattered by Shootout: Three Officers, Suspect Wounded After Roselle Bank Robbery." *Chicago Tribune* (Aug. 11): sec. 1, pp. 1, 8.

Cipriano, R.F. (1982) "Firearms and Law Enforcement Officers Killed: An Alternative." *Police Chief* (July): 46-48.

City of Canton v. Harris (1989) 489 U.S. 378, 109 S.Ct. 1197 (February 28).

Civil Rights Subcommittee of the House Judiciary Committee (1992) "Hearings on Reauthorization of the Civil Rights Division of the U.S. Department of Justice, Testimony of Assistant Attorney General John Dunne and National Institute of Justice Director Charles DeWitt." (May 7).

Clark, B. (1978) "Law Enforcement/Civil Liability: The Misuse of Force." (12-minute film, available through Aims Instructional Media, Glendale, CA).

Clark, Jacob R. (1990) "Charges Fly as Chemical and Stun Gun Lead to Flame." *Law Enforcement News* (September 30): 1, 6.

_____ (1992) "Keeping a Lid on Things: Police Officials in Four Cities Analyze What Was Done Right to Avert L.A.-Style Civil Unrest." *Law Enforcement News* (May 31): 1, 6.

Clark, Kenneth (1974) "Open Letter to Mayor Abraham D. Beame and Police Commissioner Michael J. Codd." *New York Times* (September 17).

Clede, Bill (1990) "NIBRS: The National Incident-Based Reporting System." *Law and Order* (March): 100-101.

_____ (1990a) "New Levels of Lethal Force." *Law and Order* (March): 59-60.

_____ (1991) "Colt Introduces the '2000'—A New Pistol for Police." *Crime Control Digest* (February 18): 7-8.

_____ (1992) "A Bouquet of Aerosal Sprays." *Law and Order* (September): 57-59.

Clede, Bill, with Keven Parsons (1987) *Police Nonlethal Force Manual: Your Choices This Side of Deadly.* Harrisburg, PA: Stackpole Books.

Clesca, J.M. (1992) "Letters to the Editor: Let's Take the Club Out of Police Hands." *New York Times* (May 28): A14.

Cleveland Foundation (1922) *Criminal Justice in Cleveland: Reports of The Cleveland Foundation Survey of The Administration of Criminal Justice in Cleveland, Ohio.* Cleveland: Cleveland Foundation. Reprinted 1968. Montclair, NJ: Patterson Smith.

Cloward, Richard A., and Lloyd E. Ohlin (1960) *Delinquency and Opportunity: A Theory of Delinquent Gangs.* New York: Free Press.

Coates, James (1992) "Unrest Keeps Las Vegas Near the Boiling Point." *Chicago Tribune* (May 20): sec. 1, pp. 1, 8.

Cohen, A. (1979) "Cincinnati: Torn by Grief and Anger." *Police* 2 (6, November): 46-53.

_____ (1980) "I've Killed that Man 10,000 Times." *Police Magazine* 3 (July): 17-23.

Cohen, Laurie, and Robert Blau (1992) "Pressure Mounts on Marshal's Office: Erickson's Shootout Has It On Hot Seat." *Chicago Tribune* (August 2): sec. 2, pp. 1, 3.

Cohen, Lawrence E. (1981) "Modeling Crime Trends: A Criminal Opportunity Perspective." *Journal of Research in Crime and Delinquency* 18: 138-164.

Colorado Springs Gazette Telegraph (1992) "Officers Slain in the Pikes Peak Region." *Colorado Springs Gazette Telegraph* (April 15): A15.

Columbia Broadcasting System (1979) "Stop—Police!" (15-minute film, available through MTI, Northbrook, IL, broadcast on CBS-TV).

Comment (1962) "Police—Philadelphia's Police Advisory Board." *Villanova Law Review* 7: 656.

Commission on Accreditation for Law Enforcement Agencies (1983) *Standards for Law Enforcement Agencies: The Standards Manual of the Law Enforcement Agency Accreditation Program.* Fairfax, VA: CALEA.

_____ (1988) *Standards for Law Enforcement Agencies: The Standards Manual of the Law Enforcement Agency Accreditation Program.* Fairfax, VA: Commission on Accreditation for Law Enforcement Agencies.

Concerns of Police Survivors (1988) *Support Services to Surviving Families of Line-of-Duty Death: Law Enforcement Agency Handbook.* Washington, DC: Concerns of Police Survivors.

Condon, Richard J. (1985) *Report to Governor Mario M. Cuomo: Police Use of Deadly Force in New York State.* Albany, NY: New York State Division of Criminal Justice Services.

Connelley, James, and Terry Bratton (1991) Personal communication between two Houston Police Department tactical trainers and William A. Geller (February 11).

Connelly, Michael (1992) "Holdup Victim Testifies in Suit Against Police Over Killings: A Night Manager Tells How She Waited for Officers As Robbers Broke Into the Restaurant and Threatened Her Life." *Los Angeles Times* (February 26).

Connor, Gregory J. (1990) *Vehicle Stops: Tactical Procedures and Safety Strategies.* Champaign, IL: Stipes Publishing.

_____ (1991) "Use of Force Continuum: Phase II." *Law and Order* (March): 30-32.

Connor, Gregory J., and Matthew D. Summers (1988) *Tactical Neutralization Techniques.* Champaign, IL: Stipes Publishing Co.

Cook, Dave (1992) "The Situation in Los Angeles." *Washington Post* (May 5): A13.

Cook, T.D., and Donald T. Campbell (1979) *Quasi-Experimentation.* Chicago: Rand McNally.

Cordner, Gary W. (1985) "Police Research and Police Policy: Some Propositions about the Production and Use of Knowledge." In William A. Geller (ed.), *Police Leadership in America: Crisis and Opportunity*. New York: Praeger and American Bar Foundation.

Cordner, Gary W., and Donna C. Hale (eds.) (1992) *What Works in Policing? Operations and Administration Examined*. Cincinnati, Ohio: Anderson Publishing.

Cope, J., and K. Goddard (1979) *Weaponless Control for Law Enforcement and Security*. Springfield, IL: Charles C. Thomas.

Cory, B. (1978) "Deadly Force." *Police* 1 (5): 5-14.

_____ (1979) "They're Marching Again in Birmingham (AL)." *Police Magazine* 2 (6, Nov.): 30-34.

_____ (1981a) "New Politics of Deadly Force." *Police* 4 (2, March): 6-11.

_____ (1981b) "Philadelphia: 'When in Doubt, Don't Shoot'." *Police* 4 (2, March): 12-15.

Council for Science and Society (1978) *Harmless Weapons*. Little London, Chichester, Sussex, England: Barry Rose Publishers.

Council on Scientific Affairs, American Medical Association (1992) "Assault Weapons as a Public Health Hazard in the United States." *Journal of the American Medical Association* 267 (22, June 10): 3067-3070.

Cox, Terry C., Jerry S. Faughn, and William M. Nixon (1985) "Police Use of Metal Flashlights as Weapons: An Analysis of Relevant Problems." *Journal of Police Science and Administration* 13 (3): 244-250.

Cramer, Shane J., and Gerald D. Robin (1968) "Assaults On Police." *Police* 12 (March-April): 82-87.

Crenshaw, Albert B. (1992) "Insurers Put Riot Costs at $200 Million: L.A. Payouts to Exceed Those for Watts Damage." *Washington Post* (May 5): C1, C2.

Crime Control Digest (1989) "Shooting of Innocent Bystanders Tripled Since 1986, Four-City Survey Finds." *Crime Control Digest* (July 3): 1-2.

_____ (1990a) "Street Survival '91 Offers to Share Cops' Reality with Judges and Lawmakers." *Crime Control Digest* (October 15): 2-3.

_____ (1990b) "National Crime Survey: Victims Report 19.7 Million Violent Crimes, Thefts in 1989." *Crime Control Digest* (October 29): 1-2.

_____ (1990c) "Police Foundation Study of Women Police Points Out Problems, Calls for Changes." *Crime Control Digest* (November 19): 1-6.

_____ (1990d) "Dallas Police Minority Recruiting Drops, Study Shows." *Crime Control Digest* (November 19): 3-4.

_____ (1990e) "Philadelphia Police Shooting More as Crime Increases." *Crime Control Digest* (November 16): 6-7.

_____ (1990f) "Rookie Dallas Policeman Mistakenly Kills Shop Owner." *Crime Control Digest* December 31): 7-8.

_____ (1990g) "Southwest Border Violence Against Immigrants Rising." *Crime Control Digest* (May 7): 9.

_____ (1991) "First Female Police Officer Killed in Los Angeles History." *Crime Control Digest* (February 18): 9-10.

_____ (1991a) "Settlement Reached in Black Prisoner's Jail Death." *Crime Control Digest* (February 18): 2.

_____ (1991b) "Personal and Household Crime Fell Three Percent Last Year, BJS Reports." *Crime Control Digest* (April 8): 1-5.

_____ (1991c) "FBI Reports: Serious Crime Up Slightly." *Crime Control Digest* (April 29): 5.

_____ (1991d) "Surviving Edged Weapons: Police Training Video Blamed for Jump in Shootings by San Diego Police Officers." *Crime Control Digest* (June 3): 1-2.

_____ (1991e) "AELE [Americans for Effective Law Enforcement] Calls for National Reporting System on Use of Force, Police Misconduct." *Crime Control Digest* (April 1): 1, 10.

_____ (1991f) "S&W 10mms: Pistols Used by Virginia State Police Caused Problems for Others." *Crime Control Digest* (June 17): 9.

_____ (1991g) "Detective, Two Suspects Killed in Dallas UC Buy." *Crime Control Digest* (December 23): 5.

_____ (1991h) "Hispanic Growth Change U.S. Racial Mix, Threatens Conflict." *Crime Control Digest* (June 17): 7-9.

_____ (1991i) "Virginia Officers Stunned By Weak Cap-Stun Solution Due to Mix-Up in Product."

Crime Control Digest (November 18): 10.

_____ (1991j) "In 1990: Murders Hit Record Highs in Nation's Major Cities." *Crime Control Digest* (January 14): 1.

_____ (1991k) "FBI Reports 65 Officers Killed Feloniously in 1990: Lowest Number Since 1960s." *Crime Control Digest* (April 22): 1, 5.

_____ (1991l) "Revised LAPD Policy Toward Homosexuals Could Lead to Settlement." *Crime Control Digest* (September 9): 8-9.

_____ (1991m) "Alleged Brutality...L.A. Sheriff Agrees to Set Up Advisory Panel: Will Implement Some Suggestions of LAPD's Christopher Commission." *Crime Control Digest* (September 16): 8-9.

_____ (1991n) "Shootings by LASD Deputies Up 36 Percent in One Year." *Crime Control Digest* (November 4): 7-8.

_____ (1991o) "Survey Shows Most Front-Line Police Wear Protective Vests." *Crime Control Digest* (May 13): 5-6.

_____ (1991p) "Supreme Court Narrows Definition of Seizure: Broadens Police Powers." *Crime Control Digest* (April 29): 1, 3-4.

_____ (1991q) "FBI Reports 41 Officers Killed Feloniously During First Six Months of Year." *Crime Control Digest* (November 4): 1, 3.

_____ (1992a) "Need Body Armor: Rural Missouri Police Ask for Protection." *Crime Control Digest* (February 3): 5.

_____ (1992b) "Number of Law Enforcement Officers Grew by 5.4 Percent From 1987 Through 1990." *Crime Control Digest* (February 17): 1, 6-7.

_____ (1992c) "Experts Begin Review of Dallas Police Drug Detail." *Crime Control Digest* (February 17): 5-6.

_____ (1992d) "New Memphis Police Department Shooting Policy Saves Lives, Reduces Friction with Community." *Crime Control Digest* (March 30): 1, 7-8.

_____ (1992e) "FBI Agents Shoot and Kill Suspect in Deputy's Death." *Crime Control Digest* (April 13): 9.

_____ (1992f) "BJS Reports: Personal, Household Crimes Rose Less than 2% Last Year." *Crime Control Digest* (April 27): 1-3.

_____ (1992g) "Los Angeles Riot: Gates Blames Top Brass for Slow Police Response." *Crime Control Digest* (May 11): 1-5.

_____ (1992h) "Riots 'Sicken' Bush: DOJ May Press Sec. 1983 Charges Against L.A. Officers; Rioting Spreads Nationwide." *Crime Control Digest* (May 4): 1-5.

_____ (1992i) "In Legislature: California Law Enforcement Fighting Misconduct Bills." *Crime Control Digest* (May 25): 4-6.

_____ (1992j) "House is Re-Examining How Federal Government Responds to Police Brutality." *Crime Control Digest* (May 18): 9-10.

_____ (1992k) "Verbal Judo Instructor Course." *Crime Control Digest* (May 18): 8.

_____ (1992l) "L.A. Sheriff's Department to Keep Using Taser Guns." *Crime Control Digest* (June 29): 4.

_____ (1992m) "Venue Shopping: Racially Charged Police Trial in Florida Seeks a Home." *Crime Control Digest* (August 24): 1-2.

_____ (1992n) "Four U.S. Marshals Disciplined." *Crime Control Digest* (August 24): 5.

_____ (1992o) "Non-Lethal and the Stopping Power of a 38 Special." *Crime Control Digest* (August 24): 10.

_____ (1992p) "In Maryland: Woman Killed by 'Non-Lethal' Rubber Bullet Fired by Officer." *Crime Control Digest* (September 7): 5-6.

_____ (1992q) "N.J. Prosecutors Have No Plans to Back Down from Violent Car Thieves." *Crime Control Digest* (September 7): 9.

_____ (1992r) "Commission Adopts Interim Report on Use of Dogs." *Crime Control Digest* (September 7): 10.

Criminal Justice Council (1985) "Black on Black Crime." Dade County, FL: Criminal Justice Council (cited in Alpert 1989a).

Criminal Justice Newsletter (1990) "36 Officers Were Killed During First Half of 1990, FBI Reports."

Criminal Justice Newsletter 21 (21, November 1): 4.

Crimmins, Jerry (1992) "Gunmen Work Overtime Over Holiday Weekend." *Chicago Tribune* (September 9): sec. 2, p. 2.

Croft, Elizabeth Benz (1986) "Police Use of Force: A Twenty-Year Perspective." (Paper presented at the Annual Meeting of the Academy of Criminal Justice Sciences, Orlando, FL).

Cruse, and Rubin (1972) "Determinants of Police Behavior." In *Project Report to National Institute of Law Enforcement* 194. Washington, DC: U.S. Department of Justice.

Cunningham, William C., and Todd H. Taylor (1985) *Private Security and Police in America (The Hallcrest Report)*. Portland, OR: Chancellor Press.

Cunningham, William C., John J. Strauchs, and Clifford W. Van Meter (1990) *Private Security Trends: 1970-2000 (The Hallcrest Report II)*. Stoneham, MA: Butterworth Heinemann.

Cunningham, William C., John J. Strauchs, and Clifford W. Van Meter (1991) "Private Security: Patterns and Trends." *National Institute of Justice Research in Brief* (August) (# NCJ 127594).

Dallas Police Department (1974) *Report on Police Shootings*. Dallas, TX: Center for Police Development, Southern Methodist University.

_____ (1990) "Review of Dallas Police Department's Use of Deadly Force." (Unpublished intradepartmental memorandum to the Chief by Assistant Chief Marlin R. Price) (June 4).

_____ (1991) Officer-involved shooting data compiled by Assistant Chief of the Dallas Police Department Marlin R. Price and furnished to William A. Geller January 11).

_____ (1992) Officer-involved shooting data compiled by Assistant Chief of the Dallas Police Department Marlin R. Price and furnished to William A. Geller January 14.

_____ (1992a) "Comparative Statistical Survey: 1991." (Unpublished survey of major city police departments concerning a variety of administrative and operational topics) (circulated to participating police departments April 28, 1992).

Daniels, Lee A. (1992) "The Jury: Some of the Jurors Speak, Giving Sharply Differing Views." *New York Times* (May 1): A10.

Dao, James (1992) "Amid Dinkins's Calls for Peace, Protesters Skirmish with Police." *New York Times* (July 8): A14.

_____ (1992a) "Two Are Killed in A Shootout in Queens: Hostage is Slain in Botched Robbery." *New York Times* (August 12): B1-B2.

Dash, J., and Martin Reiser (1978) "Suicide Among Police in Urban Law Enforcement Agencies." *Journal of Police Science and Administration* 6 (1): 18-21.

David, Jonathan (1991) *By Our Own Hand* (39-minute video on police suicide, directed by J. David, made in cooperation with the New York City Police Department and funded by the New York City Police Foundation).

Davis, Mike (1992) "Urban American Sees Its Future in L.A., Burning All Illusions." *Nation* (June 1): 743-746.

Day, S.C. (1978) "Shooting the Fleeing Felon: State of the Law." *Criminal Law Bulletin* 14 (4, July-August): 285-310.

del Carmen, R. (1981) "An Overview of Civil and Criminal Liabilities of Police Officers and Departments." *American Journal of Law* 9: 33-50.

_____ (1991) *Civil Liabilities in American Policing: A Text for Law Enforcement Personnel*. Englewood Cliffs, NJ: Brady Publishing.

Delattre, Edwin J. (1989) *Character and Cops: Ethics in Policing*. Washington, DC: American Enterprise Institute for Public Policy Research.

Delattre, Edwin J., and Cornelius J. Behan (1991) "Practical Ideals for Managing in the '90s: A Perspective." In William A. Geller (ed.), *Local Government Police Management* (3d rev. ed.). Washington, DC: International City Management Association.

Desmedt, John C. (1984) "Use of Force Paradigm for Law Enforcement." *Journal of Police Science and Administration* 12 (2): 170-176.

DiVasto, Peter, Frederick J. Lanceley, and Anne Gruys (1992) "Critical Issues in Suicide Prevention." *FBI Law Enforcement Bulletin* (August): 13-16.

Doerner, William G. (1983) "Why Does Johnny Reb Die When Shot? The Impact of Medical Resources Upon Lethality." *Sociological Inquiry* 53: 1-15.

_____ (1988) "The Impact of Medical Resources on Criminally Induced Lethality: A Further

Examination." *Criminology* 26: 171-179.

_____ (1991) "Police Unholstering and Shooting Behavior Under Simulated Field Conditions." *American Journal of Police* 10 (3): 1-15.

Doerner, William G., and J.C. Speir (1986) "Stitch and Sew: The Impact of Medical Resources Upon Criminally Induced Lethality." *Criminology* 24: 319-330.

Dolan, John T., and G. Dwayne Fuselier (1989) "A Guide for First Responders to Hostage Situations." *FBI Law Enforcement Bulletin* (April): 9-13.

Donahue, Michael Eugene (1983) "Halt...Police! An Analysis of the Police Use of Deadly Force in a Large Midwestern City." (Unpublished Ph.D. dissertation, Michigan State University. Available through University Microfilms, Ann Arbor, MI).

Donnelly, Peter J. (1978) "Investigating the Use of Deadly Force." *Police Chief* (May): 24-26. Reprinted in Harry W. More, Jr. (ed.), *Critical Issues in Law Enforcement* (4th rev. ed.) Cincinnati: Anderson Publishing.

Donovan, E. (1989) "List of Names of Police Officers Killed in 1988." *Police Stress* (Summer).

Doyle, James E. (1992) Unpublished presentation to the Wisconsin Attorney General's Law Enforcement Conference, Stevens Point, WI (May 21).

DuChesne, L.W., and V.L. Vasil (1983) "Responding to Use of Deadly Force: The Rollout Team." *Police Chief* (May): 34-41.

Duggan, Paul (1992) "Prince George's Officer Shoots Man in Wheelchair." *Washington Post* (May 19): A1.

Dwyer, William O., Arthur C. Graesser, Patricia L. Hopkinson, and Michael B. Lupfer (1990) "Application of Script Theory to Police Officers' Use of Deadly Force." *Journal of Police Science and Administration* 17 (4, December): 295-302.

Egan, Timothy (1992) *Breaking Blue.* New York: Knopf.

Eck, John E. (1984) *Using Research: A Primer for Law Enforcement Managers.* Washington, DC: Police Executive Research Forum.

Eck, John E., and William Spelman (1987) *Problem-Solving: Problem-Oriented Policing in Newport News.* Washington, DC: Police Executive Research Forum.

Eck, John E., and Gerald L. Williams (1991) "Criminal Investigations." In William A. Geller (ed.), *Local Government Police Management* (3d rev. ed.). Washington, DC: International City Management Association.

Eckholm, Erik (1992) "Bulges, a Slouch: This is How He Can Spot a Gun." *New York Times* (May 26): A16.

Edholm, P. (1978) "Realism in Firearms Training." *Law and Order* 26 (10, Oct.): 30, 32, 34-35, 45.

Edwards, Steven M. (1991a) "Semi-Automatic Handguns: Opposing Views on Police Firearms—Caution on High-Capacity Weapons." *Police Union News* 1 (4, February): 1-3 (Newsletter of the International Association of Police Unions, AFL-CIO, Washington, DC).

_____ (1991b) "Stick to Your Guns: Proficiency, Not Technology, Is the Key to Firearms Success." *Police* (February): 4.

Egan, Timothy (1992) "Dismissed from Army as Lesbian, Colonel Will Fight Homosexual Ban." *New York Times* (May 31): section 1, p. 14.

_____ (1992a) "Fugitive in Idaho Cabin Plays Role of Folk Hero." *New York Times* (Aug. 26): A10.

_____ (1992b) "White Supremacist Surrenders After 11-Day Siege: A Two-Year Standoff Ends Only After Blood Was Spilled." *New York Times* (September 1): A6.

Eisenberg, Terry, and D. Kent (1972) "The Selection and Promotion of Police Officers: A Selected Review of Recent Literature." *Police Chief* (February).

Elliot, I.D. (1979) "Use of Deadly Force in Arrest: Proposals for Reform in Australia." *Criminal Law Journal* (Australia) 3 (2, April): 50-58.

Evans, G., and N. Farberow (1988) *The Encyclopedia of Suicide.* New York: Facts on File.

Fairbairn, William E., and Eric A. Sykes (1987—reprint of 1942 edition) *Shooting to Live With the One-Hand Gun.* Boulder, CO: Paladin Press.

Farkas, G.M. (1986) "Stress in Undercover Policing." In James T. Reese and Harvey A. Goldstein (eds.), *Psychological Services for Law Enforcement.* Washington, DC: Federal Bureau of Investigation (pp. 433-440).

Farrell, Barry (1977) "The Deadly Sin of Police Panic." *New West* September 26: 69-70.

Federal Bureau of Investigation (1974) "Police Killings in 1973—A Record Year." *FBI Law Enforcement Bulletin* 43: 13.

_____ (1979) *Uniform Crime Reports: Crime in the United States, 1978.* Washington, DC: Federal Bureau of Investigation.

_____ (1980) *Uniform Crime Reports: Law Enforcement Officers Killed, 1980.* Washington, DC: Federal Bureau of Investigation.

_____ (1981a) *Uniform Crime Reports: Crime in the United States, 1980.* Washington, DC: Federal Bureau of Investigation.

_____ (1981b) *The Legal Handbook for Special Agents.* Washington, DC: Federal Bureau of Investigation.

_____ (1982) *Uniform Crime Reports Supplement: Law Enforcement Officers Killed and Assaulted—1982.* Washington, DC: Federal Bureau of Investigation.

_____ (1987) *Uniform Crime Reports Supplement: Law Enforcement Officers Killed and Assaulted—1987.* Washington, DC: Federal Bureau of Investigation.

_____ (1988) *Uniform Crime Reports Supplement: Law Enforcement Officers Killed and Assaulted—1988.* Washington, DC: Federal Bureau of Investigation.

_____ (1988a) "Bulletin Notes." *FBI Law Enforcement Bulletin* (July): 34.

_____ (1989a) *Crime in the United States, 1989.* Washington, DC: Federal Bureau of Investigation.

_____ (1989b) *Uniform Crime Reports Supplement: Law Enforcement Officers Killed and Assaulted—1989.* Washington, DC: Federal Bureau of Investigation.

_____ (1989c) "Bulletin Notes." *FBI Law Enforcement Bulletin* (June): 33.

_____ (1989d) "Bulletin Notes." *FBI Law Enforcement Bulletin* (August): 33.

_____ (1990) Personal communication between staff of the User Services Section, Federal Bureau of Investigation Uniform Crime Reporting unit and William A. Geller (April 10).

_____ (1990a) "Bulletin Notes." *FBI Law Enforcement Bulletin*: 59 (September): 33.

_____ (1990b) "Bulletin Notes." *FBI Law Enforcement Bulletin* (August): 33.

_____ (1990c) "Supplementary Homicide Report Coding Guide" (revised January 1980; still applicable when furnished to William Geller in October 1990 by the Uniform Crime Reporting program).

_____ (1990d) "Bulletin Notes." *FBI Law Enforcement Bulletin* (December): 33.

_____ (1990e) Personal communication between the staff of the Federal Bureau of Investigation User Services Unit, Uniform Crime Reporting Section and William A. Geller (December 11).

_____ (1990f) Personal communication between Ed Davis, an instructor in the Training and Program Development unit, Federal Bureau of Investigation Uniform Crime Reporting program and William A. Geller (December 11).

_____ (1991a) Personal communication between Ms. Nancy Carnes of the User Services Section, Federal Bureau of Investigation Uniform Crime Reporting program and William A. Geller (March 29).

_____ (1991b) *Uniform Crime Reports Supplement: Law Enforcement Officers Killed and Assaulted—1990.* Washington, DC: Federal Bureau of Investigation.

_____ (1991c) *Crime in the United States, 1990.* Washington, DC: Federal Bureau of Investigation.

_____ (1992a) "Bulletin Notes." *FBI Law Enforcement Bulletin* (February): 33.

_____ (1992b) "Bulletin Notes." *FBI Law Enforcement Bulletin* (March): 33.

_____ (1992c) Personal communication between Ms. Nancy Carnes of the User Services Section, Federal Bureau of Investigation Uniform Crime Reporting program and William A. Geller (March 6).

_____ (1992d) "Bulletin Notes." *FBI Law Enforcement Bulletin* (July): 33.

_____ (1992e) *Killed in the Line of Duty.* Washington, DC: Federal Bureau of Investigation.

_____ (1992f) "Police Policy: Line-of-Duty Death Policy." *FBI Law Enforcement Bulletin* (August): 4-5.

_____ (1992g) *Crime in the United States, 1991.* Washington, DC: Federal Bureau of Investigation.

Federal Law Enforcement Training Center, U.S. Department of the Treasury (1989) *1989 Annual Report.* Glynco, GA: Federal Law Enforcement Training Center.

Fennell, J.T. (1981) "Psychological Stress and the Peace Officer: A Cop Killer." In G. Henderson (ed.), *Police Human Relations.* Springfield, IL: Charles C. Thomas.

Ferdinand, Theodore H. and Elmer G. Luchterhand (1970) "Inner-City Youth, the Police, the Juvenile Court, and Justice." *Social Problems* 17: 510-527.

Finch, F.R. (1976) "Deadly Force to Arrest: Triggering Constitutional Review." *Harvard Civil Rights-Civil Liberties Law Review* 11 (1, Winter): 361-389.

Fingerhut, Lois A., Deborah D. Ingram, and Jacob J. Feldman (1992a) "Firearm and Nonfirearm Homicide Among Persons 15 Through 19 Years of Age: Differences by Level of Urbanization, United States, 1979 Through 1989." *Journal of the American Medical Association* 267 (22, June 10): 3048-3053.

_____ (1992b) "Firearm Homicide Among Black Teenage Males in Metropolitan Counties: Comparison of Death Rates in Two Periods, 1983 Through 1985 and 1987 Through 1989." *Journal of the American Medical Association* 267 (22, June 10): 3054-3058.

Flanagan, Timothy J., and Kathleen Maguire (eds.) (1990) *Sourcebook of Criminal Justice Statistics—1989*. Washington, DC: Bureau of Justice Statistics, U.S. Department of Justice.

Fletcher, Connie (1991) *Pure Cop*. New York: Villard Books.

Floyd, Craig (1990) Personal communication between staff director of National Law Enforcement Memorial project and William A. Geller (October 9).

Fogelson, Robert M. (1977) *Big-City Police*. Cambridge, MA: Harvard University Press.

Ford, Andrea (1990) "Muslims' Shooting Described." *Los Angeles Times* (April 18): B1-10.

_____ (1991a) "Video of Police Dog Attack on Unarmed Theft Suspect Prompts Panel Inquiry." *Los Angeles Times* (December 12): B1, B11.

_____ (1991b) "Critics Call for LAPD K-9 Unit Moratorium." *Los Angeles Times* (Dec. 24): B7.

Ford, Anrea, and Eric Malnic (1992) "Ex-Officer to Avoid Retrial in Slayings." *Los Angeles Times* (June 4): A1, A27.

Ford, Andrea, and Janet Rae-Dupree (1992) "Inmate's Death Raises Questions About Deputies' Conduct." *Los Angeles Times* (July 21): A19.

Forslund, Morris A. (1972) "A Comparison of Negro and White Crime Rates." In Charles E. Reasons and Jack L. Kuykendall (eds.), *Race, Crime, and Society*. Pacific Palisades, CA: Goodyear (pp. 96-102).

Fountain, John W. (1991) "Police Seeking More Firepower: Many Go to Semi-Automatic Pistol." *Chicago Tribune* (March 17): sec. 2, pp. 1, 3.

Fountain, John W., and Michael Kates (1992) "Victory Turns Violent as Bulls Fans Stampede Through Streets." *Chicago Tribune* (June 15): sec. 1, p. 8.

Franchine, Philip (1992) "Wounded Cop Says She'll Use Semiautomatic From Now On." *Chicago Sun-Times* (February 29): 5.

Freed, David (1989) "Boy's Suit Over Slaying is Dismissed." *Los Angeles Times* (December 5): B1.

Fridell, Lorie A. (1983) "Community Attitudes Toward Police Use of Deadly Force." (Unpublished Ph.D. dissertation, University of California, Irvine.)

_____ (1989) "Justifiable Use of Measures in Research on Deadly Force." *Journal of Criminal Justice* 17 (3): 157-165.

Fridell, Lorie A., and Arnold Binder (1988) "Police Officer Decision-making in Potentially Violent Confrontations." Paper presented at the annual meeting of the American Society of Criminology, Chicago, IL.

_____ (1989) "Racial Aspects of Police Shootings Revisited." A paper presented at the Annual Meeting of the American Society of Criminology, Reno, Nevada (November 10).

Fried, Joseph P. (1990) "Prisoner's Trial to Start in Slaying of Two Detectives." *New York Times* (June 17).

_____ (1992) "Police Say Their Gunfire Killed Hostage: Man Was First Struck by a Robber's Bullet." *New York Times* (August 14): B1-B2.

Friedrich, Robert J. (1980) "Police Use of Force: Individuals, Situations, and Organizations." *Annals of the American Academy of Political and Social Science* 452 (November): 82-97.

Fritsch, Jane (1992) "Gun of Choice for the New York Police Runs Into Fierce Opposition." *New York Times* (May 31): section 1, p. 23.

_____ (1992a) "Police Weighing Risks of Semiautomatic Gun." *New York Times* (June 15): A16.

Fyfe, James J. (1978) "Shots Fired: A Typological Examination of New York City Police Firearms Discharges, 1971-1975." (Unpublished Ph.D. dissertation, School of Criminal Justice, State

University of New York-Albany. Available through University Microfilms, Ann Arbor, MI).

_____ (1979a) "Officer Race and Police Shootings." Paper presented to the annual meeting of the American Society of Criminology, Philadelphia (November).

_____ (1979b) "Administrative Interventions on Police Shooting Discretion." *Journal of Criminal Justice* 7 (4, Winter): 309-324. Reprinted in James J. Fyfe (ed.), *Readings on Police Use of Deadly Force*. Washington, DC: Police Foundation, 1982.

_____ (1980a) "Always Prepared: Police Off-Duty Guns." *Annals of the American Academy of Political and Social Science* 452 (November): 72-81. Reprinted in James J. Fyfe (ed.), *Readings on Police Use of Deadly Force*. Washington, DC: Police Foundation, 1982.

_____ (1980b) "Geographic Correlates of Police Shootings: A Microanalysis." *Journal of Research in Crime and Delinquency* 17 (1, January): 101-113.

_____ (1981a) "Race and Extreme Police-Citizen Violence." In R. L. McNeeley and Carl E. Pope (eds.), *Race, Crime, and Criminal Justice*. Beverly Hills, CA: Sage (pp. 89-108). Reprinted in James J. Fyfe (ed.), *Readings on Police Use of Deadly Force*. Washington, DC: Police Foundation, 1982.

_____ (1981b) "Observations on Police Deadly Force." *Crime and Delinquency* 27 (3, July): 376-89. Reprinted in James J. Fyfe (ed.), *Readings on Police Use of Deadly Force*. Washington, DC: Police Foundation, 1982.

_____ (1981c) "Toward a Typology of Police Shootings." In James J. Fyfe (ed.), *Contemporary Issues in Law Enforcement*. Beverly Hills, CA: Sage (pp. 136-151).

_____ (1981d) "Who Shoots? A Look at Officer Race and Police Shooting." *Journal of Police Science and Administration* 9 (4): 367-382.

_____ (1982) "Blind Justice: Police Shootings in Memphis." *Journal of Criminal Law and Criminology* 73: 707-722.

_____ (ed.) (1982b) *Readings on Police Use of Deadly Force*. Washington, DC: Police Foundation.

_____ (1986a) "Enforcement Workshop: The Supreme Court's New Rules for Police Use of Deadly Force." *Criminal Law Bulletin* 22: 62-68.

_____ (1986b) "The Split-Second Syndrome and Other Determinants of Police Violence." In Anne Campbell and John Gibbs (eds.), *Violent Transactions*. New York: Basil Blackwell. Reprinted in Roger G. Dunham and Geoffrey P. Alpert (eds.), *Critical Issues in Policing: Contemporary Readings*. Prospect Heights, IL: Waveland Press (1989).

_____ (1986c) "*Tennessee v. Garner*: The Issue not Addressed." *New York University Review of Law and Social Change* 14: 721-731.

_____ (1988a) "Police Shooting Environment and License." In J.E. Scott and T. Hirschi (eds.), *Controversial Issues in Crime and Justice*. Beverly Hills, CA: Sage.

_____ (1988b) "Police Use of Deadly Force: Research and Reform." *Justice Quarterly* 5 (2) (June): 165-205.

_____ (1988c) "The Metro-Dade Police/Citizen Violence Reduction Project: Final Report," vol. 2. Washington, DC: Police Foundation.

_____ (1989a) "Police/Citizen Violence Reduction Project." *FBI Law Enforcement Bulletin* 58 (5, May): 18.

_____ (1989b) "Controlling Police Vehicle Pursuits." In James J. Fyfe (ed.), *Police Practice in the '90s: Key Management Issues*. Washington, DC: International City Management Association.

_____ (1989c) "The Split-Second Syndrome and Other Determinants of Police Violence." In Roger G. Dunham and Geoffrey P. Alpert (eds.), *Critical Issues in Policing: Contemporary Readings*. Prospect Heights, IL: Waveland Press. Reprinted from Anne Campbell and John Gibbs (eds.), *Violent Transactions*. New York: Basil Blackwell (1986).

_____ (1991) "Unacceptable Situation: L.A. Police Chief Accountable to His Boss—The People." *Los Angeles Times*.

_____ (1992) Memo to William A. Geller (March 18).

Fyfe, James J., and Mark Blumberg (1985) "Response to Griswold—A More Valid Test of the Justifiability of Police Actions." *American Journal of Police* 4 (2, Fall): 110-132.

Fyfe, James J., and J. Walker (1990) "*Garner* Plus Five Years: An Examination of Supreme Court Intervention Into Police Discretion and Legislative Prerogatives." *American Journal of Criminal Justice* 14: 167-188.

Gain, Charles (1971) "Discharge of Firearms Policy: Effecting Justice Through Administrative Regulation." Unpublished memorandum, December 23.

Galloway, Paul (1992) "A Bloody History: Rioting Not Sole Property of a Race, Culture." *Chicago Tribune* (May 10): sec. 4, pp. 1, 4.

Garner, Gerald W. (1990) *High-Risk Patrol: Reducing the Danger to You*. Springfield, IL: Charles C. Thomas.

Garner, Joel, and Elizabeth Clemmer (1986) "Danger to Police in Domestic Disturbances—A New Look." *Research in Brief*. Washington, DC: National Institute of Justice. Reprinted in Roger G. Dunham and Geoffrey P. Alpert (eds.), *Critical Issues in Policing: Contemporary Readings*. Prospect Heights, IL: Waveland Press, 1989.

Gates, Daryl F., and Diane K. Shah (1992) *Chief: My Life in the LAPD*. New York: Bantam Books.

Gates, Henry Louis, Jr. (1992) "Black Demagogues and Pseudo-Scholars." *New York Times* (July 20): A11.

Geiger, Steven, Michael H. Holmes, Michael Goergen, and Robert Skomra (1990) "Training: Hostage Negotiation." *Police Chief* (November): 52-57.

Geis, Gilbert, and Arnold Binder (1990) "Non-Lethal Weapons: The Potential and the Pitfalls." *Journal of Contemporary Criminal Justice* 6 (1, February): 2.

Geller, William A. (1979) "Filling the Information Gap: A Study of Police Shootings in Chicago," in U.S. Department of Justice (ed.), *Police Use of Deadly Force: What Police and the Community Can Do About It*. Washington, DC: U.S. Government Printing Office.

_____ (1981a) "Police Shootings Could be Reduced by Nearly One-Third." *The Brief* (June-July).

_____ (1981b) "Police Shootings Demystified: The Chicago Study." *Justice Reporter* (November-December): 1-8.

_____ (1982a) "The Effects of Restrictive Police 'Use of Deadly Force' Policies." (Unpublished memo to Chicago Police Board, January 28).

_____ (1982b) "Deadly Force: What We Know." *Journal of Police Science and Administration* 10 (2): 151-177. Reprinted in Carl B. Klockars (ed.), *Thinking About Police: Contemporary Readings*. New York: McGraw-Hill, 1983.

_____ (1983) "Remarks to the 22nd Annual Chicago Police Department Recognition Ceremony" (May 23).

_____ (1985a) "Officer Restraint in the Use of Deadly Force: The Next Frontier in Police Shooting Research." *Journal of Police Science and Administration* 13 (2): 153-171.

_____ (1985b) "15 Shooting Reduction Techniques: Controlling the Use of Deadly Force By and Against Police Officers." *Police Chief* (August): 56-58. Reprinted in U.S. Department of Justice, Community Relations Service (ed.), *Principles of Good Policing: Avoiding Violence Between Police and Citizens*. Washington, DC: U.S. Government Printing Office, May 1987; and in International Association of Chiefs of Police, *Operational Issues in the Small Law Enforcement Agency*. Arlington, VA: International Association of Chiefs of Police, 1990.

_____ (1985c) "Police and Deadly Force: A Look at the Empirical Literature." In Frederick Elliston and Michael Feldberg (eds.), *Moral Issues in Police Work*. Totowa, NJ: Littlefield Adams.

_____ (1986) "Crime File: Deadly Force: A Study Guide." Washington, DC: National Institute of Justice, U.S. Department of Justice (Companion to NIJ videotape entitled "Deadly Force," a discussion moderated by James Q. Wilson).

_____ (1987) "Factors Influencing the Use of Deadly Force." In Joseph J. Senna and Larry J. Siegel (eds.), *Introduction to Criminal Justice*. St. Paul, MN: West Publishing Company (p. 229).

_____ (1988) "Shootings of and by Chicago Police, 1974-September 1, 1988." News release issued by the Police Executive Research Forum in Chicago.

_____ (1989) "Civilians Shot by Chicago Police, 1974-1983, by Reason for Shooting and Civilian Race." Chicago, IL: Police Executive Research Forum (news release).

_____ (1990) Data furnished to William A. Geller by the Dallas Police Department on September 24, 1990.

_____ (1991) "Preface." In William A. Geller, (ed.), *Local Government Police Management* (3d rev. ed.). Washington, DC: International City Management Association.

_____ (1991a) "Perspectives on the Christopher Commission Report: Don't Multiply the Mixed Messages." *Los Angeles Times* (July 11): B7.

_____ (1991b) "Police Videotaping of Suspect Interrogations and Confessions: A Preliminary Examination of Issues and Practices." (November 12 unpublished draft) Washington, DC: Police Executive Research Forum.

_____ (1992) "Researching Abuse of Authority." Paper presented to the 13th Annual Contemporary Issues in Police Administration Conference, Southwestern Law Enforcement Institute, Richardson, TX (March 18).

Geller, William A., and Kevin J. Karales (1981a) *Split-Second Decisions: Shootings of and by Chicago Police.* Chicago: Chicago Law Enforcement Study Group. Portions reprinted in Harry W. More, Jr. (ed.), *Critical Issues in Law Enforcement* (4th rev. ed.) Cincinnati: Anderson Publishing, 1985.

_____ (1981b) "Shootings of and by Chicago Police: Uncommon Crises—Part I, Shootings by Chicago Police." *Journal of Criminal Law and Criminology* 72 (4): 1813-1866.

_____ (1982) "Shootings of and by Chicago Police: Uncommon Crises—Part II, Shootings of Police, Shooting Correlates and Control Strategies." *Journal of Criminal Law and Criminology* 73 (1): 331-378.

_____ (1985) Unpublished analysis of Chicago Police Department officer-involved shooting data (September 27).

Geller, William A., and Norval Morris (1992) "Relations Between Federal and Local Police." In Michael Tonry and Norval Morris (eds.), *Modern Policing* (vol. 15 in the "Crime and Justice" series). Chicago: University of Chicago Press.

Geller, William A., and Michael S. Scott (1990) "Deadly Force: What We Know," in Carl B. Klockars and Stephen Mastrofski (eds.), *Thinking About Police: Contemporary Readings* (2d rev. ed.) New York: McGraw-Hill.

Gelles, Richard J. (1972) *The Violent Home: A Study of Physical Aggression Between Husbands and Wives.* Beverly Hills, CA: Sage.

Georgia Board of Private Detectives and Security Agencies (1992) Personal communication between a staff member of the board and William A. Geller (April 10).

Gigliotti, R.J. (1977) "Guidelines for the Use of Deadly Force." *Law and Order* 25 (3, March): 48, 50-58.

Girodo, M. (1985) "Health and Legal Issues in Undercover Narcotics Investigations: Misrepresented Evidence." *Behavioral Sciences and the Law* 3 (3): 299-308.

Giuliani, Rudolph W. (1992) "Rumor and Justice in Washington Heights: Dinkins Helped Make a Martyr of a Drug Dealer." *New York Times* (August 7): A15.

Glidden, Ronald (1991) "Reducing Firearms Training Liability." *Law and Order* (May): 25-28.

Goddard, N.L. (1988) "Learning Retention and Use of Deadly Force: Police Training Programs." Master's thesis, Central Missouri State University.

Goering, Laurie, and Flynn McRoberts (1992) "Violence Against Police Doesn't Stop at City Limits." *Chicago Tribune* (April 10): sec. 1, pp. 1, 20.

Golden, Clinton S., and Virginia D. Parker, eds. (1940s-1950s) *Causes of Industrial Peace Under Collective Bargaining.* (Series of publications prepared under the auspices of the Causes of Industrial Peace Committee of the National Planning Association, Washington, DC). New York: Harper.

Goldkamp, John S. (1976) "Minorities as Victims of Police Shootings: Interpretations of Racial Disproportionality and Police Use of Deadly Force." *Justice System Journal* 2 (Winter): 169-183. Reprinted in James J. Fyfe (ed.), *Readings on Police Use of Deadly Force.* Washington, DC: Police Foundation, 1982.

Goldman, Nathan (1963) *The Differential Selection of Juvenile Offenders for Court Appearances.* New York: New York Council on Crime and Delinquency.

Goldstein, Herman (1963) "Police Discretion: The Ideal Versus the Real." *Public Administration Review* 23: 140-148.

_____ (1977) *Policing a Free Society.* Cambridge, MA: Ballinger.

_____ (1979) "Improving Policing: A Problem-Oriented Approach." *Crime and Delinquency* 25: 236-258.

_____ (1987) "Toward Community-Oriented Policing: Potential Basic Requirements and Threshold Questions." *Crime and Delinquency* 33 (January): 1-30.

_____ (1990) *Problem-Oriented Policing*. New York: McGraw-Hill.

_____ (1991) Personal communication between University of Wisconsin-Madison Law School Professor Herman Goldstein and William A. Geller (March 2).

Goldstein, Herman, and Charles E. Susmilch (1982) *Experimenting with the Problem-Oriented Approach to Improving Police Service*, vol. 4. Madison, WI: Madison Police Department and Law School, University of Wisconsin-Madison.

Gonzalez, David (1992) "Dominican Immigration Alters Hispanic New York." *New York Times* (September 1): A1, A11.

Gonzalez, Eduardo (1991) Personal communication between the deputy director of the Metro-Dade (FL) Police Department and William A. Geller (March 26).

Goodstein, Laurie (1992) "Manhattan Neighborhood Smolders After Violence: Dominican Man Killed by N.Y. Police Friday." *Washington Post* (July 8).

Goolkasian, Gail A., Ronald W. Geddes, and William DeJong (1985) "Coping with Police Stress." Washington, DC: National Institute of Justice, Office of Development, Testing and Dissemination. Reprinted in Roger G. Dunham and Geoffrey P. Alpert (eds.), *Critical Issues in Policing: Contemporary Readings*. Prospect Heights, IL: Waveland Press, 1989.

Gordon, Paul (1983) *White Law*. London, England: Pluto Press.

Gorman, John (1991) Personal communication between Captain Gorman of the New York City Police Department, who served for a number of years on the squad that handled hostage/barricade incidents and William A. Geller (March 12).

Governor's Commission on the Los Angeles Riots (1965) *Violence in the City: An End or a Beginning?* Los Angeles: Office of the Governor of California.

Graham v. Connor et al. (1989) 109 S.Ct. 1865.

Graves, Franklin R., and Gregory Connor (1992) "The FLETC [Federal Law Enforcement Training Center] Use-of-Force Model." *Police Chief* (February): 56, 58.

Greenberg, Reuben (1990) Personal communication between the chief of the Charleston, South Carolina Police Department and William A. Geller (October 8).

Greenidge v. Ruffin (1991) 927 F.2d 789 (4th Circuit U.S. Court of Appeals).

Greenwood, C. (1975) "Unacceptable to Whom, Mr. Jenkins?—Hollow Point Ammunition." Surrey, England: Police Federation.

_____ (1979) *Police Tactics in Armed Operations*. Boulder, CO: Paladin Press.

Grennan, Sean A. (1987) "Findings on the Role of Officer Gender in Violent Encounters with Citizens." *Journal of Police Science and Administration* 15 (1): 78-85.

Griffen (1969) "The Appropriateness of Deadly Force." *Howard Law Journal* 15: 307.

Griffin, James (1990) Personal communication between the former deputy chief of the St. Paul Police Department and William A. Geller (October 10).

Griswold, David B. (1985) "Controlling the Police Use of Deadly Force: Exploring the Alternatives." *American Journal of Police* 4 (2): 93-109.

Grogan, Paul S. (1992) "Los Angeles Do's and Don'ts: Miami Can Teach L.A." *New York Times* (May 13): A15.

Gross, Jane (1992) "Police Kill Protester at Berkeley In Break-In at Chancellor's Home." *New York Times* (August 26): A10.

Gudykunst, William B. (1991) *Bridging Differences: Effective Intergroup Communication*. Newbury Park, CA: Sage Publications.

Hale, Charles D., and Wesley R. Wilson (1974) *Personal Characteristics of Assaulted and Non-Assaulted Officers*. Norman, OK: Bureau of Government Research, University of Oklahoma.

Hall, Carla (1992) "The Actor, In a True Drama: Greg Williams, a Hero In the L.A. Riots." *Washington Post* (May 7): D1.

Hall, Dave (1991) "Use of Lethal Force Report." Unpublished report by Capt. Hall, Training Division, San Diego Police Department.

Hall, John C. (1988a) "Police Use of Deadly Force to Arrest: A Constitutional Standard (Part 1)." *FBI Law Enforcement Bulletin* 57 (6, June): 23-30.

_____ (1988b) "Police Use of Deadly Force to Arrest: A Constitutional Standard (Conclusion)." *FBI Law Enforcement Bulletin* 57 (7, July): 20-29.

_____ (1992) "Constitutional Constraints on the Use of Force." *FBI Law Enforcement Bulletin* 61 (2, February): 22-31.

Hanley, Robert (1990) "Second Grand Jury Indicts Police Officer in New Jersey Killing." *New York Times* (November 29): 1, A17.

_____ (1991) "Uneasily, Teaneck Aims for Healing: Striving to Close Racial Rift a Year After Youth's Killing." *New York Times* (April 12): A-9.

_____ (1992) "Another Newark Teen-Ager Shot in a Stolen Car." *New York Times* (August 31): A7.

Harding, Richard W. (1975) "Changing Patterns of the Use of Lethal Force by Police in Australia." *Australian and New Zealand Journal of Criminology* 8 (2, June): 125-136.

Harding, Richard W., and Richard P. Fahey (1973) "Killings by Chicago Police, 1969-1970: An Empirical Study." *Southern California Law Review* 46 (2): 284-315.

Hargrave, G., and J. Kohls (1984) "Psychological Screening of Peace Officers: A Clinical-Industrial Psychological Process." *Police Chief* (January).

Harmon, Clarence (1992) "A Community That Needs a Helping Hand: Successful St. Louisans Should Reach Out to Those Less Fortunate." *St. Louis Post-Dispatch* (August 6).

Harper, Tim (1992) "British Bobbies: No Longer Cops Without Guns." *Law and Order* (April): 22, 28-30.

Harring, Sid, Tony Platt, Richard Speiglman, and Paul Takagi (1977) "The Management of Police Killings." *Crime and Social Justice* 8 (Fall-Winter): 34-43.

Harris, Ron (1990) "Blacks Feel Brunt of Drug War: About 80% of Users are White, Experts Say, But the Majority of Those Arrested Are Black." *Los Angeles Times* (April 22): A1, A26-A27.

Harrison, Eric (1991) "Minneapolis Race Calm Shattered by Shooting: A Black Gang Member is Fatally Shot in the Back; Hostility Simmers Between Police and Community Activists." *Los Angeles Times* (February 12): A14-A15.

Hart, William L. (1979) "Fatal Shootings by Police Officers." (Unpublished report to the Detroit Board of Police Commissioners, October 22).

Harvie, R.A. (no date) "Police Officer's Use of Force: Law and Liability." Chicago: University of Illinois Police Training Institute.

Hayden, George (1981) "Police Discretion in the Use of Deadly Force: An Empirical Study of Information Usage in Deadly Force Decisionmaking." *Journal of Police Science and Administration* 9 (1): 102-107.

Hayeslip, David W., Jr. (1992) "Less-than-Lethal Weapons." National Institute of Justice *Research in Brief*. Washington, DC: National Institute of Justice.

Heal, Sid (1990) "Flashbangs: Effective Use of Diversionary Devices." *Police Chief* (July): 18-24.

Heaphy, John (1978) *Police Practices: The General Administrative Survey.* Washington, DC: Police Foundation.

Hearne, T.H. (1978) "Criminal Law: Self-Defense and the Right to Resist an Unlawful Arrest." *Missouri Law Review* 43 (4, Fall): 744-754.

Heiman, M.F. (1977) "Suicide Among Police." *American Journal of Psychiatry* 143: 1286-1290.

Hepburn, John R. (1978) "Race and the Decision to Arrest: An Analysis of Warrants Issued." *Journal of Research in Crime and Delinquency* 15: 54-73.

Hermann, Andrew (1991) "He Cared—Dad Recalls Slain Cop." *Chicago Sun-Times* (January 9): 1.

Hibbard, J., and B.A. Fried (1980) *Weaponless Defense: A Law Enforcement Guide to Non-Violent Control.* Springfield, IL: Charles C. Thomas.

Higginbotham, Charles E. (1991) Correspondence from Director of the International Association of Chiefs of Police Information Services to William A. Geller granting permission for the Police Executive Research Forum to reprint the IACP's model "use of force" policy in this volume (February 6).

Hill, Kim Quaile, and Michael Clawson (1988) "The Health Hazards of 'Street Level' Bureaucracy: Mortality Among the Police." *Journal of Police Science and Administration* 16 (4): 243-248.

Hilts, Philip J. (1990) "Life Expectancy For Blacks in U.S. Shows Sharp Drop: A Wider Racial Gap Seen." *New York Times* (November 29): 1, B7.

Hindelang, Michael J. (1978) "Race and Involvement in Common Law Personal Crimes." *American Sociological Review* 43 (February): 93-109.

Hinds, Lennox A. (1979) "Police Use of Excessive and Deadly Force: Racial Implications." In R.H.

Brenner and M. Kravits (eds.), *A Community Concern: Police Use of Deadly Force.* Washington, DC: U.S. Government Printing Office.

Hinds, Michael deCourcy (1992) "Ex-Mayor Writes of a Death Plot: Racist Police in Philadelphia Planned Killing in Siege of a Cult, Goode Says." *New York Times* (September 20): Y19.

Holmes, Steven A. (1990) "Puerto Ricans' Alienation Cited in Miami Disturbances." *New York Times* (December 5): A14.

Holzworth, R. James, and C.W. Brown (1990) "Follow-up Analyses of Police Judgments." *Journal of Police Science and Administration* 17: 95-104.

Holzworth, R. James, and Cathrine B. Pipping (1985) "Drawing a Weapon: An Analysis of Police Judgments." *Journal of Police Science and Administration* 13: 185-194.

Home Office (1986) *Report by the Home Office Working Group on the Police Use of Firearms.* London, England: Home Office.

Horrock, Nicholas M. (1992) "Politics of Division: A Bitter Harvest—Police Adjust to Street Rules of '90s." *Chicago Tribune* (May 11): sec. 1, pp. 1, 13.

Horvath, Frank (1987) "The Police Use of Deadly Force: A Description of Selected Characteristics of Intra-State Incidents." *Journal of Police Science and Administration* 15 (3, Sept.): 226-238.

Horvath, Frank, and M. Donahue (1982) *Deadly Force: An Analysis of Shootings by Police in Michigan, 1976-1981.* East Lansing: Michigan State University.

House Subcommittee on Criminal Justice (1989) "Police Use of Deadly Force" (Serial No. 140). Washington, DC: U.S. Government Printing Office.

Hubler, Shawn (1991) "Grand Jury to Investigate Shootings." *Los Angeles Times* (Sept. 20): B1, B7.

Huhs, M. (1978) "Seattle, Washington: Police Use of Deadly Force." Seattle: Seattle City Council.

Hull, Grafton H. Jr., and Joseph C. Frisbie (1987) "The Stun Gun Debate: More Help than Hazard?" *Police Chief* (February): 46-51.

Iannello, Lorraine (1988) "Policy Keys on Police Restraint: New Deadly Force Plan Stresses Value of Life." *Dallas Times Herald* (August 19): A-1, A-9.

Illinois Association for Criminal Justice (1929) *Illinois Crime Survey.* Chicago: Illinois Ass'n for Crim. Justice and Chicago Crime Commission. Reprinted 1968. Montclair, NJ: Patterson Smith.

Independent Commission on the Los Angeles Police Department ("Christopher Commission") (1991) *Report of the Independent Commission on the Los Angeles Police Department.* Los Angeles: Independent Commission on the Los Angeles Police Department.

Indianapolis Police Department (1992) *Annual Report, 1991.* Indianapolis, IN: Indianapolis Police Department.

International Association of Chiefs of Police (1971) *Annual Law Enforcement Casualty Report.* Gaithersburg, MD: International Association of Chiefs of Police.

_____ (1971a) "Principles of Unarmed Defense: Training Key." Gaithersburg, MD: International Association of Chiefs of Police.

_____ (1971b) *The Police Weapons Center Final Report.* Gaithersburg, MD: International Association of Chiefs of Police.

_____ (1974) "Come-Along Holds: Training Key." Gaithersburg, MD: IACP.

_____ (1975) "Examining the Hollowpoint, Part 1." *PWC Bulletin* 74 (10, April): 4-5.

_____ (1977) "Taking Prisoners Into Custody: Training Key No. 249." Gaithersburg, MD: International Association of Chiefs of Police.

_____ (1979a) "Use of Deadly Force: Training Key No. 277." Gaithersburg, MD: International Association of Chiefs of Police.

_____ (1979b) "Improper Use of Deadly Force: Training Key." Gaithersburg, MD: International Association of Chiefs of Police.

_____ (1988) "1987 Annual Law Enforcement Survey: Executive Summary." *Police Chief* 55 (1, January): 38.

_____ (1989) "Use of Force: Concepts and Issues Paper." (February 1). Prepared by the International Association of Chiefs of Police/Bureau of Justice Assistance Law Enforcement Policy Center. Arlington, VA: International Association of Chiefs of Police.

_____ (1989a) "Model Policy: Body Armor." Arlington, VA: International Association of Chiefs of Police.

_____ (1990) "A Seminar on the Causes of Excessive Force and Bad Shootings: Positive

Recommendations for Improvement, for the Kansas City, Missouri, Police Department." (photocopied hand-outs during seminar on December 6). Arlington, VA: International Association of Chiefs of Police.

_____ (ed.) (1990a) *Fear: It Kills!—A Collection of Papers for Law Enforcement Survival.* Arlington, VA: International Association of Chiefs of Police/Bureau of Justice Assistance, U.S. Department of Justice.

_____ (1990b) *Operational Issues in the Small Law Enforcement Agency.* Arlington, VA: International Association of Chiefs of Police.

_____ (1990c) "Body Armor: Concepts and Issues Paper." (June 1). Prepared by the International Association of Chiefs of Police/Bureau of Justice Assistance Law Enforcement Policy Center. Arlington, VA: International Association of Chiefs of Police.

_____ (1991) "Public Safety Officers' Death Benefit Increased." *Police Chief* (January): 20.

_____ (1991a) "Model Policy: Law Enforcement Canines." Arlington, VA: International Association of Chiefs of Police.

_____ (1992) "Law Enforcement Canines: Concepts and Issues Paper." (May). Prepared by the International Association of Chiefs of Police/Bureau of Justice Assistance Law Enforcement Policy Center. Arlington, VA: International Association of Chiefs of Police.

_____ (1992a) "Areas of Concern in Addressing Contemporary Civil Disorders." Washington, DC: International Association of Chiefs of Police (pamphlet).

International Association of Chiefs of Police/DuPont Kevlar Survivors' Club (1990) "Documented Saves Data Base: Total Documented Saves, as of 10/1/90." (Reports prepared for William Geller by Survivors' Club Administrator Helen Slavin) (letters dated October 12 and 17).

_____ (1992) "IACP/DuPont Kevlar Survivors' Club Documented Saves Database: Total Documented Saves, as of March 15, 1992." (Reports prepared for William Geller by Survivors' Club Administrator Helen Slavin) (March 15).

International City Management Association (1991) "Early Warning Signals." In William A. Geller (ed.), *Local Government Police Management* (3d rev. ed.). Washington, DC: International City Management Association (p. 297).

International Criminal Police Organization (INTERPOL) (1969) "Use of Firearms by Police to Arrest Offenders." Report submitted by the General Secretariat to the 38th General Assembly Session, 13-18 October 1969, Mexico. France: International Criminal Police Organization.

Ivans, Molly (1992) "Force, Fraud, and Favors: Politics in America." Speech to the World Affairs Conference, University of Colorado (April 8), broadcast May 12, 1992 on National Public Radio.

Jacobs, D., and D. Britt (1979) "Inequality and Police Use of Deadly Force: An Empirical Assessment of a Conflict Hypothesis." *Social Problems* 26 (4, April): 403-412.

James, Frank (1992) "Security Measures Fail to Head Off Bloodshed at the Bench." *Chicago Tribune* (July 21): sec. 1, p. 4.

James, George (1991) "Police Chiefs Call for U.S. System to Gather Data on Excessive Force." *New York Times* (April 17): A9.

Jamieson, J.P., R. Hull, and P. Battershill (1990) *Recommendations of the [British Columbia Police Commission] Committee on The Use of Less Than Lethal Force by Police Officers in British Columbia.* Vancouver, Canada: British Columbia Police Commission.

Janick, James (1990) "Fear of Fear Itself." In International Association of Chiefs of Police (ed.), *Fear: It Kills!—A Collection of Papers for Law Enforcement Survival.* Arlington, VA: International Association of Chiefs of Police/Bureau of Justice Assistance, U.S. Department of Justice.

Janssen, Christian T.L., and James C. Hackler (1985) "Police Killings in Perspective." *Canadian Journal of Criminology* 27 (2): 227-232.

Jenkins, Betty, and Adrienne Faison (1974) "An Analysis of 248 Persons Killed by New York City Policemen, 1970-1973." New York: Metropolitan Applied Research Center.

Jennings, Veronica T. (1991a) "Montgomery Leads Suburbs in Deadly Force: Chief Seeks Study of Shooting Policy." *Washington Post* (June 16): A1, A9.

_____ (1991b) "Montgomery Says It Erred on Police Shooting Data: Revised Figures Put P.G. 1st in Deadly Force." *Washington Post* (June 18): B1, B2.

Johnson, Dirk (1992a) "When Rumor Mixes with Rage." *New York Times* (May 10): 14.

_____ (1992b) "Las Vegas's Hopes Leave Blacks Bitter." *New York Times* (May 25): 7.

Johnson, Otto (executive editor) (1991) *Information Please Almanac Atlas and Yearbook, 1992.* Boston: Houghton Mifflin.

Johnston, David (1981) "When LA (Los Angeles) Police Shoot: The DA (District Attorney) 'Rolls Out'." *Police* 4 (2, March): 17-20.

_____ (1981a) "LAPD Shooting Incidents Drop." *Los Angeles Times* (January 30).

_____ (1981b) "Stop or I'll Throw My Net at You." *Police* (March): 23-28.

_____ (1990) "F.B.I. Takes Steps to Give Agents Greater Freedom in Firing Weapons." *New York Times* (June 19): A10.

_____ (1992) "Survey Shows Number of Rapes Far Higher Than Official Figures." *New York Times* (April 24): A9.

_____ (1992a) "Justice Department: U.S. May Use 1870 Statutes to Revive Case of Four Officers." *New York Times* (May 1): A12.

Joiner, Larry J. (1989) "Firearms Selection Procedures: The Reevaluation Process." *Police Chief* (May): 43-45.

Jones, Clarence E., Jr. (1989) *After the Smoke Clears: Surviving the Police Shooting—An Analysis of the Post Officer-Involved Shooting Trauma.* Springfield, IL: Charles C. Thomas.

Josephson, Rose Lee, and Martin Reiser (1990) "Officer Suicide in the Los Angeles Police Department: A Twelve-Year Follow-Up." *Journal of Police Science and Administration* 17 (3): 227-29.

Journal of Contemporary Criminal Justice (1990) "Future of Non-Lethal Weapons." (symposium issue) 6 (1): 1-43.

Kakalik, James, and Sorrell Wildhorn (1971) *Private Police in the United States,* five volumes (including *The Private Police Industry: Its Nature and Extent,* vol. 2). Washington, DC: National Institute of Justice.

Kania, Richard, and Wade Mackey (1977) "Police Violence as a Function of Community Characteristics." *Criminology* 15 (1, May): 27-48.

Kansas City (MO) Police Department (1991) *Recommendations of the Task Force on the Use of Force by the Kansas City, Missouri Police Department.* Kansas City, MO: Kansas City Police Department. (Report prepared by Major Ron Smith, task force chairman, and 8 other task force members and submitted to Chief Steven C. Bishop) (January).

Kappeler, Stephen F., and Victor E. Kappeler (1992) "A Research Note on Section 1983 Claims Against the Police: Cases Before the Federal District Courts in 1990." *American Journal of Police* 11 (1): 65-73.

Kappeler, Victor E. (1988) "Preface to Special Issue: Police Civil Liability." *American Journal of Police* 8 (1).

Kasler, Peter Alan (1992) *Glock: The New Wave in Combat Handguns.* Boulder, CO: Paladin Press.

Kass, John (1992) "Three Aldermen Want to Let Police Use High-Tech Glock 17 Pistols." *Chicago Tribune* (February 27): sec. 2, p. 3.

_____ (1992a) "Daley: City to Buy Vests for Police." *Chicago Tribune* (August 5): sec. 2, p. 3.

Kates, Michael, and George Papajohn (1992) "Shooting Victim's Fingerprints Not Found on Gun, Police Say." *Chicago Tribune* (June 10): section 2, p. 2.

Katz, B.S., and D.O. Egner (1976) "Los Angeles County District Attorney's Less-Lethal Weapons Task Force." Springfield, VA: National Technical Information Service.

Katz, Jesse (1991) "Is Training of Deputies for Deadly Clashes Adequate? Despite Extensive Instruction on When to Shoot, Critics Say Officers are Too Quick on the Trigger." *Los Angeles Times* (September 8): A1, A22-A23.

_____ (1992) "The Quiet After the Killing: Oliver Beasley's Death Set Off Mass Protest Well Before Rodney King's Beating; But Furor Fizzled, and Deputies Were Cleared. What Are the Lessons?" *Los Angeles Times* (January 31): A1, A20-A21.

Katz, M. (1974) "Violence and Civility in a Suburban Milieu." *Journal of Police Science and Administration* 2 (3, September): 239-249.

Keller, Bill (1992) "With the Police Behind Him Can de Klerk Look Ahead?" *New York Times* (June 28): E3.

_____ (1992a) "South Africa Shakes Up Top Police Command." *New York Times* (Aug. 28): A1, A6.

Kelling, George L. (1991) "Crime and Metaphor: Toward a New Concept of Policing." *NY: The City Journal* (Autumn): 65-72.

Kelling, George L., and James K. Stewart (1991) "The Evolution of Contemporary Policing." In William A. Geller (ed.), *Local Government Police Management* (3d rev. ed.). Washington, DC: International City Management Association.

Kelling, George L., Robert Wasserman, and Hubert Williams (1988) "Police Accountability and Community Policing." *Perspectives on Policing* (November). Washington, DC: National Institute of Justice.

Kennett, Lee, and James LaVerne Anderson (1975) *The Gun in America*. Westport, CT: Greenwood Press.

Kerr v. City of West Palm Beach (1989) 875 F.2d 1546 (U.S. Court of Appeals, 11th Circuit).

Kerr, Peter (1992) "Did Insurers Abandon the Inner City? L.A. Merchants Say the Big Names Refused Them, Now Their Stores are Gone." *New York Times* (May 31): section 3, pp. 1, 6.

Kerstetter, Wayne (1985) "Who Disciplines the Police? Who Should?" In William A. Geller (ed.), *Police Leadership in America: Crisis and Opportunity*. New York: Praeger.

Keve, P.W. (1979) "No Farewell to Arms." *Crime and Delinquency* 25 (4, October): 425-435.

Kiernan, M. (1978) "Shooting by Policemen in District Declines." *Washington Star* (Sept. 2).

Kieselhorst, Daniel C. (1974) *A Theoretical Perspective of Violence Against the Police*. Norman, OK: Bureau of Government Research, University of Oklahoma.

Kiley, Robert R. (1990a) Letter from the Chairman, Metropolitan Transportation Authority of New York, to New York City First Deputy Mayor Norman Steisel (August 9). Included in William J. Bratton (ed.), *Police Use of Force and the 9 mm Semi-Automatic Weapon: Background Materials for New York City Transit Police Chief William J. Bratton's Presentation to the Board of Directors, Metropolitan Transportation Authority of New York*. Unpublished reports compiled by the New York City Transit Police (November 1).

_____ (1990b) Letter from the Chairman, Metropolitan Transportation Authority of New York, to New York City First Deputy Mayor Norman Steisel (September 7). Included in William J. Bratton (ed.), *Police Use of Force and the 9 mm Semi-Automatic Weapon: Background Materials for New York City Transit Police Chief William J. Bratton's Presentation to the Board of Directors, Metropolitan Transportation Authority of New York*. Unpublished reports compiled by the New York City Transit Police (November 1).

Kindrick, Roy E. (1992) "Officer-Involved Deadly Force Incidents Report." Unpublished memorandum from Portland, Oregon, Police Bureau Training Division Captain Kindrick to Assistant Chief Inman (March 11).

Kirby, Joseph, and Andrew Gottesman (1992) "Cop, Man Killed in Fracas at Bar: Witnesses' Accounts of Fight Differ." *Chicago Tribune* (July 26): sec. 2, pp. 1-2.

Kirkham, George L., and J.D. White (1980) *Police Civil Liability: A Handbook*. New York: Harper and Row.

Kleck, Gary (1992) "Assault Weapons Aren't the Problem." *New York Times* (September 1): A15.

Klockars, Carl B. (1980) "The Dirty Harry Problem." *Annals of the American Academy of Political and Social Science* 452 (November): 33-47.

_____ (forthcoming) "A Theory of Excessive Force and Its Control." In William A. Geller and Hans Toch (eds.), *And Justice for All: A National Agenda for Understanding and Controlling Police Abuse of Force*. Washington, DC: National Institute of Justice and Police Executive Research Forum.

Knight-Ridder Newspapers (1991) "Words Worth Repeating." *Chicago Tribune* (January 2): 18.

Knoohuizen, Ralph, Richard Fahey, and Deborah J. Palmer (1972) *The Police and Their Use of Fatal Force in Chicago*. Chicago, IL: Chicago Law Enforcement Study Group.

Kobler, Arthur (1975a) "Police Homicide in a Democracy." *Journal of Social Issues* 31 (1): 163-181.

_____ (1975b) "Figures (And Perhaps Some Facts) On Police Killing of Civilians in the United States, 1965-1969." *Journal of Social Issues* 31 (1): 185-191.

Kochman, Thomas (1981) *Black and White: Styles in Conflict*. Chicago: University of Chicago Press.

Koiwai, E. Karl (1987) "Deaths Allegedly Caused by the Use of 'Choke Holds' (Shime-Waza)." *Journal of Forensic Sciences* 32 (2): 419-432.

Kolman, John A. (1982) *Guide to the Development of Special Weapons and Tactics Teams.* Springfield, IL: Charles C. Thomas.

Kolts, James G. and Staff (1992) *The Los Angeles County Sheriff's Department: A Report by Special Counsel James G. Colts and Staff* (July): Los Angeles: Office of the Special Counsel.

Konstantin, David N. (1984) "Homicides of American Law Enforcement Officers, 1978-1980." *Justice Quarterly* 1 (1) (March): 29-37.

Koop, C. Everett, and George D. Lundberg (1992) "Violence in America: A Public Health Emergency—Time to Bite the Bullet Back." *Journal of the American Medical Association* 267 (22, June 10): 3075-3076.

Korzeniowski, George (1990) "Survival City." *Law and Order.* (October): 30- 34.

Korzenny, Felipe, and Stella Ting-Toomey (1990) *Communicating for Peace: Diplomacy and Negotiation.* Newbury Park, CA: Sage Publications.

Koscove, Eric M. (1985) "The TASER Weapon: A New Emergency Medicine Problem." *Annals of Emergency Medicine* 14 (December): 112.

Koziol, Ronald, and Maria Donato (1992) "Cop's Routine Stop Would Be His Last as a Shootout Ensues." *Chicago Tribune* (April 10): sec. 2, p. 6).

Krajick, Kevin (1990) "Arms Race on Hill Street: Police Want to Pack Semiautomatic Weapons—Just as Some Crooks Do." *Newsweek* (November 19): 58-59.

Krauss, Clifford (1991) "Latin Immigrants in Capital Find Unrest a Sad Tie to Past." *New York Times* (May 8): A1, A10.

Krier, Beth Ann (1990) "Copping an Attitude: Ex-Policeman Teaches Officers the Art of Verbal Judo—Reading and Redirecting People." *Los Angeles Times* (May 8): E1 and passim.

Kroeker, Mark, and Candace McCoy (1989) "Establishing and Implementing Department Policies," in James J. Fyfe (ed.), *Police Practice in the '90s: Key Management Issues.* Washington, DC: International City Management Association.

Kroes, William H. (1976) *Society's Victim: The Policeman.* Springfield, IL: Charles C. Thomas.
_____ (1985) *Society's Victim: The Police* (2d rev. ed.) Springfield, IL: Charles C. Thomas.

Kroes, William H., and Joseph J. Hurrell, Jr. (eds.) (1975) *Job Stress and the Police Officer.* Washington, DC: National Institute of Occupational Safety and Health.

Kupcinet, Irv (1991) "Kup's Column." *Chicago Sun-Times* (January 9): 24.

Kuykendall, Jack (1981) "Trends in the Use of Deadly Force by Police." *Journal of Criminal Justice* 9 (5): 359-366.

Lacey, Marc (1992) "Riot Death Toll Lowered to 51 After Coroner's Review: Officials Say Some Counted as Victims Would Have Died Whether the Unrest Had Occurred Or Not." *Los Angeles Times* (August 12): A1, A15.

LaFave, Wayne R. (1965) *Arrest: The Decision to Take a Suspect into Custody.* (Report of the American Bar Foundation's Survey of the Administration of Criminal Justice in the United States). Boston: Little, Brown & Co.

LaFree, Gary, Kriss A. Drass, and Patrick O'Day (1992) "Race and Crime in Postwar America: Determinants of African-American and White Rates, 1957-1988." *Criminology* 30 (2): 157-185.

Landers, Ann (1991) "Sorry Son, a Policeman Has to Play for Keeps." *Chicago Tribune* (December 26): sec. 5, p. 3.

Landrum v. Moats (1978) 576 F.2d 1320 (8th Cir.).

Landsberg, Mitchell (1992) "Three of Top Ten Cities in U.S. Set Records for Murder in '91." *Chicago Sun-Times* (January 5): 24.

Langworthy, Robert H. (1986) "Police Shooting and Criminal Homicide: Temporal Relationships." *Journal of Quantitative Criminology* 2 (4, December): 377-388.

Lant, D., J. Small, and D. Wohlberg (1979) "Suing the Police in Federal Court." *Yale Law Journal* 88 (4): 781-824.

Law and Order (1990) "U.S. Murder Rate Staggering." *Law and Order* (November): 5.
_____ (1990a) "Defensive Device 'Non-Weapon'." *Law and Order* (March): 104-105.
_____ (1990b) "International News: Canada—Homicide Rate Increases." *Law and Order* (June): 6.
_____ (1991) "NYCPD Police Self-Support Group." *Law and Order* (June): 92.
_____ (1992a) "Reviewing TASER Usage." *Law and Order* (July): 112.
_____ (1992b) "Mirrors for Searching." *Law and Order* (July): 122.

_____ (1992c) "Female Officers May Need Extra Training." *Law and Order* (September): 26.

_____ (1992d) "Stun Gun Safety Disconnect." *Law and Order* (September): 117.

Law Enforcement News (1980) "Electronic Sidearm is Stunning Success Against Angel Dusters." *Law Enforcement News* (Oct. 13): 3.

_____ (1981) "NYPD May Disarm Off-Duty." *Law Enforcement News* (April 13): 3.

_____ (1990) "Jury Still Out on FBI Deadly-Force Policy." *Law Enforcement News* (July/Aug.): 5.

_____ (1990a) "Deadly-Force Policy OK'd: NYPD Doing Well, Could Do Better." *Law Enforcement News* (November 15): 3, 9.

_____ (1990b) "Bus-Stop Protest Art Riles San Diego Police." *Law Enforcement News* (November 30): 5.

_____ (1990c) "1990 Ends in a Riot as Miami Cops Are Acquitted: Tried for Fatally Beating Drug Dealer." *Law Enforcement News* (December 15): 5.

_____ (1990d) "Chemical Canister Used by NYPD Gave No Warning of Flammability." *Law Enforcement News* (October 31): 1, 9.

_____ (1991) "A Vested Interest in Policing: Survey Finds Wide Use of Body Armor by Cops—But Little Encouragement from Superiors." *Law Enforcement News* (March 31): 1, 7.

_____ (1991a) "Police Increasingly Face Public Scrutiny Through Civilian Review Boards." *Law Enforcement News* (April 15): 7, 11.

_____ (1991b) "Local Police Just Aren't Enough: Amid Concern About Rising Crime, Residents of Savannah Neighborhood Turn to Private Security to Augment Patrols." *Law Enforcement News* (November 30): 1, 14.

_____ (1991c) "Federal File: Borderline Risks." *Law Enforcement News* (November 30): 5.

_____ (1991d) "Staring Down the Barrel: Prevention-Minded Video Pulls No Punches in Look at Police Suicides." *Law Enforcement News* (December 15): 1, 9.

_____ (1992a) "Taught by Experts: After Two 'Friendly Fire' Deaths, Dallas PD Brings in a Panel of Outsiders to Look for Improvements in Drug-Squad Operations." *Law Enforcement News* (March 31): 1.

_____ (1992b) "In Portland, Community Policing Means Giving Residents a Say on Use of Force." *Law Enforcement News* (March 31): 1, 9.

_____ (1992c) "Off Duty and Armed: Iowa Shooting Raises Questions About Police Weapons Policies." *Law Enforcement News* (April 15): 1, 10.

_____ (1992d) "Thirty Days of Urban Agony: In L.A. and Other Cities, a Powderkeg Explodes." *Law Enforcement News* (May 31): 7, 11.

_____ (1992e) "Averting a Legislative Shootout: Compromise to Expand 9mm's for NYPD." *Law Enforcement News* (June 15): 5.

_____ (1992f) "Troubled Long Beach PD Seeks Fresh Start." *Law Enforcement News* (March 15): 4, 14.

_____ (1992g) "Excessive Force in L.A.: This Time County Sheriff's Department is Criticized for Policy and Practice on Use of Force; Sweeping Reforms Urged." *Law Enforcement News* (July/August): 1, 12.

Lea, John (1986) "Police Racism: Some Theories and Their Policy Implications." In R. Matthews and J. Young (eds.), *Confronting Crime*. London, England: Sage.

Lea, John, and Jock Young (1984) *What is to be Done About Law and Order?* Harmondsworth, England: Penguin.

Lee, Felicia R. (1992) "Mothers Join to End the Killing." *New York Times* (September 12): 9.

Lenhart, Jennifer (1992) "Streets Get Meaner for City Police Too: Many More Officers Being Shot At." *Chicago Tribune* (September 9): sec. 2, p. 7.

Lesce, Tony (1991) "Focus: Small Agencies—Rural Officers Face Real Hazards." *Law and Order* (June): 28-31.

Leslie, Donald R., Jr. (1992) "Compatible On- and Off-Duty Weapons." *Police Chief* (August): 20.

Lester, David (1978a) "A Study of Civilian-Caused Murders of Police Officers." *International Journal of Criminology and Penology* 6: 373-378.

_____ (1978b) "Assaults on Police Officers in American Cities." *Psychological Reports* 42: 946.

_____ (1978c) "Predicting Murder Rates of Police Officers in Urban Areas." *Police Law Quarterly* 7 (3): 20-25.

_____ (1978d) "Suicide in Police Officers." *Police Chief* (April): 17.

_____ (1981) "An Alternative Perspective: The Use of Deadly Force by Police and Civilians." *Police Chief* (December): 56-57.

_____ (1982) "Civilians Who Kill Police Officers and Police Officers Who Kill Civilians: A Comparison of American Cities." *Journal of Police Science and Administration* 10 (4): 384-387.

Lester, D., and J. Gallagher (1980) "Stress in Police Officers and Department Store Managers." *Psychological Reports* 46: 882.

Lester, D., and S.R. Mink (1979) "Is Stress Higher in Police Officers? An Exploratory Study." *Psychological Reports* 45: 554.

Levine, Robert, and Charles Stahl (1968) "Eye Injury Caused by Tear-Gas Weapons." *American Journal of Ophthalmology* 65 (4, April): 497.

Levitt, Leonard (1991) "Too Close for Comfort? DAs Need Cops Too Much to Charge Them, Critics Say." (third in a series on "Policing the Police") *New York Newsday* (November 15): 7, 30.

Lieberson, Stanley (1985) *Making It Count: The Improvement of Social Research and Theory.* Berkeley: University of California Press.

Little, Robert E. (1984) "Cop-Killing: A Descriptive Analysis of the Problem." *Police Studies* 7: 68-76.

Little, Robert E., and Max Boylen (1990) "Facing the Gun: The Firearms Threat to Police Officers." *Journal of Police Science and Administration* 17 (1, March): 49-54.

Littlejohn, E. (1981) "Civil Liability and the Police Officer: The Need for New Deterrents to Police Misconduct." *University of Detroit Journal of Urban Law* 58 (3): 365-431.

Littleton, Percy (1990) Personal communication between security consultant Percy Littleton and William A. Geller (December 18).

Long, James (1992a) "Deadly Force: Anatomy of a Shooting—The Mari Lyn Sandoz Case." *The [Portland] Oregonian* (April 26): A21.

_____ (1992b) "Police Bureau Relies Increasingly on Emergency Team: Small, Elite Unit Gets Called In to Handle High-Risk Situations Such as Hostage-Taking." *The [Portland] Oregonian* (April 27): A8.

_____ (1992c) "Deadly Force: Anatomy of a Shooting—The Leonard Renfrow Case." *The [Portland] Oregonian* (April 27): A9.

Lorch, Donatella (1991) "7 People Killed in First 5 Hours of the New Year in New York City." *New York Times* (January 2): B-12.

_____ (1992) "Police Kill a Man After a Dance, And His Friends Raise Questions." *New York Times* (May 22): B12.

_____ (1992a) "Openly Gay in Blue: Police Officers Tread Warily." *New York Times* (July 13): A17.

Los Angeles Police Department (1989) Personal communication between LAPD Deputy Chief Mark Kroeker and Michael Scott (February 17).

_____ (1991) Personal communication between LAPD Deputy Chief Mark Kroeker and William A. Geller (January 10).

_____ (1992) Personal communication between LAPD Commander Michael J. Bostic and William A. Geller (March 12).

Los Angeles Times (1986) "Study Finds TASERs Safer Than Guns: King Hospital Doctors Compare Outcomes of Victims." *Los Angeles Times* (January 16): section V, p. 22.

_____ (1992a) "Understanding the Riots, Part 1: The Path to Fury—A *Los Angeles Times* Special Report." *Los Angeles Times* (May 11): section T, pp. 1-14.

_____ (1992b) "Understanding the Riots, Part 2: Images of Chaos—A *Los Angeles Times* Special Report." *Los Angeles Times* (May 12): section T, pp. 1-8.

_____ (1992c) "Understanding the Riots, Part 3: Witness to Rage—A *Los Angeles Times* Special Report." *Los Angeles Times* (May 13): section T, pp. 1-12.

_____ (1992d) "Understanding the Riots, Part 4: Seeing Ourselves—A *Los Angeles Times* Special Report." *Los Angeles Times* (May 14): section T, pp. 1-8.

_____ (1992e) "Understanding the Riots, Part 5: The Path to Recovery—A *Los Angeles Times* Special Report." *Los Angeles Times* (May 15): section T, pp. 1-10.

Loud, Jeff (1990) "Firearms Training Tips for Problem Shooters." *Law and Order* (March): 51-53.

Luckenbill, David F. (1977) "Criminal Homicide as a Situated Transaction." *Social Problems* 25: 176-186.

Lundman, Richard J. (1974) "Domestic Police-Citizen Encounters." *Journal of Police Science and Administration* 2: 22-27.

Lunneborg, Patricia W. (1989) *Women Police Officers: Current Career Profile.* Springfield, IL: Charles C. Thomas.

Lyall, Sarah (1992) "More Police to Use Semi-Automatic Guns in New York City." *New York Times* (June 16): A13.

Madamaba, H.J. (1986) "The Relationship Between Stress and Marital Relationships in Police Officers." In James T. Reese and Harvey A. Goldstein (eds.), *Psychological Services for Law Enforcement.* Washington, DC: Federal Bureau of Investigation (pp. 463-470).

Madigan, Charles M. (1992) "Racial Stereotyping: An Old, Virulent Virus." *Chicago Tribune* (May 13): sec. 1, pp. 1, 4.

Maghan, Jess (1992) "Black Police Officer Recruits: Aspects of Becoming Blue." *Police Forum* (a journal of the Academy of Criminal Justice Sciences Police Section) 2 (1, January): 8-9, 11.

_____ (forthcoming) "The Changing Face of the Police Officer: Occupational Socialization of Minority Police Recruits." In Roger G. Dunham and Geoffrey P. Alpert (eds.), *Critical Issues in Policing: Contemporary Readings,* 2d rev. ed. Prospect Heights, IL: Waveland Press.

Maguire, Kathleen, and Timothy J. Flanagan (eds.) (1991) *Sourcebook of Criminal Justice Statistics—1990.* Washington, DC: Bureau of Justice Statistics, U.S. Department of Justice.

Major, Victoria L. (1991) "Law Enforcement Officers Killed, 1980-1989." *FBI Law Enforcement Bulletin* (May): 2-5.

_____ (1992) Personal communication between editor Victoria Major in the Federal Bureau of Investigation Uniform Crime Reporting Program User Services Section and William A. Geller (Washington, DC) (April 2).

Malcolm, Andrew H. (1990) "Many Police Forces Rearm to Counter Criminals' Guns." *New York Times* (September 4): A12.

_____ (1990a) "Change in Enforcement Is Said to Cut Violence Between Police and the Public." *New York Times* (September 2): 32.

_____ (1991) "Decisions About Life and Death." *New York Times* (November 29): A16.

Malloy, Thomas E., and G. Larry Mays (1984) "The Police Stress Hypothesis." *Criminal Justice and Behavior* 11 (2): 197-224.

Mandel, Jerry (1981) *Body Counts: The Folly of Reducing Police Killings to Statistics.* Washington, DC: National Council of La Raza (June).

Manning, Peter K. (1980) "Violence and the Police." *Annals of the American Academy of Political and Social Science* 452 (November): 135-144.

Mapp v. Ohio (1961) 367 U.S. 643.

Margarita, Mona (1980a) "Killing the Police: Myths and Motives." *Annals of the American Academy of Political and Social Science* 452 (November): 63-71.

_____ (1980b) "Police as Victims of Violence." *Justice System Journal* 5 (Spring): 218-233.

_____ (1980c) "Criminal Violence Against Police." Unpublished dissertation, State University of New York-Albany. Available through University Microfilms, Ann Arbor, MI. UM Diss. # 80-18426).

Marin, Gerardo, and Barbara Vanoss Marin (1991) *Research with Hispanic Populations.* Newbury Park, CA: Sage Publications.

Markardt, Steve (1992) Personal communication between a staff member in the Federal Bureau of Investigation's Press Office and William A. Geller (April 3).

Markardt, Steve (1992a) Personal communication between a staff member in the Federal Bureau of Investigation's Press Office and William A. Geller (July 24).

Markman, Michael A. (1992) Correspondence to William A. Geller from Deputy Chief of the NYPD (June 14).

Marriott, Michel (1992) "Police Detail Why Gunmen Came to Club: Video Poker Machines Were Said to Be Lure." *New York Times* (August 13): B1, B3.

_____ (1992a) "Police Defend Officers in Accidental Death of a Hostage: A Gunman and His Human Shield Were Killed 'By the Numbers' in Queens." *New York Times* (August 15): L22.

_____ (1992b) "On Meaner Streets, The Violent Are More So." *New York Times* (Sept. 13): 6.

Marshall, Steve (1992) "Crisis in L.A.: Poll—Case is Evidence of Racism." *USA Today* (May 1): 1A, 4A.

Martin, LeRoy (1990) Radio interview on WBBM-AM's "At Issue" program, broadcast in Chicago (November 18).

Martin, Susan (1990) *On the Move: The Status of Women in Policing.* Washington, DC: Police Foundation.

Marzuk, Peter M., Kenneth Tardiff, and Charles S. Hirsch (1992) "The Epidemiology of Murder-Suicide." *Journal of the American Medical Association* 267 (23, June 17): 3179-3183.

Maslach, C., and S.E. Jackson (1979) "Burned-Out Cops and Their Families." *Psychology Today* (May): 59-62.

Masotti, Louis H., and J.R. Corsi (1969) *Shoot-Out in Cleveland: Black Militants and the Police.* A Report to the National Commission on the Causes and Prevention of Violence. Washington, DC: U.S. Government Printing Office.

Mattis v. Schnarr (1976) 547 F.2d 1007 (U.S. Court of Appeals for the 8th Circuit).

Mattison, Scott (1990) "The Fear Factor in Law Enforcement." In International Association of Chiefs of Police (ed.), *Fear: It Kills!—A Collection of Papers for Law Enforcement Survival.* Arlington, VA: International Association of Chiefs of Police/Bureau of Justice Assistance, U.S. Department of Justice.

Matulia, Kenneth J. (1982) *A Balance of Forces: A Study of Justifiable Homicides by the Police.* Gaithersburg, MD: International Association of Chiefs of Police.

_____ (1985) *A Balance of Forces: Model Deadly Force Policy and Procedure* (2d rev. ed.) Gaithersburg, MD: International Association of Chiefs of Police.

Mays, G.L., and W. Taggart (1985) "Deadly Force as a Policy Problem in Local Law Enforcement: Do Administrative Practices Make a Difference?" *Policy Studies Review* 5: 309-318.

McAllister, Bill (1992) "Call for a Panel on L.A. Unrest Echoes Historical Response." *Washington Post* (May 4): A21.

McCafferty, Francis L., Godofredo D. Domingo, and Mary Jude McCafferty (1989) "Understanding Post-Traumatic Stress Disorder." *Police Chief* (February): 22-23.

McCarthy, Ronald M. (1990) "The Dynamics of Police-Related Fears: Reasonable and Unreasonable Fear" in International Association of Chiefs of Police (ed.), *Fear: It Kills!—A Collection of Papers for Law Enforcement Survival.* Arlington, VA: International Association of Chiefs of Police/Bureau of Justice Assistance, U.S. Department of Justice.

_____ (1990a) "Reducing the Risks in High-Risk Warrant Service." *Police Chief* (July): 26-32.

_____ (1992) Personal communication between an International Association of Chiefs of Police staff member and William A. Geller (May 22).

McCauley, R. Paul, and Steven M. Edwards (1990) "More Bullets—More Risks? Concerns with the Adoption of a High Capacity Handgun for Law Enforcement Officers." *Pennsylvania Police Chiefs Association Bulletin* (2, Spring/Summer): 35, 41, 54-55.

McClain, Troy (1989) "Firearms Selection Procedures: Revolver-to-Pistol Transition in Dallas—No Simple Matter." *Police Chief* (May): 30-38.

McCoy, Candace (1985) "Lawsuits Against the Police: What Impact Do They Really Have?" In James J. Fyfe (ed.), *Police Management Today: Issues and Case Studies.* Washington, DC: International City Management Association.

McCreedy, Kenneth R., and James L. Hague (1975) "Administrative and Legal Aspects of a Policy to Limit the Use of Firearms by Police Officers." *Police Chief* (January): 48-52. Reprinted in Harry W. More, Jr. (ed.), *Critical Issues in Law Enforcement* (4th rev. ed.) Cincinnati: Anderson Publishing.

McCrie, Robert D. (1988) "The Development of the U.S. Security Industry." *Annals of the American Academy of Political and Social Science* 498 (July): 23-33.

McErlain, Ed (1992) "Deadly Force: An Age-Old Problem, A Future Solution." *California Peace Officer* 24 (March): 24.

McFadden, Robert D. (1992) "Powerful Evidence in Police Shooting." *New York Times* (September 12): 9.

_____ (1992a) "Race, Rage, and New York Officers." *New York Times* (September 19): 32.

McGee, Jim (1992) "Ex-Justice Official Cites 'Coverup' By FBI in '78 Puerto Rico Shootings." *Washington Post* (May 9): A3.

McGraw, Carol (1990) "A Tragedy to Sort Out From a Routine Start: A Family is Suing a CHP Officer in the Fatal Shooting of a Motorist Four Years Ago." *Los Angeles Times* (March 22): B1-14.

McIver, J.P., and Roger B. Parks (1983) "Identification of Effective and Ineffective Police Actions." In Richard R. Bennett (ed.), *Police at Work*. Beverly Hills, CA: Sage.

McKinley, James C., Jr. (1992) "Angry at Dinkins's Policies, Officers Rally at City Hall." *New York Times* (September 17): A16.

_____ (1992a) "Dinkins Sees Sign of Racism In Rally by New York Police." *New York Times* (September 18): A1, A11.

McMains, Michael J. (1986) "Post-Shooting Trauma: Demographics of Professional Support." In James T. Reese and Harvey A. Goldstein (eds.), *Psychological Services for Law Enforcement*. Washington, DC: Federal Bureau of Investigation.

McMillin, Sue (1992) "Cop Training Called Key to Fewer Deaths: Officer Killings Down." *Colorado Springs Gazette Telegraph* (April 21): B1.

McMurray, Harvey L. (1988) "Police Postassault Reactions and the Buffering Effects of Social Support." Ph.D. dissertation. Rutgers, NJ: Rutgers University.

_____ (1990) "Attitudes of Assaulted Police Officers and Their Policy Implications." *Journal of Police Science and Administration* 17 (1, March): 44-48.

McRoberts, Flynn (1992) "Crusader Urges Memorial to Cops: Slain Officers Too Long Forgotten." *Chicago Tribune* (May 16): section 1, p. 5.

McNeely, R. L., and Carl E. Pope (1981) "Socioeconomic and Racial Issues in the Measurement of Criminal Involvement," 31-47 in R.L. McNeely and Carl E. Pope (eds.), *Race, Crime, and Criminal Justice*. Beverly Hills, CA: Sage.

Meadows, R., and L. Trostle (1988) "A Study of Police Misconduct and Litigation: Findings and Implications." *Contemporary Criminal Justice* 4 (2): 77-92.

Meddis, Sam Vincent (1992) "Many Blacks Think Justice Not Part of System: King Case Reaffirms Sentiment." *USA Today* (May 13): 8A.

Memorial News (1990) "The Memorial News Update." *Memorial News* (December): 3 (published by the National Law Enforcement Officers Memorial Fund, McLean, VA).

Mendez, Gary A., Jr. (1983) "The Role of Race and Ethnicity in the Incidence of Police Use of Deadly Force." Unpublished paper prepared on behalf of the National Urban League, New York City.

Merina, Victor (1992) "Sixty-two 'Problem Officers' Found in Department." *Los Angeles Times* (July 21): A1, A20.

_____ (1992a) "Handling of 'Problem Deputies' Criticized: Kolts Report—Panel Finds 'Little or No Discipline' Imposed on Officers Responsible for Bulk of Excessive Force Complaints." *Los Angeles Times* (July 22): B12.

Meyer, C. Kenneth, Cheryl G. Swanson, Charles D. Hale, and James L. Regens (1974) *An Analysis of Officer Characteristics and Police Assaults Among Selected South Central Cities*. Norman, OK: Bureau of Government Research, University of Oklahoma.

Meyer, C. Kenneth, Thomas C. Magedanz, Daniel C. Kieselhorst, and Samuel G. Chapman (1978) *A Social-Psychological Analysis of Police Assailants*. Norman, OK: Bureau of Government Research, University of Oklahoma.

_____ (1979) "Violence and the Police: The Special Case of the Police Assailant." *Journal of Police Science and Administration* 7 (2): 161-171.

Meyer, C. Kenneth, Thomas C. Magedanz, Donald Dahlin, and Samuel Chapman (1981) "A Comparative Assessment of Assault Incidents: Robbery-Related Ambush and General Police Assaults." *Journal of Police Science and Administration* 9 (1): 1-18.

Meyer, C. Kenneth, Thomas Magedanz, Samuel Chapman, Donald Dahlin, and Cheryl Swanson (1982a) "An Analysis of Factors Related to Robbery-Associated Assaults on Police Officers—Part I." *Journal of Police Science and Administration* 10 (1): 1-27.

_____ (1982b) "An Analysis of Factors Related to Robbery-Associated Assaults on Police Officers—Part II." *Journal of Police Science and Administration* 10 (2): 127-150.

_____ (1982c) "An Analysis of Factors Related to Robbery-Associated Assaults on Police Officers—Part III." *Journal of Police Science and Administration* 10 (3): 249-272.

Meyer, C. Kenneth, et al. (1986) *Ambush-Related Assaults on Police*. Springfield, IL: Charles C. Thomas.

Meyer, Fred A., Jr., and Ralph Baker (eds.), *Determinants of Law-Enforcement Policies*. Lexington, MA: Lexington Books, D.C. Heath.

Meyer, Greg (1981) "Your Nonlethal Weapons Alternatives." *Journal of California Law Enforcement* 15 (1): 126.

_____ (1991) "LAPD Brutality Incident: Don't Blame the TASER." *Law Enforcement News* (March 31): 8.

_____ (1991a) "Nonlethal Weapons Versus Conventional Police Tactics: The Los Angeles Police Department Experience." Unpublished Masters thesis by an LAPD sergeant who served as the Department's principal researcher on less-than-lethal weapons) (California State University, Los Angeles) (March).

_____ (1992) "The Sorry State of Police Tactics: What to Do?" *Crime Control Digest* (June 8): 1, 3-5.

_____ (1992a) "Nonlethal Weapons vs. Conventional Police Tactics: Assessing Injuries and Liabilities." *Police Chief* (August): 10, 12, 14-17.

Meyer, Josh, and Michael Connelly (1992) "City Council Faces Trial in Brutality Case: A Judge Rules the Officials Can be Held Liable in a $20-Million Suit Over the 1990 Police Slaying of Three Robbers in Sunland." *Los Angeles Times* (July 22): B1, B5.

Meyer, Marshall (1980a) *Report to the Los Angeles Board of Police Commissioners on Police Use of Deadly Force in Los Angeles: Officer-Involved Shootings, Part IV*. Los Angeles, CA: Los Angeles Board of Police Commissioners.

_____ (1980b) "Police Shootings at Minorities: The Case of Los Angeles." *Annals of the American Academy of Political and Social Science* 452 (November): 98-110. Reprinted in James J. Fyfe (ed.), *Readings on Police Use of Deadly Force*. Washington, DC: Police Foundation (1982).

Miedzian, Myriam (1991) *Boys Will Be Boys: Breaking the Link Between Masculinity and Violence*. New York: Anchor Books (Doubleday).

Miller, Wilbur R. (1975) "Police Authority in London and New York City, 1830-1870." *Journal of Social History* (Winter): 81-101. Reprinted as "Cops and Bobbies, 1830-1870," in Carl B. Klockars (ed.), *Thinking About Police: Contemporary Readings*. New York: McGraw-Hill (1983).

Milton, Catherine H., Jeanne S. Halleck, James Lardner, and Gary L. Albrecht (1977) *Police Use of Deadly Force*. Washington, DC: Police Foundation. Portions reprinted in Harry W. More, Jr. (ed.), *Critical Issues in Law Enforcement* (4th rev. ed.) Cincinnati: Anderson Publishing.

Milward, John (1990) "A Happy Hunting Ground for Yuppies." *Chicago Tribune* (May 16): sec. 5, p. 1, 5.

Mintz, E., and G.B. Sandler (1975) "From Police Force to Police Service: The Response to Violence." In Jack Kinton (ed.), *Police Roles in the Seventies: Professionalization in America, 1975*. Aurora, IL: Social Science and Sociological Resources.

Mirrlees-Black, C. (1992) *Using Psychometric Personality Tests in the Selection of Police Firearms Officers* (Home Office Research and Planning Unit paper). London, England: Home Office.

Missouri Association for Criminal Justice (1926) *The Missouri Crime Survey*. New York: Macmillan. Reprinted 1968. Montclair, NJ: Patterson Smith.

Monahan, John (1981a) *The Clinical Prediction of Violent Behavior*. (Part of the "Crime and Delinquency" monograph series) Washington, DC: National Institute of Mental Health.

_____ (1981b) *Predicting Violent Behavior: An Assessment of Clinical Techniques*. Beverly Hills, CA: Sage.

Moran, Julio (1992) "State Retrial of Powell is Put on Hold." *Los Angeles Times* (Aug. 8): B1, B14.

_____ (1992a) "State Case Against Powell Likely to Be Dismissed: Judge Indicates That Federal Trial of Officer Accused in King Beating Will Cover the Same Ground." *Los Angeles Times*(August 15): B1-B2.

Moreland (1954) "The Use of Force in Effecting or Resisting Arrest." *Nebraska Law Review* 33: 408.

Morgan, J.P. (1992) "Oleoresin Capsicum Policy Considerations." Unpublished paper by the Goldsboro, NC police chief, on file with the Police Executive Research Forum.

_____ (1992a) "Oleoresin Capsicum Policy Considerations." *Police Chief* (August): 22-23, 26.

Moore, Mark H., and Darrel W. Stephens (1991a) Beyond Command and Control: The Strategic Management of Police Departments. Washington, DC: Police Executive Research Forum.

_____ (1991b) "Organization and Management." In William A. Geller (ed.), *Local Government Police Management* (3d rev. ed.). Washington, DC: Int'l City Management Association.

Moorman, Charles B., and Richard C. Wemmer (1983) "Law Enforcement Officers Murdered in California: 1980-81." *Police Chief* (May): 42-54.

Moorman, Charles B., Richard C. Wemmer, and George T. Williams (1990) "A Decade of Peace Officers Murdered in California: the 1980s." *Jnl. of California Law Enforcement* 24 (1): 1-18.

More, Harry W., Jr. (1985) "The Police Use of Deadly Force," in Harry W. More, Jr. (ed.), Critical Issues in Law Enforcement (4th rev. ed.) Cincinnati: Anderson Publishing.

Morgan, James P., Jr. (1992) "Police Firearms Training: The Missing Link." *FBI Law Enforcement Bulletin* (January): 14-15.

Moriarty, Mortimer D. (1990) "Training: Undercover Negotiating—Dealing for Your Life." *Police Chief* (November): 44-47.

Morris, Norval (1981) "Foreword." In William A. Geller and Kevin J. Karales, *Split-Second Decisions: Shootings Of and By Chicago Police*. Chicago: Chicago Law Enforcement Study Group.

Morrison, Patton N., and C. Kenneth Meyer (1974) *A Microanalysis of Assaults on Police in Austin, Texas*. Norman, OK: Bureau of Government Research, University of Oklahoma.

MTI (1979) "Shooting Decisions." Northbrook, IL: MTI (30-minute film).

Muir, William Ker (1977) *Police: Streetcorner Politicians*. Chicago: University of Chicago Press.

Murphy, Dean E. (1992) "Rights Study Cites Serious Police Abuse in L.A.: Amnesty Int'l Finds an 'Unchecked' Pattern of Excessive force by Officers." *Los Angeles Times* (June 27): B1-B2.

Murphy, L. (1978) "Police Use of Force." *Military Police Law Enforcement Journal* 5 (1): 38-43.

Muwakkil, Salim (1992) "Life on the Receiving End of the Law's Long Arm." *Chicago Tribune* (August 17): sec. 1, p. 15.

Mydans, Seth (1992) "Testimony Begins on Police Beating: Defense Calls Suspect Bizarre in Incident on Videotape." *New York Times* (March 6): A1, A8.

_____ (1992a) "Police Can't Identify Them, So Looting Suspects Go Free." *New York Times* (June 3): A8.

_____ (1992b) "Los Angeles Installs Police Chief Quietly." *New York Times* (June 27): 6.

_____ (1992c) "U.S. Faces Tough Task in Taped-Beating Trial: Making a Federal Case of a Beating Won't Make Convictions Easy." *New York Times* (August 24): A6.

_____ (1992d) "Los Angeles Prosecutor Bows Out of the Spotlight." *New York Times* (September 19): 5.

Myers, Linnet (1991) "Officer Saved by Vest Recounts Brush with Death." *Chicago Tribune* (February 9): sec. 1, p. 5.

Nassau County Police Department (1982) "Commissioner's Order No. 6, January 20, Pursuit Policy and Guidelines."

Nasser, Haya El, and Jonathan T. Lovitt (1992) "Feds Indict 4 L.A. Cops." *USA Today* (Aug. 6): 1.

National Advisory Commission on Civil Disorders [Kerner Commission] (1968) *Report*. Washington, DC: National Advisory Com. on Civil Disorders. Reprinted, New York: E.P. Dutton, 1968.

National Advisory Commission on Criminal Justice Standards and Goals, U.S. Department of Justice, Law Enforcement Assistance Administration (1973) *A National Strategy to Reduce Crime*. Washington, DC: National Advisory Commission on Criminal Justice Standards and Goals.

NAACP (1981) *Organizing Guide on Police-Citizen Violence*. New York: NAACP.

National Bulletin on Police Misconduct (periodical) *National Bulletin on Police Misconduct*. Boston, MA: Quinlan Publishing.

_____ (1990) "Police Brutality/Excessive Force: 38 Lessons Learned, 1990 Edition." *National Bulletin on Police Misconduct* (special supplement, December).

_____ (1990a) "Proper Use of Deadly Force—Burden of Proof—Standard of Reasonableness." *National Bulletin on Police Misconduct* (March): 2.

_____ (1990b) "Discharge of Weapon—Respondeat Superior Claim Against City—Injuries from

Shot Through Door." *National Bulletin on Police Misconduct* (March): 4.

_____ (1990c) "Discharge of Weapon: Hamm v. Powell." *National Bulletin on Police Misconduct* (April): 2.

_____ (1990d) "Plain Clothes Narcotics Officers Open Fire on Man Sitting in Car." *National Bulletin on Police Misconduct* (May): 2-3.

_____ (1990e) "Officer Shoots Motorcycle Driver—Passenger Dies in Crash." *National Bulletin on Police Misconduct* (May): 3.

_____ (1990f) "Discharge of Weapon Justified." *National Bulletin on Police Misconduct* (July): 1.

_____ (1990g) "Police Shoot Out Suspect's Tires in Misdemeanor Arrest." *National Bulletin on Police Misconduct* (July): 2.

_____ (1990h) "Murder of Police Officer." *National Bulletin on Police Misconduct* (July): 2-3.

_____ (1990i) "Shooting Truck Tires." *National Bulletin on Police Misconduct* (October): 2.

_____ (1990j) "Accidental Shooting: Auto Theft Suspect—Officer Not Liable." *National Bulletin on Police Misconduct* (October): 4.

_____ (1990k) "Discharge of Weapon: Accidental Death—Negligence." National Bulletin on Police Misconduct (October): 4.

_____ (1990l) "Failure to Safeguard Weapon: Suspension—Three Years Loss of Pay, Benefits."National Bulletin on Police Misconduct (October): 6.

_____ (1990m) "Discharge of Weapon: Suspect Shot—Fleeing Felon Rule—Immunity." *National Bulletin on Police Misconduct* (October): 7.

_____ (1990n) "Off Duty Use of Weapon: Officer Kills Wife with Service Revolver—Gross Negligence—Supervisor's Indifference to Prior Violent Acts." *National Bulletin on Police Misconduct* (November): 5.

_____ (1990o) "Armed Man Shot by Police: Civil Rights Claim." *National Bulletin on Police Misconduct* (December): 1.

_____ (1990p) "Game Room Owner Shot During Quarrel About Loitering." *National Bulletin on Police Misconduct* (December): 3.

_____ (1990q) "Suspect Shot After High-Speed Chase—Claims Civil Rights Violation." *National Bulletin on Police Misconduct* (December): 8.

_____ (1992) "Excessive Force: Officer Shoots Drunken, Suicidal Woman—Failure to Train Alleged." *National Bulletin on Police Misconduct* (July): 1-2.

National Center for Health Statistics, U.S. Public Health Service (1967) *International Classification for Diseases, Adapted for Use in the United States* (8th rev. ed.) Washington, DC: U.S. Government Printing Office.

National Commission on Law Observance and Enforcement [Wickersham Commission] (1930-1931) *Reports.* (15 volumes). Washington, DC: National Commission on Law Observance and Enforcement. Reprinted, Montclair, NJ: Patterson Smith, 1968.

_____ (1931) *Report on Lawlessness in Law Enforcement.* Washington, DC: National Commission on Law Observance and Enforcement. Reprinted, Montclair, NJ: Patterson Smith, 1968.

National Commission on the Causes and Prevention of Violence (1969) *To Establish Justice, To Insure Domestic Tranquility.* Washington, DC: National Commission on the Causes and Prevention of Violence.

_____ (1970) *To Establish Justice, To Ensure Domestic Tranquility.* New York: Bantam Books.

National Institute of Justice (1983) *Police Handgun Ammunition: Incapacitation Effects. Volume 1—Evaluation. Volume 2—Experimental Data.* Washington, DC: Government Printing Office.

_____ (1985) "Deaths in the Line of Duty," in *NIJ Reports: Upgrading Criminal Justice Technology.* Washington, DC: National Institute of Justice, U.S. Department of Justice.

_____ (1991) "Police Killings: A Comprehensive Analysis." In National Institute of Justice, *Research Plan: 1991*: 36-40 (May). Washington, DC: Nat'l Institute of Justice, U.S. Dept. of Justice.

_____ (1992) "Police Killings: A Comprehensive Analysis." In National Institute of Justice, *Research and Evaluation Plan: 1992* (April). Washington, DC: National Institute of Justice, U.S. Department of Justice.

_____ (1992a) *Research and Evaluation Plan: 1992* (April). Washington, DC: National Institute of Justice, U.S. Department of Justice.

National Minority Advisory Council on Criminal Justice to Law Enforcement Assistance

Administration (1978) *Preliminary Report: Police Use of Deadly Force.* Washington, DC: National Minority Advisory Council on Criminal Justice (August). Also see Gwynne W. Peirson.

National Safety Council (1989) *Accident Facts—1989 Edition.* Chicago: National Safety Council.

"National Teleconference on the 9 mm Semi-Automatic Pistol—Issues and Training." (1988) A broadcast on the Law Enforcement Satellite Training Network, co-produced by the Kansas City, MO, Police Department and the Federal Bureau of Investigation (December 14).

Ndibongo, Manelisi H.F. (1990) "Apartheid and Black Policing in South Africa." Paper presented at the 14th Annual Conference of the National Organization of Black Law Enforcement Executives, Houston (July 16).

Neilsen, E. (1983) "Policy on the Police Use of Deadly Force: A Cross-National Analysis." *Journal of Police Science and Administration* 11: 104-108.

Neilsen, E., D.L. Eskridge, and E.L. Willoughby (1982) "Police Shooting Incidents: Implications for Training." *Police Chief* (July): 44.

Nelligan, K.E. (1976) "Constitutional Law: Police Officer Who Shoots Fleeing Felon Protected from 42 U.S.C., 1983 Action by State Privilege Rule—*Jones V. Marshall*, 528 F.2d 132 (2nd Cir. 1975)." *Suffolk University Law Review* 10 (4): 1294-1311.

Nelson, Deborah (1992) "Point System Rewards Cops for Arrests: Officers With Too Few Penalized." *Chicago Sun-Times* (June 7): 1, 27.

_____ (1992a) "Three Teens Say Police Used Shock Torture." *Chicago Sun-Times* (July 19): 1, 26-27.

_____ (1992b) "Cop Torture and Shock Allegations Date to '70s." *Chicago Sun-Times* (Aug. 2): 4.

Nemecek, David F. (1990) "NCIC [National Crime Information Center] 2000: Technology Adds a New Weapon to Law Enforcement's Arsenal." *Police Chief* (April): 30 and passim.

Nemeth, Charles P. (1991) "The Findings of the Move Commission and the Office of the Philadelphia Medical Examiner: By Whose Standards Was a Judgment Rendered?" *Journal of Crime and Justice* (sponsored by The Midwestern Criminal Justice Association) 14 (2): 149-173.

New York City Police Academy (1971) "Study of Reports Received During 1970 Under Authority of Standard Operating Procedure No. 9, Series 1969." Unpublished statistical report.

New York City Police Department (1988) "Firearms Discharge Assault Report for 1987." Unpublished report.

_____ (1989) Correspondence from the commanding officer, Firearms and Tactics Section, New York City Police Department to William A. Geller.

_____ (1990) "Firearms Discharge Assault Report for 1989." (Unpublished report).

_____ (1991) "Firearms Discharge Assault Report for 1990." (Unpublished report).

_____ (1992) "Firearms Discharge Assault Report for 1991." (Unpublished report).

New York City Police Department Chief of Department (1988) "Department Firearms Discharge Review Board Annual Report, 1987." Internal memorandum from chief of department to police commissioner (February 26).

New York City Transit Police (1991) *The New York City Transit Police Vision for the 1990s: Taking Back the Subway for the People of New York.* Brooklyn, NY: New York City Transit Police.

New York Newsday (1991) "Editorial." *New York Newsday* (Oct. 25). Reprinted in "The PBA Inserts Feet into Mouth," *Law Enforcement News* (November 30, 1991): 8.

New York State Commission on Criminal Justice and the Use of Force (1987) "Report to the Governor," vol. I. (Unpublished report).

New York State Police, Planning and Research Unit (1989) "New York State Police 9mm Auto-Loading Pistol Study and Evaluation." Albany: New York State Police. Unpublished study (December).

New York Times (1977a) "Los Angeles Police Scored on Shooting." *New York Times* (Aug. 15): 13.

_____ (1977b) "Killings of Chicanos by Police Protested." *New York Times* (October 12): A17.

_____ (1978a) "Houston Quiet After Violence Hospitalizes Over 12." *New York Times* (May 9): 22.

_____ (1978b) "2,000 Assail Police at Black Rally as Off-Duty Officers Meet Nearby." *New York Times* (July 17): B3.

_____ (1991) "Officer Charged with Murder After Suspect is Shot in Back." *New York Times* (January 13): 14.

_____ (1991a) "Rookie is First Policewoman to be Slain in Los Angeles." *New York Times* (February 12): A13.

_____ (1991b) "Mr. Ward's Lesson for Chief Gates: Editorial." *New York Times* (March 16): 15.

_____ (1991c) "Most Blacks Are Found to Favor Term 'Black'." *New York Times* (January 29): A19.

_____ (1992) "When Racial Tension Has Boiled Over." *New York Times* (May 1): A12.

_____ (1992a) "Philadelphia Bomb Survivor Leaves Prison." *New York Times* (May 14): A8.

_____ (1992b) "Head of Police Fights Bill to Replace Officers' Guns." *New York Times* (May 28): A13.

_____ (1992c) "Guard to Remove a Lesbian Officer: Official Reluctance Attends the Dismissal of a Colonel with 26 Years' Service." *New York Times* (May 29): C16.

_____ (1992d) "Rioting in Los Angeles Gave Arson a 'Holiday'." *New York Times* (June 11): A9.

_____ (1992e) "Four Are Shot in Phoenix Office; Woman and Gunman Are Killed." *New York Times* (June 12): A13.

_____ (1992f) "Violence Rocks Hispanic Area of Washington: A Single Arrest Ignites Hours of Disturbances." *New York Times* (May 12): A8.

_____ (1992g) "New Federal Center Will Try to Reduce Violence." *New York Times* (June 26): A12.

_____ (1992h) "Two Police Officers Indicted in Shootings of Civilians." *New York Times* (July 3): A12.

_____ (1992i) "Killing by Police Leads to Community Protest." *New York Times* (July 7): A11.

_____ (1992j) "Los Angeles Deputies Criticized in Inquiry." *New York Times* (July 22); A9.

_____ (1992k) "Expert Says South African Police Systematically Mistreat Captives." *New York Times* (July 27): A5.

_____ (1992l) "Judge Delays Officer's Retrial in Taped Beating." *New York Times* (August 8): 6.

_____ (1992m) "Marshal Slain on Mountain Where Fugitive is Holed Up." *New York Times* (August 22): 5.

_____ (1992n) "Philadelphia Gets New Police Commissioner." *New York Times* (August 21): A13.

_____ (1992o) "One Marshal Dead, Others Confront Fugitive in Idaho: Tense Standoff Goes On at a Mountain Cabin." *New York Times* (August 23): 10.

_____ (1992p) "Officer on Disability After Killing Youth." *New York Times* (August 19): A13.

_____ (1992q) "Editorial: Now, Federal Review of the King Case." *New York Times* (Aug. 7): A14.

_____ (1992r) "Citizens' Unit Urges Los Angeles Police to Curb Use of Dogs." *New York Times* (August 17): A14.

_____ (1992s) "Los Angeles Riot Toll Dropped to 51 After Review." *New York Times* (August 13): D19.

_____ (1992t) "Twenty-six Relatives of Police Slain in Punjab Separatist Strife." *New York Times* (August 11): A5.

_____ (1992u) "18% Rise in Suicides in the Army Is Found Between 1987 and 1991: Army's Suicide Rate in '91 Was Higher than National Rate." *New York Times* (September 8): A10.

_____ (1992v) "College and Police Apologize for Sweep of Black Students." *New York Times* (September 12): 9.

_____ (1992w) "Editorial: The Lesson of Washington Heights." *New York Times* (September 13): 20.

_____ (1992x) "F.B.I. Studies Action as Auto Hijackings Rise in Washington." *New York Times* (September 14): A13.

_____ (1992y) "Editorial: New York's Finest Mob." *New York Times* (September 18): A12.

_____ (1992z) "Editorial: After the Police Riot, a Subway Fight." *New York Times* (September 19): 10.

_____ (1992aa) "Newark Man Held After Car Chase: Attempted-Murder Charged After Auto-Theft Suspect Rams Police Vehicle." *New York Times* (September 19): 12.

_____ (1992bb) "Lawyer Calls Officer's Death A Suspect's Self-Defense." *New York Times* (September 19): A16.

New York Transit Police Department (1991) Personal communication between command staff in the office of the chief and in the Inspectional Services Division and William A. Geller (May 28).

Newman, Maria (1992) "After the Riots: Sequence of Funerals Ends, But Bitter Questions Linger." *New York Times* (May 13): A10.

Newsweek (1985) "A *Newsweek* Poll: Deadly Force." *Newsweek* (March 11): 53.

_____ (1992) "Counting Up the Human Cost: Scores of Lives Were Lost in the Tide of Rage, Some Heroically, and Others by a Terrible Happenstance. A Roster of the 54 Deaths Linked to the Riots So Far." *Newsweek* (May 18: 47).

Newton, G.D., and Franklin E. Zimring (1969) *Firearms and Violence in American Life.* Washington, DC: U.S. Government Printing Office.

Newton, Jim (1992) "Officers' Indictments Called Political: King Case—Prosecutors Deny Defense Attorneys' Charge That They Were Under Pressure from Washington." *Los Angeles Times* (August 7): B1, B12.

Newton, Jim, and Leslie Berger (1992) "U.S. Files Civil Rights Charges Against 4 Officers in King Case: Federal Prosecutor Says Beating 'Was an Unreasonable Use of Force;' If Convicted, Each Man Faces Up to 10 Years in Prison and Fines." *Los Angeles Times* (Aug. 6): A1, A18.

Newton, Jim, and Eric Malnic (1992) "Indictments Expected Today in King Beating: At Least Three Officers Will be Named in Civil Rights Charges Returned by a Federal Grand Jury, Sources Say." *Los Angeles Times* (August 5): B1, B8.

Nicoletti, John (1990) "Training for De-escalation of Force." *Police Chief* (July): 37-39.

Nielsen, Swen (1990) "The Need for Replicative Firearms Training." *Police Chief* (November): 36-39.

Nielson, Eric (1983) "Policy on the Police Use of Deadly Force—A Cross-Sectional Analysis." *Journal of Police Science and Administration* 11 (1, March): 104-108.

Nieves, Evelyn (1992) "The Path to Racial Harmony in Linden: Fight on the Use of Police Dogs Fosters a New Sensitivity to Minority Concerns." *New York Times* (August 12): B5.

Nilson, Dennis W. (1990) "The Anatomy of a Research Project: Double Action Service Revolvers." *Law and Order* (May): 83-86.

Noesner, Gary W. and John T. Dolan (1992) "First Responder Negotiation Training." *FBI Law Enforcement Bulletin* (August): 1-4.

Norris, Michele L., Avis Thomas-Lester, and David Von Drehle (1992) "In L.A., Death Drew Few Distinctions: Riot Victims Cut Down Randomly, Tragically." *Washington Post* (May 11): A1, A8-A9.

North, John (1992) "Cap-Stun Grows Popular Here, But Not With Those on the Receiving End." *Kansas City Star* (February 11): B-1, B-6.

Note (1964) "The Administration of Complaints by Civilians Against Police." *Harvard Law Review* 77: 499.

Note (1955) "Note." *North Carolina Law Review* 34: 122.

Novello, Antonia C., John Shosky, and Robert Froehlke (1992) "From the Surgeon General, U.S. Public Health Service: A Medical Response to Violence." *Journal of the American Medical Association* 267 (22, June 10): 3,007.

Nowicki, Dennis E., and Bernard R. Stahl (1978) "Firearms Use by Chicago Police." Unpublished intra-agency memorandum by Chicago police sergeants Nowicki and Stahl to an assistant deputy superintendent (March 30).

Nowicki, Dennis E., Gary W. Sykes, and Terry Eisenberg (1991) "Human Resource Management." In William A. Geller (ed.), *Local Government Police Management* (3d rev. ed.). Washington, DC: International City Management Association.

Nugent, Hugh, Edward F. Connors III, J. Thomas McEwen, and Lou Mayo (1989) *Restrictive Policies for High-Speed Police Pursuits.* (Issues and Practices Series) Washington, DC: National Institute of Justice.

Nulton, David P. (1991) "Less Than Lethal Force Focus Group Conference Confronts Technical Issues in Law Enforcement." *The Law Officer* (newspaper of the International Union of Police Associations) 11 (3): 28.

O'Brien, John, and Matt O'Connor (1992) "Erickson's Guards 'Were Not Remiss'." *Chicago Tribune* (July 23): sec. 2, p. 1.

O'Connell, Jim (1990) "San Diego is Fourth in Fatalities by Police." *San Diego Union* (Aug. 5): B1.

_____ (1990a) "City's Per-Capita Suspect Death Rate Soars." *San Diego Union* (December 21): A-10, A-11.

O'Connell, Richard J. (1992) "Commentary/Analysis: What Are We Doing?" *Crime Control Digest* (August 17): 1, 5-6.

O'Connor, Matt, and Linnet Myers (1991) "Cop Slaying Suspect Had Lengthy Record." *Chicago Tribune* (January 10): sec. 2, p. 3.

O'Connor, Matt, and John O'Brien (1992) "Bloody End for Erickson Saga." *Chicago Tribune* (July 21): sec. 1, pp. 1, 4.

_____ (1992a) "Erickson Beat the System at Every Turn." *Chicago Tribune* (July 22): sec. 1, pp. 1, 12.

O'Connor, Phillip J. (1988) "Fewer Civilians Shot by Cops." *Chicago Sun-Times* (September 4): 3.

_____ (1991) "Plainclothes Cops Shot More Often, Researcher Says." *Chicago Sun-Times* (January 9): 19.

_____ (1992) "Autopsy Shows Boy Shot in Side, Not Back." *Chicago Sun-Times* (June 9): 5.

_____ (1992a) "Police Will Wear Vests If City Buys, Union Says." *Chicago Sun-Times* (August 11): 5.

O'Connor, Phillip J., and Pamela Cytrynbaum (1992) "Five Hurt in Roselle Shoot-out: Bank Robbery Suspect Fires on Cops in Chase." *Chicago Sun-Times* (August 11): 3.

O'Linn, Missy K. (1992) "The Gaps in Use-of-Force Policies and Training." *Police Chief* (February): 52-54.

O'Neill, M. (1979) "Gun Retention." *FBI Law Enforcement Bulletin* 48 (9, September): 20-23.

Oakley, Robin (1990) "Police Training on Ethnic Relations in Britain." *Police Studies: The International Review of Police Development* 13 (2, Summer): 47-56.

Office of Justice Programs, U.S. Department of Justice (1991) "Discretionary Programs for Fiscal Year 1991: Notice." *Federal Register* (January 16): 1672-1695.

Osgood, Charles (1990) "Commentary." Broadcast on CBS Network Radio (WBBM-AM, Chicago) (December 2).

Ostrow, Ronald J. (1990) "FBI Easing Policy on When to Shoot." *Los Angeles Times* (June 13).

Overton, Michael (1986) *Stun Gun Use in Nebraska: Survey Results*. Lincoln, NE: Statistical Analysis Center, Nebraska Crime Commission.

Owen, I.K. (1975) "What About Dumdums?" *FBI Law Enforcement Bulletin* 44 (4, April): 3-6.

Pagano, Clinton L. (1984) "The 9mm Auto As Police Sidearm." *The Police Marksman* (January/February).

Palermo, Ray (1990) Personal communication between New York City police detective Palermo, assigned to the Bronx district attorney's squad and William A. Geller (October 26).

Paradise, Paul R. (1991) "The DEA Trauma Team." *Law and Order* (June): 97-99.

Pareles, Jon (1992) "The Disappearance of Ice-T's 'Cop Killer' Song." *New York Times* (July 30): B3.

Parkin, A. (1979) "Resisting Unlawful Police Action." *New Law Journal* 129 (August 30): 850-853.

Parsons, Kevin (1980) *Techniques of Vigilance*. Charles E. Tuttle Co.

Pate, Antony, J.W. McCullough, R.A. Bowers, and A. Ferrara (1976) *Kansas City Peer Review Panel: An Evaluation Report*. Washington, DC: Police Foundation.

Pate, Antony, and Edwin E. Hamilton (1991) *The Big Six: Policing America's Largest Cities*. Washington, DC: Police Foundation.

Paul, Gordon N. (1990) "The Climate of Fear in Law Enforcement" in International Association of Chiefs of Police (ed.), *Fear: It Kills!—A Collection of Papers for Law Enforcement Survival*. Arlington, VA: International Association of Chiefs of Police/Bureau of Justice Assistance, U.S. Department of Justice.

Pauly, Brett (1992) "L.A. Council Pays Tribute to 4 Who Braved Mobs to Aid Victims." *Los Angeles Daily News* (May 6): 1, 8.

Peak, Ken (1990) "The Quest for Alternatives to Lethal Force: A Heuristic View." *Journal of Contemporary Criminal Justice* 6 (1): 9.

Pearson (1930) "The Right to Kill in Making Arrests." *Michigan Law Review* 28: 957.

Pearson, Terry L. (1992) "Focus on Police Pursuits: The Precision Immobilization Technique." *FBI Law Enforcement Bulletin* (September): 8-9.

Peirson, Gwynne W. (1978) *Police Use of Deadly Force: Preliminary Report*. Washington, DC: National Minority Advisory Council on Criminal Justice to Law Enforcement Assistance Administration (August). See also National Minority Advisory Council on Criminal Justice to Law Enforcement Assistance Administration.

Pendergrass, V.E., and N.M. Ostrove (1986) "Correlates of Alcohol Use by Police Personnel." In James T. Reese and Harvey A. Goldstein (eds.), *Psychological Services for Law Enforcement*. Washington, DC: Federal Bureau of Investigation (pp. 489-496).

Pennsylvania v. Mimms (1977) 434 U.S. 117.

Perez, Douglas (1978) "Police Accountability: A Question of Balance." Ph.D. dissertation, University of California, Berkeley.

_____ (1992) "Police Review Systems." *MIS [Management Information Service] Report* 24 (8, August): 1-15 (published by International City/County Management Association).

Perkins (1940) "The Law of Arrest." *Iowa Law Review* 25: 201, 272.

Personal Protection Consultants (1991) "Introducing the Violence Management Training System for Police Departments." Training program brochure produced by PPC, Hyannis, MA.

Petacque, Art, and Jim Casey (1991) "Ex-Convict on Supervised Leave Held in Cop Killing." *Chicago Sun-Times* (January 9): 4.

Peter, Laurence J. (1979) *Peter's Quotations: Ideas for Our Time*. New York: Bantam Books.

Petersilia, Joan, Susan Turner, James Kahan, and Joyce Peterson (1985) *Granting Felons Probation: Public Risks and Alternatives*. Santa Monica, CA: Rand Corporation.

Peterson, Ruth D., and William C. Bailey (1988) "Structural Influences on the Killing of Police: A Comparison with General Homicides." *Justice Quarterly* 5 (2, June): 207-233.

Petrillo, Lisa (1990a) "When a Cop Shoots, Who Takes Close Look? Here, Unlike Most Cities, An Outside Probe Rarely Results When Officers Fire." *San Diego Union* (Dec. 21): A-1, A-10.

_____ (1990b) "Officers Carry Their Wounds on the Inside." *San Diego Union* (Dec. 21): A-10.

_____ (1990c) "San Diego Police Shootings: This is How a Man Became the Year's Third to Die of a Police Bullet." *San Diego Union* (December 21): A-12.

Philadelphia Police Department (1990) Deadly force data furnished by Deputy Commissioner Thomas Nestel and interpreted by Sgt. John Ferry (December 3 and December 5).

Phoenix Police Department (1986) "General Order A-11, July 1986, Operation of Department Vehicles." Phoenix, AZ: Phoenix Police Department.

Pilant, Lois (1992) "Selecting the Proper Weapon." *Police Chief* (July): 35-44.

_____ (1992a) "Equipping Your SWAT Team." *Police Chief* (January): 37-47.

Piliavin, Irving, and Scott Briar (1964) "Police Encounters with Juveniles." *American Journal of Sociology* 70 (September): 206-214.

Pilla, T.V. (1980) *Police-Community Relations in San Jose (CA): A Staff Report of the Western Regional Office of the United States Commission on Civil Rights*. Washington, DC: U.S. Commission on Civil Rights.

Plaster, John (1990) "Police Sniper Training." *FBI Law Enforcement Bulletin* 59 (9, September): 1-6.

Platt, Anthony M. (1971) *The Politics of Riot Commissions, 1917-1970*. New York: Collier Books.

Pledger, James R. (1988) "Hogan's Alley: The Federal Bureau of Investigation Academy's New Training Complex." *FBI Law Enforcement Bulletin* (December): 5-9.

Police Chief Magazine (1983) "Deadly Force to Apprehend Escaping Felons." *Police Chief* (May): 29-34.

Police Executive Research Forum (1982) "Survey of Police Deadly Force Policies." Unpublished report. Washington, DC: Police Executive Research Forum.

_____ (1991) "PERF Legislative Survey Finds Support for Bulk of Police Accountability Act." *Subject to Debate* (Police Executive Research Forum newsletter) (November/December): 4.

Police Foundation (1984) "Violence Reduction Training for the Metro-Dade Police Department." Unpublished research proposal on file at the Police Foundation, Washington, DC.

_____ (1988) "The Metro-Dade Police/Citizen Violence Reduction Project: Final Report, Executive Summary." Washington, DC: Police Foundation.

Pompa, Gilbert G. (1978) *Police Use of Excessive Force: A Community Relations Concern*. Washington, DC: Community Relations Service, U.S. Department of Justice.

_____ (1978a) "A Major and Most Pressing Concern." *Engage/Social Action* (Nov./Dec.): 10-14.

_____ (1980) "Police Use of Force: How Citizens Think It Should be Dealt With." Presentation to the League of United Latin American Citizens [LULAC] 1980 National Convention, "Hispanics at the Threshold of Economic and Political Power," Washington, DC, June 27. Washington, DC: Community Relations Service, U.S. Department of Justice.

Pope, Carl E. (1979) "Race and Crime Revisited." *Crime and Delinquency* 25 (July): 347-357.

Powell, Dennis D. (1981) "Race, Rank, and Police Discretion." *Journal of Police Science and Administration* 9 (4): 383-389.

_____ (1990) "A Study of Police Discretion in Six Southern Cities." *Journal of Police Science and Administration* 17 (1, March): 1-7).

Pratt, James (1990) Personal communication between Tulsa attorney and former Oklahoma State Bureau of Investigation agent and William A. Geller (October 11).

President's Commission on Law Enforcement and Administration of Justice (1967) *Task Force Report: The Police.* Washington, DC: U.S. Government Printing Office.

Prothrow-Stith, Deborah, and Michaele Weissman (1991) *Deadly Consequences: How Violence is Destroying Our Teenage Population and a Plan to Begin Solving the Problem.* New York: Harper Collins.

Public Interest Law Center of Philadelphia (1975) *A Study of the Use of Firearms by Philadelphia Policemen from 1970-1974.* Philadelphia: Public Interest Law Center of Philadelphia.

_____ (1979) *Deadly Force: Police Use of Firearms 1970-78.* Philadelphia: Public Interest Law Center of Philadelphia.

Purdue, H. (1980) "Escalation of Police Use of Force." *Trooper* 5 (5, September): 54-55, 57, 59, 61.

Purdum, Todd S. (1992) "Slurs From Police Not New to Dinkins." *New York Times* (September 19): 32.

Quinn, James (1990) "Robot Cop: New Weapon Can Go Places Where Humans Fear to Tread." *Los Angeles Times* (August 22): B1, B8.

Raspberry, William (1992) "When People Feel They Don't Matter." *Washington Post* (May 4): A23.

Reardon, Patrick T., and Matt O'Connor (1991) "Police Tactical Teams Tempt the Fates Daily." *Chicago Tribune* (January 9): 1-2.

Rechtschaffen, O.H. (1985) "The Use of Firearms by the European Police." *Texas Police Journal* 33 (2, March): 17-18.

Recktenwald, William (1991) "New Year Begins on the Same Old Violent Note." *Chicago Tribune* (January 2): 14.

Recktenwald, William, and Angela Bradbery (1992) "Cops at Risk When They Patrol Alone." *Chicago Tribune* (March 8): sec. 2, pp. 1, 3.

Recktenwald, William, and Linnet Myers (1991) "849 Homicides Place 1990 in a Sad Record Book." *Chicago Tribune* (January 2): 1, 14.

Reddin, Thomas J. (1967) "Nonlethal Weapons—Curse or Cure?" *Police Chief* (December): 6.

Reese, James T., and Harvey A. Goldstein (eds.) (1986) *Psychological Services for Law Enforcement.* Washington, DC: Federal Bureau of Investigation.

Regens, James L., C. Kenneth Meyer, Cheryl Swanson, Samuel Chapman, and Paul Wilson (1974) *An Analysis of Assaults on Municipal Police Officers in 46 South Central Cities.* Norman, OK: Bureau of Government Research, University of Oklahoma.

Reich, Kenneth (1992a) "Reiner Assails Kolts Report: The District Attorney Calls the Document Seriously Flawed; It Criticizes the Prosecutor for Pursing Only One of 382 Incidents Involving Shootings by Deputies." *Los Angeles Times* (July 22): B1, B12.

_____ (1992b) "Block Gives a Mixed Review to Kolts Report: Sheriff Says Study is Wrong About 'Problem Officers' But Agrees to Facilitate Handling of Complaints." *Los Angeles Times* (July 30): A1, A24.

_____ (1992c) "Guns Using Plastic Bullets Are Urged: Grand Jury Says Deputies Should Replace Electric Dart Guns." *Los Angeles Times* (June 5): B1, B8.

Reich, Kenneth, and Frederick M. Muir (1992) "Block's Cooperation Key to Reform Measures: Implementing Report Recommendations Without Agreement of the Sheriff Could Require Legal and Governmental Changes." *Los Angeles Times* (July 21): A1, A20.

Reiner, Robert (1985) *The Politics of the Police.* Brighton, England: Wheatsheaf.

_____ (1992) "Police Research in the United Kingdom: A Critical Review." In Michael Tonry and Norval Morris (eds.), *Modern Policing* (vol. 15 in the "Crime and Justice" series). Chicago: University of Chicago Press.

Reinhold, Robert (1992) "Judge Sets Los Angeles for Retrial of Officer in Rodney King Beating." *New York Times* (May 23): 1, 7.

_____ (1992a) "U.S. Jury Indicts 4 Police Officers in King Beating: Los Angeles Panel Files Civil Rights Charges." *New York Times* (August 6): A1, A12.

Reiss, Jr., Albert J. (1971a) *The Police and the Public.* New Haven: Yale University Press.

_____ (1971b) "Systematic Observation of Natural Social Phenomena." In H. Costner (ed.), *Sociological Methodology.*

_____ (1980) "Controlling Police Use of Deadly Force." *Annals of the American Academy of Political and Social Science* 452 (November): 122-134.

_____ (1991) "What is 'R&D' Really?" In William A. Geller (ed.), *Local Government Police Management* (3d rev. ed.) Washington, DC: International City Management Association (p. 339).

_____ (1992) "Police Organization." In Tonry, Michael, and Norval Morris (eds.), *Modern Policing* (vol. 15 in the "Crime and Justice" series). Chicago: University of Chicago Press.

Reuss-Ianni, Elizabeth (1983) *Two Cultures of Policing: Street Cops and Management Cops.* New Brunswick, CT: Transaction Books.

Revell, Oliver B. (1990). Personal communication between then-associate deputy director for investigations, Federal Bureau of Investigation and William A. Geller (April 12).

Revering, A.C. (1974) "Are Police Dogs Reasonable Force?" *Police Chief* 41 (9, September): 24-26.

Reyes, David (1992) "Police Chiefs Study Training Policy: Many Say King Verdict Stunned Them; They Promise to Implement Outreach Programs Spurred by the Beating." *Los Angeles Times* (May 3): B-3, B22.

Richard, Wayne C., and Ronald D. Fell (1975) "Health Factors in Police Job Stress." In William H. Kroes and Joseph J. Hurrell, Jr. (eds.), *Job Stress and the Police Officer.* Washington, DC: National Institute of Occupational Safety and Health (pp. 73-84).

Richardson, Lynda (1992) "A Suburb Seeks Clues After a Lawless Night." *New York Times* (May 13): A13.

Ritter, Jim (1992) "Gains in Comfort Help Bulletproof Vests Gain Favor." *Chicago Sun-Times* (September 6): 5.

Rivetti, Dominick J. (1987) "What is the Future of Less Than Lethal Weapons in Law Enforcement?" Unpublished paper Number 5-0086 written for the State of California Police Officer Standards and Training Command College Class V (November).

Roberts, Barbara E. (1992) "Legal Issues in Use-of-Force Claims." *Police Chief* (February): 16, 20, 22-24, 28-29.

Robin, Gerald D. (1963) "Justifiable Homicide by Police Officers." *Journal of Criminal Law, Criminology, and Police Science* 54: 225-231.

Robinette v. Barnes (1988) 854 F.2d 909 (6th Circuit U.S. Court of Appeals).

Rodriguez, Matt (1991) Personal conversation between the then-deputy superintendent, Bureau of Technical Services, Chicago Police Department and William A. Geller (December 17).

_____ (1991a) "The Risks to Police Officers from Arrestees' Undiscovered Weapons." Unpublished presentation to a midwest regional meeting of the Police Executive Research Forum, Chicago (February 6).

Rohrlich, Ted (1991) "L.A. Police Considering Reviving the Chokehold: Advocates Say Its Use is Safer than the Baton; Opponents Say It Can Kill, and Has." *Los Angeles Times* (September 2): A1, A28-A29.

Rohter, Larry (1992) "Retrial of Miami Policeman Could Test Judiciary on Race." *New York Times* (August 15): 1, 5.

_____ (1992a) "New Move Advised in Officer's Trial: Judge in Miami Says Trial in Killing of Two Blacks Should Return to Tallahassee." *New York Times* (August 18): A15.

Ronkowski, E. (1979) "Uses and Misuses of Deadly Force." *DePaul Law Review* 28 (3): 701-29.

Rossi, Rosalind (1992) "Probe Targets Source of Key to Handcuffs." *Chicago Sun-Times* (July 22): 15.

Roth, J., and R. Downey (1976) *Officer Survival: Arrest and Control.* Santa Cruz, CA: Davis Publishing.

Rousey, Dennis C. (1984) "Cops and Guns: Police Use of Deadly Force in Nineteenth-Century New Orleans." *American Journal of Legal History* 28 (1): 41-66.

Rowan, Carl T. (1989) "Media Fan Fires of Racism." *Chicago Sun-Times* (May 21).

Rubenstein, Jonathan (1975) "Cops' Rules." In Jerome H. Skolnick and Thomas C. Gray (eds.), *Police in America*. Boston: Little, Brown & Co..

Rubin, Sylvia (1992) "Street Negotiators: [Women] Police Officers Try Communication Before Reaching for Nightstick." *Chicago Tribune* (April 5): sec. 6, p. 12.

Rudd, David C., and Angela Bradbery (1992) "Schools Fear Gun Talks Could Backfire." *Chicago Tribune* (May 22): sec. 1, pp. 1, 8.

Rule, Sheila (1992) "Police Plan to Expand Time Warner Protest." *New York Times* (July 8): B1, B3.

Rummel, B. (1968) "The Right of Law Enforcement Officers to Use Deadly Force to Effect an Arrest." *New York Law Forum* 30: 749.

Russell, Harold E., and Allan Beigel (1990) *Understanding Human Behavior for Effective Police Work* (3d rev. ed.) New York: Basic Books.

Russo, Philip A., Jr., Alan S. Engel, and Steven H. Hatting (1983) "Police and Occupational Stress: An Empirical Investigation." In Richard R. Bennett (ed.), *Police at Work: Policy Issues and Analysis*. Beverly Hills, CA: Sage (pp. 89-106).

Rutledge, Devallis (1988) *The Officer Survival Manual* (2d rev. ed.) Placerville, CA: Custom Publishing Co.

Sahagun, Louis (1990) "LAPD Gets Approval to Switch Officers to Hollow-Point Ammo." *Los Angeles Times* (April 18): B1-14.

St. George, Joyce (1991) "'Sensitivity' Training Needs Rethinking." *Law Enforcement News* (November 30): 8, 12.

St. Louis Metropolitan Police Department, Planning and Development Division (1992) "Discharge of Firearms by Police Officers." (Unpublished internal study) (May).

St. Petersburg Police Department (1984) "General Order iii-12, December 1, Police Vehicle Operation."

Sampson, C. (1989) *The Use of Firearms in the [London] Metropolitan Police*. London: Her Majesty's Inspectorate of Constabulary.

San Diego Police Department (1992) Data furnished to William A. Geller (March 26).

Sanchez, Sandra (1991) "New Washington Riots Prompt Curfew." *USA Today* (May 7): 3A.

Santa Ana (CA) Police Department (1991) Correspondence and data summaries provided to William A. Geller by letter from Training Section Lt. Greg Cooper (May 29).

Santos, Michael R. (1991) "Use of Force: *Tennessee v. Garner* Revisited." *Police Chief* (October): 13-14, 16.

Sawyer, Suzie (1989) "The Aftermath of Line-of-Duty Death." *FBI Law Enforcement Bulletin* (May): 13-15.

Saxe, S., and J. Fabricatore (1982) "Using Psychological Consultants in Screening Police Applicants." *FBI Law Enforcement Bulletin* (August).

Scarman, L. (1981) *The Brixton Disorders, 10-12 April 1981*. London: Her Majesty's Stationery Office.

Scharf, Peter, and Arnold Binder (1983) *The Badge and the Bullet: Police Use of Deadly Force*. New York: Praeger.

Scharf, Peter, R. Linninger, D. Marrero, R. Baker, and C. Rice (1978) "Deadly Force: The Moral Reasoning and Education of Police Officers Faced with the Option of Lethal Legal Violence." *Policy Studies Journal* 7 (special issue): 450-454.

Scharf, Peter, R. Linninger, and D. Marrero (1979) "Use of Legal Deadly Force by Police Officers in a Democratic Society." In Fred A. Meyer, Jr., and Ralph Baker (eds.), *Determinants of Law-Enforcement Policies*. Lexington, MA: Lexington Books, D.C. Heath.

Schiller, S.A. (1978) "Use of Force by Law Enforcement Officers." *Police Law Quarterly* 7 (4, July): 5-16.

Schlossberg, H., and L. Freeman (1974) *Psychologist with a Gun*. New York: Coward, McCann and Geohagan.

Schmetzer, Uli (1991) "Philippine Cop Wages His Own War on Pushers." *Chicago Tribune* (December 29): sec. 1, pp. 9, 22.

Schmich, Mary T. (1991) "Boycott by Blacks Costs Miami." *Chicago Tribune* (January 27): sec. 1, pp. 21, 24.

Schmidt, Annesley (1985) "Deaths in the Line of Duty," in *NIJ Reports* (January): 6-8 (National

Institute of Justice, U.S. Department of Justice).

Schmidt, Wayne W. (1976) "Recent Developments in Civil Liability." *Journal of Police Science and Administration* 4 (2, June): 197-202.

_____ (1976a) "Recent Trends in Police Tort Litigation." *Urban Lawyer*: 681-692.

_____ (1985) "Section 1983 and the Changing Face of Police Management." In William A. Geller (ed.), *Police Leadership in America: Crisis and Opportunity*. New York: Praeger (pp. 226-240).

_____ (1992) Personal communication between the Executive Director, Americans for Effective Law Enforcement, and William A. Geller (September 9).

Schmitt, Eric (1991) "U.S. Seeks to Cut Accidental War Death." *New York Times* (December 9): A7.

_____ (1992) "War's 'Friendly Fire' Toll Spurs Push for Solutions." *New York Times* (June 5): A9.

_____ (1992a) "Chaplain Says Homosexuals Threaten the Military: Defending the Armed Forces' Ban on Gay Men and Lesbians." *New York Times* (August 26): A20.

Schofield, Daniel L. (1990) "Remarks: Legal Issues of Pursuit Driving." *The Police Yearbook 1990*. Arlington, VA: International Association of Chiefs of Police.

Schrader, George E. (1988) "Firearms Training/Civil Liability: Is Your Training Documentation Sufficient?" *FBI Law Enforcement Bulletin* 57 (6, June): 1-3.

Schultz, Donald O. (1990) *Police Unarmed Defense Tactics*. Placerville, CA: Custom Publishing Co.

Scraton, Phil (1985) *The State of the Police*. London: Pluto Press.

Scrivner, Ellen (1985) "Psychological Reactions to the Use of Deadly Force." *National Sheriff Magazine* (February/March).

Seibel, Tom (1992) "1,500 Attend Rites for Cop Slain by Burglary Suspect." *Chicago Sun-Times* (March 13): 4.

Senna, Joseph J., and Larry J. Siegel (1987) "Deadly Force." In Joseph J. Senna and Larry J. Siegel (eds.), *Introduction to Criminal Justice*. St. Paul, MN: West Publishing Co. (pp. 224-231).

Serrano, Richard A. (1990) "A Question of Restraint: Amid Brutality Allegations, Police in San Diego Are Using Ancient Asian Tool as Weapon in Subduing Suspects." *Los Angeles Times* (January 8): E1-E2.

_____ (1992) "Chokehold Ban Cited as Reason King Was Beaten." *Los Angeles Times* (March 25): B3.

_____ (1992a) "LAPD Revises Its Riot Response Manual: New Measures Aim at Providing A Quicker, More Effective Reaction to Civil Unrest." *Los Angeles Times* (June 3): B1, B8.

_____ (1992b) "Dreams of LAPD Class Become Tarnished: The Academy's Graduates in 1965 Had to Rebuild the Department's Image After the Watts Riots; Now, After the Rodney King Beating, 'A Lot of the Good We Did' is Gone, A Member of that Group Says." *Los Angeles Times* (January 21): B1, B8.

Sherman, Lawrence W. (1977) "Research Note on Police Homicides." Unpublished paper, State University of New York-Albany.

_____ (1979) "The Effects of Firearms Policies: A Longitudinal Analysis." Paper presented to the American Society of Criminology, Philadelphia, November 10.

_____ (1980a) "Execution Without Trial: Police Homicide and the Constitution." *Vanderbilt Law Review* 33 (1): 71-100. Reprinted in James J. Fyfe (ed.), *Readings on Police Use of Deadly Force*. Washington, DC: Police Foundation (1982).

_____ (1980b) "Causes of Police Behavior: The Current State of Quantitative Research." *Journal of Research in Crime and Delinquency* 17(1): 69-100.

_____ (1980c) "Perspectives on Police and Violence." *Annals of the American Academy of Political and Social Science* 452 (November): 1-12.

_____ (1983) "Reducing Police Gun Use: Critical Events, Administrative Policy and Organizational Change." In Maurice Punch (ed.), *Control in the Police Organization*. Cambridge, MA: Massachusetts Institute of Technology Press.

_____ (1992) "Policing and Crime Control." In Michael Tonry and Norval Morris (eds.), *Modern Policing*. Chicago: University of Chicago Press.

Sherman, Lawrence W., and Mark Blumberg (1981) "Higher Education and Police Use of Deadly Force." *Journal of Criminal Justice* 9 (4): 317-331.

Sherman, Lawrence W., and Anthony V. Bouza (1991) "Seizing Opportunities for Reform." In William A. Geller (ed.), *Local Government Police Management* (3d rev. ed.) Washington, DC: International City Management Association (pp. 358-61).

Sherman, Lawrence W., and Ellen G. Cohn, with Patrick R. Gartin, Edwin E. Hamilton, and Dennis P. Rogan (1986) *Citizens Killed by Big City Police, 1970-1984*. Washington, DC: Crime Control Institute.

Sherman, Lawrence W., and Robert Langworthy (1979) "Measuring Homicide by Police Officers." *Journal of Criminal Law and Criminology* 70 (4, Winter): 546-560. Reprinted in James J. Fyfe (ed.), *Readings on Police Use of Deadly Force*. Washington, DC: Police Foundation (1982).

Sherman, Lawrence W., Leslie Steele, Deborah Laufersweiler, Nancy Hoffer, and Sherry Julian (1989) *Stray Bullets and Mushrooms: Random Shooting of Bystanders in Four Cities, 1977-88*. Washington, DC: Crime Control Institute.

Sherman, Lewis J. (1975) "An Evaluation of Policewomen on Patrol in a Suburban Police Department." *Journal of Police Science and Administration* 3 (4): 434-438.

Sherwin, S., and K.E. Renner (1979) "Respect for Persons in a Study of the Use of Force by Police Officers." *Clinical Research* 27 (1): 19-22.

Shines, Gayle (1992) Personal communication between the chief administrator, Office of Professional Standards, Chicago Police Department and William A. Geller (April 6).

Shipler, David K. (1992) "Khaki, Blue and Blacks." *New York Times* (May 26): A15.

Shubin, Lester D. (1984) "The Next Twenty Years." *Police Chief* (April): 33-35.

Shubin, Lester D., and Daniel E. Frank (1985) "Police Handgun Ammunition." *Texas Police Journal* (March).

Silverman, David, and Monica Copeland (1991) "Cop Slain, Partner Hit; Nab Suspect." *Chicago Tribune* (January 8): 1, 12.

Sipchen, Bob (1992) "A Riot by Any Other Name...: Was It Anarchy or Uprising? The Way People Label the Unrest Says a Lot About Their Views On Its Causes and the Culpability of Those Who Took Part." *Los Angeles Times* (August 3): A1, A18-A19.

Skolnick, Jerome, and James J. Fyfe (forthcoming) *Above the Law: Why Police Use Excessive Force and What To Do About It*. New York: The Free Press.

Skolnik, Bob (1992) "15 Years Later, Officer Returns to Job." *Chicago Tribune* (March 31): 3.

Slahor, Stephenie (1992) "A New Look to 'Hogan's Alley'." *Law and Order* (March): 29-31.

Slavin, Helen (1988) Personal communication between the administrator of the International Association of Chiefs of Police/DuPont Kevlar Survivors' Club and William A. Geller (September 23).

_____ (1992) Personal communication between the administrator of the International Association of Chiefs of Police/DuPont Kevlar Survivors' Club and William A. Geller (July 23).

_____ (1992a) Personal communication between the administrator of the International Association of Chiefs of Police/DuPont Kevlar Survivors' Club and William A. Geller (September 21).

Slavin, Peter (1974) "Riots." *Networker* (magazine of the National Urban Coalition) (October/November).

Sloan, John Henry, Arthur L. Kellermann, Donald T. Reay, James A. Ferris, Thomas Koepsell, Frederick P. Rivara, Charles Rice, Laurel Gray, and James LoGerfo (1988) "Handgun Regulations, Crime, Assaults, and Homicide: A Tale of Two Cities." *The New England Journal of Medicine*.

Smith, Douglas, Christy A. Visher, and Laura A. Davidson (1984) "Equity and Discretionary Justice: The Influence of Race on Police Arrest Decisions." *Journal of Criminal Law and Criminology* 75 (1): 234-249.

Smith, Harold Irving (1992) Personal communication between the Public Information Officer for the Prince George's County (MD) Sheriff's Department and William A. Geller (September 8).

Smith, Mark (1989) *Hidden Threat: A Guide to Covert Weapons*. Boulder, CO: Paladin Press.

Smith, Paul M. (1990) "Survival Course for Border Patrol Agents." *Law and Order* (Oct.): 109-113.

Smith, Tim (1990) "Maybe It Will Help." *Arete* (June): 14-15.

Smothers, Ronald (1992) "Klan Vows to 'Have Our Say' After Mayor Cancels Permit." *New York Times* (May 9): Y5.

Snell, John (1992a) "Fear a Factor When Police Pull Trigger: Reality Defies Classic Image of Police Officer." *The [Portland] Oregonian* (April 26): A22.

_____ (1992b) "Shootings: Who, What, and How Many Shots." *The [Portland] Oregonian* (April 26): A22.

Snell, John, and James Long (1992a) "Deadly Force." *The [Portland] Oregonian* (April 26): A1, A20.

_____ (1992b) "Deadly Force: Police Training Gets Caught in City's Budgetary Crossfire." *The [Portland] Oregonian* (April 27): A1, A8.

Snell, John, and Phil Manzano (1992a) "Deadly Force: Police Watchdog Lacks Bite?" *The [Portland] Oregonian* (April 28): A1, A12.

_____ (1992b) "Complaints Against Officers Get More Than a Once-Over—By Police." *The [Portland] Oregonian* (April 28): A12.

Snow, Robert (1990) "Line-of-Duty Deaths in Small Departments." *Law and Order* (June): 34-38.

Solomon, Roger M. (1990) "The Dynamics of Fear in Critical Incidents: Implications for Training and Treatment" in International Association of Chiefs of Police (ed.), *Fear: It Kills!—A Collection of Papers for Law Enforcement Survival*. Arlington, VA: International Association of Chiefs of Police/Bureau of Justice Assistance, U.S. Department of Justice.

Solomon, Roger M., and James M. Horn (1986) "Post-Shooting Traumatic Reactions: A Pilot Study." In James T. Reese and Harvey A. Goldstein (eds.), *Psychological Services for Law Enforcement*. Washington, DC: Federal Bureau of Investigation.

Somodevilla, S.A. (1986) "Post-Shooting Trauma: Reactive and Proactive Treatment." In James T. Reese and Harvey A. Goldstein (eds.), *Psychological Services for Law Enforcement*. Washington, DC: Federal Bureau of Investigation (pp. 395-398).

Soskis, David S., and Clinton R. Van Zandt (1986) "Hostage Negotiation: Law Enforcement's Most Effective Nonlethal Weapon." *Behavioral Sciences and the Law* 4 (4): 423-435.

Southgate, Peter (1982) *Police Probationer Training in Race Relations* (Home Officer, Research and Planning Unit Papers 8) London, England: Home Office.

_____ (1984) *Racism Awareness Training for the Police* (Home Office, Research and Planning Unit Papers 29) London, England: Home Office.

_____ (1992) *The Management and Deployment of Police Armed Response Vehicles* (Home Office Research and Planning Unit Paper 67). Home Office: London, England.

Southgate, Peter, with Paul Ekblom (1986) *Police-Public Encounters* (Home Office Research Study 90) London, England: Her Majesty's Stationery Office.

Sparger, Jerry R., and David J. Giacopassi (1992) "Memphis Revisited: A Re-Examination of Police Shootings After the *Garner* Decision." Unpublished paper excerpted in *Crime Control Digest* (March 30): 1, 7-8.

Sparrow, Malcolm K., Mark H. Moore, and David M. Kennedy (1990) *Beyond 911: A New Era for Policing*. New York: Basic Books, a Division of Harper Collins.

Spaulding, W.G. (1987) "The Longest Hour: The First Response to Terrorist Incidents." *Law Enforcement Technology* (July/August): 26.

Spector, Elliot B. (1992) "Chief's Counsel: Nonactor Liability—The Duty to Not Look the Other Way." *Police Chief* (April): 8.

Spelman, William, and John E. Eck (1989) "The Police and Delivery of Local Government Services: A Problem-Oriented Approach." In James J. Fyfe (ed.), *Police Practice in the '90s: Key Management Issues*. Washington, DC: International City Management Association (pp. 55-72).

Spetalnick, Matt (1992) "U.S. Indicts 4 L.A. Cops in King Beating" *Chicago Sun-Times* (Aug. 6): 6.

Spielman, Fran (1992) "Cops to Get More Firepower: Semiautomatics OKd as Main Gun." *Chicago Sun-Times* (February 27): 3.

_____ (1992a) "Top Cop Opposes 'Hair Trigger' Pistol." *Chicago Sun-Times* (March 20): 4.

Spolar, Christine, and Debbi Wilgoren (1992) "A Year After Unrest, Marchers Show Unity." *Washington Post* (May 6): B1, B6.

Springer, John (1991) "Risk Analysis for Planned Operations." *Law and Order* (May): 29-30.

Stafford (1986) "Lawsuits Against the Police: Reasons for the Proliferation of Litigation in the Past Decade." *Police and Criminal Psychology* 2 (1): 30-34.

Stanford, Rose Mary and Bonney Lee Mowry (1990) "Domestic Disturbance Danger Rate." *Journal of Police Science and Administration* 17 (4, December): 244-249.

Steele, David E. (1992) "Police Sticks." *Law and Order* (August): 37-40.

Stein, Sharman (1992) "Chicago Officer Eulogized as a Hero." *Chicago Tribune* (March 13): sec. 2,

p. 9.

_____ (1992a) "Cops Defend Shooting of 12-Year-Old." *Chicago Tribune* (June 9): section 2, p. 3.

_____ (1992b) "Sink or Swim: Named Top Cop on the Day the Loop Flooded, Matt Rodriguez Still Faces Some Tidal Waves." *Chicago Tribune* (June 21): section 5, pp. 1-2.

_____ (1992c) "Handcuffs Behind Back Called Safer." *Chicago Tribune* (July 22): sec. 1, p. 13.

Stein, Sharman, and Teresa Wiltz (1992) "Cop Slain Questioning Suspect." *Chicago Tribune* (March 8): 1, 13.

Steisel, Norman (1990a) Letter from New York City First Deputy Mayor Steisel to Robert Kiley, chairman, Metropolitan Transportation Authority of New York (August 3). Included in William J. Bratton (ed.), *Police Use of Force and the 9 mm Semi-Automatic Weapon: Background Materials for New York City Transit Police Chief William J. Bratton's Presentation to the Board of Directors, Metropolitan Transportation Authority of New York.* Unpublished reports compiled by the New York City Transit Police (November 1).

_____ (1990b) Letter from New York City First Deputy Mayor Steisel to Robert Kiley, chairman, Metropolitan Transportation Authority of New York (August 10). Included in William J. Bratton (ed.), *Police Use of Force and the 9 mm Semi-Automatic Weapon: Background Materials for New York City Transit Police Chief William J. Bratton's Presentation to the Board of Directors, Metropolitan Transportation Authority of New York.* Unpublished reports compiled by the New York City Transit Police (November 1).

Stephens, D. (1977) "Domestic Assault: The Police Response." In M. Roy (ed.), *Battered Women.* New York: Van Nostrand Rhienhold (pp. 164-172).

Stevens, Philip, and Carole F. Willis (1979) *Race, Crime and Arrests.* (Home Office Research Study 58) London, England: Her Majesty's Stationery Office.

Stevenson, Richard W. (1992) "As Troops March Out, Courts Narrow Backlog." *New York Times* (May 8): A11.

Stewart, Robert, and Gayle Fisher-Stewart (1990) "Why Multi-Cultural Training for Police?" Unpublished paper prepared as background in connection with the preparation of *Local Government Police Management* (3d rev. ed.), William A. Geller (ed.). Washington, DC, 1991.

_____ (1991) "Managing Diversity." In William A. Geller (ed.), *Local Government Police Management* (3d rev. ed.). Washington, DC: International City Management Association.

Stillman, Frances A. (1986) *Line-of-Duty Deaths: Survivor and Department Responses—Final Report.* Washington, DC: National Institute of Justice, U.S. Department of Justice.

_____ (1987) "Line-of-Duty Deaths: Survivor and Departmental Responses." *Research in Brief.* Washington, DC: National Institute of Justice. Reprinted in Roger G. Dunham and Geoffrey P. Alpert (eds.), *Critical Issues in Policing: Contemporary Readings.* Prospect Heights, IL: Waveland Press (1989).

Stobart, R.M. (1972) "Serious Assaults on Police." *Police Journal* 45: 108-126.

Stolberg, Sheryl (1990) "Six SIS Detectives Cleared in Shooting of Bank Robbers." *Los Angeles Times* (June 8): A1, A38.

_____ (1991) "Arrests Show Decline After King Beating." *Los Angeles Times* (June 28): A1, A26.

_____ (1992) "Christopher Panel Drew Map That Showed Kolts the Way." *Los Angeles Times* (July 21): A19.

_____ (1992a) "Critics Say Kolts Report is Flawed by Bias, Errors: Attacks Come From District Attorney's Office, Deputies' Union and Civil Liberties Advocates." *Los Angeles Times* (July 28): A1, A16-A17.

_____ (1992b) "Convictions in Rights Case Could Be Difficult to Win: Main Issues Are the Same as in State Trial, But U.S. Prosecutors Must Expand Proof of Officers' Intent." *Los Angeles Times* (August 6): A1, A18.

Stone, Andrea (1992) "No Simple Answers in Rebuilding a Community." *USA Today* (May 5): 4A.

Stratton, J.G., and B.T. Stratton (1982) "Law Enforcement Marital Relationships: A Positive Approach." *FBI Law Enforcement Bulletin* (May): 6-11.

Stratton, J.G., and B. Wroe (1980) "Alcoholism Programs for Police." *Journal of Law and Order* (October): 18-24.

Strum, Charles (1992) "An Officer Admits Lies in Shooting: In Newark, A Policeman Agrees to Testify Against His Colleagues." *New York Times* (August 7): A12.

Sullivan, Joseph F. (1992) "New Jersey Panel Urges Uniform Guidelines for Police Use of Deadly Force." *New York Times* (May 11): A13.

_____ (1992a) "Officers to Face Scrutiny About Conduct at Party Before Two Fatal Shootings." *New York Times* (August 25): A13.

_____ (1992b) "At Funerals for 2 Slain by Police, a Plea to Youths." *New York Times* (August 29): 10.

Sullivan, Kevin (1992) "12 Teenagers Charged in Attack in Maryland: King Verdict Suspected Motive in Beating of Kensington Man." *Washington Post* (May 5): D1, D14.

Sullivan, Robert (1989) "Firearms Selection Procedures: Corpus Christi's Transition Methodology." *Police Chief* (May): 45-49.

Sullivan, Ronald (1992) "New York Officer Cleared in Killing: Efforts Are Pressed to Avert More Violence in Protests." *New York Times* (September 10): A1.

Sultan, Cynthia, and Phillip Cooper (1979) "Summary of Research on the Police Use of Deadly Force," in U.S. Department of Justice (ed.), *A Community Concern: Police Use of Deadly Force*. Washington, DC: U.S. Government Printing Office.

Suro, Roberto (1992) "Quiet City in Texas Hears Anger of Blacks Over Woman's Death." *New York Times* (August 10): A8.

Sutherland, Edwin H., and Donald R Cressey (1970). *Criminology* (8th rev. ed.) Philadelphia: Lippincott.

Swanton, Bruce (1985) "Shooting of Police Officers: American and Australian Hypotheses." *Police Studies* 8 (4): 231-240.

Swanton, Bruce, and Trish Psaila (1986) *Descriptions of Police Officer Murders and Woundings by Shooting and Bomb Blast, 1964-83*. Canberra, Australia: Australian Institute of Criminology.

Sweeney, Thomas J. (1990) Personal communication between the chief of the Bridgeport, Connecticut Police Department and William A. Geller (August 10).

_____ (1991) Letter to William A. Geller (April 15).

Sweetman, Sherri (1987) *Report on the Attorney General's Conference on Less than Lethal Weapons*. Washington, DC: National Institute of Justice, U.S. Department of Justice.

Sykes, Gary (1990) Personal communication between the director of the Southwestern Law Enforcement Institute and William A. Geller (September 7).

_____ (1991) Personal communication between the director of the Southwestern Law Enforcement Institute and William A. Geller (January 2).

Sykes, R.E., and E.E. Brent (1980) "Regulation of Interaction by Police: A Systems View of Taking Charge." *Criminology* 18 (2, August): 182-197.

_____ (1983) *Policing: A Social Behaviorist Perspective*. New Brunswick, NJ: Rutgers University Press.

Takagi, Paul (1974) "A Garrison State in 'Democratic' Society." *Crime and Social Justice: A Journal of Radical Criminology* 5 (Spring-Summer): 27-33. Reprinted in James J. Fyfe (ed.), *Readings on Police Use of Deadly Force*. Washington, DC: Police Foundation (1982).

_____ (1978) "Issues in the Study of Police Use of Deadly Force." Paper prepared for the annual meeting of the National Black Police Association, Chicago, IL (August). Rockville, MD: National Institute of Justice, National Criminal Justice Reference Service, U.S. Department of Justice.

_____ (1979) "Death by 'Police Intervention'." In U.S. Department of Justice (ed.), *A Community Concern: Police Use of Deadly Force*. Washington, DC: U.S. Government Printing Office (pp. 31-38).

_____ (1979a) "LEAA's Research Solicitation: Police Use of Deadly Force." *Crime and Social Justice* 11 (Spring-Summer): 51-59.

Tange, D.E. (1974) "Model Firearms Training Program for All Police Agencies: Can One be Devised?" Ph.D. dissertation, John Jay College of Criminal Justice.

Taylor, Paul, and Lou Cannon (1992) "Quiet Los Angeles Ends Curfew Today: Schools, Electricity, Buses to Resume." *Washington Post* (May 4): A1, A14.

Temkin, Jody (1988) "Civilians Shot by Police on Decline, Study Says." *Chicago Tribune* (Sept. 4).

Tennessee v. Garner (1985) 471 U.S. 1, 105 S. Ct. 1694, 85 L. Ed. 1. Lower court rulings: *Garner v. Memphis Police Department*, 600 F.2d 52 (6th Cir. 1979); *Garner v. Memphis Police*

Department, Civil Action No. C-75-145, Memorandum Opinion and Order, slip opinion (W.D. Tenn. July 8, 1981); *Garner v. Memphis Police Department*, 710 F.2d 240 (6th Cir. 1983).

Tennessee Advisory Committee to the U.S. Commission on Civil Rights (1978) *Civic Crisis—Civic Challenge: Police Community Relations in Memphis, Tennessee*. Washington, DC: U.S. Government Printing Office.

Tercek, Ray (1992) "Comparative Analysis: Officer-Involved Shootings." Unpublished memorandum from Portland, Oregon Police Bureau training division sergeant Tercek to training division Captain Roy E. Kindrick (May 6).

Teret, Stephen P., Garen J. Wintemute, and Peter L. Beilenson (1992) "The Firearm Fatality Reporting System: A Proposal." *Journal of the American Medical Association* 267 (22, June 10): 3073-3074.

Terkel, Studs (1992) *Race: How Blacks and Whites Think and Feel About the American Obsession*. New York: The New Press.

Terrill, Richard J. (1990) "Alternative Perceptions of Independence in Civilian Oversight." *Journal of Police Science and Administration* 17 (2): 77-83.

Terry, Don (1992) "Basketball Title Spurs Violence Around Chicago: Crowds Loot and Burn on a Warm Evening." *New York Times* (June 16): A8.

Terry, W. Clinton, III (1985) "Police Stress Reconsidered." In W. Clinton Terry, III (ed.), *Policing Society: An Occupational View*. New York: Wiley (pp. 400-413).

Thomas, Bob, and Randy Means (1990) "Objective Reasonableness Standard for Use of Non-Deadly Force Established." *Police Chief* (July): 45-46.

Thomas-Lester, Avis (1992) "Many L.A. Riot Suspects Found to Have Criminal Backgrounds: Records Check Challenges Assumptions About Motives." *Washington Post* (May 20): A2.

Thompson, George J. (1983) *Verbal Judo: Words for Street Survival*. Springfield, IL: Charles C. Thomas.

Thompson, Larry N. (1990) "Remarks: Police Pursuit." *The Police Yearbook 1990*. Arlington, VA: International Association of Chiefs of Police.

Thornberry, Terence P. (1973) "Race, Socioeconomic Status, and Sentencing in the Juvenile Justice System." *Journal of Criminal Law and Criminology* 64: 90-98.

Thurm, Milton (1992) "Chief's Counsel: The Post-Excessive Force Investigation—Its Effect on Your Agency's Civil Liability." *Police Chief* (February): 8, 10.

Ting-Toomey, Stella, and Felipe Korzenny (1991) *Cross-Cultural Interpersonal Communication*. Newbury Park, CA: Sage Publications.

Tobar, Hector (1992) "Sheriff's Probe Transformed Kolts' Views." *Los Angeles Times* (July 27): A1, A18-A19.

Tobar, Hector, and Kenneth Reich (1992) "Probe Finds Pattern of Excess Force, Brutality by Deputies: The Report Commissioned by County Supervisors Calls for Wide Reforms, Including Participation by Civilians; Discipline, Oversight Said to Have Broken Down." *Los Angeles Times* (July 21): A1, A18.

Toch, Hans (1965) "Psychological Consequences of the Police Role." *Police* 10: 22-25. Reprinted in A. Blumberg and A. Niederhoffer (eds.), *The Ambivalent Force: Perspectives on the Police*. New York: Blaisdell (1970).

_____ (1968) Book Review of Marvin E. Wolfgang and F. Ferracuti, *The Subculture of Violence* (1967). *Contemporary Psychology* 13: 329-330.

_____ (1969) *Violent Men: An Inquiry into the Psychology of Violence*. Chicago: Aldine. (2d and 3d rev. eds., 1980, 1984) Cambridge, MA: Schenkman Publishing.

_____ (1969a) "The Police as Minority." *The Nation* (April 21). Reprinted in G. Leinward (ed.), *The Police*. New York: Pocket Books (1972).

_____ (1970a) "Change Through Participation (and Vice Versa)." *Journal of Research in Crime and Delinquency*. 7: 198-206. Reprinted in Y.R. Snibbe and H.M. Snibbe, *The Urban Policeman in Transition*. Springfield, IL: Charles C. Thomas; and in M. O'Neill and K.R. Martensen, *Criminal Justice Group Training*. University Associates (1975).

_____ (1970b) "The Social Psychology of Violence." In E.I. Megargee and J.E. Hokanson (eds.), *The Dynamics of Aggression*. New York: Harper and Row.

_____ (1971a) "Quality Control in Police Work." *Police* 16: 42-44.

_____ (1971b) "Who Left the Bomb in Mistress Murphy's Chowder? A Comment on Violent Youth." *Youth and Society* 2: 367-377.

_____ (1975) "Reducing Violence in the Criminal Justice System." In D. Chappell and J. Monahan (eds.), *Violence and Criminal Justice*. Lexington, MA: D.C. Heath.

_____ (1977) *Peacekeeping: Police, Prisons, and Violence*. Lexington, MA: D.C. Heath and Co.

_____ (1978a) "Normatively Hostile, Purposefully Hostile or Disinterestedly Bloody Angry?" *Journal of Research in Crime and Delinquency* 15: 162-165. Reprinted in *Criminology Review Yearbook*, vol. 2. Beverly Hills: Sage (1980).

_____ (1978b) "Police Morale: Living with Discontent." *Journal of Police Science and Administration*. 6: 249-252.

_____ (1978c) "Struggling with the Violence Morass." *The Humanist* 38: 20-23.

_____ (1978d) Book Review of William Ker Muir, *Police: Streetcorner Politicians* (1977). *Contemporary Psychology* 23: 905-906.

_____ (1980a) "Toward an Interdisciplinary Approach to Criminal Violence." *Journal of Criminal Law and Criminology* 71: 646-653.

_____ (1980b) "Mobilizing Police Expertise." *Annals of the American Academy of Political and Social Science* 452: 53-62. Reprinted in Stojkovic, Klofas, and Kalinich, *The Administration and Management of Criminal Justice Organizations*. Waveland Press (1990).

_____ (1980c) "Evolving a 'Science of Violence': A Propaedeutic Comment." *American Behavioral Scientist*. 23: 653-666.

_____ (1985) "The Catalytic Situations in the Violence Equation." *Journal of Applied Social Psychology* 15: 105-123.

_____ (forthcoming) "The Violence Prone Officer." In William A. Geller and Hans Toch, *And Justice for All: A National Agenda for Understanding and Controlling Police Abuse of Force*. Washington, DC: National Institute of Justice and Police Executive Research Forum (June 1992 tentative title of essay and volume).

Toch, Hans, and K. Adams (1989) *The Disturbed Violent Offender*. New Haven: Yale Univ. Press.

Toch, Hans, and J. Douglas Grant (1990) "The Impermanence of Planned Change." In D.M. Gottfredson and R.V. Clarke (eds.), *Policy and Theory in Criminal Justice*. Farnborough, England: Gower.

_____ (1991) *Police as Problem Solvers*. New York: Plenum.

Toch, Hans, Joan Grant, and J. Douglas Grant (1982) "Police-Citizen Conflict." In V.J. Konecni and E.B. Ebbesen (eds.), *The Criminal Justice System: Social Psychological Analysis*. San Francisco: W.H. Freeman.

Toch, Hans, J. Douglas Grant, and Ray Galvin (1975) *Agents of Change: A Study in Police Reform*. Cambridge, MA: Schenkman (Halsted).

Toch, Hans, and R.M. Schulte (1961) "Readiness to Perceive Violence as a Result of Police Training." *British Journal of Psychology* 52: 389-393. Reprinted in Hans Toch and C.H. Smith, *Social Perception*. Van Nostrand (1968); and in W. Nord (ed.), *Concepts and Controversy in Organizational Behavior*. Goodyear, 1970. Reprinted, New York: Simon and Schuster, 1969.

Toner, Robin (1992) "Los Angeles Riots Are a Warning, Americans Fear: Country Must Deal with Troubles of the Cities, Many Say in Poll." *New York Times* (May 11): A1, A11.

Torres, Jane A. (1992) "Making Sensitivity Training Work." *Police Chief* (August): 32-33.

Trigoureau, Susan (1990) "Revolver vs. Auto: The Endless Debate." *Illinois Police and Sheriffs' News* (publication of the Combined Counties Police Association, Cook County, IL.

Trojanowicz, Robert C. (1991) "Community Policing and Accountability: A Proactive Solution to Police Brutality." Unpublished working paper written for the Harvard Executive Session on Community Policing, Kennedy School of Government, Program in Criminal Justice Policy and Management (November).

_____ (1992) "Director's Corner: Preventing Individual and Systemic Corruption." *Footprints: The Community Policing Newsletter* 4 (1, Winter/Spring): 1.

Trojanowicz, Robert C., and Dennis W. Banas (1985) "Perceptions of Safety: A Comparison of Foot Patrol Versus Motor Patrol Officers." East Lansing, MI: National Neighborhood Foot Patrol Center (subsequently named National Center for Community Policing).

Trojanowicz, Robert C., and Bonnie Bucqueroux (1990) *Community Policing: A Contemporary*

Perspective. Cincinnati: Anderson Publishing.

———— (1991) "Community Policing and the Challenge of Diversity." No. 21 in the Community Policing Series of papers published by the National Center for Community Policing, East Lansing, MI.

Trojanowicz, Susan E. (1992) "Line Police Officers' Attitudes Toward Community Policing." Unpublished master's thesis, Michigan State University.

Trostle, Lawrence C. (1990) "The Force Continuum: From Lethal to Less-than-Lethal Force." *Journal of Contemporary Criminal Justice* 6 (1): 23.

Tsimbinos (1968) "The Justified Use of Deadly Force." *Criminal Law Bulletin* 4: 3-34.

Turco, Ronald N. (1986) "Police Shootings: Psychoanalytic Viewpoints." *International Journal of Offender Therapy and Comparative Criminology* 30 (1): 53-58.

Turner, Maurice T. (1989) "Firearms Selection Procedures: The 9mm Conversion in Washington, DC" *Police Chief* (May): 43.

Uchida, Craig D. (1981) "Controlling Police Use of Deadly Force: Organizational Change in Los Angeles." Unpublished Ph.D. dissertation, School of Criminal Justice, State University of New York-Albany.

Uchida, Craig D., and Laure W. Brooks (1988) "Violence Against the Police: Assaults on Baltimore County Police Officers, 1984-1986: Final Report." (Unpublished report submitted to the National Institute of Justice). College Park, MD: University of Maryland.

Uchida, Craig D., Laure W. Brooks, and C.S. Koper (1990a) "Danger to Police During Domestic Encounters: Assaults on Baltimore County Police, 1984-1986." *Criminal Justice Policy Review.*

Uchida, Craig D., Laure W. Brooks, and M. Wilson (1990b) "The Neighborhood Context of Violence Against the Police." *American Journal of Criminal Justice.*

Uchida, Craig D., Lawrence W. Sherman, and James J. Fyfe (1981) *Police Shootings and the Prosecutor in Los Angeles County: An Evaluation of Operation Rollout.* Washington, DC: Police Foundation.

Uelman, Gerald (1973) "Varieties of Police Policy: A Study of Police Policy Regarding the Use of Deadly Force in Los Angeles County." *Loyola-L.A. Law Review* 6: 1-61.

Ulery, J.A. (1975) "Hollowpoint and Law Enforcement." *Police Chief* 42 (10, October): 26 et seq.

United States Civil Rights Commission (1979) *Police Practices and Civil Rights Hearing Held in Philadelphia, Pennsylvania Volume I, Testimony.* Washington, DC: U.S. Government Printing Office.

———— (1981) *Who's Guarding the Guardians?* Washington, DC: U.S. Government Printing Office.

U.S. Department of Health and Human Services (1991) *Vital Statistics of the United States, 1988.* Hyattsville, Maryland: U.S. Department of Health and Human Services.

U.S. Department of Justice, Community Relations Service (ed.) (1978) *Police Use of Deadly Force: What Police and the Community Can Do About It.* Washington, DC: U.S. Government Printing Office.

———— (1979) *National Consultation on Safety and Force: An Opportunity for Police-Minority Community Cooperation—Summary Report.* Washington, DC: U.S. Government Printing Office.

———— (1986) *Police Use of Deadly Force: A Conciliation Handbook for Citizens and the Police.* Washington, DC: U.S. Government Printing Office.

———— (1987) *Principles of Good Policing: Avoiding Violence Between Police and Citizens.* Washington, DC: U.S. Government Printing Office.

United Way of Chicago (1992) "Vietnamese Association of Illinois: Bridging Cultural, Language, Psychological Gaps." *The Bottom Line* (Chicago United Way newsletter) (Summer): 6.

Upton, James (1985) *Urban Riots in the Twentieth Century.* Bristol, IN.: Wyndam Hall.

USA Today (1992) "Four Heroes Honored: Angelenos Fought for the Fallen." *USA Today* (May 6): 3A.

Uviller, H.R. (1986) "Seizure by Gunshot: The Riddle of the Fleeing Felon." *New York University Review of Law and Social Change* 14: 705-720.

Van Den Berghe, Pierre L. (1974) "Bringing Beasts Back In: Toward a Biosocial Theory of Aggression." *American Sociological Review* 39: 777-788.

Van Maanen, J. (1974) "Working the Street: A Developmental View of Police Behavior." In Herbert

Jacob (ed.), *The Potential for Reform of Criminal Justice*. Newbury Park, CA: Sage.

_____ (1980) "Beyond Account: The Personal Impact of Police Shootings." *Annals of the American Academy of Political and Social Science* 452 (12, November): 145-156.

_____ (1980a) "Street Justice." In Richard J. Lundman (ed.), *Police Behavior: A Sociological Perspective*. New York: Oxford University Press.

Van Raalte, Ronald C. (1990) Direct-mail fundraising form letter dated September 17 on the letterhead of the Law Enforcement Memorial Foundation, Inc., PO Box 72835, Roselle, IL 60172-0835.

Vandall, F.J. (1976) *Police Training for Tough Calls*. Atlanta: Emory University Press.

_____ (1981) "Use of Force in Dealing with Juveniles: Guidelines." *Criminal Law Bulletin* 17 (2, March-April): 124-146.

Vaugh, James (1991) Personal communication between a staff member in the Uniform Crime Reporting Program, Federal Bureau of Investigation and Michael Scott (April 10).

_____ (1992) Personal communication between a staff member in the Uniform Crime Reporting Program, Federal Bureau of Investigation and William A. Geller (July 30).

Vaughn, Joseph B., and Victor E. Kappeler (1986) "A Descriptive Study of Law Enforcement Officers Killed: 1974-1984." Paper presented at the annual meeting of the Academy of Criminal Justice Sciences, Orlando, FL, March 18.

Vera Institute of Justice (1977) *Women on Patrol: A Pilot Study of Police Performance in New York City*. New York: Vera Institute of Justice.

Verbal Judo Institute (no date) "What is Verbal Judo?" Tijeras, NM: Verbal Judo Institute.

Verhovek, Same Howe (1992) "Albany Senate Passes Bill to Give New York City Police New Guns." *New York Times* (May 29): A16.

_____ (1992a) "Foes of Police-Gun Bill Say Blocking Vote May Be Only Hope." *New York Times* (May 30): 12.

Villa, B.J. (1981) "Management Control of Fatigue Among Field Police Officers." *Journal of Police Stress* (Spring): 38-41.

Vogel, Kenneth (1990) "I'm Hit, Help Me!" *Law and Order* (November): 83-84.

Volanti, John M. (1983) "Stress Patterns in Police Work: A Longitudinal Study." *Journal of Police Science and Administration* 11 (2): 211-216.

Volanti, John M., John E. Vena, and James R. Marshall (1986) "Disease Risk and Mortality Among Police Officers: New Evidence and Contributing Factors." *Journal of Police Science and Administration* 14 (1): 17-23.

Waddington, Peter A.J. (1983) *Are the Police Fair?* (Home Office Research Paper 2) London, England: Social Affairs Unit, Home Office.

_____ (1984) "Black Crime, the 'Racist' Police and Fashionable Compassion." In D. Anderson (ed.), *The Kindness That Kills*. London, England: SPCK.

_____ (1988) *Arming an Unarmed Police: Policy and Practice in the [London] Metropolitan Police*. London: Police Foundation [of the United Kingdom].

_____ (1991) *The Strong Arm of the Law*. Oxford, England: Clarendon Press.

Wade, Gary E. (1990) "Training: Undercover Negotiating—Flashroll Management." *Police Chief* (November): 48-51.

Waegel, William B. (1984a) "The Use of Lethal Force by Police: The Effect of Statutory Change." *Crime and Delinquency* 30 (1) 121-40.

_____ (1984b) "How Police Justify the Use of Deadly Force." *Social Problems* (December) 144-155.

Wagner, M., and Brzeczek, Richard J. (1983) "Alcoholism and Suicide: A Fatal Connection." *FBI Law Enforcement Bulletin* (August): 8-15.

Waite (1955) "Some Inadequacies in the Law of Arrest." *Michigan Law Review* 29: 448, 463-468.

Wakin, Daniel J. (1990) "Violence Erupts Over Teen's Death: A Town [Teaneck, NJ] That Prides Itself on Ethnic Diversity is Torn Apart by Racial Strife." *San Diego Times-Advocate* (April 12): A4.

Walker, Samuel (1976) "Police Professionalism: Another Look at the Issues." *Journal of Sociology and Social Welfare* 3 (6, July): 702.

_____ (1977) *A Critical History of Police Reform: The Emergence of Professionalism*. Lexington, MA: Lexington Books.

_____ (1985) "Racial Minority and Female Employment in Policing: The Implications of 'Glacial' Change." *Crime and Delinquency* 31 (4) 555-572.

_____ (1985a) "Setting the Standards: The Efforts and Impact of Blue Ribbon Commissions on the Police." In William A. Geller (ed.), *Police Leadership in America: Crisis and Opportunity.* New York: Praeger.

_____ (1990) "Beyond the Supreme Court: Alternate Paths to the Control of Police Behavior." *American Journal of Criminal Justice* 14: 189-204.

Walker, Samuel, and Vic W. Bumphus (1991) "Civilian Review of the Police: A National Survey of the 50 Largest Cities, 1991." Omaha, NE: Department of Criminal Justice, University of Nebraska at Omaha.

Walker, Samuel, and Lorie A. Fridell (1989) "The Impact of *Tennessee v. Garner* on Deadly Force Policy." A paper presented at the annual meeting of the American Society of Criminology, Reno, NV, November 10.

Wallen, L.M. (1976) "Professional and Bureaucratic Processes of Organizational Central Internal Discipline in the Los Angeles Police Department." Ph.D. dissertation, University of California.

Warner, John (1992) "Guest Commentary: The Improper Use of Deadly Force in Arrest Situations and Some Needed Remedies." *Crime Control Digest* (July 6): 1-3.

Warren, Susan (1992) "Second King Trial Raises Double Jeopardy Flag." *Chicago Tribune* (May 15): section 1A, pp. 23-24.

Washington Crime News Services (1982) "Commission Approves 'Defense of Life' Policy on Police Use of Force." *Crime Control Digest* (January 25).

Washington Post, The (1992) "Local Shooting, King Case Spark Clash in Toronto." *Washington Post* (May 5): A14.

Wasserman, Robert, and Mark H. Moore (1988) "Values in Policing." Part of the *Perspectives on Policing* series. Washington, DC: National Institute of Justice, U.S. Department of Justice.

Weaver, Gary (1992) "Law Enforcement in a Culturally Diverse Society." *FBI Law Enforcement Bulletin* (September): 1-7.

Weiner, Neil (1991) "Police Spark Riots." *Background Briefing: A Weekly News Feature.* Unpublished information sheet, prepared in Chicago, circulated to news industry (May 15).

Weisbourd, David and Craig Uchida, eds. (1992) *Police Innovation and the Rule of Law.* New York: Springer.

Weisel, Deborah Lamm (1990) *Tackling Drug Problems in Public Housing: A Guide for Police.* Washington, DC: Police Executive Research Forum.

Westley, William A. (1951) "Violence and the Police: A Sociological Study of Law, Custom, and Morality." (Unpublished Ph.D. dissertation). MIT, Cambridge, MA.

_____ (1970) *Violence and the Police: A Sociological Study of Law, Custom, and Morality.* Cambridge, MA: MIT Press.

Whetsel, John, and J.W. Bennett (1992) "Pursuits: A Deadly Force Issue." *Police Chief* (February): 30-31.

Whitaker, Charles (1992) "The Rodney King Wake-Up Call: Which Way America?" *Ebony* (July): 116-120.

Whitaker, Gordon P. (1982) "What is Patrol Work?" *Police Studies* 4: 13-22.

Whittingham, Michael D. (1984) "Police/Public Homicide and Fatality Risks in Canada: A Current Assessment—Serving and Being Protected." *Canadian Police Chief* 3 (10): 4-8.

Wiese, Bill (1991) Personal communications between the chief of Inspectional Services, New York City Transit Police Department and William A. Geller (May 1, 28).

Williams, C. (1987) "Peacetime Combat: Treating and Preventing Delayed Stress Reactions in Police Officers." In *Post-Traumatic Stress Disorders: A Handbook for Clinicians.* Washington, DC: Disabled American Veterans.

Williams, Gerald (1991) "Statement of Gerald Williams, President, Police Executive Research Forum, on Police Brutality Before the House Judiciary Subcommittee on Civil and Constitutional Rights" (April 17). (Available through Police Executive Research Forum).

Williams, Hubert (1991) "External Resources." In William A. Geller (ed.), *Local Government Police Management* (3d rev. ed.). Washington, DC: International City Management Association.

Williams, Hubert, and Patrick V. Murphy (1990) "The Evolving Strategy of Police: A Minority

View." No. 13 in the *Perspectives on Policing* series. Washington, DC: National Institute of Justice, U.S. Department of Justice (January).

Williams, Willie (1991) "Framing the Issues." Keynote address to a conference, sponsored by the Police Executive Research Forum and the National Organization of Black Law Enforcement Executives, on "Unfinished Business: Racial Issues Facing Policing," Arlington, VA (September 23).

Wilson, George (1991) Interview of defense analyst Wilson by a reporter on National Public Radio (February 25).

Wilson, James Q. (1970) "Movie Cops—Romantic Vs. Real." In Arthur Neiderhoffer and Abraham S. Blumberg (eds.), *The Ambivalent Force: Perspectives on the Police*. Waltham, MA: Xerox College Publishing.

_____ (1980) "Police Use of Deadly Force." *FBI Law Enforcement Bulletin* 49 (8, August): 16-21.

Wilson, Laura Ann, Gregory C. Brunk, and C. Kenneth Meyer (1990) "Situational Effects in Police Officer Assaults: The Case of Patrol Unit Size." *Police Journal* 63 (3): 260-271.

Wilson, William Julius (1992) "Imagine Life Without a Future." *Los Angeles Times* (May 6): B15.

Wines, Michael (1992) "Bush Made to Flee A Rally in Panama As Protest Erupts: Shots and Tear Gas Fired." *New York Times* (June 12): A1, A7.

Winter, S.L. (1986) "*Tennessee v. Garner* and the Democratic Practice of Judicial Review." *New York University Review of Law and Social Change* 14: 679-704.

Witkin, Gordon, with Ted Gest and Dorian Friedman (1990) "Cops Under Fire." *U.S. News and World Report* (December 3): 33-44.

Wolfgang, Marvin E., and Franco Ferracuti (1967) *The Subculture of Violence: Towards an Integrated Theory in Criminology*. New York and London: Tavistock.

_____ (1978) "Subculture of Violence." *International Annals of Criminology* 15: 27-48.

Wolfgang, Marvin E., and Margaret A. Zahn (1983) "Homicide: Behavioral Aspects." In Sanford H. Kadish (ed.), *Encyclopedia of Crime and Justice*, vol. 2. New York: Free Press (pp. 849-855).

Woollons, Norman (1992) "Re-Arming the British Police." *Law and Order* (July): 109-111.

Wright, E.J. (1978) *Police Handguns and Deadly Force: A Special Report to the Governor of the State of New York, Hon. Hugh L. Carey, February 1976*. Albany, NY: New York State Division of Criminal Justice Services.

Wright, J.D., and P.H. Rossi (1981) *Weapons, Crime, and Violence in America: Executive Summary*. Washington, DC: National Institute of Justice, U.S. Department of Justice.

_____ (1985) *The Armed Criminal in America: A Survey of Incarcerated Felons*. Washington, DC: U.S. Government Printing Office.

Wukitsch, David J. (1983) "Survey of the Law Governing Police Use of Deadly Force." *New York State Bar Journal* (January).

Young, W.M. (1978) "Official Repression and Violent Crime." Unpublished Ph.D. dissertation, University of Southern California.

Young, Steve (1992) "An Introduction to V_{50} Testing for Police Body Armor." *Crime Control Digest* (March 23): 1, 7-9.

Yount, August, and T. O'Rourke (1978) "Breaking the Ice: A Study of Accidental Discharges Among Illinois Police Officers." *Police Chief* (April): 72-76.

Zacharias, Louis (1991) Personal communication between Zacharias, a sergeant in the Kansas City, Missouri Police Department Internal Affairs Division and William A. Geller (May 6).

Zamichow, Nora (1992) "Were All Deaths in Toll Really Riot-Related?: Some Authorities Believe That Several of the 58 Slayings Listed as Part of the Violence May Have Had Other Causes; Coroner's Officer Stands by the Numbers." *Los Angeles Times* (May 6): B1, B12.

Zane, J. Peder (1992) "Weapons in Question: Glock Versus Old .38." *New York Times* (May 31): section 1, p. 23.

Zeichner, Irving B. (1990) "Inside Justice." *Law and Order* (October): 10.

Zeling, M. (1986) "Research Needs in the Study of Post-Shooting Trauma." In James T. Reese and Harvey A. Goldstein (eds.), *Psychological Services for Law Enforcement*. Washington, DC: Federal Bureau of Investigation (pp. 409-410).

Zimring, Franklin E., and Gordon Hawkins (1983) "Crime Commissions." In *Encyclopedia of Crime and Justice*, vol. 1. New York: The Free Press (pp. 353-357).

APPENDIX A:

STANDARDS ON USE OF DEADLY FORCE OF THE COMMISSION ON ACCREDITATION FOR LAW EN-FORCEMENT AGENCIES

1.3 Use of Force

1.3.1 *A written directive states personnel will use only the force necessary to effect lawful objectives.*

Commentary: The directive should encompass the use of all types and kinds of force (whether deadly or nondeadly) and all types and kinds of weapons. The directive may be issued in the form of a policy, rule, or order.
(M M M M M M)[1]

1.3.2 *A written directive states that an officer may use deadly force only when the officer reasonably believes that the action is in defense of human life, including the officer's own life, or in defense of any person in immediate danger of serious physical injury.*

Commentary: The purpose of this standard is to provide officers with guidance in the use of force in life-and-death situations and to prevent unnecessary loss of life. Definitions of "reasonable belief" and "serious physical injury" should be included in the directive.
(M M M M M)

1.3.3 *A written directive specifies that use of deadly force against a "fleeing felon" must meet the conditions required by standard 1.3.2.*

Commentary: A "fleeing felon" should not be presumed to pose an immediate threat to life in the absence of actions that would lead one to believe such is the case, such as a previously demonstrated threat to or wanton disregard for human life. **(M M M M M M)**

1.3.5 *A written directive governs the discharge of "warning" shots.*

Commentary: Warning shots pose a danger to officers and citizens alike and should not be used. **(M M M M M M)**

At its November 16-18, 1990, meeting in St. Paul, Minnesota, the Commission on Accreditation adopted and agreed to circulate to all accredited agencies for comment the commentary to standard 1.3.5 that appears above (Bentley 1990: 4). After being duly processed according to CALEA procedures, the commentary was adopted. See our discussion in Chapter 5 of this volume of an effort made at that same commission meeting by a police chief from Georgia to persuade CALEA to relax its defense-of-life standard or grant a blanket exemption from compliance with it to all police departments in Georgia seeking accreditation. As this volume went to press in July 1992, no relief from compliance with the deadly force standards had been granted to police departments in Georgia or elsewhere seeking accreditation.

---

[1] The M's are a symbol used by the Commission to indicate that compliance with the indicated standard is mandatory for a department wishing accreditation (Commission on Accreditation for Law Enforcement Agencies 1988: xiii).

APPENDIX B:

IACP MODEL DEADLY FORCE POLICY

Note: "This Model Policy on Use of Force was prepared under funding by the U.S. Department of Justice's Bureau of Justice Assistance under cooperative agreement NO. 87-SN-CX-K077 to the International Association of Chiefs of Police. Points of view or opinions stated in this document are the result of work performed by the IACP/BJA National Law Enforcement Policy Center and do not necessarily reflect the official position of the U.S. Department of Justice or the International Association of Chiefs of Police" (Higginbotham 1991).

USE OF FORCE

Model Policy

Effective Date **February 1, 1989**		*Number*
Subject **Use of Force**		
Reference **Deadly Force, Nondeadly Force, Firearms, Non-Lethal Weapons**	*Special Instructions*	
Distribution	*Reevaluation Date* **January 31, 1990**	*No. Pages*

I. PURPOSE

The purpose of this policy is to provide police officers with guidelines on the use of deadly and nondeadly force.

II. POLICY

This department recognizes and respects the value and special integrity of each human life. In vesting police officers with the lawful authority to use force to protect the public welfare, a careful balancing of all human interests is required. Therefore, it is the policy of this department that police officers shall use only that force that is reasonably necessary to effectively bring an incident under control, while protecting the lives of the officer or another.

III. DEFINITIONS

A. *Deadly force:* Any use of force that is likely to cause death or serious bodily harm.
B. *Nondeadly force:* Any use of force other than that which is considered deadly force.

III. PROCEDURES

A. Parameters for use of deadly force:
1. Police officers are authorized to fire their weapons in order to:
   a. Protect the police officer or others from what is reasonably believed to be an immediate threat of death or serious bodily harm; or,
   b. Prevent the escape of a fleeing felon whom the officer has probable cause to believe will pose a significant threat to human life should escape occur.
2. Before using a firearm, police officers shall identify themselves and state their intent to shoot, where feasible.

3. A police officer may also discharge a weapon under the following circumstances:
   a. During range practice or competitive sporting events.
   b. To destroy an animal that represents a threat to public safety, or as a humanitarian measure where the animal is seriously injured.
4. Police officers shall adhere to the following restrictions when their weapon is exhibited:
   a. Except for maintenance or during training, police officers shall not draw or exhibit their firearm unless circumstances create reasonable cause to believe that it may be necessary to use the weapon in conformance with this policy.
   b. Warning shots are prohibited.
   c. Police officers shall not fire their weapons at or from a moving vehicle.
   d. Firearms shall not be discharged when it appears likely that an innocent person may be injured.

B. Parameters for use of nondeadly force:
1. Where deadly force is not authorized, officers should assess the incident in order to determine which nondeadly technique or weapon will best de-escalate the incident and bring it under control in a safe manner.
2. Police officers are authorized to use department-approved nondeadly force techniques and issued equipment for resolution of incidents, as follows:
   a. To protect themselves or another from physical harm; or
   b. To restrain or subdue a resistant individual; or

This Model Use of Force Policy was developed under the auspices of the Advisory Board of the IACP/BJA National Law Enforcement Policy Center. A Concepts and Issues paper discussing key decision points and controversial issues pertaining to Use of Force may be purchased for $5.25 plus $1.00 for postage and handling by sending your order to the IACP/BJA National Law Enforcement Policy Center, 1110 North Glebe Road, Suite 200, Arlington, VA 22201.

c. To bring an unlawful situation safely and effectively under control.

C. Training and qualifications:
1. Deadly weapons:
   a. While on-and off-duty, police officers shall carry only weapons and ammunition authorized by and registered with the department.
   b. Authorized weapons are those with which the police officer has qualified and received departmental training on proper and safe usage, and that are registered and comply with departmental specifications.
   c. The police department shall schedule regular training and qualification sessions for duty, off-duty and specialized weapons, which will be graded on a pass/fail basis.
   d. Police officers who fail to receive a passing score with their duty weapon(s) in accordance with department testing procedures shall be relieved of their police powers and immediately reassigned to nonenforcement duties.
   e. A police officer shall not be permitted to carry any weapon with which he has not been able to qualify during the most recent qualification period.
   f. A police officer who has taken extended leave or suffered an illness or injury that could affect his use of firearms ability will be required to requalify before returning to enforcement duties.
2. Nondeadly force weapons and methods:
   a. A police officer is not permitted to use a nondeadly weapon unless qualified in its proficient use as determined by training procedures.
   b. The following nondeadly weapons are authorized: _____
   (Department should insert its own list here.)

D. Reporting uses of force:
1. A written report prepared according to departmental procedures will be required in the following situations:
   a. When a firearm is discharged outside of the firing range.
   b. When a use of force results in death or injury.
   c. When a nonlethal weapon is used on a person.
2. A supervisor will be immediately summoned to the scene and will comply with investigative procedures as required by the department in the following situations:
   a. When a firearm is discharged outside of the firing range.
   b. When a use of force results in death or serious injury.
   c. When a subject complains that an injury has been inflicted.

E. Departmental response:
1. Deadly force incident
   a. Where a police officer's use of force causes death, the officer shall be placed on administrative leave after completing all internal investigative requirements, and until it is determined by a mental health professional that the police officer is ready to return to duty.
   b. The department shall conduct both an administrative and criminal investigation of the incident.
2. Administrative review of critical incidents:
   a. All reported uses of force will be reviewed by the appropriate departmental authority to determine whether:
      (1) Departmental rules, policy or procedures were violated;
      (2) The relevant policy was clearly understandable and effective to cover the situation;
      (3) Department training is currently adequate.
   b. All findings of policy violations or training inadequacies shall be reported to the appropriate unit for resolution and/or discipline.
   c. All use of force incident reports shall be retained as required by state law.
   d. There will be a regular review of use of force incidents by the appropriate departmental authority to ascertain training and policy needs.
   e. An annual summary report of use of force incidents will be published and made available to the public.

By order off:

_____
Signature of Chief of Police

APPENDIX C:

STUDIES CONTAINING DATA ON POLICE-INVOLVED SHOOTINGS IN SPECIFIED MAJOR AMERICAN JURISDICTIONS

Jurisdiction(s) Studied	Years	Published Study (Full Cites in References)
Akron	1970-83 1970-84 1975-79 1985-89	Matulia (1985) Sherman and Cohn (1986) Matulia (1982) Geller and Scott (this book)
Albuquerque	1970-83 1970-84 1975-79 1985-89	Matulia (1985) Sherman and Cohn (1986) Matulia (1982) Geller and Scott (this book)
Alexandria, VA	1989-90	Jennings (1991a, 1991b)
Arlington Co., VA	1989-90	Jennings (1991a, 1991b)
Atlanta	1970-83 1970-84 1971-78 1971-78 1971-78 1975-79 1980-91	Matulia (1985) Sherman and Cohn (1986) Sherman (1983) Blumberg (1981) Fyfe (1988b) Matulia (1982) Geller and Scott (this book)
Austin	1970-83 1970-84 1975-79 1985-89	Matulia (1985) Sherman and Cohn (1986) Matulia (1982) Geller and Scott (this book)
Baltimore	1970-83 1970-84 1975-79 1985-89 1987-90	Matulia (1985) Sherman and Cohn (1986) Matulia (1982) Geller and Scott (this book) St. Louis Police Dept. (1992)
Baltimore County (Baltimore County Police Department)	1984-86	Uchida and Brooks (1988) Uchida, et al. (1990a) Uchida, et al. (1990b)

Jurisdiction(s) Studied	Years	Published Study (Full Cites in References)
Birmingham, AL	?	Binder, et al. (1982)
	1970-83	Matulia (1985)
	1970-84	Sherman and Cohn (1986)
	1973-74	Milton, et al. (1977)
	1973-74	Meyer (1980a)
	1975-79	Matulia (1982)
	1977-80	Binder and Fridell (1984)
	1977-80	Fridell and Binder (1989)
	1985-89	Geller and Scott (this book)
Boston	1950-60	Robin (1963)
	1970-73	Boston Police Dept. (1974)
	1970-83	Matulia (1985)
	1970-84	Sherman and Cohn (1986)
	1975-79	Matulia (1982)
Buffalo	1970-83	Matulia (1985)
	1970-84	Sherman and Cohn (1986)
	1975-79	Matulia (1982)
Charlotte	1970-83	Matulia (1985)
	1970-84	Sherman and Cohn (1986)
	1975-79	Matulia (1982)
	1985-89	Geller and Scott (this book)
Chicago	1950-60	Robin (1963)
	1950-60	Sultan and Cooper (1979)
	1969-70	Harding and Fahey (1973)
	1969-70	Knoohuizen et al. (1972)
	1970-83	Matulia (1985)
	1970-84	Sherman and Cohn (1986)
	1972-92	Geller and Scott (this book)
	1974-78	Geller and Karales (1981a, 1981b, 1982)
	1974-78	Geller (1986)
	1974-88	Geller (1988, 1989)
	1974-88	O'Connor (1988)
	1974-88	Temkin (1988)
	1975-77	Nowicki and Stahl (1978)
	1975-79	Matulia (1982)
	1977-79	Wagner and Brzeczek (1983)
	1970s-90	Reardon and O'Connor (1991)
	1970s-90	O'Connor (1991)
	1985-89	O'Connell (1990)
	1986-90	O'Connell (1990a)
	1982-92	Goering and McRoberts (1992)
Suburban Chicago	1985-92	Goering and McRoberts (1992)

Jurisdiction(s) Studied	Years	Published Study (Full Cites in References)
Cincinnati	1970-83 1970-84 1975-79 1979 1985-89	Matulia (1985) Sherman and Cohn (1986) Matulia (1982) Cohen (1979) Geller and Scott (this book)
Cleveland	1970-83 1970-84 1975-79 1985-89 1987-90	Matulia (1985) Sherman and Cohn (1986) Matulia (1982) Geller and Scott (this book) St. Louis Police Dept. (1992)
Columbus, OH	1970-83 1970-84 1975-79 1985-89	Matulia (1985) Sherman and Cohn (1986) Matulia (1982) Geller and Scott (this book)
Cook County, IL	1926-27	Robin (1963)
Dallas	? 1970-83 1970-84 1970-91 1975-79 1985-89 1986-90 1985-87	Dallas Police Dept. (1974) Matulia (1985) Sherman and Cohn (1986) Dallas Police Dept. (1990, 1991) and Geller and Scott (this book) Matulia (1982) O'Connell (1990) O'Connell (1990a) Alpert (1987b)
Denver	1970-83 1970-84 1975-79 1985-89	Matulia (1985) Sherman and Cohn (1986) Matulia (1982) Geller and Scott (this book)
Detroit	7/70-3/71 1970-83 1970-84 1973-74 1973-74 1974 1975-79 1976-81 1976-81 1985-89 1986-90 1985-89 1987-90	Knoohuizen, et al. (1972) Matulia (1985) Sherman and Cohn (1986) Milton et al. (1977) Meyer (1980a) Sultan and Cooper (1979) Matulia (1982) Horvath and Donahue (1982) Horvath (1987) O'Connell (1990) O'Connell (1990a) Geller and Scott (this book) St. Louis Police Dept. (1992)
El Paso, TX	1970-83 1970-84 1975-79 1985-89	Matulia (1985) Sherman and Cohn (1986) Matulia (1982) Geller and Scott (this book)

Jurisdiction(s) Studied	Years	Published Study (Full Cites in References)
Fairfax Co., VA	1989-90	Jennings (1991a, 1991b)
Fort Worth	1970-83 1970-84 1975-79 1985-89	Matulia (1985) Sherman and Cohn (1986) Matulia (1982) Geller and Scott (this book)
Honolulu	1970-83 1970-84 1975-79 1985-89	Matulia (1985) Sherman and Cohn (1986) Matulia (1982) Geller and Scott (this book)
Houston	1970-83 1970-84 1975-79 1980-91 1985-89 1986-90	Matulia (1985) Sherman and Cohn (1986) Matulia (1982) Geller and Scott (this book) O'Connell (1990) O'Connell (1990a)
Indianapolis	1970-83 1970-84 1973-74 1973-74 1975-79 1985-89	Matulia (1985) Sherman and Cohn (1986) Milton et al. (1977) Meyer (1980a) Matulia (1982) Geller and Scott (this book)
Jacksonville	1970-83 1970-84 1975-79 1985-89	Matulia (1985) Sherman and Cohn (1986) Matulia (1982) Geller and Scott (this book)
Jersey City	1970-84	Sherman and Cohn (1986)
Kansas City, MO	1969-78 1969-78 1970-83 1970-84 1972-78 1972-78 1972-78 1972-91 1973-74 1973-74 1975-79	Blumberg (1981) Fyfe (1988b) Matulia (1985) Sherman and Cohn (1986) Sherman (1983) Blumberg (1983, 1989) Sherman and Blumberg (1981) Geller and Scott (this book) Milton et al. (1977) Meyer (1980a) Matulia (1982)
Long Beach	1970-83 1970-84 1975-79 1977-81 1985-89	Matulia (1985) Sherman and Cohn (1986) Matulia (1982) Uchida, et al. (1981) Geller and Scott (this book)

Jurisdiction(s) Studied	Years	Published Study (Full Cites in References)
Los Angeles City	1915-91	Gates and Shah (1992)
	1970-76 &	
	1977-88	Dash and Reiser (1978)
	1970, 1975,	
	1980, 1987	Josephson and Reiser (1990)
	1877-1981	Uchida (1981)
	7/70-3/71	Knoohuizen, et al. (1972)
	1970-83	Matulia (1985)
	1970-84	Sherman and Cohn (1986)
	1974-78	Geller (1986)
	1974-79	Meyer (1980a, 1980b)
	1975-79	Matulia (1982)
	1977-81	Uchida et al. (1981)
	1980-91	LAPD (1989, 1991) and Geller and Scott (this book)
	1985-89	O'Connell (1990)
	1986-90	O'Connell (1990a)
	1986-91	Independent Comm. on LAPD (1991: 37)
	1987-90	St. Louis Police Dept. (1992)
	1991	Berger and Braun (1991)
Los Angeles County	1970-71	Uelman (1973a)
	1975-78	Meyer (1980a)
	1977-81	Uchida et al. (1981)
	1979-91	Katz (1991)
	1986-90	*Crime Control Digest* (1991n)
	1986-4/1/92	Kolts, et al. (1992: 139) and *Law Enforcement News* (1992g: 1)
Louisville	1970-83	Matulia (1985)
	1970-84	Sherman and Cohn (1986)
	1975-79	Matulia (1982)
	1985-89	Geller and Scott (this book)
Memphis	1969-74 &	Sparger and Giacopassi (1992), excerpted
	1980-89	in *Crime Control Digest* (1992d)
	1969-74	ACLU (1992: 8)
	1969-76	Fyfe (1982)
	1970-83	Matulia (1985)
	1970-84	Sherman and Cohn (1986)
	1975-79	Matulia (1982)
	1969-76	Geller and Scott (this book)
Metro-Dade Co., FL	1980-91	Geller and Scott (this book)
	1984-88	Alpert (1989a)

Jurisdiction(s) Studied	Years	Published Study (Full Cites in References)
Miami	1970-83	Matulia (1985)
	1970-84	Sherman and Cohn (1986)
	1975-79	Matulia (1982)
	1977-80	Binder, et al. (1982)
	1977-80	Fridell and Binder (1989)
	1980-86	Alpert (1989b)
	1985-89	Geller and Scott (this book)
Milwaukee	1970-83	Matulia (1985)
	1970-84	Sherman and Cohn (1986)
	1975-79	Matulia (1982)
	1985-89	Geller and Scott (this book)
Minneapolis	1970-83	Matulia (1985)
	1970-84	Sherman and Cohn (1986)
	1975-79	Matulia (1982)
	1985-89	Geller and Scott (this book)
Montgomery Co., MD	1989-90	Jennings (1991a, 1991b)
Nashville	1970-83	Matulia (1985)
	1970-84	Sherman and Cohn (1986)
	1975-79	Matulia (1982)
	1985-89	Geller and Scott (this book)
New Orleans	1800s	Rousey (1984)
	1970-83	Matulia (1985)
	1970-84	Sherman and Cohn (1986)
	1975-79	Matulia (1982)

APPENDIX C: STUDIES OF CITIES **487**

Jurisdiction(s) Studied	Years	Published Study (Full Cites in References)
New York City (City Police Dept.)	?	Blumberg (1983)
	1844-1978	Margarita (1980a)
	1857-58	Geller and Karales (1981a)
	1857-58	Geller (1986)
	1970	NYC Police Academy (1971)
	1970	Burnham (1971)
	7/7-3/71	Knoohuizen, et al. (1972)
	1970-73	Jenkins and Faison (1974)
	1970-73	Clark (1974)
	1970-83	Matulia (1985)
	1970-84	Sherman and Cohn (1986)
	1971-75	Fyfe (1978, 1979b, 1980a, 1980b, 1981a, 1981b, 1981c, 1981d, 1988a, 1988b)
	1971-75	Sherman (1983)
	1971-75	Meyer (1980a)
	1971-91	Pilant (1992: 1)
	1972-90	*Law Enforcement News* (1990a)
	1975-91	Matulia (1982)
	1977	O'Neill (1979)
	1980-91	Cerar (1989, 1990, 1991) and Geller and Scott (this book)
	1981, 1989	Witkin, et al. (1990: 38)
	1985-89	O'Connell (1990)
	1986-90	O'Connell (1990a)
	1986-91	*Law Enforcement News* (1991d)
	1989	Malcolm (1990a)
New York City (Transit Police)	1980-90	Bratton (1990a)
	1985-89	Geller and Scott (this book)
Newark	1970-83	Matulia (1985)
	1970-84	Sherman and Cohn (1986)
	1975-79	Matulia (1982)
	1977-80	Binder, et al. (1982)
	1977-80	Binder and Fridell (1984)
	1977-80	Fridell and Binder (1989)
	7/1/86-12/31/86	McMurray (1990)
Norfolk	1970-83	Matulia (1985)
	1970-84	Sherman and Cohn (1986)
	1975-79	Matulia (1982)
	1985-89	Geller and Scott (this book)

Jurisdiction(s) Studied	Years	Published Study (Full Cites in References)
Oakland	1968-70	Gain (1971)
	1970-83	Matulia (1985)
	1970-84	Sherman and Cohn (1986)
	1973-74	Milton et al. (1977)
	1973-74	Meyer (1980a)
	1974	Sultan and Cooper (1979)
	1975-79	Matulia (1982)
	1977-80	Binder, et al. (1982)
	1977-80	Binder and Fridell (1984)
	1977-80	Fridell and Binder (1989)
	1985-89	Geller and Scott (this book)
Oklahoma City	1970-83	Matulia (1985)
	1970-84	Sherman and Cohn (1986)
	1975-79	Matulia (1982)
	1985-89	Geller and Scott (this book)
Omaha	1970-83	Matulia (1985)
	1970-84	Sherman and Cohn (1986)
	1975-79	Matulia (1982)
	1975-84	Walker and Fridell (1989)
	1985-89	Geller and Scott (this book)
Philadelphia	1950-60	Robin (1963)
	1960-70	Nat'l Minority Advisory Council (1978)
	7/70-3/71	Knoohuizen, et al. (1972)
	1970-74	Pub. Int. Law Center of Phila. (1975)
	1970-78	Waegel (1984b)
	1970-83	Matulia (1985)
	1970-83	Fyfe (1988a)
	1970-84	Sherman and Cohn (1986)
	1971-75	Fyfe (1988a, 1988b)
	1971-78	Pub. Int. Law Center of Phila. (1979)
	1971-78	Fyfe (1988)
	1975-78	Fyfe (1988a, 1988b)
	1975-79	Matulia (1982)
	1970s, 1980	Blumberg (1989)
	1985-91	Geller and Scott (this book)
	1985-89	O'Connell (1990)
	1986-90	O'Connell (1990a)
	1989-90	*Crime Control Digest* (1990e)
Phoenix	1970-83	Matulia (1985)
	1970-84	Sherman and Cohn (1986)
	1975-79	Matulia (1982)
	1985-89	O'Connell (1990)
	1985-89	Geller and Scott (this book)
	1986-90	O'Connell (1990a)
Pittsburgh	1970-83	Matulia (1985)
	1970-84	Sherman and Cohn (1986)
	1975-79	Matulia (1982)

Jurisdiction(s) Studied	Years	Published Study (Full Cites in References)
Portland, OR	1970-83	Matulia (1985)
	1970-84	Sherman and Cohn (1986)
	1973-74	Milton et al. (1977)
	1973-74	Meyer (1980a)
	1975-79	Matulia (1982)
	1983-92	Geller and Scott (this book)
	1988-91	Snell (1992b)
	1983-92	Kindrick (1992)
	1983-92	Tercek (1992)
Prince George's Co., MD	1989-90	Jennings (1991a, 1991b)
Providence, RI	1971-79	Berman, et al. (1979)
Rochester, NY	1970-83	Matulia (1985)
	1970-84	Sherman and Cohn (1986)
	1975-79	Matulia (1982)
	1985-89	Geller and Scott (this book)
Sacramento	1970-83	Matulia (1985)
	1970-84	Sherman and Cohn (1986)
	1975-79	Matulia (1982)
	1985-89	Geller and Scott (this book)
St. Louis	1970-83	Matulia (1985)
	1970-84	Sherman and Cohn (1986)
	1975-79	Matulia (1982)
	1984-91	Geller and Scott (this book)
	1987-91	St. Louis Police Dept. (1992)
St. Paul	1970-83	Matulia (1985)
	1970-84	Sherman and Cohn (1986)
	1975-79	Matulia (1982)
	1985-89	Geller and Scott (this book)
San Antonio	1970-83	Matulia (1985)
	1970-84	Sherman and Cohn (1986)
	1975-79	Matulia (1982)
	1985-89	O'Connell (1990)
	1985-89	Geller and Scott (this book)
	1986-90	O'Connell (1990a)
San Diego	1970-83	Matulia (1985)
	1970-84	Sherman and Cohn (1986)
	1975-79	Matulia (1982)
	1980-91	Geller and Scott (this book)
	1984-90	Petrillo (1990c)
	1985-89	O'Connell (1990)
	1985-90	Petrillo (1990a)
	1986-90	O'Connell (1990a)

Jurisdiction(s) Studied	Years	Published Study (Full Cites in References)
San Francisco	1970-83 1970-84 1975-79 1985-89	Matulia (1985) Sherman and Cohn (1986) Matulia (1982) Geller and Scott (this book)
San Jose	1970-83 1970-84 1975-79 1976-79 1985-89	Matulia (1985) Sherman and Cohn (1986) Matulia (1982) Pilla (1980) Geller and Scott (this book)
Seattle	1970-83 1970-84 1975-79 1985-89 1987-90	Matulia (1985) Sherman and Cohn (1986) Matulia (1982) Geller and Scott (this book) St. Louis Police Dept. (1992)
Tallahassee	1990	Doerner (1991); *Law and Order* (1992c)
Tampa	1970-83 1970-84 1975-79 1985-89 1988	Matulia (1985) Sherman and Cohn (1986) Matulia (1982) Geller and Scott (this book) Stanford and Mowry (1990: 246)
Toledo	1970-83 1970-84 1975-79 1985-89	Matulia (1985) Sherman and Cohn (1986) Matulia (1982) Geller and Scott (this book)
Tucson	1970-83 1970-84 1975-79 1985-89	Matulia (1985) Sherman and Cohn (1986) Matulia (1982) Geller and Scott (this book)
Tulsa	1970-83 1970-84 1975-79 1985-89	Matulia (1985) Sherman and Cohn (1986) Matulia (1982) Geller and Scott (this book)
Virginia Beach	1970-84	Sherman and Cohn (1986)

Jurisdiction(s) Studied	Years	Published Study (Full Cites in References)
Washington, DC	?	Kiernan (1978)
	1970-83	Matulia (1985)
	1970-84	Sherman and Cohn (1986)
	1973-74	Milton et al. (1977)
	1973-74	Meyer (1980a)
	1974	Sultan and Cooper (1979)
	1975-79	Matulia (1982)
	1985-89	Geller and Scott (this book)
	7/1/86-12/31/86	McMurray (1990)
	1987-90	St. Louis Police Dept. (1992)
	1989-90	Jennings (1991a, 1991b)
Wichita	1970-83	Matulia (1985)
	1970-84	Sherman and Cohn (1986)
	1975-79	Matulia (1982)
	1985-89	Geller and Scott (this book)
Multiple-City Studies		
5 largest cities	7/70-3/71	Knoohuizen, et al. (1972)
9 cities	1950-60	Robin (1963)
Every city in which a PO is feloniously killed or assaulted	annual since 1961	FBI, UCR Supplemental Report on *Law Enforcement Officers Killed and Assaulted*
	1976-87	Malcolm (1990a)
Every city in which POs justifiably killed people	1950-73	Peirson (1978)
	1976-87	Malcolm (1990a)
50 cities in Los Angeles County	1970-71	Uelman (1973)
54 cities over 250,000 population	1970-79	Mendez (1983), published in Sherman and Cohn (1986)
57 cities over 250,000 population	1970-83	Matulia (1985)
	1975-79	Matulia (1982)
	1985-88	Malcolm (1990a)
59 cities over 250,000 population	1970-84	Sherman and Cohn (1986)
7 cities	1973-74	Milton et al. (1977)
All jurisdictions in which POs were killed	1961-89	Witkin, et al. (1990: 44)
	1970-75	O'Neill (1979)
	1972-82	Meyer, et al. (1986)
	1973-84	Bailey and Peterson (1987)
	1974-90	Geller (1991)
	1977-86	Boylen and Little (1990)

Jurisdiction(s) Studied	Years	Published Study (Full Cites in References)
50 cities over 250,000 population	1985-89	Geller and Scott (this book)
10 of the U.S.A.'s largest cities	1985-89	O'Connell (1990)
10 of the U.S.A.'s largest cities	1986-90	O'Connell (1990a)
8 large American cities	1989	Geller (1991a)
All cities in California	1980-81 1980-89	Moorman and Wemmer (1983) Moorman, et al. (1990)
All cities in Washington state	1950-71	Hill and Clawson (1988)
El Paso County & Pikes Peak region, Colorado	1896-92	*Colorado Springs Gazette Telegraph* (1992)
502 agencies in New Jersey	1990	J.F. Sullivan (1992)

APPENDIX D:

CORRESPONDENCE BETWEEN TABLES AND FIGURES IN THIS VOLUME (PRESENTING THE SAME OR RELATED DATA IN DIFFERENT WAYS)

Figure #	Corresponds with Table #	Table #	Corresponds with Figure #
1	E-11	1	---
2	6, E-3, E-11	2	---
3	E-1, E-68	3	32
4	E-46, E-68	4	28
5	E-6, E-56, E-68	5	28
6	E-14, E-68	6	2, 35, 37, 38, 67, E-2
7	E-17, E-68	7	36, 37, 38
8	E-12, E-68	8	---
9	E-20, E-68	9	---
10	E-21, E-68	10	---
11	E-52, E-68	11	---
12	E-60, E-68	12	48
13	---	13	---
14	E-19	14	---
15	E-1, E-68	15	---
16	E-1, E-16, E-25, E-68	16	60, 61
17	E-21, E-24, E-34, E-68	17	35, 49, 66
18	E-1, E-16, E-68	18	---
19	E-6, E-26, E-36, E-68	19	49, 66
20	E-20, E-27, E-37, E-68	20	---

Figure #	Corresponds with Table #	Table #	Corresponds with Figure #
21	E-28, E-38, E-46, E-68	21	---
22	E-17, E-29, E-39, E-68	22	---
23	E-30, E-42, E-68	23	---
24	E-14, E-31, E-40, E-68	24	---
25	E-12, E-32, E-41, E-68	25	---
26	E-52, E-53, E-54, E-68	26	---
27	E-59, E-60, E-61, E-68	27	---
28	4, 5, E-16, E-34, E-35, E-36, E-37, E-38, E-39, E-40, E-41, E-42, E-54, E-61	28	---
29	E-1, E-2, E-25	29	---
30	E-11	E-1	3, 15, 16, 18, 29, 71
31	E-11	E-2	29, 71
32	3	E-3	2, 35, 67, E-2
33	---	E-4	69
34	see Figure 1	E-5	E-1, E-2
35	6, 17, E-3	E-6	5, 19
36	7, E-43, E-45	E-7	---
37	6, 7	E-8	---
38	6, 7, E-45	E-9	---
39	E-15	E-10	---
40	E-22	E-11	1, 2, 30, 31, 34
41	E-22	E-12	8, 25, 57
42	E-44, E-45	E-13	---
43	E-22	E-14	6, 24, E-5
44	E-23	E-15	39, E-5

Figure #	Corresponds with Table #	Table #	Corresponds with Figure #
45	E-23, E-45	E-16	16, 18, 28
46	E-22	E-17	7, 22
47	E-22	E-18	62, 63
48	12	E-19	14
49	17, 19	E-20	9, 20
50	---	E-21	10, 17
51	---	E-22	40, 41, 43, 46, 47
52	---	E-23	44, 45
53	---	E-24	17
54	---	E-25	16, 18, 29, 71
55	---	E-26	19
56	---	E-27	20
57	E-12	E-28	21
58	E-46	E-29	22
59	E-51, E-68	E-30	23
60	16	E-31	24
61	16	E-32	25
62	E-18	E-33	---
63	E-18	E-34	17, 28
64	---	E-35	28
65	---	E-36	19, 28
66	17, 19	E-37	20, 28
67	6, E-3	E-38	21, 28
68	E-49	E-39	22, 28
69	E-4, E-68	E-40	24, 28
70	E-46, E-68	E-41	25, 28
71	E-1, E-2, E-25	E-42	23, 28
72	---	E-43	36
73	---	E-44	42

Figure #	Corresponds with Table #	Table #	Corresponds with Figure #
74	E-51	E-45	36, 38, 42, 45
75	---	E-46	4, 21, 58, 70
76	---	E-47	---
E-1	E-5	E-48	---
E-2	6, E-3, E-5	E-49	68
E-3	---	E-50	---
E-4	---	E-51	59, 74
E-5	E-14, E-15, E-68	E-52	11, 26
E-6	---	E-53	26
E-7	E-57	E-54	26, 28
E-8	E-58	E-55	---
E-9	---	E-56	5
E-10	---	E-57	E-7
		E-58	E-8
		E-59	27
		E-60	12, 27
		E-61	27, 28
		E-62	---
		E-63	---
		E-64	---
		E-65	---
		E-66	---
		E-67	69
		E-68	3, 4, 5, 6, 7, 8, 9, 10, 11, 12, 15, 16, 17, 18, 19, 20, 21, 22, 23, 24, 25, 26, 27, 59, 69, 70, E-5
		E-69	
		E-70	---

APPENDIX E:

MISCELLANEOUS TABLES
AND FIGURES

Table E-1:
Shootings by Chicago Police, 1974-91

Year	# Civilians Shot Fatally	# Civilians Shot Nonfatally	Total Number Civilians Shot
1974	35	102	137
1975	37	114	151
1976	15	71	86
1977	31	67	98
1978	15	58	73
1979	19	68	87
1980	24	76	100
1981	24	57	81
1982	18	58	76
1983	23	61	84
1984	17	51	68
1985	19	31	50
1986	14	32	46
1987	13	33	46
1988	20	44	64
1989	10	45	55
1990	10	47	57
1991	10	37	47
18-yr. Total	354	1,052	1,406
18-yr. Ann. Average	20	58	78

Source: Data collected by William A. Geller, 1977-92, from the Chicago Police Department.

Table E-2:
Rate of Shootings by Chicago Police
per 1,000 Forcible Felony Arrests, 1974-91

Year	# Civilians Shot Fatally & Nonfatally	# Persons Arrested for Forcible Felonies*	# Civilians Shot per 1,000 F.F. Arrests
1974	137	14,314	9.6
1975	151	14,397	10.5
1976	86	11,315	7.6
1977	98	9,239	10.6
1978	73	8,994	8.1
1979	87	9,733	8.9
1980	100	10,067	9.9
1981	81	9,695	8.4
1982	76	9,104	8.4
1983	84	9,190	9.1
1984	68	13,982	4.9
1985	50	7,062	7.1
1986	46	6,743	6.8
1987	46	6,463	7.1
1988	64	14,331	4.5
1989	55	16,963	3.2
1990	57	14,806	3.9
1991	47	16,309	2.9
18-yr. Total	1,406	202,707	6.9

Source: Data collected by William A. Geller, 1977-92, from the Chicago Police Department.

* *The forcible felonies used were murder/nonnegligent manslaughter, criminal sexual assault (rape), robbery, and aggravated assault—the offenses most likely to give rise to police-civilian violence.*
Note: The substantial increase in the number of persons arrested for forcible felonies in 1988 and the continuing high level of such arrests in 1989, 1990, and 1991 were partly the result of the Police Department classifying as aggravated assaults (a forcible felony) types of assaults that in prior years were classified as simple assaults (not forcible felonies). Officials in the Department's Research and Development Division explained that the new classification was, in their view, consistent with the FBI Uniform Crime Reporting program's definitions of aggravated assaults. The importance of the substantial increase in arrests, as the table shows, is that they combine with shootings (which also rose 1987 to 1988) to produce a dramatic decline in 1988 and thereafter in shooting **rate**.

Table E-3:
American Police Who Were Killed Feloniously and Who Died
Accidentally in the Line of Duty, 1960-91

Year	# POs Killed Feloniously	% POs Killed Feloniously	# POs Who Died Accidentally	% POs Who Died Accidentally
1960	28	58%	20	42%
1961	37	76%	12	24%
1962	48	62%	30	38%
1963	55	63%	33	37%
1964	57	65%	31	35%
1965	53	64%	30	36%
1966	57	58%	42	42%
1967	76	62%	47	38%
1968	64	52%	59	48%
1969	86	69%	39	31%
1970	100	68%	46	32%
1971	126	71%	52	29%
1972	112	73%	41	27%
1973	134	76%	42	24%
1974	132	74%	47	26%
1975	129	70%	56	30%
1976	111	79%	29	21%
1977	93	74%	32	26%
1978	93	64%	52	36%
1979	106	65%	58	35%
1980	104	63%	61	37%
1981	91	58%	66	42%
1982	92	56%	72	44%
1983	80	53%	72	47%
1984	72	49%	75	51%
1985	78	53%	70	47%
1986	66	50%	67	50%
1987	74	50%	74	50%

Year	# POs Killed Feloniously	% POs Killed Feloniously	# POs Who Died Accidentally	% POs Who Died Accidentally
1988	78	50%	77	50%
1989	66	46%	79	54%
1990	66	50%	67	50%
1991	71	57%	52	43%
TOTAL	2,635	62%	1,630	38%

Sources: FBI, Crime in the United States *(annual)*, Law Enforcement Officers Killed and Assaulted *(annual)*, *Behm (1992).*

Table E-4:
Persons Shot at Intentionally by Kansas City, MO
Police Officers (Shot at and Missed, Struck Fatally
and Nonfatally), by Quarter, 1972-91

Year	Qtr. 1	Qtr. 2	Qtr. 3	Qtr. 4	Total	All Hits	All Misses
1972	8	5	2	6	21	16	5
1973	11	8	9[a]	7[b]	35	13	22
1974	0	6	6	7	19	10	9
1975	3	6	5	6	20	6	14
1976	4	2	13	9[c]	28	12	16
1977	6	9	7	4	26	7	19
1978	3[d]	4	5	7	19	11	8
1979	3	4	1	8	16	7	9
1980	4	3	6	5	18	8	10
1981	5	4	2	3	14	3	11
1982	1	5	0	4	10	6	4
1983	3	5	3	3	14	6	8
1984	3[e]	3	3	4	13	6	7
1985	4	0	5	5	14	8	6
1986	4	2	4	3	13	5	8
1987	3	3	2	3	11	3	8
1988	1	3	5	3	12	6	6
1989	3	6	1	3	13	7	6
1990	7[f]	6	3	3	19	13	6
1991	3	2	4	5	14	9	5
Total	79	86	86	98	349	162	187

Sources: Kansas City Police Department (1990-92).

[a] Chief Clarence Kelley left office on July 9, 1973, and was replaced by Acting Chief James R. Newman.
[b] Acting Chief Newman ceased serving as chief on November 1, 1973, and was replaced by Chief Joseph D. McNamara.
[c] Chief McNamara left office on October 4, 1976, and was replaced by Acting Chief Marvin L. VanKirk, who was named chief on January 1, 1977.
[d] Chief VanKirk ceased serving as chief on February 7, 1978, and was replaced by Chief Norman A. Caron.
[e] Chief Caron ceased serving as chief on March 31, 1984, and was replaced by Chief Larry J. Joiner.
[f] Chief Joiner retired and was replaced by Chief Steven Bishop on March 14, 1990.

Table E-5:
Annual FBI Tally[1] of Justifiable Homicides by American
Police Officers Using All Weapons, 1950-90

Year	Justifiable Line-of-Duty Homicides by City, County and State Law Enforcement Officers (All Police Weapons)	Year	Justifiable Line-of-Duty Homicides by City, County, and State Law Enforcement Officers (All Police Weapons)
1950	282	1971	557
1951	227	1972	469
1952	256	1973	492
1953	255	1974	553
1954	244	1975	559
1955	227	1976	420
1956	226	1977	314
1957	228	1978	314
1958	229	1979	445
1959	227	1980	459
1960	245	1981	383
1961	237	1982	380
1962	184	1983	419
1963	242	1984	333
1964	278	1985	321
1965	271	1986	303
1966	298	1987	300
1967	387	1988	343
1968	395	1989	362
1969	422	1990	385
1970	412		

Sources for Table E-5: Robin (1963) for 1950-60; Matulia (1985) for 1961-68;[2] Matulia (1985) for 1969-73; FBI (1990) for 1974-88; analysis of FBI Supplementary Homicide Report computer summaries for 1989-90.

[1] *The numbers reported in this table are those provided by agencies that voluntarily reported justifiable homicides by peace officers to the FBI's Uniform Crime Reporting program. Many agencies do not report such information or do not report it completely (see discussions in Chapter 2).*

[2] *Matulia (1985: 8), in Table 2.1, listing "Justifiable Homicides by Total U.S. Police" for 1950-83, cites an erroneous source for the 1961-67 annual totals. Matulia indicates that his data for 1950-67 came from "Robin, G: Justifiable Homicide by Police Officers, J. Crim. Law Crim. Pol. Sci., 54: 225-231, 1973." In fact, Gerald Robin's article was published in the indicated journal in 1963 rather than 1973, in volume 54,*

*and discussed data only for the years 1950-60. Thus, we assume that Matulia's actual source for the 1961-68 data was some other study that compiled FBI Uniform Crime Reporting data for those years. On his Table 2.1, Matulia indicates the source for his 1968-83 data as the FBI's "Uniform Crime Records (unpublished)." Moreover, the data that Matulia published for the years 1980-83, although apparently provided by the same unit of the FBI from which we obtained our data in April 1990 and September 1990, do not agree with the numbers we were given (the numbers for 1974-79 **do** agree). The numbers published by Matulia are: 1980: 484 (this is the year with the largest discrepancy); 1981: 381; 1982: 379; and 1983: 416. Because of this concern about accuracy, we relied upon data furnished directly to us by the FBI for the years 1974-90 (earlier years not being readily available at the time of our inquiries in April 1990, September 1990, and March 1992).*

Table E-6
Civilians Shot by Dallas Police, 1970-91

Year	Shot Fatally	Shot Nonfatally	Total Shot
1970	8	23	31
1971	6	21	27
1972	11	14	25
1973	4	11	15
1974	6	12	18
1975	8	12	20
1976	5	7	12
1977	4	12	16
1978	8	8	16
1979	9	17	26
1980	17	10	27
1981	8	12	20
1982	4	14	18
1983	15	14	29
1984	10	10	20
1985	9	9	18
1986	10	19	29
1987	4	14	18
1988	8	14	22
1989	6	9	15
1990	5	6	11
1991	7	6	13
TOTAL	172	274	446

Sources: Dallas Police Department (1990, 1991, 1992).

Table E-7:
Ratio of Blacks to Whites Shot (Fatally and Nonfatally)
by Dallas Police, 1970-91

Year	# Blacks Shot	# Whites Shot	Ratio Black:White
1970	19	9	2.1:1
1971	9	17	0.5:1
1972	19	6	3.2:1
1973	8	4	2:1
1974	11	5	2.2:1
1975	12	4	3:1
1976	7	4	1.8:1
1977	11	2	5.5:1
1978	11	4	2.8:1
1979	15	8	1.9:1
1980	16	6	2.7:1
1981	9	8	1.1:1
1982	10	6	1.7:1
1983	20	5	4:1
1984	8	2	4:1
1985	9	4	2.3:1
1986	15	7	2.1:1
1987	7	5	1.4:1
1988	13	3	4.3:1
1989	9	3	3:1
1990	6	2	3:1
1991	6	4	1.5:1
TOTAL	250	118	2.1:1

Sources: Dallas Police Department (1990, 1991, 1992).

Table E-8:
Service Handguns Authorized for Use by Officers on Routine Patrol in
26 Large Municipal Police Departments, as of August 1990

City	Using 9mm Semi-Automatic	Changing to 9mm Semi-Automatic[1]	Using Revolver; No Current Plan to Change to 9mm Semi-automatic
Atlanta	yes		
Baltimore		yes	
Boston	yes		
Chicago			yes
Cleveland	yes		
Columbus, OH		yes	
Dallas		yes	
Denver	yes		
Detroit	yes[2]		
Houston	yes		
Kansas City, MO			yes[3]
Los Angeles		yes	
Miami	yes		
Milwaukee		yes	
New Orleans		yes	
New York City			yes
Philadelphia		yes	
Phoenix		yes	
Pittsburgh		yes	
Saint Louis		yes	
San Antonio			yes[4]
San Diego		yes	
San Francisco		yes	
Seattle		yes	

City	Using 9mm Semi-Automatic	Changing to 9mm Semi-Automatic[1]	Using Revolver; No Current Plan to Change to 9mm Semi-automatic
Tampa	yes		
Washington, DC	yes		
TOTAL	9	13	4

Source: Adapted from two tables in Bratton (1990a).

[1] *Departments indicated they are phasing in 9-millimeter weapons beginning with new recruits. Also, presently assigned officers have the option of purchasing 9-millimeter semi-automatic pistols following mandatory training and qualification with these weapons.*

[2] *The New York City Transit Police survey, the source of the data in this table, may be incorrect about the status of the Detroit Police Department's use of semi-automatics as of the time the survey was conducted in 1990. An article in the* New York Times *on April 23, 1991, indicated that, although Detroit Police Department officials wanted to make the shift to semi-automatic pistols, as of that date such a change had not yet been made.*

[3] *Bratton (1990a) reported that the Kansas City Police Department was currently researching the use of semi-automatics but lacked the funding to effect any change (as of August 1990).*

[4] *Bratton (1990a) reported that the San Antonio Police Department as of August 1990 was using a .357 magnum but was researching a change to 9-millimeter semi-automatic pistols.*

Table E-9:
Average Number of Shots Fired Per Incident at Suspects of Different Races/Ethnicities by Los Angeles Police Department Officers, 1974-78

Suspect's Action and Weapon	White Suspects	Black Suspects	Hispanic Suspects
Disobeying order to halt, appearing to reach for weapon, assault	2.41	2.44	1.73
Displaying, threatening use of, actually using weapon	4.99	4.85	4.78
SUSPECT'S WEAPON: None	2.42	2.62	1.50
Gun	5.16	5.00	4.95
Other Weapon	4.32	3.49	4.16

Source: Meyer (1980a: 50).

Table E-10:
Illustrative Discrepancies/Agreement Between FBI and Private*
Researchers' Tallies of Justifiable Homicides by
American Law Enforcement Personnel, 1980 and 1981

City	1980		1981	
	FBI	Private*	FBI	Private*
Akron	*no data*	*1*	0	0
Albuquerque	0	0	*no data*	*1*
Atlanta	4	4	*4*	*3*
Austin	*1*	*2*	*1*	*2*
Baltimore	*5*	*4*	*4*	*3*
Birmingham	*5*	*7*	1	1
Boston	*no data*	*no data*	*3*	*no data*
Buffalo	0	0	0	0
Charlotte	*no data*	*1*	1	1
Chicago	*23*	*24*	*26*	*23*
Cincinnati	*3*	*5*	1	1
Cleveland	*2*	*3*	3	3
Columbus, OH	*3*	*4*	*4*	*6*
Dallas	*17*	*15*	8	8
Denver	6	6	*2*	*3*
Detroit	*14*	*12*	*8*	*9*
El Paso	*2*	*1*	0	0
Ft. Worth	3	3	*3*	*2*
Honolulu	0	0	0	0
Houston	*7*	*10*	*4*	*7*
Indianapolis	*no data*	*5*	*3*	*4*
Jacksonville, FL	*7*	*6*	6	6
Jersey City	1	1	*no data*	*1*
Kansas City, MO	*1*	*3*	*no data*	*2*
Long Beach	8	8	*1*	*2*

City	1980		1981	
	FBI	Private*	FBI	Private*
Los Angeles	*17*	*15*	*18*	*15*
Louisville	5	5	1	1
Memphis	3	3	7	7
Miami	*4*	*5*	*5*	*3*
Milwaukee	*2*	*1*	1	1
Minneapolis	0	0	2	2
Nashville	*3*	*6*	*4*	*5*
New Orleans	*11*	*13*	4	4
New York	25	28	26	*40*
Newark, NJ	*3*	*no data*	*8*	*no data*
Norfolk	*1*	*0*	0	0
Oakland, CA	*3*	*2*	4	4
Oklahoma City	*2*	*4*	*2*	*1*
Omaha	0	0	2	2
Philadelphia	*9*	*13*	*5*	*6*
Phoenix	*3*	*2*	3	3
Pittsburgh	*3*	*no data*	*1*	*no data*
Portland, OR	0	0	0	0
Rochester, NY	1	1	*no data*	*2*
Sacramento	*0*	*1*	0	0
St. Louis	*9*	*no data*	*2*	*no data*
St. Paul	0	0	0	0
San Antonio	*no data*	*1*	*no data*	*3*
San Diego	*2*	*3*	4	4
San Francisco	*3*	*4*	2	2
San Jose	*3*	*1*	1	1
Seattle	1	1	*1*	*2*
Tampa	2	2	0	0

City	1980		1981	
	FBI	Private*	FBI	Private*
Toledo	3	3	*2*	*1*
Tucson	*1*	*2*	*no data*	*1*
Tulsa	*2*	*1*	*4*	*3*
Virginia Beach	0	0	1	1
Washington, DC	*1*	*2*	8	8
Wichita	4	4	0	0
TOTAL	*238*	*248*	*201*	*210*

* *The private study used for illustrative purposes is Sherman and Cohn (1986). FBI data were furnished to the Police Executive Research Forum by the FBI in the form of computer print-outs listing all agencies reporting "felons killed by peace officers" to the FBI. These deaths are a subset of the FBI's justifiable homicide data, reported to the Bureau on "supplementary homicide report" forms.*

Note: The bold, italicized entries call attention to discrepancies between the FBI and private study data.

Of the 55 cities for which Sherman and Cohn (1986) had data in 1980, the FBI tally differed in 40 cities (i.e., there was a discrepancy in 73 percent of the cities). In 1981 there was disagreement between the FBI and private tallies in 47 percent of the cities (26 of the 55 for which Sherman and Cohn had data). Where the table shows "no data" for the FBI for any given city but a number of one or larger for the private study, this is considered a discrepancy because the FBI either has received a report of zero justifiable killings of felony suspects from that city or has received no report whatsoever from the particular city.

Table E-11:
Felony Suspects Killed Justifiably by American Police,
in 50 Big Cities, 1985-89

City	YEAR					Total	5-year annual average
	1985	1986	1987	1988	1989		
Akron	0	0	0	0	0	0	0
Albuquerque	0	3	3	0	4	10	2
Atlanta	3	4	5	4	4	20	4
Austin	1	0	0	0	0	1	0.2
Baltimore	1	3	6	4	2	16	3.2
Birmingham	0	0	0	0	1	1	0.2
Charlotte	0	1	1	2	2	6	1.2
Chicago: *FBI*	0	8	1	18	7	34	6.8
Geller data	19	14	13	20	9	75	15
Cincinnati	1	0	1	2	2	6	1.2
Cleveland	2	3	5	3	1	14	2.8
Columbus, OH	0	0	0	3	3	6	1.2
Dallas: *FBI*	9	8	1	6	3	27	5.4
Geller data	9	10	4	8	6	37	7.4
Denver	3	2	4	3	2	14	2.8
Detroit	12	9	7	3	7	38	7.6
El Paso	0	0	0	0	0	0	0
Ft. Worth	1	2	0	0	0	3	0.6
Honolulu	1	0	2	1	1	5	1
Indianapolis	0	0	0	1	3	4	0.8
Jacksonville, FL	2	2	0	0	0	4	0.8
Kansas City, MO: *FBI data*	0	0	0	0	0	0	0
Geller data	2	1	2	1	0	6	1.2
Long Beach	1	0	1	1	0	3	0.6
Los Angeles	23	21	20	22	25	111	22.2
Louisville	0	0	0	0	0	0	0
Memphis	0	11	4	3	2	20	4
Miami	2	1	6	0	0	9	1.8
Milwaukee	1	0	1	2	3	7	1.4
Minneapolis	0	0	4	1	0	5	1

City	YEAR					Total	5-year annual average
	1985	1986	1987	1988	1989		
Nashville	0	0	0	1	0	1	0.2
New York	15	15	13	27	18	88	17.6
Norfolk	1	1	1	2	2	7	1.4
Oakland, CA	1	3	1	0	5	10	2
Oklahoma City	5	2	5	0	2	14	2.8
Omaha	0	2	0	0	0	2	0.4
Philadelphia: *FBI data* *Geller data*	9 --	3 5	5 6	4 8	6 9	27 37	5.4 7.4
Phoenix	3	2	3	2	4	14	2.8
Portland, OR	2	1	4	3	0	10	2
Rochester, NY	1	0	0	1	0	2	0.4
Sacramento	2	1	1	2	0	6	1.2
St. Paul	2	0	0	0	0	2	0.4
San Antonio: *FBI data* *Police Dept. data*	0 ?	0 ?	0 ?	0 ?	0 ?	0 16	0 3.2
San Diego	4	6	7	12	11	40	8.0
San Francisco	1	0	0	3	3	7	1.4
San Jose	5	0	0	1	4	10	2
Seattle	1	0	0	6	2	9	1.8
Tampa	1	2	4	0	0	7	1.4
Toledo	1	0	0	0	1	2	0.4
Tucson	0	2	1	2	0	5	1
Tulsa	3	3	1	1	2	10	2
Washington, DC	2	0	0	3	0	5	1
Wichita	1	0	0	0	3	4	0.8
TOTAL (FBI data)	123	121	118	149	135	646	129

Sources: FBI unpublished Supplementary Homicide Report file listings (all 50 cities); Dallas Police Department (1990) for Dallas data; O'Connell (1990) for San Antonio data; Chicago, Kansas City (MO), and Philadelphia Police Department data furnished by each city police department to William Geller during 1989 and 1990.

Table E-12:
Incidents* in Which Philadelphia Police Discharged Their
Firearms Intentionally and Accidentally, 1986-91

Type of Incident	Year						6-Yr. Total
	1986	1987	1988	1989	1990	1991	
Fatal	5	6	8	9	8	11	47
Injury (nonfatal)	19	15	13	24	39	33	143
Misses (noninjury)	34	29	38	35	55	36	227
Other (animals shot)	3	6	14	9	20	19	71
Total Incidents with *Persons* Shot/Shot at	58	50	59	68	102	80	417
Total Incidents (including animals shot)	61	56	73	77	122	99	488
On Duty	43	43	51	63	81	68	349
Off Duty	18	13	22	14	41	31	139
Accidental**	16	15	16	21	38	17	123
Intentional**	45	41	57	56	84	82	365

Sources: Philadelphia Police Department, Deputy Commissioner Thomas Nestel and Sgt. John Ferry (who prepared and interpreted the compilations) (December 3 and 5, 1990) and Deputy Commissioner Thomas Nestel (March 3, 1992).

* *The reader is reminded that all the Philadelphia data in this table count **incidents** rather than **persons**. Thus, for example, the count of fatals may include one or more incidents in which more than one person was killed by police. Such an incident would be counted only as one incident in this table.*
** *Incidents of accidental firearms discharges by officers and incidents of intentional firearms discharges by officers are shown separately in these two rows but are also included in all the rows above (on and off duty, fatal, nonfatal, misses, animal shootings, and the two totals rows). Thus, the numbers in the "accidental" row and in the "intentional" row include incidents with hits (fatal and nonfatal) and misses, whether the target of the shots is a person or an animal.*

Table E-13:
Incidents* in Which Philadelphia Police Officers
Were Shot at and Shot by Civilians, 1987-91

Type of Incident	Year					
	1987	1988	1989	1990	1991	5-Yr. Total
Police Shot *AT* by Civilians**	5	5	9	19	20	58
Police *SHOT* by Civilians	3	1	2	3	7	16

Source: Philadelphia Police Department, Deputy Commissioner Thomas Nestel and Sgt. John Ferry (who prepared and interpreted the compilations) (December 3 and 5, 1990) and Deputy Commissioner Thomas Nestel (March 3, 1992).

* Note: These are incident, not person, counts. Thus, in any given incident involving a civilian shooting at Philadelphia police or striking Philadelphia police with bullets, there may have been more than one officer fired upon or struck.
** Only incidents in which police returned fire are included. If police did not return fire, the figures are not available from the Police Department.

Table E-14:
Shots-Fired Incidents and Number of Adversaries Shot (Fatally and Nonfatally)
by New York City Police Department Officers, 1970-91

Year	Total Firearms Discharge Incidents	# Persons Shot Fatally	# Persons Shot Nonfatally	Total Number Persons Shot
1970	--	50	212	262
1971	--	93	221	314
1972	--	66	145	211
1973	541	58	118	176
1974	420	41	80	121
1975	391	44	87	131
1976	327	25	79	104
1977	406	30	88	118
1978	377	37	78	115
1979	360	28	80	108
1980	376	25	101	126
1981	406	33	91	124
1982	337	33	87	120
1983	288	29	63	92
1984	295	26	48	74
1985	217	11	47	58
1986	221	18	38	56
1987	234	14	36	50
1988	251	24	46	70
1989	329	30	61	91
1990	307	39	72	111
1991	332	27	81	108
TOTAL	6,415	781	1,959	2,740

Sources: Cerar (1989, 1990, 1991).

Table E-15:
Uniformed New York City Police Department Officers
Shot Fatally and Nonfatally, 1970-91

Year	Shot Fatally	Shot Nonfatally	Total Shot
1970	6	46	52
1971	11	47	58
1972	5	40	45
1973	6	50	56
1974	4	32	36
1975	6	23	29
1976	0	11	11
1977	3	20	23
1978	5	19	24
1979	4	17	21
1980	6	15	21
1981	3	22	25
1982	2	15	17
1983	1	11	12
1984	3	22	25
1985	0	12	12
1986	2	18	20
1987	1	12	13
1988	5	17	22
1989	6	22	28
1990	0	17	17
1991	2	17	17
TOTAL	81	505	584

Sources: Cerar (1989, 1990, 1991).

Table E-16:
Rate of Shootings by Chicago Police per General Population Homicides, 1974-91

Year	# Civilians Shot Fatally and Nonfatally	# of General Population Homicides	# Civilians Shot per 100 General Population Homicides
1974	137	970	14.1
1975	151	818	18.5
1976	86	814	10.6
1977	98	823	11.9
1978	73	787	9.3
1979	87	856	10.2
1980	100	863	11.6
1981	81	877	9.2
1982	76	668	11.4
1983	84	729	11.5
1984	68	741	9.2
1985	50	666	7.5
1986	46	744	6.2
1987	46	691	6.7
1988	64	660	9.7
1989	55	742	7.4
1990	57	849	6.7
1991	47	923	5.1
18-yr. TOTAL	1,406	14,221	9.9

Source: Data collected by William A. Geller, 1977-92, from the Chicago Police Department.

Table E-17:
Suspects Shot and Shot at by Los Angeles Police
Department Officers, 1980-91

Year	Suspects Shot Fatally	Suspects Shot Nonfatally	Total Shot	Persons Shot at but Missed	Total Persons Shot at
1980	14	30	44	---	---
1981	15	31	46	---	---
1982	21	31	52	62	114
1983	25	40	65	41	106
1984	19	27	46	76	122
1985	23	42	65	95	160
1986	21	27	48	71	119
1987	22	34	56	72	128
1988	23	55	78	42	120
1989	22	46	68	56	124
1990	39	34	73	66	139
1991	23	38	61	57	118
TOTAL	267	435	702	638	1,250

Source: Los Angeles Police Department.

Table E-18:
Reasons for the Justifiable Killing of Felony Suspects
by American Police, 1980-90

| Year | Reason for Justifiable Homicide (See Key Below) | | | | | | | Total w/o "G" | Total with "G" |
	A	B	C	D	E	F	G		
1980	158 39%	25 6%	5 1%	27 7%	133 33%	59 15%	52 --	407 101%	459 ---
1981	118 35%	18 5%	7 2%	34 10%	120 35%	43 13%	40 --	340 100%	380 ---
1982	111 34%	22 7%	9 3%	18 6%	128 39%	37 11%	55 --	325 100%	380 ---
1983	138 37%	37 10%	10 3%	27 7%	124 33%	40 11%	48 --	376 101%	424 ---
1984	118 42%	22 8%	8 3%	18 6%	77 27%	38 14%	52 --	281 100%	333 ---
1985	113 39%	18 6%	14 5%	18 6%	84 29%	44 15%	31 --	291 100%	322 ---
1986	135 53%	8 3%	4 2%	15 6%	64 26%	27 11%	48 --	251 101%	301 ---
1987	142 53%	12 5%	8 3%	7 3%	66 25%	33 12%	29 --	268 101%	297 ---
1988	150 50%	13 4%	12 4%	14 5%	83 28%	29 10%	38 --	301 101%	339 ---
1989	172 52%	13 4%	15 5%	16 5%	82 25%	36 11%	28 --	334 102%	362 ---
1990	179 52%	14 4%	10 3%	6 2%	89 26%	46 13%	41 --	344 100%	385 ---
TOTAL	1,534 44%	202 6%	102 3%	200 6%	1,050 30%	432 12%	462 --	3,520 101%	3,982 ---

KEY

A= Felon attacked police officer.
B= Felon attacked fellow police officer.
C= Felon attacked a civilian.
D= Felon attempted flight from a crime.

E= Felon killed in commission of a crime.
F= Felon resisted arrest.
G= Not enough information to determine reason for killing.

Note: All percentages exclude category "G" (not enough information). The data presented in this table reflect only those shootings that agencies voluntarily report to the FBI through the UCR program.
Source: FBI, unpublished supplementary homicide report file listings.

Table E-19:
Firearms Discharges by Chicago Police Compared with Arrestees Armed with Firearms, by Police District, 1976-77

Police District	# of Firearms Use Incidents	# of Arrestees Who Possessed a Firearm When Arrested in the District, 1976-77	Rate: # Shooting Incidents per 100 Armed Arrestees
1	15	629	2.4
2	52	2,435	2.1
3	34	1,638	2.1
4	39	981	4.0
5	50	1,178	4.3
6	36	1,582	2.3
7	49	1,763	2.8
8	21	394	5.3
9	29	763	3.8
10*	25	2,477	1.0
11	30	1,622	1.9
12	13	903	1.4
13	31	1,201	2.6
14	26	1,173	2.2
15	50	1,472	3.4
16	15	208	7.2
17	14	325	4.3
18	21	842	2.5
19	10	549	1.8
20	21	455	4.6
21	22	929	2.4
22	28	675	4.2
23	27	825	3.3
TOTAL (Citywide)	658	25,019	2.6

Source: Adapted from Nowicki and Stahl (1978: 14).

* A corruption scandal surfaced during the 1980s that involved several 10th District officers (who came to be called the "Marquette 10" in press coverage). The officers were convicted of shaking down drug dealers to provide large quantities of guns—or money that officers could use to purchase guns—that could be submitted to satisfy gun confiscation objectives set by commanders. As a result of this problem, we urge the reader to consider the numbers from the 10th District with even more analytic reflection than the reader should apply to any gun confiscation data coming from any police department during any time period. It is possible that the true number of arrestees possessing firearms at the time of their arrest in the 10th District was considerably lower than indicated. It is also possible that the reporting rate for off-target firearms discharges in the 10th District was lower than for other districts, although we have nothing but idle speculation to support this possibility. Hence, the distinction that the 10th District has of having one of the lowest officer firearms use rates in the entire city may not be well grounded.

A variety of mischief reportedly has been prompted in Chicago by administration demands for high numbers of gun confiscations. Another common practice has been for officers to look for armed security guards on their way to or from work (during which time they are legally authorized to have a firearm in their possession), to stop the guards in their personal cars, search the cars, and, upon locating the handgun, make an arrest for unlawful possession of a weapon, sometimes with the explanation that the security guard credentials displayed may be counterfeit. It is abundantly clear to the arresting officers that the charges will be dismissed in court because of the arrestees' lawful authority to possess the firearm, but the arresting officers have satisfied the pressure to make the Department look good by running up the number of guns "seized." Similarly, officers have relieved the pressure on them to confiscate guns by stopping out-of-state truck drivers passing through town; these drivers not infrequently have a gun for protection. Although these guns are illegally possessed, questions remain about whether such uses of police officers' time and creative energies are the best way to serve the public interest in security and safety (Nelson 1992).

At one point during the 1980s a Harvard University research team, having heard about the unusually high confiscation rate enjoyed by the Chicago Police Department, sought departmental permission to conduct a study to identify the ingredients of success. After initial indications that the request would be granted, police officials considered further the potential for embarrassment if the full gamut of gun-confiscation techniques was disclosed and declined to authorize the study. A "point system" for arrests, in which supervisors in certain units placed high priority on seizing guns, was exposed by a local newspaper and criticized by Chicago Police Superintendent Matt Rodriguez in June 1992 as skewing police energies away from meaningful crime prevention and toward sometimes meaningless arrests. Said the new Chicago Superintendent: "We have three responsibilities: To protect life. To protect property. And the third is to make arrests when we have failed at the first two.... We're just counting number three right now" (Nelson 1992: 27).

Table E-20:
Shots-Fired Incidents (Intentional and Unintentional), by
Houston Police, 1980-91, and Houston Police Officers Shot, 1980-91

Category	Year of Occurrence												TO-TAL
	80	81	82	83	84	85	86	87	88	89	90	91	
Citizen Death	9	9	13	16	9	8	7	4	4	10	13	15	117
Citizen Injury	21	18	32	29	22	23	20	17	15	25	17	20	259
Total Persons Struck	30	27	45	45	31	31	27	21	19	35	30	35	376
No Personal Injury	31	45	61	46	50	36	30	22	15	38	37	36	447
Property Damage Only	5	1	1	7	1	0	14	15	8	5	6	6	69
Total Incidents with Persons Fired at Intentionally	66	73	107	98	82	67	71	58	42	78	73	63	878
Incidents with Accidental Firearms Discharges	20	16	24	21	7	15	4	4	10	5	17	15	158
Animal Death	*	*	*	*	*	*	*	*	*	1	5	2	8
Animal Injury	*	*	*	*	*	*	*	*	*	1	2	1	4
Total Incidents with Shots Fired by HPD POs	86	89	131	119	89	82	75	62	52	85	97	81	1,048
Officers Killed	1	0	4	0	0	0	0	0	1	1	1	1	9
Officers Shot Nonfatally	7	4	9	9	3	7	11	6	6	4	9	10	85
TOTAL OFFI-CERS SHOT	8	4	13	9	3	7	11	6	7	5	10	11	94

Source: Houston Police Department. Data on shots fired and persons, animals, and property struck are from the Internal Affairs Division. Data on officers killed and shot nonfatally are from the Homicide Division.
* Data not available for these years.

Table E-21:
Persons Shot at by Atlanta Police, 1980-91

Year	Persons Shot Nonfatally	Persons Shot Fatally	Total Persons Struck	Noninjury Firearm Discharge Incidents	Total Shots-Fired Incidents
1980	8	4	12	18	30
1981	10	3	13	37	50
1982	7	3	10	49	59
1983	7	7	14	28	42
1984	8	3	11	24	35
1985	6	3	9	19	28
1986	7	3	10	28	38
1987	10	8	18	38	56
1988	10	4	14	34	48
1989	17	3	20	30	50
1990	8	6	14	45	59
1991	9	7	16	40	54
TOTAL	107	54	161	390	549

Source: Atlanta Police Department.

Table E-22:
Deadly Weapon Assaults on American Police, 1978-90

Year/ % Injured	Type of Weapon Used			TOTAL
	Firearm	Knife or Cutting Instrument	Other Dangerous Weapon	
1978 #: % Injured: # Injured:	3,065 17.8 546	1,761 35.0 616	5,485 42.7 2,342	10,311 34.0 3,504
1979 #: % Injured: # Injured:	3,237 20.7 670	1,720 34.4 592	5,543 41.1 2,278	10,500 33.7 3,540
1980 #: % Injured: # Injured:	3,295 22.5 741	1,653 34.4 569	5,415 38.0 2,058	10,363 32.5 3,368
1981 #: % Injured: # Injured:	3,334 18.3 610	1,733 34.3 594	4,803 40.6 1,950	9,870 32.0 3,154
1982 #: % Injured: # Injured:	2,642 16.4 433	1,452 27.0 392	4,879 39.1 1,908	8,973 30.5 2,733
1983 #: % Injured: # Injured:	3,067 21.8 669	1,829 31.4 574	5,527 40.2 2,222	10,423 33.2 3,465
1984 #: % Injured: # Injured:	2,654 20.1 534	1,662 30.0 499	5,148 42.2 2,173	9,464 33.9 3,206
1985 #: % Injured: # Injured:	2,793 20.8 581	1,715 27.4 470	5,263 41.1 2,163	9,771 33.0 3,214
1986 #: % Injured: # Injured:	2,852 22.3 636	1,614 29.9 483	5,721 38.3 2,191	10,187 32.5 3,310
1987 #: % Injured: # Injured:	2,789 21.7 605	1,561 30.7 479	5,685 38.4 2,183	10,035 32.6 3,267
1988 #: % Injured: # Injured:	2,759 27.3 753	1,367 32.3 442	5,573 42.1 2,346	9,699 36.5 3,541
1989 #: % Injured: # Injured:	3,154 30.2 953	1,379 30.5 421	5,778 40.8 2,357	10,311 36.2 3,731

Year/ % Injured	Type of Weapon Used			TOTAL
	Firearm	Knife or Cutting Instrument	Other Dangerous Weapon	
1990 #: % Injured: # Injured:	3,662 29.4 1,077	1,641 29.4 483	7,390 42.5 3,141	12,693 37.0 4,701
13 Yr Total: % Injured: # Injured:	39,303 22.4 8,808	21,087 31.4 6,614	72,210 40.6 29,312	132,600 33.7 44,734
13 Yr *Annual* *Average* #: % Injured: # Injured:	3,023 22.4 678	1,622 31.4 509	5,555 40.6 2,255	10,200 33.7 3,441

Sources: FBI, Law Enforcement Officers Killed and Assaulted *(annual).*

**Table E-23:
American Police Whose Lives Were "Saved" by
Soft Body Armor, 1972-91**

Year	Number Saved from Assaults	Number Saved from Accidents	TOTAL SAVED
1972	1	0	1
1973	5	0	5
1974	15	6	21
1975	25	8	33
1976	24	9	33
1977	40	8	48
1978	24	21	45
1979	33	28	61
1980	34	25	59
1981	35	39	74
1982	35	31	66
1983	29	22	51
1984	31	18	49
1985	30	27	57
1986	53	38	91
1987	56	55	111
1988	54	64	118
1989	67	64	131
1990	70	70	140
1991	60[1]	45[1]	105
TOAL	721[2]	578[2]	1,299

Source: IACP/DuPont Kevlar Survivors' Club (1992).

[1] *Preliminary figures, furnished on March 15, 1992.*

[2] *These totals are lower than the totals furnished by the IACP/DuPont Kevlar Survivors' Club on March 15, 1992 (and reflected in Tables 27 and 28 in Chapter 5). These discrepancies probably stem from the fact that most of the annual tallies reflected above in Table E-23 were provided to us by the Survivors' Club about two years ago, and during the interim the club may have been notified of additional law enforcement personnel whose lives were saved in prior years because of their soft body armor. We take the higher totals, reflected in Tables 27 and 28, as the more current of the two sets of numbers.*

Table E-24:
Demographics for Atlanta, 1980-91

Year	Resident Population	# Sworn Police	# Reported Homicides	# Violent Crime Arrests[1]
1980	422,474	1,223	201	3,884
1981	435,626	1,294	182	4,277
1982	441,103	1,340	152	4,654
1983	448,635	1,315	141	4,301
1984	442,951	1,276	135	4,345
1985	436,214	1,278	145	4,285
1986	445,617	1,326	186	4,575
1987	429,953	1,346	207	5,174
1988	444,995	1,395	217	6,818
1989	426,482	1,518	246	7,180
1990	394,017	1,560	231	7,053
1991	437,300	1,590	205	7,186

Sources: FBI (annual reports), FBI (1991a—unpublished arrest tallies for specified cities), and Atlanta Police Department.

[1] *Violent crime arrests include arrests for murder/nonnegligent manslaughter, rape/aggravated sexual assault, robbery, and aggravated assault. These arrests are used in computing rates because they provide some approximation of the frequency of potentially violent police-civilian encounters in any given jurisdiction during any particular year.*

Table E-25:
Demographics for Chicago, 1974-91

Year	Resident Population	# Sworn Police	# Reported Homicides	# Violent Crime Arrests[1]
1974	3,296,936	13,266	970	14,314
1975	3,150,000	13,039	818	14,397
1976	3,134,499	13,039	814	11,315[2]
1977	3,086,806	13,314	823	9,239
1978	3,086,699	13,020	787	8,994
1979	3,060,801	13,293	856	9,733
1980	2,986,419	12,392	863	10,067
1981	3,012,703	12,475	877	9,695
1982	3,010,862	12,562	668	9,104
1983	3,021,203	12,353	729	9,190
1984	3,012,524	11,960	741	13,982[3]
1985	2,998,841	11,871	666	7,062
1986	3,003,105	12,264	744	6,743
1987	3,018,338	12,312	691	6,463
1988	2,994,100	12,163	660	14,331[2]
1989	2,988,260	11,828	742	16,963
1990	2,783,726	12,237	851	14,806
1991	3,032,845	12,831	923	16,309

Sources: FBI (annual reports), FBI (1991a—unpublished arrest tallies for specified cities), and Chicago Police Department.

[1] *Violent crime arrests include arrests for murder/nonnegligent manslaughter, rape/aggravated sexual assault, robbery, and aggravated assault. These arrests are used in computing rates because they provide some approximation of the frequency of potentially violent police-civilian encounters in any given jurisdiction during any particular year.*

[2] *Mid-year in 1976 the Chicago Police Department stopped classifying as aggravated assaults any arrests that the Cook County State's Attorney's Office declined to prosecute as more than simple assaults, even though UCR program definitions allowed classification of assault arrests based solely on police determinations. Then, in 1988, the Police Department reversed this approach, reverting to the classification system used prior to 1976.*

[3] *The Chicago Police Department's Research and Development Division offered the opinion that the number of violent crime arrests listed for 1984 is artificially inflated by some arrests that actually occurred in either 1983 or 1985 or both. The similarity between the arrest tally for 1985 and the tallies for 1986 and 1987, however, raises some skepticism about this view.*

Table E-26:
Demographics for Dallas, 1970-91

Year	Resident Population	# Sworn Police	# Reported Homicides	# Violent Crime Arrests[1]
1970	849,000	1,635	242	---
1971	849,000	1,797	207	---
1972	816,000	1,875	192	---
1973	816,000	1,929	230	---
1974	813,000	1,939	196	---
1975	813,000	1,968	237	---
1976	829,000	2,014	230	---
1977	845,000	2,004	224	---
1978	871,832	1,997	230	2,930
1979	882,225	2,031	307	3,203
1980	900,104	1,990	319	3,131
1981	937,273	1,955	298	3,106
1982	970,624	1,996	306	3,132
1983	998,827	2,084	268	2,777
1984	987,696	2,087	294	2,215
1985	997,467	2,170	301	2,665
1986	1,016,488	2,290	347	3,737
1987	1,009,947	2,400	323	4,147
1988	1,017,818	2,381	366	3,897
1989	996,320	2,472	351	3,756
1990	1,006,331	2,763	444	4,211
1991	1,006,331	2,847	501	4,612

Sources: FBI (annual reports), FBI (1991a—unpublished arrest tallies for specified cities), and Dallas Police Department.

[1] *Violent crime arrests include arrests for murder/nonnegligent manslaughter, rape/aggravated sexual assault, robbery, and aggravated assault. These arrests are used in computing rates because they provide some approximation of the frequency of potentially violent police-civilian encounters in any given jurisdiction during any particular year.*

Table E-27:
Demographics for Houston, 1980-91

Year	Resident Population	# Sworn Police	# Reported Homicides	# Violent Crime Arrests[1]
1980	1,619,644	3,070	633	---
1981	1,621,897	3,214	701	---
1982	1,679,607	3,345	678	2,990
1983	1,728,783	3,716	561	2,694
1984	1,805,783	3,957	473	2,709
1985	1,746,375	4,363	457	2,801
1986	1,779,677	4,618	408	3,154
1987	1,739,999	4,445	323	2,828
1988	1,725,421	4,270	440	---
1989	1,713,499	4,088	459	2,565
1990	1,630,553	4,087	617	---
1991	1,665,756	4,077	671	---

Sources: FBI (annual reports), FBI (1991a—unpublished arrest tallies for specified cities), Houston Police Department, Crime Control Digest *(1991j), and Landsberg (1992).*

[1] *Violent crime arrests include arrests for murder/nonnegligent manslaughter, rape/aggravated sexual assault, robbery, and aggravated assault. These arrests are used in computing rates because they provide some approximation of the frequency of potentially violent police-civilian encounters in any given jurisdiction during any particular year.*

Table E-28:
Demographics for Kansas City, Missouri, 1972-91

Year	Resident Population	# Sworn Police	# Reported Homicides	# Violent Crime Arrests[1]
1972	511,600	1,304	71	1,601
1973	511,461	1,310	47	1,893
1974	512,267	1,280	109	2,305
1975	489,094	1,246	114	2,415
1976	488,012	1,221	95	1,737
1977	492,055	1,226	97	1,450
1978	463,931	1,192	115	1,297
1979	462,914	1,192	119	1,497
1980	446,865	1,183	132	1,678
1981	450,211	1,154	115	2,211
1982	451,397	1,145	93	1,922
1983	453,128	1,140	106	1,901
1984	450,489	1,105	88	2,148
1985	444,942	1,114	91	2,168
1986	448,237	1,097	116	2,307
1987	444,382	1,113	131	2,383
1988	447,461	1,117	134	2,375
1989	440,435	1,132	140	2,796
1990	448,160	1,162	121	3,345
1991	435,146	1,139	135	2,564

Sources: FBI (annual reports), FBI (1991a—unpublished arrest tallies for specified cities), Kansas City Police Department, and the New York Times (3/28/91: A10) for 1990 population figure.

[1] *Violent crime arrests include arrests for murder/nonnegligent manslaughter, rape/aggravated sexual assault, robbery, and aggravated assault. These arrests are used in computing rates because they provide some approximation of the frequency of potentially violent police-civilian encounters in any given jurisdiction during any particular year.*

Table E-29:
Demographics for Los Angeles, 1980-91

Year	Resident Population	# Sworn Police	# Reported Homicides	# Violent Crime Arrests[1]
1980	2,952,511	6,587	1,010	15,423
1981	3,031,090	6,867	879	15,170
1982	3,101,979	6,861	849	15,304
1983	3,158,688	6,886	820	14,812
1984	3,144,256	6,966	759	14,546
1985	3,186,459	7,051	777	15,136
1986	3,260,856	6,951	834	22,353
1987	3,341,726	7,072	811	21,992
1988	3,402,342	7,553	736	23,845
1989	3,441,449	7,893	877	27,104
1990	3,485,398	8,456	983	29,950
1991	3,536,800	8,190	1,039	28,653

Sources: FBI (annual reports) and Los Angeles Police Department.

[1] *Violent crime arrests include arrests for murder/nonnegligent manslaughter, rape/aggravated sexual assault, robbery, and aggravated assault. These arrests are used in computing rates because they provide some approximation of the frequency of potentially violent police-civilian encounters in any given jurisdiction during any particular year.*

Table E-30:
Demographics for Dade County, Florida, 1980-91

Year	Resident Population	# Sworn Police (Actual)[1]	# Reported Homicides	# Violent Crime Arrests[2]
1980	775,665	1,582	303	3,848
1981	832,784	1,785	329	4,497
1982	848,275	2,089	283	5,286
1983	858,044	2,219	229	5,769
1984	864,546	2,238	231	6,711
1985	880,952	2,256	237	7,016
1986	905,550	2,243	235	7,950
1987	931,312	2,336	230	3,595
1988	962,839	2,350	296	N/A
1989	988,344	2,461	274	5,680
1990	1,037,221	2,527	266	6,007
1991	1,055,700	2,539	223	5,535

Source: Metro-Dade County Police Department.

[1] *The numbers in this column are the number of officers employed by the Department each year, rather than the "authorized" strength of the agency (the number the agency is entitled to employ under budgetary constraints). It is not uncommon for a police department's actual strength to run somewhat below its authorized strength due to delays in hiring, the use of funds for other, unanticipated purposes, and such.*

[2] *Violent crime arrests include arrests for murder/nonnegligent manslaughter, rape/aggravated sexual assault, robbery, and aggravated assault. These arrests are used in computing rates because they provide some approximation of the frequency of potentially violent police-civilian encounters in any given jurisdiction during any particular year. The arrests, as well as the number of reported homicides, included in this table do not reflect all incidents for Dade County as a geographical whole. The data pertain only to activity within the jurisdiction of the Metro-Dade Police Department. There are 24 other municipal police departments, a state university police department, a Native American reservation police department, and five state law enforcement agencies in Dade County that generate and report their own statistics. In many instances, however, the Metro-Dade Police Department conducts the actual investigation of major crimes, especially homicide and sexual battery, for most of these jurisdictions.*

Table E-31:
Demographics for New York City, 1970-91

Year	Resident Population	# Sworn Police	# Reported Homicides	# Violent Crime Arrests[1]
1970	7,867,760	31,671	1,117	27,472
1971	7,868,000	30,685	1,466	32,473
1972	7,889,921	30,828	1,691	37,485
1973	7,843,200	29,861	1,680	36,878
1974	7,716,600	31,033	1,554	43,517
1975	7,422,506	26,640	1,645	44,371
1976	7,530,493	25,789	1,622	40,756
1977	7,481,613	24,895	1,553	39,798
1978	7,242,886	24,408	1,503	40,286
1979	7,109,420	23,310	1,733	40,017
1980	7,035,348	22,590	1,812	37,020
1981	7,070,429	22,467	1,826	39,600
1982	7,096,559	22,855	1,668	39,858
1983	7,100,063	23,339	1,622	40,770
1984	7,167,121	25,044	1,450	43,678
1985	7,183,984	26,073	1,384	42,901
1986	7,179,609	27,425	1,582	49,140
1987	7,284,319	27,523	1,672	51,924
1988	7,346,352	26,723	1,896	53,049
1989	7,369,454	25,858	1,905	56,370
1990	7,322,564	26,882	2,245	55,094
1991	7,350,023	26,668	2,154	53,506

Sources: FBI (annual reports), FBI (1991a—unpublished arrest tallies for specified cities), and New York City Police Department, Office of Public Information and Crime Analysis and Program Planning Section.

[1] *Violent crime arrests include arrests for murder/nonnegligent manslaughter, rape/aggravated sexual assault, robbery, and aggravated assault. These arrests are used in computing rates because they provide some approximation of the frequency of potentially violent police-civilian encounters in any given jurisdiction during any particular year. The NYPD calculates violent crime arrests using two different systems: the crime classifications required by New York Penal Law and those required by the FBI UCR system. Under both systems, arrests for the first three of the four offenses are counted identically. But slightly more aggravated arrests are tallied under the UCR system than under New York Penal Law, essentially because some simple*

assault arrests involving deadly weapons are not classified as aggravated assault arrests under New York Penal Law.

To the best of our knowledge, all of the violent crime arrest statistics shown in this table reflect arrests made by all three New York City police agencies—the NYPD, the New York City Transit Police, and the New York City Housing Police. Since we believe these three agencies' data are included over the entire time period, there should be no artificial change in the number of arrests from one year to the next over the period depicted in the table. But, presumably, each year, the actual number of arrests made by the NYPD alone would be lower than the numbers in the table. This means that, where we have used these arrest figures in calculating rates of shootings in this volume, those shooting rates would be higher than we would have derived if the arrest data were limited only to the NYPD. We are reasonably confident that the shooting data used to compute those rates pertain solely to the NYPD rather than also including shootings involving Transit or Housing police officers.

Table E-32:
Demographics for Philadelphia, 1980-91

Year	Resident Population	# Sworn Police	# Reported Homicides	# Violent Crime Arrests[1]
1980	1,681,175	7,454	436	9,588
1981	1,686,834	7,472	362	10,455
1982	1,687,557	7,377	332	10,886
1983	1,692,364	7,218	311	10,381
1984	1,667,545	7,075	264	10,314
1985	1,640,102	6,966	273	10,176
1986	1,645,144	6,868	343	10,566
1987	1,649,364	6,698	338	9,968
1988	1,657,285	6,063	371	10,099
1989	1,652,188	6,263	475	10,017
1990	1,585,577	6,448	500	10,302
1991	1,585,577	6,444	442	10,419

Sources: FBI (annual reports), FBI (1991a—unpublished arrest tallies for specified cities), Philadelphia Police Department, and Crime Control Digest *(1991j).*

[1] *Violent crime arrests include arrests for murder/nonnegligent manslaughter, rape/aggravated sexual assault, robbery, and aggravated assault. These arrests are used in computing rates because they provide some approximation of the frequency of potentially violent police-civilian encounters in any given jurisdiction during any particular year.*

Table E-33:
U.S. Population, Reported Murders/Nonnegligent
Manslaughters, and Arrests for Violent Crime, 1960-91

Year	U.S. Population	# Murders/Non-negligent Manslaughters	# Arrests for Violent Crimes[1]
1960	179,323,175	9,060	100,708
1961	182,992,000	8,690	119,404
1962	185,771,000	8,480	125,144
1963	188,483,000	8,590	125,137
1964	191,141,000	9,310	137,576
1965	193,526,000	9,910	151,180
1966	195,576,000	10,980	167,780
1967	197,457,000	12,170	191,807
1968	199,399,000	13,800	201,813
1969	201,385,000	14,760	216,194
1970	203,235,298	16,000	287,550
1971	206,212,000	17,780	323,060
1972	208,230,000	18,670	350,410
1973	209,851,000	19,640	380,560
1974	211,392,000	20,710	429,350
1975	213,124,000	20,510	451,310
1976	214,659,000	18,780	411,630
1977	216,332,000	19,120	435,720
1978	218,059,000	19,560	469,700
1979	220,099,000	21,460	467,700
1980	225,349,264	23,040	475,160
1981	229,146,000	22,520	490,460
1982	231,534,000	21,010	526,200
1983	233,981,000	19,310	499,390
1984	236,158,000	18,690	493,960
1985	238,740,000	18,980	497,560
1986	241,077,000	20,610	553,900

Year	U.S. Population	# Murders/Non-negligent Manslaughters	# Arrests for Violent Crimes[1]
1987	243,400,000	20,100	546,300
1988	245,807,000	20,680	625,900
1989	248,239,000	21,500	685,500
1990	248,709,873	23,438	705,500
1991	252,177,000	24,703	718,890

Sources: FBI (Crime in the United States, annual): Illustrative cites to 1985 edition—

- *Table 1: Index of Crime, United States, 1976-85 (p. 41), including national **estimates** of all murders/nonnegligent manslaughters and estimates of the total national population based on extrapolations from U.S. Census Bureau data;*
- *Table 24: Total Estimated Arrests, United States, 1985 (p. 164), including "arrest totals based on all reporting agencies and estimates for unreported areas" (national arrest data are provided here for the four violent crimes noted above, among other offenses).*

[1] *This includes arrests for murder/nonnegligent manslaughter, rape/aggravated sexual assault, robbery, and aggravated assault. These arrests are used in computing rates because they provide some approximation of the frequency of potentially violent police-civilian encounters in any given jurisdiction during any particular year. For the years 1960 through 1969, the number of arrests for violent crimes listed in the FBI's Crime in the United States is not an estimate of the total number of arrests in the nation (as the number is for all subsequent years) but instead is the actual number of violent crime arrests reported to the FBI by the law enforcement agencies then participating in the UCR program. The number of participating agencies varied from year to year, ranging from a low of 3,443 in 1960 to a high of 4,812 in 1968.*

Table E-34:
Rates at Which Civilians Were Shot (Fatally and Nonfatally)
by Atlanta Police, 1980-91

Year	# per 1,000 Violent Crime Arrests[1]	# per 100 Reported Homicides[2]	# per 1,000 Sworn Officers	# per 100,000 Population	# of Civilians Shot
1980	3.1	6.0	9.8	2.8	12
1981	3.0	7.1	10.1	3.0	13
1982	2.2	6.6	7.5	2.3	10
1983	3.3	9.9	10.7	3.1	14
1984	2.5	8.2	8.6	2.5	11
1985	2.1	6.2	7.0	2.1	9
1986	2.2	5.4	7.5	2.2	10
1987	3.5	8.7	13.4	4.2	18
1988	2.1	6.5	10.0	3.2	14
1989	2.8	8.1	13.2	4.7	20
1990	2.0	6.1	9.0	3.6	14
1991	2.2	7.8	10.1	3.7	16

Sources: Atlanta Police Department; FBI, Crime in the United States (annual); and unpublished FBI UCR program data.

[1] Arrests for murder/nonnegligent manslaughter, rape/aggravated sexual assault, robbery, and aggravated assault. These arrests are used in computing rates because they provide some approximation of the frequency of potentially violent police-civilian encounters in any given jurisdiction during any particular year.
[2] Reported murders and nonnegligent manslaughters.

Table E-35:
Rates at Which Civilians Were Shot (Fatally and Nonfatally)
by Chicago Police, 1974-91

Year	# per 1,000 Violent Crime Arrests[1]	# per 100 Reported Homicides[2]	# per 1,000 Sworn Officers	# per 100,000 Popula-tion	# of Civilians Shot
1974	9.6	14.1	10.3	4.2	137
1975	10.5	18.5	11.6	4.8	151
1976	7.6[3]	10.6	6.6	2.7	86
1977	10.6	11.9	7.4	3.2	98
1978	8.1	9.3	5.6	2.4	73
1979	8.9	10.2	6.6	2.8	87
1980	9.9	11.6	8.1	3.4	100
1981	8.4	9.2	6.5	2.7	81
1982	8.4	11.4	6.1	2.5	76
1983	9.1	11.5	6.8	2.8	84
1984	4.9[4]	9.2	5.7	2.3	68
1985	7.1	7.5	4.2	1.7	50
1986	6.8	6.2	3.8	1.5	46
1987	7.1	6.7	3.7	1.5	46
1988	4.5[3]	9.7	5.3	2.1	64
1989	3.2	7.4	4.7	1.8	55
1990	3.9	6.7	4.7	2.1	57
1991	2.9	5.1	3.7	1.6	47

Sources: Chicago Police Department; FBI, Crime in the United States *(annual); and unpublished FBI UCR program data.*

[1] *Arrests for murder/nonnegligent manslaughter, rape/aggravated sexual assault, robbery, and aggravated assault. These arrests are used in computing rates because they provide some approximation of the frequency of potentially violent police-civilian encounters in any given jurisdiction during any particular year.*

[2] *Reported murders and nonnegligent manslaughters.*

[3] *Mid-year in 1976 the Chicago Police Department stopped classifying as aggravated assaults any arrests that the Cook County State's Attorney's Office declined to prosecute as more than simple assaults, even though, according to Chicago police officials, UCR program definitions would have allowed classification of assault arrests based solely on police determinations. Then, in 1988, the Police Department reversed this approach, reverting to the classification system used prior to 1976. Thus, the rates shown for 1976 and all subsequent years until 1988 are higher than they would have been if several thousand simple assault arrests each year had been classified as aggravated assaults and had been included in the tally of violent crime arrests used to calculate the rates. Similarly, the rates shown for 1974, 1975, 1988, and subsequent years are*

lower than they would have been if several thousand aggravated assault arrests had been classified as simple
assaults and therefore not included in the tally of violent crime arrests.
[4] *The Chicago Police Department's Research and Development Division offered the opinion that the number*
of violent crime arrests listed for 1984 (13,982) is artificially inflated by some arrests that actually occurred
in either 1983 or 1985 or both. The similarity between the arrest tally for 1985 and the tallies for 1986 and
1987, however, raises some uncertainty about this view. The pertinent numbers of violent crime arrests are
presented earlier in this Appendix in Table E-25.

Table E-36:
Rates at Which Civilians Were Shot (Fatally and Nonfatally)
by Dallas Police, 1970-91

Year	# per 1,000 Violent Crime Arrests[1]	# per 100 Reported Homicides[2]	# per 1,000 Sworn Officers	# per 100,000 Population	# of Civilians Shot
1970	---	12.8	19.0	3.7	31
1971	---	13.0	15.0	3.2	27
1972	---	13.0	13.3	3.1	25
1973	---	6.5	7.8	1.8	15
1974	---	9.2	9.3	2.2	18
1975	---	8.4	10.2	2.5	20
1976	---	5.2	6.0	1.5	12
1977	---	7.1	8.0	1.9	16
1978	5.5	7.0	8.0	1.8	16
1979	8.1	8.5	12.8	3.0	26
1980	8.6	8.5	13.6	3.0	27
1981	6.4	6.7	10.2	2.1	20
1982	5.8	5.9	9.0	1.9	18
1983	10.4	10.8	13.9	2.9	29
1984	9.0	6.8	9.6	2.0	20
1985	6.8	6.0	8.3	1.8	18
1986	7.8	8.4	12.7	2.9	29
1987	4.3	5.4	7.5	1.8	18
1988	5.7	6.0	9.2	2.2	22
1989	4.0	4.3	6.1	1.5	15
1990	2.6	2.5	4.0	1.1	11
1991	2.8	2.6	4.6	1.3	13

Sources: Dallas Police Department; FBI, Crime in the United States *(annual); and unpublished FBI UCR program data.*

[1] *Arrests for murder/nonnegligent manslaughter, rape/aggravated sexual assault, robbery, and aggravated assault. These arrests are used in computing rates because they provide some approximation of the frequency of potentially violent police-civilian encounters in any given jurisdiction during any particular year.*
[2] *Reported murders and nonnegligent manslaughters.*

Table E-37:
Rates at Which Civilians Were Shot (Fatally and Nonfatally)
by Houston Police, 1980-91

Year	# per 1,000 Violent Crime Arrests[1]	# per 100 Reported Homicides[2]	# per 1,000 Sworn Officers	# per 100,000 Popula-tion	# of Civilians Shot
1980	---	4.7	10.0	1.9	30
1981	---	3.9	8.4	1.7	27
1982	15.1	6.6	13.5	2.7	45
1983	16.7	8.0	12.1	2.6	45
1984	11.4	6.6	7.8	1.7	31
1985	11.1	6.8	7.1	1.8	31
1986	8.6	6.6	5.9	1.5	27
1987	7.4	6.5	4.7	1.2	21
1988	---	4.3	4.5	1.1	19
1989	13.7	7.6	8.6	2.0	35
1990	---	4.9	7.3	1.8	30
1991	---	5.2	8.6	2.1	35

Sources: Houston Police Department; FBI, Crime in the United States *(annual); unpublished FBI UCR program data, and* Crime Control Digest *(1991j).*

[1] *Arrests for murder/nonnegligent manslaughter, rape/aggravated sexual assault, robbery, and aggravated assault. These arrests are used in computing rates because they provide some approximation of the frequency of potentially violent police-civilian encounters in any given jurisdiction during any particular year.*
[2] *Reported murders and nonnegligent manslaughters.*

Table E-38:
Rates at Which Civilians Were Shot (Fatally and Nonfatally)
by Kansas City (MO) Police, 1972-91

Year	# per 1,000 Violent Crime Arrests[1]	# per 100 Reported Homicides[2]	# per 1,000 Sworn Officers	# per 100,000 Population	# of Civilians Shot
1972	10.0	22.5	12.3	3.1	16
1973	6.9	27.7	9.9	2.5	13
1974	4.3	9.2	7.8	2.0	10
1975	2.5	5.3	4.8	1.2	6
1976	6.9	12.6	9.8	2.5	12
1977	4.8	7.2	5.7	1.4	7
1978	8.5	9.6	9.2	2.4	11
1979	4.7	5.9	5.9	1.5	7
1980	4.8	6.1	6.8	1.8	8
1981	1.4	2.6	2.6	0.7	3
1982	3.1	6.5	5.2	1.3	6
1983	3.2	5.7	5.3	1.3	6
1984	2.8	6.8	5.4	1.3	6
1985	3.7	8.8	7.2	1.8	8
1986	2.2	4.3	4.6	1.1	5
1987	1.3	2.3	2.7	0.7	3
1988	2.5	4.5	5.4	1.3	6
1989	2.5	5.0	6.2	1.6	7
1990	3.9	10.7	11.2	2.9	13[3]
1991	3.9	7.4	8.8	2.3	10[4]

Sources: Kansas City Police Department; FBI, Crime in the United States *(annual); and unpublished FBI UCR program data.*

[1] *Arrests for murder/nonnegligent manslaughter, rape/aggravated sexual assault, robbery, and aggravated assault. These arrests are used in computing rates because they provide some approximation of the frequency of potentially violent police-civilian encounters in any given jurisdiction during any particular year.*
[2] *Reported murders and nonnegligent manslaughters.*
[3] *Although in 1990 the Kansas City Police Department experienced an unusually high number of incidents in which civilians were struck by police bullets, the annual figure was driven up primarily by large numbers of shootings in the first half of the year (10 persons struck by police bullets). By comparison, only three persons were struck by police bullets during the second half of 1990; and, during the first quarter of 1991*

(the latest period for which we have data) only two persons were struck by police bullets. The two persons shot in the first quarter of 1991 compares with four persons shot in the first quarter of 1990 (Bishop 1991; Zacharias 1991). Such small numbers, of course, are highly subject to random variation.

[4] *In other tables or graphs in this volume (those showing the number of persons shot and fired upon per quarter) the total number of persons intentionally struck by police bullets is listed as 9 rather than 10. This minor discrepancy appeared in the data furnished by the agency.*

Table E-39:
Rates at Which Civilians Were Shot (Fatally and Nonfatally)
by Los Angeles Police Department Officers, 1980-91

Year	# per 1,000 Violent Crime Arrests[1]	# per 100 Reported Homicides[2]	# per 1,000 Sworn Officers	# per 100,000 Population	# of Civilians Shot
1980	2.9	4.4	6.7	1.5	44
1981	3.0	5.2	6.7	1.5	46
1982	3.4	6.1	7.6	1.7	52
1983	4.4	7.9	9.4	2.1	65
1984	3.2	6.1	6.6	1.5	46
1985	4.3	8.4	9.2	2.0	65
1986	2.2	5.8	6.9	1.5	48
1987	2.6	6.9	7.9	1.7	56
1988	3.3	10.6	10.3	2.3	78
1989	2.5	7.8	8.6	2.0	68
1990	2.4	7.6	8.6	2.1	73
1991	2.1	5.9	7.5	1.7	61

Sources: Los Angeles Police Department and FBI, Crime in the United States *(annual).*

[1] *Arrests for murder/nonnegligent manslaughter, rape/aggravated sexual assault, robbery, and aggravated assault. These arrests are used in computing rates because they provide some approximation of the frequency of potentially violent police-civilian encounters in any given jurisdiction during any particular year.*
[2] *Reported murders and nonnegligent manslaughters.*

Table E-40:
Rates at Which Civilians Were Shot (Fatally and Nonfatally) by New York City Police Department Officers, 1970-91

Year	# per 1,000 Violent Crime Arrests[1]	# per 100 Reported Homicides[2]	# per 1,000 Sworn Officers	# per 100,000 Population	# of Civilians Shot
1970	9.5	23.5	8.3	3.3	262
1971	9.7	21.4	10.2	4.0	314
1972	5.6	12.5	6.8	2.7	211
1973	4.8	10.5	5.9	2.2	176
1974	2.8	7.8	3.9	1.6	121
1975	3.0	8.0	4.9	1.8	131
1976	2.6	6.4	4.0	1.4	104
1977	3.0	7.6	4.7	1.6	118
1978	2.9	7.7	4.7	1.6	115
1979	2.7	6.2	4.6	1.5	108
1980	3.4	7.0	5.6	1.8	126
1981	3.1	6.8	5.5	1.8	124
1982	3.0	7.2	5.3	1.7	120
1983	2.3	5.7	3.9	1.3	92
1984	1.7	5.1	3.0	1.0	74
1985	1.4	4.2	2.2	0.8	58
1986	1.1	3.5	2.0	0.8	56
1987	1.0	3.0	1.8	0.7	50
1988	1.3	3.7	2.6	1.0	70
1989	1.6	4.8	3.5	1.2	91
1990	2.0	4.9	4.1	1.5	111
1991	2.0	5.0	4.1	1.5	108

Sources: New York City Police Department; FBI, Crime in the United States *(annual); unpublished FBI UCR program data; and New York City Police Department.*

[1] *Arrests for murder/nonnegligent manslaughter, rape/aggravated sexual assault, robbery, and aggravated assault (see footnote 1 to Table E-31 for an explanation of the felony arrest data used to calculate these rates). These arrests are used in computing rates because they provide some approximation of the frequency of potentially violent police-civilian encounters in any given jurisdiction during any particular year.*

[2] *Reported murders and nonnegligent manslaughters.*

Table E-41:
Rates at Which Civilians Were Shot (Fatally and Nonfatally)
by Philadelphia Police, 1984-91

Year	# per 1,000 Violent Crime Arrests[1]	# per 100 Reported Homicides[2]	# per 1,000 Sworn Officers	# per 100,000 Popula-tion	# of Civilians Shot
1984	2.6	10.2	3.8	1.6	27
1985	2.4	8.8	3.5	1.5	24
1986	2.3	7.0	3.5	1.5	24
1987	2.1	6.2	3.1	1.3	21
1988	1.8	4.9	3.0	1.1	18
1989	3.3	7.0	5.3	2.0	33
1990	4.6	9.4	7.3	3.0	47
1991	4.2	10.0	6.8	2.8	44

Sources: Philadelphia Police Department; FBI, Crime in the United States (annual); and unpublished FBI UCR program data.

[1] *Arrests for murder/nonnegligent manslaughter, rape/aggravated sexual assault, robbery, and aggravated assault. These arrests are used in computing rates because they provide some approximation of the frequency of potentially violent police-civilian encounters in any given jurisdiction during any particular year.*
[2] *Reported murders and nonnegligent manslaughters.*

Table E-42:
Rates at Which Civilians Were Shot (Fatally and Nonfatally)
by Metro-Dade (FL) Police, 1980-91

Year	# per 1,000 Violent Crime Arrests[1]	# per 100 Reported Homicides[2]	# per 1,000 Sworn Officers	# per 100,000 Population	# of Civilians Shot
1980	5.5	6.9	13.3	2.7	21
1981	5.3	7.3	13.5	2.9	24
1982	3.0	5.7	7.7	1.9	16
1983	1.9	4.8	5.0	1.3	11
1984	1.5	4.3	4.5	1.2	10
1985	1.6	4.6	4.9	1.3	11
1986	1.0	3.4	3.6	0.9	8
1987	2.0	3.0	3.0	0.8	7
1988	N/A	2.7	3.4	0.8	8
1989	1.4	2.9	3.3	0.8	8
1990	2.7	5.3	6.3	1.5	16
1991	1.3	3.1	2.8	0.7	7

Source: Metro-Dade County Police Department.

[1] *Arrests for murder/nonnegligent manslaughter, rape/aggravated sexual assault, robbery, and aggravated assault. These arrests are used in computing rates because they provide some approximation of the frequency of potentially violent police-civilian encounters in any given jurisdiction during any particular year.*
[2] *Reported murders and nonnegligent manslaughters.*

Table E-43:
Rates at Which American Police Were Feloniously Killed, 1960-91

Year	# per 100,000 Sworn POs Employed	# per 100,000 Violent Crime Arrests[1]	# per 10,000 Homicides[2]	Actual # of POs Killed
1960	14	28	31	28
1961	18	31	43	37
1962	23	38	57	48
1963	24	44	64	55
1964	25	41	61	57
1965	22	35	53	53
1966	23	34	52	57
1967	29	40	63	76
1968	23	32	46	64
1969	29	40	58	86
1970	32	35	63	100
1971	38	39	71	126
1972	30	32	60	112
1973	34	35	68	134
1974	33	31	64	132
1975	31	29	63	129
1976	27	27	59	111
1977	21	21	49	93
1978	22	20	48	93
1979	24	23	49	106
1980	24	22	45	104
1981	21	19	40	91
1982	21	18	44	92
1983	16	16	41	80
1984	14	15	39	72
1985	14	15	38	72
1986	13	12	32	66

Year	# per 100,000 Sworn POs Employed	# per 100,000 Violent Crime Arrests[1]	# per 10,000 Homicides[2]	Actual # of POs Killed
1987	14	14	37	74
1988	15	13	38	78
1989	12	10	31	66
1990	11	13	28	66
1991	12	10	29	71

Sources: FBI (annual reports).
[1] *Includes arrests for murder/nonnegligent manslaughter, rape/aggravated sexual assault, robbery, and aggravated assault. These arrests are used in computing rates because they provide some approximation of the frequency of potentially violent police-civilian encounters in any given jurisdiction during any particular year.*
[2] *Includes reported murders and nonnegligent manslaughters.*

Table E-44:
Rates at Which American Police Were Assaulted with Deadly Weapons, 1978-90

Year	# POs Assaulted		# POs Employed in U.S.	Rates: # POs Assaulted	
	with injury	w/o injury		with injury per 100,000 employed	w/ & w/o injury per 100,000 employed
1978	3,504	6,807	430,724	814	2,394
1979	3,540	6,960	436,868	810	2,404
1980	3,368	6,995	438,442	768	2,364
1981	3,154	6,716	444,240	710	2,222
1982	2,733	6,240	449,491	608	1,996
1983	3,465	6,958	496,919	697	2,098
1984	3,206	6,258	515,112	622	1,837
1985	3,214	6,557	519,218	619	1,882
1986	3,310	6,877	525,058	630	1,940
1987	3,267	6,768	530,641	616	1,891
1988	3,541	6,158	537,125	659	1,806
1989	3,731	6,580	547,315	682	1,884
1990	4,701	7,992	588,334	799	2,158

Sources: FBI (annual reports).

Table E-45:
Sworn Municipal, County, and State Police in the United States, 1960-91

Year	# of Municipal Police	# of County Police[1]	# of State Police[2]	Total # Sworn Officers
1960	175,598	5,000	24,630	205,228
1961	170,751	5,327	25,858	201,936
1962	173,753	6,014	25,591	205,358
1963	182,292	21,074	25,848	229,214
1964	181,632	22,632	27,589	231,853
1965	190,005	27,299	28,768	246,072
1966	193,661	28,248	30,872	252,781
1967	200,186	29,720	33,720	263,626
1968	211,006	30,316	36,309	277,631
1969	223,135	35,771	38,718	297,624
1970	233,562	40,471	40,470	314,503
1971	246,601	47,493	41,365	335,459
1972	268,750	62,949	42,479	374,178
1973	276,808	68,208	44,237	389,253
1974	286,973	68,219	44,802	399,994
1975	292,346	73,354	45,440	411,140
1976	287,448	86,157	44,690	418,295
1977	293,019	98,732	44,980	436,731
1978	294,579	90,237	45,908	430,724
1979	296,332	95,563	44,973	436,868
1980	294,181	99,182	45,079	438,442
1981	297,324	100,740	46,176	444,240
1982	298,334	105,073	46,084	449,491
1983	304,012	145,358	47,549	496,919
1984	309,960	157,157	47,995	515,112
1985	312,713	157,965	48,540	519,218
1986	318,484	157,369	49,205	525,058
1987	320,959	159,424	50,258	530,641

Year	# of Municipal Police	# of County Police[1]	# of State Police[2]	Total # Sworn Officers
1988	325,095	160,471	51,559	537,125
1989	322,293	174,060	50,962	547,315
1990	341,387	181,875	65,072	588,334
1991	348,070	187,559	58,859	594,488

Sources: FBI (annual reports).

[1] *The number of county officers was not listed at all in the FBI's* Crime in the United States *for 1960; we estimated the number that year based on available information for subsequent years. The number of county police jumped from 1962 to 1963, perhaps due to a dramatic increase in the number of officers employed by county agencies but very likely also due to an increase in data gathered by the FBI.*

[2] *The numbers of state police in 1960 through 1964 are extrapolations necessitated by the fact that not all states were represented in the state police tallies in* Crime in the United States *for those years. In 1960, only 6 states were represented; in 1961, 8 states; in 1962, 9 states; in 1963, 13 states; and in 1964, 17 states. Beginning in 1965 all states were represented in the FBI's published tallies of state police. The extrapolation method used was to calculate the percentage during 1965 that the states appearing in earlier years had of all state police in the nation. Thus, for example, if the six states reported in 1960 had 10 percent of the nation's state officers in 1965, then an adjustment was made in the 1960 tally in the table above treating the total numbers given for those six states that year as 10 percent of the actual total. A similar extrapolation method was used for 1961 through 1964. Although an imperfect way to arrive at a tally of America's sworn law enforcement personnel, no other method could be suggested that was superior in our consultations on this matter with the FBI, the Census Bureau, and the Labor Department.*

Table E-46:
Shots-Fired Incidents (Intentional Versus Accidental), and Persons Struck
(Fatally and Nonfatally), by Kansas City, MO Police, 1972-91

Year	Number of Intentional Shots-Fired Incidents	Number of Accidental Shots-Fired Incidents	Total Number of Shots-Fired Incidents	Persons Struck Fatally	Persons Struck Nonfatally
1972	24	7	31	5	11
1973	47	9	56	6	7
1974	19	7	26	2	8
1975	21	4	25	3	3
1976	29	9	38	4	8
1977	27	10	37	5	2
1978	20	7	27	5	6
1979	18	7	25	2	5
1980	19	9	28	3	5
1981	16	8	24	2	1
1982	11	8	19	2	4
1983	13	8	21	1	5
1984	11	6	17	3	3
1985	13	7	20	2	6
1986	12	6	18	1	4
1987	11	7	18	2	1
1988	11	11	22	1	5
1989	12	11	23	2	5
1990	19	6	25	7	6
1991	15	5	20	2	8
TOTAL	368	152	520	60	103

Source: Kansas City Police Department.

Table E-47:
Percentage of Police Officers Employed and Killed
Feloniously, by Region of the United States, 1987

Region	% of Total POs Employed	# of POs Killed Feloniously	% of Total POs Killed Feloniously
Northeast	25%	12	17%
Midwest	22%	17	24%
South	34%	28	39%
West	19%	15	21%
TOTAL U.S.	100%	72[1]	101%[2]

Source: FBI.

Note: Total number of sworn officers employed by region are not available from the FBI. Annual editions of the FBI's Crime in the United States *contain regional data on sworn police employed only for the 9,000+ cities that have been reporting employment and crime data to the FBI in recent years. The total number of officers employed by these municipal agencies in the late 1980s has been in the range of 320,000—nearly 200,000 fewer police than are estimated to be employed in the entire nation. The percentages shown in the table above for total number of police employed by region are taken from the FBI's annual report,* Law Enforcement Officers Killed and Assaulted, *and presumably are based on the numbers contained in* Crime in the United States. *The assumption the FBI is making in calculating the employment data in this way is that the uncounted 200,000 officers each year are distributed around the nation's regions in approximately the same proportions as are the identified city police officers. If this assumption is wrong, it is possible that the comparisons developed by the FBI of percentages of officers killed and employed by region are misleading. If, for example, a disproportionately large number of the uncounted sworn officers were employed in the South, then the wide gap between police killed and employed in that region would narrow.* **See rates at which officers are feloniously slain, presented in Table E-63**.

[1] *Excludes one officer killed in the U.S. Territories (in Puerto Rico).*

[2] *Does not total 100 percent due to rounding.*

Table E-48:
Percentage of Police Officers Employed and Killed
Feloniously, by Region of the United States, 1988

Region	% of Total POs Employed	# of POs Killed Feloniously	% of Total POs Killed Feloniously
Northeast	24%	7	9%
Midwest	23%	12	16%
South	34%	38	50%
West	19%	19	25%
TOTAL U.S.	100%	76[1]	100%

Source: FBI.

Note: Total number of sworn officers employed by region are not available from the FBI. Annual editions of the FBI's Crime in the United States *contain regional data on sworn police employed only for the 9,000+ cities that have been reporting employment and crime data to the FBI in recent years. The total number of officers employed by these municipal agencies in the late 1980s has been in the range of 320,000—nearly 200,000 fewer police than are estimated to be employed in the entire nation. The percentages shown in the table above for total number of police employed by region are taken from the FBI's annual report,* Law Enforcement Officers Killed and Assaulted, *and presumably are based on the numbers contained in* Crime in the United States. *The assumption the FBI is making in calculating the employment data in this way is that the uncounted 200,000 officers each year are distributed around the nation's regions in approximately the same proportions as are the identified city police officers. If this assumption is wrong, it is possible that the comparisons developed by the FBI of percentages of officers killed and employed by region are misleading. If, for example, a disproportionately large number of the uncounted sworn officers were employed in the South, then the wide gap between police killed and employed in that region would narrow.* **See rates at which officers are feloniously slain, presented in Table E-63.**
[1] *Excludes two officers killed in U.S. Territories.*

Table E-49:
Percentage of Police Officers Employed and Killed
Feloniously, by Region of the United States, 1989

Region	% of Total POs Employed	# of POs Killed Feloniously	% of Total POs Killed Feloniously
Northeast	22%	9	14%
Midwest	24%	8	12%
South	28%	32	49%
West	22%	9	14%
Territories	4%	8	12%
Total U.S.	100%	66	101%[1]

Source: FBI.

Note: Total number of sworn officers employed by region are not available from the FBI. Annual editions of the FBI's Crime in the United States *contain regional data on sworn police employed only for the 9,000+ cities that have been reporting employment and crime data to the FBI in recent years. The total number of officers employed by these municipal agencies in the late 1980s has been in the range of 320,000—nearly 200,000 fewer police than are estimated to be employed in the entire nation. The percentages shown in the table above for total number of police employed by region are taken from the FBI's annual report,* Law Enforcement Officers Killed and Assaulted, *and presumably are based on the numbers contained in* Crime in the United States. *The assumption the FBI is making in calculating the employment data in this way is that the uncounted 200,000 officers each year are distributed around the nation's regions in approximately the same proportions as are the identified city police officers. If this assumption is wrong, it is possible that the comparisons developed by the FBI of percentages of officers killed and employed by region are misleading. If, for example, a disproportionately large number of the uncounted sworn officers were employed in the South, then the wide gap between police killed and employed in that region would narrow.* **See rates at which officers are feloniously slain, presented in Table E-63.**

[1] *Does not total 100 percent due to rounding.*

Table E-50:
Percentage of Police Officers Employed and Killed
Feloniously, by Region of the United States, 1990

Region	% of Total POs Employed	# of POs Killed Feloniously	% of Total POs Killed Feloniously
Northeast	N/A	7	11%
Midwest	N/A	14	22%
South	N/A	30	46%
West	N/A	9	14%
Territories	N/A	5	8%
TOTAL U.S.	N/A	65	101%[1]

Source: FBI (data published in Crime Control Digest *1991k: 5).*

Note: Total number of sworn officers employed by region are not available from the FBI. Annual editions of the FBI's Crime in the United States *contain regional data on sworn police employed only for the 9,000+ cities that have been reporting employment and crime data to the FBI in recent years. The total number of officers employed by these municipal agencies in the late 1980s has been in the range of 320,000—nearly 200,000 fewer police than are estimated to be employed in the entire nation. The percentages shown in the table above for total number of police employed by region are taken from the FBI's annual report,* Law Enforcement Officers Killed and Assaulted, *and presumably are based on the numbers contained in* Crime in the United States. *The assumption the FBI is making in calculating the employment data in this way is that the uncounted 200,000 officers each year are distributed around the nation's regions in approximately the same proportions as are the identified city police officers. If this assumption is wrong, it is possible that the comparisons developed by the FBI of percentages of officers killed and employed by region are misleading. If, for example, a disproportionately large number of the uncounted sworn officers were employed in the South, then the wide gap between police killed and employed in that region would narrow. **See rates at which officers are feloniously slain, presented in Table E-63**.*

[1] *Does not total 100 percent due to rounding.*

Table E-51:
Intentional and Accidental Shots-Fired Incidents by Santa Ana (CA)
Police, by Type of Firearm Used, 1981-90

Year	# Discharge Incidents and Type	Type of Weapon Used by Officers		
		Revolver	Semi-automatic	Shotgun
1981	**9 Incidents**	**4**	**4**	**1**
	accidental = 2	*0*	*2*	*1*
	intentional= 7	*4*	*2*	*0*
1982	**15 Incidents**	**7**	**5**	**3**
	accidental = 8	*3*	*3*	*2*
	intentional= 7	*4*	*2*	*1*
1983	**13 Incidents**	**8**	**3**	**2**
	accidental = 4	*2*	*0*	*2*
	intentional= 9	*6*	*3*	*0*
1984	**14 Incidents**	**3**	**8**	**3**
	accidental = 8	*1*	*5*	*2*
	intentional= 6	*2*	*3*	*1*
1985	**9 Incidents**	**8**	**4**	**1**
	accidental = 5	*3**	*2*	*1*
	intentional= 4	*5**	*2*	*0*
1986	**9 Incidents**	**4**	**4**	**2**
	accidental = 6	*1*	*3*	*2***
	intentional= 3	*3**	*1*	*0*
1987	**10 Incidents**	**8**	**4**	**0**
	accidental = 4	*4**	*1*	*0*
	intentional= 6	*4**	*3*	*0*
1988	**12 Incidents**	**5**	**5**	**2**
	accidental = 4	*2*	*2*	*0*
	intentional= 8	*3*	*3*	*2*
1989	**18 Incidents**	**4**	**11**	**4**
	accidental = 3	*0*	*2*	*1*
	intentional=15	*4**	*9*	*3*
1990	**19 Incidents**	**4**	**14**	**1**
	accidental = 2	*1*	*0*	*1*
	intentional=17	*3*	*14*	*0*
Total	**128 Incidents**	**55**	**62**	**19**
	accidental =47	*17*	*20*	*12*
	intentional=81	*38*	*42*	*7*

Source: Santa Ana Police Department (1991).
* *More than one weapon used.*
** *1 accidental discharge occurred while officer was handling suspect's shotgun.*

Table E-52:
Persons Intentionally Shot at or Shot by St. Louis Police, 1984-91

Year	Persons Shot Fatally	Persons Shot Nonfatally	Total Persons Struck	Total Shots-Fired Incidents (Intentional, at Persons)
1984	7	16	23	62
1985	5	15	20	48
1986	8	22	30	86
1987	6	12	18	41
1988	3	16	19	45
1989	2	9	11	42
1990	2	20	22	59
1991	1	11	12	61
TOTAL:	34	121	155	444
Annual Average:	4.3	15.1	19.4	55.5

Source: St. Louis Metropolitan Police Department.

Table E-53:
Demographics for St. Louis, 1984-91

Year	Resident Population	# Sworn Police	# Reported Homicides	# Violent Crime Arrests[1]
1984	442,528	1,702	128	7,711
1985	431,109	1,616	169	3,962
1986	429,135	1,564	195	4,305
1987	427,161	1,535	153	4,231
1988	425,187	1,514	140	4,232
1989	405,066	1,545	158	5,901
1990	396,685	1,575	177	6,339
1991	396,685	1,513	260	6,085

Sources: St. Louis Metropolitan Police Department and FBI (annual reports).
[1] *Violent crime arrests include arrests for murder/nonnegligent manslaughter, rape/aggravated sexual assault, robbery, and aggravated assault. These arrests are used in computing rates because they provide some approximation of the frequency of potentially violent police-civilian encounters in any given jurisdiction during any particular year.*

Table E-54:
Rates at Which Civilians Were Shot Intentionally (Fatally and Nonfatally) by St. Louis Police, 1984-91

Year	# per 1,000 Violent Crime Arrests[1]	# per 100 Reported Homicides[2]	# per 1,000 Sworn Officers	# per 100,000 Population	# of Civilians Shot
1984	3.0	18.0	13.5	5.2	23
1985	5.1	11.8	12.4	4.6	20
1986	7.0	15.4	19.2	7.0	30
1987	4.3	11.8	11.7	4.2	18
1988	4.5	13.6	12.6	4.5	19
1989	1.9	7.0	7.1	2.7	11
1990	3.5	12.4	14.0	5.6	22
1991	2.0	4.6	7.9	3.0	12

Sources: St. Louis Metropolitan Police Department and FBI, Crime in the United States *(annual).*
[1] *Arrests for murder/nonnegligent manslaughter, rape/aggravated sexual assault, robbery, and aggravated assault. These arrests are used in computing rates because they provide some approximation of the frequency of potentially violent police-civilian encounters in any given jurisdiction during any particular year.*
[2] *Reported murders and nonnegligent manslaughters.*

Table E-55:
Race of Civilians Shot and of St. Louis Officers Involved, 1/1/86-9/30/90

Race of POs Who Shot	Race of Persons Shot by POs (Fatally and Nonfatally)		
	White	Black	Total
White	17	46	63
Black	3	31	34
TOTAL	20	77	97

Source: St. Louis Police Department.

Table E-56:
Persons Shot at and Persons Shot by Dallas Police, 1978-91

Year	Persons Shot at or Shot		
	Shot at and Missed	Shot at and Hit	Total Shot at
1978	30	16	46
1979	25	26	51
1980	11	27	38
1981	27	20	47
1982	9	15	24
1983	17	28	45
1984	14	19	33
1985	10	18	28
1986	25	28	53
1987	6	17	23
1988	11	20	31
1989	7	15	22
1990	9	11	20
1991	11	13	24
TOTAL	212	273	485

Sources: Dallas Police Department (1990, 1991, 1992).

Table E-57:
Race/Ethnicity of Civilians Shot and of Chicago Officers Involved, 1991

Officers' Race/ Ethnicity	Civilians' Race/Ethnicity			
	White	Black	Hispanic[1]	TOTAL
White	5	10	5	20
Black	0	21	0	21
Hispanic	0	0	3	3
Mixed Race Team	0	2	1	3
TOTAL	5	33	9	47

Source: Chicago Police Department (1992).

[1] *Although it is common for government agencies (e.g., the Census Bureau) to report Hispanics as a group that overlaps persons of other races, the Chicago Police Department treated those it identified as Hispanics as a discrete group. It is likely that some of those classified as Hispanics would describe themselves as whites or blacks and that some classified as whites or blacks would identify themselves as Hispanics if the Department had inquired about their preferences.*

Table E-58
Civilians Shot by Chicago Police and Reasons for Shooting, 1991

Reason for Shooting	# of Civilians Shot (fatally or nonfatally)	Percentage Shot
Defense of Life	35	74%
Altercation	4	9%
Apprehension	0	0%
Accidental	7	15%
Other	1	2%
TOTAL	47	100%

Source: Chicago Police Department.

Table E-59:
Demographics for San Diego, 1980-91

Year	Resident Population	# Sworn Police	# Reported Homicides	# Violent Crime Arrests[1]
1980	838,300	1,231	103	---
1981	856,900	1,317	94	---
1982	900,800	1,304	72	---
1983	914,000	1,344	77	---
1984	921,000	1,344	103	---
1985	975,000	1,383	96	---
1986	993,400	1,489	101	---
1987	1,013,000	1,579	96	---
1988	1,050,400	1,706	144	---
1989	1,082,900	1,821	121	---
1990	1,106,600	1,821	135	---
1991	1,126,700	1,855	167	---

Source: San Diego Police Department (1992).

[1] *The San Diego Police Department does not separate in its arrest statistics arrests for aggravated assault and arrests for simple assault. For certain time periods, arrests for domestic violence are also included in the tally of "assault arrests." Hence, it was not possible to derive violent crime arrests tallies for the San Diego Police Department comparable to those derived for other agencies that contributed police-involved shooting data for this volume. The San Diego Police Department was, however, able to report the number of arrests over the 12 years shown on this table for three categories of offense: murder/nonnegligent manslaughter, rape/aggravated sexual assault, and robbery. The numbers reported for these three arrest types added together are: 1980—1,347; 1981—1,327; 1982—1,086; 1983—942; 1984—1,108; 1985—1,029; 1986—1,173; 1987—1,118; 1988—1,153; 1989—1,363; 1990—1,562; 1991—1,710.*

Table E-60:
Shots-Fired Incidents (Intentional and Unintentional), Citizens Shot
(Fatally and Nonfatally) by San Diego Police, and San Diego Police
Officers Shot by Citizens, 1980-91

Category	Year of Occurrence												Total
	80	81	82	83	84	85	86	87	88	89	90	91	
Citizens Shot Fatally	3	4	8	8	5	4	7	6	9	7	12	4	77
Citizens Shot Nonfatally	5	4	6	8	9	11	11	8	15	17	17	10	121
Total Citizens Struck	8	8	14	16	14	15	18	14	24	24	29	14	198
Incidents with Citizens Fired at Intentionally (hits and misses)	30	27	37	40	30	36	25	27	34	42	29	18	375
Incidents with Accidental Firearms Discharges (hits and misses)	11	16	8	8	6	10	13	20	16	16	14	14	152
Total Incidents with Citizens Shot at (hits and misses, intentional and accidental)	41	43	45	48	36	46	38	47	50	58	43	32	527
Animals Shot/Shot at	13	8	15	13	15	17	15	22	25	20	16	10	189
Total Incidents with Shots Fired by San Diego Officers	54	51	60	61	51	63	53	69	75	78	59	42	716
Officers Shot Fatally by Citizens	0	2	0	1	2	1	0	0	1	0	0	1	8
Officers Shot Nonfatally by Citizens	3	0	0	0	1	2	2	6	8	3	5	2	32
Total Officers Shot by Citizens	3	2	0	1	3	3	2	6	9	3	5	3	40

Source: San Diego Police Department (1992).

Table E-61:
Rates at Which Civilians Were Shot (Fatally and
Nonfatally) by San Diego Police, 1980-91

Year	# per 1,000 Violent Crime Arrests[1]	# per 100 Reported Homicides[2]	# per 1,000 Sworn Officers	# per 100,000 Popula-tion	# of Civilians Shot
1980	---	7.8	6.5	1.0	8
1981	---	8.5	6.1	0.9	8
1982	---	19.4	10.7	1.6	14
1983	---	20.8	11.9	1.8	16
1984	---	13.6	10.4	1.5	14
1985	---	15.6	10.9	1.5	15
1986	---	17.8	12.1	1.8	18
1987	---	14.6	8.9	1.4	14
1988	---	16.7	14.1	2.3	24
1989	---	19.8	13.2	2.2	24
1990	---	21.5	15.9	2.6	29
1991	---	8.4	7.6	1.2	14

Source: San Diego Police Department (1992).

[1] *Arrests for murder/nonnegligent manslaughter, rape/aggravated sexual assault, robbery, and aggravated assault. These arrests are used in computing rates because they provide some approximation of the frequency of potentially violent police-civilian encounters in any given jurisdiction during any particular year. The San Diego Police Department does not separate aggravated and simple battery in their arrests statistics and hence was unable to provide the number of arrests we needed to calculate rates based on arrests for violent felonies.*
[2] *Reported murders and nonnegligent manslaughters.*

Table E-62:
Race/Ethnicity of Person Killed and Circumstance in
Justifiable Homicides by American Police, 1990

Circumstance of Justifiable Homicide	Race/Ethnicity of Person Killed					
	White	Black	Hispanic	Other	Unk.	Total
Felon Attacked Police Officer (Type A)	80	60	35	3	1	179
Felon Attacked Fellow Police Officer (Type B)	7	6	0	1	0	14
Felon Attacked a Civilian (Type C)	5	1	3	0	1	10
Felon Attempted Flight from a Crime (Type D)	3	3	0	0	0	6
Felon Killed in Commission of a Crime (Type E)	39	29	16	3	2	89
Felon Resisted Arrest (Type F)	21	17	7	1	0	46
Subtotal without Type G	155	116	61	8	4	344
Not Enough Info. to Determine Circumstance (Type G)	20	19	1	0	1	41
TOTAL	175	135	62	8	5	385

Source: Unpublished FBI supplementary homicide reports file listing for 1990.

Note: These are justifiable homicides that municipal, county, and state agencies voluntarily reported to the FBI's UCR program using supplementary homicide reports. They are not likely to be complete tallies of all justifiable homicides by police in the United States. See discussion in Chapter 2 of this volume.

Table E-63:
Number and Rate of American Police Officers Killed Feloniously, by Region, and Crime, Arrest, and Police Employment Statistics, 1990

Category	Region of the United States (FBI's UCR classifications)					
	Northeast	Midwest	South	West	Territories	TOTAL
# of Police Feloniously Killed	7	14	30	9	6	66
% of all Police Fel. Killed	11%	21%	46%	14%	9%	101%
% of all Police Employed	22%	23%	30%	22%	3%	100%
# of Police Employed[1]	129,436	135,317	176,500	129,436	17,645	588,334
Employ-ment-based Rate[2]	5.4	10.4	17.0	7.0	34.0	11.2
# Violent Crimes[3]	384,047	354,925	655,247	425,911	N/A	1,820,130
% of All Violent Crimes[4]	21.1%	19.5%	36.0%	23.4%	N/A	100%
Reported Violent Crime-based Rate[5]	1.8	4.0	4.6	2.1	N/A	3.6
# Arrests for Violent Felonies[6]	118,048	88,547	171,886	184,000	N/A	526,481
% of All Arrests for Violent Felonies	21.0	15.7	30.6	32.7	N/A	100%
Violent Felony Arrest-based Rate[7]	5.9	15.8	17.5	4.9	N/A	12.5

Sources: FBI (1991b, 1991c), Behm (1992).
[1] *Derived by multiplying the national employment figures presented in Table E-45 (in this volume) by the percentage distributions of U.S. police employees presented in FBI (1991b: 9). See the cautionary note at the end of Tables E-47 through E-50.*
[2] *Rate = number of police killed in each region per 100,000 employed in each region during 1990.*
[3] *Number of violent crimes (murder, forcible rape, robbery, aggravated assault) reported to police and, in*

turn, to the FBI's UCR program, during 1990. Calculated by multiplying the number of violent crimes in FBI (1991c: 50—Table 1) by the percentage distribution of these violent crimes across regions shown in FBI (1991c: 51—Table 3).

[4] *Percentage of the violent crimes listed in note 3 reported, by region, as indicated in FBI (1991c: 51—Table 3).*

[5] *Rate = number of police killed in each region per 100,000 violent crimes reported in each region during 1990.*

[6] *Number of arrests for violent felonies (murder and nonnegligent manslaughter, forcible rape, robbery, and aggravated assault) reported by police to the FBI's UCR program, by region of the country, as listed in FBI (1991c: 175—Table 25).*

[7] *Rate = number of police killed in each region per 100,000 arrests for violent felonies in each region during 1990.*

Table E-64:
Disposition of Investigations of Shootings by
Chicago Police, 1/1/89-9/30/91

Year	# of Ci-vilians Shot by Police[1]	# Shooting Incidents with "CR"[2] Investigation	Dispositions of "CR" Investigations			
			Sustained	Not Sustained	Exonerated	Unfounded
1989	55	*On Duty* 15	6	6	0	3
		Off Duty 6	4	0	2	0
1990	57	*On Duty* 13	11	1	1	0
		Off Duy 12	9	0	0	3
1991	47[3]	*On Duty* 4	3	0	0	1
		Off Duty 4	4	0	0	0
Total	159	*On Duty* 32	20	7	1	4
		Off Duty 22	17	0	2	3
TOTAL	159	54	37	7	3	7

Source: Shines (1992).

[1] *Civilians shot fatally and nonfatally, as reported in Table E-1 in this appendix.*

[2] *A "CR" (complaint register) number is assigned to cases subjected to full investigation by Chicago Police Department investigators (because initial review indicates that some violation of law, policy, or procedure may have occurred). Shooting incidents not subjected to this level of scrutiny have already been reviewed by the Office of Professional Standards and other departmental officials, and they have determined not to require this additional level of inquiry. Shootings not subjected to a "CR" investigation presumably were found to be justified.*

[3] *The count of 47 civilians shot fatally and nonfatally by Chicago Police in 1991 is the **full year** count, whereas the data concerning cases converted to "CR" investigations and the data on dispositions only cover the first three quarters of 1991.*

Table E-65:
Reasons that Memphis Police Officers Discharged Their Firearms
(Hits and Misses), 1969-74 and 1980-89

Reason for Shooting	1969-74	1980-84	1985-89	1980-89 Total
Defend Life and Apprehend Fleeing Persons Suspected of Violence/Threats of Violence	63	108	75	183
Apprehend Fleeing Apparently Armed Persons Suspected of Property Offenses	114	41	2	43
Accidental Discharges	11	42	43	85
Not Ascertained	10	0	0	0
Destroy Animal	13	19	50	69
Other[1]	---	1	0	1
Total Incidents *Excluding* Shots to Destroy Animals	198	192	120	312
TOTAL	211	211	170	381

Source: Sparger and Giacopassi (1992: Table 3).

Note: The reasons for shootings are worded differently than those used in the source document (Sparger and Giacopassi 1992: Table 3), but, as the researchers acknowledged (ibid.: 10), more accurately reflect the incidents contained in the categories than the headings they employed in their table.
[1] *The incident listed for the 1980-84 time period involved an officer firing his weapon "to break a car window to attempt the rescue of an unconscious occupant from a burning car" (Sparger and Giacopassi 1992: Table 3 n. 3).*

Table E-66:
Incidents in Which New York City Police Department Members Discharged
"Glock 19" Semi-automatic Pistols at Persons,[1], 5/89-12/91

Year	# Firearms Discharge Incidents			# Shots fired: all intention-al dis-charge incidents	Average # shots fired per intention-al dis-charge incident	# of Persons struck by bullets fired inten-tionally	# rounds fired in-tention-ally which hit persons
	Accidental	Intentional	Total				
1989[2]	3	6	9	27	3.0	1	1 4%
1990	2	7	9	48	5.3	5	23 48%
1991	1	3	4	13	3.3	2	5 39%
TOTAL	6	16	22	88	5.5	8	29 33%

Source: Cerar (1989, 1990, 1991).

[1] *Shots at animals are not included in this table.*
[2] *Starting in May 1989.*

Table E-67:
Intentional Firearms Discharges (Hits and Misses)
by Kansas City Police, Monthly, 1972-77

Month	Year					
	1972	1973	1974	1975	1976	1977
January	3	3	0	0	1	4
February	3	3	0	1	1	1
March	2	5	0	2	2	1
April	2	1	3	2	0	4
May	1	3	1	3	2	3
June	2	4	2	1	0	2
July	0	4	3	1	5	2
August	2	2	1	1	5	4
September	0	3	2	3	3	1
October	2	2	0	3	4	1
November	2	1	3	2	3	3
December	2	4	3	1	2	0
TOTAL	21	35	18	20	28	26

Source: Kansas City Police Department.

Note: The table indicates when new chiefs of police took office. Clarence M. Kelley served from August 28, 1961, through July 9, 1973. James R. Newman served from July 9, 1973 (as acting chief), through November 1, 1973. Joseph D. McNamara, whose tenure covers the shaded portion of the table, served from November 1, 1973, through October 18, 1976. Marvin L. VanKirk served from October 18, 1976, through February 22, 1978 (as acting chief until January 1, 1977, and then as full chief).

The monthly average number of intentional firearms discharge incidents during the administration prior to Chief McNamara's was 2.4; during McNamara's administration the monthly average was 1.8; in the next administration (including only the 15 months shown on the table) the monthly average was 2.3. The highest quarterly total (13) for intentional firearms discharges occurred at the end of Chief McNamara's tenure. A single quarter's experience obviously cannot have more than a marginal impact on diminishing or enhancing a police administration's entire track record with shootings over a considerably longer period.

Table E-68:
Changes in Shooting Levels and Rates in Selected Jurisdictions, 1980s-early 1990s

City/County/Department	# Persons Shot or Shot at in 1980[1]	# Persons Shot or Shot at in 1991[2]	Shooting Rate in 1980[3]	Shooting Rate in 1990[4]
Atlanta	12	16	6.0	6.1
Chicago	100	47	11.6	6.7
Dallas	27	13	8.5	2.5
Houston	30	35	4.7	4.9
Kansas City, MO	8	10	6.1	10.7
LAPD	44	61	4.4	7.6
Metro-Dade, FL	21	7	6.9	5.3
NYPD	126	108	7.0	4.9
Philadelphia[5]	58[6]	80	10.2[7]	9.4
St. Louis	23[8]	12	18.0[9]	12.4
San Diego	8	14	7.8	21.5[10]
Santa Ana	9[11]	19[12]	---	---

Sources: Police departments (data presented in other tables in Appendix E).

[1] *For some jurisdictions data were not available for 1980. The years are specified in notes for those jurisdictions. All data are for persons actually struck by police bullets unless otherwise indicated.*

[2] *The figures in this column match the type of figures in the column immediately to the left. If the data for the 1980s are for persons shot, so are the data for 1991; if the 1980s data are for persons shot at, so are the 1991 data.*

[3] *Number of persons shot (fatally or nonfatally) per 100 general population homicides. All rates are for 1980 unless otherwise indicated.*

[4] *Number of persons shot (fatally or nonfatally) per 100 general population homicides.*

[5] *The figures are for all shots-fired incidents, not persons struck.*

[6] *The number is for the year 1986.*

[7] *The rate is for the year 1984.*

[8] *The number is for the year 1984.*

[9] *The rate is for the year 1984.*

[10] *Given the dramatic increase in shooting rate from 1980 to 1990, we call the reader's attention to the fact that in 1991 the rate dropped to 8.4.*

[11] *The number is for the year 1981 and pertains to shots-fired incidents rather than persons hit.*

[12] *The number is for the year 1990.*

Table E-69:
Suspects Shot by Los Angeles Sheriff's Deputies and Deputies Shot, 1986-91

YEAR	86	87	88	89	90	91	Total	Annual Average
Suspects Shot by Deputies	*35*	*43*	*31*	*37*	*50*	*56*	*252*	*42.0*
Deputies Shot	*6*	*4*	*5*	*4*	*6*	*10*	*35*	*5.8*

Source: Kolts (1992: 139).

Table E-70:
Race/Ethnicity of Suspects Shot by Indianapolis Police, 1970-91

Year	White	Black	Hispanic	Total Shot Nonfatally	Total Shot Fatally	Total Shot
1970	2	0	0	2	0	2
1971	3	4	0	5	2	7
1972	2	13	0	14	1	15
1973	3	8	0	10	1	11
1974	10	19	0	17	12	29
1975	13	14	0	20	7	27
1976	4	15	0	13	6	19
1977	6	7	0	9	4	13
1978	5	5	0	8	2	10
1979	4	2	0	5	1	6
1980	6	9	0	10	5	15
1981	3	6	0	5	4	9
1982	1	13	0	11	3	14
1983	3	8	0	10	1	11
1984	2	7	0	8	1	9
1985	4	4	1	6	3	9
1986	2	1	0	2	1	3
1987	1	1	0	1	1	2
1988	3	0	0	2	1	3
1989	2	4	0	3	3	6
1990	3	5	0	5	3	8
1991	3	7	0	8	2	10
Total	85	152	1	174	64	238

Source: Indianapolis Police Department (1992: 8).

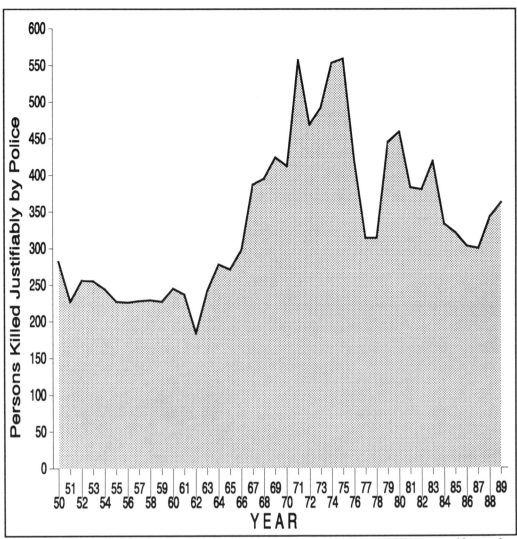

Figure E-1: Justifiable Homicides by American Police Using All Weapons (Agencies Reporting to FBI), 1950-89

Source: FBI (annual unpublished supplementary homicide report data).

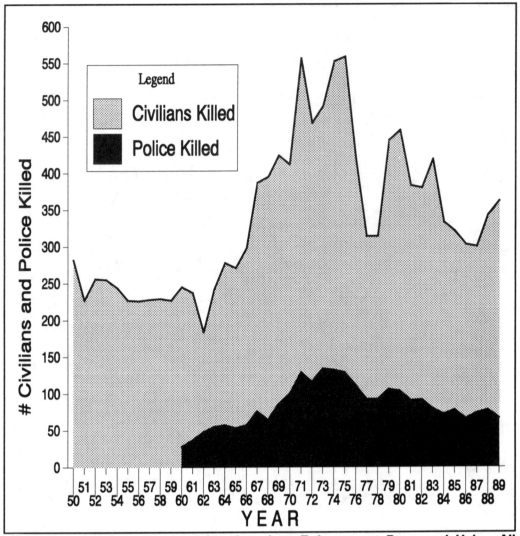

Figure E-2: Killings of and by American Law Enforcement Personnel Using All Weapons, 1950-89 *Source: FBI.*

Note: The number of law enforcement personnel killed is likely to be accurate and complete due to the multiple data sources used by the FBI to tally these events. But the number of civilians justifiably killed by police in the United States is an undercount. Only those agencies (in the range of 9,000 per annum in recent years) that voluntarily report the killing of felons by police may be reflected in the FBI data used to generate this line graph. Moreover, findings by Sherman and Cohn (1986) and our own more recent findings show substantial undercounts to the FBI even by police departments that participate more faithfully in other aspects of the UCR program. Thus, it is not at all unusual to find that a major city police department has fully and accurately reported on crime occurrences and arrests to the UCR program but has not reported all (or sometimes, any) of its justifiable homicides by police officers, despite the UCR program's call for such reporting. By contrast, these same police agencies typically do report fully and accurately on police-involved shootings (fatal and nonfatal) when asked to do so by responsible private research organizations. For a discussion of the possible reasons for the undercounts provided to the FBI by local police agencies, see Chapter 2.

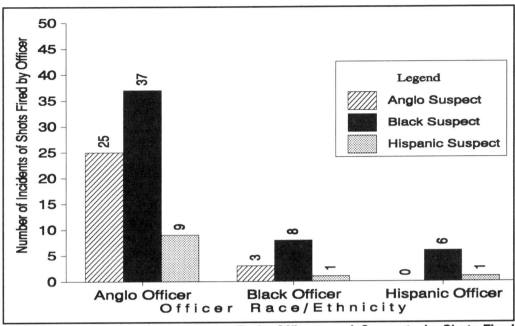

Figure E-3: Race/Ethnicity of Metro-Dade Officers and Suspects in Shots-Fired Incidents, 1/84-6/88

Source: Alpert (1989a).

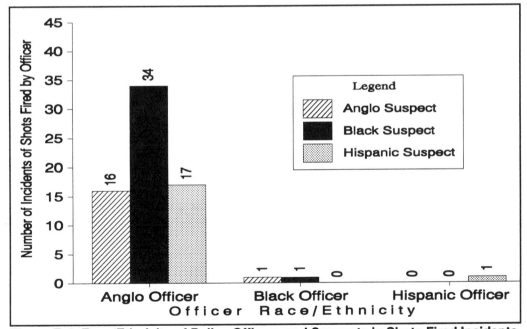

Figure E-4: Race/Ethnicity of Dallas Officers and Suspects in Shots-Fired Incidents, 1/85-6/87   *Source: Alpert (1987b: 24).*

Note: During the period 1985 through June 1987, Dallas officers discharged their weapons in 128 incidents, but the race/ethnicity of both the officers and those at whom they fired were identified for only the 67 incidents represented in this figure (Alpert 1987b:19, 24).

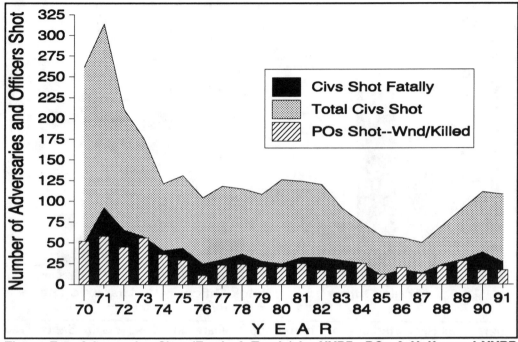

Figure E-5: Adversaries Shot (Fatals & Totals) by NYPD POs & Uniformed NYPD POs Shot in the Line of Duty, 1970-91
Source: Cerar (1990, 1991)

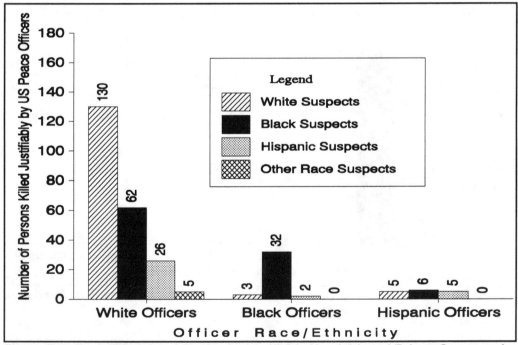

Figure E-6: Race/Ethnicity of Parties in Justifiable Homicides of Felony Suspects by American Police, 1989
Source: FBI.

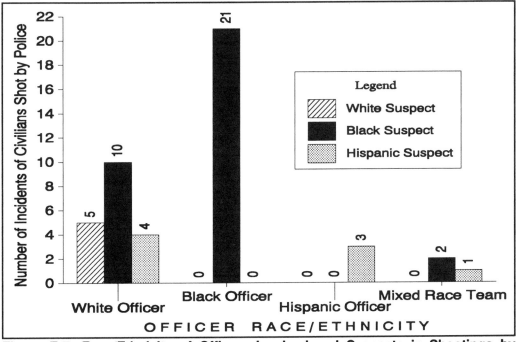

Figure E-7: Race/Ethnicity of Officers Involved and Suspects in Shootings by Chicago Police, 1991   *Source: Chicago Police Department.*

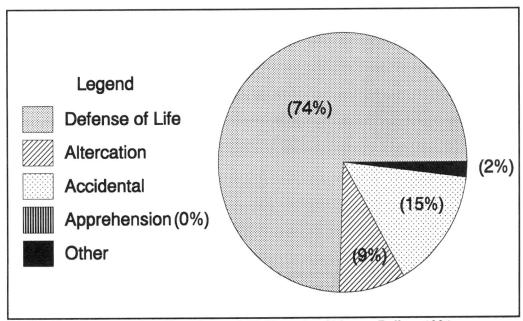

Figure E-8: Reasons for Shootings of Civilians by Chicago Police, 1991
Source: Chicago Police Department.

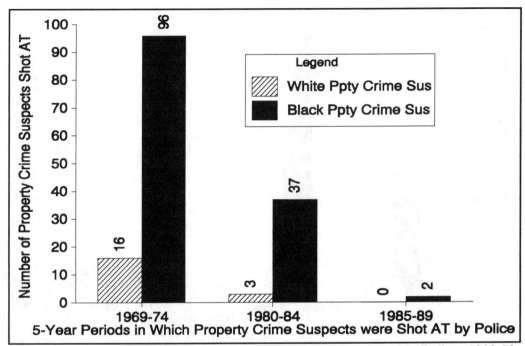

Figure E-9: Race of Property Crime Suspects Shot at by Memphis Police, 1969-89
Source: Sparger and Giacopassi (1992: Table 4).

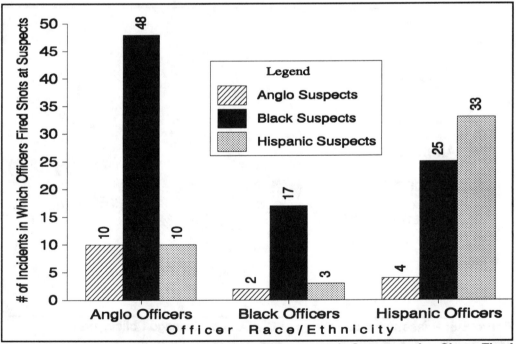

Figure E-10: Race/Ethnicity of Miami Officers and Suspects in Shots-Fired Incidents, 1980-86   *Source: Alpert (1989b: 489).*

APPENDIX F:

DATA COLLECTION INSTRUMENT OF THE IACP/DUPONT KEVLAR SURVIVORS' CLUB

IACP/Du Pont
KEVLAR Survivors' Club*
Assault/Accident
Report

Please fill out only those sections that apply to your life-threatening incident. Also please note that Part X must be completely filled out in order for this application to be considered.

PART I: ABOUT THE AGENCY

1. Name of reporting agency:

   _____

   A. ____ City police department
   B. ____ Sheriff's office
   C. ____ Highway patrol
   D. ____ State police
   E. ____ County police
   F. ____ University police
   G. ____ Other (please specify)

   _____

2. Population served by reporting agency:
   A. ____ 250,000 & over
   B. ____ 100,000 - 249,999
   C. ____ 50,000 - 99,999
   D. ____ 25,000 - 49,999
   E. ____ 10,000 - 24,999
   F. ____ Under 10,000
   G. ____ Suburban counties
   H. ____ Rural counties

PART II: ABOUT THE OFFICER

1. Name: _____

2. Sex: A. ____ Male   B. ____ Female

3. Years of police service: _____

4. Rank:
   A. ____ Patrolman, deputy, trooper
   B. ____ Detective
   C. ____ Sergeant or field supervisor
   D. ____ Above sergeant
   E. ____ Other (please specify)

   _____

5. Race:
   A. ____ White
   B. ____ Hispanic ethnicity
   C. ____ Black
   D. ____ American Indian
   E. ____ Other (please specify)

   _____

6. Height: _____ Feet _____ Inches

7. Build:
   A. ____ Slender
   B. ____ Medium
   C. ____ Heavy

8. Date of birth: ____/ ____/ ____
                  mo. day year

9. Assignment:
   A. ____ Auto patrol
   B. ____ Foot patrol
   C. ____ Traffic
   D. ____ Juvenile
   E. ____ Narcotics/drugs
   F. ____ Detective
   G. ____ Jail
   H. ____ Other (please specify)

   _____

10. Duty status:
    A. ____ On duty
    B. ____ Off duty

11. Dress at time of assault:
    A. ____ Uniform
    B. ____ Plain clothes

12. Was officer in:

A. ____ One-man unit

B. ____ Two-man unit

C. ____ Other assignment (please describe)

_____

PART III: ABOUT THE BODY ARMOR

1. Threat level or protection level offered by the body armor:

A. Concealable personal body armor:

1. ____ I

2. ____ IIA

3. ____ II

4. ____ IIIA

5. ____ Unknown

6. ____ Other (please specify)

_____

B. Tactical or special purpose armor:

1. ____ IIIA

2. ____ III

3. ____ IV

4. ____ Other (please specify)

_____

5. ____ Steel inserts

6. ____ Ceramic inserts

2. Year armor was purchased: _____

3. Style of body armor:

A. ____ Concealable—no side protection

B. ____ Concealable—side protection

C. ____ Concealable—other (please describe)

_____

D. ____ Tactical or special purpose (please describe)

_____

PART IV: ABOUT THE LIFE-THREATENING INCIDENT

1. Type of incident:

A. ____ Assault

B. ____ Automobile accident

C. ____ Motorcycle spill

D. ____ Fall

E. ____ Fire

F. ____ Other (please describe)

_____

2. Date of incident: ____/ ____/ ____
                        mo. day year

3. Day of week:

A. ____ Sunday

B. ____ Monday

C. ____ Tuesday

D. ____ Wednesday

E. ____ Thursday

F. ____ Friday

G. ____ Saturday

4. Approximate time:

_____ am   _____ pm

5. Incident place:

_____ City _____ State

6. If incident was assault, please answer:

A. ____ Disturbance calls:

1. ____ Bar fights

2. ____ Family quarrels

3. ____ Man with gun

B. ____ Arrest situations:

1. ____ Burglary in progress

2. ____ Robbery in progress

3. ____ Drug-related arrest

4. ____ Attempting other arrest

C. ____ Civil disorder (mass disobedience, riot, etc.)

D. ____ Handling, transporting, custody of prisoners

E. ____ Investigating suspicious persons/circumstances

F. _____ Ambush situations:
    1. _____ Entrapment/premeditation
    2. _____ Unprovoked attack
    3. _____ Bombing
G. _____ Mentally deranged
H. _____ Traffic pursuits/stops
I. _____ Hijacking:
    1. _____ Airlines
    2. _____ Mass transportation (buses)
    3. _____ Commercial vehicles (trucks)
J. _____ Other (please specify)

_____

7. From:
  A. _____ Front
  B. _____ Side
  C. _____ Rear

8. If incident was a vehicular accident, please answer:
  A. Patrol vehicle:
    1. _____ Automobile
    2. _____ Motorcycle
    3. _____ Other (please specify)

_____

  B. Driver:
    1. _____ Yourself
    2. _____ Partner
  C. Accident situations:
    1. _____ Pursuing a suspect
    2. _____ Responding to emergency calls for help
    3. _____ Responding to non-emergency calls for help
    4. _____ High speed pursuit
    5. _____ Traffic stop
    6. _____ Directing traffic
    7. _____ Other (please specify)

_____

D. Weather/road conditions:
    1. _____ Clear/dry
    2. _____ Rainy/wet
    3. _____ Snow/ice
E. Please describe accident: _____
_____
_____
_____
_____
_____
_____
_____
_____
_____

9. If incident was non-vehicular accident, please describe circumstances: _____
_____
_____
_____
_____
_____
_____
_____
_____
_____

PART V: ABOUT THE SUSPECT

1. Suspect:
  A. _____ Known
  B. _____ Unknown

2. Age: _____

3. Sex:
  A. _____ Male
  B. _____ Female

4. Race:
   A. ____ White
   B. ____ Hispanic ethnicity
   C. ____ Black
   D. ____ American Indian
   E. ____ Other (please specify)
   _____

5. Height:
   ____ Feet ____ Inches

6. Employed?
   A. ____ Yes
   B. ____ No

7. If Yes, give usual occupation:
   _____

8. Build:
   A. ____ Slender
   B. ____ Medium
   C. ____ Heavy

9. Did the officer know the identity of the suspect prior to the assault?
   A. ____ Yes
   B. ____ No

10. Did suspect appear to be under the influence of alcohol?
    A. ____ Yes
    B. ____ No

11. Did suspect appear to be under the influence of drugs?
    A. ____ Yes
    B. ____ No

12. Did suspect appear mentally deranged?
    A. ____ Yes
    B. ____ No
    C. ____ Don't know

13. Had suspect been drinking?
    A. ____ Yes
    B. ____ No
    C. ____ Don't know

14. If suspect was arrested, specify charge(s):
    _____
    _____

15. Criminal history:
    A. ____ No previous criminal history known
    B. ____ Prior criminal arrest, not convicted
    C. ____ Prior criminal arrest, convicted
    D. ____ Prior arrest for crime of violence, not convicted
    E. ____ Prior arrest for crime of violence, convicted
    F. ____ Convicted on criminal charges, granted leniency
    G. ____ On parole or probation at time of assaulting the officer
    H. ____ Prior arrest for assault
    I. ____ Prior arrest for assaulting police officer or resisting arrest
    J. ____ Prior arrest for weapons violation

16. Disposition of suspect:
    A. ____ Arrested and charged
    B. ____ Fugitive
    C. ____ Justifiably killed
    D. ____ Committed suicide

17. Arrested and charged:
    A. ____ Found guilty of assault on the officer
    B. ____ Guilty of lesser offense related to assault
    C. ____ Guilty of crime other than assault
    D. ____ Acquitted or otherwise dismissed
    E. ____ Committed to mental institution
    F. ____ Case pending or disposition unknown
    G. ____ Died in custody

PART VI: ABOUT THE WEAPON USED

1. Firearms used by suspect:
   A. ____ Officer's own handgun
   B. ____ Officer's shotgun
   C. ____ Officer's rifle
   D. ____ Suspect's handgun
   E. ____ Suspect's shotgun
   F. ____ Suspect's rifle
   G. ____ Other handgun or rifle
   H. ____ Set bomb or trap

2. Caliber of handgun:
   A. ____ .22 caliber
   B. ____ .25 caliber
   C. ____ .32 caliber
   D. ____ 9 millimeter
   E. ____ .357 magnum
   F. ____ .380 caliber
   G. ____ .38 caliber
   H. ____ .41 magnum
   I. ____ .44 caliber
   J. ____ .45 caliber
   K. ____ Caliber not reported
   L. ____ Other (please describe)

   _____

3. Rifle size:
   A. ____ .22 caliber
   B. ____ 9 millimeter
   C. ____ Caliber not reported
   D. ____ Other (please describe)

   _____

4. Shotgun size:
   A. ____ 12 gauge
   B. ____ 16 gauge
   C. ____ 20 gauge
   D. ____ Gauge not reported (please describe)

   _____

   E. ____ Type shot (please describe)

   _____

   F. ____ Other (please describe)

   _____

5. Was suspect using a stolen firearm?
   A. ____ Yes
   B. ____ No
   C. ____ Unknown

6. If firearm used, how many shots? _____
   From what distance? _____

7. Other weapon:
   A. ____ Knife
   B. ____ Club
   C. ____ Broken bottle
   D. ____ Other (please specify)

   _____

PART VII: ABOUT THE INJURIES

1. Was the officer injured?
   A. ____ Yes   B. ____ No

2. Was officer hospitalized? _____
   If Yes, how long? _____

3. If officer injured, where injured?
   A. ____ Front head
   B. ____ Rear head
   C. ____ Front upper torso
   D. ____ Rear upper torso
   E. ____ Front below waist
   F. ____ Rear below waist
   G. ____ Arms/hands

4. Was injured area protected by body armor?
   A. ____ Yes   B. ____ No

5. Degree of injuries in area protected by body armor:
   A. ____ Superficial bruises
   B. ____ Superficial laceration
   C. ____ Severe bruises
   D. ____ Severe lacerations
   E. ____ Fractured or broken bones
   F. ____ Cut or puncture
   G. ____ Gunshot wounds
   H. ____ Other (please describe)

   _____

PART VIII: TRAINING COURSES

Please indicate below those training courses that saved officer had completed, indicating whether that training was completed during the past 6 months, 12 months, or longer:

Course Title	Last 6 Months	Last 12 Months	Longer
Basic Recruit Training	1. ____	2. ____	3. ____
Firearms Training	1. ____	2. ____	3. ____
Arrest Procedures	1. ____	2. ____	3. ____
Prisoner Handling	1. ____	2. ____	3. ____
Riot Control	1. ____	2. ____	3. ____
Police Community Relations	1. ____	2. ____	3. ____
Defensive Tactics	1. ____	2. ____	3. ____
Defensive Driving	1. ____	2. ____	3. ____
Pursuit Driving	1. ____	2. ____	3. ____
Never had any Police Training	1. ____	2. ____	3. ____

PART IX: WHAT WAS UNUSUAL? Further Description

In the following spaces, please write in any information you have about unusual weapons, unusual assault techniques, notable circumstances (unusual events, particular people present, situational factors, etc.), or anything you believe is important that is not covered elsewhere or that needs further explanation. You may wish to attach a copy of the Police Incident Report.

_____
_____
_____
_____
_____
_____
_____
_____
_____
_____

Thank you for completing this summary. This information will be used to help you and your fellow officers. The information you have given in this summary will be assimilated with information submitted by other officers and computer analyzed to determine causes and counter measures for assaults on police officers.

PART X: NOMINATION OF SAVED OFFICER TO IACP/DU PONT KEVLAR SURVIVORS' CLUB*

I. FROM SURVIVOR

It is recognized that some individual officers and/or police departments might be willing to share the above information for the benefit of other police officers, but might not wish to participate in the IACP/Du Pont KEVLAR Survivors' Club*. Please complete the information requested below to participate.

____ I wish to participate in the IACP/Du Pont KEVLAR Survivors' Club*

_____
Signature   Date

_____
Exact Name For Plaque

____ I want my story to benefit other officers and will be happy to have my name used.

_____
Initial

____ I wish to remain anonymous.

II. FROM NOMINATING OFFICER

____ Our department will participate in the IACP/Du Pont KEVLAR Survivors' Club*

_____
Signature   Date

_____
Rank

Please forward IACP/Du Pont KEVLAR Survivors' Club* membership package to: (Fill in name & address of chief or other police executive who will be presenting award.)

_____
_____
_____
_____

Telephone: _____

Please return this form to:

IACP/Du Pont KEVLAR Survivors' Club*
Room X-50680
Wilmington, DE 19898

If you have any questions, please call 800/441-2746.

APPENDIX G:

THE FBI'S PROPOSED REVISION OF
ITS DEADLY FORCE POLICY
AND
THE NATIONAL ORGANIZATION OF BLACK LAW
ENFORCEMENT EXECUTIVES' JULY 18, 1990, RESOLUTION
OPPOSING THE FBI'S PLAN

[FBI] DEADLY FORCE POLICY (REVISION III)[1]

Agents may use deadly force when any of the following three justifications is present. Whenever feasible, verbal warnings should be given before resort is made to deadly force.

1) TO PROTECT FROM PRESENT DANGER

Agents may use deadly force when they have reasonable grounds to believe such force is necessary to protect themselves or others from the present danger of death or serious bodily harm.

2) TO PREVENT THE ESCAPE OF A DANGEROUS PERSON FROM A SCENE OF VIOLENCE

Agents may use deadly force when they have reasonable grounds to believe such force is necessary to prevent the escape of a person from the vicinity of a confrontation or violent crime during either of which that person is reasonably believed to have caused or attempted to cause death or serious bodily harm to the Agent(s) or other persons, or to have threatened death or serious bodily harm to such persons while displaying a deadly weapon or device. *The use of deadly force is not authorized to prevent the escape of a person who without displaying a deadly weapon or device has only threatened the infliction of death or serious bodily injury.*

3) TO PREVENT THE ESCAPE OF A DANGEROUS PERSON UNDER OTHER CIRCUMSTANCES

Agents may use deadly force when they have reasonable grounds to believe such force is necessary to prevent the escape of a person who is reasonably believed to have committed an offense in which he caused or attempted to cause death or serious bodily harm and who is either reasonably believed to be armed or who is reasonably believed, considering the

---

[1] This version of the proposed policy was current as June 1991.

timing and nature of the previous offense(s) and other facts, to be likely again to cause death or serious bodily harm if his apprehension is delayed. *Where a person is not escaping from a scene of violence, the use of deadly force is not authorized to prevent his escape where the person has only threatened the infliction of death or serious bodily harm.*

WARNING SHOTS

The use of warning shots is discouraged. However, it is recognized that there may be limited circumstances where the use of a warning shot is a reasonable alternative to the immediate application of deadly force. A warning shot is permissible only where *all* of the following conditions are present: 1) the use of deadly force is justified under FBI policy; 2) the warning shot poses no foreseeable risk to innocent persons; and 3) the use of a warning shot does not endanger the lives of Agents or others by delaying the use of deadly force. *The use of a warning shot is never required under this policy.*

NOBLE RESOLUTION, ADOPTED JULY 18, 1990

"WHEREAS,   The National Organization of Black Law Enforcement Executives and other professional police organizations joined with the Commission on Accreditation for Law Enforcement, Inc. in 1979 to establish a voluntary national body of standards to govern law enforcement agencies; AND

WHEREAS, N.O.B.L.E. was in the forefront of developing the 'use of force' policy which states: 'An officer may use deadly force only when the officer reasonably believes that the action is in defense of human life, including an officer's own life, or in defense of any person in immediate danger of serious physical injury'; AND

WHEREAS, A 'fleeing felon' should not be presumed to pose an immediate threat to life in the absence of actions that would lead one to believe such is the case, such as a previously demonstrated threat to or wanton disregard for human life; AND

WHEREAS, Officers shall not use firearms when the discharge of the firearm is solely intended as a warning, since warning shots pose a danger to officers and citizens alike, AND

WHEREAS, The Supreme Court in 1985, *Garner v. Tennessee* [sic], struck down the Tennessee law permitting police to use 'all necessary means' to apprehend fleeing suspects,

NOW, THEREFORE, BE IT RESOLVED THAT the National Organization of Black Law Enforcement Executives strongly opposes any efforts to change current policy on when an officer may use deadly force, and the use of warning shots that are inconsistent with existing national standards."

APPENDIX H:

FBI UNIFORM CRIME REPORTING PROGRAM DATA COLLECTION FORMS:

"Law Enforcement Officers Killed or Assaulted"

"Supplementary Homicide Report"

4-931 (Rev. 8-7-89)

Form Approved
OMB No. 1110-0006

LAW ENFORCEMENT OFFICERS KILLED OR ASSAULTED

It is requested this report be completed and transmitted with monthly crime reports to: Director, Federal Bureau of Investigation, Uniform Crime Reports, Washington, D. C. 20535. This form should be used to report the number of your officers who were assaulted or killed in the line of duty during the month. Additional information concerning officers killed will be requested by a separate questionnaire.

OFFICERS KILLED

Number of your law enforcement officers killed in the line of duty this month.	By felonious act _____
	By accident or negligence _____

Officers Assaulted (Do not include officers killed) - See other side for instructions.

Type of Activity	Total Assaults by Weapon A	Type of Weapon				Type of Assignment							Police Assaults Cleared M
		Firearm B	Knife or Other Cutting Instrument C	Other Dangerous Weapon D	Hands, Fists, Feet, etc. E	Two-Officer Vehicle F	One-Officer Vehicle		Detective or Special Assign.		Other		
							Alone G	Assisted H	Alone I	Assisted J	Alone K	Assisted L	
1. Responding to "Disturbance" calls (family quarrels, man with gun, etc.)													
2. Burglaries in progress or pursuing burglary suspects													
3. Robberies in progress or pursuing robbery suspects													
4. Attempting other arrests													
5. Civil disorder (riot, mass disobedience)													
6. Handling, transporting, custody of prisoners													
7. Investigating suspicious persons or circumstances													
8. Ambush - no warning													
9. Mentally deranged													
10. Traffic pursuits and stops													
11. All other													
12. TOTAL (1-11)													
13. Number with personal injury . . .													
14. Number without personal injury .													
15. Time of assaults . . AM PM													

12:01 2:00 4:00 6:00 8:00 10:00 12:00

DO NOT WRITE HERE

	Initials
Recorded	
Edited	
Punched	
Verified	
Adjusted	

DOJ/FBI

Month and Year	Agency Identifier	Prepared by	Title
Agency	State	Chief, Sheriff, Commissioner, Superintendent	

FBI/DOJ

INSTRUCTIONS FOR PREPARING REPORT

When an officer is assaulted in the line of duty, an entry should be made on the appropriate line for type of activity (lines 1-11), under type of weapons used (columns B-E), and under type of assignment (columns F-L). An entry should also be made in either line 13 (injury) or line 14 (no injury). Also count the assault by the time of day on line 15.

When any of these assaults are cleared, an entry should be made under column M for appropriate activity.

At the end of the month, add all lines under columns B through E and enter in column A. The total of columns F through L should equal the total of columns B through E as entered in column A. Also add all columns down and enter in line 12.

Columns B-E:

If more than one type of weapon is used to commit a single assault, the column encountered moving from left to right (B to E) which shows one of the weapons used should be selected for the entry. Do not enter any of the other different types of weapons which were used.

Columns F-L:

Column F (Two-Officer Vehicle) and columns G and H (One-Officer Vehicle) pertain to uniformed officers; columns I and J (Detective or Special Assignment) to non-uniformed officers; columns K and L (Other) to officers assaulted while in a capacity not represented by columns F-J such as foot patrol, off duty, etc.

Column M:

In column M count the number of "assault on officer" offenses cleared. Do not count the number of persons arrested for such offenses. Include exceptional clearances.

Lines 1-11:

Indicate the type of police activity the officer was engaged in at the time of assault.

Line 12:

Enter the total of lines 1-11.

Line 13:

Enter the number of assaults from line 12 which resulted in personal injury to the officer.

Line 14:

Enter the number of assaults from line 12 in which there was no injury to the officer.

Line 15:

Enter the total number of assaults on police officers occurring within the appropriate two-hour intervals.

4-918 (Rev. 3-7-89)
Form Approved
OMB No. 1110-0002

SUPPLEMENTARY HOMICIDE REPORT

This report is authorized by law Title 28, Section 534, United States Code. While you are not required to respond, your cooperation in using this form to list data pertaining to all homicides reported on your Return A will assist the FBI in compiling comprehensive, accurate data regarding this important classification on a timely basis.

1a. Murder and Nonnegligent Manslaughter

List below specific information for all offenses shown in item 1a of the monthly Return A. In addition, list all justifiable killings of felons by a citizen or by a peace officer in the line of duty. A brief explanation in the circumstances column regarding unfounded homicide offenses will aid the national Uniform Crime Reporting Program in editing the reports.

Incident	Situation*	Victims**				Offenders**				Data Code		Weapon Used (Handgun, Rifle, Shotgun, Club, Poison, etc.)	Relationship of Victim to Offender (Husband, Wife, Son, Father, Acquaintance, Neighbor, Stranger, etc.)	Circumstances (Victim shot by robber, robbery victim shot robber, killed by patron during barroom brawl, etc.)
		Age	Sex	Race	Ethnicity	Age	Sex	Race	Ethnicity	\multicolumn{2}{c}{Do Not Write In These Spaces}			

** - See reverse side for explanation

Month and Year _____   Agency Identifier _____   Prepared By _____

Agency _____   State _____   Title _____

Chief, Sheriff, Commissioner, Superintendent

DO NOT WRITE HERE
Recorded
Edited
Punched
Verified
Adjusted

SUPPLEMENTARY HOMICIDE REPORT (Continued)

1b. Manslaughter by Negligence
Do not list traffic fatalities, accidental deaths, or death due to the negligence of the victim. List below all other negligent manslaughters, regardless of prosecutive action taken.

Incident	Situation*	Victim**				Offender**				Data Code (Do Not Write In These Spaces)	Weapon Used (Handgun, Rifle, Shotgun Knife, etc.)	Relationship of Victim to Offender (Husband, Wife, Son, Father, Acquaintance, Neighbor, Stranger, etc.)	Circumstances (Victim shot in hunting accident, gun-cleaning, children playing with gun, etc.)
		Age	Sex	Race	Ethnicity	Age	Sex	Race	Ethnicity				

* - Situations   A - Single Victim/Single Offender
                  B - Single Victim/Unknown Offender or Offenders
                  C - Single Victim/Multiple Offenders
                  D - Multiple Victims/Single Offender
                  E - Multiple Victims/Multiple Offenders
                  F - Multiple Victims/Unknown Offender or Offenders

Use only one victim/offender situation code per set of information. The utilization of a new code will signify the beginning of a new murder situation.

** - Age   - 01 to 99. If 100 or older use 99. New born up to one week old use NB. If over one week, but less than one year old use BB. Use two characters only in age column.
     Sex   - M for Male and F for Female. Use one character only.
     Race   - White - W, Black - B, American Indian or Alaskan Native - I, Asian or Pacific Islander - A, Unknown - U. Use only these as race designations.
     Ethnicity - Hispanic Origin - H, Not of Hispanic Origin - N, Unknown - U.

APPENDIX I:

HOUSTON POLICE DEPARTMENT'S
DEADLY FORCE POLICY

(Number 600-17: Issued February 15, 1987;
still current as of April 1992)

POLICY

The Houston Police Department places its highest value on the life and safety of its officers and the public. The department's policies, rules and procedures are designed to ensure that this value guides police officers' use of firearms.

The citizens of Houston have vested in their police officers the power to carry and use firearms in the exercise of their service to society. This power is based on trust and, therefore, must be balanced by a system of accountability. The serious consequences of the use of firearms by police officers necessitate the specification of limits for officers' discretion; there is often no appeal from an officer's decision to use a firearm. Therefore it is imperative that every effort be made to ensure that such use is not only legally warranted but also rational and humane.

The basic responsibility of police officers to protect life also requires that they exhaust all other reasonable means for apprehension and control before resorting to the use of firearms. Police officers are equipped with firearms as a means of last resort to protect themselves and others from the immediate threat of death or serious bodily injury.

Even though all officers must be prepared to use their firearms when necessary, the utmost restraint must be exercised in their use. Consequently, no officer will be disciplined for discharging a firearm in self-defense or in defense of another when faced with a situation that immediately threatens life or serious bodily injury. Just as important, no officer will be disciplined for not discharging a firearm if that discharge might threaten the life or safety of an innocent person, or if the discharge is not clearly warranted by the policy and rules of the department.

Above all, this department values the safety of its employees and the public. Likewise it believes that police officers should use firearms with a high degree of restraint. Officers' use of firearms, therefore, shall never be considered routine and is permissible only in defense of life and then only after all alternative means have been exhausted.

RULES

The policy stated above is the basis of the following set of rules that have been designed to guide officers in all cases involving the use of firearms:

Rule 1:   Police officers shall not discharge their firearms except to protect themselves or another person from imminent death or serious bodily injury.

Rule 2:   Police officers shall discharge their firearms only when doing so will not endanger innocent persons.

Rule 3:   Police officers shall not discharge their firearms to threaten or subdue persons whose actions are destructive to property or injurious to themselves but which do not represent an imminent threat of death or serious bodily injury to the officer or others.

Rule 4:   Police officers shall not discharge their firearms to subdue an escaping suspect who presents no imminent threat of death or serious bodily injury.

Rule 5:   Police officers shall not discharge their weapons at a moving vehicle unless it is absolutely necessary to do so to protect against an imminent threat to the life of the officer or others.

Rule 6:   Police officers when confronting an oncoming vehicle shall attempt to move out of the path, if possible, rather than discharge their firearms at the oncoming vehicle.

Rule 7:   Police officers shall not intentionally place themselves in the path of an oncoming vehicle and attempt to disable the vehicle by discharging their firearms.

Rule 8:   Police officers shall not discharge their firearms at a fleeing vehicle or its driver.

Rule 9:   Police officers shall not fire warning shots.

Rule 10:   Police officers shall not draw or display their firearms unless there is a threat or probable cause to believe there is a threat to life, or for inspection.

APPENDIX J:

NEW YORK CITY POLICE DEPARTMENT FIREARMS DISCHARGE/ASSAULT REPORT FORM

COMPLETE ONLY APPLICABLE BOXES

(Where "Other" is checked and insufficient space to explain, enter on Line 16)

TEAR OFF TOP SHEET AND USE AS WORKSHEET

1. FIREARMS DISCHARGE / ASSAULT REPORT

| 3 (Office Use Only) | 7 Incident A-[] Assault Only Involved D-[] Discharge Only (Officer) B-[] Both Assault and Discharge (Officer) | 11 Pct. of Occ. |

2. PD 424-151 (Rev. 12-90) H1
Ref. P.G. 116-20

| 14 Date of Incident | 20 Time of Incident | 24 Day of Week |

3. Place of Occurrence | 25 Type Premises *(Specific)*

4. 26 Weather Conditions: 1 - [] Clear   3 - [] Rain   5 - [] Fog   2 - [] Cloudy   4 - [] Snow   6 - [] Other

27 Lighting Conditions: Outside 1 - [] Day   2 - [] Dusk   3 - Dark   Inside 4 - [] Good   5 - [] Poor   6 - [] Unlighted

5. 28 Rank   Name *(Last, First, M.I.)*   Shield No.   29 Tax Reg. No.

6. 36 Command | 39 Mo. - Yr. Aptd | 43 Height Ft. In. | 46 Weight | 49 Sex | 50 Race | 51 Duty Status 1 - [] On   2 - [] Off

7. 52 Type of Assignment: 1 - [] RMP Solo   3 - [] Foot   5 - [] Traffic   7 - [] Anti Crime   2 - [] RMP Other   4 - [] Scooter   6 - [] Inves.   8 - [] Other *(Specify)* | 53 Partner's Sex 1 - [] Male   2 - [] Female

8. 54 Type Incident: 1 - [] Disturbance   3 - [] Robbery   5 - [] Traffic   7 - [] Prisoner   9 - [] Other Arrest   11 - [] Other   2 - [] Burglary   4 - [] Ambush   6 - [] E.D.P.   8 - [] Civil Dis.   10 - [] Susp. Person/Condition | 56 How Received? 1 [] Radio   2 [] Pick-up   3 [] Other *(Specify)*

9. 57 Attire 1 - [] Uniform   2 - [] Civ. Clothes | 58 At Time Of Incident 1 - [] Alone   2 - [] Police Assisted | 59 First At Scene 1 - [] Yes   2 - [] No | 60 Number Prior Firearms Discharges

10. 61 Reason For Discharging: 1 - [] Protect Self   2 - [] Protect Citizen   3 - Accidental   4 - [] Animal   5 - [] Protect Other MOS   6 - [] Other *(Specify)* | 62 Shooting Position: 1 [] Supported (Two Hands)   2 [] Unsupported (One Hand)   3 [] Close Combat (Hip Position)

11. 63 Flashlight Used: 1 - [] Yes   2 [] No | 64 Officers Weapon: 1 [] Service Revolver   2 [] Off Duty   3 [] Other *(Specify)* | 65 Second Weapon: 1 [] Carried   2 [] None   3 [] Firearm was Fired

12. 67 No. Shots You Fired-Double Action | 69 No. Of Hits | 70 No. Shots You Fired Single Action: | 71 No. Of Hits

13. 72 Firearm Drawn Beforehand? 1 - [] Yes   2 - [] No | 73 Distance To Opponent When First Shot Fired: Ft. | 75 Sights Used? 1 - [] Yes   2 - [] No | 76 Required to Reload During Confrontation? 1 - [] Yes   2 - [] No

14. 77 Mace Used? 1 - [] Yes   2 - [] No | 78 Mace Effective? 1 - [] Yes   2 - [] No | 79 Officer Injured By 1 - [] Perp's Weapon   2 - [] Other Manner | 80 Officer Hospitalized 1 - [] Yes   2 - [] No | 81 Bystanders Killed Or Injured 1 - [] Yes   2 - [] No

15. 82 Protective Cover Used? 1 - [] Yes   2 - [] No   If Yes, Describe | 83 Vest Worn: 1 [] Department   2 [] If Personal Vest. Issued   List Manufacturer _____   Threat Level _____

84 Prior Knowledge Situation Involved Dangerous Weapon 1 [] Yes   2 [] No | 85 Shot at by Sniper? 1 [] Yes   2 [] No

16. ADDITIONAL DATA *(In Addition To Providing Information Where "Other" Is Checked, Also Include Information That May Be Useful in FIREARMS TRAINING, such as, What Segment of FIREARMS TRAINING was Prominent In your Mind During the Confrontation?)*

17.

	INJURIES					POSITIONS					VESTS	
	Not Inj.	Inj.	Criti cal	Killed	Unk.	Stand ing	Sit ting	Crouch ing	Lying Down	Other *(Specify)*	Worn	Defeated Projectile
18. 11	1 []	2 []	3 []	4 []	5 []	12 1 []	2 []	3 []	4 []	5 []	13 1 [] Yes 2 [] No	14 1 [] Yes 2 [] No 9 [] N/A
19. 15	1 []	2 []	3 []	4 []	5 []	16 1 []	2 []	3 []	4 []	5 []	17 1 Yes [] 2 [] No	18 1 [] Yes 2 [] No
20. 19	1 []	2 []	3 []	4 []	5 []	20 1 []	2 []	3 []	4 []	5 []	21 1 Yes [] 2 [] No	22 1 [] Yes 2 [] No

	Height	Weight	Sex	Race	Age	Past Crim History	Arrest Made	If Gun Cal/MM	If Fired Shots	Hits	If Handgun, Give Type
22. P1	25 Ft. In.	27	30	31	32	34 1 [] Yes 2 [] No	35 1 [] Yes 2 [] No 3 [] Check If E.D.P.	36	40	42	43 1 - [] Rev. 2 - [] Semi-Auto 3 - [] Other
23. P2	44 Ft. In.	46	49	50	51	53 1 [] Yes 2 [] No	54 1 [] Yes 2 [] No 3 [] Check If E.D.P.	55	59	61	62 1 - [] Rev. 2 - [] Semi-Auto 3 - [] Other

24. 63 Describe Weapon(s) | 64 Weapon Recovered? 1 [] Yes   2 [] No | 65 Second Weapon? 1 [] Yes If Yes, 1 [] Carried 2 [] No   3 [] Used | 66 Total No. of Perps

25. 67 Describe Weapon(s) | 68 Weapon Recovered? 1 [] Yes   2 [] No | 69 Second Weapon? 1 [] Yes If Yes, 1 [] Carried 2 [] No   3 [] Used | 70 Total No. Arrested

26. Describe Incident

27. 71 M.S. Control No. From Line Of Duty Injury Report: | 76 Arrest No. | 85 Complaint No.

28. Prepared By: Rank   Signature   Command

29. Reviewed By: Rank   Signature Of Desk Officer   Date Forwarded

DISTRIBUTION: 1 WHITE - Chief of Department (I.R.S.)   2 PINK - Firearms And Tactics Section
3 GREEN - Personnel Safety Desk   4 BUFF - Precinct File

APPENDIX K:

GEORGIA BOARD OF PRIVATE DETECTIVE AND SECURITY AGENCIES "WEAPONS DISCHARGE REPORT FORM"

GEORGIA BOARD OF PRIVATE DETECTIVE AND SECURITY AGENCIES
166 PRYOR STREET, S.W.
ATLANTA, GEORGIA 30303

WEAPONS DISCHARGE REPORT FORM

ALL INFORMATION MUST BE PROVIDED.   **ALL INFORMATION MUST BE TYPED OR PRINTED IN INK!!!**

Employee's Name:_____ Registration #:_____
              (Last)   (First)   (Middle)
Type of Weapon Permit: ( )Exposed   ( )Concealed

Employer's Name:_____ Co. License #:_____

Employer's Address:_____
              Street Number/Street   City/Zip Code

Supervisor's Name:_____ Phone #:   /_____
****
DATE OF DISCHARGE:_____ TIME OF DISCHARGE:_____ ( )AM   ( )PM

Give exact location as well as city where weapon was discharged:_____
_____

Type of Weapon: ( ).38 Caliber   ( )12-gauge shotgun   ( )Other:_____

Give a detailed account of the circumstances surrounding the discharge of weapon. Use
additional pages as needed.

_____
_____
_____
_____
_____
_____
_____
_____
_____
_____
_____

Were the police notified of this incident? ( )Yes   ( )No
If you answered yes, attach copy of police report.

Were there any injuries resulting from the weapons discharge? ( )Yes ( )No
If you answered yes, explain:_____
_____

Name of Injured Party:_____
Address of Injured Party:_____
****

I certify and declare that the above information is true and correct. I further declare
that I have recounted the weapons discharge incident to the best of my knowledge.

_____   _____
DATE OF REPORT   EMPLOYEE'S SIGNATURE

_____   _____
Notary Public   SUPERVISOR'S SIGNATURE
(SEAL)

APPENDIX L:

LOS ANGELES POLICE DEPARTMENT FORM FOR REPORTING USE OF NONLETHAL FORCE

01.87.2 (8/84)

LOS ANGELES POLICE DEPARTMENT
USE OF FORCE REPORT

DR
NO

PAGE ___ OF ___

DATE	TIME	LOCATION OF OCCURRENCE

SUSPECT'S NAME (LAST, FIRST, MIDDLE) | BOOKING NO. | CHARGE

SEX	DESCENT	HEIGHT	WEIGHT	DOB	AGE	CONNECTING REPORTS

SOURCE OF ACTIVITY
___ OBSERVED   ___ RADIO CALL   ___ CITIZEN CALL   ___ STATION CALL   ___ OTHER

CONDITIONS (CHECK ALL THAT APPLY)
___ PCP   ___ MENTAL   ___ FOOT PURSUIT   ___ FAMILY DISPUTE   ___ ASSAULT ON OFFICER

___ OTHER DRUG   ___ DUI   ___ OTHER TRAF. VIOL.   ___ BUSINESS DISPUTE   ___ ASSAULT ON CITIZEN

___ ALCOHOL   ___ VEH. PURSUIT   ___ 415   ___ NEIGHBOR DISPUTE   ___ OTHER: _____
SPECIFY

TYPE FORCE (CHECK ALL THAT APPLY)

PHYSICAL FORCE

BATON/SAP   **PAIN COMPLIANCE**

___ STRAIGHT   ___ TWIST LOCK

___ MONADNOCK   ___ WRIST LOCK

___ KUBATON   ___ OTHER: (SPECIFY)

___ SAP   _____

(MOTION USED):   **UPPER BODY**

___ STRIKE   ___ CAROTID

___ BLOCK   ___ MODIFIED CAROTID

___ CONTROL   ___ LOCKED CAROTID

OTHER

___ KICKS

___ PUNCH

___ MARTIAL ART TECHNIQUE

___ MISCELLANEOUS PHYSICAL FORCE

___ OTHER: (SPECIFY)

_____

CHEMICAL SPRAY

NO. TIMES SPRAYED _____

TYPE SPRAY USED (BRAND): _____

(MODEL NO.): _____   (EXPIR. DATE): _____

DISTANCE FROM SUSPECT

1 ___ FT.   2 ___ FT.   3 ___ FT.

DURATION OF SPRAY

1 ___ SECS.   2 ___ SECS.   3 ___ SECS

WAS SPRAY EFFECTIVE? ___ YES   ___ NO
IF NO, REASON (STATE IF UNK.)

_____
_____
_____
_____
_____
_____
SHADE AREA(S) SPRAYED

TASER   VIEW FROM

TASER SERIAL NO _____   FRONT ___ BACK
                             SHOW DART
NO. OF CASSETTES FIRED ___   CONTACT (1, 2, 3)

DISTANCE TO SUSPECT

1 _____

2 _____

3 _____

DID DARTS PENETRATE

SKIN? ___ YES   ___ NO

WAITING TIME FOR TASER

TO ARRIVE _____ MINUTES

WAS IT EFFECTIVE?

___ YES   ___ NO

IF NO, REASON
(STATE IF UNK.)

_____
_____
_____
_____
_____

ENTER THE ONE LAST TYPE OF FORCE THAT FINALLY CONTROLLED THIS SUSPECT.

EFFECTS (Check all that apply)

WAS SUSP. INCAPACITATED? ___ YES   ___ NO   TIME REQUIRED TO INCAPACITATE SUSPECT: _____ SECONDS

___ NONE APPARENT   ___ CHOKING   ___ FELL TO GROUND   ___ CONT. SOME RESISTANCE   ___ STOPPED RESISTANCE

___ EYE CLOSURE   ___ COUGHING   ___ ATTACKED OFCR.   ___ INCREASED RESISTANCE   ___ OTHER: _____

RESIDUAL EFFECTS ON OFFICERS: ___ NONE   ___ CHEMICAL   ___ ELECTRICAL SHOCK

INJURIES (RESULTING FROM USE OF FORCE)   TYPES: A - MAJOR (USUALLY HOSPITALIZED)   B - VISIBLE (NOT HOSPITALIZED)   C - COMPLAINED OF ONLY   N - NONE

	LAST NAME	TYPE INJURY	BRIEF DESCRIPTION OF INJURY	HOSPITALIZED YES / NO	OFF. TDS YES / NO	LIGHT DUTY YES / NO
OFCR.						
OFCR.						
SUSP.						

ADDITIONAL (USE OF OTHER DEVICE; I.E., FIELD TEST; ADDITIONAL OFFICER INJURED; SUSP. INJURIES UNRELATED TO USE OF FORCE; ANY OTHER PERTINENT INFO

INVOLVED OFFICERS	SERIAL NO.	SEX	DESCENT	DIVISION/DETAIL	ON-DUTY?	IN UNIFORM?
					YES ☐ ☐ NO	YES ☐ ☐ NO
					YES ☐ ☐ NO	YES ☐ ☐ NO

USE CONTINUATION SHEET IF NECESSARY.

DATE AND TIME REPRODUCED	DIVISION CLERK	INVESTIGATING SUPERVISOR	SERIAL NO.	DIV./DETAIL	W/C OR OIC APPROVING	SERIAL NO.

ALSO COMPLETE REVERSE SIDE

DISTRIBUTION: 1 - ORIGINAL, COMMANDING OFFICER, PERSONNEL & TRAINING BUREAU;   1 - EMPLOYEE'S COMMANDING OFFICER;
1 - EMPLOYEE'S BUREAU COMMANDING OFFICER;   1 - COMMANDING OFFICER, TRAINING DIVISION
(ATTACH A COPY OF ALL RELATED REPORTS)

INDEX

About the Authors

WILLIAM A. GELLER is an associate director of the Police Executive Research Forum and director of its midwest office. Previously, he served as project director of the American Bar Foundation; special counsel for public safety and internal security to the Chicago Park District; executive director of the Chicago Law Enforcement Study Group; and law clerk to Justice Walter V. Schaefer of the Illinois Supreme Court. He has written and consulted extensively on a variety of police matters, including the reduction of officer-civilian violence, community policing and problem solving, the control of corruption and enhancement of integrity, the use of video technology to document criminal suspect interrogations and confessions, and police chief selection. Mr. Geller is director of the Police Executive Research Forum's study of police use of excessive force, funded by the U.S. Justice Department's National Institute of Justice after the beating of Rodney King in March 1991. His recent books include the edited volumes *Police Leadership in America: Crisis and Opportunity* (1985) and the International City/County Management Association's (ICMA's) *Local Government Police Management* (golden anniversary edition—1991). His study of Chicago police-involved shootings (*Split-Second Decisions: Shootings of and by Chicago Police*—1981) was cited by the U.S. Supreme Court in support of its landmark 1985 ruling in *Tennessee v. Garner*.

Mr. Geller has worked with numerous police departments, municipalities, and community leaders to address policy, operational, training, and public-information problems associated with police-involved shootings. Among the organizations he has addressed on deadly force matters are the International Association of Chiefs of Police, the National Organization of Black Law Enforcement Executives, the Hispanic-American Police Command Officers' Association, the Police Executive Research Forum, the U.S. Treasury Department's Federal Law Enforcement Training Center, Northwestern University Traffic Institute, Southwestern Law Enforcement Institute, the Wisconsin Attorney General's Conference on Law Enforcement, and the U.S. Attorney General's Conference on Less-than-Lethal Weapons.

Mr. Geller was commissioned by the Justice Department's National Institute of Justice to write the study guide for the "Deadly Force" segment of the *Crime File* videotape series, hosted by James Q. Wilson. In 1983 he was awarded the City of Chicago's "Richard J. Daley Police Medal of Honor" for initiating and co-chairing a $1.5 million fund-drive that purchased soft body armor for the entire 12,500-officer Chicago Police Department. In 1986 he was awarded the New York City Police Department's Certificate of Commendation by Police Commissioner Benjamin Ward. Among his public service appointments, he served for three years as a member of the Wilmette, Illinois, Board of Fire and Police Commissioners and as a member of the American Bar Association's Committee on Standards for Criminal Justice (which wrote the *Urban Police Function* standards). Mr. Geller holds a J.D. from the University of Chicago Law School.

MICHAEL S. SCOTT is special assistant to the chief, St. Louis Metropolitan Police Department. Previously, he served as director of administration for the Ft. Pierce, Florida, Police Department; senior researcher for the Police Executive Research Forum; legal assistant to the police commissioner of the New York City Police Department; adjunct professor in the School of Public Affairs at American University in Washington, D.C.; and as a police officer in the Madison, Wisconsin, Police Department. Mr. Scott has published on police leadership and is a consultant on police management and organization. Among his writings is *Managing for Success: A Police Chief's Survival Guide* (1986). He has worked at the University of Wisconsin with Professor Herman Goldstein and at the Police Executive Research Forum developing a problem-oriented approach to policing. Mr. Scott holds a B.A. in Behavioral Science and Law from the University of Wisconsin-Madison and a J.D. from the Harvard Law School.

Police Executive Research Forum

The Police Executive Research Forum (PERF) is a national professional association of chief executives of large city, county and state police departments. PERF's purpose is to improve the delivery of police services and the effectiveness of crime control through several means:

- the exercise of strong national leadership;

- public debate of police and criminal justice issues;

- research and policy development; and

- the provision of vital management leadership services to police agencies.

PERF members are selected on the basis of their commitment to PERF's purpose and principles. The principles that guide the Police Executive Research Forum follow.

- Research, experimentation and exchange of ideas through public discussion and debate are paths for development of a professional body of knowledge about policing;

- Substantial and purposeful academic study is a prerequisite for acquiring, understanding and adding to the body of knowledge of professional police management;

- Maintenance of the highest standards of ethics and integrity is imperative in the improvement of policing;

- The police must, within the limits of the law, be responsible and accountable to citizens as the ultimate source of police authority; and

- The principles embodied in the Constitution are the foundation of policing.